BEYOND ONENESS
AND DIFFERENCE

SUNY series in Chinese Philosophy and Culture

Roger T. Ames, editor

BEYOND ONENESS AND DIFFERENCE

Li 理 and Coherence in
Chinese Buddhist Thought and Its Antecedents

BROOK ZIPORYN

STATE UNIVERSITY OF NEW YORK PRESS

Published by
STATE UNIVERSITY OF NEW YORK PRESS, ALBANY

For information, contact
State University of New York Press, Albany, NY
www.sunypress.edu

Production, Laurie Searl
Marketing, Anne M. Valentine

Library of Congress Cataloging-in-Publication Data

Ziporyn, Brook, 1964-
    Beyond oneness and difference : Li and coherence in Chinese Buddhist thought and its antecedents / Brook Ziporyn.
        pages cm. — (SUNY series in Chinese philosophy and culture)
    Includes bibliographical references and index.
    ISBN 978-1-4384-4817-6 (alk. paper) 978-1-4384-4818-3 (pbk alk. paper)
    1. Li.   2. Philosophy, Chinese.   3. Truth—Coherence theory.   I. Title.

B127.L5Z565 2013
181'.112—dc23   2012045682

10 9 8 7 6 5 4 3 2 1

This book is dedicated to the memory of my grandfather, one I. Ziporyn, immigrant, autodidact, Spinozist, and author of *Cosmo-Retardation: A Brief Introduction To A Theory Which Shows The Possibility Of Cosmic Function In A Continuum Devoid Of Energy*, a work that received, as far as I know, a total of one printed review, in the journal *Philosophy of Science*, published by the University of Chicago, July 1940.

Here is the entire review, consisting of a single sentence: "The mystic use of scientific terms prevents making head or tail of anything in this book. W. M. M."

On second thought: this book is dedicated collectively to I. Ziporyn and this reviewer, "W.M.M.," in the Borgesian hope that they have by now turned out, in the afterlife, to be two aspects of a single soul.

CONTENTS

ACKNOWLEDGMENTS

The acknowledgments section is the customary place in books such as this where the reader, perhaps out of some benevolent combination of default ritual indulgence and behind-the-music curiosity, is prepared to let the author rattle off an invocation of all his or her debts to those persons, places, and things that made the book possible. This is an author's opportunity to reflect a little on how humblingly enormous a portion of what has come about in his or her work has depended on unpredictable external factors, the seemingly almost infinite chain of encounters and supports necessary to bring any finished thing into the world. Though wary of the cringe-making awkwardness that seems likely if not inevitable in such public displays of the private, I will gladly comply with this custom. In addition to those specific persons and institutions I thanked at the beginning of the previous volume, *Ironies of Oneness and Difference*—and whom I thank anew, with renewed fervor, here and now, adding to the list also Jonathan Sim and Hiromi Okaue for their help preparing the manuscript—I feel these days an ever more insistent impulse to honor this noble tradition of acknowledgment in a more expansive or even global way; for there are so many more acknowledgeable facts and circumstances and things and fortuities left out of such specificities, and though these abstract inanimates and accidents don't care, I still want to acknowledge them, to thank them, to extend some kind of gratitude, or whatever is the equivalent of gratitude when applied to unintentional and inanimate abstract quasi-entities, to the whole mysterious and random concatenation of forces that has made it on the one hand *possible* and on the other hand *permissible* for me to write books such as this at all.

Gratitude, however misplaced, is also a fact to be acknowledged. I can only gape in wonder at this seeming stroke of dumb luck, the fact that, having somehow against all odds stumbled upon something I feel both inclined and able to do, I've so far also been permitted to continue to do it, even to get paid for it, rather than being arrested or lynched or tarred and feathered for it. How many lifeforms ever get so fortunate, to find themselves seemingly unchangeably and unjustifiably constituted in a certain way, and yet also to live in a time and place in which that way of being is viewed as an acceptable way to be, rather than as an atrocity that warrants community wrath, destruction, quarantine, or ridicule? Imagine a person who, for reasons as yet unanalyzed but quite possibly mildly pathological, seems to have always had some kind of ironclad mental block in every situation against doing "the assigned reading," as it were—who was too autistic or distracted or arrogant or cowardly or shy or contrarian to listen to anything any living person was trying to teach him, especially persons such as teachers in classrooms. Some kind of nonnegotiable resistance to the very idea of receiving instruction—rooted in an obscure but unshakeable doubt that human minds are alike enough for any single mind's desires and truths to be likely to be applicable to those of another—drives him to the written word, where the sample size is larger and the distance is greater.

But the ban falls quickly also even on books written in the past hundred years or so, in any language he has heard spoken in the flesh; the familiarity of the methods and assumptions of the authors make them too easily imaginable as living presences, and therefore repellent. Here is this person who can only listen to and learn from people who have long been safely dead for a long time, who don't remind him of anyone he knows (i.e., of anyone who, as he sees it in his paranoia, assumes it's perfectly fine to try to impose their ideas of what is true and what is good, their facts and values, on him), a person who can only dialogue with people who are far enough away from him in every sense. In the self-imposed intellectual isolation that comes with this condition, after many dismal experiments, it turns out there is only one thing that brings intellectual enlargement and some mental companionship: walking around in solitude, preferably in a city or country where no one knows who he is, reading classical Chinese texts, looking up characters in dictionaries, trying out various possible hypotheses to resolve the seemingly endless thrilling ambiguities, pondering them, trying to make sense of them, then making alternate sense of them, then growing the eyes to look at the world through the blossoming of each of these sets of new ideas that erupt as a result of these phantom encounters.

That was me. At some point in those years I got lucky enough to have the opportunity to read closely through some of the texts I loved most with some great old-school footnote-free classical-type scholars; it was the deep rootedness in the careful procession through these texts, which were already a part of my private universe, and the new vistas the greater expertise of these mentors opened up in this already beloved territory, that made this a newly viable way to learn to think new thoughts. The slow and methodical burrowing into the texts was an end in itself, with a very large noncoercive space for working through implications and connections that spontaneously emerged from this kind of extended simmering. I internalized the example of those teachers: one went about one's work, one's encounter with the text, looking neither right nor left, neither criticizing nor praising anyone else's encounter with the text, which would be noticed, reluctantly, only when one's own already internalized resources, the backlog of associations already crystallized from reading hundreds of other such texts, came to a snag, which happened only rarely. For the first and only time, I got knowledge and pleasure from being a student of another human being, and could imagine exchanging ideas with another person in a way that didn't drive me to despair over the abyss of incommensurability concealed in aggressive assumptions about some form or other of "common sense" or "good will" or "shared goals" or "universal truths."

What I thought I was doing, and what I loved to do, didn't feel as if it had anything to do with finding out the truth, becoming more rigorous, joining the ongoing conversation of an existing field of research or inquiry, getting anything right, clarifying history, improving the quality of anything, coming to a consensus, or, god forbid, learning any facts or values from anyone else or making them learn them from me. I liked having new ideas, being able to think new thoughts; tarrying long and intensely with these old Chinese texts seemed to be what facilitated that effect better than anything else I could find. Slowly, as part of this same walk-around-foreign-city-reading policy, a handful of old and long-backburnered European philosophical works also entered my orbit, and, since no one was telling me to read them and it was not my responsibility to do so, and the authors were all good and dead by then, they started to have analogous effects on me, became objects of obsessive study, and I fell in love with them in exactly the same way. My motivation was still very naive and simpleminded: to forge new lenses for looking, to find ways to think about everything I encountered in the world, alternatives to the ways I had previously been thinking about them. This did not at all mean I wanted to replace that first set of ways-of-thinking and lenses-for-looking, as one would replace an error with a truth. It was not an endeavor to fix my vision with a new prescription for my mental spectacles, or a kind of laser surgery to fix my organ of intellectual vision for good, but a greed to acquire as many cool new pairs of elaborate bifocals, trifocals, quadrifocals as I could find. . . .

Then someone told me I could do something like this all the time and not have to get a real job if I went to graduate school. So I did that. My goal was then as now simply to have available more, not fewer, ways of thinking. Why? Because otherwise I would die of boredom. All these years later, it's still the same, and I still love doing this. And I am insanely grateful that I am allowed to do this for a living, and that it has somehow or other turned out that some other people also like to get jostled around in this kind of process. It is true that the institution of formal education, with its notion of rewards and punishments meted out for one way of thinking over another, still seems to me intrinsically obscene, and the idea of one mind standing in judgment over another mind still instinctively revolts me, as much in a classroom as in the idea of a theistic cosmos. But to my surprise, I find that being in this environment—schools—which I detested so much as a student is now sometimes a place to meet really smart, interesting people, both students and colleagues, with strange and intricate minds that in certain places intersect and resonate and ricochet with mine, and that to watch and interact with these people sometimes, if I keep the right distance and the right closeness, can have something of that old new-thought-evoking effect. There's a tension and a contradiction there, and in the formal setting I've still felt it necessary to avoid too much involvement in precisely those fields of inquiry in which I personally have the most mental investment, but nonetheless, I cannot but be grateful for this mysterious circumstance. So that's gratitude number one.

On the other hand, this puts me in a funny situation sometimes, and I suspect, or at least hope, that I am not the only one in this funny situation. I still don't want the truth about things to turn out to be only a single way, or for any philosophical position to be so right that it puts all other positions out of business. I fear any monopolizing convergence of truth that would eliminate errors and mistakes and alternatives. I still think of thinking as Spinoza did, as a kind of activity, a skill, a power to do more and more stuff, correlative to a way of moving one's body in more ways, rather than as a means of arriving somewhere or getting something ("truth"? "the right answer"? "the best theory"?). I still don't like this assumption that thinking is a means by which some ideas are found to be truths and entirely other ideas are found to be errors, the former to be honored and preserved and the latter to be reviled and dispelled, such that the possibilities of moving around, mentally and physically, are reduced rather than expanded. I still have no sympathy with the academic goal of consilience of knowledge, or what strikes me as the totalitarian yearning for everyone to share the same view of what is so and of what is good, of what is true and of what they should be doing, to construct arguments and marshal evidence with the purpose of compelling everyone to agree about as much as possible. And I still can't read or learn anything someone else tells me to read or learn. Though it's now my job, a lot of the time the professionalization of philosophy (or of sinology, or of Buddhology) leaves me feeling the way I imagine a nymphomaniac who has chosen to make her living as a prostitute must feel—someone who had foolishly thought, Hey, what better way to beat the system, my job will be the exact thing I love doing anyway! It turns out, duh, that making a rent-paying job of something you had originally loved, so that now it must be done on demand, under coercion, in a style dictated by the desires of strangers with their own alien libidinal agendas, can, um, kind of ruin it. One of my main concerns in reading, in writing, in teaching is to find a way to steer clear of this fate.

Which brings us to this book. At the beginning of the previous volume, I made some general methodological clarifications that were not unrelated to these concerns—addressing matters of polyessentialism, presentism, truth-as-interest, hermeneutics as a kind of shelf-handy rhyming dictionary, maximal neglect of fallacy as excavation of ever-present but never-complete coherence, and so on—and these same considerations apply to this volume, which continues the work begun there. But I would here like to reinstate some further remarks that I deleted from that discussion, at the time due to a perhaps misguided desire to avoid causing embarrassment to various people, including but by no means limited to myself. These remarks have to do with the always touchy topic of a writer's relation to other writers. Quite often, people who find themselves engaged in this kind of work—professional scholars, I mean, who labor long and intensely with certain texts and ideas—have a vague but understandable hope to see their own works universally accepted, or, failing that, at least acknowledged with approval. Or failing that, at least cited. It is thus very human, and very forgivable, for an academic, when faced with a work that purports to discuss a text or topic he or she has spent years researching and writing about, to turn immediately to the index or bibliography in search of his or her own name. I do it too. It is frustrating not to find that name there, after laboring so long, and it would be churlish to censure anyone too harshly for venting a bit of this frustration, either as global hostility or as an ad hoc self-advertisement offered in refutation, when evaluating those works that seem to snub them.

And no one would deny that the "literature survey," where a student is supposed to demonstrate mastery of what is quaintly referred to as "the field" by reading all available secondary literature on a given topic, summarizing and perhaps evaluating all the positions previous scholars have put forth on a given text, is a valuable exercise in postgraduate training. It is perhaps for these reasons that it remains an academic custom, richly punished in the breach, to go through the motions of citing all one's contemporary colleagues when taking up any much-researched topic, respectfully acknowledging the positions put forth there, but then giving a reason why one rejects them in favor of the one currently being advanced. I've made some ritual deference to this custom in this book and the prequel, but have tried to keep it to a minimum. For there is good reason to think this practice is—in addition to being enormously onerous, insincere, and self-serving—a wasteful allocation of time and energy. The pretense is that, being a member of one and the same "field," one has objectively considered the alternate arguments about all the topics that comprise it, and decided on some mutually agreed-upon grounds that a certain argument—one's own, naturally—is better than the others. This may, indeed, be possible for some cases in some fields. But it is not likely to be possible for all cases in all fields.

More to the point, and putting aside all my personal reasons for disliking this sort of practice as rehearsed above, I am not at all convinced that adopting these procedures of compulsive citation and review of all prior interpretative expositions would serve, in disciplines other than the hard sciences, as a mechanism to ensure the cumulative advance of knowledge, even if that were something we all agreed we wanted. When it does, as in the narrowing of range of possibilities through the exclusion of failed and discarded approaches, or through the handy clarification of philological and historical confusions, it is mainly as a device for the saving of unnecessary labor, whose value is therefore mainly economical in the broadest sense of helping to allocate wisely our limited resources of energy and attention, rather than a positive building block in the constructing of a system of knowledge that either can or should progress in a single direction and toward an ideal completeness and unanimity. So I have tried to cite and discuss only those works that I have found genuinely pertinent to the task of clarifying, rather than justifying, my readings of the texts at hand; I have tried to avoid citing for citing's sake, or even pointing out the obvious radical divergences of my interpretative framework from some others that have been advanced.

I find it necessary to declare in all sincerity that this is not meant as a sign of disrespect or criticism of the interpretations developed by my esteemed peers. Rather, it is my hope that it will be apparent to readers just how pointless it would be, in the context of the present project, to express an opinion about every one of these interpretations. These works may well be very useful, successful, intelligent, persuasive, and in all ways good for the human race. They may connect in interesting ways with the approach I am taking here, or conversely, raise points that conflict irreconcilably with the conclusions I draw here. But in either case, it is very likely too soon for such conclusions to be drawn, and it is doubtful that any of the participants in a debate of this type have the necessary critical distance to give a useful overview of the issues involved. These are things to be decided by readers of both this work and those works not now, but maybe fifty years from now, by a future generation of scholars who are competent in reading the original texts for themselves with the benefit of all the conflicting hypotheses in their arsenal of interpretative tools—if they are still interested, which of course no one can force them to be. I hope I will be forgiven for expressing the heretical suspicion that, in reality, contemporaneous scholars don't really write for each other: we write for the future, for the fresh readers who will take up these problems with their own enthusiasms and their own fresh encounters with the original texts.

What proves useful to future readers survives; what does not, does not. It is for these future students to read and study and consider the possible interactions between parallel interpretations of a given era, if they so desire.

We, and our own first-generation students, are probably too close to the matter to say anything meaningful about it. It requires a "big picture" perspective. A point-by-point comparison of two alternate present-day interpretations, for example, of a particular line in the *Analects* would be not altogether meaningless, but likely an expenditure of time and energy more fruitfully applied elsewhere; both interpretations belong to a total orientation, with its own set of assumptions, goals, methods, which alone conveys its coherence, its persuasiveness, its value—and which is at present still a work in progress, the final contours of which are not yet discernible.

I propose what to my mind is a more "Confucian" alternative, with all due respect, to my colleagues: let us no longer feel honor-bound to read each others' work merely out of a concern for base covering, professional obligation, or obsessive scorekeeping. It is not an insult, it is not a disgrace, it need no longer be a shameful secret for us to need to close our ears to each other at times. The type of work we are involved in here is different in kind from the sorts for which it is important to pool knowledge and adjudicate between error and accuracy. If we were training engineers to do mathematics, there would be both a clear standard and a strong motive for stern policing: it would *be determinable* and would *matter* whether we did it right or wrong, whether our conclusions were accurate or not, because someone might build a bridge or a helicopter on the basis of our calculations. Lives would be at stake.

No such condition applies to work in the humanities—or at least, if in some loosely analogous sense there are reasons why it might matter which interpretation prevails, it would involve an exponentially slower and subtler set of parameters. Indeed, it could be argued that the thriving of a multiplicity of interpretations is actually a healthier outcome, from an analogously pragmatic point of view. I propose that we drop this whole charade of having a duty to be each others' watchdogs, and regard ourselves instead as an eccentric guild of obsessives who happen to be smitten with the same compulsion. We can agree to disagree, or even to simply neglect each other while observing all the signs of mutual ritual respect—and do so in all sincerity, as fellow enthusiasts, fellow lovers, and adventurers of the same seas—and leave the hashing out of the better or worse to coming generations.

It goes without saying that there is a danger of abuse in granting this exemption to oneself and one's peers, an opening for laziness, shoddy workmanship and self-righteous ignorance on the one hand or fruitlessly frenetic wheel-reinvention on the other. But these dangers are perhaps outweighed by the worry that our premature compromises and mutual translations into one another's idioms will snuff out the buddings of innovations that will prove to have unsuspected ramifications when allowed to grow unhindered into their full bloom, and indeed that a wheel reinvented from its first foundations may end up rolling somewhat differently from its unnoticed prototype. To assume otherwise, I think, presupposes precisely the kind of uniform "sameness" among wheels that I would like to bring into question in this very work. In any case, I have tried to steer a middle course between obsessive engagement and hubristic disregard, and I hope the results will be found neither irrelevant nor obstructive to the works of my fellow-enjoyers, both now and in the future. To them, for that hope, for letting me do this kind of thing, for their distant company, for their very cacophony of incompatible views and their strident resistance to each other, for their will to victory and the effulgence of multiplicities that are its unintended side effects, I offer my gratitude. The spaces between us, but also that between which the spaces are, have made this book possible.

LI 理 AND COHERENCE

Recap *of* Ironies of Oneness and Difference *and Terminological Clarifications*

In a previous work, called *Ironies of Oneness and Difference,* I tried to unravel the development of notions of coherence in early Chinese thought as an alternative to models of thinking, mainly Greek and European in origin, that build upon the assumption that words such as "same" and "different" describe facts about the world and refer to real attributes of things, that the distinction between "sameness" and "difference" is in some way absolute—in other words, that things, or certain aspects of things, or facts, or qualities, simply *are* the same as certain other things or facts or aspects, and different from certain other things or facts or aspects. It was necessary to trace the various alternatives to this way of viewing things in Chinese thought in such a seemingly abstract and thoroughgoing manner, I believe, in order to comprehend the later development of various understandings and usages of the term Li 理[1] in Chinese thought. Most students of the Chinese philo-sophical tradition have probably noticed that again and again they come up against a repeated tendency toward two kinds of counterintuitive claims that present persistent interpretive problems: first, assertions concerning the relation between oneness and manyness, which do not seem to be applied consistently or intelligibly, or to separate from one another neatly, and sec-ond, the surprising importance everywhere—in metaphysics, epistemology, ethics, and axiology—of *negations and negative formulations,* which are given a positive value, serving often as groundings of affirmations.[2] These are the two main problems I am hoping to clarify with the concepts of "ironic coherence" and "non-ironic coherence" and their relation to Li; for I hope

1

to show that the one-many problem and the negation problem, and also the related problem of omnipresence, are all closely intertwined, and that this intertwining is most evident in the interplay of ironic and non-ironic coherence that comes to be embodied in the term *Li*. That is what I'll be trying to do in this book. So before launching into the discussion of Li, I would like to repeat the summary of my conclusions about "coherence" from that earlier work.

In that work I attempted to draw attention to several emergent conceptions of coherence in early Chinese thought, conceived of as a fundamental category accounting for the presence, value, sustainability, and intelligibility of things. This involved delineating two intertwining variants of this conception, the non-ironic and the ironic. In both, we identified coherence as a founding, fundamental category, from which sameness and difference are negotiable, non-ultimate derivatives. Why are things what they are, as they are, able to continue being what they are, and having the values they have? Because of the way they cohere. If they cohere differently, they are different things, have different identities. Harmonizing in a certain way allows things to manifest in a particular way, and this is the ultimate category beyond which no further specification of their ontic status can be made. Their "value," on the other hand, is itself merely another kind of coherence: a function solely of the relation between these manifested identities and certain human desires and endeavors, a second-order coherence between two first-order coherences. In sum, to be seen, known, shown as having a certain identity and value derives from a relation to a particular context, most centrally a context of human desires and the discerning, exemplary eye of a sagely person steeped in coherence with a tradition of other such persons. These reflections will put us in a position to see how "centrality" and "coherence" converge into the meaning of Li, and how this sort of notion developed through various partial prefigurements in Confucian and Daoist thought.

In the *Analects*, we saw Confucius described as "not having any constant teacher" 何常師之有, and yet finding his teacher everywhere. Here we see already the structure of centrality and coherence. Confucius himself is the "center," the determinant of the coherence, the "pattern," the "principle," the value. But he neither subjectively creates this value *ex nihilo* nor acts as a mere passive mirror of an objectively existing truth. The value he creates is a coherence, a readable converging, of aspects available everywhere, combined by the selective filter of Confucius's own responses and evaluations. His discernment is a selective frame that creates/finds coherence, the value-endowed style of culture, which is omniavailable, present in more than one place, not strictly reiterable except in the special sense of being continuable. We have here already the sprout of a model of a multilocality that is neither nominalist (i.e., denying the existence of any causally relevant multiply instantiated entities in our final ontology) nor realist (i.e., asserting the existence of causally relevant and repeatably instantiatable selfsame entities in our final ontology), manifesting in a cognition that is neither a correspondence with univocally preexisting objective facts nor a baseless projection of subjective fancies. These teachers are really there, and really making available a multiply instantiated something called the Dao of Kings Wen and Wu with its own independent causal relevance, providing models, standards, justifications and even psychological rewards, and constituting a whole that has a constitutive role to play in the essential characteristics inhering in each of the parts that comprise it. But that causal relevance overrides alternative available relevances only when Confucius sees it there, links up to it, names it, desires it, coheres with it, continues it.

The *Mencius,* we saw, continues this trend in the key passage at 7B24, awarding the honorary normative title "the Nature [of human beings]" (性 *xing*) to only a subset of the existing inborn capabilities of the human animal, which is thus neither a preexisting objective fact about humans (one could equally have selected out a different subset of these existing tendencies to be named "human nature," i.e., our defining inborn essence) nor a subjective projection (since this subset too is indeed really there). The criteria for making this selection were made more explicit here: precisely those spontaneous human tendencies that allow for coherence, that is, those that are appealing to (valued by) and discernible to other humans, and that create interpersonal cohesion among humans, are to be called the Nature. Examining the usage of the term *xing* in the rest of the text, we found that these are, more specifically, the desires that can be satisfied independently of external material conditions, that allow for the other (for example, material) desires to be equally nurtured and developed, the enjoyment of which is increased rather than decreased when shared, and so on. The desires for sensory gratification, on the other hand, are to be called "the Decree" (*ming* 命) only because they are not conducive to coherence in this sense: they isolate, they create strife because their satisfaction depends on external material resources, which may be in short supply, their enjoyment is decreased when shared, and so on. Thus, the class name "Human nature" is for Mencius neither objective nor subjective, neither nominalist nor realist; and here again we have a "center" embodied by a living human agent, the sage, whose manifestation of these virtues makes him the hub, the center, around which this style of being, humanity, converges. The presence of this center literally actualizes the normative coherence "humanity," the quality of humanness and equally the really existing community of human beings, just as Confucius's presence actualized the presence of his "teachers" in all people in his environment.

In the *Xunzi*, we find a seeming conflict between a nominalistic and a realist theory of naming, which is resolved once again by recourse to a human center, in this case the tradition of the sages and exemplary persons who literally give order to the cosmos through mandated ritual. But this too is neither creation nor passive reflection of coherence, neither purely objective nor purely subjective: in Xunzi's view, there are an overabundance of real distinctions, groupings, coherences in the world, for which the sages serve as a selective filter, propagating some while ignoring others, enforcing their standardized names in the same way that weights and measures are to be enforced in the marketplace. Omnipresence is here no longer mere "omniavailability" as it had been for Confucius and Mencius, but the "great coherence" (*dali* 大理), the value present in all parts of the organized whole that results from the exemplary man's selective ritual regulations determining which of the really occurring groupings of nature may be grouped into a valued whole, that is, a whole that creates the maximal compossible satisfaction of the entire range of human desires. Although this Great Coherence is not present without human cultural intervention, it is, once created, a causatively non-inert entity which really exists, instantiated in noncontiguous particular events and things, not merely normatively but descriptively, for it includes in its order not only the human but also the natural world. When seen and named so as to become coherent with the maximally coherent set of human desires, the natural cosmos becomes not merely seen and named in a coherent way, but actually endowed with a kind of order that is fully present in more than one instance and also has causal efficacy, such as contributing to keeping the world going in the way that suits human need, inspiring exultations of awe and aesthetic joy, guiding action, and serving as a standard, support, ground, encouragement and guarantor of human virtue.

In the *Laozi* tradition, we have the advent of ironic coherence: the idea of a form of *togetherness* (coherent) which is necessarily also *unintelligible*, unreadable (incoherent). The unhewn is the source, the stuff, the course/orienter and the end of all intelligible, determinate "hewn" entities, from which they emerge and toward which they all converge, negating them all and supporting them all, and through this negation and the course of arising from and return to this negation of themselves, it is also what *unifies* them all. This unity of all possible names, forms, values, entities brings them all together but only by being itself unhewn, unnamed, that is *indiscernible*. This is the ultimate cohering, also the ultimate value, from which lesser values/coherences emerge. The motif of the center is here transformed from the exemplary center of Confucianism, the model that inspires those around it to modify themselves because it is seen and valued, to the invisible center, which creates togetherness and value precisely by not being seen, not being valued. To be valued is to inspire imitation, which is to inspire competition, which is to create strife, which is to undermine ultimate coherence. To be seen is to be cut out from a background that is unseen, which means again a loss of the greatest coherence. Coherence is "ironic" in that the true coherence (value, togetherness, the unhewn or devalued from which the valued grows, which is inseparable from the valued, which accounts for the cycle of reversal from value to anti-value, and which is omnipresent in both the valued and the devalued) is by definition incoherent (indiscernible, invisible, indeterminate).

The writings of Zhuang Zhou present to us an overabundance of differing perspectives, each positing its own standard of rightness (是 *shi*), which is intrinsic to being anything at all, to being a particular something, to being a "this" (also 是 *shi*) at all. Being a "this," it is intelligible (coherent) only by virtue of its contrast to some "that," which is itself also a "this," and hence its own new perspective. This positing of the other perspective is *intrinsic* to being a perspective at all: to be a this is to also contradict being this. This and not-this thus necessarily "cohere," and it is only by doing so that they are intelligible (coherent). But this is again a specifically *ironic* coherence: any determinate entity (this) is coherent as what it is (this) by cohering with its own intrinsic positing of not-this. The coherence of any entity is thus always an ironic coherence. Zhuang Zhou's "wild card" perspective "responds but does not store": it reflects and affirms the "rightness" presented by each new situation, but does not consider this rightness, which is always both a *shi* and a *fei* (非), to be mutually exclusive with the opposite perspective, the opposed *shi/fei*, since the latter, the negation of itself, is intrinsic to its very intelligibility. *Shi* is "this," which is coherence, value, intelligibility; but in positing its own negation, which in turn negates "this," every coherence is also necessarily an incoherence, which again affirms Laozi's ironic coherence: value which is togetherness which is unintelligibility: what Zhuangzi calls "the torch of slippage and doubt" (滑疑之耀 *guyizhiyao*). The "togetherness" here comes in not as an overriding convergence of all things in a single vision (as in Xunzi's "Great Coherence" or even the ironic version in Laozi's "unhewn") but resides in a new application of the motif of the center, already prefigured in Mencius's critique of "clinging to the center but without altering by circumstance." (執中無權 *zhizhong wuquan*) (7A26). Zhuang Zhou introduces the idea of the pivot of Dao (道樞 *daoshu*), which is also the pivot of daos: the point where opposed *shi/feis* are not opposed, not mutually exclusive, precisely because of their mutual positing, and hence, in not "storing," they flow freely into one another. The center allows one to "travel two roads at once" (兩行 *liangxing*): this special kind of value bilocality is Zhuang Zhou's distinctive contribution to the problematic of coherence, universality, and omnipresence (as omniavailability of value) in Chinese thought. In the ironic conception of coherence, in both the Laozian and the Zhuangzian versions, the value, sustainability, and identity of things is seen as coming from their connection with other things (i.e., their own negation, in Laozi), or with particular human perspectives (in Zhuangzi). But here the aspect of *intelligibility* is denied: the true value and cohesion of things precludes their intelligibility as definitive particular identities. When identified definitively, they are falsified, and indeed lose the cohesion with all things, the value, the sustainability they originally enjoyed. The true X, then, is a non-X.

A notion is thus here developed of a kind of invisible center and its derivative totality that unifies (makes coherent) and brings entities to identifiable being (makes coherent) and gives value (makes coherent with human desire), but is itself coherent only in an ironic sense, that is, unifies and yet is itself unseen, unmanifest, unintelligible. In *Liji* texts such as the "Daxue" and "Zhongyong," as also in the Yin-Yang systems of the commentaries to the *Zhouyi* and Yang Xiong's *Taixuanjing*, we find a domestication of this notion of an unseen centering that functions for each emergent coherence as a creator and preserver, thereby accounting for and legitimizing all observable order and consistency (coherence). Overall coherence works through local pockets of invisibility or ironic coherence: the as-yet-unseen sprouts, the unmanifest but constant Inner Coherence (誠 *cheng*) which reveals itself in all individual affects and actions but never shows itself *simpliciter*, or as the least manifest aspect of a hexagram-situation, or as the Yin side of a Yin-Yang dyad which, however, works toward and is subordinated to the manifestation and purposes of the Yang. Yin-Yang represents a cohesion between ironic coherence-as-unintelligibility, value as necessarily nonexplicit (Yin), and non-ironic coherence-as-intelligibility, value as explicit (Yang). In all these systems (even, contrary to appearances, Yang Xiong's *Taixuanjing*, which gives definite values to things in spite of emphasizing the unintelligibility, *xuan* 玄, of the ultimate whole), the role of the unintelligible, the background, the unreadable togetherness in which value is rooted is here acknowledged and integrated into the system of Great Coherence, Xunzi's univocal view of a maximally coherent whole. These are non-ironic integrations of the ironic: the final word, the ultimate value, lies with the non-ironic, the definite and normative values and identities of nonnegotiable individual and collective coherences. We have thus begun to see the development of one form of *compromise* between these two positions, finding a place for this built-in mysteriousness pertaining to all possible identities without thereby conceding the possible nihilistic consequences of the ironic tradition, which would seem to undermine the value of tradition, moral instruction, and human endeavor, or at least make it troublingly negotiable.

These conclusions rested on certain theoretical considerations about coherence as such, and the peculiarities of classical Chinese conceptions of it. One trope that was particularly useful for illuminating this issue was based on a passage in the writings of Qian Mu, my translation of which I will reproduce here:

> Wherever there is a circle or a pendulum range, there will be what can be called a center. This center is not on the two sides, nor anywhere outside, but rather lies within [the range of the swing of the pendulum]. A pendulum swing or a cyclic progress never actually comes to rest at that center, but the center is always there, and is always still and solid as a center. It is as if the center were controlling the motion. The ceaseless and infinite motion seems eternally to be under the command of the center, completely controlled by the center, and thus we can say that it is perfectly moving and perfectly still, perfectly changing and perfectly constant. . . . Confucians want to point out a fixed center in this infinite cyclical back and forth, and they call this center "human nature." This is also what the Neo-Confucians of the Song and Ming dynasties liked to call "the Center which has not yet become manifest," "knowing the resting place," "stillness," "the master," "the constant." The Song Neo-Confucians said that this human Nature is precisely Li [coherence], but were unwilling to say that the Nature is qi [vital energy], because qi is just the motion, whereas Li is the Center of that motion. If there were truly pure qi with no Li, it would be like an unbridled horse—no one knows where it will run to. Heaven and earth would not be able to become heaven and earth, humans and things would not be able to become humans and things. There would be absolutely no way of handling or explaining the myriad different types and forms of things. The reason we now have this "Heaven and Earth," and these "humans" and these "things," is because within the qi there is this Li. Because there is Li in qi, there is constancy and predictability, which is called "the Nature" when viewed as active and emerging from within, and as "the Decree" when viewed as passive and coming from without. But in reality this one motion is at once active and passive, internal and external, indivisibly, which is why the Nature and the Decree are seen to have a common source. Both are ways of describing this motion itself, but emphasizing different aspects of it.
>
> "The Good" is what we call the constancy in this eternal change, the center in this unceasing motion, this relatively easily

grasped and known nature. Good is just the constant tendency of this motion. . . . Whatever is separated from it by a great distance is called bad. Good is just the center of this motion, evil is nothing but going beyond it or not coming up to it. . . . Although human affairs also go through endless transformations and never stay the same, there is a constancy or a center to them. If you try to separate yourself from this constancy or center and just move straight forward, you will find that it is impossible. For example, peace and struggle are phenomena that arise alternately in human life; they usually form a cycle, a back and forth, moving from peace to struggle and then from struggle back to peace. Within this process too there is a center or a constancy. Struggle must search for peace, and peace must resist struggle (that is, must not be afraid of struggle). So peace which is close to struggle and struggle that is close to peace are both capable of continuing, and both can be called good. But struggle that is far removed from peace and peace that is far removed from struggle are both far removed from the center, so that neither can form a constancy or attain any continuity. Going too far and not coming up to it are equally bad, and both of these can be called evil. Evil is just whatever cannot be constant (sustainable). The same is true of sickness and health. Usually people think a healthy person is free of sickness, but in reality if there were no sickness, how could there be the work of metabolism, assimilating and excreting? The function of excretion is a type of sickness that is not far removed from health (and hence is good). The same is true of work and rest; to rest so much you can no longer work is evil and not good, and to work so much you can no longer rest is equally evil and not good. But people usually think of life as positive, death as negative, peace as positive and struggle as negative, health and work as positive and sickness and rest as negative, and then they start thinking that the positive side is good and the negative side is evil. But according to the theory we are developing here, as long as evil stays close to good, it is no longer evil, and indeed, if good is too far removed from evil it is no longer good.[3]

I will repeat what I said there about this trope, which I will refer to henceforth as "Qian Mu's Pendulum." I quote this passage at length because we will have many occasions to refer back to it in the pages that follow. I do not claim that this model applies perfectly for all Chinese thinkers.[4] Rather, I would like to suggest that in considering each Chinese thinker we are better off searching for something like this model and the ways in which he diverges from it than assuming something along the lines of the universal/particular model, or a whole/part model, or a substance/accident model, and the particular handlings of sameness into difference that they tend to imply. For this brilliant metaphor gives us a key by which to unlock many of the problems that we will find confronting us there, to be contrasted with the basic metaphors of mimesis, or imposing a shape onto a material that informs the Greek speculations. It is crucial to note, first of all, that the sort of "coherence" indicated here necessarily includes both *sustainability* and *value*, which are here seen as one and the same, as *synonyms*, and inseparably connected to the idea of intelligibility (the graspability of the still, virtual center as opposed to the motion of the pendulum itself) and to "centrality," a neutral point connecting to two extremes conceived as a dyadic opposition. It also provides us with a strong sense of why it is preferable to speak of "coherence" for such ideas, rather than simply some form of "harmony." For what is at stake here is literally the holding together of the parts, their grouping with one another as a condition of their being present at all, their identifiability as what they are. If any part flies off to too great a distance from the center, and from the opposite extreme, it ceases to be sustainable as itself, ceases to be itself (e.g., health too far from sickness ceases to be health). It is the coherence between the parts that not only sustains the whole, but sustains each of the parts as what it is, or as anything at all (whatever it may become after "flying off" would, on this model, be determined by its relation to *some other* center and the corresponding opposite to which it would thus be connected). And this coherence with the whole, and with the center, is really just a shorthand way of designating the relation to the other parts, or better, the opposite part. The "center" is picked out and privileged because it alone provides "coherence" in the other sense: intelligibility, identity, definite characteristics. The whole can be identified, grasped, predicted, only through the center. The center is what "shows up" to observing awareness of the circulation between the extremes.

We might note also the rather *approximate* nature of this center as a summing up of the motion involved: it is determinative, in that "too great" a distance from it will lead to a part's demise. But this does not necessarily specify the exact range of each motion, which might be more or less distant in any case, swinging a little erratically from time to time, as long as it doesn't exceed a certain range. In other words, the "control" of the center, on this model, allows for a certain randomness. It is not conceived here as control in the sense of the issuing of a command that must be exactly obeyed, or laying down a track guiding every detail of the activity. Note also the manner in which this centrality is both immanent and transcendent: it is a function of the two poles, does not really preexist them, and has only a virtual existence, but at the same time it is their "controller" in the sense that their behavior and determinate identities are derivable from their relation to this virtual center. In this sense it plays a role similar to that of a "transcendent" fundamental reality, the independent variable that determines the behavior of everything related to it. But the pendulum model also allows us to intuit the manner in which it is simultaneously not transcendent at all. The center does not belong to a separate ontological realm, being itself merely a certain fact about the two poles, namely, a way of describing their relation to one another.

In *Ironies of Oneness and Difference* some effort was also made to address some of the founding metaphors underlying the classical Greek methods of conceiving the relations among things in terms of their sameness and difference. These typically had to do with notions of a strictly and precisely repeatable Form being imprinted into a formless Matter, or of a selfsame Substance underlying a multitude of diverse Accidents or Attributes—some notion of a particular self-standing entity with a variety of aspects "belonging" to it as "properties," or, grammatically and logically, a single identical subject with various genuinely distinct predicates. All such notions offer us certain presuppositions about the relation between sameness and difference. In the case of Form and Matter and the various derivatives of this notion, such as the concepts of "essence" and "instantiation," we noted that while Form as such irreducibly involves in itself both a sameness and a difference, it is at the same time a device for keeping this sameness and this difference perfectly separate: a shared self-same essence remains mathematically one and the same in every instantiation, while maintaining absolute difference from every other essence. This attempted perfect continence among essences, however, cannot be maintained absolutely, for the commonality between diverse essences continues to leak into any thinking process that attempts to relate them, to wit, in any instance of thinking qua thinking. Hence, we have the stopgap of subsuming species into genus, of nested essences arranged in a single unchanging hierarchical taxonomy, imagined as a downward-branching tree. By means of this expedient, the aspect of sameness and the aspect of difference among any entities can be made to appear to remain perfectly distinct facts. Hence "Dog" and "Horse" are "the same" *in that* they share the selfsame essence of "Animal, Vertebrate, Mammal," etc., but differ *in that* each has a specific essence modified by its distinguishing feature. By introducing the notion of various "respects" as if it were an ontological fact, by distinguishing "the respect in which" they are the same and "the respect in which" they are different, the ontological ultimacy of sameness and difference as final facts can be maintained. The essence is the same, simpliciter, in every instantiation, but this essence is different, simpliciter, from every other essence, and from its instantiations qua instantiations.

Indeed, we may go so far as to suggest that the entire idea of the so-called "law" of non-contradiction is a further expression of this tendency.

The Law of Non-Contradiction is given by Aristotle in three forms, according to the accepted doxa: the ontological form, the logical form, and the psychological form. The "ontological version" (*Metaphysics* IV 3 1005b19–23) concerns what predicates can belong to the same subject. "The same attribute cannot at the same time belong and not belong to the same subject and in the same respect." The logical version (*Metaphysics* IV 3 1011b13–14) concerns two contradictory propositions: they cannot both be true at once. The psychological version (*Metaphysics* IV 3 1005b23–25) concerns two beliefs: one cannot believe both two contradictory claims at once. The latter two versions are dependent on the first version; if the first version were false, the other two would also be false. But in the context of our present discussion, we might notice an enormous red flag in Aristotle's: it is the words translated "at once," "at the same time," and "in the same respect." With these words, the entire principle puts itself under the suspicion of being a world-historical instance of gerrymandering hand waving.[5] What is a "respect"? A "respect in which something is asserted" is, perhaps, the part or side or aspect of some matter that is to be considered of relevance in a particular instance, as determined by a set of relations, or a context, abstracting one aspect or part of the item in question and addressing that alone, in isolation from the other aspects or parts of that very same thing or fact or topic. How do we determinate which among all the characteristics and relations of the thing, and how many of them, get to count as a single "respect"? Answer: only those relations and characteristics that produce a non-contradictory set of predicates count as a single respect. Therefore, "in the same respect" is a circular condition. I allow only as much into a "respect" as can turn out to be non-contradictory. Whatever leads to a contradiction I simply relegate to another "respect." The same can be said, *mutatis mutandis*, for what it means to say something is true "in one sense" and untrue "in another sense." Indeed, less intuitively but nonetheless just as damagingly, the same can be said about the qualifications concerning time, that is, that something might be true "at one time" and untrue "at another time." How long is one "time"? Unless moments are dimensionless simples, which would present insuperable metaphysical difficulties, the duration of a "time" in this sense must be variable, and the same problems about their definition applies: however much time can include a set of events or predicates or actions that are non-contradictory in whatever sense is under examination will be what counts as a single time in that case. The Law of Non-Contradiction is true only in the same way that the "law" that there are twelve inches to a foot is true. Whatever exceeds twelve inches is considered part of the next foot. This gives us no ontological information at all. We should be no more amazed to find it always true than we are amazed to find that, no matter where we might search throughout the cosmos, however many billions of light-years away, we always find that every foot of space has exactly twelve inches in it, no more and no less. It tells me nothing about the world, other than the finitude and conditionality of anything determinate (i.e., that there are always more inches than twelve available for counting). The Law of Non-Contradiction does not tell me that the world, or any actual entity in the world, or any truth about the world, is non-contradictory, nor that there are really samenesses and differences, simpliciter, in the world. It just tells me that wherever I can describe two contrary characteristics as coexistent in some composite, I will describe that coexistence as a non-contradictory complexity of a single entity, and whenever the elements in a composite entity fail to be capable of coexisting, due to a conflict between them, I will simply define the elements as no longer belonging to a single entity. As a matter of policy, we separate out whatever can be subsumed into a single concept as a sameness and name that the essence, and call whatever is leftover the difference. Every thing is thus both the same and different from every other thing, but "in different respects."

Thus, we see an entire logical system built up on this circular law, which requires us to separate the shared essence from the differing instantiations. The "Realist" interpretation of this arrangement will emphasize the reality of the sameness of the shared essence, which will have to be considered some kind of genuinely selfsame entity that can be instantiated unchanged in more than one time and place, and which continues to be exactly what it is whether or not it is so instantiated. This would mean that its existence has a kind of availability that is independent of whether one or more human beings ever makes mentions or experiences it. Moreover, the Realist essence must be causally relevant, that is, it must be real at least in the sense of playing some actual causal role in making at least some actual entities be what they are and do what they do, while the "Nominalist" will emphasize the difference between individual species or individual members of a species as what is ultimately real, denying that there are any nonparticular or nonconcrete entities that are as ultimately real or that are as causally relevant, in our final ontology of both the natural and human worlds, as particular and concrete entities. But in either case, what is the same and what is different really pertains to these existing things, a definitive, nonnegotiable something that has an unchanging identity in all contexts.

It is useful to consider, in contrast, how same and different are to be conceived on the pendulum model. Again, although of course it would be *possible* to describe this situation in terms of a sameness (what the two extremes "have in common" is the characteristic of "not being too far from the center"), this description is clearly less useful here than one that stresses a certain sui generis manner of interfusion of same and different. We have an alternate way of organizing sameness and difference here, which is reducible neither to the dividing off of sameness and difference in the manner of Form and Matter, nor of Substance and Accident, nor again of Whole and Part or of a Totality and its Aspects. Nor do we have a total transcendence of all pairs of opposites typical of negative theologies or philosophies of the Absolute (i.e., where all finite determinations, including same and different, are deemed inadequate to describe the truly real, the Absolute, which as infinite can be neither "this" nor "that"). For built into the idea of the extremes and the center in Qian Mu's pendulum model is the sense that what constitutes the *difference* between these two extremes is precisely *continuity* with its opposite, the fact that they *share* a neutral connecting center. Conversely, what constitutes their own specifiable *identities* and sustainability as what they are, as well as their continuity with one another, is precisely their concrete *non-exclusion* of their opposites, their continual tendency to veer back toward their opposites, their connection to and contact with the difference that excludes them, their interaction, interface, and overlap with difference. What joins them as members of this coherence is not so much sharing a certain characteristic, but rather precisely the harmonic coherence of their differences from one another. What makes health health? Its non-exclusion of sickness. What makes sickness sickness (rather than death, which would be the end of sickness)? Its non-exclusion of health. What makes health and sickness belong to the same coherence? Not their sharing of a single essence, but rather their complementarity. On this model, are health and sickness absolutely different from one another, "different" as the total exclusion of sameness? They cannot be, because a health from which all sickness is expunged here ceases to exist as health, and vice versa. The same? But if the two sides are the same, there is no swing, and thus no center, and thus no two sides. Are they different from the center? But the intelligibility of each is merely an aspect of the intelligibility of this center: what we see is only this one thing, identified by the character of the intelligible center; the rest is an unknowable blank. The same? But the center is a merely virtual, approximate point defined by the swing between the extremes, such that a pendulum resting at the center point would cease to function as the center. If it were "all center," it would be "no center." What this single concrete image perhaps most clearly shows us is how profoundly inappropriate these questions about same and different are to the case at hand.

Perhaps more to the point, if we consider closely the point about intelligibility, we can see how this notion inevitably tends toward an idea of nested identities that connects to what we will be calling the ironic model of coherence. For whatever is identifiable, on Qian's model, is always a center. Activity that does not yet turn around, that does not revert into a finite range, that is continually moving forward and hence is constitutively unfinished, cannot be identified and known. Knowing per se depends on the presence of cycles, oscillations, which are intelligible only as their approximate centers. But this means that when we speak of "health" and "sickness," say, as the two extremes within one cycle, identified perhaps as the center intelligible as "physical life," each of these two extremes must be a kind of center in its own right (for they have been identified, and identification is only of centers). Hence, within the larger vortex of "physical life," we have the two smaller vortices of "health" and "sickness." This sort of nesting would have to go on indefinitely, as long as there are identifiable elements. As an aid to visualizing this, we might expand the pendulum model into three dimensions, somewhat along the line of the Rutherford model of atomic structure (it should go without saying that this is merely a heuristic device; I do not mean to suggest that the early Chinese had in any way anticipated the knowledge of atomic structure—quite the contrary). The cloud of vibrating electrons is knowable only as a unit, which is located at and as the nucleus. But if we focus on trying to identify any further component, say an electron, on this model we will find another swarm of vibrations grouped around a virtual center, as which this swarm is identified. Expanding outward, we will find that the entire "atom" is an electron—in this case, one of two extremes of a pendulum swing—in a larger "atom." Each element is a vortex. Its center is the vertex by which it is grasped and known. This sense of mutual inclusion might play out, as in the non-ironic conception of coherence later found in, for example, the schematic charts of the sixty-four hexagrams of the *Zhouyi* broken down into their Yin-Yang line components, as a one-way subsump-tion model, superficially similar to the taxonomy of species and genus we find on the universal/particular model, or set and set-membership model. But the composition of each level by means of the vortex of mutually entailing opposites, each of which is also composed of some pair of opposites, skews this comparison decisively, particularly with respect to the highest level, but also in terms of the interconnections between the lower levels. In the full-blown ironic version, this will be pushed to the point of undermining any fixed or nonnegotiable knowability concerning the ultimate identity of any of the components. But even in the non-ironic version, there will be many interesting complications to the conception of sameness and difference among the component parts, which we will be examining in detail on a case by case basis in the pages that follow.

Centrality in this sense is itself *value*, is itself the *connection* of diverse and opposed particulars, is itself *intelligibility*: the three meanings of coher-ence with which we have been grappling. Only a center is what unifies, is discernible, and bestows value (sustainability), as Qian's analysis suggests. As we shall see in the pages that follow, whenever we talk about Li, we will have to think first and foremost about this idea of a *center*.

We should thus highlight two points about coherence as so conceived. Coherence means both "balance" or equilibrium and "productivity" or the ability to continue in new forms into the future. As balance, a quantitative relation is implied here, a proper proportion, as between the two extremes in the swing of Qian's pendulum. When either goes too far quantitatively, it disrupts the balance, loses its connection to the center and to the other extreme. Maintaining this proportion, and the ability to revert to the opposite, is precisely what allows both sides to continue forward in time, and it is this that constitutes value. The resulting vaguely quantitative but never strictly quantified sense of balancing of contrasted elements has been justly described as an "aesthetic order,"[6] in contrast to "logical order." For it involves an aesthetic sense of *altering quantitative proportions* "by feel" in order to produce a qualitative change, as in the cutting of jade to make it a marketable product, or the adjustment of mixtures of ingredients in a recipe, or the adjustment of tones into an experienced harmony. It is especially noteworthy that this balance is generally conceived, as in the pendulum model, in terms of the proportioning of two opposite qualities, a dyad of terms. This sense of coherence as the production of quality by changes in quantity is of great significance, and it is in this sense that we will understand harmony and equilibrium here.

Second, the quantitatively *produced* qualities are said to be *productive* of further coherences—of more equilibrium, or more life, in a state of intelligible continuity with the past—the production of progeny, culturally and biologically. Equilibrium implies here both life (preservation of the currently intelligible coherence) and continuity (furtherance of related coherences in the future, forming among them another intelligible coherence). It also means the production of larger, more inclusive coherences, as between members of larger and more complex social groups, as we tried to show in the discussion of the *Mencius* and the *Xunzi* in the previous volume.

Coherence in the sense used here is thus not merely consistency among elements of a whole, in the sense that they can coexist without interfering in one another's continued existence, or are mutually compatible and not contradictory. It is also not merely the relation of coherence in the logical sense of mutual support or mutual entailment of a number of elements. Among available conceptual constructs, our notion of coherence perhaps comes closest to the notion of a Gestalt, which is a combination of elements which form a relation that emerges as a single readable figure, an intelligible whole, which also has some sense of value attached to it, which attracts the eye and the mind through the release of tension and reduction of dissonance, and through its relatively easy assimilation into the current project of the viewer ("a strong Gestalt"). There is also an important element of ambiguity to a Gestalt, as illustrated by the well-known images of the vase faces, or Wittgenstein's duck-rabbit, which can point us toward the development of the ironic sense of coherence. It is possible but not so inevitable to include a sense of continuance to the value implication of the strong Gestalt. But the quantitative balance between dyadic opposites (the opposite poles of the pendulum swing), and with it the sense of temporal periodicity, does not seem to be as clearly a part of the basic notion of a Gestalt as it will be in the Chinese notions of coherence to be dealt with here. Nor indeed does the idea of a Gestalt lend itself quite so easily to the notion of inclusion of the observer, and thus the multiplication of further inclusive Gestalts growing around the original one. A Gestalt is more usually conceived as something viewed from outside, as an objective presence. The Chinese ideas of coherence would be more like a Gestalt that includes not only, say, the lines on the page that can form the emergent figure of a triangle, but also the eyes, nervous system, and prevailing desires of the living being experiencing that triangle. A coherence would then be a sort of 3-D Gestalt, but with the dyadic periodicity, the ability to create further Gestalts which form a larger Gestalt with the original one, the inclusion of the observer, and the value element stressed and developed to a much greater degree. With these adjustments, we can perhaps view coherence as a modified version of the notion of Gestalt.

One of the key themes of the discussion of coherence in the aforementioned work was the distinction between *ironic* and *non-ironic* coherence, and the various sorts of compromises between them that emerged in the early Chinese tradition. This has been briefly alluded to already, but given its prominence in the analysis to follow, it seems worthwhile to repeat the more thorough exploration of these terms and their implications.

We can note in the above reflections an implicit tension in the idea of coherence, which will serve as an engine of many further developments. For what after all is the criterion for coherence? It is not just any set of items that stick together. In early Chinese thinking, it must always be a set of things that *form a coherent grouping also with some human desire*. This will give us two criteria for coherence:

1. A grouping counts as a coherence when it creates pleasure, like the harmonious enjoyment of a flavor or a musical harmony. This pleasure may be described as a further coherence, a meta-coherence, for it is the cohering of this togetherness with some human desire. Usually, it is associated also with (a) stability, balance, or equilibrium (since to join with what destabilizes the health and stability of the organism would be experienced as displeasure), generally conceived as a balance of two opposite qualities in a *roughly quantitative but not strictly quantified*

sense, and (b) progeny, growth, continuance. Indeed, this sense of coherence as implying life, continuation, and growth runs through the tradition in various forms, from Mencian reflections on *xing* or Human Nature, on the one hand, into the Neo-Confucian glosses of Li as ceaseless production and reproduction (生生不息 *sheng sheng bu xi*), as derived from the "Great Commentary" to the *Zhouyi*. It is a balancing of contraries that must keep within a certain "distance" of one another, "neither too far nor too near," in order to maintain their existence, which is to say, less metaphorically, which must be able to change into one another, with neither too much nor too little resistance to this transformation. This is what makes it intelligible as possessing some particular identity, and this is also the source of its value, its ability to sustain itself and create beyond itself.

2. But there is, as it were, a flip side of the notion of continuance and ceaseless progression—seen instead as an infinite regress. In terms of coherence as readability, we notice immediately that when a discernible characteristic becomes fully intelligible, one passes smoothly over it, it is no longer noticed. Since its presencing as coherence depends on desire, interest, human concern, *once it is entirely unproblematic, it ceases to be noticed.* Phenomenologically, perfectly intelligible presence erases itself; perfect presence passes into non-presence. Removed from its instability, its flow back toward its opposite, the problem of maintaining its delicate balance, it ceases to be present at all. What is stably present is no longer present. In terms of coherence as grouping, the irony can be discerned in a related but slightly different way: when parts cohere perfectly, they become a whole forming a part in a larger whole, demanding a larger context, until the largest whole is reached. But the largest whole is necessarily incoherent, unintelligible, for it has no further outside context from which it can be distinguished and to which it can be contrasted—and distinguishing and contrasting are alone what make a thing intelligible and coherent as some particular essence rather than another, as having any characteristics at all. Perfect togetherness and harmony of parts presses forward to a greater whole, and points already toward the all-inclusive largest whole, which must itself be indeterminate, since determination derives from contextualization within a whole. In terms of coherence as pleasure: when a specific desire is consummated, it is no longer desired, but enjoyed,

incorporated into experience rather than held out as an object
of pursuit and attention; the desire as such thereby dies. Perfect
harmonic coherence between a human desire and some object
eliminates the relationship between them altogether.[7] Once all
the parts cohere into a single something, readable as a "one,"
this means that it has been absorbed as a single unit into something else, a part of another, larger whole. The search for ever
more coherence is, in other words, inherent in coherence, and
thus ceaseless. Each coherence cries out for further context.
The parts can only cohere if the whole coheres with a greater
context, and then this context becomes a new whole in search
of a yet larger context. We judge something to be coherent
only when it coheres with an outside (in the first example,
with some of our desires)—but this proposition alone ensures an
infinite regress, for once the new coherence is found it becomes
the inside seeking a new outside. Since the most all-inclusive
totality is necessarily incoherent (i.e., unintelligible, unname-
able, devoid of determinate identity or characteristics, all of
which necessarily derive from contextualization within a *larger*
whole), and the identity of all lesser coherences depends on
their relation to this larger context, the ultimate intelligibility of *any* definitive identity must be questioned. I call this
"ironic" because it means that any attribution of identity can
only be meant ironically, since all of them depend on relation
to a context that is itself necessarily incoherent (the whole),
such that every coherence is itself ultimately incoherent, and
this incoherence is not added on to the original coherence, but
is the actual principle of its being coherent in the first place,
its relation to its context: each identity, fully realized, reveals
itself to be an effacement of its original putative identity. It is
this "ironic" treatment of coherence that we will find in the
Daoist works, where suddenly we find a spate of claims about
how any positively valued (i.e., coherent) term (e.g., accomplishment, influence, long-lastingness, knowledge, virtue) is
accomplished only in its apparent *negation*, for example, most
famously in slogans such as the *Daodejing*'s "doing nothing and
yet thereby leaving nothing undone" (無為而無不為 *wuwei er
wubuwei*), "Guiding courses can be taken as guides, but if so
they fail to reliably guide" (道可道非常道 *daokedaofeichangdao*),
"noticeable values can be valued, but if so they fail to have reliable values" (名可名非常名 *mingkemingfeichangming*), and "the
highest virtue attains no virtue" (上德不德 *shangde bude*) and

the hundreds of similar claims found in these works.[8] What all
these claims have in common is a doubled structure which at
once affirms and denies the same term, denying X in its literal
sense and affirming *thereby* the ironic sense of X as it emerges
from this very lack of literal X. I suggested in the prequel that
the double irony of these claims can best be understood on the
model of a prospective picnic goer on rainy day sayings, "Oh,
this is *great* weather for a picnic!" "Great weather" is meant
ironically: the pouring rain is precisely *not* great weather for a
picnic. But even this irony is itself ironic: for ultimately rain *is*
in fact great weather for a picnic, "in another sense": without
such weather, there could be no picnics, for there could be no
food, for there could be no growth of plants, on which all our
picnics depend directly or indirectly. So because this weather
is not literally great weather, it is great weather. It fulfills the
original demand set up by the term "great," but does so precisely
by failing to satisfy it in the original, non-ironic sense. The
same is true of Dao, the ironic Dao which is the failure of all
literal small-d daos: it does what small-d daos are suppose to
do (bring order, sustainability, harmony, satisfaction) but does
so precisely by not providing them literally in the expected
way. Real values are attained by failing to attain value as originally conceived: this is ironic value. Real virtue, the virtuosity
implicitly promised by the ideal of virtue, is attained by failing
to attain that ideal virtue literally. This is ironic virtue. Real
coherence (sticking together, harmony, value, continuance,
sustainability) is attained, ironically, by failing to attain literal
coherence (intelligibility, definite togethernesses of particular
groupings, literal harmony, literal virtues, literal continuance
as some particular thing). Ironic coherence will continue to
be the central theme of interest in Neo-Daoism and Chinese
Buddhism works as well, finally made into an explicit principle of all experience in Tiantai Buddhism, under the name of
the Three Truths, where (local) coherence and (global) incoherence are literally identified as synonyms, alternate ways of
stating the same fact. But Confucian texts such as the "Great
Learning" and "Doctrine of the Mean," and indeed the entire
Yin-Yang system of the *Zhouyi* commentaries, sketch out some
non-ironic solutions to the same kind of difficulty, non-ironic
incorporations of ironic motifs. *Ironies of Oneness and Difference*
can be consulted for a fuller and more detailed exposition of
these categories and their range of application. In the pages

that follow we will trace out the various convergences of ironic
and non-ironic coherence, which take many forms, including
the opposite compromise, namely, the ironic incorporation of
non-ironic motifs.

Now that we have reviewed the stage-setting, we may turn to the
problem of Li in Chinese thought.

ONE

LI 理 AS A FUNDAMENTAL CATEGORY IN CHINESE THOUGHT

The term Li has a strange history. It came into prominence as the central metaphysical category rather gradually, seemingly through the intervention of Buddhist uses, taking on its decisive role only in the thought of the Cheng Brothers (Cheng Hao 程顥, 1032–1085, and Cheng Yi 程頤, 1033–1107), and further developed by Zhu Xi (朱熹, 1130–1200), read back into the pre-Buddhist tradition, although its actual appearance in the early texts is sparse and problematic. Thereafter, the term Li becomes the focus of several explicit controversies in the history of Chinese philosophy. These are well known. Cheng-Zhu Neo-Confucians (i.e., those following the line developed by Cheng Yi and Zhu Xi) critique Buddhists for understanding Li as only Emptiness. On the other hand, they critique Lu-Wang Confucians (i.e., those following the approach of Lu Xiangshan 陸象山, 1139–1192, and Wang Yangming 王陽明, 1472–1529) for understanding Li directly as Mind. Cheng-Zhu Confucians themselves, according to the standard interpretation, understand Li as the "principle" of all things, manifested more or less clearly and completely in each instance according to the balance and purity of the constituent *qi* of that thing. It is present in its entirety in each thing as that thing's true nature, accounting for the vitality and integrity of that thing as such. In man, it is the good human nature, the nature of heaven and earth, which is not the mind per se but discoverable as an aspect of mind, its pure unmanifest and balanced underpinning, from which the empirical human mind may deviate. As we shall see presently, it is this Cheng-Zhu usage, and its various aftermaths, that has been the primary target for modern writers trying to make sense of the term in the context of the encounter with Western philosophy that began in the twentieth century. Finally, the Qing Confucians, such as Dai Zhen 戴震 and Duan Yucai 段玉裁, critique *both* the Cheng-Zhu and the Lu-Wang Neo-Confucians for understanding

Li as an omnipresent universal principle of all things (whether Mind or the Nature), whereas its real, original meaning, they claimed, on the basis of classical etymological studies, was of the differentiating, particular forms of individual things, the "cuts" between them, not the bridges over these gaps. It is less known that a controversy about the unity and multiplicity of Li also emerges within Tiantai Buddhism, with the so-called Shanjia 山家 or "Home Mountain" school, represented most vocally by Siming Zhili 四明知禮 (960–1024), asserting that Li is both a unity and as multiplicity (known respectively as 理總 *lizong* and 理別 *libie*), and each phenomenon similarly serves both as a unifier and as one of many items unified in any other phenomenon (known as 事總 *shizong* and 事別 *shibie*, respectively), while his opponents, the so-called Shanwai 山外 or "Off-Mountain" school, take Li purely as unity, with diversity accounted for solely by 事 *shi*, as in Huayen thought (that is, allowing only 理總 *lizong* and 事別 *shibie*, though as we shall see later in this book, what is really lacking here is only 理別 *libie*; both Huayan and the Off-Mountain Tiantai writers do actually acknowledge 事總 *shizong*). The term Li clearly has not only exceptional importance, but also exceptional ambiguity. What has allowed it to play these multiple roles?

Before making our own attempt to answer this question, we need to examine a few of the previous attempts at understanding this problem, on some of which we will be building, and the history of the term Li in classical Chinese texts prior to the advent of the brand-name philosophers. In particular, we must make clear what we mean when offering "coherence" as a way of explaining the meaning of Li, and the related problems, or absence thereof, of universals and particulars, form and matter, classes and class membership, nominalism and realism, relativism and natural-kinds, and so on.

Fung Yulan 馮友蘭 famously and rather rashly declared that the Cheng-Zhu Neo-Confucian notion of "Li" 理 was the traditional Chinese equivalent of the Platonic Forms, based on their putative transcendence to their instantiations, and their essence-like role as a criterion by which to define the identity of these instances.[1] This suggestion quickly aroused refutations, as the many points of disharmony between the two doctrines became apparent. Most obvious among these is the fact that, while the Platonic forms are many, although perhaps somehow grounded in a greater unity, the Neo-Confucian Li seem to be simultaneously both one and many. Zhu Xi, for example, states at times both that there is only one Li, and that each thing has its own specific defining Li, and that somehow all these particularized Li are one and the same Li (which is also called the Great Ultimate, 太極 *taiji*). The entire supreme Li is contained in each differentiated entity, Zhu Xi tells us in other contexts, as the reflection of the moon is reflected completely in a multitude of bodies of water. It is not just that Li per se is both one and many; the multiplicity of it is not limited only to the multiple universals, but also to each and every particular thing. It is not just that Li is at once equivalent to the all-inclusive "Form of the Good" *and* to the particular universals "Blue," "Red," "Justice," "Love," but that it is also the specific Li of this blue chair and that red hat, including also man-made objects as much as natural objects. Li includes as much every individual existence as it does universals—Du Fu's collected works, for example, or the existence of a particular individual person: all these things have their Li.[2] The Li of this boat is what makes this boat this boat, while the Li of boats is what makes boats boats. Li are not in any straightforward sense universals. Indeed, as we shall see, the one-many distinction is precisely what the concept of Li has the least use for, in keeping with the lack of a grammatical distinction between singular and plural in the language in which the idea was developed. If these statements are taken as assertions of definitive doctrine, we have an obvious mismatch with the concept of Platonic ideas. The handling of the one-many problem in Plotinus may be less of a problem here than it is in Plato himself; for in Plotinus, the oneness of The One seems to also be instantiated precisely as the Form-ness, so to say, of the many Forms that collectively comprise its first emanation. Even here, however, the forms remain self-identical across their many instantiations in particular things, unaffected by how or where they are instantiated, and thus do not seem to be able to include indifferently both classes and individuals on equal footing as Forms. That is, the unity or oneness formed by an individual entity instantiating many Forms, which are themselves many diversified instantiations of oneness, cannot be a oneness in the same sense, as would appear to be the case for the Cheng-Zhu Neo-Confucians.

Another discrepancy lies in the fact that the Platonic forms may or may not have an evaluative force to them. They do when they define, for example, a virtue, but a universal quality such as "redness" seems to be purely descriptive. There is, of course, a derivative though perhaps pervasive axiological sense in that a putative instantiation of a given form will be judged to be deficient if it fails to meet the definition embodied by the form; a chair is not a "good" chair, which is to say, a real chair, unless it accords with the Form of the chair. This axiological dimension is perhaps reflected in the role given to the sun-like Form of the Good in the *Republic,* and the implied equation between Being and Goodness that is easily derived from the Platonic position. Still, the axiological dimension of the Neo-Confucian Li is clearly front and center, to such an extent that they have been cited as a classic example of the traditional Chinese "fusion of fact and value."[3] The Li of a thing is both "what makes it so" (所以然之理

suoyiran zhi li) and "how it should be" (當然之理 *dangran zhi li)*, and ethical norms are derived directly from this fusion of "is" and "ought." As Graham astutely notes of Li as used by the Cheng brothers, it accounts "not for the properties of a thing but for the task it must perform to occupy its place in the natural order."[4] Not its passive qualities, but an activity to be done; not the properties it has in isolation, but its ways of relating to what is around it; not solely what it is, but a task, what it must do to continue to occupy the role it plays in the context of the whole. Here, we have the properties of thing only to the extent that properties are considered to be relations, the essence of a thing only to the extent that it is considered a conatus to continue to perform the task of maintaining a certain set of relationships. It is this in which the "chairness" of a chair is seen to reside: the "ness" is not a Platonic essence or a universal of "chair" that iterates identically in all chairs, but the possibility of doing the work required to continue to coexist in a certain set of relations. This could apply either to an individual entity performing the task of maintaining the individual relations that allow it to continue to perform the role of being what it is, or to a class of thing maintaining its relation with other classes, or with individual instances of that class, or with the whole of all objects and purposes.

For these and many other reasons, it has been notoriously difficult for Western interpreters to find a fitting interpretation for Li. Leibniz was the first Western thinker to try to do so, and with results as problematic as Fung's later attempt from the other side. Leibniz records that the Jesuits had learned that Li is described by "the Chinese" (actually, the canonical Cheng-Zhu Neo-Confucian sources) as equivalent to the following philosophical categories: the first principle, Reason, the foundation of all nature, the most universal reason and substance, the supreme being than which nothing is greater nor better. Li, Leibniz tells us, is pure, motionless, rarefied, without body or shape, and can be comprehended only through the understanding. It is the law that directs all things and is the intelligence that guides them. It is the Law and universal Order, according to which Heaven and Earth were formed, the origin, source, and principle of all things. It is the sole cause which moves Heaven in a uniform motion, sufficient unto itself, giving all species of being the ability to reproduce their kind, "this virtue not being in the nature of the things themselves and not depending at all upon them but consisting and residing in this Li." It has dominion over all, is present in all things, governs and produces the world as its absolute master. It is Being, Substance, Entity, infinite, eternal, uncreated, incorruptible. It is the principle of both physical and moral existence. It is indivisible and yet contains the most perfect multiplicity; it is the Grand Void but also the sovereign plenitude. It is compared to a circle, it is the Nature of things, it is truth and goodness. In short, it is the supreme being, endowed with "all manner of perfections, so that there can be nothing more perfect."[5]

Some of the Jesuits had argued that, in spite of these attributes, Li in the Chinese conception does not mean what the Christian tradition means by God, because it also is said to lack will, activity, life, design, and consciousness. Rather, it is Primal Matter, or at best the Primal Form, the Soul of the World in the sense employed by classical pagan thinkers.

Leibniz, however, argues that this cannot be so, that Li is indeed precisely what Christian philosophers mean by divinity. Leibniz asserts that, given the supreme attributes ascribed to Li, the denial that it has life, consciousness, will, and activity "must" mean merely that it lacks these things in their ordinary sense. It means that Li actually has these attributes in a much greater degree, in what theologians call the "eminent" sense, just as some negative theologians had denied "Being" to God, calling him instead beyond Being, or super-ens, *hyperousia*. The unquestioned assumption on both sides of this debate is that there is an excluded middle between activity and passivity, spirit and matter, dependence and transcendence. If something is active, it cannot be passive; if it is spiritual, it cannot be matter; if it is transcendent, it cannot be dependent on the world. In all his arguments, Leibniz relies on the assumption of the excluded middle, and presumes that the philosophical categories into which Li is being translated are the only ones possible. "I do not at all see how it could be possible for the Chinese to elicit from prime matter—as our philosophers teach it in their schools, as purely passive, without order or form—the origin of activity, of order and of all forms. I do not believe them to be so stupid or absurd."[6] Given the qualification offered in the phrase between the dashes ("purely passive, without order or form"), this is quite true. But it also begs the question. For the real issue here, of course, is whether there could be any other sets of assumptions with which to consider these questions, not premised on a prior separation of form from matter, active from passive, order from chaos, for instance, a separation that requires an absolute ontological difference with no overlap. (Ironically, as we shall see in the "Conclusion" to this book, Leibniz himself introduced a concept into philosophy that, in my view, comes much closer than any other in the European philosophical lexicon to actually describing the character of Li specifically in Cheng-Zhu Neo-Confucianism: not *hyperousia*, much less *divinity*, nor anything like *consciousness, design*, or *will*, but rather the concept of *compossibility*. Important qualifications are of course necessary concerning the nature of the *com-* here, and the absence of a God who stands above and beyond compossibility and, for Leibniz, must then go on to make a choice to make the preexisting compossibles actually exist, which will be addressed at the end of this book.)

The word *Li* is indeed an odd one, with an odd history. Without attaching undue importance to it, readers not proficient in Chinese might get some sense of the semantic range of this term by looking at the compounds in which it appears in the modern Chinese language, remembering that this cannot be used as reliable evidence for its meaning in the classical language of any particular period.[7] Pondering these usages, we may notice the range of senses spanning over our notions of "knowing," "noticing," "reason," "thinking," "rightness," "reasonability," "ordering," "pattern," "managing," and "standard of value." The connection between "noticing," "responding to," and "ordering" should particularly pique our interest here. We should note also that the standard modern translation of Plato does indeed use the term *lixing* 理型 (Li-form) to translate "Idea" in the Platonic sense. We should note also the easy transference of the nominal and verbal usage of the term in modern language.

The most useful starting point for probing more deeply the philosophical implications of the term Li is perhaps still Tang Junyi's seminal essay "Yuan Li" (原理 Tracing the Origin of Li), originally published in 1955 but later used as the opening chapter of the first volume of Tang's massive history of Chinese Philosophy.[8] In this work, Tang attempts a comprehensive overview of the usages of Li throughout the history of classical Chinese philosophy, separating out six distinct meanings of the term while also tracing its etymological bases. Tang's six senses of the term are: *wenli* (文理 Li in the context of cultural activities), *mingli* (名理 Li in logical reasoning about abstract philosophical attributes, considered by Tang to be synonymous in its usage with 玄理 *xuanli*, abstruse or metaphysical Li), *kongli* (空理 Li as Emptiness), *xingli* (性理 Li as Human Nature), *shili* (事理 Li pertaining to events or affairs), and *wuli* (物理 Li pertaining to concrete empirical things). Tang's discussion is illuminating, in particular his discussion of the role of human activity in the definition of Li even in its apparently most concrete and objective usages; the distinction between "pattern" as a simple fact found in an object and Li as a kind of interface between human subjectivity and the structure of the surrounding world will be crucial to our discussion below. Tang also brings into focus the problem of *unity versus multiplicity* that formed one of the essential points of contention between Song-Ming Neo-Confucians on the one hand (Li as the unifying principle of all things) and their later critics among Qing Confucians on the other (Li as the separating, distinguishing forms of individual things). Tang's analysis is rooted, quite reasonably, in one of the earliest extant usages of the term *Li*, a passage from the "Minor Odes" 小雅 section of the *Shijing*, 詩經 ("The Book of Songs"), Ode 210, "Xin nanshan" 信南山, where we find the following verse:

信彼南山、維禹甸之。畇畇原隰、曾孫田之。我疆我理、南東其畝。
Truly, the region of that southern hill
Was governed so as to bring forth crops by Yu.
The lands of those marshes and plains
Are now made into fields by his distant descendants.
We separate them, we *divide* them
Into acres stretching to the south and to the east.

Li is here used as a verb, not a noun. It is parallel with the term 疆
jiang, "to divide or make a border." Li here seems to be a verb meaning
"to separate into groups, to divide into sections," but with an implication
of doing so for a particular purpose: in this case, the division of a field in
order to cultivate crops, and the creation of pathways of access to these
fields. The implication is that here Li means "to cut and divide in a way
which is consistent with a particular human value," or *a coherence that also
necessarily coheres with some human desires or inclinations.* Hall and Ames also
make much of this passage, but seem to blur this crucial aspect when they
characterize this usage as meaning, "dividing up land into cultivated fields
in a way consistent with the natural topography."[9] But the point here is surely
not that the field is simply being cut "in a way consistent with the natural
topography." Rather, what is most evident is the human action and desire
and valuation involved. We would perhaps be closer to the implication if
we said, "cutting in a way that is consistent with both the topography and,
even more decisively, with human need, desire, valuation, and response."
Indeed, this is closer to the "Nominalist" implication Hall and Ames wish
to see in the tradition, as we shall discuss in more detail presently.

Tang notes this point as well in his discussion of this ancient usage,
stressing above all the subjective and active/temporal sense of Li as primary,
with its objective and static/spatial aspects as derivative: Li as a verb rather
than as a noun. He also notes, importantly, the role of human will, a human
project, in all these early usages of Li; that is, the essential connection with
value and valuation. Tang sees Li in its earliest meaning above all as the
purposive, humanly motivated *act* of cutting, tailoring, which connects its
various aspects and phases as means toward this end. It is primarily a human
activity, and only derivatively the patterns that emerge from this activity.[10]
However, Tang's discussion is excessively beholden to the mutually exclusive
categories of subjective and objective, concerned in an almost Bergsonian
way with establishing Li as subjective *rather than* objective (in certain primary usages) and temporal/active *rather than* spatial/passive. But in fact it
is obvious that both sides of what we would call the subject/object split
are necessarily involved. Li is here "cutting in a way which is consistent

with *both* the topography and human value," or the overlap of the two. We have here again the inclusion of human response in the overall pattern of coherence. And this is how we will be understanding Li in almost every case throughout the tradition, including Buddhist and Neo-Confucian uses. Li always means, "coherence between a set of disparate items, which necessarily includes both nonhuman reality and human responses to that reality (desires and cognitions)."

This implication is very much in evidence in the definition of Li in the earliest Chinese dictionary, Xu Shen's 許慎 *Shuowen jiezi* 說文解字. Li is there defined simply as "the treating of jade" (治玉也 *zhi yu ye*). But jade is not "treated"—i.e., cut, polished, and shaped—merely in accordance with its "natural topography" or its own "inherent lines of pattern," as we would understand "its own" under the force of the ontological split between the subjective and the objective. Rather, as the great Qing commentator Duan Yucai 段玉裁 says of this entry, "When jade has not yet been treated (理 *Li*), it is called *pu* 朴, the unhewn raw stuff. Li here [is a verb and] means to cut it open and break it apart. Although jade is supremely hard, it is not difficult for it to be made into a vessel (器 *qi*) if one can find its lines of division along its edges and corners (腮理 *saili*),[11] and this is what is meant by Li."[12] Duan is writing with a very specific polemical intent here: he wants to distinguish the original meaning of Li, and its proper sense in true Confucian thought, from the Buddhist and Daoist uses of the term, and the corruption of the term in the perverted Buddhified Confucianism of Zhu Xi and others. The crux of this polemic, however, lies in his imputation of "separation"—cutting, dividing, differentiating—as the primary sense of the term Li in its verbal sense, which brings with it the stress on the sense of differentiation and division of proper roles when it is used in its nominal sense. This is contrasted to the Buddhist, Daoist, and latter-day Confucian interpretation of the term as pointing above all to "unity," to what is shared, to what is in fact omnipresent. Whatever we may think of Duan's polemic purposes, it must be admitted that he has identified an unmistakable shift in the meaning of the term. And here we have the crux of our present problem: *How is it that a term meaning cutting and differentiating comes to mean the undifferentiated omnipresent?* And with this comes a related problem: *how does a term meaning originally deliberate human shaping of raw material come to mean the state of the thing prior to human intervention?* For Li develops not only from meaning "divided" to "all-inclusive," but also from "to order" to "the interface between human intentions and the material to be ordered," and finally to "the true state of the thing prior to deliberate human interference, free of one-sided, private bias." It is in this last sense that Li tempts the translation "objective Truth" as opposed to subjective emotion. In this it seems to run from the subjective to the subjective-objective and finally to the objective.

Of course there is no reason why a term cannot in the course of time, or even in different contexts, change its meaning, and indeed take on an opposite meaning, although "meaning" is such that it must do so by pivoting off continuity with its preexisting denotations and connotations in some way or other. But the fact is that the term Li points to a notion of separation and differentiation that runs smoothly into a concept of undifferentiated omnipresence, and from subjectivity to objectivity. It points to a set of concepts of "coherence" which structures these apparently opposed ideas of differentiated finiteness and undifferentiated omnipresence in a distinctive intertwining, a notion of separation that also points to a joining and vice versa, a notion of subjectivity that also points to objectivity and vice versa. The point I will be trying to make here is that these terms *one, many, subjective, objective*—are of very limited value when walking about Li, and need to be superseded if we want to understand its history.

Tang Junyi's analysis is particularly astute on this point. For if the primary sense of Li in pre-Qin texts is what Tang calls 文理 *wenli*, taken to mean initially the *action* of making cultural patterns, as expressed especially in social interactions but also in pragmatic skill-activities such as field division and jade treating, then we have in hand a powerful model for understanding the intertwining of unity and differentiation in this concept, as Tang notes in his critique of the Dai Zhen/Duan Yucai "division-only" position. The unification here refers to the *end*, the goal of the activity, as present in each differentiated and even contrasting particular operation in the procedure. The diversity refers to the various individual means used to achieve this end. Tang stresses, importantly, that the unity here is temporal, not the joining of an array of differentiations but the unity of a single orienting intention governing a complex process. So in treating jade I may sometimes cut and sometimes polish, sometimes sharpen a corner and sometimes dull an edge. "Sharpening" and "dulling" are diverse opposite operations, but they are unified, not as objects in space as in an enveloping container, or instantiations of a universal to which they bear some morphological mimetic similarity, but as immediate phases of the total process of shaping the jade. The presence of the unifying "universal" orientation, the willed, value-informed human activity of creating a coherent pattern, is *wholly* present in each of these aspects of the process, not partially present, but it is not for that reason replicated as distinct instances of this orientation. Li implies both unity and differentiation in this distinct sense: it is temporal, purposive human activity, orienting means around a definite intended end.

Tang's comments here are a crucial starting point. But again, I believe he has overstressed the sense of subject/object dichotomy, and with it the means/end dichotomy, which I think is alien to the case. We make more progress by following his further implication that what we are talking about here is not really the subjective so much as the intersubjective, the social interactions of humans within a given community. But this changes the contours of the situation decisively, and allows us to conceive the relation of subject and object, and of unity and differentiation, somewhat differently. We can begin to pick up the thread of the problem from Duan's comment above. *Pu*, the unhewn, and *qi*, vessel, are key terms in the *Laozi*, as explored in *Ironies*, and part of Duan's intent here is to contrast his reading of Li with a "Daoist"- or "Buddhist"-leaning reading that identifies it with the one undivided universal universal, the unhewn, the whole, the encompassing background, the unifying, the omnipresent, as contrasted to individualized vessels. For a "vessel" is a *culturally valued object* which has been cut out of the unhewn raw material for a particular reason—i.e., because it has an intersubjectively recognized "market value" (whether ritual or economic), to put it crudely.

In many early Daoist works, this cutting of culturally valued "vessels" out of the natural unhewn raw material is seen as a kind of violence to that raw material, damaging it and destroying its true value. Duan's point here is that *certain* of the patterns—not necessarily all of the patterns—found "naturally" in the raw material can be used as guidelines to facilitate the creation of a vessel with human cultural value. Both the "objective" and "subjective" sides of coherence are relevant here, but it is the points at which these two types of coherence themselves "cohere" or overlap which makes Li. *Li would then mean "second-order coherence between found coherences in the world and coherent clusters of human evaluation."* The question of to what degree these "found coherences" are really in the world, or are themselves effects of the organizing teleology of human evaluations, is left open here, and, as we shall see, to a large extent rendered irrelevant.

Before pursuing these points through a textual analysis of the early philosophical usages of the term, however, it is worthwhile to clarify our approach to some of these points by taking a quick tour of some of the most suggestive of the attempts to reinterpret and translate the term by recent Western sinologists, which are of especial relevance here since our primary concern is with the mismatch of the Chinese and the Western categories, Of particular interest will be the works of Joseph Needham, Chad Hansen, A. C. Graham, Willard Peterson, and Roger Hall and David Ames, all of whom have contributed crucial insights to the present approach to be taken in the pages to that follow.

NEEDHAM AND ORGANIC PATTERN

As noted, Fung Yulan had suggested that Li be translated as "Platonic Form," and Form in the Aristotelian sense has also been proposed as a translation, along with Reason, and Law of Nature. Joseph Needham, in his classic work

Science and Civilization in China, rejects these suggestions, again with mainly the Neo-Confucian usage in mind, in developing his own overall account of the distinctive nature of traditional Chinese thinking. For Needham, all of these terms are misleading in that they suggest a heteronomous source of order, either form as imposed upon passive matter, or natural law as enforced by God as legislator, in both cases implying a transcendent source of order standing outside the things that are ordered, bearing a different ontological status. He suggested instead the terms *organization*, or better, *organism*, as modeled on the interrelation of parts in an animal organism, viewed as spontaneously interacting and organizing themselves around each other. In the West, Needham said, even organism always had to have an extrinsic "guiding principle," due to the basic belief in a personal god or gods who directed things. In the Chinese context, Needham thought, "cooperation of the component parts was spontaneous, even involuntary, and this alone was sufficient."[13] As Hall and Ames point out, this is a rather unusual understanding of the English word *organism.* In Western thought, even in Whiteheadian thought, which informs Needham's understanding, organic order is understood as profoundly teleological: "[T]his term is most generally associated with living things conceived as complex arrangements of parts function with respect to some end or aim."[14] This characterization leads, they note, to "a classification of ends or aims which would then undergird a [single, unambiguous, synordinate] taxonomic organization of 'natural kinds.' "[15]—precisely what is lacking in the Chinese case. Still, Needham's intention is clear; he wants to understand Li as spontaneous pattern brought to bear not by extrinsic coercion, even by a "guiding principle," but by the spontaneous, involuntary cooperation and reciprocal adjustment of the members in any group. The antitranscendentalist perspective is stressed here. It is not clear, however, that this model can do all the work Needham wants it to do. In particular, the normativity, definiteness, simultaneous oneness and manyness of Li, and its application to human ethics, remain for the most part mysterious on this reading.

HANSEN AND THE MASS NOUN HYPOTHESIS

Chad Hansen, in a controversial study of ancient Chinese logical paradoxes, suggests one reason why the question of universals might not have developed in China in a way that is at all comparable to its development in the West. It should be noted that Hansen was not directly addressing the question of how to interpret or translate Li, whether in Neo-Confucianism or elsewhere, but the more general issue of classes and their members in Chinese thought. Hansen suggests that classical Chinese nouns function more like mass nouns than like count nouns. Mass nouns (e.g., "water") refer to one pervasive amorphous entity that is spread out in various places, and can be divided up in various ways, while count nouns (e.g., dog) come with predetermined units for counting. I can have "one dog, two dogs, three dogs" and so on, but "one cup, one quart, two pools" *of* water. This suggestion has caused some consternation in that it fits better the grammar of modern Chinese (where indeed nouns are generally preceded by a special measure word to indicate the amount of that noun which is being indicated) than classical Chinese, where countable entities can be indicated without recourse to measure words. The lack of special forms indicating singular and plural in both ancient and modern Chinese, however, remains significant in this context. The point is that if a noun indicates primarily the entire mass of that substance, everywhere in the world, the problem of relating individual members to the general class disappears. There is no need to unify individual dogs with a universal canine essence if each dog is really just one dog-shaped scoop of the dog-substance spread out throughout the world. The implication is that rather than an additive class derived cumulatively by assembling individuals and collating their similarities, we are "dividing down" from the whole and provisionally selecting out subdivisions for closer consideration. There is no need for a two-level ontology here, where abstract essences or universals or forms, accessible to the intellect but not to the senses, "participate in" and unify concrete particulars; rather, the mass and each chunk of the mass are equally concrete and available to the senses.[16]

Hansen's insights are particularly important for setting the agenda of the present work. He notes in particular the circumvention of both Platonic ideas and mentalist ideas in classical Chinese thinking. The mind is not a representational faculty that entertains ideas or perceives the intelligible realm of ideas. There are no universals, just stuff-kinds. The mind is a faculty of actively distinguishing among these real kinds. The epistemology functions on the basis of only names and stuffs; no other entities, such as properties, attributes, essences, universals, or particulars, are necessary. However, in spite of his affirmation of stuffs as real kinds, Hansen continues to speak of this view as a kind of nominalism. He notes that the notion of "a class" is employed by nominalists as a way of avoiding these abstract entities beloved of Realist epistemology. But, Hansen adds, classes, with the exception of Russell and Lesniewski's mereological notion of class, are themselves abstract entities. A class is not necessary to the whole-part stuff ontology, he thinks.[17] But the stuff-kinds are at least viewed by Hansen as real kinds existing in nature, independently of the distinguishing function of the dynamic human mind, which can thus divide either correctly or incorrectly. They are thus real in a strong sense, and not merely conventional, although still for Hansen fully concrete. But this concreteness ends up being of a very strange kind, indeed of so strange a kind that it raises questions about all concreteness. For like a universal, it is instantiated in multiple noncontiguous times and places, and it seems to allow of no distinction between being partially instantiated and being fully instantiated (it is not claimed that it is only "partially present" when it is identified as present in any of its "parts"). The same oddness would then pertain even to contiguous applications of "the same" name to all the parts of any concrete object (for every object is actually multilocal, spanning more than a mathematical point of space), if the name can be applied in whole to each part. The problem is again exactly what we could possibly actually mean by oneness and difference, conceived as mutually exclusive, as we have argued is the real problem lurking at the back of all questions of nominalism and realism. But the assertion of the view that the stuffs are entities present in their entirety, rather than only partially, in every place they are present, and which are capable of warranting so strong a naturalism of real kinds, raises questions about whether it is not misleading to still call it a nominalism in any normal sense. For as we argued in the prequel, the nominalism/realism issue is interestingly readable as ultimately an offshoot of the more fundamental issue of the relation of oneness and otherness, of what constitutes actual sameness and difference and whether these can be thought of as mutually exclusive. A real oneness of any kind that is thinkable in abstraction from and exclusive of otherness, which could be undividedly present in more than one location, is, we would claim, ipso facto an abstract entity in the relevant sense.

GRAHAM AND THE ABSENT COPULA AND CORRELATIVE THINKING

A. C. Graham slightly amends Hansen's suggestion, in a passage we also quoted in *Ironies of One and Many*:

> We might say that while the English translations use count nouns for individuals or classes, the Chinese uses mass nouns which carry with them instructions as to where the primary division is to be made. There are also words, some of them important in philosophy (*chi'*, *tao*, *li*) which carry no such instructions, so that there is no contradiction in dividing out Yin and Yang as "the 2 ch'i" yet also picking out as "the 5 ch'i" the Five Phases, or the 5 atmospheric influences, whatever one chooses to select from the mass. On this approach a *lei* "kind," such a *jen* "man" or *ma* "horse," is a mass like cattle exhaustively divisible into similar parts (like Greek *genos* "genus" in its original sense of a race which could die out, not a class which may become empty of members): the *shih* "object" which . . . we described as "concrete and particular" is a chunk

out of a mass which is no less concrete than itself. This does not of course alter the fact that, irrespective of language, discontinuous and constant objects enforce on us a priority over divisions we can make as we please. Even if a *shih* "object" is a chunk out of a mass, the most convenient examples of it will be individuals—in the Mohist account of naming . . . not a pool or drop of water but a horse. But that the objects are indeed conceived as divisions is confirmed, as Hansen notices, but the fact that where we would speak of class and member or whole and part the Mohist logic uses only a single pair, *chien* and *ti,* and defines *ti* as a "a division in a *chien*" (Canon AC *ti, fen yu chien ye*).[18]

As noted in the previous volume, Graham here accepts the implication that the Chinese tendency is to divide down from the whole, adding however that these wholes often come with *built-in instructions* about where the main "cuts" or divisions were to be made, and that *in several important cases there are more than one possible way to legitimately make these divisions.* The idea of "built-in instructions about how to cut something up" will be quite a useful hint for us in considering the ways in which coherence comes to be understood, and all the more so the idea that several alternate, even incompatible, sets of instructions might be not only applicable, but indeed built in, with the full authority of objectivity, as it were.

Graham makes another suggestion relating to this question. The Chinese language, he notes, lacks any collapse of existential and predicative sense of "being" such as is peculiar to Indo-European languages. The broadest term for "being" (有 *you*), literally "having, possession," implies primarily "presence in the world," and does not neatly apply to abstract entities, predicates, or uncontextualized substances. Moreover, its use to say "X exists" actually puts the "X" in the object position of the sentence, thereby positing an implicit subject, a further entity that "possesses" X:

> [T]he subject of the English "is" corresponds to the object of the Chinese *yu* [有 *you*]. In Indo-European Languages a thing simply *is*, without implying anything outside it, and it is the most abstract entities which the Platonic tradition most willingly credits with being. In Chinese, on the other hand, one approaches the thing from outside, from the world which "has" it, in which "there is" it. From this point of view, the more concrete a thing is, the more plainly the world has it; for example, one can emphasize the absolute non-existence of X by saying . . . "The world does not have X" (more literally, "There is no X under the sky"). In this respect, as in the absence of the copulative function of "to be," *yu* is like "exist,"

which also implies a concrete thing with a background from which it stands out (*exsistit*). But there remains the difference that "exists," like "is," is attached to a subject and not to an object. . . . This is the source of one of the most striking difference between Chinese thinking about *yu* and *wu* and Western thinking about Being. In English, a table is a thing, exists, is; Beauty is not a thing, does not exist, but we can still say it is. Having the verb "to be" (*esse*), we can form a noun from it and say that Beauty, although not a thing, is an "entity" (*ens, entitas*). We can also form an adjective from "thing" (*res*) and say that it is "real." To indicate the kind of being which is not existence we can invent "subsistence." Beauty, that real, subsisting entity, is assimilated as closely as possible to the table, that real, existing thing. As a last refinement, we may find reasons for claiming that such an immaterial entity more truly is, is more real, than the phenomena perceived by the senses. . . . In Chinese, on the other hand, the word *yu* is used primarily of concrete things. . . .[19]

This relates directly to our problem. In classical Chinese we literally cannot say something exists without simultaneously positing something larger in which it exists. This has obvious implications for the question of the Omnipresent, and with it the notions of unconditioned determinateness and the relation between classes, as discussed in the previous volume. It also discourages the development of a two-tiered metaphysic and any decontextualized absolutes. It points us further directly toward the "dyadic a priori," discussed in *Ironies*, and the self-overcoming of coherence into its ironic effacement, as we'll see below.

We may note another use of the "to be" verbs in some Indo-European languages which is notably and importantly absent in Chinese: the use of "to be" in passive constructions. In English, for example, we transform the active "to see" into the passive "to *be* seen." It is worth pausing to consider what kind of connection between being and passivity, or perhaps objectivity, is implied by this grammatical peculiarity. In classical Chinese, purely passive constructions might be expressed by auxiliary verbs indicating receiving, wearing, carrying, bearing or, a bit later, being the locus of the action of a main verb (e.g., 被 *bei* and 所 *suo*). But in many cases the same verb is used to indicate both passive and active aspects of the same action without morphological distinction, or with an alternate pronunciation that continues to attribute the action to the supposed recipient. "To see" (見 *jian*), for example, is written in classical texts in the same way as "to be manifested, to be seen" (見 *xian*). We also have the important and often misconstrued usage of *xiang* 相 to make a verb transitive without indicating its object.[20]

It is interesting to note that the passive construction does later come to be written with *wei*, beginning in translations from Buddhist sutras, possibly to try to echo the use of the copulative "be" construction for passive voice in Indic source languages.[21]

Putting these points together, we may suggest that to say that something exists in Chinese always implies that it is *actively present* and that it is so *in some context*. The general tendency to divide down from the whole, noted by both Hansen and Graham, is again in evidence here. While it is true, as Graham points out, that this makes Chinese thinkers particularly hesitant to attribute "being" to abstract or nonsensory entities (such as Li), preferring to call them 虛 *xu* "tenuous," 空 *kong* "empty," 無 *wu* "nothingness," or 非有非無 *feiyoufeiwu* "beyond being and Non-Being," it does not positively exclude the abstract from the category of being. But it does make the notion of pure transcendence, or unconditionality, problematic: it is immediately obvious that anything *determinate* (i.e., divided down from a larger context and deriving its identity from contextualization in that whole) cannot be unconditional. It ensures, in effect, that even abstract entities will be thought of as primarily contextualized, perhaps making the later Buddhist idea that abstract entities are perceived by the intellect in a way not fundamentally distinct from the way the senses perceive their objects easily assimilable: the mind is a sense organ that perceives ideas and thoughts, which also always come with a context, and are therefore not simply and completely determinate. This circumvents the "determinate but unconditional" paradox noted in the previous volume.

Graham translates Li as "pattern," which he specifies as meaning the "recurring" patterns in which things are organized, the sorting out of which is the thinking which belongs to the realm of man. We will have to return to the question of recurrence below. The possibility of iterability of "the same" anything in different times and places is, in normal Western usage, predicated on the existence of some kind of universal that can subsume and recur identically in many instances. For this reason, I would like to bracket "recurrence" in the strong sense for the moment. For a Daoist, Graham thinks, these Li-patterns would include things such as "the relative positions of heaven and earth and the alternations of Yin and Yang, rise and fall, birth and death; they do not include standards of conduct, which a [Daoist] denies in principle."[22] He describes Li in Cheng-Zhu Neo-Confucianism as "the universal pattern branching by division from the Supreme Ultimate (T'ai-chi) [太極 *taiji*], setting the lines along which things move," which is opposed to 氣 *qi* as the "universal fluid out of which things condense and into which they dissolve, freely moving when fine or inert when coarse, active as the Yang or passive as the Yin."[23] Li in this system are "the patterns which regularize things and events."[24] Again we may reserve judgment especially about the implications of the term *regularize* here.

Graham provides a distinctive solution to the descriptive/normative problem. In general, he asserts, Chinese thought assumes that we are already spontaneously moved in various directions before any prescriptive moral discourse comes to us. But these spontaneous promptings are alterable; they change when we are aware of more or other things. The point of ethical culture in China then was to expand awareness of all relevant implications, so that we would be spontaneously moved in a different way. The ultimate standard was the way the wisest and most fully aware persons, the sages, were spontaneously moved. In terms of Li in Neo-Confucianism, this helps Graham explain why struggle is needed to attain the sage's lucid spontaneity, and why Li can be spoken of both as "what makes things what they are"—a matter of simple fact—and "how things should be"—a prescriptive norm (the "fact/value fusion" alluded to above). Graham says, "To the extent that I remain ignorant, the dense *ch'i* [qi] of my organism runs blindly in the broad channels of the *li* where it happens to be; but by moral training I refine my substance to greater transparency and penetrate into the finer veins of the universal pattern, so that my spontaneous reactions change as the rarified *ch'i* out of which the denser goes on being generated adjusts to newly perceived *li*. The assumption is that if I still fail to respond in the full light of my knowledge, it is because a *li* has permeated just far enough to awaken a spontaneous inclination along its path, but not yet to articulate the motions of the organism as a whole."[25] One is always proceeding according to some portion of the overall Li however one is moved and whatever one is doing; moral value attaches only to how much or little of the Li one has penetrated. Right and wrong is a matter of greater and lesser penetration of Li. If one continues only in the "coarser veins" of Li where one "happens to be," one has failed to live up to the Li of being a human being, which is exemplified by the sages, who have shown that man's mind is able to penetrate the entirety of Li. When one fails to do so, one is a "not really a human being"—not fully realizing the Li of being a human, but only the less comprehensive Li of being an animal, for example. We will be returning to, and partially adopting, this interpretation of Li's ethical implications in the pages to follow.

Graham describes Zhu Xi's Li as

> a vast three-dimensional structure which looks different from different angles. In laying down the lines along which everything moves, it appears as the Way (*Tao*); in that the lines are independent of my personal desires, it imposes itself on me as Heaven (*T'ien*);

as a pattern which from my own viewpoint spreads out from the sub-pattern of my own profoundest reaction, it appears as my own basic Nature (*hsing*). Looking down from the Supreme Ultimate, at the apex of which its branches join, it first divides as the Way of the first two diagrams of the *Changes*, Ch'ien and K'un, patterning the *ch'i* in its Yang and Yin phases; but from my own viewpoint, the major lines which connect me with the whole are the principles of conduct, Benevolence, Duty, Manners, Wisdom [i.e., 仁義禮智, *ren yi li zhi*, the four cardinal Mencian and Neo-Confucian virtues]. Each person, peering into the vast web from his own little corner of it, may, if his *ch'i* is perfectly transparent, see all the way to the Supreme Ultimate at its farthest limits.[26]

Of crucial importance in this interpretation, which makes admirable sense of the "one-many" question, is Graham's claim that the "subjectivising, Chinese" assumption that "the knowing of a *li* [is] inseparable from the reactions it patterns."[27] The organic pattern is not merely an objective network to be observed and studied from without; our own reactions are also parts of this network of connections. The mind is not set aside as a separate ontological category, but is part of the whole. This insight will serve us well in the considerations below.

Graham also develops a notion of Chinese thinking, particularly from the Han on, as marked by "correlative" or analogic, rather than "analytic" or "causal" pattern formation. We will return to this suggestion in the discussion of the treatment of these problems by Hall and Ames below.

PETERSON AND COHERENCE

In his 1986 article "Another Look at Li," Willard Peterson made a breakthrough suggestion on how to translate, and understand, the term Li in Neo-Confucianism. The translation he suggests is the English word *coherence*. By coherence, Peterson means "'the quality or characteristic of sticking together,' with the connotations of varying according to context."[28] The contextualizing implication is perhaps not analytically derivable from the notion of "coherence" as such, but it is a qualification that fits well with the points we have considered above, and indeed the two parts of this definition bring into sharp relief the crux of the problem. For indeed, coherence does suggest contextualization, if "sticking together" is meant to apply not only to the parts of the entity in question, but to the way the entity as a whole "sticks together" with what surrounds it. Coherence, then, means both the coherence of the parts of any whole with each other and the coherence of

this whole with all other things that are related to it, which contextualize it. Peterson notes that this interpretation allows many of the mysteries
surrounding the Cheng-Zhu use of Li to disappear. He makes the following
points about the Cheng-Zhu use of Li as coherence:

1. "There is coherence for each and every thing, whether that
   thing is taken as heaven-and-earth as a whole, or a thing smaller
   than a cricket, an ant, or a blade of grass."[29] Each thing, to be
   the thing it is, must have its own coherence, and this applies
   both to any whole as a whole and to each part as a part.

2. "Coherence is unitary." This solves the one-many problem:
   "[W]e can speak of the coherence of my puppy, the coherence of
   all dogs, the coherence of all living things, and so on, without
   involving ourselves in a verbal dilemma over the relationship
   between the 'different' levels or envelopes of coherence."[30]

3. "Coherence of object or phenomena is not locatable independently of ch'i."[31] Here we have the immanence of Li to qi.

4. "Coherence is categorically distinct from the ch'i of which
   things are constituted."[32] Here we have the transcendence of
   Li to qi.

5. "Coherence is transcendent as well as immanent."[33] This is a
   restatement of the previous two points.

6. "Coherence is that by which a thing is as it is."[34] It is descriptive, and also explanatory, in the sense of being "that by virtue
   of which a thing is what it is, rather than any other thing."

7. "Each phenomenon has its associated ultimate or 'perfect coherence' (*chih li* [*zhi Li*]), which may or may not be attained."[35]

This is meant to solve the problem of the simultaneous descriptive
and normative use of "coherence." Peterson explains his understanding of
this connection as follows: "The logic is simple. There is the coherence of
all that is. There is the coherence of what will be or ought to be, usually
expressed as the perfect coherence. As an aspect of that which we now are,
we have the coherence of what we ought to be and the allied capacity to
attain that ultimate, the full realization (*ch'eng*) of our potential. The puppy
becomes a dog, what it ought to be, if it acts in a manner congruent with
fulfilling that potential coherence within it (e.g., if it does not run under
the wheel of a truck) and is not otherwise interfered with."[36]

This last point is the only part of Peterson's rather brilliant exposition of Li as coherence, which I will otherwise be adopting and building from here, with which I will be taking issue. The imputation of a distinction between "potential" and "actual" coherence invoked here, it seems to me, implies an abstract transcendentalism that undermines the power of the coherence model. Peterson tries to circumvent this implication by suggesting that the former is an "aspect" of the former, and indeed, both can be subsumed under the concept of "coherence." As Peterson puts it, Zhu Xi is "urging us to understand as a coherent whole both what a man is now and what he might be in the future."[37] This restatement continues to rely on the distinction of "is" and "might," but the whole point of having recourse to the concept of coherence is surely that it reaches across these putatively separate categories of potentiality and actuality.[38] Indeed, Peterson makes the point that Li must be understood as standing on both sides of the pair "potential" and "realized or actualized."[39] But the implications of this claim remain to be explored, and we will have to pay careful attention to the question of Li as potential, particularly in the Buddhist contexts, later.

HALL AND AMES AND THE FOCUS/FIELD

Hall and Ames also have a problem with the putative "transcendentalism" of Peterson's notion of coherence, which was of course intended only as an explication of the term's use in Cheng-Zhu Neo-Confucianism, not in the entire tradition of Chinese thought, early and late. Hall and Ames state that they wish to adopt this interpretation for pre-Qin thought, but leaving out the transcendentalism, which they take to be applicable only to post-Buddhist, Neo-Confucian uses of the term.[40] (This radical separation of Buddhist uses from other Chinese uses, which in fact dates back to the Neo-Confucian critiques of Buddhism, is one of the issues the present work hopes to reconsider.) Hall and Ames's discussion of Li comes in the context of their overall interpretation of the dominant modes of "Han thinking" as a whole, which they characterize as privileging what Graham had identified as the "correlative, analogical, metaphorical" mode of classification over the "analytic, causal, metonymic" mode, as we discussed at length in *Ironies of One and Many*. Correlative groupings are loose, metaphorical, and ad hoc in character, producing concepts that are "image clusters in which complex semantic associations are allowed to reflect into one another in such a way as to provide rich, indefinitely "vague" meanings. Univocity is, therefore, impossible. Aesthetic associations dominate."[41] These associations are nominalist, pragmatic, historicist, thus always necessarily ambiguous and negotiable. Hall and Ames see one of the most important examples of this in the "seemingly ubiquitous distinction between yin and yang," which is "no more than a convenient way or organizing 'thises' and 'thats.' This is clearly a consequence of the nominalistic character of Chinese intellectual culture."[42] Correlative thinking, we are told, allows a freeform association of items that might "cohere" with a given class, again very much including the subjective or cultural axiological reactions to things experienced together with them.

It is in this context that Hall and Ames adopt and modify Peterson's notion of Li as coherence. Li, they say, is "the inherent formal and structural patterns in things and events, and their intelligibility. In expressing this notion of coherence and intelligibility, no severe distinction is made between 'natural' coherence (*tianli* [天理] or *daoli* [道理]) and 'cultural' coherence (*wenli* [文理] or *daoli* [道理]) . . . each is integral to *li*. . . . [It is] the fabric of order and regularity immanent in the dynamic process of experience . . . li in defining order confounds the familiar distinction between rational faculty and the underlying principles it searches out. Li has neither an exclusively subjective nor objective reference."[43] Moreover,

> Li establish the ethos of a given community. As such li may never be considered as independent of context. There are no transcendent li. . . . In the absence of teleological guidance, there is only an ongoing process of correlation and negotiation. . . . Things are continuous with one another, and thus are interdependent conditions for each other. In a tradition which begins from the assumption that existence is a dynamic process, the causes of things are resident in themselves as their conditions, and the project of giving reasons for things or events requires a tracing or mapping out of the conditions that sponsor them. . . . Li constitutes an aesthetic coherence in the sense that it begins from the uniqueness of any particular as a condition of individuation, and is at the same time a basis for continuity through various forms of collaboration between the given particular and other particulars with which, by virtue of similarity or productivity or contiguity, it can be correlated.[44]

This antitranscendental emphasis on process, and on reciprocal action (to which we will resort again at length in what follows) gives a different implication to the notion of "coherence":

> Process entails uniqueness, and makes any notion of strict identity problematic. As such, coherent unities are characterized in terms of a relative continuity among unique particulars. And such continuity is open-ended rather than systematic; it is contingent rather than necessary; it is correlative rather than causal. This is can include

aspects which, if entertained simultaneously, would seem inconsistent or even contradictory, yet when entertained in process, are well within the boundaries of continuity.[45]

The stressing of contextualization, mutual determination of the focus and the field, negotiability, provisionality, reciprocity, and immanence of coherence here, in a correlative cosmology, are crucial insights for understanding Li. However, I would like to stress an aspect of the ad hoc nature of Li which is underplayed a bit here, although it can be seen as an extension of the claim that Li has neither an exclusively subjective nor objective reference. For taken in all seriousness, this statement allows us to avoid a misunderstanding of the previous claim that Li includes equally cultural and natural patterns, *as if these were two different realms included within the larger set of Li*. This cannot be correct, even by the standards set by Hall and Ames themselves. As we shall see, there simply are no natural Li that are not also cultural, and no cultural Li which are not also natural. If we must divide these two ideal sets of possible coherences, we would perhaps do better to speak of Li as a kind of intersection or overlap between the two. But this is really a backward way of putting it. For what is at stake here, as we shall see, are the full implications of the inclusion of "subjective" reactions in the overall pattern of Li, as noted by Graham: the nondistinction between the concrete and the abstract, and the necessity of contextualization.

We can sum up in advance what we will adopt and what reject from the giants on whose shoulders we stand here, and what we will find, in the readings that follow, needs to be added.

From Needham we accept that Li is somehow autonomous rather than heteronomous, not a principle imposed from without. But we reject the idea of organism and the idea of pattern; organism implies a fixed ends-means teleology of organs, while pattern implies strict repeatability, neither of which can be found in Li.

From Hansen we accept the claim that the Chinese notion of knowledge tends to be primarily of a dividing out from a context, connected to an ontology based on dividing down rather than accumulation of distinct particulars. We also adopt the staunch rejection of the necessity of any two-tiered metaphysics that this model implies. But Hansen's model seems to leave the vicissitudes of the dividing process up in the air, susceptible to the usual conflict between nominalism and realism, which we do not find to be applicable as a strict either/or in the Chinese case.

From Graham we adopt the emendation of Hansen, the "built-in instructions" for dividing, which we call "perforations." We will make much of the possible multiplicity and incompatibility of these perforations within any stuff. We also wish to amplify on his insight about the inclusion of human inclinations within the scope of the given, and the clue this provides to solving the descriptive/normative problem for Li. But we will amend his notion of "pattern," "regularizing," and "reiterability," as well as the depiction of Li as a sort of passive channel in which qi may flow. Our emendation comes from further emphasizing the perforation idea, combining it with the notion of Li. Li are these perforations, and the flowing of qi is also its rearrangement. Li must include also the notion of dividing and unifying, not just as a network branches apart but also interconnects, but rather as material is rearranged, divided into groups, so as to cohere, stick together, in a certain way. The "flow" of qi must be understood as the way Li reorganizes it.

From Peterson we adopt the crucial idea of Li as coherence, meaning both the sticking together of the parts of a thing and its way of sticking together with its environment. The multiple levels of nesting this conception allows will be crucial to developing Graham's "perforation" idea, as well as the unity/multiplicity and immanent/transcendent dilemmas concerning Li, along with the negotiable identities of all terms that are so crucial to Hall and Ames's insights on this matter. The use of this paradigm to solve the third crucial dilemma—the descriptive/normative—is, we feel, not yet accomplished in Peterson, and it is this angle we would like to augment.

From Hall and Ames, we adopt the addition of the sense of coherence as "intelligibility" to Peterson's model, the inclusion of human and natural within its scope (continuing Graham's point), and the greater emphasis on the ad hoc nature of these coherences, their shifting and always negotiable character. We also would like to build on the focus/field model, and the *ars contextualis* that goes with it. However, we would like to add several things to this model, while substantially agreeing with its overall intent. First, to the senses of "coherence," we add and stress a fourth: value. Coherence, in Li, must cover at least these four senses: sticking together of parts, sticking together with the environment, intelligibility, and value. In stressing this point, we find that the ad hoc and purely nominalist rendering of the model is perhaps misleading; for these coherences are genuinely multilocal, instantiated in many separate events, and have actual causal efficacy as the wholes that play a decisive role in the constitution and character of their parts, albeit in an unusual way that does not amount to a realism either, and does indeed invite the kind of shifting focal contextualization that Hall and Ames concentrate on. For us, Li is neither nominalist nor realist in character, neither an absolute objective presence nor a subjectively projected invention. Li are neither purely invented nor purely discovered, and the extent to which we continue to think of these as mutually exclusive and exhaustive of all possible relations to coherent experiences will be the extent to which we still struggle with the meaning of Li. The Li, too, are really there, and really transcendent to any concrete instantiation, and have real causal efficacy in their multilocality precisely as determining wholes, which always involves also a relation to some human conation as part of the determining holistic totality of the coherence in a way that a purely nominalist description tends to obscure. There can be many patterns in the world and many intelligible togethernesses that are *not* Li: those that a human being, in according with, will not come together with the world in such a way as to satisfy his specifically human desires. That is, unless cohering with it allows you to cohere with the world more coherently, it is not a Li. This is perhaps the crucial emendation: we would like to assert that Li is beholden to a reference to a *second-order* coherence. That is, it is only those coherences that cohere in a certain way with certain other coherences (i.e., human beings) that qualify as Li. This is to some extent already implicit in Peterson's use of the term, and implied strongly by Graham. But it is still far too easy to imagine Li simply as some sort of pattern to be apprehended, without considering the subjective position of the apprehender. Li is not just any togetherness: it is a valued togetherness. Value, however, is also a togetherness: it is a relation between a desire and its object. The valuer is already implicated. The intelligibly coherent thing must cohere with certain human inclinations, which must themselves cohere with other inclinations in a valued way—i.e., as we shall see, "harmoniously."

Lastly, we would like to augment the Hall and Ames field/focus model with a reference to Qian Mu's pendulum model. This is to some extent already adumbrated in the idea of "focus" as a point that serves as a *center* toward which there is a *convergence,* as Hall and Ames already note. We may regard this idea of convergence as the crucial paradigm shift that unlocks much of Confucian thought, and returns in the Tiantai identification of "Centrality" (中 *zhong*) per se with Li. Li—valued coherence—*means* center in this sense, as Zhiyi also tells us. Centrality is itself value, is itself the connection of diverse and opposed particulars, is itself intelligibility: the three meanings of Li as coherence with which we have been grappling. A center unifies, is discernible, and is value (sustainability), as Qian's analysis suggests. With the identification of the terms *Li* and *Center* in Tiantai, we have the bridge to the Neo-Confucian usage of the term Li to denote this kind of centrality. We will return to this in our discussion of Tiantai below and also when we briefly discuss the status of Li in Neo-Confucianism in the Conclusion.

That is, there is a dyadic character to the force field, a certain circular form and rotating motion, which must be further stressed. Fields come in dyads, with two extremes ranged around a center. Hall and Ames perhaps allude to this in their discussion of Yin and Yang as a "this/that" pair, but it seems insufficiently integrated into their field/focus model, and their description of Li, still, as a kind of "pattern." To stress the dyadic character of the field and the "centrality" of the focus, as well as some sense of a pull of force, a center of gravity, in the organizing process, I will suggest instead a model of *vertex and vortex*. This vortex must be thought of as intrinsically dyadic in structure, bringing together *opposed* ingredients on the model of Qian Mu's pendulum, but taking place in several nested dimensions at once: a sort of multi-dyadic vortex. Taking a further step, we stress that these vertices are lines of perforation inviting human action, the action of making a division, hence making something intelligible and articulate, organizing the material at hand in a particular way, grouping it. By dividing along a certain perforation, a Li, we join the totality into a certain harmonious whole—harmonious in the sense that it harmonizes with our senses (perception) and inclinations (actions and values). Here, the further model of the acupuncture meridian must be used to supplement the still too objectivist picture of vertex and vortex. In this way we can perhaps return to the notion of a "coherence" in general as developed prior to the advent of Li, modeled on the *three-dimensional Gestalt* that incorporates also the cognitions and desires of the human observer as part of the same Gestalt. A Li is a vertex making coherent a multi-dyadic vortex of which we are ourselves a constitutive part.

Above and beyond these emendations, we will be identifying an ironic and a non-ironic usage of all the key terms concerning coherence, without which the apophatic adaptations of these terms in Taoist and Buddhist thought cannot be understood, rendering the grain of Chinese intellectual history unintelligible.

From the above considerations, I will be able to offer a general schema that can be applied to many of the diverse usages of Li to be considered below, broad and indeterminate enough for us to trace the continuities in usage without asserting that the word literally "means" the "same" thing in all eras, traditions and texts: *Li will be viewed as a harmony which, when harmonized with by a human being, leads to further harmonies.* These further harmonies may involve the original harmony, the human being, or both. I can restate the definition by replacing the word *harmony* with *coherence* in each instance, emphasizing thus that one of the ways in which a harmony can harmonize with a human being is for the human being to know it, to be aware of it, to pick it out and identify it, for it to be intelligible to him. Both terms imply a togetherness of diverse terms. Harmony emphasizes the experience of pleasure, and the quality of balance implied in this togetherness. Coherence implies the intelligibility in this togetherness. So more completely, but less elegantly, we may say: *Li is a harmonious coherence, which, when a human being becomes harmoniously coherent with it, leads to further harmonious coherence.*

In its simplest sense, Li is "how to divide things up so they fit together well." Not "how they are divided up," but "how to divide them up." "To fit together well by being divided up in a certain way" is the basic idea of coherence. But the little word *well* in this definition leads to a further wrinkle, for "well" here means another fitting together: to "fit together *well*" is to "fit together in a way that is desired," which is to say, "that fits together in a way that fits together with a desire or ideal." Hence, this "fitting together" always involves (1) the dividing up of the parts of an object into dyadic balances so that the object as a whole fits together sustainably, creating an object that can reproduce itself and continue into the future; (2) the dividing up of value and desire so that they fit together pleasurably and lastingly satisfyingly, creating a sustainable object of desire; and (3) the dividing up of known and knower so that they fit together intelligibly, creating an intelligible object of knowing. Hence, we note that three distinct levels of harmonious coherence are thus necessary for any item, X, to qualify as Li. At each level there is a requirement of harmony, but this already introduces the broad variability involved in the many usages of the term: for *what* must be harmonized with at each level can vary widely. Above all, one of these levels is always a coherent harmony between some given human desires and some situation; since these desiderata can vary extremely in different systems of thought, the implications of Li will vary just as broadly. The three levels can be spelled out more explicitly as follows:

1. The harmonious coherence (togetherness) of

    a. the parts of X with one another, and

    b. X as such and as a whole with its environment.

2. The harmonious coherence between X and a desiring human perceiver:

    a. The given desires of the human being must harmoniously cohere with X; that is, X must satisfy *some* human desires or other.

    b. Human awareness harmoniously coheres with X; that is, X is intelligible to human awareness.

3. The harmonious coherences that result when "1" above harmoniously coheres with "2" above. These can be of any number of types:

    a. Marketability or social utility of X (X adheres with economic demand and market desires);

b. Harvest of crops (nutrition available to humans, which harmonious cohere with their needs);

c. Progeny and continuation of the clan or species (harmonious coherence of past and present);

d. Grouping together of the clan or species (harmonious coherence of its members);

e. Skill in human relations, or practical prowess or skill of any kind (coherence of ends and means);

f. Liberation from suffering (Nirvana), and enlightenment into further intelligible coherences ("wisdom").

Li is any harmonious coherence of the type described in 1 that can harmoniously cohere with human beings in the sense of 2, leading to further harmonious coherences of the type described in 3.

In its earliest uses, Li is a verb meaning to organize raw material by dividing it up in some particular way, including dividing it up by cutting something away from a background, and to shape it into a coherent object that further coheres with some human values. When used as a stative verb it can usually be translated as "ordered" and when used as a transitive verb as "to put in order," with the qualification a particular notion of order is implicit in the term: the arrangement of the parts of a thing, separating them into groupings and regions, so that it becomes a coherent whole, meaning a whole that more effectively interfaces—coheres—with human needs and human awareness. It means to put something into a humanly palatable form. In its earliest nominal usages, Li seems to be translatable roughly as "a valued way of cohering," or "value-laden coherence." This can mean the lines along which the cutting, articulation, and divisions must be done in order for the thing to be "ordered" in the above sense, its implicit perforations, or by a further extension, the resulting network of articulations. In this case, we can speak of "following" (循 xun) or "tracing" (緣 yuan) along the Li, which in this context translates easily as "pattern," if we again recall that this implies a humanly valuable pattern, not necessarily any configuration that happens to repeat at regular intervals. Nor does it in any way imply strict repetition: instead, what matters is continuity, which is to say, coherence. This pattern of articulations is valuable or healthy for humans; it is also intelligible to humans, and healthy for humans to pay attention to. A further item that fits into the same set of articulations in an equally healthy way may be said to be part of the same Li, and to recognize this interconnection or harmony between these two items, or events, is to recognize the "same Li." We could also in this sense speak of "the Li of X," which would denote the way of

viewing X so that its organizing articulations are evident, the ways in which
·it is optimally divided and grouped. To see the Li of X would be to see it
subdivided in that optimal way for our understanding and handling of it,
our integration (coherence) of it into our other experiences and purposes,
rather than in some alternate way. In this sense, the term *principle* can be
a tempting and often appropriate translation. We can restate this, as noted
above, given the relativistic and pragmatic concept of value in play here, as
a coherence that coheres also with human desires and inclinations, or ways
of being together that are in harmony with some human evaluative stance.
This may also imply an effect on the relation among those desires—making
them, of course, more harmoniously coherent with one another in just this
sense. Also implied is some reciprocity or mutuality between these desires
or inclinations and these forms of togetherness in the world.[46]

It is in this context that the idea of the Omnipresent emerges, not as
either the universal universal or as what is left out of all universals, as we
saw (in *Ironies of Oneness and Difference*) underlie the competing notions
of omnipresence in Western thought, but rather as the Great Coherence,
which is non-ironically called Dao, the guiding course; or, alternately, the
Incoherent Coherence, which is *ironically* called Dao. The former simply
means the maximum coherence fitting the above definition, allowing human
tradition, human society, natural groupings, and human desires to cohere,
with a particular notion of human desires as the defining criterion. It is
omnipresent in the sense of omniavailable, and in the sense that whatever
falls outside of it cannot be said to really exist in any meaningful way for
human beings. The latter, ironic coherence, is the literal inclusion and
togetherness of all possible contents and contexts, the raw material and
background from which they are cut and which is therefore itself never the-
matizable except as the detritus left over after any given cutting something
out of raw material to make value, any act of Li-ing, of making usably coherent; it is therefore necessarily incoherent, valueless, and unintelligible, but
which is all the more the great coherence in the sense of the togetherness
and value of all things. At various times and places we have the attempted
appropriation of one of these sense of omnipresence by the other; but this
oscillation is in any case quite different from the oscillation and mutual
refutation between the two opposite senses of the Omnipresent derived from
the occidental notion of universals.

Let us now turn to the slow development of this notion, growing from
the soil of the prior conceptions of coherence already considered in *Ironies
of Oneness and Difference*, in the work of particular thinkers and traditions.

TWO

THE ADVENT OF LI,

IRONIC AND NON-IRONIC

I have mentioned that Li is not yet a central philosophical category in the earliest texts from the formative years of the Chinese philosophical traditions. However, there are some relatively nontechnical but nonetheless telling uses of the term in those contexts, prior to its self-conscious adoption as a specialized philosophical term, which it will be useful for us to consider. We will thus begin with those texts, with an eye specifically to the gathering storm of Li as it is taking shape in the gradual thickening of the associations of the term in its still vague ordinary meaning of "order." The discussion is organized thematically rather than strictly chronologically. In this chapter I will address relatively undiluted expressions of what I take to be the non-ironic usages of Li from the *Xunzi*, and in late Warring States texts such as the "Yueji" ("Record of Music") in the *Liji* and the canonical commentaries to the *Zhouyi*, and even the works of Dong Zhongshu (179–104 BCE) in the Han. In the next chapter, we will consider ironic appropriations of non-ironic themes as expressed around the usages of Li, considering them responses to non-ironic trends, even though some of the texts treated there certainly predate some of the texts treated here. The assumption is that we can thus trace a trajectory within the non-ironic line of thinking that exists in some form, and thus is capable of serving as a stimulus to thinkers with an orientation toward the ironic tradition, even before some of its written expressions, and even before all its ramifications have been fully developed.

LI AS "GREATEST COHERENCE" IN THE *XUNZI*

In *Ironies of Oneness and Difference*, I noted in passing that among the texts of the non-ironic tradition, it is in the *Xunzi* that we see the beginning of the advent of Li as an important and common term, with an exponential surge of frequency of usage as compared with earlier texts: a total of 106 appearances in the text as a whole.[1] Prior to this, we do have the key non-ironic, though sparse, usages of the term, still completely unflagged as any kind of special term, in the *Mencius*, in which the term occurs a whopping total of seven times. Four of these occur in the phrase 條理 *tiaoli*, "stripelike orderliness," used to describe the harmony of music in both its beginning and its end, a way to praise the timeliness of Confucius as expressed in his "wisdom" and his "sageliness," signifying the starting and finishing harmony respectively (*Mencius* 5B7). The meaning here is simply orderliness, with the important implication of harmony, as related to music, and of a coherence not only synchronically (harmony of various instruments and tones at any given time) but also diachronically (between the beginning and end of the piece), related explicitly to the combination of dyadically opposed virtues in the timeliness of Confucius.

The other significant usage compares the way delicious flavors please the mouth with the way "coherence and rightness" (理, 義 *li,yi*) please the heart/mind (*Mencius* 6A7). The close linkage of these two terms is to be noted here: coherence is, as we shall soon see in detail, in the non-ironic sense directly related to "rightness" in the sense of the fulfillment of one's specific role and its duties. The coherence of parts is related to their separation into their separate duties, and their ability to discharge those roles without overstepping them. Note also that for Mencius the term is unabashedly related here, as in the musical example, to a kind of visceral pleasure.

Let us now turn to Xunzi's much more frequent deployments of the term *Li*, to unearth what kind of thinking required him to begin reaching for this word so much more often than any of his predecessors had. Xunzi most commonly uses the term Li as a stative verb, meaning "ordered" or "coherent" in a positively valued way; it is one of his words for the order that counts as Xunzi's highest *nonnegotiable* value. That is, while Xunzi treats many things as having a variable value, there are a small number of things that are for him nonnegotiable, and Li makes its appearance as one of those items. As I argued in *Ironies*, "order" per se is for Xunzi a near-synonym for value: as I read him, when Xunzi says "bad," he means disordered, that is, incoherent in the sense of self-conflicted. This applies also to Xunzi's famous claim about human nature. When he says it is bad, he does not mean there is nothing that can be put to good use in it; he just means that in its native state it is disordered, incoherent, self-conflicted, thus self-weakening. Hence, there is no contradiction in Xunzi saying both "Human nature is bad" and "The source of goodness lies in human nature." An incoherent whole can have some elements that are good or neutral or ambiguous. Ultimate value for Xunzi is very simply the maximal satisfaction of human desires. This can only be achieved by human strength over other creatures and over nature, which can only be achieved by human teamwork, which can only be achieved by division of labor and privileges among humans, which can only be achieved by social ritual. These are the nonnegotiable values, including both the ultimate value (the satisfaction of desires being a self-justifying autotelic value) and the instrumental values leading thereto. Ritual is non-negotiable, but it has value because it leads to social divisions that lead to human togetherness and teamwork. These are the non-ironic coherence that Xunzi prizes. It is of value because it means being free of self-undermining social conflict, so that humans can be strong enough to get what they want. But all those qualities that might or might not contribute to ritual can be good or bad; whatever contributes to ritual coherence at some time or place is in that time or place good; whatever obstructs it is bad. These are the negotiable items, which include all sorts of human dispositions, emotions, institutions, habits: if properly fitted into the ritual coherence, they are good, but if not, they are bad. This allows Xunzi to give the most comprehensive possible picture of coherence, the Greatest Coherence, which can incorporate a wide range of apparently conflicting qualities and tendencies and behaviors: ritual itself serves as the "center" that unifies the two extremes of any given exemplar of Qian Mu's pendulum swing: advance and retreat, heaven and man, softness and hardness, cultural refinement and material austerity.[2] The negotiable items are valued differently according to how well or poorly they serve the nonnegotiable items; their desirability is purely a function of how well they cohere with the latter. It is this coherence itself, however, that really constitutes the nonnegotiable values.

A typical but maximally simple example would be this description of the noble person (君子 junzi): "When he is joyful he is harmonious and orderly, when he is worried he is still and orderly" (喜則和而理, 憂則靜而理 xi ze he er li, you ze jing er li).[3] This comes in a list of descriptions of the junzi, showing how in each of two apparently oppositely valued situations or moods he is still exemplifying value, that is, order. He can be either joyful or worried, but each is part of a larger whole that alters its resultant moral quality, which allows it to succeed in being Li, coherent or orderly, and thus a positive rather than a negative characteristic. Li in this passage is parallel to the following stative verbs: 道, 節, 類, 法, 止, 齊, 明, 詳 (dao, jie, lei, fa, zhi, qi, ming, and xiang), meaning "guiding," "regulated," "classified," "lawful," "still," "even," "clear," and "well-articulated." When expansive he is heavenlike and serves as a guide; when small-minded or careful he is fearful of rightness and regulated, and so on. All of these describe forms of *value* for Xunzi: one may be expansive or careful, clever or dull, successful or unsuccessful, joyful or worried, but as long as one is orderly, so that all one's parts and functions form one coherent whole and this whole coheres harmoniously with the world and with the ancient traditions in these ways, it is still a positively valued aspect of the noble man's existence. Li is one way of describing this orderliness; some of its other aspects are acting as guide, being regulated, classifying into types, being stable, and being intelligible—all ideas folded into our non-ironic notion of coherence: value, intelligibility, and orderly unification of diverse elements, balance of contrasted qualities, such that continuance is possible.

It is significant that among these parallel terms we here see, for the first time, the notorious *lei*, that is, "categorization," the division into types. Xunzi spells out the relation between Li and *lei*-types more explicitly elsewhere: "Viewing things exhaustively by means of the Way, past and present conform to a single measure. When types do not contradict each other, then even over a long span of time they form the same Li [類不悖雖久同理 *leibubei suijiu tong li*]. Hence, one can face deviations and twists without being confused."[4] A *qualifying condition* is provided here, indicating that *some but not* all types may come together to form a Li: if they cohere with one another over a sufficiently long period of time, they can be considered a Li. Not all *lei* count as Li. At the same time, it is not the repetition of a pattern that serves as the criterion that classifies them as Li, not a strict sameness or the participation in an isomorphic standard. It is rather a horizontal consistency, a coherence, between parts: the parts are not in revolt against one another, they do not contravene one another: the coherence of a Li is a harmony, not a sameness.

But this is an abbreviated way of describing the criterion for making a Li out of the available *lei*. Xunzi gives us a little more detail elsewhere: "The benevolent man uses loyalty and trustworthiness as the material of which he is made [質 *zhi*], dignity and respect to form his controlling unifier [統 *tong*], ritual and rightness to form his patterned ornamentation [文 *wen*], and human relations and type-categories to form his Li. [忠信以為質，端愨以為統，禮義以為文，倫類以為理 *zhongxin yiwei zhi, duanque yiwei tong, liyi yiwei wen, lunlei yiwei li*]."[5] We are being told here precisely how one goes about *making Li*, that is, forming an intelligible and harmoniously coherent order capable of serving as a guideline for action, a perforation along which to cut so as to sustain and continue this order: it is formed from (1) human relations and (2) types existing in the world. In other words, where these two contrary and pressing demands overlap, the benevolent man makes a Li. When human social relations on the one hand and natural groupings of feeling and response in nature come together, he makes a selective judgment call, thereby producing the value-laden orderliness of coherence, Li. The parallelisms with *zhi*, *tong*, and *wen* also help us fill out the notion of Li here: *zhi* and *wen* are a standard opposition, as in *Analects* 6:18, while *wen* and Li are commonly linked as closely related terms. This suggests that *zhi* and *tong* stand together here against *wen* and Li, and each pair bears roughly the same internal relation. *Zhi* is to *wen* as *tong* is to Li. *Zhi* is the foundation of *wen*, *wen* gives aesthetic expression to *zhi*; so controlling unification is the foundation of Li, and Li gives aesthetic expression to this unification. Li is the intelligible, discernible, visible expression of this totalizing unification. *Wen* and Li are visible to the eye, discernible, coherent, while *zhi* and *tong* are internal and hidden, to be inferred rather than perceived. Li is the *intelligible* aspect of value-bearing coherence.

Xunzi speaks repeatedly of Li as something that can be "threaded together" (貫 *guan*),[6] as something that can be followed (循 *xun*),[7] and as something that simplifies a complex situation and makes it intelligible, or easy to discern (簡然易知 *jianran yizhi*).[8] Threaded together, various smaller coherences form the "Greatest Coherence" 大理 *dali*, Xunzi's word for the largest coherent whole. Coherence here functions like a mass noun, as both Hansen and Peterson would predict. Many coherences together still form coherence—for the "together" is precisely the coherence. That Li can be followed and easily discerned go with the meaning of coherence as intelligibility; the common trope of "following" Li further supports our understanding of Li as harmony rather than sameness. One does not repeat it, one rather traces its contour and continuity among diverse instances; this is done not by matching to a model isomorphically, but by moving along the channel, tracing the path of contiguity. Where various elements join together harmoniously, allowing for a smooth transition from one to another, we have a "traceable" Li.

Li is for Xunzi a harmonious continuity, a discernible, valued coherence, but it is not simply "found" in the world; rather, as we described in our discussion of Xunzi's notion of coherence in *Ironies*,[9] it is formed and chosen from among all available groupings by the selective act of the authoritative sage. We saw there a seeming contradiction in Xunzi's "Rectification of Names" chapter, which seemed on the one hand to affirm the existence of real samenesses and differences distinguished by human sensory perception—something like "natural kinds"—and on the other an affirmation of the social construction, or regulation, of what words designate and distinguish. The naturalism of the former point would, in isolation, seem to rest on the recognition of some entities called Natural Kinds, which I claim would have to be in some sense genuinely identical wherever they are instantiated, possessing the causal efficacy not only of warranting their recognition as noncontiguous instantiations of the selfsame thing, but also of constituting genuine holistic totalities upon whose characteristics the identities of their parts are ontologically dependent, thus implying a kind of Realism. The conventionalism of the latter point, in isolation, would seem to recognize only the individual entities as objectively real, and their unity, their grouping under a particular name, as something that has reality only if applied from outside of these individual entities themselves, that can be added or withdrawn at will without changing anything about their real character, and hence implies a kind of Nominalism. To resolve this tension, interpreters sometimes suggest that Xunzi embraces a sort of "weak nominalism": the distinctions actually exist once and for all in the physical world, but human convention decides what particular *sound* and *symbol* is used to denote them. The groupings remain the same, and admit of a strict dichotomous right and wrong, but social regulation needs to determine which particular words denote each grouping in each community. We found in our analysis, however, that this solution oversimplifies the text. Xunzi is saying something somewhat more interesting. Our conclusion in *Ironies* was that for Xunzi there is an overabundance of possible ways to group things in the world, all of which have some warrant in the actual behavior of the objective world, but which stand in potential conflict with one another: the world as such, prior to human intervention, forms no single synordinate coherence. To recap that example, there is a real grouping in the physical world that puts whales in the same class as fish—to wit, they all really live in the water; there is another real grouping in the physical world that puts whales in a class with mammals—that is, they all really give birth to live young and produce milk. Both of these groupings are genuinely present, and both of them constitute genuine unities that, considered in themselves, are multiply instantiating and causally real in providing warrant for accurately naming these entities in this way. Indeed, as coherences, they are multiply instantiating entities that have causal efficacy also in actually holding the members of the coherence together in this way and enabling their relations in the manner described. That is, the totality of aquatic animals is, say, a holistic ecosystem, a genuine coherence in which the identities of its members are constituted only by their participation in that ecosystem, and the same is true, in another way, of the holistic totality of milk-producing and live young–bearing organisms. Both are coherences in the sense of wholes that can be accurately viewed as having a determining role to play in the actual constitution of the existence and identities of their members, bestowing a multiply instantiated character that inheres in each of these members.[10] Modern biology seems to imply that the former is an erroneous grouping, missing the true essence of these animals, while the latter is the true grouping that uniquely carves nature at its joints. Xunzi would say that both can be true, but that a human society, guided by regulations from a king guided by the tradition of sage kings, must choose one or the other— somewhat in the way kilograms and pounds both pick out physical realities, and yet if both systems are used, or if values are randomly or inconsistently assigned to them without being regulated by social conventions and even sanctions, the marketplace will be in chaos. The Greatest Coherence is the maximal coherence that can be created, not by the world alone nor by human beings alone, but by a certain selective overlap of the two: those among all nonhuman systems of grouping which can form a second-order coherent harmony with human desires and cognitions. But again, not all human desires and cognitions: only those that can form a coherent whole with those of the traditions of the sage-kings on the one hand and the surplus-ordered (i.e., chaotic, because it is possesses an overabundance of competing orders) nonhuman world. The Greatest Coherence is the *intersection* of the ways in which things are grouped by the nonhuman world, the tradition of the sage-kings and the present sensory and affective experiences of living human beings. This is the locus of true value. As Xunzi remarks, "Human trouble is always a matter of being restricted to one corner of things and ignoring the Greatest Coherence [大理 *da Li*]."[11]

This can perhaps be more clearly grasped from the connections drawn between Li and *tong* and *lei,* as well as *xing,* Human Nature, in the following passage:

> That which knows things is Human Nature [人之性 *ren zhi xing*]. That which can be known is the coherences of things [物之理 *wu zhi Li*]. If we seek to know the coherences of things with this human nature which is able to know, without any point of consolidation or resting point [i.e., point of orientation], then even if one continues to study all one's life one will never get all of it. Even though one may string together coherences numbered in the millions, it will never be sufficient to go through all the changes of the ten thousand things, and one will still be no better off than the ignorant. . . . Thus study must have its endpoint, its point of orientation. Where shall it come to rest? In the perfect sufficiency. And what is this perfect sufficiency? The sage kings. "Sage" means those who penetrate to the utmost the relations of things, and "king" means those who regulate things to the utmost. When these two are both brought to the utmost, it is adequate to serve as the utmost standard of the world. Thus in our study we must take the sage kings as our teachers, according with the regulations of the sage kings as our patterns, emulating these patterns in order to unify types [統類 *tong lei*], and to come to resemble them as people.[12]

There is no end to the multiplicity of possibly relevant coherences out there in the world; the only way to select out from among them that are relevant is to follow the sage-kings. It is this alone that makes of them a single overarching, synordinate coherence, with genuine value. The point is driven home most emphatically in a passage that has caused interpreters great trouble: the question has tended to be, Is the order of the universe discovered—a preexisting normative code—or is it invented by the noble man? Xunzi seems to be saying both. But in fact he is saying neither: order neither preexists nor is it created ex nihilo by the sages. Rather, it is that overlap of the man and nature that forms the Greatest Coherence. Here is one of Xunzi's most striking formulations of this point, which recapitulates the seeming tension between realism and nominalism, between preexisting order to be discovered and the human creation of order in the universe:

> Thus Heaven and Earth produce noble men, and noble men bring coherence to [li] Heaven and Earth. Noble men are those who join into and form a triad with Heaven and Earth, the controlling unifiers of the ten thousand things, the fathers and mothers of the people. Without noble men, Heaven and Earth would be incoherent [buli], ritual and rightness would fail to form a totality. There would be no rulers and teachers above, no fathers and sons below. This is what is called the utmost disorder. The relation of lord and minister, of father and son, of elder and younger brother, of husband and wife—these begin and then end, end and then begin, joining in the same coherence [tongli] with heaven and earth, joining in the same lastingness with ten thousand generations.[13]

> 故天地生君子, 君子理天地; 君子者, 天地之參也, 萬物之摠也, 民之父母也。無君子, 則天地不理, 禮義無統, 上無君師, 下無父子, 夫是之謂至亂。君臣、父子、兄弟、夫婦, 始則終, 終則始, 與天地同理, 與萬世同久。

It is tempting to identify this specific passage in Xunzi as the precise place in Chinese thought where the term Li is elevated from among the throng of possible words with which to denote some of the various forms and dimensions of the coherence and its sometimes conflicted implications, which had preoccupied thinkers up to that time, as we traced in detail in *Ironies of Oneness and Difference*, to its candidacy for a more specific, technical term by which to indicate a specific second-order form of coherence among coherences, providing a wedge that opens the way to many future developments, problems, and solutions. Noble men produce the coherence of Heaven and Earth, and yet the system they create also "joins in the same coherence" as Heaven and Earth.

Heaven and Earth are a first-order coherence in the sense in which we have defined it: a dyadically conceived whole that is continually productive of what become new parts of itself, nonidentical continuations of itself which continue to cohere with the initial coherence, neither same nor different from it, both adding to it and included within it. The relationship each new part has to this whole is what gives those parts their existence and identity, and each of these parts has some way of organizing its activity toward this whole, and thus organizing this whole around it; this manner in which each part coheres with and continues the whole, extending the whole in a new way but also included within it, is what constitutes each part's proto-evaluative act, as it were, its way of prioritizing and organizing and valuing the other elements of the whole in such a way that it is maximally sustaining to itself, although these different ways of valuing may or may not be consistent with one another. One of their parts, their productions, their continuations, is the noble man, a certain kind of human being, who also continues and coheres with the whole in his own way, thereby organizing it around his own self-maximizing evaluative orientation.

But Heaven and Earth themselves are not yet an example of the second-order coherence between coherences that Xunzi calls a Li, or of the greatest totality of these, the *da Li*, the Greatest Coherence. If they were, the noble men could not themselves be said to produce this Li. But nor are they definitively excluded from being included in the subsequent Greatest Coherence; they form an element that can be integrated into a Greatest Coherence once it has been created. At least some subset of what exists prior to human beings, some elements of the productive coherence of the physical world that produced them, can be incorporated into the fabric of this second-order continuity, which is the Greatest Coherence created by the noble men. Thus is the tension between apparent Realism and apparent Nominalism resolved here, just as in the case of Natural Kinds in general, as discussed in Ironies and recapped above.

This coherence of Li is real, multiply instantiated, and has a determinative power retrospectively even on the nature of its elements and on the conditions of its own production, which makes it genuinely productive of the new identity of Heaven and Earth as they exist within the value-producing coherence and continuity of this new whole. Heaven and Earth are now, as instantiations of this Li created by the noble men, elements that causally contribute to the sustaining of the physical world in the specific form that is maximally sustaining to human beings, as well as serving as genuine moral guidelines, serving actively as cooperative guarantors of model normativities. In fact, the noble men unify existing coherences, groupings, in the physical world, existing *lei*, selectively, and thereby create the Greatest Coherence. This is a way of "joining in" the same coherence as Heaven and Earth, which is to be clearly distinguished from following a preexistent coherence. This coherence coheres with some subset of those coherences, forming the Greatest Coherence possible. This is where the dichotomous conception of "same and different" that we struggled to dispel in *Ironies* can lead to such interpretative havoc: the "same" (*tong*) here is prevented from being a dichotomous sameness by its connection with the "join" (*yu*) and the "coherence" (Li). It does not mean following a single preconstituted principle that is "the same" in all instantiations. This would make the claim that "noble men produce" this principle, this order, this coherence (Li) incomprehensible. Xunzi means rather a joining up with a single unbroken continuity, which is constituted by both sameness and difference: the overlap of some part of what is coherent in tradition, some part of what is coherent in human cognition, and some part of what is coherent in the physical world to form the greatest available coherence.

Note also that maintenance and continuance here again go hand in hand with finding those coherent relations in humans that in turn cohere with some aspect of the world. Human social codes are those among the natural coherences that must not be altered: "Music/joy refers to those harmonies [和 *he*] which must not be changed; ritual means those coherences [Li] which must not be changed. Music joins the same, while ritual divides the different. The unity of ritual and music is controlled by the heart-mind of man."[14] The parallelism between "harmony" and "coherence" should be especially noted here. Xunzi contrasts and pairs ritual and music by noting that ritual stresses division, while music stresses harmony, or difference and sameness, which where at the heart of his theory of general terms and his theory of real but conflicting groupings in the world. Here again, he states explicitly that their unity lies in the mind of man. This jibes closely with our analysis of the problem above. Li is here still the divisions, the fixed roles, the determinate particularities, as opposed to the harmonizing, the joining and merging, of harmony. But Xunzi's intertwining of the two reveals the manner in which this dividing is also a joining, and this joining is also a dividing. Both harmony and coherence are a matter of separating into interrelated groups. When we divide, we unite; when we unite, we divide.

This passage is also of particular interest to us here because of the way it determines the relationship between ritual and Li. Ritual is a *subset* of Li. Among all the possible Li, *those which cannot be changed* are the authoritative rituals. If Li meant anything like "reason" or "truth" or "principle" or "order," we would expect the exact opposite claim: Li would be those eternal truths that can be culled from human rituals, the unchangeable moral principles. Xunzi's view is the reverse. There are many many types of coherence out in the world, many ways in which things group together. Among these, man chooses out some subset that are crucial to maximizing his own power. These are the authoritative rituals, and they cannot be changed in the sense that they *must* not be changed. This claim, of course, has a brother: the other coherences *can* be changed. They do not form a single consistent synordinate system applying at all times. Xunzi allows for timeliness of the application of "principles," the grouping into coherences, as long as they do not violate the nonnegotiable subset of coherences, the socially mandated rituals. I may call the whale a fish or a mammal as the situation demands, as long as I do so in the ritually prescribed manner, and these will be true descriptions of real coherences in nature in either case. This is one of the strongest pieces of evidence for the rejection of the idea of Li as principle or law of nature in Xunzi.

Xunzi says elsewhere: "When Benevolence is maintained with a sincere heart, it becomes externally manifest. When manifest it becomes spiritual, when spiritual it is able to transform others. When Rightness is practiced with a sincere heart, there is second-order coherence [Li]. When thus coherent, it becomes manifest [明 *ming*], and thus able to transform with circumstances."[15] The internal coherence of one member of the group becomes outwardly apparent, and this makes it capable of forming larger coherences within the group, both by inspiring others to emulate it and by gaining the ability to coherently contextualize itself (transform with circumstances). In sum, Xunzi exhorts us, "In whatever you do, establish what is beneficial to creating coherence [Li], and discard whatever is not beneficial to creating coherence."[16] Li has here become a word for ultimate, nonnegotiable value.

"HEAVENLY PRINCIPLE" (天理 *TIANLI*) IRONIC AND NON-IRONIC IN THE "INNER CHAPTERS" OF THE *ZHUANGZI* AND "THE RECORD OF MUSIC"

With the Inner Chapters of the *Zhuangzi*, we are squarely in the heart of the hardcore ironic tradition, as discussed at length in *Ironies of Oneness and Difference*. The term Li plays very little role in this development, as we have noted; where the term really explodes into its full development is in the incorporations of non-ironic themes into the framework of the ironic tradition, as expressed in the "Outer" and "Miscellaneous" Chapters of the *Zhuangzi*, as will be analyzed at length in the next chapter. But Li does occur in the "Inner Chapters" (1–7) of the *Zhuangzi*, exactly one time. This is the only occurrence of the character in either the *Laozi* or the "Inner Chapters," the core texts of the ironic tradition. It is a very important usage, the very first time in the tradition that the two characters 天理 *tianli* are used together, giving the appearance of what would later become a set binome and a very central term of much of later Chinese philosophical Confucianism and Daoism, a term that is sometimes translated "heavenly principle." In the "Inner Chapters," however, this would be a rather misleading way to construe the phrase. The meaning of *tianli* here is perhaps closer to something like, "spontaneous (nonfabricated, nonarranged, nonteleological) coherence." This term still seems strongly to suggest the existence of genuine natural kinds or real coherences in the world, but we have argued at length, in the prequel, that Zhuangzi's perspectivism entails a thoroughgoing rejection of natural kinds. Is this consistent?

Yes. The reason is simple. Zhuangzi's perspectivism is not the denial of natural coherences, but the assertion of an overabundance of real coherences, which cannot be combined into an exhaustive single synordinate meta-system of non-ironic coherence (a point accepted and responded to by Xunzi). The passage in question is Cook Ding's description of how he cuts up an ox: "I meet it with my spirit and don't look with my eyes; my organ-knowledge [官知 guanzhi, teleological deeming knowledge, more or less equivalent to the 知 zhi or eye-knowledge of the Laozi] stops and my spiritual desires [roughly equivalent to Laozi's stomach-"clarity" 明 ming] proceed. I depend on the heavenly coherences [依乎天理 yihutianli] and cut through the large gaps, guided by the big channels; I go by the inherent rightnesses [因其固然 yinqiguran]."[17] I am inclined to read "depend on the heavenly coherences" and "go by the inherent rightnesses" as roughly parallel, and thus as mutual glosses. Li would then be parallel to ran, which we have seen to mean, in the "Qiwulun," "to affirm as this and as right." The nonarranged, nonteleological coherences would then be the same as the inherent rightness of each position, perspective, and thing, and hence none other than their "heavenly," untidied state prior to deliberate interference: what Zhuangzi calls "the radiance of drift and doubt" (滑疑之耀 guyi zhi yao). To "go by the inherent rightnesses" (因固然 yin guran) of each perspective is precisely "to go by the this," (因是 yinshi), that is, the coherence set up temporarily by each perspective on the basis of its own self-affirming thisness. They are "heavenly" or "nonarranged" in the sense that they are not made to cohere with any single, overarching, synordinate coherence of a uniquely privileged whole. The practical implication is simply that there are natural coherences, and that by following them in each case one can flow along without contention in each particular case, and then go on to follow an entirely different noncontrived coherence when encountering the next "this." Each "this" brings with it its own coherence, necessarily. This implies nothing about a single overall system of "overall coherence" or "heavenly principle," singular. Each position creates, indeed is, the coherence of all that is around it; the coherent whole is formed within each particular member, not around or above them. Zhuangzi's tianli is not Xunzi's dali. It is, rather, its ironic counterpart—the inescapable parody of overall coherence. With this ironic usage of tianli, we have made the step into what appears to be the "objective" sense of Li. It is what is opposed to individual, private bias, to preconceived ideas, to clinging to a particular perspective. We are told to follow it rather than impose something upon it. In these points, it sounds like "objective truth," the real as opposed to the merely apparent, the objective as opposed to the subjective. But my point here is that in this usage we are witnessing what Richard Rorty would call a live metaphor, and in particular, a still stinging irony. *Tianli* is initially a deliberate contradiction in terms. *Tian* is what things are like before they are Li-ed. The Li of Tian are like the Dao that cannot be a dao. To follow them is to follow the unfollowable. They are anything but objective truths; rather, we are told to follow them the way the monkey trainer is told to follow along with the monkeys in Zhuangzi's second chapter. This is not because the monkeys are objectively right—quite the contrary. The monkeys are as subjective as they can be—one-sided, biased, irrational. As we discussed at length in *Ironies*, the reason for following their values is not that they are objectively true, but because that is how the wild card works, and sustains itself. This is how the term *Li*, originally meaning the imposition of order onto a raw material, comes to bleed into what sounds like a sense of the suspension of one's own deliberate intentions to follow along with something external. What looks like the advent of a notion of objective truth is rather an instance of sovereign Zhuangzian irony. We will see this sense developed further in the Guo Xiang commentary to the *Zhuangzi*, and reinvested with a stronger sense of normativity by some Buddhists and Neo-Confucians. But despite appearances, objectivity in its usual sense is never what is meant by this term.

"The Record of Music" (樂記 "Yueji"), which forms part of the 禮記 *Liji*, is the site of the one other classical use of this same term *tianli*, "heavenly coherence." The text shows signs of being a relatively late Warring States work, certainly later than both *Zhuangzi* and *Xunzi*, with clear influences from the latter. The passage in question gives a general theory of man's relation to the external world, using a phraseology similar to that of both the *Xunzi* and the "Great Commentary" to the *Zhouyi*:

> Thus the reason the former kings created ritual and music was not to extend to the utmost [極 *ji*] the desires of the mouth, stomach, ears and eyes, but to teach the people to even out their likes and dislikes and return to the proper Way of human beings. Human beings are in a state of stillness when born; this is their Heavenly nature [天性 *tianxing*]. They are touched off by [external] things and [only then] move; these are the desires belonging to their nature [性之欲 *xing zhi yu*]. But after things arrive, the [faculty of] knowledge [知 *zhi*] apprehends them—only then do likes and dislikes take shape therein. If likes and dislikes have no regulation within, and the [faculty of] knowledge is enticed from without, [human beings] can

not reflect upon themselves, and the Heavenly coherence [天理 *tian li*] is destroyed. Now if the touching off of human beings by things is without limit, and their likes and dislikes have no regulation, then this is a matter of things arriving and people being transformed by things. For people to be transformed by things is to destroy the Heavenly coherence and for [their truly] human desires [i.e., the "desires belonging to their nature, mentioned above] to meet with exhaustion [i.e., failure to be fulfilled].[18] Because of this they have the disposition for rebellion and deception, and the activities of excessive indulgence and creation of disorder.[19]

It would seem that "the nature" and even "Heaven" are positively valued here, but not unambiguously so; in a somewhat Xunzian manner, it is merely asserted that man's initial quiescence and his response to external things with desire are Heavenly, inborn, unavoidable. The value dimension is flagged by the term *Li*, the coherence that can be made from these desires, particularly through the education in coherence as harmony and division that comes through music and ritual. That this Li is nonetheless called Heavenly may seem un-Xunzian, or an extension of Xunzi's prior concession to the ironic tradition, as is the emphasis on the initial stillness of man when undisturbed by external things. The solution here, however, is not a reclaiming of this initial stillness, which is presumably regarded as impossible, but a regulation of the responses to the world so that they cohere with real values, so that man remains true to the coherence—the balance and harmonious self-sufficiency—of this stillness, not the stillness itself. As the text says later, even music is to be considered "still" or quiet because "it comes from within." The regulated desires are "still" in the same sense, that is, consistent with the inner nature of man. We may think here again of Qian Mu's comment about the "stillness" of the Center of the pendulum swing, which means not that there is no swinging but that the swinging is balanced and regulated by its relation to this constant center.

Nonetheless, the sense of prior existence of this Heavenly coherence may be interpreted as indeed privileging this original stillness in a way that Xunzi would not. For the idea seems to be that in the regulation of the desires, man regains the coherence he had when he was still and not "transformed by" external things, by the likes and dislikes created when the interaction of things is directed by the faculty of knowledge as subordinated to external things. Note that, at least as I am reading it, the passage asserts that the loss of this Heavenly coherence makes it impossible for the truly human desires to be fulfilled, namely, the desires that remain consistent with the original stillness of man's nature, the proper Way of man, the desires of his nature. A very similar idea occurs in the opening lines of another

Liji text, the famous "Zhongyong," as discussed in *Ironies*: the central balance 中 *zhong* prior to the activation of the emotions (presented in the form of pairs of contrasted opposites, joy and anger, sorrow and pleasure) is regained or mirrored in a modified form in the post-activation state by "hitting the proper measure" (中節 *zhongjie*—note the echoing pun on *zhong*). The extremes of the pendulum swing maintain their "centrality" by each finding the proper measure, the extent that will allow them to swing back and retain the capability of the opposite state. In the "Record of Music," the "regulated" version of these interactions between desires and external things is described as Li, a harmonious coherence in our sense, for precisely the reason given in the lines that follow: desiring in the way that has lost man's proper path interferes with the harmonious coherence of the social group, leading to rebellion and disunity. Li here again means a coherence that must cohere with a given set of human desires to produce further coherences.

The text goes on to describe music and ritual as creating unity and differentiation, respectively. Unity brings intimate togetherness, differentiation brings mutual respect. Music comes from within, and so is still; ritual comes from without, and so is culturally patterned. Great music is "easy," great ritual is "simple" (易, 簡, *yi, jian*)—a trope used also in the "Great Commentary" to the *Zhouyi* for Qian and Kun, pure Yang and pure Yin, respectively. Music shares in the "harmony" (和 *he*) of heaven and earth, ritual in their "regulation" (節 *jie*) or "sequential orderings" (序 *xu*). Benevolence is close to music, righteousness is close to ritual. This unity and division are the two sides of the creation of the groupings and coherences of nature. As in the "Great Commentary," we are told that things group according to type; here this is said to be the function of the "differentiations of heaven and earth" (天地之別 *tiandi zhi bie*), which ritual embodies. Indeed, the text echoes the proclamation we noted in the *Xunzi* that "Ritual is those coherences [*Li*] which must not be changed." Ritual is a subset of coherence, the one that a society cannot afford to alter. At the same time, the mutual chafing of the Yin and Yang, the harmonies that transform all things, are the workings of the harmony of heaven and earth, and are embodied in music. We are told that the coherences (Li) of the remote and intimate, the young and old, the male and female, are all manifested in music. The stress here is once again on Li as the divisions of these pairs of opposites, but significantly these Li are said to be manifested in the harmony of music. Li once again suggests then the harmonious coherence of divided groups, and these Li account for the mutual responsiveness and harmony in the whole. "Harmonization responds to singing, so that the turning and perverse, the twisted and straight all return to their own allotments, and so the coherence of the ten thousand things [萬物之理 *wanwu zhi Li*] all move each other according to type [類 *lei*]." Here we have a usage of Li that might seem not to be directly related to value. Even the twisted and perverse have their "Li" which account for the mutual response of members of a type, so that perverse music creates a harmful effect in people hearing it. But the point is that Li here is that by which the negative can be known and effectively dealt with. By perceiving the mutual responses, and knowing the psychological effects that will inevitably be created by such and such a music, one can make the adjustments—in this case, prohibiting such music—that will allow for greater human social coherence and harmony. Li even in this sense still accords with our definition of Li as a harmonious coherence (evil sounds with evil emotion) that, if cohered with (known), leads to further harmonious coherence (adjustment leading to greater social harmony). The accord between evil sound and evil emotion is still a "harmony" within its own sphere. The problem with it is that it fails to cohere with the context that surrounds it, unless properly known and responded to. It is a Li because, if accorded with (that is, known), it leads to responses that allow one to handle it so as to create these broader harmonies. Hence, there is no contradiction when the text goes on to explicitly link "harmony" and "coherence" (Li) in a parallelism, describing the way in which music "moves the harmonies of the qi of the four [seasons] and manifests the coherence [Li] of the ten thousand things."

We have seen the further application of this type of nesting of levels of coherence in the discussion of the *Zhouyi* in *Ironies*. Let us turn back to that text now with an eye to its role in the development of the meanings of Li.

LI IN THE "WINGS" TO THE *ZHOUYI*

In *Ironies of One and Many*, we presented an analysis of the thinking of the "Great Commentary" to the *Changes*, focusing on its concept of ultimate value: "The great virtuosity of Heaven and Earth is generation" (天地之大德之謂生 *tiandi zhi da de zhiwei sheng*) (II.1). And again, "Constant generation and regeneration is what is meant by Change" (生生之謂易 *shengsheng zhiwei yi*) (I.5). As I indicated there, the crux of the value theory operating in the "Great Commentary" is indicated in the following well-known passage: "One Yin and one Yang—this is called Dao. Its continuance is the Good. Its completion is human nature. The benevolent see it and call it benevolent; the wise see it and call it wise; the ordinary folk use it every day and yet are not aware of it. Thus the way of the exemplary man is rare indeed. It manifests as benevolence, but is concealed in all processes [or activities of the ordinary folk]. It drums the ten thousand things forward and yet does not worry itself as the sage must. This is the ultimate of flourishing virtue and great vocation!"

The meaning of this is made clear in a key passage of the commentary, which after much analysis we translated as follows: "The process of alternation of the emergence of intelligible coherences and the necessary incoherence with which it must cohere, of the active and the structive, of beginnings and finishes, such that they are always leading to each other, implying each other, and mixed with each other, is called the Way. When this alternation occurs in a proportion that is consistent with its own continuance, so that it does not get caught in a dead-end of unceasing dominance of either one side or the other, this harmony is called goodness, or value. What completes this harmony, both in the sense of being its pinnacle and of being the agent of its completion in the universe, is human nature. This principle of value is most obvious in what is called benevolence and wisdom, which is why the Way may one-sidedly be called benevolent or wise by those focused on these qualities, but it is the source and foundation of all activity in the cosmos, in a less obvious form, even in the daily activities of the common folk."

This was explained in terms of non-ironically valued coherence and its relation to disvalued unintelligibility with which it must nonetheless cohere. Valued coherence is a proportion between Beginnings and Finishes, between the active and the responding-structive, or, we may say, between the apparently positively valued (Yang, coherence in the first-level, naive sense, which brings things into being) and the *apparently* negatively valued (Yin, first-level, naive incoherence, which brings things to their finishes, marks an end of a given continuity), a proportion that allows both to continue to exist in a proportion that will allow them to continue to coexist, and so ad infinitum. It so happens that this proportion is one that usually involves the (non-quantitative) dominance and primacy of the apparently positive over the apparently negative, giving a ruling and superior role in the hierarchy, while at the same time, perhaps, granting the *quantitative* predominance to the apparently negative, modeled on the small number of rulers contrasted to the large number of the ruled. But this is of value only because it allegedly allows *both* to flourish. Beginnings and finishes should be arranged such that beginnings and finishes, that is, the creation of things and situations, continue to occur afterward, so that, in other words, *no finish is final*. The dominance of a finish, Yin, would spell the end of both beginnings and finishes, for to finish is to bring a coherence into incoherence, to end a continuity. Likewise, the total dominion of beginnings (Yang) that never lead anywhere, are never picked up, given structure, brought to completion, would also disturb the formation of things, the process of beginning and finishing, of making coherent. For to finish is also to make fully formed, to make fully coherent.

This gives us a clear understanding of how Yin is both negative in itself (the finish, death, the end of all being) and a part of the necessary process of creation of things (since "finish" here has both the sense of "to make an ending" and "to bring to its final form"—to complete or perfect, to bring to its *proper* end). It brings us to a way of understanding a form of "complementarity" that could be complementary with, and not in conflict with, "conflict." The complementarity of Yin and Yang presupposes their conflict. They are both conflicting opposites and two necessary parts of a single process, and there is no conflict between these two levels. Yin, as "finishing," is both negatively valued (in conflict with Yang and with the whole process) and positively valued (complementary to Yang and the whole process).[20]

The implication is that a dominance of Yin would kill off both Yin and Yang, and this alone is the source of its ultimate disvalue. The continuance of both is the determinant of what sort of relationship between them is desirable. Humanity's role is to make sure that this proportion prevails, lest the cosmos go askew, veering into a dominance of Yin that would end the alternating process of Yin and Yang. This, and not the eradication of Yin, nor even its suppression in every situation, is the aim of moral endeavor. Moreover, and crucially, there exist situations where the dominance of Yang would endanger the continuing flourishing of both, when it would lead to a monopoly that would eradicate Yin or itself. In these cases, the dominance of Yin is identical to value. The "one thread" running through all value is then: the relationship that will allow relationships to continue to exist, coherence that coheres with further coherence.[21]

The implications of all this for the way the order of things in the world is to be conceived are nowhere more stunningly portrayed than in another of the classical "Wings" to the *Zhouyi*, the "Shuogua" ("Explanations of the Trigrams"), as we discussed at length in *Ironies*. The text attempts to sum up the implications of the system of trigrams and hexagrams comprising the *Zhouyi*. Here is how the general statement of the procedure used by the sages to devise that system:

> Viewing the transformations of Yin and Yang [in the sky, i.e., Heaven], they established the trigrams. Developing the further implications of the hard and soft [of the Earth], they produced the individual lines. Harmonizing it to make it comply [和順 *heshun*] with the [human] Dao and its Virtue, they separated into coherent groups what was appropriate to each [理於義 *li yu yi*]. Fully exhausting this coherence they plumbed the depths of Human Nature, until it reached the Decree [Fate]. In ancient times when the sages created the *Changes*, they were attempting to comply with these coherences of human nature and its Decree, and so they established the Dao

of Heaven, calling it Yin and Yang; established the Dao of Earth, calling it the soft and the hard; and established the Dao of Man, calling it Benevolence and Rightness. Encompassing all three primal powers and applying this doubleness to each, they exchanged the six lines [in all possible ways] and made them into the hexagrams. Dividing Yin from Yang, alternately applying the soft and the hard, they transformed six positions [in various ways] and made them into the visible figures.

A two-termed "pendulum range" is here observed in three parallel realms: Heaven, Earth, and Man. Each has its own Dao, its "course," by means of which it proceeds. In each case, a dyadic alternation is observed as what is necessary to its sustainability. Heaven alternates between dark and light, night and day, Yin and Yang. The terrain of the earth alternates between soft and hard (e.g., mountains and waters, obstructions and passages). Human action alternates between the accepting lovingness of Benevolence and the judgmental severity of Rightness. It is the *overlap* of these three subsystems that yields the final system: those elements of the natural processes of celestial and earthly oscillations that can be made to "harmonize and comply" with the human course of benevolence and rightness, the course and its virtuosities, by means of the hexagram system. This is what is meant, it seems, by "separated into coherent groups what was appropriate to each [理於義 *li yu yi*]." That is, a "Li"-grouping emerges wherever the oscillation of the moral-pragmatic needs of *man* and the oscillations of the light and dark of the sky and the obstruction and passages of the earth overlap and coincide; we can imagine this as a kind of interference pattern of three types of waves, perhaps along the lines of the "double-slit experiment" used to demonstrate the wave-function of photons. Where these three types of oscillation "sync up," we have a Li, a valued coherence. I have briefly discussed the details of the sorts of things that count as this sort of "Li" in this text in the prequel to this book, *Ironies of One and Many*. Just how far from any familiar notion of "reason" or indeed of "order" this turns out to be can be easily observed from that discussion. This text, particularly its concluding statements about the ways the trigrams help to classify things in the world, seemed to its earliest occidental readers to be the pinnacle of ridiculous nonsense.[22] But we can now begin to understand in just what sense these classifications are meant to exemplify something called "separating things into coherent groups as appropriate." The appropriateness in question has to do with the matching or fitting between these three heterogeneous systems of oscillation: the temporal rhythm of the sky, the variations of the terrain of the earth, and human moods, intentions, and moral dispositions. When all these things come together, we have Li.

LI AND CENTRALITY IN DONG ZHONGSHU (179–104 BCE)

Let us skip ahead to take a quick look at the way some of these ideas take shape in the thought of Dong Zhongshu, the great systemizer of Han ideology and of what becomes the default non-ironic position, in resistance to which later theorists resurrect the ironic tradition. Dong's calendrical and geomantic model for understanding Yin and Yang, typical of Han thought, leads to a further development of the idea of Centrality and Harmony, explicitly linking them with Li, as will often be the case in the development of this term. Here again we see the force of the conception of coherence as harmony around a center. In Chapter 77 of the same work, entitled "Following the Way of Heaven," Dong writes:

> Following the Way of heaven in order to nourish one's person is called the Way. Heaven has two Harmonies, which complete its two Centers [中 zhong]. When the year establishes its Centers, its function is endless. That is: the function of the Center of the North joins with Yin, and only then do things begin to move what is below. The function of the Center of the South joins with Yang, and only then does its nourishment begin to beautify what is above. The motion below cannot be produced without the Harmony of the East, namely, the Mid-spring (Spring Equinox, literally Center of Spring). The nourishing above cannot be completed without the Harmony of the West, namely, the Mid-Autumn (Autumn Equinox, Center of Autumn). So then what does the beauty of Heaven and Earth reside in? In the place of these two Harmonies, which accomplish and complete the activities of the two Centers when the latter return to them. Thus the East generates and the West completes, and thus the Harmony of the East is generated. What the North brings forth is completed by the Harmony of the West, and thus what is nourished by the South grows. What arises cannot be generated unless it reaches the Harmony. What is nourished and grows cannot come to completion unless it reaches the Harmony. What is completed in Harmony must have Harmony also at its inception. What is begun in Centrality must have Centrality also in its ending. The Center is what makes for all the ends and beginnings of Heaven and Earth. And Harmony is what makes for all the generations and completions of Heaven and Earth. For generally speaking, there is no greater virtuosity than Harmony, and no Way more correct than the Center. The Center is the unobstructed Coherence of the beauties of Heaven and Earth [中者天地之美達理也 zhongzhe tiandizhimeidali], and what the Sage

preserves and holds to. The *Odes* say, "Neither firm nor yielding, he spreads forth his governance in all its excellence." Is this not referring to the Center? For this reason, the virtuosity of he who can use Centrality and Harmony to coherently order [Li] the empire [以中和理天下 *yi zhonghe li tianxia*] will flourish, and the longevity of he who can use Centrality and Harmony to nourish his person will reach its ultimate of his allotted span.

The quotation from the *Odes* brings us a coded reference to Yin and Yang, here interpreted through their calendrical and geomantic associations, with some typical Dongian punning, to present an equation of Li with centrality as such, the point of balance that harmonizes the extremes of Yin and Yang. In this sense, in spite of his exaltation of Yang, the real ultimate value of Dong's system is not Yang but Centrality, which he explicitly links with Li, a particular kind of coherence between the apparently valued and the apparently disvalued, the Yang and the Yin. Here as before, the criterion for what counts as Li is that it must be a coherence (in this case, between Yin and Yang, and also between their concrete forms as the four seasons and the four directions) which with humans can cohere (knowing it, using it to order the empire and the body) to bring about a further coherence (sustainability, continuance, longevity, flourishing). Here we have the full consolidation of the cluster of ideas around Li, and most notably, its direct association with the idea of the Center, the key non-ironic trope, which will subsequently be reclaimed for newly ironic purposes in Chinese Buddhism.

This quick overview of the development of Li within the non-ironic tradition should put us in a position to understand the challenges faced by the ironic tradition in assimilating this development. Li is closely associated with the kind of division into groups that allow for a single overarching "Greatest Coherence" to operate as the locus of the highest value, constituted by an overlap of prior human and natural coherences. Li are here intelligible and plural, a way to talk about the specificities of particular coherences as an element in value. This is in contrast to the earliest ironic conception of coherence, which as yet allowed scant role for specific explanatory or moral intelligibles, locating highest value instead in precisely the abrogation of the same. It is to the integration of these two disparate visions that we now turn.

THREE

THE DEVELOPMENT OF LI
IN IRONIC TEXTS

We have turned back to the earlier texts of the non-ironic tradition to find the gradual emergence of the term Li, and its connection to the notion of coherence understood in the non-ironic sense there, also tracing the development of the non-ironic notion of Li a few steps forward in time. We now turn our eyes to Li in the late Warring States ironic texts. The term appears only the once in the "pure" ironic texts, the *Daodejing* and the Inner Chapters of the *Zhuangzi*. But we find it emerging as a key term in the later developments of that tradition, which we may regard as a kind of mirror image of the "appropriations of the ironic into the non-ironic" considered in *Ironies of Oneness and Difference*, namely, the *Liji* texts "Daxue" 大學 and "Zhongyong" 中庸 and the Yin-Yang compromise as developed in the canonical commentaries to the *Zhouyi* 周易. In those works, we saw ironic themes and insights adopted and integrated into a non-ironic framework, enlisted to serve non-ironic ultimate values. In the later ironic texts, we find the parallel situation in reverse: they make a place for some of the concerns and insights of the non-ironic tradition, arriving at a compromise position of their own, where non-ironic values are subordinated to ironic ultimate values. Li turns out to be a central tool in effecting this form of the *rapprochement* of the two traditions. However, as we shall see, this development spans a number of distinct phases, which can be found scattered throughout these works.

LI AND NON-IRONIC COHERENCE IN THE LATER PARTS OF THE *ZHUANGZI*: INTEGRATING THE NON-IRONIC

The perspectivism of Zhuangzi's "Inner Chapters," as we saw in *Ironies of Oneness and Difference*, entails a strong denial of the existence of unique, univocal natural kinds: the world considered in isolation of human beings possesses no privileged ways of cohering. The predictive and normative functions of knowledge are there dismissed; what was so in the past is no guide for what will happen in the future, and what happens here, or for me, is no guarantee of what happens there, or for you. There can be no generally formulized rules about things or actions, not even in the rough and ready, pragmatic sense. In the *Laozi,* Dao did have a weak "predictive" and "normative" sense; it suggested that a general and predictable course for all things was the reversing rise and fall from not-being-there to being-there to not-being-there, and that this told us something important on how best to deal with things in general. Still, the nature of this single course was necessarily ironic with respect to any more specific determinate (coherently intelligible) course or generalizations about particular things. Only coherence in the new, ironic sense of the term is left.

As we have already seen, this was not an insurmountable problem for those who wished to defend the non-ironic sense of coherence. One reason for this was because coherence already involved a perspectival element from the beginning, even in the non-ironic tradition, in that it always implied coherence with human desires in particular. Another reason is that Zhuangzi's argument doesn't really entail the denial of real coherences, but rather the overabundance of them, and the impossibility of combining them into a single mega-coherence. This implication is granted and responded to by Xunzi, as we saw above: the sage-kings simply pick out the best coherences from the multitude of coherences really available in the world, best here meaning those which lead to the maximal coherence with those desires within human psychology and tradition that are themselves maximally coherence-making for human society.

But several other positions were developed in the early Chinese traditions to accommodate both the ironic and non-ironic applications of coherence, forming new syntheses. In this chapter I will discuss several compromises between ironic and non-ironic coherence that can be described as attempting to accommodate the latter to the former. These can be divided into three types, all found already within the later parts of the extant *Zhuangzi* text. In all of them, as in the *Xunzi,* the term Li plays a newly prominent role.

FIRST TYPE: LI AND DAO BOTH NON-IRONIC

The first type of combination of ironic and non-ironic in the *Zhuangzi* that begins to make use of the term Li is a simple extension of a slightly modified non-ironic. We see this non-ironic incorporation of the ironic in some of what Graham calls the "syncretic" chapters of the *Zhuangzi.* In Chapter 16,

"Shanxing" 繕性 ("Mending the Nature"), we can see clearly how Li begins to be deployed in this context. Here we find a positive and noninverted relationship between (real, non-ironic) Li and the traditional non-ironic virtues:

> The ancient practitioners of the Course used placidity to nourish their knowledge. To refrain from action based on knowledge once this knowledge is born [from this placidity] is called nourishing the placidity together with that knowledge. When knowledge and placidity thus nourish one another, harmony and coherence grow out of the inborn nature [知與恬交相養, 而和理出其性 zhi yu tian jiao xiangyang, er he li chu qi xing]. Virtuosity is harmony. The Course is what makes coherent. When Virtuosity is all inclusive, it is Benevolence. When the course makes everything coherent, it is Rightness. Virtuosity is harmony. The Course is coherence. [夫德, 和也; 道, 理也 fude, heye, dao, liye] When Virtuosity is all-inclusive, it is Benevolence. When the Course makes everything without exception coherent, it is Rightness. [德無不容, 仁也; 道無不理, 義也 dewuburong, renye, daowubuli, yi ye][1]

Here Dao is equated directly with Li, with De, the Virtuosity that is the attainment of Dao, is equated with harmony. Dao is straightforwardly the orderliness with which all things cohere, and there is no hint of any indeterminacy, irony, self-cancellation, or unintelligibility to Dao, Li, De, or harmony: all can be known and practiced. Dao is the coherent whole of coherent Li. Li is here consistent with and expressed by yi, the rightness of each thing keeping to its own place within the coherent whole, rather than necessarily undermined by these definite norms of rightness, as we will see in the properly ironic usages of Li. Here the role of knowledge is problematized: knowledge and non-knowledge are to nourish each other, but while non-knowledge ("placidity") nourishes knowledge directly, serving as the source from which it emerges, knowledge only nourishes non-knowledge by *not interfering in it* after emerging from it—by not trying to control it or indeed know it. This way of thinking, and the use of Li within its exposition, is consistent with the general outlook of the *Guanzi* chapters, as we shall see in the next chapter.

SECOND TYPE: DAO IRONIC, LI NON-IRONIC

But something new begins to happen in the second type of ironic/non-ironic relation we find in the later parts of the *Zhuangzi*: the assimilation of Li in the non-ironic sense into an *ironic* sense of coherence. That is, in this second stratum, we find an attempt to make room for some kind of generally assertable modes of togetherness with some rough and ready pragmatic reliability, as applied to particular things in the realm of experience, but retain a strong sense of the provisionality and limitedness of these groupings and rules, subordinated to the ironic sense of coherence in general which makes its appearance in the consideration of the uppermost category, Dao—which one could almost describe here as universally applicable irony itself. In more old-fashioned and approximate language, here we will be looking at Daoist assimilations of Confucian ideas, to be contrasted with the previous volume's examination of exactly the opposite case as seen in the technical Yin-Yang systems: Confucian accommodations of Daoist irony.

I have in mind in particular certain passages from the later chapters of the *Zhuangzi* itself. The later sections of the present *Zhuangzi* text develop some of the ideas of the "Inner Chapters," and sometimes diverge from them. The radicalism of Zhuang Zhou's relativistic perspectivism is effaced, sometimes in favor of a fixed picture of the distinction between benefit and harm, or of the division between the spontaneous and the deliberate—the standard fault lines of older Daoism. The text includes both critiques of Confucian values and praises of them, syncretic systems and extremist primitivisms, anarchism and conservatism, "rationalizing" and "irrationalizing" tendencies (as Graham put it), all of which stand side by side in the text as a whole as it currently exists.

For example, in the chapter "Autumn Floods" (秋水 "Qiushui"), characterized by Graham as a "rationalizing" chapter, we find a systematic expansion of the relativism of the Zhuang Zhou writings. Nothing is big or small or good or bad in itself, in this exposition; we call something big when it is bigger than something else, and thus "big" is a predicate that can apply to anything at all, and does not pertain to the thing itself. The same goes for all predicates. Similarly, each thing affirms itself and negates all others, meets its own standard and fails to live up to the standards embodied in other things—an idea derived from the "this/right" conflation in the "Inner Chapters" of the Zhuangzi, convincingly attributed to Zhuang Zhou himself. But at the end of this discussion in the "Autumn Floods" version, we are told that these considerations give some real knowledge about how things are (namely, things are free of intrinsic characteristics, susceptible to relative valuations and attributions, etc.), and that this *knowledge* aids a person in living well in the world, in understanding what is truly harmful and beneficial. This is a step back from the Zhuang Zhou writings, a subtle shift that nonetheless alters the significance of this whole line of thought significantly. The text then, in direct contradiction to Zhuang Zhou, sets up a fixed division between the "human" and the "heavenly" (or natural), that is, the deliberate and the spontaneous, as if these could be known in a way that was not purely perspective-dependent. The text asserts this categorically: the heavenly is "the internal," the human is the "external," and we are to privilege the heavenly over the human, which alone is the source of all virtue. The distinction between them is perfectly clear and unambiguous: a horse has four feet—that is the natural, the spontaneous, the heavenly; a horse has a saddle on its back and a bit in its mouth—that is the human, the artificial.[2] Where Zhuang Zhou had said, "How do I know that what I really call heaven is not man, and vice versa?"[3] and even "How do I know that what I call knowing is not not-knowing, and vice versa?"[4]—the author of this chapter tells us once and for all what is spontaneous and what not. Where Zhuang Zhou had, after suggesting that the human not be allowed to interfere with or try to help along the spontaneous, gone on to describe the state of the Genuine Person where, as Zhuang Zhou's sixth chapter puts it, "neither heaven nor man wins out over the other" (天與人不相勝

tianyuren buxiangsheng),[5] this later chapter, evidently from another hand, stops at the first step without taking the second.

The term Li is crucial to this discussion, and we should pause to look at how it is used here. The Xunzian binome 大理 *dali* appears non-ironically: "Now you have come out of your little river and seen the great ocean, thus knowing your own ugliness. Now I can speak to you about the Great Coherence [*dali*]."[6] When the content of this great coherence is indicated, however, we find it closely connected with the perspectival relativism of the Inner Chapters, as formulated here, however, in terms of the Yin-Yang pair: "If you try to take right [是 *shi*] as your master and eliminate wrong [非 *fei*], or take good-order as your master and eliminate disorder, that would just mean you were unclear about the coherence of heaven and earth [天地之理 *tiandi zhi Li*] and the real condition of the ten thousand things [萬物之情 *wan wu zhi qing*]. This would be like taking heaven as your master and eliminating earth, or taking Yin as your master and eliminating Yang; the impossibility of it is obvious."[7] Here the necessary coupling and inseparability of each coherence with its paired opposite, including the contextualizing of coherence per se by what undermines it into incoherence, is taken as the Great Coherence itself. This is how the balance of both sides of each dyad, which in the Inner Chapters entails also the non-dominance even of the Heavenly, is appropriated here: coherence-incoherence is given a metalevel definition as Great Coherence itself. This is indeed the standard ironic move, used to make the very notion of coherence ironic. That this is here in contrast meant, oddly, non-ironically is clear from the following: "The Dao has no end or beginning, but things must go through death and life, and their completion as such-and-such can not be depended on. Now empty, now full, their forms not holding to any one position. The years cannot be held on to, the times cannot be stopped. Things wax and wane, fill and empty, ending and then bringing a new beginning. *This is the means by which we can speak of the method of the Great Rightness* [大義之方 *da yi zhi fang*], *and discuss the Li of the ten thousand things* [萬物之理 *wan wu zhi Li*]."[8] The parallelism of *fang* and Li is susceptible to several interpretations here: *fang* can mean "direction," "locus," "recipe," or "method," and also "square," that is, with clearly delineated edges and sides, as opposed to the more amorphous shape of a circle, which cannot be so simply divided into separate parts. The sense of "direction," "method," or "recipe" resonates with Li in the sense of a guideline to be traced, the built-in way in which something can be divided and carved, the perforations along which work is to be done to create maximum value (i.e., maximum coherence). The sense of "locus" and "squareness" brings out the sense of coherence as "definite intelligibility." At the same time, we have an association (through a kind of skewed parallelism) of the typical unironic coupling of Li and *yi*, coherence and rightness, just as we see in the *Mencius* and *Xunzi,* and in the *Guanzi* "Techiniques of the Heart/mind."

The final non-ironic use of Li in this passage is even more instructive. In answer to the question, "What then is valuable about the Dao," we get, "He who knows the Dao will necessarily comprehend the coherence of things [必達於理 *bi da yu Li*]; he who comprehends the coherence of things will necessarily be clear about the shifting balances of things [權 *quan*]. He who is clear about the shifting balances of things will not allow things to harm himself. . . . He investigates the safe and the dangerous, is at peace in both disaster and good fortune, is careful in what he approaches and avoids, and so none can harm him."[9] Understanding of the Great Coherence, that is, the way things fit together, what was just described as the principles of constant change and the inseparability of each coherence and its negation, leads to careful calculation of what goes with what, where and when harm will come, and how to maintain the shifting balances, *but always in reference to the unchanging perspective of harm to oneself.* We see here an attempt to combine the inseparability of coherence and incoherence typical of the ironic approach, the copresence of any perspective with the opposed perspective, which negates it and undermines its original coherence, with a single Great Coherence and a single unchanging perspective, which, as in the Confucian context, has mainly to do with a certain stable set of human desires of the observer. It seems that the assumption is now once again, as in the *Mencius,* that humans share the same basic desires, or at least that any person over time will have some desires that necessarily apply at all times (i.e., concerning his personal benefit and harm)—two premises that are both rejected by the more radical perspectivism of the Inner Chapters. One could argue perhaps that only temporary definitions of benefit and harm, as dependent on any given perspective, are meant by the present passage too, but the overall treatment of the Great Coherence seems to militate against this reading.

This sort of containment of the ironic has practical consequences as well. Another set of texts collected in the current *Zhuangzi*, characterized by Graham as the "Primitivist" chapters (Chapters 8–10 and the first part of Chapter 11), adopts a similarly fixed definition of the spontaneous and the artificial, buttressed somewhat by some of the anti-civilization riffs in the *Laozi*, considering all pursuit of objects of conscious knowledge or valuation as disruptions or disturbances of man's original spontaneous nature. This applies equally to material gain and to morality, both of which are "external" to man's true nature. Here the division between "inner" and "outer," and between "natural" and "artificial," is regarded as knowable and fixed. Zhuang Zhou had suggested that by following along with the shifting perspectives, "the radiance of drift and doubt" 滑疑之耀 *guyi zhi yao*, one could "do good while remaining far from the reach of fame, do evil while remaining far from the reach of punishment" 為善無近名, 為惡無近刑 *weishan wujinming, wei'e wujinxing*. By this he meant, it seems, that one might find oneself doing what is defined as good or evil according to some perspective at any given time, but that one would not be committed to any single course of action to the extent that would bring one to the extremes of either fame for goodness or punishment for evil in any case, either of which would require cumulative, extended, consistent behavior according to a particular fixed value perspective. The author of the "Primitivist" chapters of the *Zhuangzi*, on the other hand, tells us that he would be ashamed to commit *either* good or evil, understood here in the fixed conventional sense of benevolence and righteousness on the one hand and "excessive or perverse conduct" on the other; both disturb his true, spontaneous nature, identified with the Dao as a metaphysical absolute.[10]

From these examples we can see some of the ambiguities involved in the Zhuangzian line of thought, and the variety of conclusions to which it can lead when subtle shifts are made in its premises. With these shifts, it becomes possible to incorporate a more non-ironic respect of definite coherences and fixed goals, the lineaments of common sense in general. We have a definitionally incoherent Dao, the largest and most unsurpassable whole, the togetherness of all things that is necessarily incoherent; all of that is standard ironic fare. But here a compromise has been struck which allows this incoherent whole to ground and support intelligible specific, coherent patterns and guidelines that make for successful activity as construed by commonsensical values. It should be noted in passing that this structure mirrors that found in *HuangLao* texts which view Dao as the source of Law or authoritative regulation (法 *fa*)—a point we will return to in discussing the Hanfeizi below. Li is in these examples precisely a way of indicating this intelligible pattern that is grounded in and somehow expresses the unintelligible whole, accessing it and providing the ideal way of inhabiting it.

We see echoes of this type of thinking scattered throughout the later chapters of the *Zhuangzi*, though expressed less intricately and extensively. In the "Tiandi" ("Heaven and Earth") chapter, for example, we find the following passage:

> In the Great Beginning there existed non-existence, without existence and without name. From this the One arose. The One existed but had no form. When things obtain it [得 *de*] and thus came to life, this is called the thing's Virtuosity [德 *de*]. When the formless divides into separate parts, with some temporary rough continuity [且然無間 *qieran wujian*] to each, it is called the ordained Life [命 *ming*] of each thing. From the stopping and moving creatures were born, and when these creatures form in such a way as to generate a coherence [物成生理 *wu cheng sheng Li*] it is called physical form [形 *xing*]. In the physical form spirit is preserved, each with its own rule, which is called its nature [性 *xing*]. If the nature is cultivated so it returns to the Virtuosity, the Virtuosity can be made to be the same as the Beginning. In being the same, it is empty. In being empty, it is vast, joining with the chirpings of the birdbeaks. When the birdbeak chirpings are joined, one has joined with heaven and earth. This joining is muddled and dim, as if stupid or half-conscious. This is called the Dark [hidden, unintelligible] Virtuosity, which means being the same as the Great Flow.[11]

Individual entities are here depicted as deriving from a division within the original Non-Being, the unintelligible whole. Each entity obtains this formlessness, which becomes its Virtuosity (virtue), from which derives the coherence of its physical form, from which derives its internal regularity, its "nature." It is noteworthy that the determinate nature of a thing is derived from its physical form, not vice versa. Virtuosity would seem to be not any specific form or nature, but merely the concretized version of the formlessness of Dao itself, formlessness that has been "obtained." We may perhaps think of this simply as formlessness as seen from the perspective of any particular form, the unintelligibility standing at the root of, and in the past and future of, any intelligible coherence, regarded by that coherence as its own root, beginning and end. We will have a further development of this idea in the *Guanzi* chapters and in the *Hanfei* commentary on the *Laozi*, to be discussed momentarily. If this Virtuosity is "returned to," the individual being is reconnected with the formless, unintelligible Beginning, entering a state of dimness, and muddledness, which can join together in a new way with the determinate entities of the formed world (the "birdbeaks" here perhaps referring to the expression of various determinate words and positions as described in the "Qiwulun"). Coherence here is formed from and by incoherence, and has as its goal the reappropriation and reintegration of this original incoherence; in this version of the ironic tradition's appropriation of non-ironic coherence, the real coherence is rooted in incoherence.

THIRD TYPE: DAO AND LI BOTH IRONIC

An interesting contrast to these non-ironic usages of Li can be found in other later chapters of the *Zhuangzi*, where we find the third type of usage of Li in the text, bringing the meaning of coherence itself, even on the specific micro-level, fully into the realm of the ironic. Chapter 22, 知北遊 "Zhibeiyou" ("Knowledge Wandered North") is among the chapters classified by Graham as representing an "Irrationalizing" development of Zhuangzian themes, as contrasted to the "Rationalizing" tendency of the "Autumn Floods" ("Qiushui") chapter—a contrast that we can reframe in terms of our ironic/non-ironic schema. In this chapter, the term Li appears in several interesting contexts, very helpful for understanding the implications of the "ironic" deployment of this term. The first of these runs as follows:

> Heaven and earth have great beauty [大美 *da mei*], but do not speak of them. The four seasons have unconcealed regularities [明法 *ming fa*] but do not dispute about them. The ten thousand things have perfectly completed coherences [成理 *cheng Li*], but do not explain them. The sage traces the beauty of heaven and earth back and arrives at the coherences of the ten thousand things [緣天地之美而達萬物之理 *yuan tiandi zhi mei er da wanwu zhi Li*]. Thus the perfect man has no deliberate action, the great sage does not initiate anything, which is what is meant by watching heaven and earth. . . . Once things have died or been born, become square or round, no one knows their root. Floatingly the ten thousand things emerge from the past and have their certain existences. The vastness of the six directions is still within [this root], and tininess of an autumn hair relies on it to form a particular body.[12]

Beauty, regularities (i.e., regulations, patterns to be followed, statutes) and coherence (*mei, fa, Li*) are all standard non-ironic values, and are presented as parallel here. Each is here contrasted with some form of intelligible expression: speaking, disputing, explaining. The contrastive "and yet" in each phrase suggests that normally beauty, regularity, and coherence would be expected to be accompanied by intelligibility. The "great" beauty, "unconcealed" regularizations, and "perfectly formed" versions, however, are precisely those that lack intelligible expression. Note that "great," "unconcealed," and "fully formed" are all normally terms for visibility or ease in apprehension, the state of things easily seen—forms of coherence. This is exactly the point of the contrast: the real coherence is incoherent. This is a clear indication of the wedge between the valuable/balanced/togetherness aspect and the intelligibility aspect, the wedge that marks the ironic usage of these terms in Daoism. The truly valuable, balanced and inseparable coherence is that which is nonintelligible, and it is this that is instantiated in the non-action of the sage described in the remainder of the passage.

The second example comes a few passages later in the same chapter, put into the mouth of Laozi, speaking to Confucius. After explaining that the bright (intelligible) comes from the dark (unintelligible), the formed from the unformed, and that the sage preserves that which remains unaugmented when added to and undiminished when taken from (i.e., the indeterminate unhewn Dao), he says:

> This Middle Kingdom is populated with "*human beings*," but such creatures are ultimately neither Yin nor Yang. For they dwell between heaven and earth only temporarily assuming the form of a human being, always just on the verge of returning to their source. From the point of view of its root, life is just a temporarily congealed thing. Although some are long lived and some die young, how much of a difference is there really? It's all a matter of no more than a single instant—what room is there for the rightness of Yao and the wrongness of Jie? Every fruition has its own coherence [果蓏有理 *guo luo you Li*]. Although humans encounter difficulties in their interactions with one another, this is precisely how they are able to interlock. The sage meets them without rebelling, lets them pass without holding on to them. To respond to them after harmonizing them is a matter of Virtue, but to respond to them as if it were pure happenstance is a matter of the Way.[13]

The difficult, passing reference to Li here is one of the few places in the pre-Qin corpus where the term is used with an implication of its all-pervasiveness, as a term for the Omnipresent, a notion to be of great importance in both Buddhism and Neo-Confucianism, where Li serves as the totalizing "universal universal" which is present everywhere. This passage is followed immediately by Zhuangzi's famous "Dao is everywhere, even in the piss and shit" passage, further lending support to this interpretation, albeit circumstantially. It is important, however, that the text does not say simply that every insignificant object, no matter how small or neglected, has "Li" in it or to it, but that every "fruition" does. The term translated here as fruition is the binome *guoluo*. *Guo* denotes the fruits that grow on trees, *luo* those that grow on vines. If this is chosen not as a haphazard random example of any given object, the implication is perhaps that there is coherence to anything that comes to completion, to fruition, that, in other words, fruition is coherence. This would mean that when anything—whether a sage such as Yao or a villain like Jie—reaches its completion, it has its own sticking together, its intelligibility, its balanced harmony, its connection to its environment, and its value. The implication is brought home by the otherwise rather obscure following line: "Although humans encounter difficulties in their interactions with one another, this is precisely how they are able to interlock." This is to say that "the difficulties," like the villain Yao, are themselves a kind of fruition, a kind of coherence. What seems to lack inner harmony and balance, and doesn't seem to cohere smoothly with the environment, which are not experienced with pleasure as non-ironic coherence is supposed to be, also have their coherence—they are the very means by which the humans interlock, that is, cohere (literally, interlock like teeth). This means that every formation and situation in a context, no matter how discordant, is also a way of cohering with a context, and this is the real (ironic) coherence that brings about the more readily recognizable forms of non-ironic coherence.

The full thrust of the ironic conception of Li is spelled out even more explicitly elsewhere in our text:

> To delight in clear vision is to be corrupted by visible forms. To delight in sharp hearing is to be corrupted by sounds. To delight in Humanity [ren] is to disorder Virtuosity. To delight in Rightness [yi] is to violate Coherence [Li].[14]

Notice here how the wedge is driven between Rightness and coherence, which were so intimately linked in the *Mencius,* and as we shall see again in the *Guanzi* texts and in the non-ironic tradition generally, where they tend to function as aspects of one another, and in the "Qiushui" passage of the *Zhuangzi* quoted above. Here, ironically, the explicit form of coherence, namely, Rightness, the separation into appropriate divisions, is a direct violation of genuine Coherence, which is necessarily unarticulated.

In another late chapter, we are told:

The sage's birth is the process of Heaven, and his death is the transformation of things. At rest he shares in the Virtue of Yin, in motion he flows in the waves of Yang. He does not make himself a precursor of good fortune or an initiator of ill fortune. He responds only after feeling a stimulus, moves only when forced to move. He starts things only when there is no other choice. He discards knowledge and precedent, following only the coherences of Heaven [天理 *tianli*].[15]

Here the "coherences of Heaven" (*tianli*) are explicitly contrasted with "knowledge and precedent," which would be aspects of coherence and intelligibility in the non-ironic tradition. To follow genuine coherence means to discard the apparent coherent; real coherence is ironic coherence. These examples may be considered consistent with the "Irrationalizing" trend but at odds with the "Rationalizing" trend.

Many further examples of this turn of thought could be adduced within the developed ironic tradition; in all of them, we find a practical application, from the point of view of the individual existences, of the overall incoherence of real coherence. This is a compromise position that allows for a guideline to be established for action, circumventing the full-fledged Zhuangzian skepticism, but a rule that incorporates the non-ironic notion of coherence only to undermine it at the highest level, or to use this irony itself as a guiding rule for creating real coherence—value—in the world.

In the "irrationalizing" passages, then, we see a radical extension of the ironic usage that is, I think, consistent with the *Laozi* and Inner Chapters approach. Nonetheless, I classify it here as a "compromise" usage because of its willingness to suggest specific individual coherences with some application to particular things and classes, while excluding others, or at least the general acceptability of certain middle-level generalizations located somewhere between the unintelligibility of the Dao and the momentary coherence of individual experiences.

INTEGRATING TYPES TWO AND THREE

This tendency is most explicitly marked in one more dialogue from the later parts of the *Zhuangzi* that must be considered here, since it addresses the question of natural kinds and coherences straight on, and may perhaps be regarded as an attempt to reconcile these two opposed attitudes—the rationalizing and the irrationalizing—toward local coherences within an ironic context. It comes in Chapter 25, and is considered by Graham to belong to the same school of thought as the "Autumn Floods" dialogue. However, we shall see that its treatment of the problem at hand differs significantly.

The "Community Words" dialogue[16] begins by explicitly raising the question of what categories are, how things of the same type are grouped together into a single coherence:

> Know-little asked Great Universal Reconciliation, "What is meant by 'Community Words' [丘里之言 *qiu li zhi yan*]?"
>
> Great Universal Reconciliation replied, "A community is the joining of ten (family) surnames and a hundred (individual) names to form a set of customs [風俗 *fengsu*]. The different [異 *yi*] is joined into the same [同 *tong*], the same is dispersed into the different. For example, you can point to the hundred parts of a horse's body and never come up with a horse, and yet the horse is right there, tethered in front of you; it is precisely through establishing the hundred parts that we call it 'horse.' For this reason, hills and mountains pile up the low to make the high, the Yangtse and the Yellow River join the small[17] to make the large. The great man joins and brings [things] together to make the universal [公 *gong*].

An observation is here made about recognizable grouping of things into types that share a single name—what we'd be inclined to call class names, general terms, universals, types, or natural kinds. These are explained, very significantly, by *comparing words to communities*. Communities, we are told, are the joining of individual human beings into a collectivity, forming *customs* that have a discernible identity. This is "the joining of the different into a unity," which at the same time can be viewed in terms of its elements, the individuals that make up the community. As we have seen, it is characteristic of early Chinese thinking that in considering how singularities can be joined into a coherent unity, even when the ultimate topic of the discussion is the logical concepts of difference and sameness (異, 同 *yi, tong,* terms used commonly by both the Mohist and the non-Mohist logicians), and "universal" or general terms, the initial concept is derived from the workings of human society, the interpersonal relations that take place in the social realm. Indeed, one of the most fundamental meanings of the word which I take loosely to mean universality or generality here (公 *gong*) is "public," and its immediate sense has more to do with the lack of bias or partiality pertaining to the social totality, what is public, common or *generally accepted* (as opposed to the views or practices of some subgroup or individual), than with the logical notion of universality as a category or Form embracing a set of particulars. The undeniable fact that individuals gather together and come to form coherent social unities that in some sense transcend the sum of their parts is here used as the starting point for a discussion of how the same process occurs also in nature (e.g., in the horse and its parts), in language, in the state, and finally, by way of contrast, in something called "Dao."

The primary model for thinking of the relations between things here is not that of inert parts of an objective whole, a thing from which the observer stands abstracted, a whole whose parts are closely interrelated but still mutually exclusive, but rather the relation between members of a community. These interrelate in a very different way from members of a class of objects, particulars subsumed under a universal, or even parts of a whole. The whole/part relation here is cast in terms of the relation of a community's customs, the forms of conventional behavior that allow its component members to communicate and cooperate and characterize it for other groups, pervading the individual participants and their specific social role identities. Each individual in a community in a sense fully instantiates, by virtue of his unconscious absorption and execution of generally accepted norms of behavior (風俗 fengsu, customs), the specific identity of this entire community. These customs are internal to and constitutive of each member's behavior and identity. This involves more than just a shared characteristic or shared membership in a whole, or indeed the mere fact of harmonizing coherently: what makes them part of this whole is not only that they all are able to continue being a part of it, but that each has the total system of customs within himself. This is a way of describing how each part is in a certain sense the whole: as a son who internalizes the customs and norms of the father-son relation is joined to that relationship by the total system of norms, including those that pertain to the father to which he must respond, and the same is true of the father. Being a father requires an internalization of the entire father-son relation, and the same is true of being a son. Something like this model is applied more broadly here to an entire community: each one keeps to his role, but in so doing each is saturated with all the roles. The individual members share beliefs, ideas, customs, practices, which constitute each of the members differently and yet in such a way that they are not prevented from being a part of the content of one as much as of another.

This socially conceived convergence of oneness and difference of the parts joined into a whole is further compared to a horse's body, which can be analyzed into its component parts, or seen as a totality, a horse. When thinking of it as merely these hundred parts, we cannot perceive how it can be a single unified horse, for these parts appear to be disparate and mutually exclusive; nonetheless, it is due to these very parts that we get the horse. As Graham points out,[18] this is an explicit rejection of the adequacy of the whole-part relation as usually conceived, and amounts to saying that the whole, the horse, is more than the sum of its parts, and can never be understood in terms of analysis into these parts, which, thus analyzed, remain exclusive of and separate from one another. Nonetheless, we can identify and separate these parts in thought, and at the same time see that these differences are joined, and in fact do in some sense equal the whole, for there is no whole apart from these very parts. What is more, to anticipate what is to come, the very functioning of the parts together in terms of their interactions with one another may be said to express the "horsiness" of each of the parts, just as the interactions of the role identities in the society are expressive of the customs that characterize that society. This is the second step of the argument, another vivid example of how differences are joined into coherences, and the paradoxes to which this relation leads when thought about in overly rigid terms, in terms of the mutual exclusivity of objects. We can understand the joining of these parts into a whole that is greater than their analyzable sum, the dialogue suggests, only by analogy to the joining of individuals to form customs in a community. To apply the original analogy, the community is not the sum of its members; on the contrary, there is something more to the community than the atomistic and disparate individual members considered in themselves. This something more is precisely the customs (*fengsu*) which are part of the makeup of each of them, which bind them into one organically functioning whole, a whole that is complete, in an adumbrated form, in each of its parts. This is how it comes about that "the different is joined to make the same, the same scattered to make the different."

Grand Universal Reconciliation continues by extending this principle to other natural phenomena, and finally to the "Great Man" himself. Mountains are a unification of the low into the high, rivers are the unification of the small into the great. These natural things are described here as the unification of qualitative opposites, of small and large, or rather as the unification of the small to form the large, just as a community collects the different to form the same. It is of the essence that we strive to understand this strange assertion. This comparison works on a number of levels; small and large are opposites, as are different and same, individuals and communities; the two poles are joined in each case by showing how one pole actually consists of the other: the large is just the unification of the small, oneness is just the joining of the diverse. What is essential in all this is just this *ability to join* the things in question, and thereby to create a completely new quality: the joining of the small produces, not just more smallness, but its *opposite*, largeness, just as the joining of individual identities yielded not just a bunch of individuals, but something quite different, a community distinguished by an identifiable set of customs, or as the unity of parts yielded not just a collection of parts, but its opposite, a whole. Behind both these images is the primary sense of joining individuals human beings together to form collective groups with pervasive norms, that is, something that comes to be shared *within* each of them, and indeed is as constitutive of them as they are of it, but involves a transformation thereby into the *opposite*: this is the essence of the *ironic* move (by being more X, more coherently X, it ceases to be X). We may view it as a development of the "balance of opposites" entailed in the non-ironic view of the Center, of the type seen in Qian Mu's pendulum example, into something more radical, an actual convergence of the opposites.

The role of man, and thus of language, is brought back explicitly in the next line, stating that the Great Man joins disparate things together and arrives at universality, generality, impartiality, publicness (*gong*, echoing the name of the imaginary being who is speaking). This term may be taken to imply, as we shall see in more detail below, the unbiased totality of a community that shares customs which in their entirety are lodged in each member, interfusing and constituting the identity of each, as well as enabling their interactions.[19] The Great Man brings this interfusion to all things, joining them all into a whole that is constitutive of all its parts. Here we have the introduction of a particular kind of coherence of all things, *gong*, a relation explicitly compared to that between the customs of a community and the members of that community. The Great Man embodies the coherence of these customs, dwelling within them, and thereby bestows a greater coherence on the community itself, as we saw in the *Mencius*, and beyond the human also into the community of nature, as we saw in the *Xunzi*.

But here this involves a necessary reversal, irony, incoherence to this greatest coherence. To see what is here meant by this joining of all things into coherence, and how the Great Man goes about it, we must read on:

> For this reason, that which comes in [to him] from without has a host to receive it without being [exclusively] clung to. What comes from within [him] is able to rectify [affect other things] without being rejected.

The great man joins all things into universality, 公 *gong*: this is the "community word" par excellence, one that also describes the characteristic function of communities and of community words. Here we see the further implications of his mastery of these community words, and the universality they bring with them. In light of the entire passage, I interpret the "for this reason" here to mean, "Because the Great Man has grasped this idea of *gong*, i.e., interfusing and constitutive totality, the relation of customs to a member of a community . . ." Here I believe the discussion is returning to the original topic, namely, words. The words of a great man are community words, they are *gong*, and thus he interacts with his community in the way described here. "That which comes in to him from without"—that is, the words other members of his community address to him—"has a host to receive it"—that is, can be understood and properly apprehended, since the customs and conventions underlying these words are present in both the speaker and the listener—"but is not exclusively clung to"—since he has apprehended the totality and its constitution of all the parts, he is not misled by a partial perspective from one particular member of the community, but sees also its connection to the whole, to the words and beliefs of the community, which may include contrary beliefs or ideas from the ones explicitly expressed at any particular time. "What comes from within him"—i.e., his own words—"has that which it rectifies"—again, because the entirety of the community's customs and conventions is complete in each of its members, so that the custom-based universality in his words corresponds with that in the listener, and is able to affect and transform, to influence other members of the community—"and is not rejected"—for his words tally with those customs and accord with the sentiment of the whole; hence, all the members of the community accept his words. These are community words in two senses; they are words that are in actual practice *gong,* since they are accepted and practiced by the total group. They are also community words in that they bring all things together, gather the individual inanimate objects of various kinds and unify them into single terms and expressions, what we would be tempted to call universals. But even here it is to be stressed that this universality has the primary significance of being a shared part of the experience of the community, rather than any indication of a real kind or abstract class of objects in the world. Moreover, this *gong* is explicitly linked with its instantiation in the person of an authoritative individual; it is the entirety of the community not as such, but as made coherent via his gaze. A user of words has correctly grasped them as "community words" if he understands them as corresponding in this unbiased manner with the total usage of the word in the community, so that as a listener he is impartial and undeceived, and as a speaker he is convincing. These, and not any kind of correspondence or accuracy, are the standards by which the appropriateness of his words are to be judged. We may be reminded here of Xunzi's proposed regulation of general terms; they are right when the community agrees upon them. In Xunzi's case, of course, this was to be effected by directives from above, whereas in the current passage the suggestion is that the Great Man finds the real commonalities of reference of his community within himself, and speaks accordingly, thereby creating a discourse that has real efficacy within that community—indeed, making that community cohere to an extent (i.e., his words are not rejected, a coherence between himself and his community is created) through his own verbal continuations of its incipient commonalities.

In sum, the Great Man is here depicted as a part *within* the whole who nonetheless represents or encompasses the whole, that is, the universal, custom, identity of whole, and *hence* he fosters the effective interaction between the parts of the whole, via the analogy of these words/information which serve as tokens of the universal/custom/identity of the whole. A similar doubleness to the meaning of "universality" is discernible, as we have seen, in the *Mencius,* where the "nature" (*xing*) proper to the human species is both (1) what all humans have in common at birth, and what distinguishes them from other species, and (2) what actively *unifies* them as a group, in that the perfect exemplification of this nature, its complete development and display as accomplished by a sage, necessarily attracts, binds, subdues, and transforms all the other members of this group, inspiring them to rally around him and become a true community which shares the salutary customs he embodies. A similar conception, structuring the concept of universality on the model of the "universal man" within the community, can be discerned in many Warring States works, which perhaps suggests that we may single it out as a premise shared widely, which can partially account, as it does here, for some of the unexpected turns of thought in works from this period.

It is in this context that the text finally introduces the term Li, and drives home the irony of the overriding conception of Dao at work in this exposition of the "unbiased":

> The four seasons have their different breaths, but Heaven is not partial[20] to any of them, and thus the year comes into being. The five bureaus of government have their different duties, but the ruler is not partial to any of them, and thus the state is well governed. Literature and war [are different skills],[21] but the Great Man is partial to neither, and hence his virtue is complete. All things have their different coherences, but Dao is not partial to any of them, and thus it has no name [萬物殊理，道不私，故無名 *wanwushuli daobusi guwuming*]. Since it has no name, it has no activity. It has no activity, but there is nothing it does not do.

At this point, the argument undergoes a slight shift in direction. We have just been speaking about the behavior of the Great Man, how he joins things together in words, and how these words tally with the community at large, thus bringing them together as well. Now, however, we are told of the processes of nature and government, and from there of Dao itself. These are all asserted to be analogous to the behavior of the Great Man just adduced, to wit, his use of community words. Specifically, they are analogous because these things also come to completion by means of "not being partial" to any part. The Great Man, in his use of language, apprehends the whole (the total set of linguistic customs and their entire unifying scope embracing all things as they cohere with this particular community) inherent in each of the parts (a particular word spoken by a particular member of the community at a particular time), and his words tally with this totality, thereby not being biased toward any one part, and including the opposite side of each particular that happens to be before him. This is because the model of part/whole relations here is still that of the member to his community, where the *entire* set of customs is embodied, intuitively known, and enacted by each individual member. In the same way, in the "community" of words, each single word or linguistic act has "within" it, as its meaning context, the entire system of speech and names, the "customary" behavior of the words and their custom-based unifications within that linguistic community. The opposite of this particular word is involved in that this opposite is also included in the whole adumbrated therein; whatever *else* besides the particular part being explicitly articulated at the moment is in the totality is also in each of the parts, and this is what is expressed in the community words of the Great Man. To the Great Man, all words spoken by members of the community have ultimately only one referent: the coherence of this community itself, the customs that makes this community a coherent whole. Thus, the parts are not mutually exclusive, since each contains within itself the totality, including the opposites of itself. Here we may see an expansion on Zhuang Zhou's point in the "Inner Chapters" about opposites as entailing one another, where each part contains the entirety of the opposition.

Similarly, the text suggests, the total year is in the spring, in that it was the year as a whole, the alternation of all four seasons, that make spring what it is; the same is true for each of the other members of the group, the other three seasons. The year is to them what the totality of customs of the community are to each individual member of the community, or what the total community's language is to a single speech act. By allowing each of these partial manifestations, showing no special preference to any, hence applying this "universality" or generality, this principle of impartiality and constitutive totality complete in each part—the principle reflected in the Great Man's use of community words—nature makes the totality of the year. The same pattern is visible in the relation between the ruler and the bureaus of government, and to the Great Man himself in his cultivation of particular virtues; the opposites and contrasts are seen as complementary, mutually implicating and interpenetrating, and thus partiality is avoided. All this is the same principle as that implicit in the Great Man's use of words, which likewise embrace the universality of things, the totality of customs and conventions of the community and its collective apprehension of things, and thus his words, the names he uses, are unifiers of opposites, bring all things and people into oneness, are *gong* like Heaven and the ruler of the state.

But then, when we begin to speak of Dao, there comes an important difference. At first the relation between Dao and all things, with their coherences, is exactly parallel to that of the last three cases. But the conclusion is somewhat surprising: we are told, not that Dao is complete or universal due to its not being partial to any one principle, but rather that it *therefore* "*has no name.*" Here, unlike in the "Autumn Floods" dialogue, we are dealing with coherence in its ironic sense. This is a jump; for were we not just told that precisely *names* had the ability to be impartial, to join things together in this special way? Why then does Dao's comprehensiveness preclude name, since words, in the arguments so far advanced, are precisely the conveyers of comprehensiveness, of intercommunication and interpenetration of the community and of the objects of its experience?

The answer is that this assertion acknowledges another property of words; not the integrating function of language as a communal unifier, but the specifying function of any one particular word qua particular—Zhuang Zhou's point about terms such as "this" and "I." To put it another way, this assertion acknowledges the flip side of the integrating function of language, its "shadow," which is the fact that in language this unification must always be accompanied by simultaneous division and separation. To specify any one determination in particular is to contrast it to what it is not, to negate something. To identify a given class or universal (hence *unifying* a group of particulars), by means of a name, is to distinguish (hence *separate*) it from other classes; to use a word is always simultaneously to compare and contrast things, two meanings conveniently summed up in the Chinese word *bi*, as we shall see below. What we see in this turn of the argument is a sort of bringing of the principle so far elaborated as pertaining to community words, namely, the ability to join individual members into a whole, enabling their interactions, sustaining them as a comprehensive entity, to its logical conclusion: What about the most comprehensive unity of all? Does the same thing still apply? Here a self-generated surprise emerges: in the case of Dao, the largest comprehensiveness or *gong*, the very same process implies its own opposite (a sort of metalevel joining of opposites). What combined individuals into some distinctive "name" (an indwelling comprehensiveness unifying the members, and identifying the whole) now results precisely in "namelessness." Dao's comprehensive inclusivity necessarily precludes the assignation of any one name to it. Since Dao is "not partial" to any given intelligible coherence (*Li*), it can have no particular name, for this would specify one particular meaning to the exclusion of all others and hence be an instance of just such partiality. Thus, the comprehensiveness of the community words used by the Great Man, which brings differences into oneness, is still only a partial comprehensiveness, dependent still on contrast to what is outside itself in any given instance; when this principle of all-inclusivity is extended to its logical conclusion, in the case of the Dao, it overcomes itself into namelessness, into unintelligibility, indiscernibility. So far here, as in the second type of ironic incorporation of non-ironic themes seen above, we have Li and Dao in a kind of part/whole relation, where Li are the individual, discernible, limited coherences, and Dao is the overarching coherence of these coherences, which is for that reason unlimited and indiscernible, incoherent, nameless. Dao is ironic coherence, but Li are non-ironic coherences.

This namelessness, moreover, is here asserted to be somehow analogous to the completion of the year, the governing of the state, and the perfection of individual power or virtue. And the relation of Dao to individual coherences is analogous to the relation between heaven and the seasons, the ruler and the bureaus, the Great Man and his virtues. This suggests what is confirmed in the following lines, to wit, that this namelessness is not yet the total eradication of language, but rather another particular case of inclusivity, which includes other such cases, all of language and all particularity, within itself—hence, "there is nothing it does not do." The impartiality of nature in making the year does not eradicate spring and autumn; it merely eradicates the mutual exclusion or sunderedness of each of them with respect to the other. The same is true of Dao and language, or specific names, accomplishments, or non-ironic intelligible coherences. "Because it has no name it does nothing. It does nothing, but there is nothing it does not do." The latter is one of two instances in the entire *Zhuangzi* where this famous phrase of the *Laozi* is quoted, but the context gives this familiar Daoist truism new implications. To be everything and nothing, to be all names and no names, to accomplish everything and nothing is here asserted to be analogous to being a horse and yet the parts of a horse, or being the customs of a community and yet being the role behavior of all its individual members. Because it has no particular name, nothing particular can be predicated of it, hence it cannot be said to "do" anything in particular. But this non-doing is unnamable precisely because it is a doing and being of everything, and is partial to none; hence, it has no negation, nothing outside itself with which to be contrasted, and thus no determination, no name. This non-doing is not the exclusion of all activity, but precisely the inclusion of all activity, just as the customs are not the exclusion of the behavior of the individuals, the year is not the exclusion of the seasons and the namelessness is not the exclusion of all meanings, but rather their comprehensive impartial inclusion, and indeed the glue immanent in each member which enables them to function together. It is their coherence, in the sense of their sticking together, and in the sense of what makes them function "coherently" as themselves, as particular coherently intelligible identities. The inclusiveness of community words here reaches its ultimate culmination, which also happens to be the apparent contradiction of itself—and indeed, the joining of such contradictions is precisely what can be accomplished by the unities brought about by the Great Man's community words and Dao's nameless nonactivity which does everything.

To sum up, we are told here that "Universal/custom/identity" means "unbiased to any part," and moreover that it is precisely the presence of this in each of the parts which allows the communication between parts, the intelligible identity of each part, and the effective function of the whole. The whole is a whole because it is inherent in each part. Given this premise, Dao is adduced as the largest of all categories, the universal of universals, the universal/impartial/public/custom/identity *present in each being and unifying all beings,* that is, all actions, things, principles and names, that is, all parts, which enables them to function together, to interact, to form a whole. But, as the customs are not identifiable with any family or individual customary roles in the community, nor the horse with any part or combination of parts of horse-parts, Dao, as unbiased, can have no particular name, action, or identity. Thereby it enables all actions, names, identities. The function of names and words, as unifying, here reaches its ultimate term and in so doing negates and overcomes itself: the ultimate unifying word, "community word," Dao, can be no word. The ultimate coherence cannot be coherent. It can only be adduced in an ironic sense. We have here the ironic idea of omnipresence combined with a non-ironic ideal of sagehood, the Great Man, who is able to embody the totality through other means, as in the pre-ironic texts.

To appreciate the distinctiveness of what has been asserted so far, we may construct the following table, showing all the "whole/part" relations that are here claimed to be strictly analogous:

WHOLE	PART
Customs/Community	Families and Individuals
Same	Different
Horse	Horse Parts
High	Low
Large	Small
Universal/Public/Unbiased (*gong*)	[Particular Things?]
Heaven's Year	Qi of Seasons
Ruler's State	Government Bureaus and Duties
Great Man's Virtue	Civil Culture and Warfare
Dao	Coherences of Things
Namelessness	Names
Swamp	Trees and Plants
Mountain	Rocks and Trees

It is the counterintuitiveness and leaps involved in moving the analogy from one of these pairs to the other that has led us to the conclusions about words and Dao we have reached so far, and which has located the presence of Dao in each thing, as that which gives them their life. As we shall shortly see, the presence of Dao manifest precisely as the Dao-like paradoxicality operative in each thing, and it is just this that gives all beings their being: the ironic use of Li as pertaining to individual coherences. The text continues:

> The seasons have their ends and beginnings, generations have their alternations and transformations. Disaster and prosperity, paired together, come flowing over; whatever is thwarted is also [in some other sense] suited. Each particular thing spontaneously follows a different direction; whatever is just right is [in some other sense] deficient. [Alternate translation: Whenever something is thwarted, something (else) is suited; whenever something is just right, something (else) is deficient.] It can be likened to a great swamp, where all the different trees alike dwell;[22] one can see this also in contemplating a great mountain, taken as a foundation for trees and rocks alike. This is what is called Community Words.

This passage is a bit more straightforward than the last, but still rife with interpretative possibilities and significant points. Again, the general idea is a description of the joining of contraries (disaster and prosperity, thwarting and suiting, just right and deficient, trees and rocks) into one totality. This seems at first to be a description of Dao's doing all, in spite of its doing nothing in particular; since it does nothing in particular, and is not determined as any particular action, it negates no action, and hence includes all contraries in its activity. However, this is only partly true. In my opinion, the focus switches from the Dao and its nonactive activity, described in the first two lines, to the position of the individual, and his community words, within this process of change. This switch of focus from the activity of Dao to the words and experience of the individual comes with the lines I have rendered as "Whatever is thwarted is also [in some other sense] suited . . . whatever is just right is [in some other sense] deficient."[23] Disaster and prosperity can only pertain to parts, not the whole. The point here is that, to the extent that either of the two applies to any part, the other will as well; what was disaster to part X will be prosperity to it in the due course of transformation; or is prosperity to part Y, or is already in one sense prosperity and in another disaster.

I take the meaning of the passage to be as follows: Dao, in its nameless, nonactive activity, brings about the turning of the seasons and the generations without partiality. From the individual human perspective, this means that disaster and prosperity are both included, bundled up together, so that where there is one there is the other, where there is thwarting there is also suiting. One's situation at any given time is in one sense thwarted with respect some particular aspect, but is also always necessarily suited to something else. This interpretation is in keeping with the ironic sense of coherence and the perspectivism of the "Inner Chapters." Each of these things goes off in its own direction, but wherever it goes, it cannot escape being at all times both just right and deficient, for Dao is not partial to either of these, gives both to each entity. We saw before that the real presence of the whole in the part was not only what identified the whole but, on the model of customs to the individuals in the community, is what in fact allows the parts to function at all, and to interact effectively with one another. We were then told that the ultimate whole, Dao, is necessarily paradoxical, a name that is no name, a doing which does nothing. Here we see the consequence of bringing these two premises together. Thus, it is not only Dao itself that is like a great swamp or mountain, which necessarily includes opposites within it; *the same is true of each individual within this totality*. Each individual includes the totality, just as each member of the community possesses the totality of its customs within him—this, again, is the paradigm, not that of objective whole and parts, the former being impartial and the latter partial and finite. Because the individual has this union of opposites necessarily within him, his words can be community words, words that embrace the totality and join the members together, all of whom contain completely within themselves the same body of customs and conventions. After the previous passage, which described the presence of the whole in the parts as what enabled the activity and interaction of the parts, we are here given a description of this enabled function, of the "nothing it [Dao] does not do." Dao, as the ultimate *gong* which must *therefore* be nameless and meritless, is thus paradoxical in that it does all and does nothing. Its presence within the parts, therefore, which enables them to live and function, is manifested as this paradoxicality pertaining to the parts themselves. Hence, we have an emphasis on polar, temporal transformations, contradiction, balance, and ultimate irresolvable *ambiguity* pertaining not only to the whole, but also to each part.

The text up to this point acknowledges the relative value of words as a unifying force, and as something that has legitimacy within the realm of things; indeed, we may say that language is here given a kind of cosmic significance, as being at least isomorphic with Dao and with the whole-making of nature itself. Words are to social man what Dao is to nature, in a very precise sense: they are the imminent totalizing whole within the parts which binds the parts together. But, as we see in what follows, the text goes on to sharply repudiate the suggestion that words are in any way adequate to describe Dao, which is much more than simply the unification of opposites and particulars accomplished by community words:

> Know-little said, "This being the case, are [these Community Words] sufficient to be called the Dao?" Great Universal Reconciliation said, "No. If we calculate the number of things, it does not stop at ten thousand, and yet we set a limit by calling them 'The Ten Thousand Things'—this is just to speak of them with a provisional name due to their great quantity. Thus Heaven and Earth are the vast among forms, Yin and Yang are the vast among forces [氣 qi], the Dao is the impartiality and unity among activities [為之公 wei zhi gong].[24] To use [the word Dao] as a provisional name for the vastness involved is permissible; but once you have [these words] you take [Dao] as being comparable and contrastable [比 bi] to something! To dispute and distinguish on this basis is to compare [the Dao to a class outside itself], like [the comparisons between finite categories like] dogs and horses [in the manner of the logicians]. This misses it by a wide margin.[25]

This passage, on my interpretation, asserts that although words—local socially determined and intelligible coherence—and Dao—global, unintelligible, incoherent coherence—are similar in that both embrace opposites, universalize, combine things into a oneness, they are different in that Dao is truly universal, not only a particular universality such as the meaning of any given word, but also each individual contingent thing, and all things, with nothing outside to which it could be compared or contrasted. No word, even a community word such as *gong* or "namelessness" or "Dao," is sufficient for this true universality, since any word gets its meaning from comparison and contrast (*bi*), from encompassing less than all and more than one, and the true universality of Dao is by definition not comparable or contrastable to anything, as we have already suggested in establishing the inherent paradoxicality of Dao, above. Comparison implies that there must be something external to be compared to, which is impossible for a true universality that includes everything within itself, partial to no particular meaning or principle, as our text pointed out above. In the other direction, Dao will embrace the irreducible uniqueness of individual events, as we shall see below, which words can never reach, since words are always the bringing-together-into-a-class of similars. Dao cannot be named simply with the name of universality, even though to universalize is part of what it does, for this name still contains comparison and contrast in its meaning—the name *universal* is not universal enough, the name *unbiased* is too biased. Comparisons like those to the swamp and the mountain above (introduced with the same word, *bi*) are only provisionally adequate; they work for the universality of community words, but not that of Dao. Even the name *namelessness,* as shown above, is simply a name for this universality, for the lack of partiality toward any particular meaning, comparable to the universality of heaven with respect to the seasons and the community with respect to its members, and thus even this name is to be considered inadequate, as we shall see below.

A sharp distinction is here still being drawn between the finite and the infinite. Words—which exemplify the type of universality or non-partiality similar to the community and its customs' universality with respect to the individual members of the community, joining them all together and appearing complete in each—can indeed resemble Dao; indeed, the Great Man's words, and the words he receives, penetrate perfectly, so that they reach to others without being refused. But this is a far cry from the real omnipresence of Dao. To use words, even a word meaning omnipresence, is still to miss omnipresence; for to have meaning a word must be particularized. This is the case in the logician's disputes, where an attempt at all-inclusiveness, such as Huizi's "Great Unity," which has "nothing outside it," is the closest one can come to the all-inclusiveness of Dao. But this merely corresponds to the concept *universality,* which is given its meaning according to the function of general terms such as *dog* and *horse,* standard examples of the Mohist logicians, given meaning by contrast to one another. To take Dao as simply one such general term is to reduce it to the status of finite things. We call it Dao because it is *gong* as the ten thousand things are "ten thousand." It certainly is *gong,* but it is not limited to this, as the ten thousand things are ten thousand but not only ten thousand. If we take *gong,* its universality, its relation to individual things as customs of the community relate to individual members of the community, as its definitive mark, we will be badly mistaken, just as if we were to insist that there were only ten thousand things. We may take this as a strong denial of the apodictic standard of knowledge in general, and also of the reality of determinate universals, that is, anything short of "the universal universal." Any claim of knowledge is to be understood in this sense; when I say, "The sky is blue," or, "Filial piety is good," it is no more literally or apodictically true than the statement that there are just ten thousand things. This does not mean we should never say such things, or that there are no coherences to be spoken of any more; rather, every statement and every coherence is to be regarded as tentative, merely pragmatic, or, better, ironic, always indicating also its opposite.

What then are the things about which words can speak, if they cannot speak of Dao itself? What is there to say strictly within the realm of the finite? The dialogue continues:

Know-little said, "[In that case,] within the four directions and the
six realms, how does the arising of the ten thousand things come
about?" Great Impartial Reconciliation said, "Yin and Yang shine
on each other, injure each other, heal each other. The four seasons
replace each other, give birth to each other, slaughter each other.
Desire and aversion, dismissal and approach arise bridged between
these. The joining of male and female like paired halves becomes
a regular presence amidst these. Safety and danger replace each
other, disaster and prosperity give birth to each other, leisure and
hurry grind against each other, aggregation and dispersal complete
one another.[26] This is the realm of which names and objects can
be recorded, of which even the most subtle can be registered. The
coherent mutual ordering of things as they follow in succession
[隨序之相理 suixu zhi xiangli], the mutual influence of things in their
bridge-like motions, that they revert when they reach exhaustion,
that they begin again when they come to an end, this is what there
is inherent in the realm of things, what words can exhaust, what
knowledge can reach to—it gets to the ultimate limit of things and
no further. He who sees the Dao doesn't follow after them when
they are discarded nor trace them back to where they arise—this
is where discussion comes to an end."

This is the realm of things, and what can be said with words. Surprisingly, it is quite a lot, and still represents a retreat from what Lee Yearly has
called the "radical Zhuangzi"—the hardcore ironic position. For here, words
can indeed be accurately and legitimately used to describe a certain amount
of what goes on in the world. Here we see the nature of the compromise
between the ironic and non-ironic senses of coherence, once again pivoting
on the Yin-Yang dyad and the "constructive" application of the inescapable
self-undermining dyadic structure so crucial to the ironic position. Dao, the
ultimate ground of things, does not enter into this discussion of "how" things
come to be. We are told rather literally the *manner* in which they come
to be, and this manner once again points to the Dao-like paradoxicality
which also inheres in things themselves. Nonetheless, words, as themselves
creators of coherence among disparate parts, are able to accommodate a
certain amount of this paradoxicality: words, as "community words," have
some of this paradoxicality built into them, as we saw in the opening of
the dialogue. There are certain linguistically identifiable patterns to things,
patterns also derived from the idea of the joining of opposites so important
in the first part of the dialogue. These more or less follow the conception in
the *Laozi* of what is assertable about individual things: they return, they go
back and forth, they follow a bell-shaped curve. They go through patterns

of alternation and mutual response of opposite poles, they arise bridged between these various sets of opposites. This image of the bridge is apt: all things rise and descend, supported over an abyss by having one foot on each of two opposite shores, by being rooted in both Yin and Yang, growth and decline; if either were removed, they would collapse.[27] The existence of things is, in fact, a rising and falling joining of opposites—a bridge. The self-undermining dyadic alternation is now asserted as a generally adequate way of describing what will take place in the empirical world, and constitutes about all we can reliably assert. That is what we can know about them, and that is, for human purposes, adequate. That, however, is not Dao. As we recall, the coherence accomplished by words is merely a local or restricted version of its own principle, the principle of universality, the harmonizing of the different. When the principle involved in all words is extended to its logical conclusion, the most comprehensively coherent type of coherence, we have Dao, which by that very token has no name, is unintelligible, incoherent. What we have here then is, as it were, merely a "horizontal" explanation of the arising of things, and how they "cohere by ordering one another" (相理 xiangli); any kind of vertical explanation, that is, in terms of how existing things per se come to exist, the ultimate reason why there is any Being at all, rather than how individual things bring each other to be, is not, according to the author of this passage, possible within the realm of discussion, of words. Dao, as that which is "doing all while doing nothing," would seem to be a likely candidate for first cause or vertical explanation of all beings, but it cannot be legitimately invoked in this way. It cannot be asserted to exist as a coherent named identity. He who sees Dao does not search after this kind of explanation, inquiring into what becomes of things after their disappearance or before their arising. No single unifying quality/name/determinacy can be applied as the explanatory principle for the existence of things, in the "vertical" sense. The unbiased/undifferentiated whole, which is what one would logically wish to adduce as the ultimate cause of the being and function of all the parts, cannot be adduced as the "cause" of the parts, for the very reason that it is truly unbiased and comprehensive, and hence not identifiable as anything in particular. Nor do the parts cause the whole. Again we see an emphasis on contradiction, joining of opposites, balances, polar transformations, for this alone is the true presence of Dao in things, which, like the presence of any whole in its parts, operates like customs and language in a community: it is what allows them to be and to function at all.

Special notice should be taken of the appearance of the character Li in this context, in the phrase "the coherent mutual ordering of things as they follow in mutual succession" (suixu zhi xiangli). The word is unambiguously a verb here, and applied specifically to the reciprocal limiting of things in the horizontal dimension, especially the relation between the two members of any opposed dyad. In terms of our previous discussion, we can interpret this phrase to mean, "the reciprocal making-coherent of the two sides of each dyad as they succeed each other." They limit each other, cut each other out from the whole, make the quantitative adjustments of one another that provide each with its qualitative value. The original meaning of Li is very much in force here, and its application to the horizontal interaction of the poles of a dyad is to be recalled, particularly when we come to consider the Hanfeizi commentary on the *Laozi*, which will have something similar to say about the relation between Dao and Li.

The next exchange in the dialogue runs as follows:

> Know-little said, "Between Jizhen's theory that no one does it and Jiezi's theory that something causes it, which contention is right on the mark about the real conditions of these [things] [正於其情 *zheng yu qi qing*], and which is a partial apprehension of their coherence [偏於其理 *pian yu qi Li*]?" Great Impartial Reconciliation said, "Chickens squawk, dogs bark—this is something people know. But even someone with the greatest knowledge cannot describe in words that from which they come to be thus, nor can he plumb by thought what they will do next. We can go on splitting and analyzing things further, until 'the subtlety reaches the point where there are no more divisions possible, the vastness reaches the point where it cannot be encompassed.'[28] [But even so], the theories that 'something causes it' or 'nothing does it' don't yet get out of the realm of things, and in the end fall into error. 'Something causes it' implies something substantial; 'Nothing does it' implies total emptiness. The idea of having a name and a real substance refers to the presence of things; the idea of namelessness and emptiness depends on the spaces between things. One can speak and think about these, but the more one talks the farther away one gets."

Before taking a closer look at this, we should pause to note the use of the term Li in the posing of this question. As a way of inquiring "Which is right and which is wrong?" we have instead, "which contention is right on the mark about the real conditions of these [things] [*zheng yu qi qing*], and which is a partial apprehension of their coherence [*pian yu qi Li*]?" Two criss-crossing contrasts are used here: *zheng* (right on the mark, upright, straight, balanced) versus *pian* (one-sided, biased) and *qing* (real condition) versus *Li* (coherence). The use of Li to mean a true proposition that can be an object of knowledge or understanding, moreover—the Li of X or Y, meaning an idea about X or Y that one can "get" or "not get," and which it is deemed to be important to understand—is also destined to become more and more prevalent. We have an opportunity to see both of these standard tropes used here when they were still startling, still live metaphors. In Buddhism, as we shall see, *qing* will mean something like deluded partial attachments, with a decided implication of passion and emotion (which soon becomes a standard meaning of the word), and Li will mean liberating truth. In this passage, however, the double parallelism suggests that *qing* and Li are synonyms, and the difference between getting it right and getting it wrong resides purely in *zheng* and *pian*, balanced on-the-mark comprehensiveness as opposed to lopsided bias or partiality. This is, of course, especially significant in that the topic under discussion here is the extent to which a comprehensively balanced coherence can be intelligible at all. This is also the standard of truth and falsehood found in the "Jiebi" chapter of the *Xunzi* and in the "Tianxia" chapter of the *Zhuangzi*: comprehensiveness versus one-sidedness. Comprehensiveness, however, implies balance, the relation to a center, an idea that will become more and more important in the implications of Li as time goes by. A balanced apprehension of *qing*, real condition of all beings (including, we may say, the passions and emotions—the desires—of human beings), is the apprehension of their coherence, their "truth," their "principle." Here we have the advent of a usage of Li that tempts the translation as "truth." But fundamentally, it still means "the Great Coherence," *dali*. Here, the question is, which statement fits into the Great Coherence of Heaven and Earth, or Dao, or of all things, or the function of all things: does someone do it, or does no one do it? The possessive pronoun *qi* is important here, even if its exact reference is somewhat ambiguous. The question is, which description is balanced with, takes in all relevant sides of, the "genuine state," meaning, the state of a thing before being manipulated for some specific (i.e., partial) deliberate purpose. Something might be genuine, the *qing* or indeed a coherent Li, without quite being the "truth": to be the truth, it must also be *zheng* with respect to that *qing* or Li. A partial apprehension of some limited coherence, or some limited genuine state, would not yet be "true" on the *gong/si* epistemology of this passage and many like it. So either of these alternatives might "have" coherence (*you Li*), but still be "one-sided" with respect to (all relevant) Lis, and thus still would not count as an acceptable proposition.

In this passage, two alternatives are posed with respect to the ultimate question, the question left over after the answer to the previous query has been given, about the mutual ordering—making coherent—of individual things as the reciprocal limiting of opposites. A "vertical" explanation is asked for about the existence of the universe as a whole, the Great Coherence. But this passage rejects the possibility of providing a coherent answer to any such ultimate question about Dao, and even, be it noted, about the origin of individual things in the universe.

To indicate the inadequacy of any ultimately intelligible explanation of the world, the text first cites, not the self-contradiction of reason when confronted with ultimate questions, but the squawking of chickens and the barking of dogs—i.e., immediate, everyday experiences, particular finite parts of the infinite totality. Unlike the more general rules adduced in the previous section, these concrete particulars are asserted to be themselves ultimately mysterious, unsusceptible to verbal accounts of their origin and destiny. The ultimate mysteriousness of the world is apparent not only in the fact that we cannot get a grasp on whether time has a beginning or not, but more viscerally, in the fact that we cannot even comprehend or predict a chicken's squawk. Here we find that both the totality, Dao, and individual things, a chicken's squawk, are similar in that both can be partially described by words but ultimately cannot be accounted for verbally. In particular, the question of their arising and passing away is in both cases unfathomable. Words work for *the intermediate realm* of specific universals—the general laws of Yin/Yang interactions described in the previous passage. But the two extremes, the real totality and the real particulars, the limit cases of the union of opposites evident in a less radical form in the general laws, overflow this realm of words. Both the greatest and the smallest coherences turn out to be ultimately incoherent.

The whole passage thus breaks conveniently into four sections: first, the extent to which words are adequate to describe the operations of Dao (as *gong*, etc.), followed by a caveat about the inadequacy of these verbal determinations for the real fullness of Dao (the word *Dao* being like the "ten thousand" of the "ten thousand things"). Then the same pattern in the discussion of things, namely, what can be said about them and then what cannot. The realms of Dao and things, then, after being strictly separated, do not remain separate. On the contrary, they serve almost as aspects of one another. Dao is the indescribable aspect of things, things are the describable aspect of Dao. Dao qua thing is describable; Dao qua Dao is not. Things qua things are describable; things qua Dao are not. This last category is the most surprising, and it is just this that depends on the special whole/part relations we have been discussing. For the individual entity shares this quality of doubleness with the totality. It both can and cannot be spoken of, it is in the realm of words and out of it, just like Dao. All things are coherent only in an ironic sense. Once again. the individual shares the quality of the whole. Words work for general rules and tendencies, for classes of more than one and less than all. For it is these classes that both bind together individuals into groups and contrast these groups with groups outside themselves. This is what community words are good for; they tell us that Dao unifies all contraries in itself, and that all things arise generally from the interaction of these contrary forces. But this cannot explain the fullness, nor the arising and perishing, of either (1) a single one or (2) the whole, that is, what is not yet unified in these words, or what has nothing outside itself, in contrast to which it can be defined. At the same time, both of these extremes interface with the intermediate level of general terms, and to this extent are speakable—as *gong*, on the side of Dao, and as the individual joining of opposite forces, determinate general tendencies, on the side of individual things. But the living, particular spontaneity of a particular chicken's squawk cannot be described in words or predicted in thoughts. For these "community" words and thoughts describing the horizontal relations and general principles of these things relate to individual instances only as the collective customs relate to individual members of the community. They do indeed join together opposites and particulars, but at the same time they miss the main thing, the unsearchability of the origin and outcome of this chicken's squawk here and now, the actuality of the interface between this particular coherence and its manner of cohering with the context that makes it what it is. Here we return to Zhuang Zhou's sensitivity to the unknowability of the origin or beginning of any particular event. Community words may tell us the general "customs" that are present in each member of the community called "chickens"—i.e., they squawk at dawn, or when hungry, or when seeking a mate. The words *chickens squawk* unify a vast number of chickens and a vast number of squawks, and the experiences of a vast number of members of the linguistic community who use such words. The words unify the community's customs with respect to these chickens and squawks, and the unification accomplished by them is an aspect of the unity of these customs. This type of unity of particulars into a whole, implicit in the universalization accomplished by socially accepted words, is adequate to a certain extent, but not fully adequate. It is as adequate to the description of these chickens as "ten thousand things" is adequate to describe all things in the world. In the present case, our knowledge of chickens does not get us inside any particular squawk, in its contingency at this particular moment, as the untraceable impulse of a particular chicken in a particular time and place. And why is this? Because whatever laws or tendencies may accurately apply to the being and behavior or this chicken, these tendencies themselves are subsumed under Dao, which is nameless, that is, devoid of positive non-ironic identity, saturated with irony. This chicken here may instantiate the smaller general categories (transformations of Yin and Yang, etc.), as determinate and specifiable unities of contraries, but in so doing it must also be instantiating the comprehensiveness that comprehends even these lesser tendencies, namely, Dao. To instantiate Dao, however, is to instantiate paradoxicality, namelessness, doing all which doing nothing, being all which is being nothing. Hence, what makes this particular chicken live, Dao, is also what makes it slip out of whatever determinate categories might be partially applicable to it. What makes it describable—membership in some "community" or general tendency as a whole immanent in each part which unifies particulars—is also what makes it indescribable—membership therefore in the largest community, the immanence of Dao. When the word *chicken* is used, all other members of the community of words suddenly appear implicit within it. It is thrown into relation with those other things, made "universal" (*gong*), and this leaves us back in the horizontal question, the question that is answered by the interrelation between opposites implied by this (custom-like) universality implicit in all particular parts. It is indeed true of this particular squawk that it is a union of contrary forces, just as it is true that Dao is universal. But it is also something more than this, something that cannot be spoken in words. The vertical question, concerning the ultimate source of this particular squawk, remains unanswered for the particular thing as it does for the whole, whereas it is answerable for general tendencies—Yin comes from Yang, Yang comes from Yin, etc. (indeed, this is just what we mean by a "horizontal" explanation). The particular is more like the whole than the intermediate general terms are.

The assertion is made that both the alternative answers to the question about the origin of things are merely restricted to the realm of things. Even to speak of nothing is just to speak of the spaces between things. That is to say, the concept "nothing does it" is completely conditioned by thinking about things. It merely means a conception of where the things are not, which is still described by the shape of the things themselves. The mind cannot conceive of a nothingness except in contrast the presence of existent things. Both the things and the spaces between them are interwoven to form the fabric we call "the realm of things." To focus on one rather than the other as the ultimate source does not get us outside this realm. Moreover, it is one-sided, since the totality, the "universal community" of this realm is based on the "bridge-like" interaction of the two extremes of spaces and substances. Both being and not-being are in the category of being. Hence, these two views each occupy only one corner of the realm of things. It is here that we are told also that total "namelessness" is just as inadequate to Dao as having a particular name. Namelessness, cited as actually merely an example of a community word above, simply a conceptualization of the lack of partiality of Dao, is also only one extreme, complete Non-Being, the side of "Nothing does it," the spaces between things, which thus does not get beyond "the realm of things," and remains in only one corner of things. Namelessness, we may say, is the space between names, just as nothing was just the space between things—that is, namelessness is completely defined

by the outlines of the names, an integral part of the realm of names and
unable to get us outside it. Silence, in the end, is no better than speech.[29]
     The dialogue continues:

> "What has not yet been born cannot be prohibited from coming,
> what has already died cannot be stopped from going. Life and death
> are not distant, and yet their coherence [Li] cannot be apprehended.
> These theories that 'something causes it' or 'nothing does it' are
> merely what doubt avails itself of. I gaze at its root, and its ante-
> cedents go back without end; I seek its furthest developments, and
> their coming stretches forward without stop. Having no end and no
> stop—these are negations within the scope of language, and thus
> share the same coherences [Li] with things themselves. 'Something
> causes it' and 'Nothing does it'—these are attributions of the root
> [of things], which remain within the scope of language, and thus
> they merely end and begin with things.[30] Dao cannot be considered
> existent, nor can it be considered non-existent. The name 'Dao'
> [Way] is what we avail ourselves of so as to walk on it. 'Something
> causes it' and 'Nothing does it' each occupy only one corner of
> things. What do they have to do with the Great Method?"

     The passage goes on to cite something else that is very commonplace
and nearby, and yet inexplicable and unalterable, to undermine the adequacy
of words and wordlessness: life and death, the origin and disappearance of
individual entities. The coherence even of something as close and omnipresent as life and death cannot be apprehended with speech and thought,
nor even by the total negation of these by such terms as "namelessness"
and such hypotheses as "Nothing does it," which ultimately remain still
within the realm of words and thought. Li of individual events here is also
ironic coherence, unintelligible coherence, a sticking together that cannot
be described. Why? In looking at the antecedents and consequences of any
individual things, we find them stretching out infinitely into the past and
the future, in spite of the appearance and disappearance of this particular
entity. This endlessness, the text tells us, is what we are referring to when
we negate the existence of an origin of things, or assert Dao to be "nameless," but this endlessness is merely something about things themselves, and
has not yet gotten us beyond the realm of things to the question of their
source. This refers to positing nothing at all about the origin of things—but
even this cannot be thought of as a way of getting beyond the finitude of
things, for it only reflects the formulable principle of things themselves.
On the other hand, definitive theories about the root of things, such as
"Something causes it" and "Nothing does it," also merely end and begin

with things, also do not get us beyond their finitude. Neither words nor silence is adequate. Hence, Dao cannot be taken to be either existent or nonexistent—such is the inadequacy of words. On the other hand, we still depend on the word *Dao,* meaning a way or path, in order to walk it, in order to position ourselves in the world—our need to avail ourselves of this name indicates the inadequacy of silence.

Hence, the passage finishes with the following words:

> If words were completely adequate, one could speak all day and all of it would be about Dao. If words were completely inadequate, one could speak all day and all of it would be about things. The ultimate reaches of Dao and things cannot be carried by either words or silence. Only where there is neither words nor silence does discussion really come to its ultimate end.

We saw above that words were accepted as adequate for describing the general behavior of things; here however, we are told that they are inadequate, not only to describe the infinite Dao or the origin of all things, but to describe even the quite finite squawking of a chicken. Here, the strict division between the two realms, established earlier in the passage, is finally broken down. The immediate behavior of the individuals, outside what can be described in community words of their general laws, is also the inexplicableness of Dao. Here we see that the part still adumbrates the whole, just as in the paradigm of community/member we began with. The beyond-words-trans-universality of Dao is present also in each of its parts, such that each of them is also indescribable in words in certain aspects, while being describable in others (i.e., on the question of "in what manner" things in general arise). Thus, any given entity is both beyond words and describable in words, just like Dao itself, which is both describable by the word *gong* and not merely *gong.* The squawking of a chicken is both a thing and not merely a thing, that is, not merely what is referred to by the community word *thing.* This is what the end of the passage refers to as the "the ultimate reaches of Dao and things"; this margin is the self-transformation of all things, their forming of themselves, their irreducible individuality and unpredictability in spite of general categories and laws. As things (i.e., the referent of some community word), they are some already-completed entity, and members of some general community or class; as Dao, each is an inexpressible coming to be and transformation of this particular thing happening here. The joining of these two, the ultimate reach of both which is also their interface (際 *ji*), is the squawking of a chicken, that is, a particular unpredictable act, both linked to the general laws and beyond them. This is what we face at every moment of our experience, this is in fact our entire world. For this, neither words nor silence are adequate. Silence is adequate for the wholly abstract Dao, which is partial to no one principle and has no name. Words are adequate for the communal laws of the interaction of things, their alternations and unifications of opposites. If words were completely adequate, we would always be speaking of nothing but Dao; if they were completely inadequate, we would always be speaking of nothing but things. But the fact is that we are always talking about both, no matter what we do: our speech never gets beyond the finitude of things, and yet we also indicate something beyond what we say when we speak of the squawking of chickens, point to the general manner of their arising and vanishing, which is the Dao we speak of in order to walk it. Things are beyond any determinate identity because identity is the presence of an opposite-unifying whole within the part. Things are beyond any identity because of their identity, and have an identity because they are beyond any identity. Things are speakable because they are unspeakable, and unspeakable because they are speakable.

With this, we have reached a new level of thought on the question of coherence, a type of convergence of ironic and non-ironic conceptions of Li that eliminates the strict division between the whole and the part. Here, it is not that the overriding coherence is ironic while the individual coherences are non-ironic, as in the second type of treatment of Li above, nor that both overriding coherence and individual coherences are both fully ironic, as in the third. Rather, both the overriding and the particular coherences, Dao and Li, are at once in one sense ironically coherent and in one sense non-ironically coherent. Both are speakable and both are unspeakable. It is in the direction of this intensified interfusion of ironic and non-ironic, their convergence and ultimately the overcoming of their mutual exclusivity, that we will see the term Li developing through the works of Xuanxue and Chinese Buddhist thinkers in the chapters that follow. But first we must consider the advent of self-conscious deployments of the term Li as a special philosophical term, and the attempts to give it a formal definition, which we will find in a few texts on the periphery of the Legalist tradition, that is, in certain sections of the *Guanzi* and the *Hanfeizi*.

FOUR

THE ADVENT OF LI AS A
TECHNICAL PHILOSOPHICAL TERM

We have seen the gradual thickening of associations around the term Li, first in non-ironic usage, as in the *Xunzi*, and then a parallel development among writers within the ironic tradition, using this term as an increasingly important token by which to formulate a response to the non-ironic tradition and by which to incorporate some its elements into the universe of ironic discourse. We have seen within the variety of texts collected in the *Zhuangzi* several ways in which this seems to have been attempted, each with its own distinctive usage of Li: (1) the extended non-ironic usage with a beginning of ironic tendency in the emphasis on mental stillness and quietude, where both Dao and Li are used in a basically non-ironic sense; (2) a fully ironic usage that takes both Dao and Li ironically, regarding both—the totality of coherence and each particular coherence—as intrinsically self-undermining, accomplished only by their subversion, each being a coherence as a value-bearing grouping of opposed elements found only in unintelligibility; and (3) a compromise position that incorporates a non-ironic notion of Li, intelligible specific coherences, as somehow operating under and even deriving from the ironic unintelligible coherence of Dao. A further development from the last of these moves forward another step: (4) a view of both macro and micro coherence, Dao and Li, as each being at once in a sense intelligible and in a sense unintelligible. We may view these developments as reverse mirror images to the incorporations of ironic notions of coherence into a non-ironic framework, as seen in some of the *Liji* texts such as the "Daxue" and "Zhongyong," and in the "Great Commentary" to the *Zhouyi*, as discussed in *Ironies of Oneness and Difference*. Although Li seems to be an increasingly important focal point in framing these discussions, we still have not witnessed its advent into a consciously singled-out philosophical term, considered abstractly and as such, and given an abstract and general

definition. This seems to happen first in some texts of a syncretic character, mainly in the interface of Legalist and Daoist thinking as found in the
Guanzi and the *Hanfeizi,* continued in later texts of mixed provenance such
as the *Huainanzi.* It is to this development that we now turn.

TOWARD THE IRONIC: LI IN THE PRE-IRONIC DAOISM OF THE *GUANZI*

In *Ironies of Oneness and Difference,* I attempted a tentative dating of certain
chapters of the *Guanzi*—"Neiye" 內業 ("Inner Training"), "Xinshu shang"
心術上 ("Techniques of the Heart/mind, Part 1"),"Xinshu xia" 心術下
("Techniques of the Heartmind, Part Two"), and "Baixin" 百心 ("Purifying
the Heart/mind")—characterizing some parts of them—namely, the "Neiye"
and the first part of "Xinshushang"—as belonging to what might be described
as a kind of "pre-ironic Daoism."[1] If this early dating is correct, placing these
texts well prior to the *Xunzi,* it would make these texts among the earliest
texts to make extensive use of the term Li in its non-ironic sense. Since I
am by no means certain about this early dating, however, the conclusions
of this part of the discussion must be regarded as highly speculative. But
even if these texts postdate the *Xunzi,* and thus are not to be taken as
indicative of the early formation of the non-ironic sense of Li, they are
all the more notable for the microcosmic use of the crypto-Xunzian sense
of Li, modified by a proto-ironic notion of how that coherence is created,
which brings us insight right into the heart of the thinking that would later
produce the full-fledged ironic turn. For these reasons I leave the question
of dating tentative, but treat these texts after treating the *Xunzi* and the
Zhuangzi, in spite of the strong possibility of an earlier date for at least some
of the material therein, to highlight and unravel the gradual move toward
the ironic implications of Li, which can only be made intelligible on the
basis of a firm understanding of the kind of straight non-ironic usage of the
term of the kind we have spelled out in the case of the *Xunzi* and "Yueji."
Based on the development of the ideas in these works, and in particular the
developments of thinking on Li through a deepening complexity of ironic/
non-ironic interaction, my best guess on these texts is that the "Neiye"
and first part of "Xinshu shang" could predate the *Xunzi* and *Zhuangzi,* perhaps, as some scholars have speculated,[2] representing the thought of Jixia
Daoism or in particular Song Xing 宋銒, the famous laugher mentioned in
Zhuangzi's first chapter (who thus obviously predates both Zhuangzi and
Xunzi) or a member of his school. Here, Li is still an ordinary, nontechnical term. The *second* half of "Xinshu shang," which begins to give explicit
glosses on the terms and statements used in the first half, would then read
as a somewhat later commentary on the first half, written *after* some of the

developments we have covered in the last two chapters. For it is here that we find the first explicit attempt at a real *definition*, in the formal sense, of Li as a philosophical term. The "Xinshu xia," on the other hand, looks like a loose commentary on the "Neiye." So we will examine the earlier stratum ("Neiye" and "Xinshu shang") as one unit, coming before the development of the full ironic and non-ironic usages of Li, and their various intertwinings as seen in the last chapter; then we will look at the ascension of the term into a conscious and explicit philosophical term in the second stratum, notable in the latter part of the "Xinshu shang."

The "Neiye" starts by presenting the idea of the "vital essence" (*jing*) as what produces and gives life (*weisheng*) to all things: the stars above, the grains below, the spirits flowing between heaven and earth. "Life" is here clearly understood in a very broad sense, including the movement and brightness of the heavenly bodies and the growth of crops; it seems to be a generally vitalistic notion of life energy, which can manifest in a great variety of diverse forms. The sage is a person who holds this vital essence, in its full potency, within his own breast (藏於胸中 *cang yu xiongzhong*). As the text proceeds, it casually redescribes this vitality as "this *qi*" (*ciqi*)—it is one certain type of *qi*, it would seen, the quintessential form of *qi* in its full potency. Now for anyone who wishes to become a sage by holding this *qi* in his own breast there is a difficulty: it cannot be held onto or retained within oneself by force, but only by "Virtuosity." (是故此氣也，　不可止以力，而可安以德 *shigu ci qi ye buke zhi yi li, er ke an yi de*). This Virtuosity, when accomplished, produces wisdom, and all the other traditional virtues that spring therefrom. How can one accomplish it? By eliminating the emotional disturbances—worry, joy, anger, desire—that interfere with the spontaneous self-formation of the harmony (*he*) of the mind in its full Virtuosity and potency.

The text then introduces the term *Dao*, which seems to be another redescription, with a slightly different emphasis, of the "vital energy" or *qi* just discussed. We are told that this Dao is "that by which the form is filled" (夫道者所以充形也 *fudaozhe suoyi chong xing ye*). This term has been discussed in the previous volume; here I'd only like to say that "form" seems to mean not only the physical body but determinate mental states and attitudes, which are described in similar terms, but more specifically as a process of spontaneous formation and filling out, earlier in the text. The problem is, again, that human beings are unable to keep the totality of this Dao or vital essence or energy in its self-forming power, its power to generate life, whole and intact within themselves, due to their emotional disturbances. The text offers a definition of the Dao as what is abundantly overflowing everywhere, born together with oneself, but systematically elusive, with no fixed sound or form, and yet which "accomplishes things in an orderly sequence" (而序其成謂之道。 *er xu qi cheng wei zhi dao*). It is in this context that the text asserts a relation between Dao and Li: "All Dao is without particular locus, but he who is skilled in using the mind dwells in it peacefully:[3] when the mind is still, and the qi is [thus] coherently ordered [心靜氣理 *xinjing qi Li*], Dao comes to stay in it."[4] Qi, the energy that constitutes the living body, is made "orderly" (Li) by the stillness of the mind, and this is the precondition of the experience of Dao coming to dwell in the mind, or is perhaps synonymous with it. The formlessness and elusiveness of Dao, its having no "locus" (所 *suo*) and thus being inaccessible to the ordinary modes of acquisition and knowing, has been noticed and accentuated here. It "has no locus" both in the sense that it has no one particular form, cannot be located in one sound or sight, and also in that "people are unable to hold it fast" in its full potency by means of intention and force. This systematic elusiveness to knowledge of Dao is here, however, only a minor problem, not yet something that pushes all the way into the ironic tropes of "knowing only through non-knowing," "obtained only by not being attained," "taught only by non-teaching," and so on. Rather, its elusiveness as a specific cognitive object can be overcome by a certain state of mind, possibly associated with some kind of yogic practice: the "Virtuosity" of an undisturbed mind. When the mind is stilled, the *qi* is "Li"-ed automatically in response, and this orderly *qi* (note the intimate Li/*qi* pairing!) is the attainment of Dao. Li here is still a stative verb: it means something like, "ordered in a desirable way." *Qi* being ordered in this way seems here to be a synonym for Dao, at the very least the specific dao, right way, of *qi*. *Qi* following its dao, its way of optimal function, is for *qi* to be ordered/Li. Dao is the spontaneous form-giving life force that fills the body and gives shape to the mind, forms the body and mind. Li is how Dao forms things when not interfered with by emotional disturbances and desires, above all by the desire to attain it. We have a straightforward non-ironic conception here, naturalized and tilted slightly by the emphasis on systematic elusiveness and the slightly paradoxical need for not-seeking of Dao in order to attain Dao that qualifies this text as "proto-ironic." Li is still a nontechnical term here meaning "harmoniously ordered," but with an emphasis on this as a result of spontaneity, of not being disturbed. Note that in this context, as contrasted to what we will see in the "ironic" appropriations such as the *Hanfeizi* commentary to the *Laozi*, Dao is associated only with life and success: "[B]y losing it people die, by gaining it people live; by losing it affairs fail, by gaining it, affairs succeed" (人之所失以死, 所得以生也。 事之所失以敗, 所得以成也。 *renzhisuoshi yisi, suode yishengye; shizhisuoshi yibai, suode yichengye*).

This general picture is expanded upon in the opening trope of the "Xinshu shang," representing what I regard as the oldest material in the text:

The mind's position in the body is that of the ruler; the different jobs of the nine apertures [of qi-flow] have the divided roles of the organ-functionaries [官 guan]. When the mind is rightly positioned in its Dao, the nine apertures follow the divisions that allow them to cohere harmoniously [循理 xun Li]. When preferences and desires overflow, however, the eye cannot see forms and the ear cannot hear sounds. Thus it is said that when the one above departs from his Dao, the ones below lose their proper tasks.[5]

心之在體，君之位也。九竅之有職，官之分也。心處其道，
九竅循理。嗜欲充益，目不見色，耳不聞聲。故曰：上離其道，
下失其事。

The mind is the lord, the other parts of the body are its "officials" or functionaries. The role of the mind is then described here as in the "Neiye" as consisting in quietude, as not interfering or trying to do the jobs of the other parts. It is to be quieted, made still, cleared, emptied of desires and emotional attachments: this is "its Dao." This Dao is "not far" but difficult to bring to fruition, copresent with human beings but hard to attain, again as in the "Neiye." It is only when the mind is "made empty" that "spirit"—another casual synonym, it seems, for Dao, jing and qi,—comes to "reside" in it (虛其欲，神將入舍 xu qi yu shen jiang ru she).

The text continues to assert that it is this "emptiness" that is the true origin of the traditional virtues, of all the things humans desire, which it lists and defines:

People all desire wisdom, but they never seek out how wisdom comes about. Wisdom! Wisdom! It is what he who casts about for it beyond the oceans can never snatch, what he who seeks it can never succeed in dwelling in. The upright person rather does not seek it at all, and thus is able to be empty and totally bereft. Emptiness which it totally bereft of any form is called Dao. What transforms and grows all things is called Virtuosity. The human tasks of lord and servant and of father and son are called Rightness (Duty). Properly bowing and yielding while ascending and descending so that there is a distinction between noble and base, so that those more and less closely related form a single body, is called Ritual. Simplifying all things down to the smallest so that they follow a single Dao, using violence, prohibition and punishment, is called Law.[6]

Note that Dao is here only the emptiness of mind itself, the proper Way of the mind in its role as Lord of the body. The function of nourishing and transforming all things is attributed rather to Virtuosity, which grows out of the mind properly following its own role of emptiness and stillness. The list of virtues are depicted as what comes forth from this process, fully articulated, as the content of the "wisdom" that can only be attained by this emptying of the mind which depends on not seeking wisdom—constituting the proto-irony of this conception. This picture of the human body as a social hierarchy in microcosm, which persists in the *Mencius* and all the way down the centuries into Song and Yuan dynasty Daoist Internal Alchemy (內丹 *neidan*) and thereafter, is extended to assert that the mind need only be quiet, "nonacting," to put the organs of perception and interaction with the world, the nine apertures, "in order" (Li) spontaneously. Like a sage ruler who has mastered either the ritual *wuwei* of Shun in *Analects* 15:5 or the later Daoist anti-ritual extension of the same idea, the mind should not overstep its bounds and start meddling in the individual affairs of the various organs. Taken with the statement just quoted from the "Neiye," this suggests that the *qi* becomes Li—coherent, harmonious, organized—as a spontaneous correlative to the stillness of the mind. This coherence among the parts, their formation of a coherent whole, seems closely related to the idea of each of the organs doing only its own job, following "the division of individual roles" (分 *fen*), just as in Xunzi's conception of social coherence. Indeed, Li here means nearly the same thing: the *division* of individual roles. The following of Li means staying within its proper limits. Li is, we might say, the articulations of these limits, the grain of the body that separate its organs into specific jurisdictions of *qi*-flow. Note that the mind is in the position of the unifying totality, and thus is said to follow "its Dao"; the individual organs are in the role of specific functions, and what they follow is their Lis, the divisions that allow them to cohere. We will encounter this whole/part picture of the Dao/Li relation many times below, conceived in various ways. Here, the organs and the *qi* "follow the guidelines making for coherence (Li)" when the eye can see sights and the ear can hear sounds, when these are not interfered with by the *purposive desires and preferences* of the mind, which is failing to be properly still and *wu-wei* (無為). Conscious willing and purpose are a problem because they interfere with the stillness of the mind. This stillness is what makes the *qi* genuinely Li-ed—orderly, coherent, harmonious. This in turn creates the virtuosity (德 *de*) which is the presence and attainment of Dao, and this is the true source of real values, including here the traditional Confucian virtues: they are attained by not actively seeking them, but rather stilling the mind so that the *qi* is made into the kind of coherence that serves as their spontaneous matrix, which is what truly produces them.

   Note that the engine for full ironic Daoism is already in place here: we want the Dao (here meaning explicitly the proper role of the mind as ruler, but clearly also still implying that this must be the basis of the full course of traditional virtues, as their listing demonstrates), but we can only get it by not willing it, not trying to attain it. Our purposes are achieved by renouncing our purposes. We cannot "Li" our *qi* by trying to manipulate it directly, arranging it so that it runs in its proper channels, but rather by ceasing to attempt to so regulate it. But the full consequences of this paradox are not yet drawn. There is still something we can apparently straightforwardly "do": still the mind. In these texts this "order" seems to mean specifically the *separation* into specific groupings, forming a coherent whole: unity of the whole via division of the parts into separated roles.

Expanding on this, the "Neiye" gives an interesting disquisition on the topic of what "unity" means as coherence and harmony of differentiated roles, giving us perhaps the earliest explicit crossing of the "division" and "unification" motifs intertwined in the notion of Li:

> A single thing that is capable of transforming other things is called spirit. A single affair that is capable of changing other things is called wisdom. But to be able to transform and change things without altering one's own vital energy or wisdom can only be accomplished by the noble man who holds to unity. Holding to unity without losing it, you can rule over the ten thousand things. The noble man controls things and is not controlled by them: this is the ordered coherence among things that comes from his attaining unity [得一之理 *deyi zhi li*]. With an orderly mind within, orderly words issue from his mouth, and orderly deeds are applied to others, and it is thus that the world becomes orderly. When by attaining a single word the world submits, when by fixing a single word the world obeys, this is what is meant by being unbiased (*gong*).

> 一物能化謂之神，一事能變謂之智，化不易氣，變不易智，惟執一之君子能為此乎！執一不失，能君萬物。君子使物，不為物使。得一之理，治心在於中，治言出於口，治事加於人，然則天下治矣。一言得而天下服，一言定而天下聽，公之謂也。[7]

Note that Li here means not the "principle" of holding to unity, but the condition of controlling rather than being controlled by things. This is precisely the meaning of the unity, the coherence, here. This is what is attained by stillness of mind: the mind takes its proper role of the mind as ruler, and thereby rules. "Holding to unity" could mean either "keeping concentrated on its own proper task, undistracted by anything else: in this case, the task of the mind, which is to maintain stillness." It could also be read as referring to the unity that is attained among all the organs of the entire mind when the mind does this: they become unified as a single coherent whole. "Attaining the unity" can thus mean both the keeping to the proper role of the part and the resultant continuity and coherence of the whole. Li thus could conceivably still be read here as meaning "the specific, divided-out role, limitation"—in this case, the proper role of the heart/ mind or of the ruler, which is to hold to unity and thus maintain stillness, and thus bring order—the playing of their proper roles—to the rest of the organs of the body. Coherence is at the same time a *result* of "holding to unity," which is to say, the stillness of the "ruler," the mind, which causes the other organs to unify around it by being still, by not interfering in their functions. Li here means both the limited role of one part—the ruler/ mind—and also the omnipresent effect of this holding-to-the-limit evident in the unity of the body as a whole: it makes all the organs keep to their separate roles, their Li, the guidelines of separation into groups that allow for coherence. It is coherence in the sense of division, clear articulation, that leads to coherence in the sense of unity, omnipresence, coming-together. This trick is performed by means of the special character of the limited role of the mind specifically: stillness, non-doing, the eschewing of any specific contents or purposes beyond the purely formal one of *not* interfering in any other role, not doing any other organ's job for it. Here we have another version of the basic motor of Daoist thought that continues *mutatis mutandis* straight through the hardcore ironic writers all the way into the Guo Xiang commentary to the *Zhuangzi*. In the case under discussion here, it is a coherence that is also hierarchical—a ruling and organizing of all the types around a single center, to which they are unambiguously subordinate. This is clearly non-ironic coherence. The unity of coherence, of each playing its role harmoniously, is manifested as the ruler's relation to his various subordinates, or the mind to the various organs and the *qi*: because of its unity (concentration, stillness), they form a coherent oneness that serves it, rather than making him a servant of it. Again, this is present as a direct and unproblematic consequence of the mind constraining itself to its proper Li-limitation, to wit, playing the role of a noninterfering and purposeless ruler, thus attaining stillness and unity.

Li is here the order that is taken by *qi* when it is not interfered with or manipulated by mental purposes and desires. It is the arrangement of *qi* when no purposive arrangement is made to *qi*, when there is no human (i.e., subjective mental) interference in it. As such it may seem to be a good analogue of a kind of objective order: the order of things when not manipulated by and subordinated to the one-sided subjective purposes of any particular agent. I have claimed, however, that Li is never simply the order of nature, but always the overlap or interaction between human coherence and nonhuman coherence, as we have seen prototypically in the case of the

Xunzi above. But even in this case, examined carefully, we really do have a form of human-nonhuman overlap in the notion of Li; it is confusing, however, precisely because it is a proto-ironic version of this overlap. That is, the order of non-purposive *qi* in the role-divisions of the organs and their functions is not a simple fact, nor a pure normative ideal, but is in fact the *result* of a human disposition: that of stillness and noninterference of mind. To make the paradox more stark: the spontaneous order of *qi* as it is when free of subjective purposive human interference is the result of the condition of the human. It is not just "so" irrespective of what humans do or think; it exists only when humans do and think in a certain way, namely, non-doing and non-thinking. This is of course precisely the irony so central to the politics of the *Laozi*: to cite the most obvious of many examples, the highest ruler is the one who makes the people say "We did it ourselves!" (我自然 *woziran*) (*DDJ* 17). This lack of a felt presence of the ruler, and the resulting perfect and spontaneous order, is due to the way the ruler is. The natural order of the *qi*, the spontaneous nondisturbed Li, is a *conditional* state: it is conditioned by the presence of a mind, but one which is in the state of "non-mindlikeness," that is, stillness and freedom from desire. In this irony we see the coherence of the human and the natural again, but in its proto-ironic form as the ironic attainment of (human) purpose through purposelessness—just as rain is "great weather" for a picnic.

What is this coherence that is brought about by noninterference of mental purpose? The text states flatly: "The life of man is formed by the joining of the essential qi from heaven and a shape from earth. With harmony, there is life. Without harmony, there is no life. Seeking out the Dao of harmony, we find that its subtlety is invisible, its minuteness is beyond any categorization."[8] Life, continuation, is a result of harmony. The "Neiye" makes this most emphatic: "The real condition of that thing called the heart/mind is such that its ease is benefited by quietude. Just don't disturb or disorder it, and its harmony forms of itself." Harmony here is, like Li, the state into which things settle if freed of disturbances; Li is just this harmonious self-coherence. We may again note the self-forming durability and continuance that are attributed to harmony here. Similarly, the "Neiye" states flatly: "The life of man is formed by the joining of a seminal quintessence (精 *jing*) put forth by Heaven and a physical shape put forth by Earth. When there is harmony [between them], there is life. Without harmony, there is no life."[9] Moreover, this harmony is intrinsically related to pleasure; repeating the same sentence structure, the text goes on to state, "The life of man necessarily depends on his pleasure [凡人之生，必以其歡 *fanren zhi sheng, bi yi qi huan*]. With sorrow he loses the proper measure, with anger he loses the starting point. When he is disturbed by sorrow, misery, joy or anger, Dao has no place to dwell in him."[10] Dao is here again a spontaneous result of the removal of disturbance: it is the Li-ing or ordering of *qi* that results when the mind is no longer disturbed by purposes that interfere in the separation of roles of the various organs. This harmony is already characterized here quite concretely as a following of the Mean, the Center: in the matter of nutrition, to be specific, it is a result of eating neither too little nor too much. Harmony and pleasure (though not excited joy and active desire) is here conceived as a quantitative but unquantified center that balances two extremes, and is here given a foundational role as the basis of life.

This introduces a crucial point that will come back again and again in many forms. I have spoken about coherence with human desires as a criterion of Li. However, here we have a distinction between some human affects and others. In this case at least, certain human desires and emotions are apparently not among those with which these external coherences must cohere to count as Li. What is the criterion by which we can make this judgment? The "Inner Training" says that these emotions "disturb" the stillness that allows the qi to settle, to become "Li"-ed. This is further described as a losing of the proper "measure." Here we see a very obvious answer taking shape: just as some but not all of the available coherences out in the world count as Li—i.e., those that cohere with human desires—likewise, some but not all of human desires count as Li-ed: those that cohere with the world, and with each other, in a balanced way. Anything that knocks the grouping of human drives out of balance, or resonates and overlaps with no groupings in the world, is to be excluded or moderated or modified. The Center is here already the implicit criterion. Failing to cohere with existing conditions in the world will upset the balance between extremes, the centering. But any pair of extremes implies a center; how do we locate the relevant center? Given the equation between balanced coherence and pleasure, smoothness of activity and continuance, this line of thinking expands easily into a related criterion: the spontaneous, non-premeditated springs of action are in a state of inner and outer coherence, while the deliberate, stubbornly object-pursuing desires are not. We see these two lines of thinking, *mutatis mutandis*, and with various degrees of emphasis, put to many diverse uses, from Laozi's "stomach/eye" (腹／目 *fu/mu*) distinction (*DDJ* 12), to Zhuangzi's distinction between "preferences and desires" (嗜慾 *shiyu*—the same term is already used in the "Xinshu shang" to name the harmful human affects) (in *Zhuangzi*, Chapter 6), or "goal oriented organ knowledge" (官知 *guanzhi*) on the one hand and "the spontaneous springs of Heaven" (天機 *tianji*) or "spirit-like desire" (神慾 *shenyu*) on the other (as in *Zhuangzi*, Chapter 3), all the way up to sharp divide between the "human desires" (人慾 *renyu*) or "selfish desires" (私慾 *siyu*, literally one-sided or private desires) and "the Li of Heaven" (天理 *tianli*) in Neo-Confucianism. It is only that subset of both the internal inclinations and the external groupings that "cohere," thus requiring no deliberate scheming and seeking, that counts as Li. The excluded category generally means, whatever desires I may have that impede either my own harmony as a psycho-physical whole, my harmony with my environment (unattainable desires with which no object corresponds, which cause me longing and frustration), or the coherence of my social group (attainable but with antisocial consequences). Again and again, we will see this related to the idea of balance and moderation as opposed to bias or one-sidedness, and to the spontaneous and non-purposive as opposed to the deliberate and purposive.

The early part of the "Xinshu shang" text includes another very telling remark about the relation between Dao and Li:

> Strength cannot succeed in all cases; wisdom cannot plan all affairs successfully. Things have their definite forms, and forms have their definite names. One who names them properly is called a sage. Thus it is only after one knows the deed consisting of wordlessness and nonactivity that one can know the ruling string of Dao. It diversifies their shapes and tendencies, but does not join in/differ from the different coherences (Li) of the ten thousand things [殊形異勢, 不與萬物異理 shuxingyishi, buyuwanwuyili]. Thus "it can be considered the beginning of the world."[11]

Note that I give two exactly opposite interpretations of the last line of this passage: it can be read to mean either "it does not 'participate' (yu) in the different Li of the ten thousand things" or, just the opposite, "it does not take any Li (coherence) that is different from (yu) the ten thousand things." It is of great interest that these two opposite grammatical options yield the same metaphysical picture for us—a mark of the ironic structures into which we are beginning to enter here. Note that it mirrors exactly the ambiguity of unity and division noted above with respect to the role of the mind: by keeping to its proper role as a particular part (stillness), it unifies the whole and affects all the other parts. By keeping away from them, and limiting itself, it pervades and participates in them. If we may venture an interpretation of the thought of this passage, it would seem to imply that Li refers to the differences of the forms and tendencies of individual things, while Dao is the all-pervasive beginning of these differences, which both diversifies them and remains aloof from their differences. Here again we have Li meaning the division of roles, the limitations between things. And yet, to do justice to the other reading, this amounts to no more than saying that it forms no coherence of its own apart from them, that it shares in all their coherences: by its silence and noninterference, it lacks any agenda of its own, any coherent character, any Li, and yet it is just this that accomplishes the coherence of the whole, each playing its separate role. By being *completely different* from them all, from every specific Li (since as stillness, as the work of wordlessness and non-doing, it is a nothingness, a total lack of Li) it is able to be *no different* from any of them: there is nothing there to differ from them, it is able to join into them all unobstructedly. Its transcendence is its immanence and vice versa. That is the true hallmark of the ironic notion of Dao, as we analyzed it in the discussion of *Laozi* in the previous volume.[12] Dao, like the non-doing mind discussed above, remains still and does not interfere in them; it is, for this very reason that which gives—allows?—them their diversification. Here again we have the same structure of unity and division. The Dao does not participate in the individual limited Lis, and thus it makes these separate Lis, and their coherence into a whole, possible. The later "commentarial" section of "Xinshu shang" interprets this to mean that ordinary people are moved by "precedent" (故*gu*), which along with "wisdom" is contrasted to "following things" and "not acting in advance of things" in the rest of the text. The commentarial section states that it is in being free of precedent that the sage is *different* from all other things and people. It is this difference that allows him to be "empty," and it is this emptiness which is the Dao, the beginning of all things.

We begin to press further toward the ironic implications here. Names, and the purposive values that they betoken—such as strength and wisdom—do not cover everything; the wordless teaching and the non-doing activity are needed to attain comprehensiveness, which, as it were, bridges and connects, as well as giving coherent being to, these individual instances. The true origin of the formed/valued is in the formless/valueless, which overflows them. It makes them differ, but does not itself become different along with them. Li denotes their differences, while Dao denotes the overflowing background that bestows these differences, stays out of them, and thereby unifies them into a coherent whole. Note again that sagehood consists of both a grasp of namelessness and the ability to bestow and use the proper names for things. We will see divergent echoes of this kind of thinking in the ironic treatment of these themes in the *Hanfeizi* commentary to the *Laozi* and its interpretation of "yielding" and "pliancy."

LI DEFINED: THE LATER TWO-AND-A-HALF CHAPTERS OF THE *GUANZI*

Now let us take up the remaining two-and-a-half chapters: the second part of the "Xinshu shang," the "Xinshu xia," and the "Baixin." These take an approach roughly consistent with that of the "type two" appropriations in the *Zhuangzi*: Dao is ironic, Li is non-ironic. Both linguistically and doctrinally, it seems reasonable to assume that they come from a later stratum of thought than the "one-and-a-half chapters" of pre-ironic Daoism discussed above. It is in this later part of the "Xinshu shang," as noted, that we find what is probably the earliest attempt at a formal definition of Li, marked off with the "X 也者 yezhe . . . 也 ye" form. This is an expanded commentary on the first section of the older section, quoted above, including the attempted definition of the traditional virtues of a ruler up to and including Law as deriving from the emptiness and stillness of the mind. One additional term is added in this later stratum, however: the term Li. The passage is worth quoting at length:

Dao in the midst of Heaven and Earth is so vast that there is nothing outside it, so small that there is nothing inside it. Thus it is said to be "not far and yet difficult to fully realize." Empty space is never separated from human beings, and yet only the sage can attain the Dao of empty space. Thus it is said that "it is copresent with us and yet difficult to attain." . . . The Dao of Heaven is empty and formless. Empty, it cannot be conquered; formless, it has no position or obstruction.[13] Having neither position nor obstruction, it flows through all things but never changes. Virtuosity [德 de] means the dwelling of the Dao [in oneself]. Things attain it to live and continue [生生 sheng sheng]; knowledge attains it to know[14] the vital essence of Dao. Thus virtuosity means to attain it [得 de]. Attainment here means what they attain in order to be what they are. Non-doing is Dao, and dwelling in it [so that Dao dwells in oneself] is Virtuosity. Hence there is no separation between Dao and Virtuosity, and the two are spoken of here together without any distinction. The coherences [Li] that stand between them [間之理 jian zhi Li], however, refer to what allows [Dao] to have a [specific, individuated] dwelling place. Rightness means each thing being positioned appropriately. Ritual means according with unpremeditated human dispositions [人之情 ren zhi qing], following along with the coherence of their rightnesses, and creating restraining proportions and patterns [節文 jiewen][15] from them. Thus Ritual means to have coherent articulations [which allow coherence among the things articulated] [禮者謂有理也 lizhe youli ye]. *Coherence [Li] means the divisions made explicit so as to disclose rightness* [理也者 明分以諭義之意也 liyezhe mingfen yi yuyi zhi yi ye]. Hence ritual derives from rightness, rightness derives from Li, and Li follows appropriateness [禮出乎義, 義出乎理, 理因乎宜 li chu hu yi, yi chu hu li, li yin hu yi]. Law is that whereby sameness is produced, and what cannot be otherwise. Thus violence, prohibition and punishment are used to

unify them. Thus deeds must be overseen by Law, which emerges
from the power to make judgments [權 quan], which emerges from
Dao.[16]

In the earlier sections of the Guanzi texts, Dao is still non-ironic,
signifying the harmony of qi; it has no fixed "locus," to be sure, but this was
only a minor problem for anyone seeking to obtain it: all that was needed
was mind as ruler of the body taking its proper role as quietude, which
would allow all the other parts of the person to settle into their own roles,
thereby producing a coherence of the whole body which would produce the
traditional virtues of a ruler, including the recourse to Law. The emergence
of specific roles and identities from the Dao was not a problem, in spite of
its "having no locus"—for this meant only that it was found in no single
place, and thus could not be gained by force, but rather pervaded the totality
as their harmonious order, attained only by emptying the mind of desire to
attain it in one particular form. In this passage, on the contrary, the transition has become more problematic and requires a specific and convoluted
explanation. We have an attempt at a transition from the purely ironic Dao,
unintelligible and indeterminate, to the definite and determinate forms of
coherence, signified by the term Li. These include the patterns of concrete
behavior—ritual, Confucian virtues, coercive laws—seen as rooted somehow
in this formless indescribable Dao.[17] That indescribability has here been
intensified, so that the simpler solution offered in the pre-ironic stratum of
these texts is no longer sufficient. There, Dao had no one locus, meaning
that it, as the life force engendering all types of being, could not be located
in any particular practice or role that one might desire and adopt; the
problem was to find a specific role or task for the mind that could at the
same time effect this order in the totality, and that task turned out to be
the mildly ironic one of not desiring and thus settling into quietude. Here,
Dao has neither position nor form, no specific identity, not even directly as
the orderly harmony of the parts; but human and concrete beings relate to
it, position themselves in it, via "Virtuosity." Virtuosity is the concretization
of Dao, giving it a definite non-ironic shape and form, perhaps something
like a scoop or vessel that gives shape to the formless Dao, like a vessel that
scoops up water and makes it shaped and useful. But it also means the way
of "obtaining" Dao so that it *does* dwell within oneself, which was impossible through deliberate activity and a busily desiring mind. *De* originally
relates to "*daos*" in the non-cosmic sense as virtuosity relates to a course
of study that is guiding one's endeavor, a *dao*; *de* means mastery of a Dao.
Here we have the formless Dao that is positioned nowhere, made concrete
by the mastery or virtuosity of beings that live and know by dwelling in,
and thereby "attaining," this Dao, so that it dwells in them. In themselves

there is no separation between the two. Dao is compared to the empty space that surrounds us, the clarity and non-obstruction that is an image of the sage's desire-free mind, always immanently at hand but resistant to possession and not limited to any one locus. It is the Dao of this emptiness, the Way of becoming empty, that is the Dao of the mind of the sage. It is only indirectly, through the associations developed in the rest of the discussion, that this can play the role of life-giving vital essence for all things. For as we have seen, it is by being completely different from them, not participating in their affairs, that it is able to generate, sustain, and give life to them: it is the ruler that does not interfere in their specific roles and activities. The specific activities of these concrete beings, including their needs and desires, are thus contrasted sharply to the formless, empty, omnipresent Dao. This is where the term Li is introduced: what stands at the interface between Dao and its simultaneous participation and absolute difference from De, its concrete instantiation dwelling as the life force in individual things, is here said to be Li, the specific coherences of each of these individual things in their divided separate roles. Here this is not a betrayal of its formlessness and omnipresence, as in the more radical forms of ironic Daoism, but rather a derivation of it. The term used to denote this transition to the concrete division into roles is Li. This is what allows them to dwell in it and allows it to dwell in them—what makes for the possibility of De or virtuosity, which is originally no different from Dao and thus absolutely distinct from any particular role or activity.

Division, pattern, restraining proportions: these are the ideas we get packaged with Li here. We are told that there is a Li within "appropriateness" (宜 yi), meaning a "fit" between a thing and its environment, directly pointing to the notion of Li as coherence with a context. Li has to do with limitation, with constraint and positioning within a specific role. Moreover, the centrality of unpremeditated human disposition and response[18] to this context is made quite explicit here. The equation is that ritual is the division, pattern, and restraining measures that result when unpremeditated human emotion and desire are added to the appropriateness of things in their contexts, in their proper places. This is the adding of a further coherence, that which factors in human desire, to the original coherence between a thing and its proper environment. Ritual divisions of roles, forming a harmonious coherence of parts in a whole, is what makes Li, value-bearing coherence, present; this is the making of formless Dao present, palpable in the coherence of the whole.

We have here almost the transformation from the verbal to nominal sense of Li in process, as it were. Life is harmony, coherence, equilibrium, and continuance. This is what is made present by the embodying of Li in ritual and rightness: appropriateness between a thing and its environment, the fitting together of real human responses with the appropriateness of a thing in its own role, in its own environment. The final statement, however garbled it may be in the received text, is particularly telling: Li means following along with appropriateness. Coherence that brings value, the sticking together of human emotions (pleasure) and the divisions between things, is what is meant by Li. It is the interface between Dao and Virtuosity, which at once separates and joins them. Li is the transition between the formlessness of Dao and the usable form of virtuosity. This is present as the divisions between individual roles forming a coherent whole around the nonacting mind of stillness, or the formless Dao. The "making intelligible of rightness" (明義 mingyi) accomplished by these role divisions points again to the human intentionality, the inclusion of subjectivity, in the formation of these apparently objective patterns of division. Li are the coherences that make appropriate (1) fits among things and (2) between those things and human responses (3) intelligible and clear to human minds—each of these three being a form of coherence.

This linkage between Li and 情 qing is found repeatedly in these texts, as in the "Community Words" dialogue. Qing in early texts signifies the actual unpremeditated condition of things, and later comes to denote human emotions as what are genuine, not yet subjected to deliberate manipulation in accordance with conscious purposes.[19] The "Xinshu shang" states: "Because his hates do not lose their Li, and his desires do not go beyond [過 guo] their qing, he is called an exemplary man [junzi]."[20] We have a parallelism here that suggests that the emotions of hate and desire have their own proper Li, coherence or balance, and qing, real spontaneous condition, which must be matched harmoniously by "not going too far" (guo). This is reminiscent of the contrast of 正 zheng and 偏 pian in the final question of the "Community Words" dialogue.

The "Baixin" says, "By tracing things back to their beginnings their reality can be calculated, which stands as the foundation of what it generates. Knowing their image we can seek out their palpable form, tracing their Li we know their qing, searching out their beginning we know their names."[21] In this passage, Li are something that can be "traced" (緣 yuan— often the verb used for apprehension of Li, suggesting lines of pattern) to attain the deeper knowledge of their qing, their actual state prior to consciously purposive interference. But this linkage of qing and Li suggests again the overstepping of any neat subjective/objective division. For qing is not "real" in the sense of objective, but in the sense of sincere: the condition of a thing prior to intervention, prior to deliberate, purposive manipulation. Li stands to qing here as image to form, and beginning to name. In each case we have a typical sprout-blossom type of manifestation structure: what begins obscurely as Li later becomes fully manifest as qing.

Makeham translates this passage as follows: "Trace things back to their origins and determine what their *shi* (actualities) are; make one's foundation that which gave birth to things. If you want to know something's image, then you search its form; if you follow something's distinguishing marks, then you will come to know its essential qualities; if you search back to its starting point, then you will come to know its name." Note that he translates Li as "distinguishing marks," and *qing* as "essential qualities."[22] The "reality" referred to in the first line is not the "names," as Makeham wants to say in order to claim an essentialist theory of language here. Rather, it is the unseen, the unmanifest. It is typical of the ironic appropriation of the non-ironic that we have here an intermediate level of unmanifestness grounding, and making coherent, the more crudely manifest. In straight ironic Daoism, the grounding unmanifestness is simply the Dao—nothing, the nameless, and the like. It cannot be multiple or specific. Here, we have multiple specific groundings for particular things, which themselves further trace back to the even more unmanifest Dao. Images, beginnings and Li: these form the intermediate stratum between the fully unintelligible Dao and the fully intelligible and concrete world of palpable forms, real conditions, and names. Li here seems to take on the sense of a kind of potentiality, a principle, a blueprint according to which realities come to be produced. But the parallelism points us toward the way this is consistently understood in the ironic appropriations of the non-ironic sense of Li: the cutting is the *beginning* of the cut thing. The cut thing, the finished product, is the result of the cutting. The Li is this cutting, or the lines along which this cutting must occur to provide the coherence of the finished product. It is intelligible, but *less* distinctly intelligible than the final, chiseled out product. Li is the intermediate state between the pure formlessness of Dao and the finished separation of individual forms.

Indeed, it is possible to read this passage as referring not to inanimate things, but to quasi-animate creatures; indeed, in early sources, the *qing* of a thing generally refers to the way it behaves, what it tends toward and away from, rather than a static characteristic,[23] in which case it might mean something like, "When we see the way something 'Li's—the way it divides and groups things into coherences for its own consumption—we can thereby come to apprehend its *qing,* its spontaneous unmanipulated condition and responses to the world." Conversely, we can interpret this to mean, "When we see the way this object groups in order to cohere with our own coherence, for our own consumption, we will come to apprehend the true condition it has in our world, the truly relevant facts about it for us, what it, left to itself, *does* to or for or in relation to us." In either case, a direct link between the way things are grouped and the way the groupers of those things feel about them is established. We have encountered similar ideas in the *Liji* texts ("Great Learning," "Doctrine of the Mean," "Record of Music") in *Ironies of Oneness and Differences*. We see here both the intermediate position of Li in the ironic appropriations of the non-ironic, the semi-manifest intelligibility of the act of division or perforations in accordance to which divisions will produce coherence, and the manner in which this oversteps the objective/subjective distinction.

These *Guanzi* texts have sometimes been regarded as representing a kind of intermediate position between Daoism and Legalism, closely related to the "HuangLao" tradition, and perhaps even the work of the crypto-Daoists or proto-Legalists Peng Meng, Tian Peng, and/or Shen Dao. We have seen the direct linkage of Law to Dao in the *Guanzi* texts, deriving the former from the latter via the medium of Li. The HuangLao texts famously declare that "Dao generates the Laws," which has sometimes been seen as an assertion of a real, objective cosmic law rooted in the absolute Dao, something akin to the European notion of "Natural Law." In light of the above analysis, however, we have serious reasons to doubt this reading. For what we have seen in the above passages is very consistent with the words put into the mouth of the same Peng Meng, found in the text *Yinwenzi*: "The person of the Sage comes from himself; the Laws of the Sage, however come from Li. Li comes from his self, but his self is not Li. His self can put forth Li, but the Li are not himself (理出于己，己非理也。己能出理，理非己也。 *Lichuyuji, jifeiliye. Jinengchuli, lifeijiye*). Thus the rule of the person of the sage puts only himself in order, while the rule of the Laws of the Sage puts all things in order." The first sentence here seems to assert a strict division between the person of the sage and the Laws; one is subjective, the other is objective. But the following explanation undermines this neat division. Law comes from Li, but Li itself *comes from the sage*. Peng Meng is not asserting that the Li, or the Laws that derive from them, are purely objective, inscribed in nature, as opposed to the person of the sage. Rather, he as stating that, although the Li come from the person of the sage, they are not one and the same as the person of the sage. They are, as we have said, the interface between his particular sagely viewpoint and the realities of the world, between individual Virtuosities and the formless empty Dao, which is the role of the mind as desireless ruler that brings coherence to them by not interfering in them. They are neither subjective nor objective. They continue to be dependent on the sage, as he who is able to discern, embody, and actualize them—indeed, in an important sense, to create them, selectively whittling down from among the available groupings in the world, as we saw also in the *Xunzi*. They are the coherences between his own coherences and the coherences of the world. This is not inconsistent with the claim that "Dao generates the Laws." For the sage too is not separate from Dao. The sage is the one who perfectly *practices* Dao, embodies it, actualizes it. The Laws in question are not "Natural Law": they are the punitive laws used by the Daoist-Legalist ruler in his society, which in the "Xinshu shang" are directly related to his "power to make judgments," 權 *quan*.

THE *HANFEIZI* COMMENTARY ON THE *LAOZI*: LI AS DIVISION AND THE YIELDING DAO

Many of the later chapters of the *Zhuangzi* include quotations from the existing *Laozi* text, and function as glosses to them. A more direct and formal commentary on parts of the *Laozi*, the earliest in the tradition, is found in the *Hanfeizi* text.[24] There we find the following attempt to define the relation between Dao and Li as used in the "ironic tradition," where Dao is ironic but Li is non-ironic, a way of relating specific determinate coherences to the necessary incoherence of the Dao's indeterminacy:

> Dao means that by which all the ten thousand things are as they are, where all the ten thousand coherences [Li] join and meet, and become discernible [所稽 *suo ji*].[25] Coherence means the patterns found in fully formed things, while Dao means that by which things come to be formed. Thus we say, Dao is what "separates and coheres" them [道理之者也 *Dao Lizhizhe ye*]. Each thing is coherent, so they do not infringe upon one another. Thus coherence is the cutting and limitation [制 *zhi*] between things. Each thing has its own different coherence, and Dao joins together, making intelligible, the coherences of all things. Hence they necessarily transform. Because they must transform, none can maintain the same form of activity for long. Because of this, the energies of their life and death are received from it, various types of wisdom are scooped and poured from it, various affairs arise and collapse into it. . . . Dao is wise with Yao and Shun, is crazy with Jieyu, perishes with Jie and Zhou, flourishes with Tang and Wu. . . . The real condition of Dao, in all cases, is without any limit or special form of its own; it is yielding and supple, following along with the times, according with each coherence. All things attain it to accomplish both their defeats and their successes. Dao can be compared to water; the drowned are those who die by drinking too much of it, while the thirsty may live by drinking of it in the proper amount. . . . Thus it is by gaining it that they die and by gaining it that they live, by gaining it that they fail and by gaining it that they succeed. . . . Coherences mean the divisions between square and round, short and long, coarse and fine, firm and fragile. Thus only when coherences are fixed can Dao be attained. Thus the fixed coherences [定理 *dingli*] divide existing from perishing, death from life, flourishing from declining. For

things now sometimes survive and sometimes perish, suddenly die
or suddenly come to life, first flourish and then later decline; they
cannot be called constant. Only that which was born together with
the separation of Heaven and Earth and which does not perish
even when they are destroyed can be called Constant. The constant
never alters but has no fixed coherence [無定理 *wudingli*]. Having
no fixed coherence, it has no constant locus and thus cannot be
expounded. . . . It is contrasted dyads of long and short, large and
small, square and round, firm and fragile, light and heavy, white
and black that are called "coherences." It is when their coherences
are fixed that things are made easy to cut and tailor. . . .[26]

In this passage, Li, coherence, is defined as the differentiating limits,
or as the determinate marking off of the two sides of each determinate dyad.
Li are differentiated cuts, pointing to the limits and differences between
things. Dao is the name for the totality that transcends these limits, and
for that reason has no definite intelligible identity and cannot be named as
the one or the other of any contrasting pair. Dao is for this reason here also
identified as the *process* of formation, while Li are the specific completed
formations. Dao is the process of becoming coherent, and the undifferentiated incoherence from which they emerge, while Li is the coherences that
result. These coherences are balanced proportions, quantitative measures
and limits that make each thing what it is, here as always presented in terms
of pairs of opposites. As the last line of the citation stresses, this still very
much implies a coherence with human purposes and desires; the coherences
in things show where they can easily be "cut" to suit human purposes.

Li here is very clearly construed as the quantitative/qualitative *limit*
of X, beyond which it ceases to be X, is destroyed, becomes non-X. Li is
the regulative division between the two members of a matched, inconstant
pair. This implies a cycle and a condition of reciprocity, reciprocal limiting,
which is reminiscent of the term 相理 *xiangli*, mutual ordering or mutually
making coherent, which we encountered in the "Community Words" passage
from the *Zhuangzi* cited in the previous chapter.

Dao, on the other hand, is what goes beyond these proper defining
measures, but produces and grounds them. Dao is the indeterminacy that
undermines each particular determinacy, each half of a dyad, and in this
sense is what cuts them into coherent chunks. The undermining overflow
of any determinacy is Dao, and this undermining is how they are limited,
divided off from the opposite number of the dyad. Dao in this sense contributes to the division of things into coherent chunks. Li are those coherent
chunks. But Dao is also that from which they are cut, the unhewn. This follows closely the logic of the *Laozi*, as we have analyzed it in the prequel: Dao

is both the "stuff" and the "source" of all things, as the unhewn is both the stuff and the source of the hewn. It is thus also their "course"—the process of return embedded in each of them, which is simply the undermining of each coherent identity embedded in each identity. All knowable identities, all coherences, are thus relative, partial, unstable. Dao alone is sustainable (常 *chang*) and comprehensive, overreaching the limits of any given identity or coherence in both space and time. Li implies value and coherence. Dao has more value than value, it coheres more than coherence, it is more Li than Li, but for that reason it is unintelligible. This is the ironic double meaning typical of the *Laozi* text: true "order" negates/transcends order.

Note here that Dao and Li are contrasted: one is ironically coherent, that is, incoherent, while Li are now the locus of all the specific coherences of things, including all that can be said and known about them and also how best to deal with them, how to tailor them for human purposes. For this reason Dao is beyond value, has only an ironic meta-value. Unlike what we saw in the "Neiye" from the earliest pre-ironic Daoism, Dao is now what brings both death and life, both failure and success. The difference, as the example of water to the drowning suggests, is in how it is doled out, the measure and limitations, the quantities: in other words, the value of Dao is entirely on the side of the Li, which are what makes it digestible to human purposes. Dao is ironic: it has "value" because it is beyond value; Li are non-ironic, have value for human beings. The "Inner Training" described Dao as what is gained in life and what is lost in death. The *Hanfei* commentary, on the other hand, tells us that Dao flourishes with the flourishing and perishes with the perishing; it is as present in failure, death, and insanity as it is in success, life, and virtue. It is what all these things, positive or negative, must depend on and attain in order to be what they are. We may regard this as a more thoroughgoing conception of omnipotence that overcomes the *qi*-as-life force derivation of pre-ironic Daoism, and the axiocentric omnia-vailability of non-ironic Confucianism. On the other hand, as we shall see, it does not exactly make of Dao a value-neutral creator or source of all things that eliminates all possibility of value, as in a thoroughgoing pantheism. We are told here that Dao is "supple and yielding" in that it follows the particular coherences of things—in the sage it is wise, in the fool it is folly. This is why "all things attain it to accomplish both their defeats and their successes." Dao does not "cause" things to be wise or foolish, or to display any other particular coherence—to serve as a cause in this way would be to act as master, commander, *wei*-ing, being rigid and assertive rather than soft and yielding. Rather it is "attained" by whatever coherences are there, and accords with them, making them "coherent" but not determining which coherence they will be. In other words, the role of Dao in cutting out coherences is severely limited. Dao is the indeterminate, Li are determinate. What is the transition from the indeterminate to the determinate? Indeterminacy is inherently process, since it is an undermining of any given determinacy. But it is not a controlling process, and thus does not lead to a deterministic cosmos. Dao is not a creator: it is that which enables self-creation. It is that which is constantly available, and even mandatorily always impinging upon any limited determinacy, forcing it beyond its limits and into new limits, a kind of internal pressure to overflow divisions, to swing back to the other side of the pendulum, and in that sense is a motive force. But it would seem to be the prior determinacy of things themselves that does the "scooping and pouring" from this ever-present source of energy and action. Dao must be channeled by Li to become determinate. When the text says that Dao is the process by which they cohere, it seems to mean that Dao provides only "coherence" as such, not the specificity of each particular coherence. They might cohere in any other way, but these coherences would not be Li, the specific overlap of that set of possible coherences in nature and the coherence with human desires, the need to divide things so that they are "easy to cut." Dao is an opportunity for Li, the availability of Li, but is "weak and yielding": it does not provide the determinacy in any given case, but rather is the infinite ability to "follow along" with any specific determinacy, to enable and accomplish it.

Where do these specific determinations come from? This problem had already been vaguely touched on in Chapter 51 of the *Laozi*, which stresses the double status of Dao in the ironic tradition:

> Dao generates them; Virtuosity husbands them; things form them; tendencies[27] complete them. For this reason, all things honor the Dao and esteem Virtuosity. But the honoring and esteeming of Dao and Virtuosity are not brought about because someone commands them, but are always spontaneous. Dao generates them, husbands them,[28] grows them, nourishes them, houses them, matures them, feeds them, shelters them. [Dao] generates them without possessing them, makes them but without being depended on. It grows them without being their master. This is called the Unmanifest Virtuosity.[29]

This passage begins by giving us a division of labor; Dao merely generates, no more. As for the specific forms of things, this comes from Virtuosity, things, tendencies—all activities from the agency of *already formed individual things*. In the case of the emergence of any new determinacy, there are prior determinacies that serve as determinants of this newly emerging determinacy. We are speaking, then, not about a *creation ex nihilo* of all things at the beginning of time, but rather of the constant and beginningless process of creation, focusing on the beginning and emergence of any particular entity. Virtuosity is here somewhat like what the *Hanfeizi* commentary calls Li, particular coherences, what each generated thing has "attained" (*de*), its particular coherent form of continuance and function. So Dao, here as in the "Inner Chapters" of the *Zhuangzi,* is just a name for indiscriminate generation as such, where the particular determinacies are due to the agency of the things so generated themselves. It is not merely a receiving, but an "attaining" from Dao, and it is the things themselves that do the attaining which makes them so. As the "Qiwulun" put it, "The Heavenly piping blows forth the ten thousand differences, allowing each to be itself. But since they all choose themselves, who is the blower?"[30] If we give a cosmological read to the famous "windstorm" story in the second chapter of *Zhuangzi*, it would seem that the "wind" represents Dao, and the sounds of the indentations represent individual creatures. The wind just makes sound sound; it does not determine what the particular sounds are. This is done by the shape of the holes themselves. The universal Universal of Dao is just the process of manifesting newness as such, of generation per se (生而已 *sheng er yi,* as Chapter 6 of the *Zhuangzi* says of "what Heaven does"), but does not make them thus and so—they accomplish that themselves. But since the individual determinacies all make themselves and are not commanded or determined to be so by Dao, what is this Dao? It cannot be a determinate something at all, cannot even be said to have any intelligible content, even definitely to "exist" or "be there" at all, and thus reduces in the *Zhuangzi* into the "vague," ironic "Who?" Thus far, this might seem like a radical dualism: the shapes of the holes are derived from a source unrelated to the wind, at least within the confines of this metaphor. Even if we were to suppose that they were created by the wearing-away effect of wind upon the objects in the forest, the differences would still have to be accounted for by the initial conditions of the objects blown upon. But the ironic "Who?" addresses this dualism, the indeterminacy of the Dao, its weakness and yielding. For this dualism holds only as long as we take "indeterminacy" as itself some definite determinacy, that is, as an unchanging "one" that is *the same* everywhere: then we have the unsolvable problem of transitioning from the same to the different. But the indeterminacy of Dao is precisely *not* some one determinate characteristic—just as, in Zhuangzi's metaphor, the wind is not "the same" everywhere, but would presumably blow differently at different times and places. But this difference is random fluctuation, simply an implication of that very indeterminacy that is Dao's constancy. The constancy, in other words, is not a monolithic "one," a sameness. It is indeterminable as any particular characteristic (it has no Li of its own), and thus any particular Li can be its direct expression. Precisely because Dao "produces without owning," because it "issues no commands" on how it is to be used, because it is "soft and yielding" and accords with whatever use individual creatures put it to, will cohere this way or that at their pleasure, it is "spontaneously honored by them in all their activities." Thus, Chapter 51, quoted here, finishes by contradicting itself, delivering a typical Laozian ironic twist: it turns out that, precisely because the Dao does not account for the particular coherences, it does so: Dao generates them, but also husbands them, grows them, nourishes them, houses them, matures them, feeds them, shelters them. The Dao does all the things that Virtuosity, things, and tendencies were said to do above, more or less. It does them by not doing them. It gets credit for them by taking no credit. The initial division of labor is abrogated by the indeterminacy of Dao, which is the doer of all that it does not "do," of all that other preexisting determinacies of things themselves "do."

So what makes each coherence what it is? Literally, it would seem, just chance, circumstance, other things, other coherences. But because each of these things is generated by a noncommanding Dao, the deeds of these others are also construable as the nonaction/action of the incoherent coherence of the Dao. Dao is their stuff, their source, their end, and their tendency to revert into each other. It is what limits them in this sense, and this limiting is what determines what they are. The intervention of another thing to limit this thing is thus also readable as this thing's internal limiting of itself when it reaches its extreme, which is thus also readable as its inherent tendency to revert—which is Dao.

Concomitant with this careful differentiation of the meanings of Dao and Li in the *Hanfeizi* commentary, specifying the former as indeterminate and the latter as the locus of all determinacy, we find the advent of the binome 道理 *daoli*, occasionally used in *Xunzi* and other earlier texts but without yet attaining there the full force of a definite bit of terminology. This might surprise us at first glance: Dao and Li are, after all, here *opposites*; how can they then be combined into a single term? But the ironic structure we have just elucidated should dispel this surprise. Dao and Li are indeed opposites, and it is just for this reason that they now become a definite explanatory principle. *Daoli* are the Li of things as rooted in Dao, which has the specific ironic meaning of "the determinacies of things as emerging from and always embodying their own undermining, their inconstancy, their reciprocal relation to their opposites and tendency to revert into each other, their way of fitting together, determinacies as a departure from the indeterminacy of Dao which, because of that very indeterminacy, turns out to also be accomplished by the indeterminacy from which they depart"—the ironic appropriation of non-ironic coherence. *Daoli* as such is always inherently a union of opposites.

COSMOLOGICAL DAO AND ITS LI IN THE *HUAINANZI*

We may discern a development of this line of thinking in the cosmological reflections of the first chapter, the "Daoyuanxun," of the *Huainanzi*, a text compiled by Liu An (180–122 BCE), grandson of Han dynasty founder Liu Bang, in 139 BCE, possibly written partially by Liu himself but most likely compiled in consultation with a large group of syncretically inclined Daoist thinkers patronized and supported by him, who may have written the individual chapters themselves.[31] As such, the first chapter of this text gives us a nice overview of the "state of the field" of Daoist-leaning speculation in the early Han dynasty, and the ways in which the scraps and fragments of the pre-Qin Daoist ironists were being assembled into systematic pronouncements, attempting to present an ordered univocal picture of the universal cosmological process. Here as in the *Hanfeizi*, and in contrast to the earlier *Guanzi* texts, Dao is the what must be attained to attain both life and death, both success and failure, not merely life and success; we are squarely in realm of ironic appropriations of the non-ironic. Any coherence qua coherence is rooted in the indeterminacy of Dao, and yet specifications are now possible about these determinate coherences, which can serve as reliable guides for behavior. Li plays a prominent role in the deliberations of the whole *Huainanzi* collection, both as a mental object to be cognized—X *zhi li*, the Li "of" something or other, that is, the guideline this something provides, as well as the entrenchment of Hanfeizi's term *daoli*. This is the sense of the term normally translated as "the principle of X." We also find a near-verbatim recapitulation of the use of *tianli* in the sense it has taken on in the "Record of Music," discussed above, namely, *tianli* as something that can be destroyed by overindulgence in programmatic likes and dislikes. Common also are many applications of Li in its original verbal sense, meaning "to put in order." The most telling usage, however, occurs in this first cosmological chapter, and provides its own version of the linkage between these opposed terms Dao and Li that we saw in the *Hanfeizi* commentary to *Laozi*, denoting the formless oneness and the formed divisions respectively. Indeed, the first *Huainanzi* chapter twice uses *daoli* (道理) as a binome:

> Thus if you depend on the abilities of a single person, it will be insufficient to manage even a holding of three acres' extent. But if you work with the measure of the specific coherences as rooted in their incoherence [修道理之數 *xiudaoli zhi shu*], following the self-so of Heaven and Earth, none in the six directions will be able to equal you.[32]

The contrast here, as in the *Hanfeizi* commentary, is between one-sided limitations on the one hand (the skills of a single person) and a system for integrating all opposed limitations into their mutual relations, as centered in the indeterminacy that undermines them. What is new here is the association of these *daoli* with *shu*, literally "number," signifying "calculability" and more specifically "measure." This points to a determinate quantitative limit that is fully intelligible, and thus can be known and relied upon. Harold Roth translates the key phrase, "But if you comply with the norms of the Way."[33] "Norms" is meant to translate *shu*, as Roth's footnote 17 to the same chapter indicates: "The norms (*shu* 數) appear to be the characteristic patterns of things. For example, in 12.1, the 'norms' of the way are detailed as follows: 'Non-action responded, "The way that I know can be weak or strong, can be soft or hard, can be yin or yang, it can be dark or bright, it can embrace or contain Heaven and Earth, it can respond to or await the Limitless. These are the norms by which I know the Way."'"[34] *Shu* here obviously means the mutual limiting of opposites in any dyad, the two extremes of the pendulum swing. It indicates their *measure*, the quantitative limits that mark them off from one another and at the same time ensure their reciprocity and their tendency to veer into one another. "Norms" is thus a rather misleading translation. Even "balance" might be better. The point, of course, is that Li are specifically these mutually limiting coherences rooted in Dao, that is, in the indeterminacy that forces all determinacies to undermine themselves and transform into their opposite. But these determinacies are now truly *grounded* in the indeterminacy, as in the *Hanfeizi* commentary, and thus are truly discernible, truly reliable, truly determinate: they have a definite "calculable measure" (*shu*) to them. They have become definite and knowable—real coherences, genuinely intelligible. Non-ironic coherence has been integrated into an ironic overall cosmology.

The other occurrence of this binome comes in the context of a recommendation for "following," that is, responding rather than acting first, being behind others rather than in front of them, reacting rather than taking initiative. The text then says, qualifying this recommendation:

> What I call being in the rear does not mean being stagnant and doing nothing, congealed and tied up and unflowing; rather it is a way of valuing a comprehensive relation to all measured limits (*shu*) which can thus always match the needs of the time. For if you pair up with every change by firmly holding to the determinacies-rooted-in-indeterminacy [執道理以耦變 *zhidaoli yi oubian*], then the one in front can control the one in the rear, and the one in the rear can also control the one in the front. Why? Because you

don't use that by means of which one is able to control others, and thus no one can control you.[35]

Here again, the usage of *daoli* is specifically associated with the matching of opposites and their tendency to transform into one another: it is the limitation of coherent things—Li—as rooted in and embodying the overflow of that limitation in indeterminacy, Dao, thus providing the point outside either of the two extremes from which to accomplish the proper (human) management of them. Here, as in the *Guanzi* texts, we have this associated with "controlling others without being controlled by them." This undermines the one-sided attachment only to following and staying in the rear; the text makes clear that this is really only a means of finding the central point beyond both front and rear, which can transform freely into either, and thus remains in command of them, the central indeterminate point between the two swinging extremes of a dyadic pendulum. It is a coherence that is rooted in its own incoherence, and yet provides a guideline by which to enable successful and definite activity in the world—the coherence with human cognition and desire. It is an ironic appropriation of non-ironic coherence.

This idea plays a newly important role in the *Huainanzi*'s more comprehensive cosmological reflections, particularly in the meaning it gives to the idea of "unity" or "oneness." The opening chapter tells us:

> Formlessness is what we call the One. What we call One is what has no counterpart in the world, which stands toweringly alone, a solitary mass onto itself, above permeating the Nine Heavens and below threaded through the Nine Regions, round but not charted by any compass, square but not charted by any carpenter's square, for all are vastly mixed together to make up this One, free of all restraints and resting on no root, bagging together all of Heaven and Earth as the open gate of the Dao. Mysterious, vague, hidden, dark, its unmixed Virtuosity is preserved in solitude, spreading out without finish, functioning without exhaustion. Thus it is not found when looked for, not heard when listened for, no identity is found for it when sought. It is the formlessness in which form is generated, the silence in which the Five Tones resound, the flavorlessness in which the Five Flavors take shape, the colorlessness in which the Five Colors come to be. Thus beings arises from Non-Being, the substantial emerges from the Empty. Encircling the world, all names and realities coexist within it. The number of tones does not exceed five, yet their variations are inexhaustible. The harmony

of the flavors does not exceed five, yet their transformations are inexhaustible. The number of the colors does not exceed five, yet their variations are inexhaustible. For among tones, when the *gong* tone is established, all Five Tones take shape; among flavors, when sweetness is established, all Five Flavors take their places; among colors, when white is established, all Five Colors come to be. Dao means that when this One is established, all things are generated. For this reason, the Coherence [Li] of the One is put into effect everywhere within the four seas, and the division of the One separates Heaven and Earth [是故一之理施四海，一之解際天地 *shigu yizhili shi sihai yizhijie ji tiandi*]. Its wholeness is pure, like unworked wood; its scattered parts are confused and mixed, like turgid water. It turgidity slowly clears; its emptiness slowly fills.[36]

Both the solitariness and the inclusiveness of the One are stressed here, the inexhaustible ramifications and variations that emerge out of the most formless, the smallest number, the one. This is possible because the One is formlessness per se, the indeterminacy of the ironic Dao. It has no identifiable form, no specific identity; it overflows all individual forms, like Laozi's pre-cut unhewn raw material, the unworked wood. Its oneness is ironic; in fact it is neither one nor many, it has no specific determinations, and for this reason is it is omnipresent in all particular forms, murky like turgid water. The establishment of this peculiar n/oneness brings with it the generation of all specific, limited, identifiable things. It makes them what they are in the sense discussed above, precisely by being formless, not interfering, being soft and yielding, not contributing to their limitations. The establishment of the one "background" tone, flavor, or color is here like Laozi's unhewn which is at once "B as opposed to A" and "both A and B" and "neither A nor B," as we saw in *Ironies*, both one among many, the totality of all the many, and the none which stands beyond any, and thus entails the formation of all the other tones, flavor, and colors, because of its irony: its simultaneous determinacy and indeterminacy, the non-Dao which is also a Dao, which guides by not guiding, which is ironically good by not being good, the source and the course and the whole of the others. What is new here, in the explicit incorporation of the new developments of non-ironic coherence as Li, is the specification that this oneness is thus also a kind of separating, an ordering, a Li-ing, and it is precisely this kind of Li-ing that is capable of being omnipresent throughout the world, indeterminacy as present in all determinacies through their mutual limiting and overflowing into one another, the way they interlock through their inconstancy, the Dao that is present in Li, *daoli*. Note that Li is here parallel to 解 *jie*, also meaning to untangle or separate, and the omnipresence is presented as an omnipresence of division, the omnipresence of a grouping, an ordering, a coherence: the function of the Li of oneness is parallel to the "separation" of Heaven and Earth. The act of separating them, their mutual limitation, their finitude, is what is omnipresent, what unifies them. Note also that the wholeness, the oneness/noneness as such, is unhewn, unidentifiable, but again it functions in the individual limited entities as their "mixed-up-ness," their inability to be purely what they are and stay cleanly within their own limitations. This is another way of indicating their tendency to return, to overstep their borders, the function of the formless Dao as reversion, as a course of behavior, as their constant Way.

So Li and related terms throughout these ironic appropriations of non-ironic coherence signify the limit beyond which a thing reverts or crashes, the limit of coherence that the Dao both forms and undermines. This notion of reversal when a thing reaches its "limit" combines a notion of balanced proportion—proper measure—with an idea of reciprocity, the mutual limiting of individual things. A comparative note is perhaps in order here. Measure, for Hegel, was the most sophisticated and complete idea possible for monistic philosophies that posited no intelligible realm or reality behind appearances. Reciprocity, similarly, was the most sophisticated and complete category by which two-tiered metaphysical systems could think about the world—encompassing and sublating ideas of identity and difference, appearance and reality, substance and attribute, cause and effect and so on. Beyond both of these was the realm of the Concept (*Begriff*), which dealt with syllogistic thinking and thinking itself, Reason, as the ultimate reality, a realm reached only by the comprehension of the Idea, the realm of forms in their true signification as understood by Hegel, namely, pure thought as the self-positing purposive activity of the absolute as both subject and substance. But in the ironic tradition in early China, "Measure" and "Reciprocity" are matched with Dao as a third dimension unknown to Hegel, not a crypto-Platonic intelligible realm, since it is by definition indeterminate, but something that nonetheless "does the work" thereof (that of which one should remain cognizant in order to come to grips with something, cognitively or pragmatically), the indeterminate source and encompasser (which unifies, includes them) of all the specific, contrary Li. Its relation to particular Li is soft and yielding, making them only by generating and allowing them, and present in them only in according with their own mutual limiting. This is the relation between the Dao and individual coherences, to be contrasted sharply to "instantiation" or "inclusion" in the sense of a universal, form, or whole, or determination (formal "cause") as in the case of an essence, form, or Idea in Greek thought. These convergences of coherence and its incoherence will be the focus of development of the further intensified role of the term Li as we move into the world of post-Han thought, in particular in the representative "Xuanxue" thinkers, Wang Bi and Guo Xiang.

FIVE

LI AS THE CONVERGENCE OF COHERENCE AND INCOHERENCE IN WANG BI AND GUO XIANG

Xuanxue 玄學, literally "dark" or "mysterious" learning, sometimes translated as "Neo-Daoism" or even "Metaphysical Studies," is the name traditionally given to the Post-Han revival of speculative thought, taking its name from the renewed interest in reinterpreting the *Laozi*, *Zhuangzi*, and *Zhouyi*, known at the time as the "Three Abstruse (Texts)" (三玄 *sanxuan*). The movement is seen as in some manner attempting to fill the void left by the fall of the Han dynasty, and with it the undermining of the official cosmological and political ideology, rooted in the thought of Dong Zhongshu. The *Zhouyi*, of course, played a major role in this ideology, but only as subjected to a particular esoteric mode of interpretation, closely linked to calendrical and political correlative schemes. Characterizing this text as "abstruse" and also linking it with the *Laozi* and *Zhuangzi*, the key sources of ironic thought, viewed as heterodox by the Han ideologues, Xuanxue rejects the previously prevailing "clarity" of interpretation of the text: it had been seen as something already comprehended and incorporated, now it is again asserted to have unplumbed mysteries parallel to those of the ironic texts, which had already been relegated to husks whose few useful insights had already been harvested and incorporated harmlessly into the Yin-Yang correlative schemes (Yin having its origin as a mark of non-ironic incorporation of ironic coherence, as we have seen in *Ironies of Oneness and Difference*). Xuanxue can thus be seen as a reclaiming of the untamed implications of the *Zhouyi*, and an attempt to read that text in close dialogue with the *Laozi* and the *Zhuangzi* instead of through the lens of the correlative schemes of the Han. As such, we have here a rethinking of the relation between the two streams of the tradition, a reshuffling of the ironic and non-ironic cards to produce a new attempt at a synthesis—one that of course makes use of some of the moves devised by former attempts at mediation of the two trends, but makes significant innovations.

We have already seen some of the developments of the notion of Li in non-ironic traditions, and their incorporations into ironic systems, taking place in the Han. Recapping them chronologically, we had the *Huainanzi's* continuation of the use of Li as part of the ironic incorporation of non-ironic coherence in the *Hanfeizi* commentary to the *Laozi*, itself a continuation of one of the trends found in the later parts of the *Zhuangzi*, where Li serves as the word for limited non-ironic coherences contrasted to but also deriving from the largest coherence, Dao, which is, however, ironically coherent, that is, definitionally unintelligible and unknowable. We had also the revival of the straight non-ironic use of Li, with the ironic element safely incorporated into a highly rigidified version of the Yin-Yang system, in Dong Zhongshu, where both the Great Coherence of the whole and particular intelligible coherences were both construed as ultimately non-ironic. And we saw in Yang Xiong's *Taixuan* system an ingenious new mode of incorporation of the ironic notion of coherence as unintelligible—the "Great Mystery" of the title of his work. In Yang's system, the necessarily contrarian aspect of all coherence, Laozi's bell-shaped rise and fall structure of reversal, was accepted by Yang but systemized as the triplicity of (1) incipience, (2) development into intelligible coherence, and (3) contravening decline. There, this originally ironic structure is assimilated into a system of non-ironic Great Coherence. Lip service is given to the unintelligibility of the Great Mystery as the greatest whole, but far from undermining the knowability of particular coherences, this unknowable is present in them as their very triadic structure and interrelations. In this way, although the unknowable is called "unknowable," it is arrayed in a perfectly determinate manner: it is Yang's book itself. This set of determinations is presented as cohering much more directly with nature than the system of determinations found in the *Zhouyi*, in that the intermediary of coherence with the tradition of the sages is annulled by the fact that Yang Xiong creates his own system from scratch. The overabundance of coherences chosen out by human sages is no longer an issue here. We have a single-ordered cosmos, which incorporates the self-contravening of each coherence and hence its inevitable rootedness in unintelligibility into a single coherence, as process rather than as relativity. In contrast, in the *Huainanzi*, developing tendencies found in the "Community Words" dialogue and other later sections of the *Zhuangzi*, the *Hanfeizi* reading of *Laozi*, and the later parts of the *Guanzi* chapters, we found non-ironic coherence, marked explicitly as Li and defined as the separating boundaries between things in dyadic pairs which confer on them their determinacy, explicitly incorporated into an ironic overall structure, maintaining the ironic incoherence of Dao and thus emphasizing the changeability even of the non-ironic coherences derived therefrom, while still allowing a recognizable workable coherence to them.

Historians like to point to the new political situation of the unified Han empire to account for divergences like this. Although I am deeply uncomfortable about positing a direct causal relationship between these kinds of correlated developments, it is perhaps worth noting that, while Yang's work, coming in the middle of the Han, shows no particular innovations in the actual usage of the term Li per se, we do see some decisive changes taking place during this period. In particular, as Mizoguchi Yûzô has pointed out, Liu Xiang (77–76 BCE) seems to be the first person to use Li as a self-standing, independent term, functioning as an unmodified subject rather than implicitly as the predicate of something else. It is no longer the verbal "to Li," meaning "to order," nor the patterning that results, nor "the Li of something," nor the opposite counterpart of Dao in the pair Dao-Li, the limited as opposed to the limitless, as in the *Hanfeizi* commentary, nor as a derivative intermediary of Dao in its intersection with particular things and with human needs, as in the "Xinshu shang."[1] Nor is it just the "Li of X" posited as an object to be cognized, analogous to "the principle of X," as we have also begun to see here and there. In Liu Xiang's 戰國策 *Zhanguoce,* "Qiguo," we find the statement: "The event that necessarily arrives is death [or alternately: What all events necessarily arrive at is death]. The Li that is fixedly so [or: what all Lis fixedly accept as so] is that wealth and status are what one strives toward and poverty and lowliness are what one avoids. This is what is necessarily so of events, what is fixedly so of Li" (事之必至者死也。理之固然者富貴就之，貧賤去之。此事之必然，理之固然 *shizhibizhizhe siye, lizhiguranzhe fuguijiuzhi, pinjianquzhi, ci zhizhibiran, lizhiguran*). Here, Li is a stand-alone noun. Elsewhere in that work, a military victory is explained by saying, "It was all a case of the strategy taking shape and the tendencies working advantageously. The Li was spontaneously that way—how could it require the presence of any spirits?" (皆計形勢利，自然之理，何神之有 *jiejixingshili, ziranzhili, heshenzhiyou*). In the *Hanshu,* Emperor Wen is depicted as declaring, "Death is the Li of heaven and earth, the self-so of things (死者天地之理，物之自然 *sizhe tiandizhili, wuzhiziran*), and hence should cause us no extreme sorrow."[2] This extends the same sort of parallelism to the term *ziran,* self-so, seemingly as a gloss of Li. Elsewhere, the same text states, "In general, that a thing which flourishes must decay is a self-so Li (夫物盛必衰，自然之理 *fuwushengbishuai, ziranzhili*)." Mizoguchi is right to note a new usage in these examples, Li as unmodified subject—and also apparently one of the first usages of the phrase *ziranzhili,* and of the coupling of Li and 事 *shi.* But he is perhaps too quick to identify it with a concept of Li as a metaphysical principle in its own right, serving as a causal determinant of events and serving to explain why they are as they are. Mizoguchi's reading would seem to interpret the phrase *lizhiguran* from the first-cited *Zhanguoce* passage as "This is what is definitely so (because of the) Li," or perhaps, "This is a definite principle." But the parallelism in the first statement, and particularly the use of 之 *zhi* rather than 然 *ran* the first time through, shows us the contours of this still formative sense of Li. That is, there is still an implicit plurality to both the "events" and the "Lis" here. We would do better to interpret this statement literally, either as, "What all events must come to is death," or, alternately, "The one event that necessarily comes is death." Similarly, "What all Lis definitely share in affirming is self-interest," or alternately, "The Li that is always definitely affirmed is self-interest." The *ran* implies both a sense of "being so" and "being accepted, being affirmed as right." There is still something perspectival about this statement, and an implication of the active participation of those who do the affirming. It is because they are as they are that they can cohere with this coherence, and this "being as they are" is still something independent of what is made so by the Li in question. They are not simply passively determined to be so, to posses this attribute, by the presence of this metaphysical principle. The latter reading does imply something like universality, but it still presupposes that there are more than one Li. This particular Li of self-interest is the one that is affirmed from everywhere. This coherence is the one that *coheres* with every other coherence, and every other event. This is not the same thing as positing something called "the Li," or even "a Li of self-interest," and then saying that what it makes so is that all beings are self-interested.

The linkage to 固然 *guran* and its parallel 必然 *biran*, and further, to 自然 *ziran*, is indeed quite significant. This brings us closer, I think, to the implication of the term here. It is indeed no longer merely something like "valued way of grouping" or "order," but neither is it a principle determining phenomenal events. Rather, it is the way things go when left to themselves, what they tend toward (e.g., wealth and status, death), the way they must, as long as they are themselves and because they are themselves, go. That is, it is still what they cohere with, what their being-themselves coheres with. This is "necessary" because as long as they are themselves, they will do what they themselves do; it is somewhat like the statement, "Wherever I go, there I am." But a kind of continuity and exceptionless reliability is attributed to this tendency, which is rooted not in the Li but in what the "self" in question is here, and hence the "self-so." We may note that the term is contrasted with the intervention of a spirit. It is what is so when no particular agent deliberately makes something so, when things are left to themselves. Significantly, this is still clearly a question of coherence—for example, the coming together of things and that which they tend toward, or of tendencies and strategies. The idea of a convergence of multiple events, as opposed to a single particular agency, and hence the idea of something beyond the deliberate control of either intentions or conscious desires of any particular being, is what pushes us toward the idea of Li as something like "objectivity" and even "truth" here: that is, it is indeed what is so whether you like it or not, what is inescapable in all cases, what is necessary and universal. But this is to a significant degree a deceptive appearance, as can be seen by the development of this usage of Li—as convergence and as "the Li of the self-so"—in the post-Han Xuanxue thinkers, Wang Bi and Guo Xiang.

Let us begin with Wang Bi, author of what became canonical commentaries to both the *Zhouyi* and the *Laozi*, whose work may also be classified as a non-ironic incorporation of the ironic, but with significant structural innovations. Wang is thus the architect of a new reading of the *Zhouyi* in light of the *Laozi*, and vice versa, which opens up the way to a new approach to thinking about the relation of the ironic and non-ironic traditions. Wang too finds a way of bridging the gap between the Omnipresent, the universal universal, the great coherence, where the problem of unintelligibility is most pressing, and the individual coherences of particular situations and things, thus putting the ironic tradition to use in creating and predicting coherences. The inner mechanism of this move in Wang's case is most clearly enunciated in his interpretative strategy with respect to the *Zhouyi*. The essence of Wang's approach, his key insight, lies in his view of each hexagram in the *Zhouyi* as a yin-yang chart depicting a temporary mini-cosmos with its own mini-Dao, a move that bears considerable resemblance to Yang Xiong's approach. In the opening section of his 周易略例 *Zhouyilueli*, "Illuminating the 'Judgments,'" his methodological mission statement for the reading of the *Zhouyi*, Wang puts his key point this way:

> What is the Judgment of a hexagram? It is the overall discussion of the whole hexagram's structure [體 *ti*], illuminating the master that it follows. The many cannot rule the many; the many are ruled by the fewest of the few. The moving cannot control the moving; all the world's motions are controlled by the stable and unified [and thus still]. Thus it is only because their master necessarily makes them one that the many can coexist, and it is only because their source necessarily is not-two that all the various motions can proceed. Things do not happen haphazardly; they necessary all proceed from their particular coherence ["principle," Li]. There is a source and master that unifies them, an origin which brings them together [統之有宗,會之有元 *tongzhi you zong, huizhi you yuan*]. Thus they are complex but not chaotic, manifold but not confused. Thus the way the six lines of any hexagrams impinge upon one another can

be made intelligible by one [among them] The way the firm and the yielding support one another can be fixed by setting up their master. . . . For the scarce is what the abundant esteem; the few is what the many take as their source and master. When a hexagram has five Yang lines and one Yin line, the yin line is its master. If it has five Yin lines and one Yang line, the Yang line is its master. For Yang is what is sought by Yin, and Yin is what is sought by Yang.[3]

A hexagram, in Wang's view, is a graphic representation of the yin-yang structure of a given situation in which a person might find himself, a given moment in time. A hexagram that, viewed as a whole from without, has the pervasive character of being "Yang," is in its inner structure precisely lacking in Yang. As a whole it relates to other hexagrams in a Yangish manner precisely because it lacks inner Yangness, and thus all its elements seek Yang, cohere around Yang, express the emergent total character of Yangishness. Its coherence both as the togetherness of its parts and as its togetherness with things outside it (its effect on them and the way it appears to them) is a direct effect of what is least intelligible, least findable and discernible, in its parts. The more Yin a hexagram is quantitatively, the more Yang it is qualitatively. The more Yang it is, the more Yin it is. What is *least* in evidence in that situation, the *least* prominent element in that hexagram, is the master of that situation, which truly determines its character. Like Dao in the world, what is least manifest is most powerful; what is least discernible is the source of the discernibility of all the other things in the world, the principle of their convergence. What is least coherent (least intelligible) is what makes all the elements cohere intelligibly. But these incoherent elements are themselves given a name and described as having a character in the "Judgments" to the Hexagrams. Moreover, there is not just one unintelligible incoherent coherer of the world; there are *many* of them, one for each of the sixty-four hexagrams, at least. It is not an absolutely incoherent and unintelligible void, then, but merely the *least* evident force in the situation. All elements in that particular situation flow toward it, "seek" it, orient themselves around it. This is what gives it unity, consistency, what makes its parts cohere as this rather than anything else. This is its coherence. It is not the visible and intelligible coherence as such which is their real organizing structure. Rather, each situation has its "coherence" (Li) in what is least apparent in it, what it most lacks. Li here begins to function somewhat like the term *principle*, which from here on becomes a marginally feasible translation of the term, in that it is called the *zong* or ancestor of the situation, and is its "master," as *arche* is the "first form" or "beginning" and "ruler" of a thing in Greek thought. There is an immanent teleological element implied as well, in that Wang speaks of the hexagram lines as "seeking after" their opposite, their master, which applies to them both severally and as the newly emergent coherence as a whole. Still, it is clearly not temporal priority that is meant by "source" here, not even to the degree that it had been in Yang Xiong, and even "logical priority" does not seem to be an accurate description of what Wang has in mind. The principle is not a self-standing element to which the totality is ultimately reducible, as in the pre-Socratic first principles of fire, water, and the like. Rather, the notion of a convergence is here not a reducibility into a primal stuff, but a *center* which unifies heterogeneous elements into an organizational unity. It is as if the Laozian Dao is particularized into the sixty-four hexagrams, with mini-Daos for each situation and thing. These mini-Daos are called Li. Li are explicitly what "unify" 統 and "bring together" 會 the elements of the situation: they make it "cohere," and they make it cohere "coherently." They are what order that situation, unify it, make it intelligible, knowable as having this particular character. Moreover, they are unlike Aristotelian principle most centrally in the sense in which "to rule," a characteristic closely associated with *arche* as well, is understood here. *Arche* in Greek has an etymological link to *archos*, "ruler," signifying sovereignty, power, domination (still found in English words like "monarchy," "patriarchy," and so on). We may note that "principles" are etymologically related with "principalities" and "princes," just as "patterns" are to "paternal." Wang's metaphor is also political and genetic, speaking of "masters" and "ancestors." But the derivative notion of a "principle" will bear the mark of the political ideal from which the metaphor is drawn. For Li in Wang's view do not rule except in the Daoist sense of not-ruling, by being scarce and invisible, by being the lacked object of desire sought by the rest, even if they are unaware of it, that is, even if it is their "stomach desire," which genuinely orients them. Aristotle's Unmoved Mover is also a ruler that brings all things toward it by doing nothing, by letting them converge in its direction rather than by directly "ruling" them by "rules" imposed upon them, and thus a daring interpretation of even the particular rules that characterize teleological final causes as rules to particular beings might be attempted on the same model, though I believe this would be an unconventional reading of Aristotle. Nonetheless, the attraction exerted by the unmoving Good does seem to be conceived of as something cognized, or at the very least *cognizable*. The ruling attraction it exerts is dependent on its *definiteness* as something that can be desired. The opposite seems to be the case for the form of "teleology" operative in Wang Bi's thought. For an "object" of desire that is nonetheless invisible is the Dao, the correlate of "stomach desires." Wang says "scarce," of course, not "unintelligible" "invisible," or completely lacking, and this is what allows him to particularize his mini-Daos, and put them to use. Coherence (Li) had always implied value, as we have seen, and here this is incorporated into the "valuing" of the scarce line by the abundant lines, and by the ethical implications of the hexagrams. The Li is what all the parts of the situation value, what they lack, what they want, and this is what makes them what they are. But this wanting is not a conscious wanting of an object first cognized as desirable; it is, rather, desirable in the Daoist manner precisely because of its unintelligibility, its incoherence, the "empty space" it provides to beings for them to move into with their own particular coherences intact. As mini-Dao, the Li are here like the "womb" or the "valley" or the "empty hub" of the *Laozi*, which attract and unify by providing an empty space for other things to move into, a slot into which they can enter and thereby connect with one another coherently.

The aspect of coherence as intelligibility is thus given a twist, in that any situation or thing can indeed be known, but only precisely as what it is not, what it lacks, what organizes all its parts around their desire for it. It can be known from the outside, in the context of a greater coherence of this situation with the knowing consciousness and with the entire sequence of situations, only as the particular "coherence" that generally names the whole hexagram. But this is precisely, quantitatively or materially speaking, what it is "not," what it lacks. An example from optics might be helpful here: when an object appears red to us, it is because that object is absorbing all the colors of the spectrum except for red; hence, the red is bouncing off of it, rejected, reflected, and deflected outward to our eyes. Hence, the way it appears externally is an index of exactly the opposite of what it contains. The color that it "has" least of internally is the color that it, as a totality seen from outside, "is."

This example, however, loses the most distinctive part of Wang's analysis, the idea of the parts of a situation "seeking" what is least, or what is lacking. "Is" and "ought" are brilliantly combined here, for the "is" equals "what it is knowable as," which in this case equals precisely "what it is not, but wants to be." All things are the opposite of what they appear to be, but the precise and determinate opposite, as a thing appears red because it absorbs all colors except red. The twist to the one-many relationship is along the same lines: all "principles" are the same principle—nothingness, lack—but different, in that they are, as it were, holes in different things. In the *Hanfeizi* commentary, the knowable Li were opposed to the unknowable Dao. The Li were the individual coherences of particular things and situations, their finiteness, their limits, while the Dao was the limitless, the overflowing of all limits. The former were knowable, describable, coherent, while the latter was unintelligible, incoherent. The incoherent Dao was what made the coherent Lis what they are, and also what undermined them, but the determinacy and the indeterminacy of the two sides of the relationship remained very clear-cut. Wang has devised a way of bringing the indeterminacy right into the heart of the determinacy, so that they are no longer opposed, no longer two different things. Rather, the way in which the unintelligible causes the intelligibility has become immanent; the absence of what is lacking is the presence of what is present. From the outside, it is intelligible as X; from the inside, everything is oriented around and derives from its flagrant non-Xness. Xness, in all its specificity, means precisely "the ruling presence of non-Xness as the specific absence of X." This is a huge and decisive step in the integration of the ironic and non-ironic traditions.

Implicit in this conception is the call for a new kind of knowing, which is, as in the "Great Commentary" to the *Zhouyi* itself, once again asserted to be possible only through the hexagrams and the sagely judgments on them, the coherence of and with the tradition. Nonetheless, the idea of necessity (必 *bi*) in the hard sense is certainly more evident in Wang Bi's description than it was in the "Great Commentary" itself, where the appeal to the specific wisdom of the sages is presented as the ultimate guarantee of the coherence of the text in the face of its multiple sets of contradictory rules. Wang Bi's Li are necessary in a more built-in, less "culture-specific" way. Again, the *Hanfeizi* gave us a fairly simple whole/part relation between Dao and Li, where the Dao is the indescribable limitless and the Lis are the describable contents between limits. The Dao's participation in the individual Lis of things, their knowable coherences, derived from the *Laozi*'s raw material/vessel relation, where the raw material is nameable as none of the particular vessels, but is identical with them nonetheless as their stuff, and as the source, end, and course of their activities. By being none in particular, it was present in all, but only as a "gentle and yielding" material that allowed itself to be temporarily shaped and determined by whatever vessel it formed a part of, and the shaping course of their inevitable overflow back toward it, producing their dyadic relation to their own opposites. Because it is nothing (in particular), its addition to any particular something does not add any further determinations to it: it goes along with the Li, enabling strength in the strong, weakness in the weak, life in life, death in death, success in success, failure in failure. For Wang Bi, in contrast, this nothingness has taken on a new, more vital, structuring function. Its ironic non-ruling isn't presence merely as "following" or "yielding" or "pliancy," it doesn't just let itself be shaped; rather, it is the center of gravity of the shaping process, the process of converging and cohering. Each Li is the Dao of its situation. The *Hanfeizi* commentary already hinted in this direction with its claim that the Dao is *what makes* Lis, or what forms the divisions between things, but this is still depicted as a vague process of mitosis in the context of the overall orienting and cohering activities of the Dao in its relation to the world as a whole. These individual coherences are the by-products of the global course of rise and return which is the process of the Dao in the world, fully present in them only in the ironic sense pertaining to its nothingness, its unnameability: the "whole" nothingness is present in each particular in the form of its yielding to it, allowing the particular's name to be affixed to it. We will see a similar line of thought in the Huayan school of Buddhism. For Wang Bi, on the contrary, it is not just "the" Dao that makes coherences; it is Daoishness, namely, whatever aspect of the situation is playing the Daoish role of being the least, the most invisible, the lowest. The entire quality of Daoishness is now fully, not partially, present in and as each situation, in all its specificity. The Dao is at once one and many, not just in the sense of being divided up into specific entities to which the One Dao remains immanent, but in that, in a very real sense, there are *many Daos,* diverse and specific Daos that are nonetheless also Dao, the "leastness" per se. The many Li are now literally many Daos. There is a different hole in each being which is its Dao, but all holes are the same hole, precisely, lack, which is everywhere indistinguishable. The distinguishable and indistinguishable, the coherent and the incoherent, the non-ironic and the ironic begin to really converge here. This is a decisive step toward the working through of another, more thoroughgoing, kind of omnicentrism, which we will see developed in the Tiantai school.

Tang Junyi's comments on the passage cited above are particularly useful for our purposes here. Tang notes:

> This passage on "Illuminating the Judgments" originally comes simply from an attempt to say that in interpreting a hexagram one should stress the whole hexagram's essence, and seek out its smallest and most condensed line as the ruling line, and thus makes the point that all things have their Li which serves as "a source and master that unifies them, an origin which brings them together." People always try to speculate about what this Li is, but this approach does not accord with Wang Bi's text. Actually, if we read this text carefully, we can see that this Li is precisely "the many tending toward the few, the abundant tending toward the least, the complex tending toward the simple" itself. This "tending toward the few and the simple" is precisely "tending toward the master, toward the origin." We need not seek any other Li to serve as the "master that unifies them, the origin which brings them together." Thus when Wang Bi says, "Things do not happen haphazardly; they necessary all proceed from their particular Li," he means that the reason a particular thing is actually like this or like that is because of the principle [Li] of "the many tending toward the one, the abundant tending toward the few, the complex tending toward the simple and

thus interacting and converging." Guo Xiang, in his commentary to Zhuangzi's "Dechongfu," says, "Things do not happen haphazardly; they are all the coming together [會 *hui*] of heaven and earth, the convergence [趣 *qu*] of the ultimate coherence [Li]." This comment, explaining Li in terms of convergence [*huiqu*], precisely grasps Wang Bi's idea, and serves as good evidence for my claim here. Precisely this convergence [*huiqu*] is what makes a thing what it is. It is also what makes an activity or and event what it is. . . . It is unnecessary to go beyond this master or origin and try to think about a single original qi or heavenly deity, or any objectively existing metaphysical substance, or a self-subsistent metaphysical principle, to serve as this master or source of things. The things or events formed by this tendency of the many converging toward the one and so on are each individual concrete events and activities, that is, concrete situations, like the "difficult" situation described in the Tun hexagram. But this situation, or any situation, is always a single convergence, "a many tending toward a one, an abundance tending toward the few, a complexity tending toward a simplicity." But in calling it *a* convergence, we note that it possesses a singularity, which constitutes its fewness or its simplicity. Whenever people look squarely at a situation as a whole, they always unify it, reduce it to fewness, simplify it, which is to say, they unify it in a single master or source, and thus know the Li that it comes from. This Li is just "what it comes from," just as Dao is a "what things come from." Where we find the sense in which it is a motion "from" the many to the few, "from" the abundant to a one, "from" the complex to the simple, we find the Li, the principle, the Dao of Change. Thus we can say that this "fromness" resides in neither the complex nor in the simple, not in the one nor in the many, not in the abundant nor in the few.[4]

Tang's point about Li is extremely important: for Wang, Li is really not that which "controls" these convergences, or a separate realm of the One, but rather a way of describing these concrete processes of convergence toward the least represented element in each situation. "One" here is not *the* One, but the lowest number, the least. There is not any single "One," then, but rather a different one, least, simple, implicit in any situation, which structures that situation. "Ones" are multiple, not one. Tang is surely right to further stress the implications of Wang's view in the stress on "stimulus" (感 *gan*, as reflected in his commentary to the 咸 *xian* hexagram) and interactivity, with its emphasis on "emptiness" (i.e., psychologically and morally speaking, humility) as a development of this idea of "seeking" and "wanting" embedded in the hexagram structures. It is this mutual seeking, interacting, responding to stimulus that allows things to structure themselves around the least present aspect of the situation, the object of desire. This in turn provides a novel insight into the problem of stimulus and response (感應 ganying), which is now conceived as neither response to the same type nor to different type; the emptiness (虛 xu) of the participants allows them to manifest as their opposite, across types. As Tang says, commenting on Wang's commentary to the xian hexagram, for the male and female to interact, the male must temporarily abandon his maleness and take the role of the female (e.g., in humbling himself to go forth and receive his bride).[5] This sort of reciprocity, convergence, interactivity is the locus of Li for Wang, which is thus different in each situation, and manifest in a multitude of ways along with the multitude of situations. There are many Lis, each serving as a miniature Dao for that particular situation.

Unfortunately, in discussing Wang Bi's interpretation of the Laozi as opposed to the Zhouyi, Tang backpedals a bit on his interpretation, reverting to a "Single Dao" reading, which he compares to the trackless space in which airplanes or birds may fly, but which is not for that reason the path of airplane or bird. On this reading, Dao is once again transcendent to individual situations, unaffected by them, a single encompassing universal emptiness in which many different particulars may come and go.[6] But I would like to claim here that Tang would have done better to recall his own interpretation of "emptiness" and "oneness" in his discussion of Wang's hexagram interpretation and applied this to his understanding of Wang's Laozi commentary. Indeed, the idea of oneness as "the least" rather than as "the all-encompassing One" is already present in the Laozi, but with a stress on the "least" in the world as a whole, rather than to each situation. We see this for example in Chapter 39 of that text, the most extensive discussion of "the One" therein, which after describing how various entities gain their own specific coherent characters by "gaining the One" (note that again they themselves attain the One, rather than merely receiving some determinacies from it) goes on to conclude explicitly by saying, "Thus the esteemed take the humble as their base, the lofty take the lowly as their foundation" (故貴以賤為本，高以下為基 gu gui yi jian we ben, gao y ixia wei ji). The "humble" and "lowly" is the One: it is the lack of the specific value represented by each of these entities themselves. This allows this "least" to also serve, ironically, as the all-encompassing One, as the unity both of the parts of each entity cohering so as to make it sustainably what it is, and also its way of linking to the coherence with its opposite, and with all other entities, through its contact with what is least itself, least represents its own value, its own opposite. In the same sense, for Wang the "least" in any situation, since it structures the whole situation, is what is all-encompassingly present in that situation, what that situation appears to be "when viewed squarely as a whole," as Tang puts it. Indeed, Wang even describes this coherence of what a situation wants but is not, what it tends toward, in the full ontological sense as "the coherence that makes it what it is" (所以然之理 suoyiran zhi Li): "When one recognizes the motion of things, the coherences [Li] that make them what they are can all be attained."[7] That is, the convergence around what is lacking in them is the Li that makes them what they are. The Li is both this process of converging and this least-present element, just as Laozi's Dao was both the unintelligible background of raw stuff and the process of reverting to this raw stuff. To clarify the implications of this, let us now look at Wang Bi's approach to the Laozi.

SUBJECTIVE PERSPECTIVISM IN WANG BI: THE ADVENT OF TI AND YONG 體用 AS IRONIC STRUCTURE

Somewhat surprisingly, Tang Junyi characterizes Wang Bi as stressing the "subjective" meaning of Dao in the Laozi, pushing this beyond what he sees as the strictly political and more objective sense of Dao in the interpretation of the text by HuangLao Daoists, in his concept of "embodying Non-Being" (tiwu 體無). It is here that Tang sees the most distinctive feature of Wang's apparent stress on the Dao as "substance" (ti): not as a reference to what Tang calls the objective and transcendent metaphysical substance of Dao (道體 daoti), but as a subjective mode of relating to the Non-Being of Dao. Wang's interpretation is loftier than the earlier ones, Tang says; in a sense, he says, Wang thus overestimates Laozi, seeing only his loftiest meaning. For Wang's reading is not an accurate reclaiming of the objective sense of Dao as metaphysical reality that Tang sees in the Laozi itself; Tang praises Wang for going beyond the previous types of interpretations, but also criticizes him for reducing the full complexity of Laozi's Dao, shortchanging the multiplicity of its original objective implications.[8]

This critique may seem out of place, given the generally accepted doxa on Wang's development of a theory of "original Non-Being" (benwu 本無) as the origin of all things, which seems to suggest an objective orientation to Dao. But a close reading of Wang's commentary actually reveals the acuity of Tang's analysis. This is nowhere more evident than in the apparent advent of the categories of 體 ti and 用 yong as a paired dyad in Wang's commentary to Laozi 38. This is the text to which we are most commonly directed when searching for the origin of this pair of categories, which would have such an important role to play in subsequent Chinese metaphysics, crucial particularly for what Tang would call the formulation of objective metaphysics; Tang calls this chapter's commentary the summary of Wang Bi's thought on the relation between Dao and De. But when we turn to this text, we find that Wang has not presented the familiar ti/yong pair as metaphysical categories at all. In fact, *ti* and *yong* are not yet used systematically as technical philosophical terminology by Wang Bi. Rather, as Tang's analysis notes, the use of both terms in this passage is thoroughly *subjective*. Tang does not explain, however, the exact way in which Wang is tweaking the crucial tropes in the passage. The *Laozi* (11) had suggested, in a set of striking metaphors, that Non-Being (*wu* 無) gives all things their "function" (*yong* 用), just as it is the empty space in a room, or at the hub of a wheel, that gives these things their function, their "use." This is contrasted, not to "body" or "substance" (*ti* 體), but to "advantage" (*li* 利), which derives from the presence or Being (*you* 有) of these things. Since their function derives from the Non-Being, the empty hubs and passages that make a space for other things, we practitioners of the Way must ourselves "make use of" of the receptive empty spaces, the Non-Being, in ourselves in dealing with things.

Wang Bi pairs this with *ti*, adding a third level beyond the preferred *yong* and less-favored *li*, in his commentary to *Laozi* 38. He pushes the trope of "making use of Non-Being" a step further by combining it with another theme in the *Laozi*, non-deliberate action (*wuwei* 無為). The Daoist tradition in general, as we have seen, views the deliberate and explicit embrace of ideals, and the purposive action that follows from it, as an obstacle to the truly spontaneous and richest realization of those very ideals. *Laozi* 38, as Wang reads it, warns against taking even *Daoist* virtuousity (*de* 德) as an explicit ideal, a mental object held in mind as a maxim of behavior, to be taken as a guide for action and consciously followed, of which one might deliberately make use, saying, "The highest Virtue does not do Virtue" (*shangde bude* 上德不德), and so on. For as the highest Dao is a Dao that is not known or deliberately embraced as a Dao, the highest use or function of Dao is not a deliberate "making use of" the Dao, or Non-Being. Wang thus suggests in his commentary that it is necessary rather to merge thoroughly with Non-Being, to the point where it is no longer an object of deliberate use: "Although it is valuable to take Non-Being as function [i.e., as something to be used], it does not enable one to let go of it [as something deliberately 'made use of'] so that one can [instead] embody it as one's own substance. If one is unable to let go of Non-Being so as to [instead] embody it as one's own substance, it loses that which makes it truly great" (雖貴以無為用，不能捨無以為體也。不能捨無以為體，則失其為大矣 *sui gui yi wu wei yong, buneng she wu yiwei ti ye. Buneng she wu yiwei ti, ze shi qi wei da yi*). The crucial thing to notice in this passage, often glossed over but effectively underlined in Tang's analysis, is that in this, their earliest usage as a pair in the entire Chinese philosophical tradition, *ti* and *yong* though technically used as nouns are really best understood through the sense of these words as verbs. This verbal sense of *ti* 體 is occasionally used in pre-Qin texts. It is usually translated as "embody," meaning to merge with, to form one body with, or simply, as Alan Chan has suggested in his discussion of this passage, to "be one with" something.[9] But this remains an obscure metaphor: What does it mean to be "one with," or to "form one body with" something such as Non-Being, or Benevolence, or Dao? An examination of the contexts in which this usage of *ti* is deployed in early texts can help us specify at least three implications of this interesting term. To "embody" means (1) "to give concrete form to (to concretize, to body forth),"[10] (2) "to fully integrate and present in its completeness,"[11] and, most crucially to Wang Bi's usage, (3) "to stand in the position of, and to see and act from that position."[12] This last sense implies embodiment in the sense of taking something as one's own body, *inhabiting* something rather than confronting it, so that we see and respond to the world "from the position of" this thing, such that it is not an object in our world but rather in the "subject" position.

What is important here is to see the way this metaphor plays into the deployment of *negation* in the *Laozi* passage, the effacement of thematic or explicit appearance of something, meant as an explanation of why the "highest virtue" is "non-virtue." That is, "forming one body" with X does not merely mean integrating X into one's preexisting body or self, so that it becomes, as it were, an organ of one's own body, like one's hands and feet; nor does it mean simply that one is integrated into it, becomes a part of it. Rather, concomitant to this integration is the capacity for a *reversal of position*, where the object becomes, as it were, the subject. One stands in the position of X, sees the world, including oneself, as X sees the world. Virtue does not see virtue. Thus, when a person "is" Virtue, there "is" [to that person] no Virtue.

When Wang Bi speaks of "taking Non-Being as" either function or substance, he means just that: to subjectively take them as such. It is not a reference to "the function of Non-Being (Dao)" and "the Substance of Non-Being" as objective or metaphysical realities. They are not descriptions of aspects of existing things, nor of the Dao, but rather of two subjective ways of relating to the Dao: inhabiting it or using it. The former phrase, in fact, is exactly equivalent to Wang's explicit use of the verbal sense of the word *ti* in other places, with Non-Being as its object: "embodying Non-Being" (*ti wu* 體無). This refers to a full internalization, a non-deliberate identification with Dao. The three verbal senses of *ti* all apply here: it means "standing in the place of" Non-Being, "giving it concrete form" as its embodiment, and "presencing Non-Being in its integrated totality," leaving out no aspect of it, rather than grasping it in some partial form from some specific angle. It means standing in the place of Non-Being as its full living embodiment—being Non-Being in the flesh, as it were, inhabiting

Non-Being and acting "from" there, rather than "using" it in one's actions as a standard or guide. "Using the Dao," or Non-Being, or any of the Virtues listed in Chapter 38, is the deliberate, purpose-driven application of this Dao to specific uses, necessarily standing at a distance from it, separated from it, so that it is before us, among the objects confronting us "at-hand." We do not, after all, exactly "use" our own body as we use other things: we do not have to make a plan and devise a strategy to beat our own hearts, or to lift our hands. We "inhabit" our bodies effortlessly, without noticing it (if it is functioning well). It is things outside of ourselves that we notice, identify, and deliberately make use of for one purpose or another. In the same way, Wang Bi tells us we must "embody" or "inhabit" (ti) the Dao, thereby effacing it as a definite and determinate entity. It is this full inhabiting of the Dao as one's own body that truly allows it to function well; this is the "mother" of the function or use of the Dao, and hence of all things.

The best gloss on the meaning of this verbal use of ti can be found in the famous anecdote in Wang Bi's biography where he compares Laozi unfavorably to Confucius, a watershed in the history of Chinese thought, precisely this phrase is used: the Sage, Confucius "embodied Non-Being" (tiwu 體無), which is why he did not have to talk about it, making him superior to Laozi, whose failure to embody it was what compelled him to discuss it.[13] Non-Being, when fully embodied, ceases to appear as an object to be "used," discussed, analyzed—even known. Similarly, as Chan Buddhists would later never tire of saying, the eye does not see itself: "embodying" the eye, being the eye, means never seeing the eye. The absence of the eye from one's experience is the proof that one is oneself the eye. The absence of Non-Being from one's experience is the proof that one is oneself Non-Being, has embodied it. Here, the full realization of something, conceived on the subjective praxis and ethical cultivation, is exactly equivalent to its phenomenological absence. We have here a dialectic of self-negation that superficially resembles the contours of negative ontology, that is, the notion that the Absolute or the infinite, as an objective reality, is a kind of nothingness, transcends being, since all predications of being are relative and finite. To this extent, we must agree with Tang's judgment that Wang's comments, even when seemingly focused on the metaphysics of nothingness, are ultimately derived from and oriented toward the subjective and the ethical.

Oddly, however, Tang does not seem to appreciate the distinction between ti and yong in Wang's commentary, treating "embodying Non-Being" and "using Non-Being" as nearly synonymous.[14] Tang understands "embodying Non-Being" to be merely an emphatic way of saying, "using only Non-Being, following only Non-Being," and the like, rather than seeing "embodying" and "using" as two strictly contrasted modes of relating to the Non-Being. In my humble opinion, this is an enormously consequential oversight. Hence, we must agree with Tang on the importance of this passage, and on the ultimately subjective meaning of *ti*. But we must insist, against Tang, on the importance of the distinction and contrast between the two terms, and seek here the solution to some of the shortcomings Tang sees in Wang's reading, as well as the source of some of the most distinctive moves in later Chinese metaphysics.

This contrast between "embodying" (*ti*) and "use/function" (*yong*) is developed, through some complex turns in Wang's discussion, into the mother/child relation: the *manifest* usefulness or function of Non-Being (seen in the space of a room or the hub of a wheel) is *derived from* the more thorough embodiment of Non-Being, which does not make of it a "something" to be used. The phenomenological absence of Non-Being, that is, the inhabiting of Non-Being, is the *source* of its phenomenological presence as Non-Being used. But for Wang this is not merely a deriving of one thing from another where the "offspring" can exist separately from its foundation. Rather, in accordance with *Laozi* 52, Wang goes on in this passage to assert that the mother and child are here inseparable, like an infant at the mother's breast. Hence, Wang pushes the metaphor another step, comparing embodiment/mother to the *root* of a plant, and use/offspring to its *branches*. The goal is still to make these roots, these children, these functions, maximally effective. But the way to do so, ironically, is not to simply use them, but to turn one's attention to their root, their mother, their embodiment, *in which they are seemingly effaced.* A dialectic of *maximization through negation* takes shape, but in a thoroughly practical sense. In this way, a kind of root/branch relation is sketched between *ti* (body, substance) and *yong* (use, function). The branches are many and the root is one. The branches depend on, grow out of, and express the root. At the same time, the root is the *negation* of the branches, the opposite of the branches, the phenomenological absence of the branches, their effacement as determinate objects.

The branches and root taken together form one whole; they are complementary. They are also, strictly speaking, opposites, and mutually exclusive: the branches are the embodiment of Non-Being, where Non-Being ceases to manifest as any kind of object to awareness, while the branches are Non-Being as an object, a guide, a goal to be used. Thus far, we have, already, a quite odd philosophical structure: a complementary but asymmetrical set of parts, where one part depends on the other but not vice versa, forming a single whole, which are moreover mutually exclusive and opposed. This coincides with Laozi's image of the spokes of a wheel and its empty hub in *Laozi* 11.

However, there is another, seemingly opposed implication to Wang's use of these terms. The root/branch idea suggests complementary and inseparable parts of a single whole, a fundamental and unified root and diversified and derivative branches. But at the same time, in Wang's original usage, both the root and the branch were the *same* (non-)entity, simply viewed in two different ways, through two contrasted modes of relating: Non-Being, viewed either as embodied or as deliberately put to a particular use. Wang understands this Non-Being, according to Tang, in a primarily subjective sense: it is the stillness and emptiness, the flavorless, the purposelessness at the root of every particular purpose, which alone gives them their function. To put this to use, objectifying it, is to *actively and purposefully employ* stillness and purposelessness, a secondary or even inauthentic application of the purposelessness, emptiness and Non-Being that is the Dao. But this is not only derivative of Dao-as-embodied—true purposelessness and stillness—and the opposite of it (phenomenologically present as "stillness and emptiness" rather than absent): it is even, in some sense at least, *the selfsame thing*, in two different modes or contexts.

Here we see the problem before us: *ti* and *yong* are both (1) two complementary parts of a larger whole; (2) mutually exclusive opposites; and (3) two names for the same thing, viewed in two different contexts or applications. These categories would go on to become an omnipresent tool in later Chinese metaphysics, especially Chinese Buddhism and Neo-Confucianism. We will often see Li as part of a pair of terms formulated on this model: Li and *shi* in Chinese Buddhism, and sometimes also in Neo-Confucianism, where we also find, most notably, the Li/qi pair at times explicated as a kind of *ti/yong* structure. It is crucial to see here at the advent of this pair of categories the intrinsic subjectivity involved in the notion of *ti*, for this will help us guard against construing Li too as a kind of objective law or principle. Affect and perspective, and a certain ironic self-undermining structure endemic to subjectivity, remain deeply woven into this category, and the same will be true for the various deployments of Li that we will find in the later tradition. Here we may note the way Wang's original deployment of *ti* and *yong* as a pair echoes the structure of Li as derived from his reading of the structure of the hexagrams. In both cases, we are looking at a *center of convergence* that at once *makes the whole coherent* and is *the negation of that coherence*. That is, it is structurally necessary that this unifying center *not* be intelligible in the same way that the whole it unifies is. In the case of *ti* and *yong*, *ti* is the unifying single "mother" or "root" of a set of diverse expressions, but is also the subjective internalization of the character of those expression which does not appear to itself as any of them, which is not visible to itself; it is the locus of any X where X disappears, where even its identifying Xness is seen as an alienated and partial view of it from outside, premised on a distortedly deliberate attitude toward that X. The *ti* of X will be non-Xish, will be the unifying center where it does not "read out" as X, with the understanding that it really means to *be* X. *Yong* will be the deliberate deployment of this same quality in some particular situation as a *partial expression*, mistakenly made the object of a deliberate intention and cognition, which will thus always be susceptible to crashing back into the center, the *ti*, where that expression and that coherence is effaced. For some help in intuiting what might be meant here, we may think again of Qian Mu's pendulum. In the case of Li, we have the lack or hole at the center of vortex, the vertex around which it converges and takes shape, again necessarily lacking precisely what is coherent as the resulting whole. The opposition between coherence and incoherence, or between the non-ironic and ironic senses of coherence (as intelligibility and unification), approaches a new level of clarity here; they are given a structural inseparability built into the key terminology, which will shape the future of the Chinese metaphysical tradition.

APPLICATIONS OF THE MULTIPLICITY OF LI IN WANG'S *LAOZI* COMMENTARY

Let us now turn back for a closer look at Wang Bi's actual usage of the term Li. It is most significant that Wang speaks of Li, coherences, in the plural, in spite of his alleged interest in the encompassing, the omnipresent Dao. This is the contribution made by his interest in the *Zhouyi*, which here combines with the Laozian influence to create room for the individual coherences and principles of particular things, which are at once both situational expressions of the single incoherent unintelligible universal Dao and coherent, differentiated, particular principles of the sixty-four hexagrams. It is perhaps significant in this connection to note the use of Li in its *verbal* sense that predominates in Wang's commentary to the *Laozi*. Combined with the overall sense of the noninterfering and nonintelligible (nonapparent) universal coherence of Dao, as variously expressed in particular things and events, this brings to the fore the sense of "reciprocal ordering" in the use of Li as a verb, connected closely with the sense of "balance," which can be noted in the concept of Li/coherence throughout the tradition. Dao makes coherent by its own incoherence and by not actively making anything coherent, by not interfering, so it is evident only in the mutual making-coherent of individual things, as in the *Hanfeizi's* notion of the manner in which opposite terms limit and order each other. Hence, Wang says in his commentary to *Laozi* 5, "Heaven and Earth follow the self-so, doing nothing and creating nothing. The ten thousand things thus naturally order and limit each other/make-each-other-coherent [萬物自相治理 *wanwu zixiang zhili*]. Thus [Heaven and Earth] are described as 'not benevolent.' . . . When one abandons himself and goes along with the things themselves, all of them are ordered/made coherent [棄己任物則莫不理 *qiji renwu ze mo bu li*]."[15] The connection of this to the ironic tradition's *problematik* of intelligibility is made clear in a comment to *Laozi* 15: "When darkness is used to order [Li] things, they attain their brightness [明 *ming*]." That is, when they are not forced into coherence from above, when no overall principle of coherence is evident interfering with them and working to make them cohere, they attain their particular intelligible coherence through spontaneous mutual limitation. Even in this verbal use of Li, we see Wang Bi's distinctive notion of Li as the opposite of the intelligible aspect of each particular thing: by making darkness the Li of a thing, that thing as a whole attains its brightness. The ironic is assimilated to the non-ironic here: the unintelligible Li is what makes present the particular intelligible Lis, or rather, the unintelligible Li of each situation—its least visible aspect—is what makes it intelligible as this situation. The use of the darkness to make-bright and make-cohere means allowing the process of convergence around the unseen least present element.

This verbal sense of the term allows us to understand Wang's occasional use of the *nominal* sense of the term in this commentary. "I do not force others to follow, but rather use their self-so, adducing their own perfect coherence [用夫自然舉其至理 *yong fu ziran, ju qi zhi li*]. Following it necessarily leads to good fortune, while transgressing it necessarily leads to bad fortune" (42). The Li of each thing is its self-so, what it is like when unforced, *their* way of cohering and converging. But in this usage we see Li deployed in a way that is amenable to the "Great Coherence" sense of the non-ironic tradition, as the overriding principle that one must know to operate effectively, to attain one's value, and as an object of understanding. Elsewhere in the commentary, Wang even states, "The Dao has a great constancy, and coherences have a great consistency [道有大常，理有大致 *dao you da chang, li you da zhi*]. . . . If one can attain the place things tend toward [之 *zhi*], they can be known through consideration even if one does not go forth to them. If one recognizes the ruling ancestor [宗 *zong*] of things, the coherence of their right and wrong [是非之理 *shi fei zhi li*] can be attained and named even if they are not seen."[16] Here we see the connection to Wang's conception of the Li as the mini-Daos of the particular hexagrams in the *Zhouyi*: the principle of a thing, as a noun, an intelligible object of knowledge and understanding, is this thing it lacks and tends toward, which rules its motion, its own mini-Dao, which discloses its own right and wrong, the values implicit in it. One attains one's own desires, one's own right and wrong, by going along with this inherent right and wrong of the things themselves, their own values, their tendencies to seek the thing they lack. This tendency toward the opposite of itself is the grounding for the verbal use of the term as reciprocal ordering. We see this also in the comment to Chapter 79: "If one does not comprehend the Li [does not make the coherence intelligible, 不明理 *bu ming li*], one's contractual agreements will cause great resentment." Wang's unexpected reach for the term Li in this humble intersubjective context, in discussing the interaction of conflicting points of view on what is right and what is wrong, is revealing, and perhaps can help us tie together the new implications he gives to the term, with its roots in his notion of the crypto-social convergence of the various lines, construed as desiring Yin-Yang beings, of a hexagram toward their center. That is, the violation of the rights and wrongs of those with whom one enters into agreements will lead to resentment. The Li in question here is what the parts of the situation want, what they lack. This determines what they consider right and wrong. Wang Bi's new conception of Li here allows him to make a kind of non-ironic incorporation even of Zhuangzian perspectivism of multiple rights and wrongs of the ironic tradition, which, in its notion of the "axis of Dao" (道樞 *daoshu*) standing at the "center of the circle" of various contrasting rights-and-wrongs but thereby enabled to respond to and harmonize with them (in the manner of the famous monkey keeper of Zhuangzi's second chapter) had established perhaps the earliest prototype of this notion of a *center* which unifies by being at once a *negation* and a *harmonization* of that which it unifies. In the unalloyed ironic vision of Zhuangzi, this center was mirrorlike, empty, devoid of any specific determinations. Wang Bi has taken this same structure and put it at the heart of each particular entity, as the *ti* that is this entity being what it is in its specificity, embodying it and unifying it around itself as the unseen center, but only by negating that specificity. Each thing and each situation has its own axis, making for a multitude of axes that are neither one nor many, and the name of these axes, forming the unifying center in which each situation is truly embodied and thus verges into its own negation, is Li.

CONVERGENCE OF COHERENCE AND INCOHERENCE IN GUO XIANG: LI AS "JUST THE WAY IT IS," AS LIMIT, AND AS VANISHING CONVERGENCE

Let us now turn to the usage of the term Li by the other great luminary of the Xuanxue movement, Guo Xiang. With Guo Xiang, we come to a real turning point, a kind of limit case of the indigenous development, where the ironic and non-ironic traditions converge to a sort of "singularity" in the sense in which that term is used in physics. Guo is famously the person who brings the ironic cosmology of Daoism to its completion, reaching its most explicitly ironic summit in an actual *ironic ontology*. Where the traditional Daoist irony focused on value, action, guiding, coherence, and order, Guo's focuses on existence per se and knowledge per se. The Dao of Laozi and Zhuangzi is ironically a dao; it is a Dao that ironically guides only because

it does no guiding ("dao"-ing), an order that orders because it orders nothing, a coherence that makes things coherently intelligible by remaining
unintelligible, a unity that holds things together by being utterly unlike
them, a source of value because it has and gives no value. But the Dao of
Guo exists as a source of all being only because it is literally nonexistent:
it is only *ironically existent*. It is what exists and produces all things only by
not existing: it exists only in the ironic sense that its nonexistence is what
allows any event to take place at all. Dao, in Guo's view, is not the origin
of things. It is, rather, a way of asserting the absence of any such entity:

> The Dao has no power. When the text says, "They attained it from
> the Dao," this is merely to show that they spontaneously attained
> it. It is simply spontaneously auto-attained; the Dao cannot make
> them attain it. What I have not attained, I cannot make myself
> attain. Thus whatever is attained [i.e., whatever qualities one has],
> externally do not depend on the Dao, internally do not come from
> my self; it is simply abruptly self-attained and self-right [自得 *zide*]
> and transforming on its own [獨化 *duhua*].[17]

It is not just that the Dao is powerless. Guo rejects any existence for
any first cause, a point argued most explicitly in his rejection of a creator
of things (造物者 *zaowuzhe*), in spite of Zhuangzi's allowance for some of
his characters to use this fanciful phrase as one of many shorthand terms
for Dao (though one that is quickly replaced, in the same dialogue, by
alternate nicknames of exactly opposite connotation). But the argument
Guo uses would apply just as well to a primal impersonal first cause as to
a conscious creator:

> Some in the world say that the penumbra is dependent on the
> shadow, the shadow is dependent on the physical form, and the
> physical form is dependent on the Creator. But I ask: As for this
> Creator, is he existent, or is he nonexistent? If he is nonexistent,
> how can he create things? If he is existent, having a definite form
> himself, then he is not qualified to form all forms. Thus only after
> you understand that all forms form themselves can you understand
> what is meant by creation. Hence of all things involved in the realm
> of existence, even the penumbra, there has never been one that
> did not transform itself entirely on its own, constantly positioned
> in the realm where all agency vanishes. Thus creation is without
> any lord or master, and each thing creates itself.[18]

A creator of all existence, or even a real preexistent source of things
such as the Dao of earlier Daoism, would have to be prior to all existing

things. Prior to all existing things, it could not be an existent thing itself, for then it would fail to be prior to *all* existing things, not being prior to itself. Not existing, it could not do anything of any kind at all. Unable to do anything, it could not be a creator of anything, much less of all existence. The notion of a creator of all things is, Guo thinks, inherently self-contradictory. But rather than conclude therefore that there is one all-embracing priorly existing indestructible monistic Being that creates or transforms into all particular beings, that has the special status of self-creation and thus can at least produce all beings other than itself, Guo seems to take this as having implications for being per se: if the notion of a self-creating being is unavoidable in thinking about beings, then beings might as well all be granted this character of self-creation, for the notion of being is for Guo univocal. The problem necessarily arises in the very idea that things must be formed by something other than themselves. Hence, the problem is solved by dropping this assumption entirely. For Guo, this implies that being per se is necessarily ungrounded in anything else, and this ultimately applies to any individual instance of being as much as it does to Being-as-a-whole. Though there may be a particular chain of connection between some particular being and prior beings, since ultimately this chain can never lead back to any ultimate grounding, the entire process of trying to ground one thing on another comes to naught, and we are better off abandoning it entirely when considering what things ultimately are; in the end the totality of things and *thus* each thing turns out to be causeless.

The upshot of this is that, thought through to the bottom, being qua being is groundless, uncaused, beyond reason or purpose. Each entity can thus ultimately be described only as self-so (自然 *ziran*). This fact is equivalent to the fact that there is no Dao, that no creator and no source exists. This fact of its nonexistence is the ironic "existence" of the Dao. The existence of Dao is like the goodness of rain for the picnic: where the valuelessness of Dao was always ironically its real value, now its literal absence is its real presence. The self-so of entities is the absence of Dao, which is ironically the only real presence of Dao.

Concomitantly, the only real "itself" of any given entity is just this self-so: its true essence is its unknowability in terms of chains of causality or networks of explanation and description. No fact coheres with any other fact as its explanatory context or cause or goal, and thus all facts remain incoherent. Leaving such connections aside, it is a self-so event. No more can or need be said or known about it. It is not made the way it is by connection to some other thing (a goal or purpose) that is supposed to follow it, nor by some other thing (a cause or reason) that is supposed to precede it, nor even through its position in the midst of a totality of other entities (a context). To be self-so is to have nothing to do with such cognizable connections to other entities, either as conscious will or as a relation to a definitely knowable external cause or precedent or context.

This results in a fully ironic epistemology and axiology to go with Guo's ironic ontology. There is really nothing to be known about where anything comes from or where it's going or what it should do or what it is. But precisely this is non-knowing is, ironically, true knowledge of the thing: knowledge of its self-so. This is also its real value, which means only its perfect coincidence with whatever is unintentionally happening and its freedom from beholdenness to any outside standard or cause or purpose. This pertains both to its being and to its value. For the self-so in this sense is its self, and also its being right (然 ran) to itself, which is testified to by its being comfortable and fit (適 shi), and therefore not conscious of itself. Non-knowledge of it is correct knowledge of it; and its own non-knowledge of itself is the source and sign of its own value. This last line of reasoning derives from the following passage in the Zhuangzi:

> To forget the feet indicates the fitness [or comfort, shi] of the shoes; to forget the waist indicates the fitness of the belt; when consciousness forgets right and wrong it indicates the fitness of the mind. . . . He who begins in fitness and is never unfit has the comfortable fitness of forgetting even fitness.

Guo comments:

> When all the parts of the body are fit, one forgets the body. . . . Right and wrong are born from unfitness. . . . He who still has consciousness of fitness is not yet really fit.[19]

To be conscious of anything indicates a problem, a lack of fit, a mismatching deviation of some kind. Hence, the sign of anything's self-so as its rightness (然 ran) to itself (自 zi) is precisely the lack of reflexive consciousness of it, knowing that embeds one thing in a chain of causes, reasons, and purposes. This relating of "one thing" to "other things" is a function of regarding not the self-so, but the "traces" (跡 ji) left by prior self-so events. It is this kind of knowing that leads to the positing of explicit values and goals as well as the kind of knowledge that attempts to identify and account for things by placing them in a causal or contextual network of "other" entities. These values and this knowledge, however, are the antithesis of real value and knowledge, which resides precisely in forgetting identities, causes, purposes: the fitting comfortableness of the traceless self-forgetting self-so. But Guo's critique of the invalidity of trace-cognition means not only that knowledge is never the efficient cause of anything actually happening; it's that no *possible object of knowledge* is ever the efficient cause of anything actually happening. Both the subject and the object of knowledge are hopeless alienations from the self-so, and as such both are entirely without real efficacy, which rests entirely in self-so process. What are objects of possible knowledge? They and they alone are *determinate facts*. It follows that no single determinate fact is the actual cause of anything being so. This would very much include abstract facts such as the "nature" or "essence" of something, or a "principle." Such things cannot be what makes anything so.

Thus, Guo's key notion of "self-so" (自 然 *ziran*) pertains, again, both to the being and to the value of things. Both are now fully ironic: the real identity of things is their lack of any definite being, and ironically this does provide what was originally sought when we sought their being; what is really valuable is not having any specific value, which ends up providing what the effort to find value was seeking. It is crucial, then, to understand that when Guo says "self-so," then, he emphatically does not mean, "What I myself make so, by an act of volition or knowledge." There is no self, no identity, above and beyond the unidentifiable and incoherent self-so. Guo tells us:

> My life is not generated by me; thus my whole life long, within [my] hundred years, whether I sit, stand, walk, stop, move, or stay still, whatever I take or renounce, all my feelings, my innate determinacy, my knowledge, my abilities, whatever I have, whatever I don't have, whatever I do, whatever I encounter, none of it is [because of] me; it is all simply self-so.[20]

Thus even that which I knowingly "do" ultimately rests not upon not knowing and willing, nor on my "self." "These merely come to be of themselves; they are not made so by their selves" (自生耳。非我生也 *zisheng er; fei wosheng ye*).[21] Now it is true that "not made by me" initially signifies a negation of Guo's two archenemies, knowledge and deliberate intention. Hence, this kind of claim is taken to mean that things are not made what they are by (1) Heaven or Dao or any transcendental creator, or (2) my own will, intention, and action. Both of these are correct inferences. But it is too often assumed that this means they are instead made by something neither totalizing (Heaven and so on) nor consciously intentional (such as a "self" or "knowledge" or "intention") but rather by a singular, unconscious "principle" or "nature" of each individual. This is thought to escape Guo's strictures about what can make something else. But in fact this is an enormous mistake. For Guo rejects not only the knower and willer as a determinant, but also the *willed and known*. That is, Guo's epistemology of traces excludes not only the subject of knowledge, but also the object of knowledge; anything that *could* be known, any knowable fact, is excluded as a potential determinant. For knowables are merely traces, just as much as knowers are. To be knowable means to be determinate, to have a definite essence waiting to be known, which one could be correct or incorrect about. In denying trace-knowledge as providing any information about efficient causes, Guo is denying that there is any entity (i.e., something knowable even at least in theory) such as fixed nature or principle even of individual things that makes them so. This means there is no definite and determinate thing, whether a Li ("principle"?) or Nature (*xing*) that accounts for things being as they are. "Self-so" means not made so by *any* determinate (i.e., knowable or knowing) other entity. "Self-so" means not done by me, nor by anyone or *anything* else. This distinction is to be kept in mind whenever Guo speaks of things "creating themselves." This term has a purely negative significance for Guo; it means simply that nothing cognizable as an entity makes it so. Thus, he says:

> Although [the text] has the term, "What makes things what they are" [物物者 *wu wu zhe*], this is meant merely to show that things make themselves what they are [物之自物 *wu zhi ziwu*]; ultimately there is no thing that makes things what they are. . . . Once we have understood that there is no thing that makes things what they are, we should also understand that neither can things make themselves what they are [物之不能自物 *wu zhi bu neng ziwu*]. But then who is it that does it? They are all unconsciously and abruptly thus[22] and self-so.[23] (Guo 1983, 754)

Thus, we see that when Guo says that all things are "self-so" he means that they are what they are without being made so by *anything* apprehendable by any consciousness, be it their own conscious volition or a transcendental Dao, or anything else that may be taken as a cause as a definite entity, which can only be a figment of trace-cognition. Principles are excluded as much as intentions or knowledge or a Creator or a Dao or Heaven.

At the same time, this unconsciousness of their becoming so, their becoming so as rooted in what is *necessarily* inaccessible to any trace-cognition, is precisely what makes this becoming self-so in the other sense, namely, self-right, and what gives it its intrinsic, self-forgetting, uncognized value to itself. This applies also to a "nature" or a "principle": no nature or principle makes things as they are. It is this point that is crucial to the understanding of Guo's use of the term Li. These considerations must also make us reconsider the charges of a fixed predetermined fatalism that are often leveled against Guo Xiang. But Guo is definitely no fatalist. In fact, he is said to have authored, in addition to the *Zhuangzi* commentary, a work entitled 吉凶由己論 "Jixiong youji lun," ("Good and bad fortune come from oneself") as an explicit repudiation of fatalism, a work that is, unfortunately, no longer extant. But in this capacity, we should note the relevant multiplicity of senses of the term *self-so* (*ziran*) in his writings. For self-so means equally necessity, freedom, and chance. Guo uses it to mean all three, but in each case the other two are also implied. It is not merely that these three aspects can be identified for each and every thing, but that the three notions themselves are in their deepest meaning identical: for what these three concepts have in common is their self-so. Here *ziran* signifies the free necessity of chance, and all of these may be regarded as nothing but three different ways of viewing and describing what is at bottom one simple concept, that of being self-so. To be self-so means not to be grounded in anything—that is chance. It means to be what one is without being grounded in anything else, hence not contingent on or changeable by anything else—that is necessity. It means in this sense to be grounded only in oneself, or only in one's present moment of action and determinacy, and that is a definition of freedom. Entities are self-so; this means they are what they are and cannot be otherwise: self-so is necessity. There can be no ultimate explanation of their being-so: self-so is chance. They themselves are being-so, not made so by others and themselves experiencing this spontaneous becoming-so from within: self-so is freedom.

As in the case of the *Xunzi*, we see in Guo's text, in purely quantitative terms, an exponential increase in occurrence of the character Li per se: according to Kitahara Mineki's concordance, a total of 174 occurrences, far outstripping the occasional usage in Wang Bi or in the *Zhuangzi* text upon which Guo is commenting. I am in full agreement with Mizoguchi that Guo's usage of Li marks a decisive watershed in the development of the tradition, but my interpretation of this sea change is directly opposed to the position taken by Mizoguchi, who sees Li as denoting an immanent determinative principle within each thing. This interpretation, which is shared by many modern interpreters who see Guo as positing something called "the Nature" or "the Principle" of each thing as what makes it what it is, clashes sharply with Guo's insistence that there is no ruler of things, no Dao that makes things so, as well as Guo's specific statements about what this "Nature" or "Li" actually refers to. Mizoguchi is aware of this problem, and tries, following Togawa Yoshiro, to solve it simply by saying that, while Guo denies an *external* determinative principle controlling things, he posits in its place an *internal* one. But this solves precisely nothing; as long as there is a determining of one fact by another fact, a relationship of control and determination, we have, strictly speaking, an external relationship. The "internal" here ends up meaning nothing at all. It is a failure to think through the meaning of "immanence" of Li to things themselves, which

Mizoguchi correctly identifies as one of the most distinctive contributions of Six Dynasties thinking, particularly that of Guo Xiang. Mizoguchi thus ends up admitting that the sense of "principle" as an independent agent in Guo's usage of Li is "still very weak," overshadowed by the stronger sense of patterning and ordering, but this leads to an even starker contradiction with Guo's antimetaphysical immanentism in that Mizoguchi claims that this ordering is an attribute of an absolute substance of some kind.[24]

The problem with all such interpretations is that they completely misunderstand the meaning of the term 自然 ziran in Guo's thought. Guo takes Wang Bi's reconfiguring of the Dao/Li relation a step farther, playing out in a new way the incipient association of Li and ziran already seen in the Han sources quoted above. With Wang, full Daoishness comes to operate as the very coherence of each individual situation. For Guo, the Li *is* the situation itself. It is strictly synonymous with ziran, which is not a principle but the equivalent of the empty tautological phrase, "The way it is." Its function is not to provide an explanation of anything, nor to denote that which determines anything, controls anything, or makes anything so. It is rather precisely the opposite, *a way of asserting the uselessness and impossibility of any such explanation*, and why we humans are better off relinquishing any attempt to find one.

This has been poorly understood in recent studies of Guo's thought. Many readers have been misled, I believe, by the fact that Guo tells us *ad nauseum* that each thing has its own "nature" (性 xing, perhaps better translated here as "determinacy"), "allotment" (分 fen), "limits" (極 ji)—and also, it would seem, its own Li. The first three terms come to be more or less synonymous in Guo's usage. In fact, they give us precisely the meaning of Guo's usage of the term Li. Perhaps forgivably, many scholars have taken these terms to have their more usual meaning here: a *fixed* nature, allotment, limit, or principle that serves as the determining underlying character of a thing, persisting over time and standing behind the phenomenal flux of appearances. This is then taken to be Guo's substitute for the Dao as determining creator, which all scholars admit he banishes from his thought. Guo's outspoken and virulent opposition to any metaphysical unity or Absolute would make him the least likely candidate for the use of Li in the sense of a single overriding "Great Coherence." Indeed, Guo often unambiguously speaks of what appear to be "principles" (Li) in the explicit or implied plural, for example, in the expression 萬理 wanli, "ten thousand coherences/ principles," or when he uses it as a parallel with 物 wu (things) or 事 shi (events). In this sense, we must admit the truth of the standard doxa that Guo stresses multiplicity rather than the single overriding Li (the latter usually attributed to Wang Bi), at least superficially. As Guo says, "What [Zhuangzi] calls leveling [齊 qi]—why should it require making their forms and shapes uniform, all matching the same compass and T-square? Thus vertical and horizontal, ugly and beautiful, things ribald and shady and grotesque and strange, each affirms what it affirms [各然其所然 *ge ran qi suo ran*], each considers acceptable what it considers acceptable, and thus although there are a thousand differences between their various principles/coherences [*Li*], they are one in attaining and being right in their own determinacies [性同得 *xing tong de*], thus [the text] says, 'The Dao unifies them all.'"[25] In this sense, it is correct to note that Li is used in the plural, and denotes for Guo Xiang the multiple Lis of individual things, which would seem to differ from one another. As in the *Hanfeizi* commentary, Lis play the role of indicating multiplicity and specificity, the limitations of particular things, separation, finitude, difference.

But the view that Li are for Guo therefore fixed individual natures or principles that stand inside or behind existent things, determining them, is insupportable. Guo tells us explicitly, again and again, that what a thing "encounters" (遇 *yu*) *and* what it "does" are in exactly the same boat when it comes to the "nature" or "Li" or "limits" of the thing—they are both internal to it, and *neither can ever be changed*. This refutes the idea that there is some "internal" principle behind the flux of an entity's experience, making it what it is. His insistence that the limits, nature, Li, and allotment of a thing can never be changed is matched by his equally shrill insistence that everything is constantly changing, instant by instant, to the point where even identity is not continuous between moments: the former me is not the present me: "The previous I is not the I of the present moment. 'I-ness' moves along together with the present moment; how could one constantly hold on to the old?" (向者之我非復今我也。我與今俱往。豈常守故哉 *xiangzhezhiwo feifujinwoye, woyujinjuwang, qichangshouguzai*). There is no particular content to selfhood, either as a Nature or as an "immanent" Principle that remains the same behind its changes and which would therefore determine what those changes are. Rather, "selfhood" is purely a form, meaning whatever is going on at the present moment, regarded as "self" in Guo's distinctive sense of the self-so. Thus, Guo later says, of the various changes that might be encountered *or* undergone: "I 'self' them all [吾皆吾之 *wujiewuzhi*], and hence there is no loss of selfhood; since there is nothing I do not consider myself, the inner and outer are obliteratingly unified, past and present are strung along one thread, I am daily renewed along with all changes; how could I know wherein resides my 'self'?"[26] The self in question here is again the self-*so*, which means simply whatever is going on right now apart from what is made so by either objectified objects of knowledge or deliberate acts of will. To "self" them, as a transitive verb, means just to merge into them comfortably, to vanish them and oneself into the self-so, forgetting the determinate traces of both, for whatever is forgotten is the self(-so).

It is not a true self, a real or original Nature, that persists beneath appearances and remains the same. Even being some particular thing, for example a human, is itself "just one encounter amongst the ten thousand changes [人形乃是萬化之一遇耳 *renxing naishi wanhua zhi yi yu er*]."²⁷ The idea of a metaphysical essence, or set of multiple essences, behind changing things that makes them what they are or makes them change as they do would also make a hash of Guo's insistence that each principle is self-so (自然 *ziran*)—indeed, is *ziran*-ness itself—and reestablish the same metaphysical quandary cited by Guo to overthrow the notion of the Dao as a real entity, a creator, or an actual source of all things. So on the one hand the nature, limits, or allotment of each thing can never be changed, and are absolutely separate and different; but on the other, everything is constantly changing, and all are simply self-so. How is this apparent contradiction to be resolved?

The answer is surprisingly simple. A "thing" is, as with Zhuangzi and Yang Xiong and Wang Bi and, later, Wang Yangming, a situation. For Guo, this idea is radicalized: the situation lasts only one moment: it is an "encounter." It has certain limits. It is an eternal fact. That I am here doing this right now at this exact moment in time and nothing else cannot be changed; by the time I am aware of it, and exert my will toward it, it is already gone. This means it is what it is, and it can never *be* changed. It can transform into something else, and it must transform, but it cannot *be* transformed. That is, it can never be the object of deliberate or determinate alteration brought about by some other thing, some other situation. Guo regards all knowable objects, all non-ironic coherences, as "traces"—the effect of one spontaneous event or moment on another, held over due to erroneous valuation and thereby potentially disturbing the second entity's self-so nature, its own character, limits, allotment, coherence. Any arrangement of determinate entities into a greater, synordinate whole, for example, as a discernible causal nexus, would be, for him, merely projection of this illegitimate epistemological confusion, based on the imposition of one moment onto another, creating aspiration, purpose, will, and valuation, all of which he calls "knowing" (知 *zhi*) and its concomitant, deliberate doing (為 *wei*). Guo sometimes calls this unchangeable but always changing fitting-and-thus-uncognized-way-it-is-happening-now "the allotment," which also means "division," (*fen*), because it is just this much and no more. Its "nature" is its "limits" is its "allotment"—*which is this thing—this situation, this encounter—itself*. Each thing has its own limits, its own nature, its own allotment; but once purposive knowing and doing are eliminated, this "having" of limits is simply being self-so, and the self-so is the real pre-trace "self" of any event, its vanishing convergence with all other unintentional, unnoticed pre-trace self-so events going on at the time.

Hence, Guo says, "The heavenly nature (天性 *tianxing*) that each one receives has its original determinate portion (本分 *benfen*); it cannot be escaped, nor can it be added to" (Guo 1983, 128). At first glance, such statements suggest the most inexorable predetermined fixity. But we must read carefully; Guo does not say that one's determinacy stays always the same, that it does not change; he says explicitly that it cannot be "escaped" or "added to"—both of which terms unmistakably point to conscious deliberate activity, attempts to change what one is, acting upon oneself as an agent upon a patient. One's determinacy changes, but it cannot be changed by extrinsic action upon it. Deliberate action cannot change it; it is "fixed" within a given moment, and that moment cannot be otherwise. However, as Guo is wont to repeat, "(Things) take self-attainment as 'right' and self-loss as 'wrong,' take what suits their own determinacy comfortably as good order and what loses such harmony as disorder. But things have no fixed limits [物無定極 *wu wu ding ji*], and selves have no constantly comfortable fits [我無常適 *wo wu chang shi*]; different determinacies come to have different conveniences, and thus right and wrong have no constant master."[28] What is right or so in a particular moment is just what fits the determinacy of that moment, and this rightness changes as that determinacy changes, which it must, since things have no fixed limits or determinacies. Things always "follow their allotted determinacies [分 *fen*], and thus what they do is not constant."[29] Sticking to their own "allotted determinacies" necessarily implies change. Hence, Guo says, "When we examine the alternations of fullness and emptiness, we come to understand that there is no constancy in the attainments of allotments [分 *fen*]."[30] The point is that all things are always changing of themselves, and hence do not require extrinsic activity upon them to change them. Their changes, even when apparently coming from outside, are to be considered the intrinsic and spontaneous transformations of their allotted determinacy: "He whom the age regards as worthy becomes a lord; he whose talents do not match his generation becomes a vassal. This is like heaven's being high of itself, earth being low of itself, the head spontaneously being above and the foot spontaneously being below; how could they replace each other? Although they take no pains to be right they are necessarily self-right."[31] In saying that the above and the below cannot change places he does not mean they are fixed in their places for all time, or that they are destined to be where they are by the material they are made of; rather, he states that they are given their positions purely due to their chance relation to the times in which they happen to live, and whether the present generation esteems them. Circumstances at this particular point in time happen to put every one in some particular place, and when Guo states that they cannot be otherwise, he merely means that in this moment they cannot be otherwise. Further, this circumstantial becoming such is what Guo calls "self high, self low," and so on; precisely this is self-so. The constancy of things means only that they self-transform in Guo's sense, they spontaneously change into what they become rather than being deliberately changed, not that they do not transform at all.[32] As Guo puts it elsewhere, "If one acts upon or [deliberately] refrains from acting upon them, this ruins their self-transformation."[33]

UNINTELLIGIBLE COHERENCE:
VANISHING AND MERGING INTO THINGS

Before trace-cognition, the explanation of a thing's source or nature in terms of "other" things, is applied to it, a self-so even is what Guo describes as a "vanishing merging" (冥 *ming*) of all things, the comfortably uncog-nized encounter itself. "Vanishing" means it is unknowable as a determinate object, because it is entirely within its own limits. "Merging" means that all of heaven and earth are involved in producing it, not as determinate objects of consciousness, but simply as the prereflexive coming-together, the event of an encounter:

> Although man's body is small and insignificant, it takes all of heaven and earth to collectively offer it up. Thus of the ten thousand things in heaven and earth, each entity cannot lack any one of the others for even one day. If even one thing were not present, then whatever comes to be would have no way to come to be. If even one coherence [Li] failed to arrive, then its heavenly years would have no way to reach their proper end. But Knowing [*zhi*] does not know everything that is present in the body, and Doing [*wei*] does not accomplish everything that is kept in coherence. Thus what Knowing knows is little but what the body possesses is much; what Doing does is few but what coherence keeps is many.[34]

Here we have perfectly conveyed the ironic concept of coherence: unknowability, convergence, and value. As in Wang Bi, knowing pertains what a thing is for-others, the outside, and Li to what it is to-itself, the inside. Here as there, these two are directly and perfectly opposed. But for Guo the outside is the realm of "traces" and is always mistaken and perni-cious, and *all determinate content without exception* falls into this category. The inside has no determinate content at all: it is the self-so, which is the strict antithesis of the traces, what is so outside of the interference of knowing and doing. This, simply stated, is the meaning of Li for Guo Xiang: whatever is not known or done.

We can see how easily this notion could be confused with an idea of objective truth or real principles independent of the subjective, that is to say, what is not done by any particular agent. The point here, though, is that nothing makes it so, and nothing explains it; thus, there is nothing to say about what is "so" of it. Here we see also the advent of a further implication of the term Li, which was to have great influence in subsequent Buddhist usages: Li as potentiality. Since Li is defined in opposition to knowing and deliberation action, whatever is present—converging to be present here—but is not explicitly known to awareness is Li. If we add the sense of value always associated with the term, we have here the derivation of the idea of Li as an unrealized potential for the value, something that is present but as yet unutilized. This is, of course, not far from the first stratum of nominalized meaning of the term: those fault lines, among all that may be present in nature, that, if cut along, create a coherent—i.e., intelligible and valuable—object. Those perforations are present, but as yet uncut. Hence, the Li is present, the value is "here," but it is unrealized until Li in the verbal sense—the selective cutting—is applied to it.

Indeed, for Guo Li means precisely "the cut," the limitation of the event, its absolute separation from all "others." This is, however, the full incoherent merging with all things qua *ziran*. Because each event is limited, it is not infringed on by anything else, and hence is self-so. This is called Li because it is divided out from all else, is absolutely singular, and also, as we'll see, because it is of value for us to pay heed to this aspect of the situation. It is called our "nature" because it cannot *be* changed—by knowing and doing. The term *nature* is here used in its usual sense, as we see also in the *Xunzi*: it is the opposite of purposive activity (為 *wei*) or the artificial (偽 *wei*)—hence, Guo also sometimes calls it the "genuine nature" (真性 *zhenxing*). Whatever happens without purpose and unmotivated by purposive knowing is the nature. It is neither within nor without, and makes no distinction between what is encountered and what is emitted. It is called "the allotment," which also means "division," (*fen*), because it is just this much and no more. It is called the limit because it is finite. Its "nature" is its "limits" is its "allotment" is its "coherence"—which is this thing, this situation, this encounter itself. Each thing has its own limits, its own nature, its own allotment, its own coherence; but once purposive knowing and doing are eliminated, this "having" of limits is simply being self-so, and the self-so is the real pre-trace "self" of any event, its vanishing merge of all that is so without anyone doing it: "I self whatever I encounter." The object of *ming* can be almost anything; Guo speaks repeatedly of "merging with the time," "merging with change," "merging with things," "merging with one's own nature," "merging with one's own allotment," "merging with one's own limits," "merging with whatever one encounters," and *these expression are strictly synonymous.* To vanishingly merge with whatever one encounters is to vanishingly merge with one's own nature, with one's own limits, with one's own allotment. In this sense the term *the nature* or *the coherence* is an ironic empty term for Guo, just as "Dao" or "nothingness" is. The Dao is literally nonexistent, and thus ultimately "a collective name for all things." Similarly, the Nature, Li, the self-so, is really nothing more than a collective name for all encounters, all vanishing merges, all particular events themselves: they are ways of indicating the fact that nothing and no one controls or determines or gives value to events, and that this fact is itself what makes them what they are and gives them their inalienable value.[35]

IRONIC LI AS NON-IRONIC LI IN GUO XIANG

But Guo pushes this one step farther: after making the distinction between knowing/doing/traces on the one hand and the self-so/determinacy/limits/vanishing on the other, he annuls it at a higher order of abstraction:

> One cannot do by "doing" Doing. Doing does spontaneously. One cannot Know by "doing" Knowing. Knowing knows spontaneously. It is just this spontaneous self-so Knowing, and thus it is really non-Knowing. Thus Knowing comes out of non-Knowing. It is just this spontaneous self-so Doing, and thus it is really non-Doing. Thus Doing comes out of non-Doing. Doing comes out of non-Doing, and thus non-Doing is the master. Knowing comes out of non-Knowing, and thus non-Knowing is the source [*zong*]. Thus the True Man discards Knowing and yet knows; he does not Do and yet does. Things are self-so generated, attained through sitting and forgetting. It is for this reason that the name "Knowing" is cut off and the term "Doing" is discarded.[36]

Here, Guo is asserting that even Doing and Knowing are themselves self-so. Although actions and cognitions still take place, they are not properly called Doing and Knowing, since they are ultimately still subsets of non-doing and non-knowing, that is, of *ziran*. One cannot decide to decide, one cannot deliberately determine to have a deliberate purpose. This would lead to an infinite regress of the kind Guo rejects in his critique of a creator. One just spontaneously finds oneself having deliberate purposes and making decisions. The free-will theorist might say, "Since it is possible to regard one's own sense of freedom as either illusory or true, there is a choice involved even in the adoption of the idea that one has no choice: freedom cannot be escaped even in the attempt to deny it. I cannot abstain from deliberate purposes and actions, from making choices; even so abstaining is itself a choice." Guo accepts this and draws the opposite conclusion: since whether I choose or do not choose I am in either case actually choosing, I have no choice: I cannot but be choosing, and therefore I cannot choose between choosing and not-choosing. I am not free to decide to be free. Because I am "condemned to be free," my freedom is itself a spontaneous fact not of my choosing. Hence even when I am doing, I am really, ultimately, non-doing, and even when I am knowing, I am really, ultimately, non-knowing. This means there is no need to actually eliminate knowing and doing, or to change one's behavior in any way whatsoever. The acknowledgment of the Li, the self-so, is simply a noticing of this *second-order* spontaneity that pervades even my deliberate activity and knowing, a focusing on a different level of the doing and knowing itself. To focus on the self-so aspect of any situation, the beyond-knowing-and-doing process that it is, its vanishing convergence that cannot go outside itself to any external objects of knowing or goals of doing, its limitedness to its own limits, even in its doing and knowing, is to know its Li, no more and no less.

This is why, although Guo can speak of many Lis or of the one Li of the self-so, he means the same thing in either case. It is in Guo that Li seems to take on the sense of "principles," but we can now see that these Lis or this Li be spoken of as "principles" only in the most ironic possible sense. When we probe more deeply into what is actually meant by these "principles," we find that in all cases they resolve immediately into a single principle, that is, the self-so, and given our definition of what a "principle" is, this makes the "many principles" claim deeply problematic. A principle, in the normal sense of the word as used in ordinary English speech, would have to be a reliable linking of *at least two entities*, a way of predicting a replication or a constancy. What applies to one entity only is not a principle. Guo's use of Li is the *ne plus ultra* of a certain ambiguity: it applies to all entities without exception, but only by limiting itself so extremely to each particular entity that it has no specific content, can never be applied to another case, and thus ceases to be a principle at all. It is omnipresent, but only in the sense of absolute non-replicable limitation to each moment. The Li of the event is really just the event itself, not a principle added to explain or describe the event. But it is a Li in the normal Chinese sense, for Li means a coherence not only in the sense of a coming together, but in the sense of something that can serve as an object of consciousness, and which is worth paying attention to, inasmuch as it will lead to the optimal way of relating to that thing. Guo's Li is not really a "coming together" of discernible and determinate entities, for these, considered as others, are for him merely traces. It is, rather, the vanishing of things into each other when they follow their own self-so and ignore the traces of one another. It is thus a greater togetherness and a lesser togetherness, and it is greater because it is lesser, lesser because it is greater. But it is still naturally describable as Li in that it is the practical object to be focused on in the sense that it is what we should be aware of in order to live most effectively. It is the locus of real value. However, there is only one thing to know, and it is precisely the effacement of any possibility of knowing of principles in the ordinary sense. The absolute uniqueness of each individual thing means that its principle collapses into itself; this does not amount to multiple principles, but no principles at all. If asked why something is the way it is, Guo would answer like one of Vonnegut's Tralfamadorians: "There is no why. The moment is just structured that way." This "structure," which is the very opposite of an answer to "Why?" is what Guo means by Li.

Thus, we must not be misled when we find Guo using the term Li, quite frequently, in the sense of an intelligible object of knowledge, again smoothly but rather misleadingly translatable as "principle." For examining the context and implications again, we find that the principle to be so recognized is always the principle of "self-so," *which for Guo signifies precisely ultimate unintelligibility*. The 自然之理 *ziran zhi li* which one is called upon to recognize is not "the coherence of the self-so" in the sense of "the way nature hangs together spontaneously," except in the limited sense of the reciprocal ordering and reciprocal limiting of entities in individual cases. Much less is it "the principle of Nature" or "the principle of Spontaneity" in the sense of some definite fact that is meant to explain things. The "coherences of self-so" are in one sense multiple; we are to recognize *each* thing's self-so. But "multiplicity" in the sense of the presence of "others" is precisely what self-so is a way of denying. So this very multiplicity is the effacement of multiplicity. We might say that the multiplicity is so extremely multiple that it is utterly incommensurable, and thus effaces the matrix of togetherness of discrete othernesses that is required for "multiplicity." Multiplicity, pushed to its extreme, overcomes multiplicity. Division, pushed to its extreme, is the only cure for division. Here again, we find a crucial precursor for Tiantai thinking. A thing's self-so is none other than that thing itself; it is its true self, the very process of its becoming what it is without intending to and without reference to any *intelligible* causal matrix, efficient or final. The thing that fits into the causal nexus, or hangs together with other things, is not the real thing itself, not its self-so; it is rather its "trace," which is the way this process of spontaneity impacts on other spontaneities, other moments, other beings. The thing itself is not even a "thing": it is just the self-so, and no further predications can be made about it. All predications about things, and all the moreso about principles describing the ways in which things are related to each other, are by definition a matter of the traces, which are a distortion of the reality of the self-so. The self-so is in this sense described as a "vanishing" (*ming*) into things, which is also a vanishing of the identifiable individual "things" themselves—that is, of their traces.

In the context of Guo's overall philosophy, we often find him speaking of *ziran zhi Li* in a way that does superficially suggest that he is providing some sort of an explanation for why things are so. For example, we find him telling us that "it is a self-so Li that there are some things that are brought to completion by the accumulation of habitual practice."[37] Or again, "It is a self-so Li that there are also some things that require smelting and forging to become implements."[38] But it is important that we not allow the form of these pronouncements to confuse us as to what is really being intended here. For when Guo tells us such things—"It is the Li of the self-so that all things follow each other," and the like—he is really not trying to give a reason why these things are so *but rather to reject the very possibility of giving a reason for them*. This is made clear in the following passage, among many others:

> It is a self-so Li [i.e., a fact of things with no explanation, *ziran zhi li*] that when one moves, a shadow follows, and when one speaks, an echo follows. When one smoothly follows along with things [順物 *shun wu*], traces in the form of names are established; but he who was going along with things did not do it for the name. Not doing it for a name is perfection, but ultimately the name could not be avoided; who then could release him (from this consequence)? Thus names are shadows and echoes; and shadows and echoes are the fetters of forms and sounds. When one understands this, the name-traces can be done away with; once this is done, the esteeming of others [尚彼 *shangbi*] can be cut off, and once this is done, one's own nature and life can be kept whole.[39]

The point of recognizing that this is a "self-so principle" is not to understand its inner structure so as to allow us to utilize it in terms of some teleological project of our own, as is the case for the non-ironic usage of Li, and indeed even for Wang Bi's synthesis of the ironic and non-ironic usages. Rather, it is to allow us to abandon any attempt at an explanation, or of fitting this thing into an account of the universe as a whole, or into our own project as a whole, or indeed to make it "cohere" into any kind of whole at all. It is to allow us to "follow along" with things, and thus keep our own nature and life intact, which means to preserve the self-so-ness of one's own present determinacy, which is indeed for Guo the only thing really worth doing. Following along is ironic coherence; the esteeming of others is non-ironic coherence. By dropping all attempts to locate particular things within a global matrix of meanings and explanations, we eliminate any value-implications of the thing, any need to either emulate or avoid it. Emulation or suppression of external things is what disturbs our own self-so. Hence, to recognize the unintelligibility and meaninglessness of things, we preserve ourselves, attain true value: recognizing a principle is, ironically, a way of realizing the "principle" (self-so-ness) and value of our own existence. "Principle" or coherence here is thus not a ground that makes things so, but the fact that it is important for us to recognize that there is no way to know what makes them so, that the category of "ground" or "principle" is both meaningless and harmful—the ironic tradition of unintelligibility as real coherence given a new twist. Realizing this particular fact about any thing is what will allow one to adopt the maximally satisfying attitude toward it. Li simply means here what it is good to notice about a thing: always the fact that it is self-so.

This is true even when Guo seems to be asserting a global orderliness or necessity pertaining to the universe as a whole; here too, the purpose is to free us from the need of assigning meanings and values and knowable characters of things—for this is the only way to attain value, which is what the recognition of a Li is supposed to do, thus giving us a perfect example of the ironic notion of Li. For example, Guo asserts:

> The Li of things is inherently right, and cannot be avoided. Man, in being born, is never mistakenly born, and whatever there is in his life is not there senselessly [非妄有 *fei wang you*]. . . . Thus whatever is not encountered cannot be encountered, and whatever is encountered cannot not be encountered; whatever is not done cannot be done and whatever is done cannot be not done; thus we give all things over to their self-rightness [自當 *zidang*].[40]

The point here is not to assert the rationality of the cosmos for its own sake, as something that could and should come to be understood in its particular, necessary relations. Rather, the point is given in the last line of the citation: seeing this fact about things allows us to give all things over to their self-rightness, and thus preserve our own self-rightness. Seeing Li accomplishes value. But there is only one thing one need notice, no matter what the thing or situation facing one may be: the self-so of the thing, the fact that it has no discernible cause, meaning, identity, or goal. To recognize this one fact is the sole locus of value. The particularities of the structure of the thing are irrelevant: what is truly Li, namely, the coherence that it is valuable to focus on, that allows one to deal with things in the ideal way, is always the same: the self-so. In this sense, Guo Xiang really recognizes only one Li.

We can see that it is difficult to speak of Guo as either an ironic appropriation of the non-ironic, or vice versa. For in Guo, the idea of non-ironic definite coherence as such and of ironic unknowable coherence as such come to be identical. For the first time in Chinese thought, we can state directly that coherence as such is incoherence as such, that the unity of things is also their separation, that determinacy and indeterminacy are synonymous—which will be, as we shall see shortly, the foundation stone of Tiantai thinking. The term Li is central to this development, and here its two opposed directions converge: to know Li has always meant to know what it is most valuable to know, and it still means that for Guo. But what is valuable to know is now that there is nothing to know, and that no knowledge has value. To know the Li about any thing is to know there is nothing to know about it: this is the Li of the self-so. Since this means absolutely isolating any event from any connections that will make it intelligible or valuable, this signifies a kind of absolute division. But at the same time, it is the most radical unity, cohering, of all events; this is not only because the self-so is the one fact that is universally true of every event without exception, but more crucially because for Guo it also signifies "vanishing merging," an ironic form of togetherness of all events, which is no longer seen through the lens of mutual externality, which he sees as resulting purely from the ignorance of the self-so and the involvement of trace-cognition. Thus, the self-so is also in a sense a complete unity. Coherence in the non-ironic sense meant, at the very least, (1) harmonious unification of a thing with its environment, (2) value, and (3) intelligibility. In the ironic sense, it meant at the least harmonious unification that had value because of its unintelligibility as harmony or unification or value. For Guo, the value of each thing is its forgetting of value, the only thing to be intelligibly known about it is its lack of intelligibility, and it joins together with other things harmoniously only when it recognizes no other things as causes or contexts. Li now becomes the marker of this coherence qua incoherence, incoherence qua coherence.

Li, for Guo, always means *ziran*, which is called Li because it is what is best to notice about any thing. Li in other Chinese texts means what is intelligible, what brings together the elements of an object coherently, the locus of its value, and what human activity should focus upon when dealing with the thing in question. It is in these senses that the self-so is Li. What makes human interaction with things maximally effective is to notice their freedom from any explanatory principle that is knowable, and which makes them come together to be what they are: this then is their "principle." Hence, Guo tells us:

> That which causes no harm to things does not do so because it is practicing benevolence, but the trace "benevolence" moves in it; that which makes every principle hit the mark is not practicing

righteousness, but the effect "righteousness" appears in it. Thus hitting the mark and causing no harm are not brought about by benevolence and righteousness. But the world goes running after [these traces], discarding themselves to follow others so that they lose their ever-so [i.e., their self-so]. Therefore the disordering of the mind does not come from what is ugly but always from beautiful appearances; the disruption of the world does not come from evil, but always from benevolence and righteousness. Thus benevolence and righteousness are tools for the disruption of the world.[41]

The non-ironic "principles" of benevolence and righteousness are not the true principles; in fact, they are the precise opposites of the sole real principle, the ironic principle, the self-so, the lack of any explanation or teleology or determining principle of things: the lack of any principles. To see a thing and deal with it, without reference to its value or any explanatory account of its coming-to-be, is to correctly relate to it, to allow oneself to vanish (into) it and maintain the optimal human condition.

This does not prevent Guo Xiang from sometimes seeming to address specific principles. In a small number of cases, and in a manner that can be described as very ad hoc, Guo appears to be invoking the term "Li" as the explanation for some specific connection between facts in the world, something that is closer to a "principle" or "account" that actually serves as a determining law and can be used to explain some fact. In this sense, we can discern the sense of Li as "division," its older sense, and the one which so many scholars single out as distinctive to Guo's position. For example, we find Guo saying, in explanation of the differences in the natural habitats of massive Peng and the little birds who ridicule him in Zhuangzi's first chapter: "This is all to explain that Peng flies so high only because of his huge wings. A being of small substance cannot depend on the large for its support, and *thus* a being of large substance cannot depend on the small as its provisions. *Thus principles have their perfect divisions; things have their fixed limits* [理有至分, 物有定極 *Li you zhi fen, wu you ding ji*]. Since each is sufficient to the task at hand, the assistance they respectively provide to these beings is equal."[42] I have provided emphases for two items in this citation. One is the connective "thus," and the other is the sentence that suggests the idea of principle as individual separate principles of particular things. In the latter, we find "principle" used parallel to "things," which does indeed suggest that both terms should be read in the plural and as indicating something case-specific. The principle of entity A would here seem to differ from the principle of entity B, with a "perfect division" between them, just as these two entities themselves have a fixed limit between them. But the *fen* can also be understood not as the division but as what lies between limits, that is, a role. In this sense, we might perhaps venture to interpret the first four characters, 理有至分, as still referring to Li in the singular, that is, to the one Li, *ziran*: "Li, the self-so, has perfectly continent roles and divisions within it." More simply, we can naturally read this to mean, "Each Li entails a perfect division into its role." Li as *ziran*, free of interference from traces of otherness, is precisely that separation into allotted divisions. That would mean, it is self-so, "principle," for things to be perfectly different from one another, not that there are separate principles for each thing. This question is what makes Guo's odd "thus," also italicized in my translation, significant. For he does not just state that "the large need large things, the small need small things," but rather that "because the small need small things, therefore (we can infer) the large need large things." This "thus" actually refers to the same principle being operative in both cases, just as the "assistance" to the two types of beings is equal, as stated at the end of the citation. The same principle, *ziran*, is all that ever applies anywhere. This is the *only* kind of hanging-together of the world that Guo acknowledges; not an array of individual, knowable principles, but rather the same operation performed over and over again. Because this is self-so, we can deduce that that is self-so: this is the true application of what we would call a "principle," but it turns out to be an ironic principle: the principle here is always the same principle: the self-so, which means no-principle.

Guo makes this explicit, employing the traditional terminology of root and branch, but in such a way as to make eminently clear the negligibility of specific principles: "The root includes the branch, just as the arm includes the hand. If the body as a whole is harmonious, all the individual joints will be at ease; if the Way of Heaven goes smoothly, then both root and branch will be unobstructed. Thus as soon as we have the single [Li of] non-doing, all the many Lis are simultaneously present."[43] This could perhaps be read to imply that these many principles are all present in the one principle of the self-so; but in fact Guo's point is reductive. There is no need to bother with the other Lis, for the single Li "self-so" covers them all. It is what all so-called principles resolve into, and indeed all that provides the "principle-ness" of any principle. It is all one needs to know.

In this connection, we should consider the following passage:

> Nothing but the dark ocean would be sufficient to move his body; nothing but ninety thousand miles would be sufficient to support his wings. How is this worth considering strange? It's just that a big entity is necessarily [必 *bi*] self-born [自生 *zisheng*] in a vast location, and a vast location will necessarily self-generate this vast

entity. The Li is definitely self-so [理固自然 *li gu ziran*]; one need not fear it failing to be the case. So what need is there to work one's mind through these things?[44]

Here again we may be tempted to consider this a statement about a definite, particular principle about things in the world, which differs from other principles, that is, Li here meaning "the principle that things are adapted to their environments, such that large creatures live in large habitats." This would be a justified inference, particularly given Guo's use of the robust "necessarily" (*bi*) and his unusual reversal of the terms *principle* and *self-so*, such that the former is the subject and the latter an adjectival description of it. Usually, for Guo, Li *is* the self-so, or we are told about "the Li of self-so-ness" (自然之理 *ziran zhi li*), where *ziran* seems to be the more substantial and prior term. Here, however, principle is something that is described as self-so, which gives the impression of hypostasizing principle in a stronger sense. This impression is strengthened by Guo's revelation of what it means for a principle to be "definitely self-so": it is a reliable predictor: one need not fear it failing to be the case. All these factors suggest definite individual principles.

However, Guo's characteristic insertion of the modifier "*zi*" self, a shorthand for self-so, before the crucial verb (to generate), complicates this picture considerably. We can interpret this to mean that a large place "naturally" or "spontaneously" or "self-so-ishly" generates a large entity. But Guo's use of this term, as I have argued elsewhere,[45] has a more intricate significance; this *zi* is the true self of the being in question, it is "self-generation" when it generates "self-so-ishly," because its real self is just the process of vanishing of any determinate self into the traceless process of self-so itself. "A big place" is not the true self of a big place, but rather just the "traces" of the big place on *other* entities. The generation of a big entity there is really not a linking of two distinct entities, but a revelation of the self-so, namely, the true, indeterminable self of both. In this sense, it cannot be a principle in the strict sense, in that a principle must reliably link the behavior of at least *two genuinely distinct* entities. The real import of Guo's invocation of this "necessary" principle is thus not to provide a reliable guideline for making deductions, but rather to put an end to any such deductions, and this is exactly indicated in the last line of the citation: the upshot of knowing that a "self-so principle" will never fail to be so is not that one should thus use this as a guideline for making predictions, or for refining one's thinking process, but to assure one that there is no need to worry oneself about it. A Li, by being self-so, means the end of thinking about it. What's good about Li is that it leads *away* from intelligibility, not toward it. The point here is to keep an eye on *both* implications when Guo uses the term Li: in this instance, we could translate *li gu ziran* (inelegantly) as "The absolutely separate coherence of this entity joining mergingly with its large place is reliably self-so and thus something that no inquiries or explanations need be applied to" *or* "this principle is definitely spontaneously so, and thus absolutely reliable," and they would *mean the same thing*. It is in this sense, and only in this sense, that we can speak of "definite principles" in the thought of Guo Xiang: a complete convergence of coherence and incoherence, of togetherness and separateness, of intelligibility and unintelligibility.

Of particular interest for understanding this point is Guo's unusual use of the term Li together with a modifier, which seem to point to specific principles or Li. The three most notorious examples are 人理 *renli*, 和理 *heli*, and 我理 *woli*, denoting, respectively, the principle/coherence of human beings, of harmony, and of the self. In all cases, these are ad hoc coinages glossing a phrase from the Zhuangzi; *heli* is used when the text says something about harmony (*he*); *renli* when a the texts speaks of humanity, for example, in contrast to Heaven; and *woli* is used as a gloss on a text referring to the self. For example, commenting on Zhuangzi's line, "Thus it is not sufficient to distort his harmony," Guo says, "If one understands that one's own character and life are necessarily right, then through all the thousands and ten thousands of changes, through life and death, success and failure, one remains blandly oneself, and possesses the principle of harmony [*heli*] within himself."[46] The other examples all follow this ad hoc pattern. Nonetheless, we find Guo making some interesting assertions here:

> Each thing attains its Way, and the principle of harmony [*heli*] spontaneously fits it comfortably.[47]

> Knowledge without doing does not harm one's tranquility; tranquility combined with doing that comes of its own accord does not harm knowledge. This can be called their mutual nourishing [of knowledge and tranquility]. When these two nourish each other, how could the allotment of the principle of harmony [*heli*] come from the outside?[48]

"The principle of harmony" here seems to be synonymous with "harmony," a way of nominalizing the concept of harmony. But we could equally say that harmony is joined with Li here as a kind of synonymous binome; the two terms are meant to meant the same thing. That is, when the text says *he*, Guo wants us to know that this harmony is just what he means by Li: the incoherent merging of all things in the self-so of any event. For harmony is very closely related to the idea of Li as coherence; we have mentioned the sense of Li as a coming together, and Guo's distinctive twist on this sense of the term: the vanishing (into) things, which is the function of the self-so once it is freed of its involvement in "traces" (teleological and foundational explanatory structures). "The principle of harmony" is just a word for the self-so itself.

A more likely candidate for an individual principle is the term *renli*. Guo says:

> In terms of the self-so, there is no difference between great men and petty men. But in terms of the principles of humanity itself [*renli*], he who depends on heaven may be called an exemplary person.[49]

Here a contrast is clearly being made between the self-so (or the heavenly) and *another* principle: the principle of human beings as such. In terms of the self-so, there are no distinctions of greater and lesser value: all are equal, each is perfectly right to itself, because all are equally self-so. But here Guo introduces another standard by which things might be judged. Explaining Zhuangzi's own expression of praise, he gives an explanation. "Human principles" would seem to denote what is truly valuable to man himself, that is, what is "coherent with" human interests, what is conducive to optimal human experience. And what is it that is the human principle? Recognizing the self-so, to wit, "following heaven." Here we have an early form of a paradox that takes form often in Chinese Buddhism. In terms of the self-so itself, it makes no difference whether or not we recognize or live according to the self-so, or ignore it and get lost in the traces. Both of these are equally self-so, both of these are equally self-right. The only difference between them is how they affect *us*. What is healthy for humans is "human principle," which means not only *being* self-so (which is in any case unavoidable), but *recognizing* the self-so as a principle, which means to see the futility of all principles, all explanations. "Human principle" means to free oneself from emulation of traces, abandon all value judgments and explanations of the causes or purposes of things, follow along with the self-so. Once again, we find a convergence between an individual principle and the sole real principle, the self-so. This is also the singularity, the convergence, of the ironic and non-ironic senses of coherence, or determinacy and indeterminacy. Hence, Guo says explicitly:

> If one moves in accordance with the heavenly nature, then the human principles [人理 *renli*] are also kept complete.[50]

This is in keeping with the "root-branch" metaphor cited above, and is equally reductive. Guo certainly will allow for "human principles"—such as the divisions between ruler and subject, father and son, and the like, in other words, conventional morality, which Guo elsewhere calls 明教 *mingjiao*, the teaching of names. But that is arguably not what he means by *renli* here. Rather, whenever he uses this term, he links it to the human accord with the overriding "principle," principle proper, the self-so. Li always means what it is important to notice, and *renli* means what is important for human beings to notice. What is supremely important for human beings to notice is not the specific principles of human life, but once again the self-so. Attention to the self-so will make those specific human relationships function smoothly; hence, there is no need to pay any special heed to them as principles in their own right. They are not worth noticing, and hence are not Li.

This same reversal from the particular to the universal is found in Guo's use of an even more particulate sounding term, *woli*, the coherence or principle of the self: "When one turns back and holds to the principle of self (我理 *oli*), this principle of self spontaneously penetrates all."[51]

It would seem as if the "principle of self" might be a specific individual principle. But the conclusion points us right back to the self-so: the principle of "selfness," its truth, is just its self-so, which means its lack of intelligibility, its freedom from the causal nexus of explanations and principles that constitutes the world of traces. This is why the principle of self "spontaneously penetrates all" other entities, for all of them have only this one "principle," the self-so, as their true being, their true selves, which are no knowable self at all.

We may have noticed in these usages a kind of two-tiered structure, where Li-proper is the self-so as such, and X-li is X considered in its self-so nature. I insist that Li always means self-so because it is the self-so-ness of X that makes it a Li. But this can then be applied on any level to any particular thing, for each is indeed the self-so. We have here an incipient version of the problematic of the one and the many in later Chinese Buddhism and Neo-Confucianism, most famously the Huayan-Tiantai "one is many" idea and derivatively Zhu Xi's notion that there is only one principle—the Great Ultimate (太極 *taiji*)—which is, in its entirety, also manifest in each thing, as the particular individuating Li of that thing, which defines both its character and its inner teleology. We can perhaps discern the contours of a similar way of thinking, *mutatis mutandis*, in Guo's use of the idea of the "perfect" or "ultimate principle," literally the "arrived principle" (至理 *zhili*),[52] which is contrasted with any more local or limited type of principle, that is, what would normally be called a Li by someone besides Guo Xiang. The perfect Li is what is like those Lis (a coherent and intelligible coming together, a harmonizable harmony, which can lead to value if harmonized with, i.e., recognized), but *moreso* what really does what the term Li promises: the ironic Li as the fulfillment of the non-ironic Lis. This is the standard move of the ironic tradition: the real Dao is the non-"Dao," the ultimate Li is the non-Li. It is significant that this term is also reversed, suggesting that "perfect Li" also means the "arrival of Li" (理至 *lizhi*). Perfect Li is *ziran*, in relation to any lesser particular non-ironic Li. But here again, the point is the collapse of all Lis into this one Li. Hence, we find Guo saying, "Just go along with allowing to it be itself, and the Li will arrive of itself." And again, "The perfect Li is exhausted in self-attainment"[53] (the latter phrase being another mutation of self-so). Or again, "Things have their self-so, and Li have their ultimate perfection; in following along with this they move directly forward [直往 *zhiwang*][54] and thus vanishingly self-cohere [冥然自合 *mingran zihe*]."[55]

In all these cases, the "perfect Li" is self-so, which is precisely non-principle, the negation of what would normally be called a principle. This is what leads to vanishing self-cohesion, self-attainment, moving directly forward, and so on, all of which are synonyms for value here. By recognizing a principle, one attains value. To recognize the perfect principle is to ignore all other so-called principles (as the constant Dao is the Dao that is no Dao, and so on). In doing so, one attains value—the arrival of principle (Li as value).

The standard textbook doxa on the understanding of Li ("principle," "pattern," "coherence") in Wang Bi and Guo Xiang is still perhaps that suggested long ago by Wing-tsit Chan: "The major concept [in Guo Xiang] is no longer Dao, as in Chuang Tzu [Zhuangzi], but Nature (Tzu-jan) [*ziran*, self-so]. Things exist and transform themselves spontaneously and there is no other reality or agent to cause them. Heaven is not something behind this process of Nature but is merely its general name. Things exist and transform according to principle, but each and every thing has its own principle. Everything is therefore self-sufficient and there is no need of an over-all original reality to combine or govern them, as in the case of Wang Pi [Wang Bi]. . . . While Wang Pi emphasizes the one, Kuo [Guo] emphasizes the many. To Wang Pi, principle transcends things, but to Kuo, it is immanent in them."[56] The implication seems to be that for Wang "principle" (Li) is one, but for Guo it is many—each thing has its own "principle." This suggests that for Wang there is one overriding Dao, a shared principle of all things, while for Guo, each thing has its own particular principle, its own Li. We have here, to say it again, an embryonic form of the controversies over the status of Li in later Buddhism and Neo-Confucianism, focused on the question of whether Li is to be understood as the unifying principle of all things or the distinguishing principles of each individual thing, what unifies or what divides. We have seen, however, that in an important sense it is truer to say that it is Wang Bi who develops a theory of distinctive individual principles of things, while Guo puts forth only a single principle for all things without exception: the principle of the self-so, *ziran*. On the other hand, as we have also seen, there is indeed a sense in which this amounts to an assertion by Guo of each thing having its own unique principle: but a truly *unique* principle is no longer a principle at all, it is unshared with any other entity, and in fact it is not even the essence of this one thing, but rather *is that thing itself* in its very unidentifiable becoming as the merging and vanishing of all things into it. Hence, we must take exception to Wing-tsit Chan's understanding of the difference between Wang and Guo, namely, that Wang emphasizes "the One" while Guo emphasizes "the many." Our analysis here shows that just the opposite is closer to the truth: for Wang, there are many actual, specific principles, the knowable and intelligible mini-Daos embodied in the hexagrams, which determine the nature of qualitatively different situations, while for Guo, there is really only one Li, one coherence-worth-noticing, namely, the self-so of any situation or thing, which is always characterized precisely as an effacement of intelligibility and knowledge. We can also see now the irony of Tang Junyi's citation of Guo's gloss on Wang's statement that "things never happen haphazardly," from which Tang extracts his crucial term "convergence" (會趣 *huiqu*). It applies more directly to Wang's understanding of Li as the mini-Dao of any situation, the convergence toward the "least," which is also the valued or the desired. For Guo himself, however, it is less obvious in what sense the single principle of self-so has anything to do with convergence toward the lacked and therefore valued. Nonetheless, there is perhaps a way to understand this. The self-so, for Guo, is the operation of all things in separation from their "traces," the objects of consciousness left by one self-so occurrence on another. This is the type of "convergence" which for Guo is a "small" principle, the non-ironic principle of individual things, that is, explanatory connections elucidating cause and effect, or ends and means relationships. The real principle, the self-so, is the contrary of this, the omission of all reference to traces. But this too is a kind of convergence: an ironic convergence. This is what Guo calls "vanishing (into) (*ming*)," which is indeed a kind of coming together, but one that effaces the specific identities of individual entities above and beyond their self-so, which is at once the most general and the most uncompromisingly unique in each case. So the real principle (self-so) is the absence of all so-called principles, and the real convergence (vanishing into each other) is the absence of all so-called convergences (interconnections between traces). The real Dao is the non-Dao, and the real value is the absence of all valuation. Li means a convergence that is intelligible and important to notice for the attaining of value. But for Guo it is an ironic convergence, an ironic intelligibility, an ironic noticing, and an ironic value. Principle is one in the sense of none, which is why Guo's "one" seems so much like a "many," and indeed it does point to an emphasis on individual uniqueness pushed to the point where no principle is any longer possible, nor indeed any discernible identifiable differences (traces), which is why his "many" seems so much like a "one."

In sum, Wang's development of the idea of Li in his *Zhouyilueli*, expanding on ideas put forth in the *Hanfeizi* commentary to the *Laozi* and Wang's own understanding of the *Zhouyi*, introduces the idea of multiple individual Lis as "mini-Daos," bearing the same relation to each discrete situation that the Dao bears to the world as a whole. The overriding principle of organization here is based on the idea of "rule by the fewest," rooted in a social-political paradigm in which all elements of a situation actively "seek" whatever is most scarce among them. The unseen, the absent, the Dark, being the most scarce in any situation, is the principle of that situation's coherence. But this is particularized by the individual mode of scarcity relevant in that time and place, thus yielding a multiplicity of determinate principles, all of which converge in the overriding Dao. In the case of Guo Xiang, on the contrary, we have a critique of explanatory principles as such, ostensibly in order to affirm the uniqueness of each individual self-so event; but the theoretical result of this turn away from metaphysics, within the realm of discourse at least (as opposed to praxis), is in fact that affirmation of a single, abstract metaphysical principle that applies indiscriminately to all possible situations: the self-so. This continues to be the case for most of Chinese Buddhism, where the one coherence worth noticing is Emptiness, dependent co-arising. The one exception to this, as we shall see, is the Tiantai school, which posits also a sense in which Li is simultaneously multiple. It is to the Buddhist usages of Li that we now turn.

SIX

BEYOND ONE AND MANY

Li in Tiantai and Huayan Buddhism

HOW EMPTINESS BECAME LI

I will be considering mainly the Huayan and Tiantai schools of Chinese Buddhism here, as the two most elaborately systematic and also most "sinitic" of the Chinese traditions of Buddhist doctrine, and also because it is here that the term Li is given its most distinctive, elaborate, and influential developments. Prior to the advent of these schools, Li had begun to be used grammatically in the sense of notice-worthy coherence, as intelligibility, and, in this extended sense, as a "principle" or idea that is to be known and understood, as something that is so prior to the intervention of deliberate volitions, and thus in some cases as a pervasive fact which may or may not enter consciousness. This is true even in the more specialized and highly developed usages of Wang Bi and Guo Xiang just examined, though with important ironic twists. In Guo's contrast of Li to "knowing" and "doing," as what is so within the limits of a thing prior to its overstepping these limits by means of trace-cognition and trace-volition, the implication of a potentiality that has not yet been realized or brought to awareness is especially highlighted, a dimension of the term that will come to play a larger role in the Buddhist usages. For Guo this aspect was pushed to the point of a kind of ironic self-overcoming: Li was not merely as-yet-unknown, but literally unknowable, and thus this "potential" and "principle" ended up being no principle at all, not even a genuine "fact" with any determinate content, but merely noncognizability per se. The Tang Daoist apocryphal text 關尹子 Guanyinzi opens with a gloss on the first line of the Daodejing that effectively summarizes the position to which Guo's innovation has brought philosophical Daoism: "It is not that there is a Dao which cannot be spoken or thought: unspeakableness and unthinkability are themselves Dao" (非有道不可言，不可言即道；非有道不可思，不可思即道 *feiyoudaobukeyan, bukeyan ji dao; fei you dao bu ke si, bu ke si ji dao*).[1] For Guo, Li is this very unthinkability and nothing more. Similarly, and again with highly intensified irony, this meant that in a sense it was not merely potential, but always actual: the self-so operates even in its opposite, in deliberate activity and knowledge. But it must be remembered especially that these usages never for an instant depart from Li's connection with value, with soteriology in the broad sense. It is not just a principle, a common fact, a potentiality, or a coherence among and applicable to a number of particulars, but rather is one that is being asserted to be worthy of notice and attention because of the role it can play in attaining a specific human goal.

In the Buddhist case, this is generally the soteriological goal of transcending samsâra, attaining Nirvana, overcoming suffering. As Aramaki Noritoshi has shown, early Chinese Buddhist thinkers such as Zhu Daosheng (360?–434) and Xie Lingyun (385–433) began to use the term Li as synonymous with "dharmatā"—法性 dharma-nature—and by extension, Buddha-nature: it is that which must be realized in order to become a Buddha.[2] Kan'no Hiroshi has further pointed out that a certain conflation of Li with Ultimate Truth, and with Buddhahood itself, also occurs in Zhu Daosheng's writings, mapping the 理事 Li/*shi* pair onto the Ultimate Truth/Conventional Truth structure of Indian Mahayana Buddhism.[3] Li is the fact about things—in this case, about all things without exception, hence the omnipresent universal universal—attention to which will lead to liberation. For those schools that consider Emptiness to be ultimate truth, or what needs to be realized in order to obtain the optimal human value—Buddhahood—Li is accordingly Śūnyatā, Emptiness, conditioned co-arising, and with it the consequent facts of impermanence, suffering, the Four Noble Truths, and so on. It is as non-ironic value-laden intelligibility that this is called Li, coherence, here, but it also happens that this intelligibility is asserted to be intelligible in every single instance of experience without exception, thus bringing in the sense of coherence as unification and universality. But that the value-aspect in particular is what qualifies this particular fact about things to be called Li is made most clear by 吉藏 Jizang (549–623), the great theoretician of the 三論 Sanlun (Three Treatise) school, who here as in many cases addresses the root issue with unusual clarity. In Jizang's 大乘玄義 *Dasheng Xuanyi* (Abstruse Meaning of the Mahayana) we find the following question and answer:

> Q: In the first [of the above] explanations, you specified Existence [有 *you*] as the Substance [體 *ti*] and Emptiness [空 *kong*] as its

Function [用 yong]. Can we also then take Existence as Li and
Emptiness as its Function? [A:] Substance is simply another name for
Li; so when we specify Existence as the Substance, we are already
specifying Existence as the Li. *But all realize the Way [i.e., Bodhi,
enlightenment] by perceiving Li.* If we were to say that Existence is Li,
it would mean that perceiving Existence [leads to] realization of the
Way. But in fact all the sages cut off their karmic entanglements
by perceiving Emptiness, so we know clearly that Emptiness is Li.[4]

The point here is eminently clear. Here as in Wang Bi, *ti* is already expected
to be in some sense synonymous with Li. *Ti* is paired with *yong,* and when
correlated with Existence and Emptiness, Existence is the real omnipresent
term, hence the *ti,* while Emptiness is one aspect of all existence that is
being picked out and focused upon in a particular context, and thus goes
in the *yong* position. Emptiness is simply one fact among many about every
Existence. But this is where the synonymity with Li and *shi* breaks down: Li
is specifically *ti as value.* If it were merely a matter of objective omnipresence, or ontological grounding, Existence would be a predicate as worthy of
the name Li as Emptiness; it is synonymous with Substance, and Existence
is Substance in the sense of what function depends upon, or what is given
concrete particular (partial) expression by function. This means simply that
wherever the function in question is found (in this case, Emptiness), it will
be associated with some traceably prior Existence. Existence is a universal term as much as Emptiness is; it is applicable everywhere, and is thus
equally qualified to be the omnipresent universal universal. But the term Li
indicates precisely the dimension of value and intelligibility: it is not just
what is universal, or universal within a given class or group, but what it is
worthwhile to notice about that class, or about all things. In the Buddhist
case, it is usually Emptiness that one must understand in order to be liberated, and *therefore* Emptiness is called Li.

It is important to understand, then, how this seemingly very abstract
usage of the term Li, which lends itself rather persuasively to translation as
something such as big P "Principle," or as "potential," still accords with the
definition of Li in the indigenous tradition as we have characterized it above.
We said that Li is a harmonious coherence that, if harmoniously cohered
with by a human being, leads to further harmonious coherence. Emptiness
is Li because it is a potential object of knowledge and practical realization.
It can be "accorded with" in one's cognitions and behaviors. When this is
done, one achieves liberation from the disharmony of samsâra, from suffering. So although it is true that Emptiness is the omnipresent "common
trait" shared by all existences, and in that sense the unifying category that
joins them, this is not what qualifies it to be called Li. The unification and

oneness of all things denoted by the term *Emptiness as Li* is rather a sort
of by-product. The point is the way in which a human being may himself
"cohere harmoniously" with all existences without exception (in this case,
apprehending them without attachment), merely by harmoniously cohering
with (knowing, realizing) this one particular, Emptiness, Li. Li becomes
the omnipresent universal universal, the abstract trait or category shared
by all things, here as in Guo Xiang, only secondarily. Nothing is implied
here about Emptiness as a kind of "night where all cows are black," the
undifferentiated oneness that is the real reality into which all other things
are reducible, in contrast to which all things are illusion, except in this
derivative, pragmatic sense.

That said, it is also true that the specific content of this particular Li,
Emptiness, is precisely nonduality, itself an effacement of apparent separateness, a kind of unity. This is the first level of coherence in our threefold
definition of Li: sticking together. For Emptiness means the absence of any
definitive self-nature for any entity, the unintelligibility of the borders that
separate it from what is other than it. It so happens that in Buddhism this
is regarded as what needs to be seen in order to achieve liberation. The
reasons for this, and the implications of "unity" in this more radical sense
in the Chinese Buddhist understanding of Li, must be clearly understood
before we continue. For in Tiantai and Huayan, we will see the deployment
of Li as implying first and foremost "nonobstruction" between differentiated
parts of existence, in a way that affirms both unity and differentiation; it is
here that it becomes feasible to simply cut straight to the chase and translate Li as something such as "Wholeness" or "Whole," as James Behuniak
has recently suggested: the wholeness of the whole which is whole at every
locus, manifesting as the wholeness of any possible individual being, which
exists thereby as an individual whole that is at once a part within the overall
whole.[5] To understand what kind of whole this is, and why this is important,
however, we must examine the basic Buddhist problematic of soteriology,
which here gives Li its meaning as liberating. For as we shall see, we have
here to do with a kind of wholeness that forms no total static whole with
definite characteristics, an *ironic* wholeness that does have the efficacy of
wholeness (the subsumption, transcending, and integration of the parts)
precisely by not being any determinate whole at all. But this will come in
at least two distinct types in the Tiantai and Huayan cases: the former will
present us with a vision of local coherence and global incoherence rooted
in the indigenous Chinese mereologies of whole and part, developing some
of the ironies and ironic-non-ironic relations derived therefrom, while the
latter will present something quite new in China, something perhaps closer
to the Indo-European roots of Buddhist thought: a two-tiered ontology not
of wholes and parts but of real (though ironic) conceptual universals (or

rather, one such universal: the universal universal, the indeterminate as such) straining to become a form of radical immanence by means of the uniquely ironic nature of its universal (not "whole"). We will see, however, that the Huayan project arguably never really breaks totally free of the kind of dichotomous transcendence encoded in its origins in two-tiered ontological thinking, as is most evident in the dichotomy it continues to maintain, in sharp contrast to Tiantai, between reality and appearance, a typical concomitant of two-tiered universal-particular as opposed to one-tiered whole-part thinking.

If we take Abidharma as an accurate representative of early Buddhist thinking, we can say that we have there one of the most radical assertions of "simple location" in the history of the world, and one that does not shrink from drawing the full consequences of this doctrine and denying any reality to universals or coherences or unities at all. The Abidharmic conception of the momentariness of dharmas, for example, stipulates that each moment of experience is genuinely separate from all others, that putative continuities in matter or mind are merely misperceived pluralities, such that not even a meager universal such as "this table" exists (in reality, there are a stream of similar but not identical experiences that are erroneously grouped together to form the conception of the stable table here), let alone some kind of Platonic Table as such. For "thing" is itself, in this sense, just another universal, as is "this." Each dharma disappears as soon as it appears, and these are the ultimate constituents of reality. Given this state of affairs, we might consider the emergence of Mahayana doctrines that could countenance either the universal universal (the omnipresent) or any other real coherence in the world with some wonderment. How did this come about? The story is indeed an amazing one.

To understand the way Chinese Buddhist use the term Li, which is intrinsically linked to what is valued, and why it is identified with omnipresent characteristics such as Emptiness, or with other forms of omnipresence, we first have to grasp what *value* is for the Buddhist tradition. Sentient beings experience both suffering and pleasure. These happen at different times. Simply stated, value in Buddhism always means something about ending the suffering of sentient beings. Early Buddhism, however, claims that all conditional things are suffering—not merely that they are marked by suffering, which would already be quite radical when predicated of *all* possible experiences, but that finite, conditional things, to the extent that they are finite and conditional, are ipso facto suffering itself: "When a dharma arises, it is only suffering that arises; when a dharma perishes, it is only suffering that perishes" (Samyutta-Nikâya III.134). Why is this claim made? It is the arising and perishing itself that is the suffering. Abidharmic literature expresses this with the doctrine of the three types of suffering, which together cover the whole range of temporal experience: (1) The suffering of suffering (dukkha-dukkha, 苦苦 kuku); (2) The suffering of decay (viparinama-dukkha, 壞苦 huaiku); (3) The suffering of conditionality per se (saṅkhāra-dukkha 行苦 xingku) The first is literal suffering. The second is all experiences that are not suffering: pleasure and neutral sensations. These are called suffering because, inasmuch as they are conditional and therefore impermanent, they will necessarily decay, and the decaying of nonsuffering is by definition to that extent the advent of suffering. The third is the global term for this state of alternation itself, the fact that pain and pleasure alternate, their intrinsic instability, inasmuch as suffering has just been shown to pervade the entire suffering-nonsuffering spectrum. Their instability signifies that they cannot be controlled, that they are something beyond the power of any will, and thus that they are imposed upon experience, they are literally suffered. Thus, suffering is merely a restatement of the other "marks of the Dharma" in early Buddhism: "impermanence" (anicca) and non-self (anatta). "Non-self" simply means that no single cause can account for the arising of any fact. If one could, that cause would ipso facto be a self, for self here signifies above all control. This possibility is excluded by the key theoretical insight of early Buddhism, "dependent co-arising" (pratītyasamutpāda). This signifies not merely that all events are causally conditioned, but that no single cause produces an effect on its own. Heterogeneous causes and conditions are required for the arising of an effect, a premise accepted in early Buddhism and given a more rigorous theoretical justification in Mahayana theory. So whatever arises cannot be in the control of any single cause, and thus will necessarily contravene, and thus cause suffering to, any single willed agenda, sooner or later.

Obviously, from the other side, since the point is that an absolutely continent separation between suffering and pleasure can never be enforced, that neither can be in control of the entire range of experience, we could equally say that pleasure pervades the entire field, and, in a way, this is just what the Mahayana will go on to do. But pleasure is not the problem. Suffering is. Hence, the focus is on suffering as a given fact, and value is defined as the ending of suffering. Conditionality per se is suffering. Hence, the definition of what alone is really valuable, in Buddhism, is unconditionality. This is called Nirvana, the ending of the conditional, of the impermanent, of suffering. In early Buddhism, it is conceived of as what is left over when the conditional is allowed to fade away, the negation and elimination of the conditional. As such, it is strictly indeterminable, for a determination is by definition conditional; indeed, determination is itself conditionality per se. Hence we get only apophatic characterizations of it in early texts: it is not greed, hatred, or delusion, it is not earth, air, fire, or wind, it is not this world or any other world, it is not this, not that.

However, there remains the problem that the unconditional is thus contrasted to the conditional, which it seems to exclude. Strictly speaking, this makes the unconditional itself conditional: it is conditioned by the absence of the "conditional." Mahayana philosophy can be seen in part as an attempt to reconsider this problem, taking the unconditioned as truly unconditional, and therefore in some manner copresent with or inclusive of the conditional. Nirvana is no longer the negation of samsâra: instead, the Mahayana sutras begin to assert that Nirvana and samsâra, form and Emptiness, sentient beings and Buddhas are nondual. In some sense or other, the unconditional is already present: as the Emptiness (lack of self-nature) that is the ultimate characteristic of all conditioned states, as Buddha-nature, which is already everywhere, as the preexistent Original Mind, or what have you. The unconditional is, hence, in any of these versions, truly omnipresent in all times, places, and states. For to be present in only some times, places, and states would mean to depend for its presence on the condition of "being in those times, places, and states," hence to be conditional. *Hence, value and omnipresence become synonymous.* Omnipresence is a kind of continuity between apparently separate things, a togetherness, a bringing together, a unification: a kind of coherence. It is also, as unconditioned and not limitable to any particular predicate as contrasted to that predicate's exclusion, beyond the reach of ordinary speech and perception: the unintelligible. Here we have all the ingredients of the traditional Chinese concepts of Li: value, the cohering of apparently diverse things (non-ironic cohering), unintelligibility (ironic coherence), that which the attention is to focus on for ultimate value to be attained (intelligibility). Of course, this presents new theoretical and practical difficulties, which the each of the Chinese Buddhist schools attempt to handle in their own distinctive ways.

Typically, however, even when this coextension of the conditioned and the unconditioned was aggressively asserted in Indian Buddhism, as in the works of Nāgārjuna, a different kind of distinction between them was made by means of the notion of "Two Truths." The question of what kinds of statements may count as *legitimate* is the only standard of truth in this Buddhism, and this is thoroughly determined by the overriding soteriological aims of the entire Buddhist tradition. Every statement and every practice are justified *solely* in terms of their utility for the goal of *diminishing suffering.* That means that both Buddhist epistemology and Buddhist ethics are thoroughgoingly pragmatic: what is *true* is what is conducive to ending suffering, and what is *good* is action that is conducive to ending suffering. In early Buddhism, we may conceive these along the lines delineated in the "parable of the raft": what helps one get across is good, is useful, is valid, is to be clung to for the duration of one's journey. What is on the other shore is neither true nor untrue, neither good nor bad; all such terms pertain only

to the intermediate realm of what is relevant for the goal of ending suffering—and, of course, this means mainly Buddhist doctrines and practices.
This is the realm where it is meaningful to speak of good and bad or true
and false, and in which one is pragmatically faced with a choice between
them. True is different from false, as clinging to the raft is different from
sinking. But this has nothing to do with contradiction; it has to do with
utility in the goal of ending suffering, which is accomplished by ending
attachment to desire and definitive views about reality.[6]

When this model develops in the hands of Nāgārjuna to the full-fledged
Two Truths model, we have the same structure expanded and articulated
with greater precision. Here too, "conduciveness to ending suffering" is the
sole criterion for "truth." But in Conventional Truth, Nāgārjuna includes
two things: ordinary speech (I, you, cause, effect, world, time, entities, etc.)
and specifically Buddhist doctrines (Four Noble Truths, no-self, nirvana,
suffering, dependent co-arising, etc.). The criterion for including both of
these under the heading of "truth" is exactly the same: *not* that they correspond to an external reality or can be consistently unpacked without
self-contradiction, but that speaking and acting in accordance with them
is conducive to the ending of suffering. Without ordinary language, it is
impossible to give instructions on how to end suffering, to point out the
problem of suffering, to point out the doctrines and practices of Buddhism,
even those that contradict them.

Then there is ultimate truth. Ultimate truth cannot be spoken or
conceptualized, but can only be experienced: it is the end of suffering itself,
liberation of mind, rather than any cognitive information about the world.
Liberation of mind is not allegiance to any picture of how the world is. In
fact, it is described only negatively, precisely as the lack of any identifiable predicates. The possibility of a definitive right view about reality, the
bare "being-so" of any state of affairs, falls with the belief in self-nature.
For "being-so" would have to be something that is warranted by the state
of affairs itself, acting as a single cause, and this is just what the denial of
self-nature, of a definite essence, denies. The state of affairs would be the
cause, the fact that the state of affairs is thus and so, is unambiguously one
way or another, would be the effect—a one to one causality that is definitely excluded by all Buddhist theory from the Abidharma on. "This cup
is red," means, "this cup alone is the cause of the redness attributed to the
cup." Essence is singlehanded causality. Emptiness of essence really means
simply *ontological ambiguity*: not the usual epistemological ambiguity, where
we assume that *in itself* each thing is simply what it is, but our perception of
it is vague or admits of multiple readings; rather, *ontological* ambiguity, where
any possible something is in and of itself incapable of simply being one way
or another to the exclusion of other ways, where to be is to be ambiguous.

Definitive views about reality—that any given thing simply *is* one way or another, is this or that, in isolation from a relation to other things—are shown to be incoherent, and actually meaningless. We are told not to "cling to" the view of Emptiness, that to regard Emptiness as a view describing how things really are is worse than self-views as vast as Mt. Sumeru (as the *Vimalakīrti Nirdeśa Sūtra* says). Those who cling to the view of Emptiness are declared incurable (*Mūlamadhyamakakārikā* 13:8). Emptiness is the ultimate truth, but "emptiness" is only the highest (i.e., most powerfully effective) conventional truth. Emptiness is itself not a description of any facts, and regarded as a description it is merely a conventional truth. Ultimate truth is neither "emptiness" nor "not-emptiness." These are, as they say, mere "concepts." But a concept of a certain type (a "true" one) is precisely what we normally call a *truth*: a proposition about what predicates *actually, unambiguously, in all contexts, from all perspectives*, apply to a particular entity: the essence or marks of that thing, which it alone, simply by being what it is, makes so. This is what "objective" means: that things are so *on their own*, without the participation of some *other*, some observer, some perspective. To regard the cup as red, or as empty, is clinging, is delusion. Redness is something that emerges momentarily through the cooperation of the cup and my cognitive apparatus. Emptiness, as a concept, is also something that emerges momentarily through the cooperation of the world and my cognitive apparatus. To regard reality as contradictory, or non-contradictory, is delusion. Clinging to emptiness, *attachment* to emptiness means no more and no less than *regarding emptiness as objectively true*. "Clinging" and "regarding something to be objectively [i.e., more than pragmatically] true" are synonyms. There is of course an obvious self-contradiction *here*, the usual relativism paradox: Is it *true* that there is no truth? The answer is: it is true only in the way in which truth is defined in Buddhism: saying so is conducive for the liberation from suffering of living beings.

But here we have the older conditioned/unconditioned problem reconstituted in a new way: the divide between apophatic real truth and all possible determinations is now absolute. That real truth still has to be unconditional to be the end of suffering, and thus really should somehow pervade all conditional determinations. Although Nāgārjuna will say that the extent of Nirvana (the unconditional, the end of suffering) and the extent of samsâra (the conditional, suffering) are identical, this is interpreted in Indo-Tibetan Buddhism in terms of the Two Truths: the *referent* of the two is the same, the entire realm of experience, but they say absolutely different things about that same referent. Unconditional Truth says nothing about it, while all possible determinations about it are relegated to either falsehood or Conventional Truth. We have the same problem in a new, more elaborate form. It is this problem that Tiantai sets out to solve.

TIANTAI ON TRUTH, THREEFOLD

We will begin with the usage of Li in early Tiantai, primarily in the works of the de facto founder of the school, Zhiyi 知顗 (538–597), since these develop earlier in time than the Huayan usages, although the latter are, as we shall, considerably more straightforward and easier to grasp. My account of Tiantai will mainly draw from the works of its three key figures, as it has traditionally defined itself, namely, Zhiyi, Jingxi Zhanran 荊溪湛然 (711–782), and Siming Zhili 四明知禮 (960–1028). Tiantai thinking begins, we may say, by adapting the above Nagurjunian ideas about Emptiness, and their translation into the terminology of Li by Zhu Daosheng, Jizang, and others, to ideas about the relation between provisional and ultimate truth as suggested by the *Lotus Sutra* (*Saddharmapuṇḍarīkasūtra*, 妙法蓮華經). This text appears to be the product of some sectarian infighting, between a still relatively new Mahayana movement and the "Śrāvakas" or disciples of the "Hinayana" (a pejorative Mahayana term meaning "Small Vehicle"), aggressively selling the idea that, contrary to the "Hinayana" claim, the goal of Buddhist practice is not the extinction of individual existence and suffering in Nirvana, thereby becoming an Arhat, but rather to be a Bodhisattva, to practice the Mahayana ideal of the Bodhisattva path, to work toward eventually becoming a Buddha, which means to be endlessly engaged in the project of knowing, interacting with, relating to, guiding, educating, and liberating all sorts of sentient beings, coming up with lots of different ways of edifying them in accordance with their particular dispositions and desires. But the polemic takes an odd turn in that the claim is not that the Śrāvakas are just plain wrong, but rather that they themselves, *precisely in denying the goal of Bodhisattvahood,* are in fact practicing the Bodhisattva path, are on their way to becoming Buddhas, are in fact already educating, transforming, setting an example for sentient beings, and at the same time working their way step by step toward Buddhahood, without knowing it. This disjunction between "what you are really accomplishing" and "the goal you have in mind in order to make that accomplishment possible" is the distinctive contribution of the *Lotus Sutra,* a motif that may remind us of Guo Xiang's disjunction between goal-oriented Knowing and Li. The sutra proceeds to suggest, in effect, that all beings are Bodhisattvas, that being and Bodhisattvahood are in a way convertible terms, and, further, that there is really no difference between a Buddha—the end of the process of the Bodhisattva path—and a Bodhisattva—the means; the Buddha himself is eternally a Bodhisattva, being born, taking on various forms, educating beings, striving to find the truth, becoming enlightened and dying over and over again. This is significant because of the collapsing of the ends-means relation implied, made possible by the content of Bodhisattvahood (and thus, here, also Buddhahood): it means (1) to assume an infinity of forms, in accordance with the needs of *other* sentient beings, in order to (2) liberate and enlighten them so that they may do the same, thereby (3) educating oneself and moving toward Buddhahood. If all of these are going on at the same time, it means that both participants in any relation are simultaneously in the role of the deluded sentient being and of the enlightening Bodhisattva, taking on this deluded form *without knowing it,* as the *Lotus* says is possible, to enlighten in all directions, both self and others. The possibilities opened up here for reconceiving the relation between affirmation and negation, self and others, and oneness and manyness, are to be noted. This is also where a new solution to Guo Xiang's problem is offered. Guo attempted to reunite Li and goal-oriented knowing by reducing both to Li, the non-deliberate self-so, at their ultimate level. The *Lotus,* on the other hand, reunites them by asserting that deliberate goal-oriented activity, while it is always ipso facto alienated from the truth, is also actually realizing the truth by means of that very alienation. The Śrāvakas affirm, embody, practice Bodhisattvahood, not in spite of denying it, but *by* denying it, neglecting it, knowing nothing about it, or even actively rejecting it. That *is* (a part of) their Bodhisattva practice. They are Bodhisattvas in the form of the antithesis or rejection of Bodhisattvas. They are Bodhisattvas *as* non-Bodhisattvas. This is precisely how they are going about doing the three things listed above which constitute the work of a Bodhisattva: taking on various forms (in this case, as a Śrāvaka), enlightening other beings, and working toward Buddhahood.

Tiantai takes the clue from this sutra, filters it through the category of Emptiness developed by Nāgārjuna, and arrives at what it calls the Three Truths: Emptiness, Provisional Positing, and The Center (空諦 *kongdi,* 假諦 *jiadi,* 中諦 *zhongdi*). It is important to note that the textual tradition from which Tiantai derives its understanding of Nāgārjuna's thought differs decisively from the Indian and Tibetan traditions due primarily to the existence in Chinese of the 大智度論 *Dazhidulun,* a text attributed to Nāgārjuna (although most likely written in Chinese by its ostensible translator, Kumārajīva), which was regarded as offering the most extensive and authoritative interpretive lens through which to interpret Nāgārjuna's treatment of topics treated more cursorily in the *Mūlamadhyamakakārikā.* Of particular interest for us is the relation between the Two Truths, which bears directly on how we are to interpret key *Mūlamadhyamakakārikā* texts such as 23:6, stating that both self and non-self are preached by the Buddha. Read without the context of the *Dazhidulun,* this claim was usually understood in Indo-Tibetan Buddhism to mean that "self" is taught in Conventional Truth and "non-self" in Ultimate Truth, and these remain unambiguously separate and hierarchically valued. The *Dazhidulun* approaches these issues rather differently. Most simply stated, it sets the stage for the collapse of Conventional Truths into the rubric of *upāya*, "skillful means," the freely created and extremely various methods used by a Bodhisattva to instruct all the many diverse varieties of sentient beings. This collapse of *upāya* and Conventional Truth is one of the key moves of the Tiantai tradition. One of the key procedures by which this is done is found in the *Dazhidulun's* doctrine of the Four Siddhantas.[7] We should note here that the second and third Siddhantas already take the step of completely relativizing Conventional Truths: there is no single univocal internally consistent set of Conventional Truths spoken by the Buddha, but rather an unlimited array of situational possibilities that may count as "appropriate speech," that is, soteriologically useful, liberative speech. If someone believes the world is made of bleu cheese or was created by God, the Buddha may preach to him in those terms, accepting the premise of a bleu-cheese-composed or God-created world, according to the Second Siddhanta, or in a polemically anti-bleu-cheese or anti-God way according to the Third. The authorized conventional truths preached by a Buddha may thus contradict one another; the contradiction is not only between Conventional Truth and Ultimate Truth, but necessarily exists among Conventional Truths—i.e., in this conception, *upāyas*—themselves. The second thing to note here is that the Fourth Siddhanta is still a Siddhanta, that is, is included unproblematically among the rhetorical strategies of a Buddha's preaching: "Ultimate Truth," including the preaching of Emptiness and so on, is also a pragmatic soteriological device. The upshot of this approach to the Two Truths is well expressed in the second chapter of the "Sutra of Infinite Meanings" (無量 義經 *wuliangyijing*) another Chinese forgery unknown in India or Tibet, but often quoted by Zhiyi and traditionally read as the "opening sutra" for the *Lotus Sutra* in many Tiantai and Tendai inspired traditions:

> The dispositions and desires of various sentient beings are innumerable, and thus the modes of preaching of the Dharma are also innumerable. Because the modes of preaching of the Dharma are innumerable, its meanings are also innumerable. These innumerable meanings are generated by a single dharma. That dharma is simply freedom from [any single fixed] attribute. Such freedom from fixed attribute enables every attribute without exception to be attributed [i.e., manifests as every manifestation]. Being predicable neither by attributes nor by the exclusion of attributes [i.e., neither manifesting nor not-manifesting], this is called the Real-Attribute.[8]

The result here is that there is not only one type of Conventional Truth, nor merely several progressively transcending sets of Conventional Truth, but literally *infinite* numbers of potentially mutually contradictory Conventional Truths. But something more has happened here, which is very relevant to our problems of oneness and difference. For these infinite contradictory Conventional Truths are at the same time described as being merely different aspects of a single truth, seen in different ways. Any single dharma has all these infinite contrasting meanings: these alternate meanings are meanings *of the same thing*. The sutra later states this emphatically in the paradigmatic case of words and meanings: "The words used are identical, but the meanings differ [in the ears of different listeners]" (文辭是一, 而義差異 *wenci shi yi, er yi chayi*).[9] Any one word means many contrary things. One must note also that there are only meanings in contexts—specifically, in *intersubjective contexts*. There are only truths where there are meanings, and there are only meanings where there are sentient beings. Since sentient beings differ in innumerable ways, meanings and truths will also differ in innumerable ways. But all these meanings are the meaning of attributelessness, the Emptiness of any essential attributes belonging to any entity—all these meanings are what "attributeless" *really* means—for that is the only kind of meaning there is, the only kind of meaning that means anything. Put otherwise, the essence of any thing is to be essenceless—which means also to have infinite contradictory essences.[10] Any determination is one particular thing, no particular thing, and infinitely many things, all possible things. This provides us with a good template for the Tiantai Three Truths: provisionally posited, empty, and the Center (空 *kong*, 假 *jia*, 中 *zhong*).

To understand this, we must see how this *Lotus Sutra* angle on truth changes things decisively, and in ways that are quite relevant to our current discussion. Simply stated, if we assume this Nāgārjunian model of truth, the distinction between the *three* categories of Nāgārjuna's Two Truth system fall apart (not to be confused with the Tiantai Three Truths). Again, those three are: (1) *just plain false* statements, such as the metaphysical and religious theories of non-Buddhists, absolutist claims of science, etc.—all theory, in short; (2) untheorized commonsensical everyday language, which says I and you and cause and effect but without claiming a theory or systematic objective worldview to unpack them consistently, fuzzy around the edges; and (3) Buddhist rhetoric. The criterion of truth, recall, was "what is conducive to liberation from suffering"—which means, what will, if given full play, contradict and cancel itself, serving as a vehicle by which to pass beyond itself, like a raft. So 2 and 3 are both truths (Conventional Truth), while 1 is just false. Ultimate Truth, on the other hand, *is* the end of suffering, and thus also given, honorifically as it were, the name of truth, though it has no determinate propositional content. So it stands for Nāgārjuna.

In Tiantai, however, this same criterion is now applied across the boards. Category 1 also *can* serve as a "raft"—and in fact, all purported

metaphysical systems, while claiming to arrive at a consistent, non-self-con-
tradictory complete objective view of the universe, can *all* be shown to fail
in their own terms: they can be shown to contradict themselves when taken
absolutely seriously and when their key theoretical terms are absolutized.
Tiantai theory uses the Nāgārjunian method to perform these reductio ad
adsurdums on all existing theories. But these are not to show that they are
false; this is precisely what shows that they are *true*. For "true," as we've
seen, means simply, "capable of leading beyond itself, capable of destroying
itself, conducive to the move beyond all clinging to fixed views, conducive
to ending suffering." When a metaphysical view is shown to involve contradictions, it is shown to be a conventional truth rather than a mere falsehood:
it serves as a raft to the abandoning of views. Furthermore, categories 2 and
3 are also not *always* effective as rafts. There are infinite sentient beings
with infinite differing needs, and in some circumstances one view will work
(i.e., will bring about both its own cancellation and the elimination of all
other views) while in other circumstances others will work. Even "ordinary
speech" and "Emptiness" are not *always* true (for true means only "conducive
to . . ."). All three categories *can* serve as rafts leading beyond themselves,
while none of them *always* does so. So the Buddha preaches self and non-self,
not because one is conventional and the other is ultimate truth: *both* are
conventional truths, meaning both can, in given circumstances, lead to the
dropping of both views. Neither is intrinsically more true than the other
(for to be "intrinsically" anything would be to have a self-nature). Hence,
we have the other enormous change in Tiantai: ultimate truth is no longer
"beyond" conventional truth, no longer a "higher" truth. They are equal,
and in fact the very idea of "ultimate truth" is itself a conventional truth.
However, they are not only equal. The most radical Tiantai move is that
conventional and ultimate truth are *identical*. They have *exactly the same content*. Whatever is conventional truth is also ultimate truth, and vice versa.

This point is illustrated nicely in the Tiantai interpretation of the
story of the lost son from the *Lotus Sutra* (Chapter 4).[11] The key point
to note here, in the context of our present discussion, is, as Zhiyi points
out, that the status of the "skillful means" is configured here very differently than it is in the Two Truths schema of Emptiness theory, the "raft"
model, where the means are transcended and discarded once the goal is
reached. The resources of the estate are what the father uses as a skillful
means to draw his son to the final recognition of his own status, to his final
enlightenment—the servants, the buildings, the treasury. But these are not
abandoned when the son finally does come into his inheritance. On the
contrary, these *are* the inheritance. This means that what one is enlightened
to when one is enlightened is not the dropping away of all skillful means,
the letting go of the raft, the transcendence of all determinate phenomenal

concepts, ideas, practices, forms. Rather, these things are the very content of enlightenment. Enlightenment is not the renunciation of skillful means. Enlightenment is the *mastery* of all skillful means, the integration of skillful means, the more thorough possession of them rather than the discarding or elimination of them. Conventional Truth is not what you renounce when you reach Ultimate Truth, as in the parable of the raft and the Two Truths theory. The Other Shore to which the raft rafts us, allowing us to renounce the raft, turns out to be another raft, which rafts us to an infinity of other rafts—and we ourselves, who are rafting on these rafts, are like all other entities only raft-rafting rafts. Conventional Truth is what you *get* when you reach Ultimate Truth. The content of the two is the same. Ultimate Truth is simply a name for the totality of conventional truths, and the virtuosic mastery of being able to move from one conventional truth to another unobstructedly, as the situation demands, the comprehension of the way they fit together or can function together, or the way in which they are each, as it were, "versions" of each other. Ultimate truth is the nonobstruction between conventional truths, the fact that they all inter-penetrate, that in their non-absoluteness each is simply a different way of saying what the others say. Ultimate truth is the free flow of conventional truths, their copresence in spite of their apparent oppositeness (e.g., you are a poor worker, you are a rich son).

But the Tiantai view is not only that are they identical in content: it turns out, further, that once the very idea of conventionality—"provisional positing"—is unpacked, it reveals itself to *mean* nothing more or less than what the very idea of ultimate truth—"Emptiness" of any intrinsic attri-butes, indeterminacy—means. What they both mean, unpacked, is the Center, the very convertibility between provisional positing and emptiness, between determinacy and indeterminacy, such that by adducing any one of these three, all three are implied. It is only this that enables the free convertibility between any one conventional truth and any other. Whatever determination can be adduced is nothing more than a conventional truth (= is valid, leading to the reduction of attachments, in some but not all contexts), but therefore is also empty (not valid in all contexts, not solely and context-independently able to maintain its characteristic effects) and is also neither-provisional-nor-empty, something that can be read either in its affirmative aspect ("*valid* in some contexts") and its negative aspect ("*not valid* in some contexts"), which both mean the same thing ("valid in *some* contexts"). But this "Centrality" also implies something more profound, which stands as the solution to the paradox of Nirvana and omnipres-ence in earlier Buddhism: for "Center" here also means "absolute," uncon-ditional as conditional, conditional as unconditional. We will have much to say about the implications of the Tiantai Three Truths and their precise content below; but put simply, we have here a formulaic crystallization of the affirmation/negation relation described above in the *Lotus,* where to be something (first and foremost, a Bodhisattva) and not to be that thing (to be a Śrāvaka and avoid being a Bodhisattva), and of their reversible "asness" (being a Bodhisattva as a Śrāvaka and being a Śrāvaka as a Bodhisattva). This "asness" of the two extremes, each being expressible as the other, is what is here called the Center (中 *zhong*). We must pause here to note the resonance of this notion of Centrality with the "empty hub" in the *Laozi,* and various notions of ironic coherence we have seen emerging from it, including Wang Bi's mini-Daos as *ti* and Li, and Guo Xiang's incommensurable-singularity-which-is-nothing-determinate-but-all-things-converging as the Li of the self-so.

Where Nāgārjuna had Two Truths, with a clear hierarchy between them, based on a one-way means-end relation—conventional truth is subordinate to ultimate truth, deriving its value solely therefrom, by being a means thereto, which is to be dispensed with once the end is attained—which allowed a third category (plain heretical untruth), Tiantai claims the Two Truths are exactly equivalent in value, equally ultimate, identical in content, and ultimately synonymous, and that this constitutes the third truth about them. In fact, they are not two separate realms or claims at all, but two alternate restatements of the same fact, namely, conditioned co-arising itself. "Provisional Positing" implies "Emptiness," and vice versa, just as "equilateral triangle" and "equiangular triangle" are merely different ways of describing the same fact, emphasizing now one and now another aspect.

This means the differentiations between things, their conventional designations, *as well as any crazy philosophical or religious theory or personal illusion about them,* are just as ultimately true and non-true as their Emptiness or their beyond-conceptualization Suchness, and also that both of these aspects are just as ultimate as the fact that these two aspects are simply aspects of one another. This is the interfusion of the Three Truths, which means even the Center is not more ultimate than the other two. To indicate any of the three is to indicate all three; they are three ways of saying the same thing. Hence, Tiantai goes beyond what it calls the "Exclusive Center" (但中 *danzhong*), which sees the Center as a sort of *tertium quid* beyond the two extremes of Emptiness and Provisional Positing, which grounds them both and expresses itself as both, to the point of the "Non-exclusive Center" (不但中 *budanzhong*), which makes it possible to say that any of the three, taken alone, already says all there is to say about the other two, and entails all the functions of the other two. The Center is the convertibility of the truths of Emptiness and Provisional Positing, their mutual reducibility, which also maintains their distinction, as we shall see below.

Each of the Three Truths is a way of talking about the fact that all determinate entities are dependently co-arisen (緣起 *yuanqi*). That is, each determination necessarily appears in experience "together with" other such determinations, upon which it depends for its existence. This observation is developed into the assertion of the Emptiness, Provisional Positing, and Centrality of each entity. Provisional Positing means they are dependently co-arisen, necessarily arise together with othernesses, that is, with something that is qualitatively different, with an alternate determinateness. The othernesses that necessarily arise with a particular determinacy are either (1) its components (which are qualitatively other); (2) its antecedents in time or efficient causes; or (3) its conceptual or perceptual concepts, the background of "not-this" which makes any "this" experienceable as such. Its coherence is dependent on these other coherences as conditions, but if all other coherences whatsoever are taken into account, as they would have to be if this same consideration were now applied to these other coherences (they have their own necessary othernesses), the original coherence is effaced; it is coherent as such only locally, in relation to a limited set of such conditions. Their Emptiness means that such arising therefore is never derived from an essence as single cause: one fact is never enough to make it so. Therefore, its being thus-and-so is always variable according to what other entities contribute: it is context-dependent. This means it is never the arising of an unambiguous particular entity with a uniquely decidable nature. That is, every putatively determinate "this" arises together with its "not-this," but the interface separating and joining these two discrete entities cannot be construed coherently in any unambiguous terms, or as a particular self-determining existent. To be determinate, full stop, requires being self-determining, and this is impossible.

We may restate this by noting that all coherences are only *locally coherent*. It is what it is only because the horizon of relevant contexts has been arbitrarily limited, but the fact that all being is necessarily contextualized (arises with qualitative othernesses) means that any such limit is ultimately arbitrary, and there are more relevant contexts that can be brought to bear in every case. Hence, each coherence is intelligible as such and such only when all the relevant contexts are not taken into account. Any entity's being determinately thus and so is dependent on its being experienced within a limited horizon of relevance. It is coherent as this rather than something else only *locally*. Provisional Positing means that all coherences are merely *local coherences*.

Emptiness, on this interpretation, means that all local coherences are *globally incoherent*, and indeed that local coherence as such just is global incoherence. What is determinate when viewed in some particular local context turns out to be ambiguous, indeterminate, lacking any definitive self-nature, when all relevant contexts are taken into account: it is onto-logically ambiguous, not merely epistemologically ambiguous. As a simplistic example, we may consider the way the figure "O" may be read as the letter "oh" when seen in the local context of a string of letters, or as the number zero when seen in the context of a string of numbers, but if both contexts are taken into account simultaneously, the figure no longer has any single identity. Locally, it is coherent, but globally, it is incoherent, it has no single consistent identity. For its identity is entirely dependent on context, and at every moment it is in more multiple contradictory contexts.

To put this point another way, let us say that to "be" originally means to be definitively, to be determinate, to be finite, to have simple loca-tion—to have borders or boundaries. To appear in experience at all, X must be "non-all," must be contrasted to some non-X, must have an "outside." Otherwise, it cannot be experienced or felt, it cannot be experienced in any form or on any level (even "abstractly"). To be present is to be determinately, which is to "be-with" an outside. But to *necessarily* have an outside means the outside is not really outside. The relation between the internal and the external is itself internal. We can always ask of the border, Is it part of the inside or the outside? Does the outside come to an end before making contact with the inside or not? If there is a gap, what is the relationship between them? Does this "relationship" exist or not? If it exists, it must be a determinate something with borders of its own, separating it from what is other than it. This means there must be another border between the relationship and the things of which it is the relationship. But then we have the same problem over again, an infinite regress, and the necessary relationship is lacking. If there is no gap between the boundary and the bounded, what makes this the boundary rather than the bounded? Does one end before the other begins? Is there another border between the boundary and the bounded? There is no coherent way to answer these questions, if "to exist" is assumed to mean "to be located in some specifiable time and place, within some specifiable limits."[12] Hence, the interface always proves unintelligible, and the outside proves both ineradicable and paradoxically impossible, since it always proves to really be equally internal, and hence not an outside at all. Therefore, the determination of the inside, the X, is equally ineradicable and impossible. Since it is only its borders that make this X what it is, that provide its determinate coherence, the unintelligibility of these boundaries is tantamount to the (global) incoherence of this (local) coherence. It cannot have any one particular fixed identity or coherence. It is ontologically ambiguous.

"The Center" signifies that these two are merely alternate statements of the same fact, which necessarily appears in these two contrasted ways.

We may rename it the intersubsumption of coherence and incoherence, or of determinateness and indeterminateness, entailing their necessary mutual reducibility. It is the "center" between these two extremes, coherence and incoherence. The Center signifies that determinateness, thought through to the end, turns out to be ambiguity, and vice versa. This means ambiguity and determinateness are no longer "other" to one another, and hence each is itself, just as it is, "absolute," that is to say, free of dependence on a relationship to an outside. Where this determination ends is its negation; but if there is no way to distinguish the determination from its negation, the determination is as present where it is supposedly present as where it is supposedly absent: it is omnipresent, unconditional, absolute. Therefore "determinateness" is a synonym for "ambiguity," and either, further, is a synonym for "the Center" itself. Any of these always signifies all three aspects: determinateness, ambiguity, and absoluteness. If anything is determinate, it is therefore also ambiguous and absolute, and, moreover, its determinateness *is* its ambiguity and its absoluteness, and vice versa.

It is from the idea of the Center that the Tiantai tradition derives the key ideas of interpervasion (互遍 *hupian*), interinclusion (互攝 *hushe*), mutual entailment (互具 *huju*), the claim that all things are everywhere at once, that every possible determination pervades all times and places, is copresent in and as every other, and vice verse. The motivation for this move must be understood: every entity must be omnipresent because only then can it be genuinely *unconditional*. Unconditionality is value in Buddhism, as we have seen. The Tiantai Center signifies this absoluteness, this unconditionality, this value. It is this idea of the simultaneous omnipresence of all possible entities that overcomes the Abidharmic notion of the simple location and absolute separateness of moments of experience (rather than the idea of universals or forms, which can be in more than one place at a time, which is used to compensate for atomism in Greek and subsequent occidental thought), and with it solves the "paradox of Nirvana" in early Buddhism and the isomorphic "paradox of the mutual exclusivity of the Two Truths" of later Indo-Tibetan Buddhism. It is this key idea that will be the focus of further developments and modifications by Huayan Buddhists, as we shall see presently.

The Tiantai notion of "Center" signifies not only the center transcending and encompassing the two extremes of coherence and incoherence (determinateness and indeterminateness), and their intersubsumption; it also signifies that each coherence is the "center" of the entire array of other coherences, the intersubsumption between any two local coherences. For if to be definitively X and not-to-be definitively X are merely alternate ways of stating the same fact about X, the contrast between the absence and presence of X is annulled, and X is no more present "here and now" than it is present "there and then." It is "simply located" at neither locus, but "virtually located" at both. It pervades all possible times and places to exactly the extent that it is present here at all. It can be read into any experience, and is here and now only because it has been so read into the here and now. X, in other words, is eternal and omnipresent, but only as "canceled," divested of the putative opacity of its simple location. It is necessary and universal, precisely because it is not empirically discoverable or unambiguously "present" at all, like "space." Hence, coherence X and coherence Y are both equally present at any locus. Each is the center of all existence, which can be read as any and all coherences, all of which are reducible to this coherence, revealed as aspects of it, expressing it, *as* which it is appearing.

The Tiantai tradition speaks of the interpervasion not just of "all things," but specifically of "the Three Thousand," a number derived from the multiplication of certain traditional Buddhist scriptural categories: the ten realms, each of which possesses these same ten realms again, multiplied by the ten suchnesses, multiplied again by the three worlds. The "Three Thousand" means all possible determinacies, with all their specific differences, divided according to various levels of greed, anger and delusion, suffering and pleasure, transcendence, compassion and comprehension, and also the copresence of all these specific different determinacies in one another, as experienced from all possible perspectives. Specifically, Zhiyi pulls ten "realms" or conditioned states of sentient beings from the scriptures: purgatory, hungry ghosts, animals, Asuras (belligerent egotistical titans), humans, gods, ascetic Buddhist disciples of the Śrāvaka vehicle who attain transcendence of life and death through renunciation, independent cultivators who attain transcendence of life and death through contemplation of conditionality, Bodhisattvas who reenter life and death out of altruistic compassion, and Buddhas, who are beings who are aware that their wisdom, liberation, eternity, freedom, bliss, and beauty transcend the categories of finitude that define them, and hence pervade all times and places and express themselves in the other nine realms. These ten are multiplied by the ten "Suchnesses" from the *Lotus Sutra*: Such appearances, Such natures, Such substances, Such powers, Such activities, Such causes, Such conditions, Such effects, Such responses, and Such equality from beginning to end. We now have one hundred types of determinacy. These are further multiplied by three: each of these in terms of components of the sentient being in question, in terms of the illusory sentient being himself, and in terms of his specific environment. Note that already each sentient being has been counted *twice*, as a whole and as its constituent parts. We are counting not a flat array of simply located objects, not the actual substances that make up the world, but all ways of experiencing multiperspectival reality. We now have three hundred types of determinacies. But now we go on to multiply *again* by the ten realms of sentient beings. This is because each realm inherently entails the other nine. So we have hell as hell, hell as animal, hell as hungry ghost, and so on, up to hell as Buddha. Similarly, we have Buddha as hell, Buddha as hungry ghost, and so on, up to Buddha as Buddha. Hence, the finite number three thousand is meant to indicate not only a simply flat array of particulars, but also the necessary interpervasion of these particulars. The use of this term, the Three Thousand, emphasizes the specificity of the actual existents in the world, the ineradicability of all the various subjective aspects of these existents—purgatories are as real and as interpervasive as the Buddha-realms, a point that will be of some importance below in contrasting this view to the Huayan understanding of interpenetration.

This term also brings with it also the "traditionalism" of the non-ironic tradition—i.e., these are the ten realms and ten suchnesses that are pointed out by the Buddha in the scriptures as being particularly relevant for human practice. We might think here of the way the authority of the ancient sages worked in the *Zhouyi* tradition to narrow down which set of interpretative rules were applicable in any given case. We may also note the continued importance of the factoring in of human desire here; as in the earlier tradition, what is truly "coherent" is not merely what is objectively there, but what forms a coherence harmonious with human need, desire, and praxis. Zhiyi states that this Three Thousand could equally be called any number—three billion, three trillion, infinity, zero—but this particular number is used in accordance with what is beneficial to sentient beings trying to achieve liberation, in accordance with the wise guidance provided in the scriptures by the Buddhas.

The ends-means loop, and the peculiar epistemology involved, where "provisional" and "ultimate" truth end up being identical, so that the provisional is never simply dispensed with, but instead is "made ultimate," (i.e., themselves absolute and unconditional) is handled in a distinctive way in Tiantai exegesis. Crucially, this means that "identity" here also always involves a moment of difference: we have a oneness which is also a difference, a difference which is also a oneness. The two "aspects" are after all first distinguished, and only then, and only *because of* this distinguishing, can they be identified, just as the Śrāvakas are only identical to Bodhisattvas by means of their denial of it, their separation from it. This is a peculiar type of "sameness," and we cannot understand in what sense this sameness implies "all possible entities converge into and are findable in" the Mean, the second of the new ideas in Tiantai Three Truths theory, unless we understand in just what sense these two are "the same." This peculiar mode of sameness is explained in the Tiantai doctrine of "opening the provisional to reveal the real" (開權顯實 *kaiquan xianshi*). This is a way of further specifying the relation between local coherence and global incoherence, illustrating the way in which they are not only synonymous, but also irrevocably opposed, and indeed identical only by means of their opposition. Provisional truth is the antecedent, the premise, and indeed in a distinctive sense the *cause* of ultimate truth, but only because it is the strict exclusion of ultimate truth. This effect is itself none other than the cause recontextualized. The Center is Ultimate Truth is Provisional Truth recontextualized: unchanged but simultaneously radically different.

The Tiantai exegetical technique is a process of bringing this out for any given content. "Opening the provisional to reveal the ultimate" (開權 顯實 *kaiquanxianshi*) consists of a recontextualization of provisional propositions to reveal their further implications, which allow them to *always already have been* saying the ultimate truth, without having to be changed in the least. The *Lotus Sutra* tells us precisely this kind of story again and again. We have children who think they are running toward promised toys, but when more of the situation is revealed, these very steps toward the toys, which don't really exist, turn out to have been steps out of the danger of a fire and toward a much more magnificent reward (Chapter 3). We have, as mentioned, a worker whose toil for minimum wage turns out to be, when the full context is revealed, actually a process of preparing himself to accept his status as son and heir to the household, who was already in possession of the treasury from which his meager salary was doled out (Chapter 4). We have travelers whose steps toward an illusory city are revealed to have been steps toward a treasure beyond it (Chapter 7). We have of course the Śrāvakas whose practice of "Hinayana" Buddhism is revealed to be part of a larger Mahayana Bodhisattva practice (Chapter 2). All activities are to be regarded as recontextualizable to reveal that they have always been Bodhisattva practices both expressing and leading to Buddhahood; hence, a Bodhisattva says to the Śrāvakas who scoff at his prediction that they will become Buddhas, "I do not disparage you, since you are thereby practicing the Bodhisattva path, and will all become Buddhas" (Chapter 20). That is, their very practices, even the rejection of Bodhisattva, can be recontextualized *by this very claim* to be revealed to be Bodhisattvahood. In Tiantai exegesis, we find a method that corresponds to this feature of the sutra, which is first to make intricate divisions and contrasts, establishing various qualities and characteristics of things by means of their differentiations, and then "opening them up" to reveal their identity in and by means of this very division. They are identical only because of, and as, their very difference.

The clearest way to explain this structure is to compare it to the contrasting relation between the setup and the punch line of a joke. To use a suitably silly example:

Setup: It takes money to make money.

Punch line: Because you have to copy it really exactly.

Let's talk about that structure. When I said, "it takes money to make money," it seemed as if, and it was interpreted as, a serious remark, a real piece of information, perhaps about investment strategies or the like. It had the quality of seriousness, of factuality, of non-ironic information. It does not strike anyone as funny; there is nothing funny about that statement. But, when the punch line comes, retrospectively, that setup is funny. That setup is funny because it has been recontextualized by the pun on the word *make*, which is made to have more than one identity when put into a new context.

The interesting thing here, most closely relevant to relation of identity between Conventional and Ultimate in the Tiantai Three Truths, is that it is precisely by *not* being funny that the setup was funny. In other words, if it were already funny, if you didn't take it seriously for at least a moment, the contrast between the two different meanings of this thing could never have clashed in the way that is necessary to make the laughter, to create the actual effect of humorousness. We have a setup which is serious and a punch line which is funny, but when you look back at the setup from the vantage point of having heard the punch line, *that setup is also funny*. After all, we don't say that just the punch line is funny. We say the whole joke is funny. The setup is funny, however, in the very strange mode of "not being funny yet." It is only funny because it wasn't funny. This is the sense in which the Third Truth, the Mean, reveals the "identity" between Provisional Positing and Emptiness. Provisional Positing *is* Emptiness only inasmuch as it is the very opposite of Emptiness, the temporary exclusion of Emptiness. It is by being Non-Empty (i.e., something in particular) that it is Emptiness (i.e., devoid of any unambiguous or unconditionally self-determining self-nature). It is only because it is Locally Coherent that it is Globally Incoherent. Its Global Incoherence is present *as* Local Coherence, just as Humor is present in the deadpan setup *as* seriousness. This same form of "identity"—really neither identity nor difference, or both identity and difference—then applies at the metalevel between the Mean itself and the other Two Truths: they "are" the Mean precisely because they are not the Mean, because they are the two opposed extremes.

The same structure is applied in the Tiantai reading of the *Lotus Sutra*. You're Enlightened! That is what Mahayana Buddhism keeps saying in one form or another: everyone is Enlightened! Everybody is a Buddha! Samsara is already Nirvana! All Dharmas are Nirvanic! But the way in which you are a Buddha is the way in which the setup of a joke is funny: you are a

Buddha precisely by *not* being a Buddha. By struggling toward buddhahood, toward something *else*, toward something you are *not*, but by revisualizing or recontextualizing or expanding awareness, which has been the preferred technique in Buddhism all along, those very things that are the details of daily life, of the struggles to interact, to deal with conditions and suffering and lack of control are not just a means to buddhahood. They are themselves buddhahood qua the life of a sentient being, expressing itself in the form of the life of a sentient being, as the funniness of a joke is expressed in, present in, the serious unfunniness of its setup.

The "provisional," conventional truth, local coherence, is the setup. The "ultimate truth," Emptiness, global incoherence, ontological ambiguity, is the punch line. What is important here is to preserve *both* the contrast between the two *and* their ultimate identity in sharing the quality of humorousness that belongs to every atom of the joke considered as a whole, once the punch line has been revealed. The setup is serious, while the punch line is funny. The funniness of the punch line depends on the seriousness of the setup, and on the contrast and difference between the two. However, once the punch line has occurred, it is also the case that the setup is, retrospectively, funny. This also means that the original contrast between the two is both preserved and annulled: neither funniness nor seriousness means the same thing after the punch line dawns, for their original meanings depended on the mutually exclusive nature of their defining contrast. Is the setup serious or funny? It is both: it is funny *as* serious, and serious *as* funny. Is the punch line serious or funny? It is both, but in an interestingly different way. It is obviously funny, but is it also serious? Yes. Why? Because now that the setup has occurred, both "funny" and "serious" have a different meaning. Originally, we thought that "funny" meant "what I laugh when I hear" or something like that, and "serious" meant "what gives me non-funny information" or something similar. But now we see that "funny" can also mean, "what I take to be serious, what I am *not* laughing about, what I am earnestly considering, or crying over, or bewailing even." But this means also that "serious" means "what can turn out to be either funny or serious." So both "funny" and "serious" now both mean "funny-and-serious, what can appear as both funny and serious." Each is now a center that subsumes of the other; they are intersubsumptive. As a consequence, the old pragmatic standard of truth is applied more liberally here: all claims, statements, and positions are true in the sense that all *can*, if properly recontextualized, lead to liberation—which is to say, to their own self-overcoming. Conversely, none will lead to liberation if not properly contextualized.

We can restate the above somewhat more formulaically as follows:

Every phenomenal object is a coherence. That is, it is a joining (cohering) of disparate elements—either (1) the factors that comprise it, its internal parts, or (2) its temporal antecedents, or (3) its contrasting conceptual contexts (i.e., its qualitative contrast to whatever it is "not," which is regarded as essential to its determination as this particular entity). Context and content are in the same boat on this view, in that for this object to appear phenomenally—to be "coherent" or legible, discernible—requires the coming together of multiple factors: figure and ground, elements in a structure, causal conditions. All that is necessary here is that these factors are heterogeneous, and phenomenally differ in some discernible way from the object they come to constitute. The conditions that make something so are distinct from what they make so.

Provisional Positing (*jia*) means conditionality, pratītyasamutpāda: it means that the conditions must thus always be not only distinct from the conditioned, but heterogeneous among themselves, and hence no solitary cause can have an effect, and hence no entity has any essence. Whatever they appear to be is posited only provisionally, and since this applies to any essence-candidate, all determinations are only provisional posits, indicating no essences. Whatever is so is so merely "in a manner of speaking." All claims are implicitly parameterized. This means that every coherence is a local coherence: it remains coherent as such and such only within a limited horizon of relevance (i.e., taking into account some but not all of the possible manners of speaking, which are by definition not limitable to any finite set). That is, its legibility depends on the fixing of a certain scale, frame, or focal orientation; its identity as this precise thing depends phenomenally on restricting the ways in which it is viewed, or the number of other factors that are viewed in tandem with it.

Emptiness (*kong*) also means conditionality, pratītyasamutpāda: it means that every local coherence is globally incoherent, that it is thus and so in some manners of speaking but not in others. There are always further parameters. If all parameters (senses, respects, times) were taken into account at once, and all applications and aspects brought to bear, the original coherence would vanish into ambiguity.

The Center (*zhong*) also means conditionality, pratītyasamutpāda: it means that Provisional Positing and Emptiness are alternate statements of the same fact, which is conditionality. It is a further insight into the nature of conditionality as such, showing that it is *necessarily* always also unconditional, and that conditionality and unconditionality are always copresent, and that this can be derived from a close examination of the nature of conditionality per se. It means that conditionality is unconditional, that every conditional state is interchangeable with its own absence and thus as present when absent as when present, and thus that every conditional thing is always also unconditionally present.

The Non-exclusive Center (*budanzhong*) also means conditionality, pratītyasamutpāda: The arising of any coherence is the arising of every other coherence, as any attempt to limit it to a finite set of determinations will fail: any totality, if determinate, will imply a further totality beyond it. Any coherence plus its constitutive context is a new X, which requires, and thus in the same way again "is," a further context, and so ad infinitum. Any conditional thing is not only copresent in its absence as such, but in every other possible coherence. Conditional X is not only also unconditional because it is also always present in and as an abstract "non-X," but because it is also always present in and as every Y, Z, A, B, C. Every determination expresses every other determination. Every globally incoherent local coherence subsumes all other local coherences. Every subsuming is an intersubsumption. Each entity is readable as every other entity, as part of every other entity, and as the whole that subsumes all other entities as its parts. Each entity is identifiable, ontologically ambiguous, and as all-pervaded as all-pervading.

LI IN EARLY TIANTAI: CENTER AS CONVERTIBILITY OF DETERMINATE AND INDETERMINATE

From the above, we can perhaps guess what the primary usage of Li in Tiantai will be. For Zhiyi, the basic meaning of Li is "Centrality" per se. Here we have a decisive step in the development of the concept of Li in Chinese thought, picking up a set of associations and meanings we have already seen slowly taking shape in previous chapters. Li is still what must be seen in order to achieve value. But here we are told what it is that needs to be perceived in order to achieve value, in this case Buddhist liberation: Centrality. Centrality means here *unconditionality*, which is the only ultimate value in Buddhism, the only end of suffering. It means absoluteness, inextricability from all possible conditions, omnipresence. The Center means what is tipped neither toward one extreme nor the other, which is equally present in the two opposite extremes, remains unchanged in and as either. In this sense, the center is the overcoming of oppositeness per se, of all oppositions: it is what is as present on both sides of any apparent mutual exclusivity, any divide. Hence, it is the unlimited, the absolute, the omnipresent. As such, it is what is virtually present throughout the vortex that is centered around and by it. For Tiantai, all things are Central: this means literally that every possible determination is unlimited, absolute, omnipresent, unconditional, present in and as all other entities, and conversely, as that in which all other entities can equally be found, their place of convergence.

This is value because it implies omnipresence, hence unconditionality: a Center is what is present indirectly but discernibly in all the peripheral elements it incorporates. To say that X is a Center is to say that all non-X entities are also versions of X; hence, X is omnipresent, unconditional, and in the Buddhist sense, therefore, value: liberation from suffering. They are "versions" of X, meaning they are X *as* some non-X determination. They are both X, the Center itself, and a particular non-X "expression" of Xness. We may note that the ruling image by which the notion of class membership or the application of a "principle" would have to be understood here is not the arraying of terms under a heading, or the inclusion of particulars within a circumscribed region, but of balanced sets of peripheral terms organized around a center, and deriving their character, both in their specific difference from the center and their copresence with and expression of the center, from their relation to this center. "All things are central" means all things are coherences that organize other things around themselves, which express themselves in the form of other things, as other things: to say X is central is to say that X is a "principle," a Li, in this sense. The cup as Central is the cup as Li, which means the cup as the principle of all other beings, as that which they are all reducible to, toward which they converge, which is expressing itself in them and is the inner secret of their determinate presence. Li as principle and Li as a bringing-together and Li as what is needful for salvation and Li as omnipresent potential are all seen as one and the same here. We may consider this as the essential Tiantai insight into the matter. That is, to be Li is to be what is present in more than one place, what remains itself in spite of instantiation in difference—doing in this sense what is normally done by what we call a principle, a universal, a form, and essence. This is itself what is salvific, because in this way the conditionality which Buddhism identifies as the true kernel of all suffering, the simple location in one place opposed to its other, is overcome.

The image of Centrality is to be understood in terms of a metaphor that goes back to the *Zhuangzi*'s idea of the "pivot of Dao" (道樞 *daoshu*) the center of a circle of opposed "thises" and "thats," rights and wrongs, points of view, where none of them "find their opposites" (是非莫得其偶 *shifei mo de qi ou*), that is, where fixed oppositeness per se has been transcended. This idea is well expressed by Qian Mu's metaphor of the pendulum, as quoted earlier, rooted in the non-ironic adaptation of the notion of centrality in the "Zhongyong" ("Doctrine of the Mean"). Center means balance, impartiality, not limited to any one side of a pair of opposed terms, and also is associated with the point by which these erratic and ex-centric particulars can be grasped, understood, and used toward human value purposes—in the Buddhist case, liberation. Centers are what unify particulars, transcend simple location and hence conditionality, make things intelligible, and embody value. That is, Centers are the locus of coherence, centers are Li.

To see the Center is to see not only the Center but all three of the Three Truths, and not separately but rather in their intersubsumptive relationship. In the Tiantai case, then, Li is sometimes described simply as Center, and sometimes as "the Three Truths." But the Three Truths are related to each other, and to all things, by means of the *upayic* structure of the *Lotus Sutra*, which complicates the picture considerably. We will find that in Zhiyi's works, the term Li is used in at least the following diverse senses:

1. The Three Truths as what it is valuable to realize, a cognitive object waiting to be understood and accorded with. It is in this sense that it is "eternal," independent of the knower, something like a preexistent "truth" to be known, a preexistent perforation in the world as guide for possible optimal action: "Whether a Buddha exists or not, the Nature [性 *xing*] and Li are constantly abiding. Because one is confused about this Li, the delusions of life and death arise. If one contemplates in accordance with Li, it is called wisdom."[13]

2. Potential as opposed to realization, as in the Tiantai doctrine of the "Six Identities" (六即 *liuji*), or anything merely known rather than fully realized. Here again we may think of perforations waiting to be recognized and utilized. "The Six Identities: identity in Li, in name, in contemplation in practice, in similarity, in partial realization and in ultimate realization. . . . The identity in Li is that one moment of experience is identical to the Li of the Storehouse of the Thus-Come [i.e., the *tathāgatagarbha*] [一念心即如來藏理 *yinianxin ji rulai zang li*]. Because it is Such [如 *ru*] it is Empty, because it is a storehouse [藏 *zang*] [of multiplicity] it is Provisional Positing, *because it is Li it is the Center*. . . . The identity in name means the state in which, although one is identical in Li, and one uses it everyday without realizing it, for one has not yet heard of the Three Truths and is completely ignorant of the Buddhadharma. . . ."[14] But "potential" is really a misleading term here. This usage in fact still means simply "a coherent object of true knowledge," or "the truth." It means something that is now in fact truly so, not merely potentially so, but which we do not see clearly. If there is a lump of gold buried in my back yard right now, which I cannot see, it is not merely "potentially" there. It is a fact yet to be known. When someone tells me about it, I might half-believe it or totally accept this, which would be equivalent to "identity in name." If I went out to the back yard and noticed a strange lump in a certain place, or began to dig and hit something hard with my shovel, it would be equivalent to the identities in practice, and when I see it myself, remove it, polish it, bring it to the jeweler's for appraisal, it is fully

realized, but the gold has always actually, not potentially, been there and legally mine. We are identical to the Buddha (and all other beings) in fact now, not merely potentially, but this is called "only in Li" in the sense that is a fact to be known which is not yet known.

3. Li as the second-order interpervasive unity of the Three Truths themselves, as opposed to the misapprehension of them as non-synonymous. This is evident, for example, when Zhiyi singles out the Center as Li, as against the other two truths, in the exegesis of the Identity of Li in the previous citation. This converging of the two other truths into the Center is the interpervasion of Provisional Positing and Emptiness, local coherence and global incoherence. But it is also the converging of all local coherences into any particular local coherence. As noted above, this is what gives us the clearest sense of what qualifies something as a Li for Zhiyi: Centrality per se is Li-ness. Centrality of X means that, in the formula seized upon by Zhili from the Kumārajīva's translation of the larger *Prajñâpâramitâ Sutra* in this connection, "All dharmas converge ultimately into X, but never go beyond it" (一切法趣X，是趣不過 *yiqiefaqu X, shiqubuguo*).[15] This applies to every conceivable X. The converging-around-a-center is what defines Li. It is Li in the traditional sense: an intelligible coherence and a value. It is a coherence as a coming together. It is intelligible as this particular X. It is a value because for Buddhists unconditionality is defined as value, and this can only be possible if entities are interpervasive, readable *as* each other. It further absorbs the ironic conception of value, for in this mutual readability, the original coherence—intelligibility—of X is both established and effaced. In the Three Truths, moreover, we see precisely that the non-ironic coherence and the ironic coherence are inter-subsumptive: any determination as coherent is identical to its indetermination, its positing as X is its emptiness of X, its local coherence is its global incoherence. As the formula from the *Prajñâpâramitâ* passage continues: "All dharmas converge into X, but never go beyond it. And why? Because X itself is unobtainable [i.e., Empty]—how much less, then, is there any convergence or non-convergence into it?" For Zhiyi, this means the Three Truths: any determination is ambiguous, readable always as (1) intelligible as some particular X, as (2) the absence of that X, and (3) all other determinations as expressions of or

aspects of that X, such that X is the ultimate unconditional fact about them, that they have no being beyond X.

4. What a practitioner should *think about* or keep in mind while performing a ritual, as opposed to what one's body is doing during it. "The repentance of event [事 *shi*] pertains to the path of suffering and karma, while the repentance of Li pertains to the path of delusion."[16] Note here that, in terms of the Three Tracks, this means Li pertains to Emptiness and the track of Contemplation and Reflection (觀照軌 *guanzhaogui*, pertaining to the experience of realization), as opposed to Provisional Positing (the track of Conditions for Completion 資成軌 *zicheng'gui*, pertaining to practice leading to realization) and the Center (the track of the Real Nature 真性軌 *zhenxing'gui*, pertaining to the preexistent truth to be realized). Li is here again an intelligible coherence to be recognized by the mind.

5. Any object of cognition, inasmuch as all are ultimately Central, and thus all ultimately unconditional, and all of them are what it is necessary to recognize and realize in order to be liberated from suffering. This is where the truly distinctive Tiantai conception of Li is especially evident. Zhiyi says, "If we open up the gate of skillful means and reveal the ultimate reality [of them], [we see that] precisely the former bodies are the perfect eternal body, the previous teachings are the Integrated teaching, the previous practices and the previous Lis are all precisely the true ultimate reality."[17] Note that Li are plural here, but also ultimately one, or as Zhiyi says elsewhere, "Li is not even one, how much less is it many?"[18] This is the application of the specifically *Lotus Sutra* problematic to the question of Li, which is indeed the heart of the matter in Tiantai. Zhiyi's view is systematized in his doctrine of the "Four Onenesses" (四一 *siyi*) and the Root and Traces (本跡 *benji*), developed most directly in the *Fahuawenju*. For these will allow us to see just what is meant by "oneness" in this context—i.e., how far it is from implying a homogenous sameness. Let us consider these in turn.

The Four Onenesess refer to the four aspects of Buddhist teaching just mentioned: the person practicing, the teaching he or she has heard, the practice he or she is doing, and the Li or ideas he is entertaining and striving to realize. Śrāvakas are Bodhisattvas, according to the *Lotus Sutra*. This is the oneness of person (人一 *renyi*); there are not Śrāvakas as opposed to Bodhisattvas, but rather precisely this person here being a Śrāvaka is that person there being a Bodhisattva, and indeed the Buddha that this Bodhisattva will eventually become. As the Buddha tells Śāriputra in the *Lotus Sutra*, after describing the glorious Buddha that he *will become in the future*, "precisely that person there is you yourself" (彼即是汝身 *bi jishi rushen*).[19] The tenseless form of the Chinese here is important: not "he will be you" or "you will be him," but "just he is you." You "are" your own future, in the way that a setup "is" the funny like the punch line: precisely because it is *not* funny. You are "one" with that Buddha because you are doing what you are doing now, namely, being a Śrāvaka, specifically *not* trying to become a Buddha. Indeed, he is a Bodhisattva even while a Śrāvaka, precisely by being a Śrāvaka. This is not the Upanishadic "tat tvam asi" ("thou art that!"), which points to each diverse creature and asserts that the real essential self of each of them deep inside is the very self that lies deep inside yourself, one and unchanging in each being beneath all illusory differences as manifested in their diverse present thoughts, deeds, and situations. Here, they are one by being different, different by being one. It is not the inner essence of the Śrāvaka that is secretly really a Buddha in essence: it is the Śrāvaka-cognitions, Śrāvaka-beliefs, Śrāvaka-deeds that are themselves also readable as Buddha-thoughts, Buddha-beliefs, Buddha-deeds, as the setup both brings about and is retrospectively readable as funny, precisely by means of its contrast to the funniness. But this means not only that the same person who is here a Śrāvaka is actually all along also a Bodhisattva and a Buddha, but also that the very same teaching he has accepted, the Śrāvaka teaching of the Hinayana, is the teaching of the Bodhisattva vehicle (the different teachings are, precisely as different, one and the same teaching), that his Śrāvaka practices themselves are Bodhisattva practices (the different practices are, precisely as different, one and the same practice), and finally that the truths he was realizing (Suffering, Impermanence, Emptiness of person, Nirvana as extinction, transcendence of Nirvana, self-benefit, and so on) are themselves, in their difference, one and the same as the truths of the Bodhisattva vehicle (the six perfections, the original vow to save all beings, Emptiness of dharmas and persons, the Emptiness of Emptiness, the Middle Way Buddha-nature, Mind-only, and so on)—this last being the sameness of Li. The structure to be recalled here is the setup/punch line interpervasion of difference and sameness explained in the previous section: they are the identical (both setup and punch line pervaded by both the seriousness of the setup and the funniness of the punch line) only by being different. The truth of the statement "all conditioned things are suffering" is the same as the truth of the statement "all dharmas are Emptiness." These turn out to mean the same thing. The same goes even for diametrically opposed truths: for example, "Nirvana is extinction" and "Nirvana is not extinction." The truth of both statements is the same truth; they differ and yet are equally Li, the same coherence (valued harmony-producing object of cognition) the recognition of which is necessary for liberation. Zhili thus criticizes the notion that only the truth to be realized by the Mahayana can be called Li: "Since you call the fruition of the Mahayana the Great Li [大理 dali], why would you not take the fruition of the Hinayana as small Li [小理 xiaoli]? The opponent (Guangzhai) defends his view by saying, 'Since the fruition aimed at by the Hinayana is not actual [according to the Lotus], we should not consider this fruition be any sort of Li.' But if so, the same is true of the provisional teaching, practice and person: none of these is actual, [considered as such]. But if nonetheless we can speak of the provisional teaching, practice and person, we can also speak of the provisional Li. Moreover, if there were no Li to the provisional, the Conventional would not be called a Truth."[20] Zhiyi's interpretation, of course, also extends this to all persons, all teachings, all practices, all truths or cognitive objects. This is what makes it impossible to say if Li is one or many, or to limit its reference once and for all to any particular level. Greater and lesser swaths of coherence are all interpervasive and intersubsumptive, requiring precisely the ignorance of the larger and the concomitant limitation to the smaller in order to manifest later as the larger, as in the Lotus. A Bodhisattva must also at times limit his practice, his teaching, his person, his own understanding to the lesser, the truths of the Śrāvakas, in order to be a Bodhisattva at all: both as a phase of self-forgetting sometimes necessary in his Bodhisattva practice, as in the Lotus stories, and as a mastery of the viewpoints and truths accepted by the benighted sentient beings whom it is necessary to communicate with in order to practice the Bodhisattva Way. All objects of cognition are Li because all without exception are what is to be realized to liberate oneself from suffering, to become a Buddha.

This level-shifting character of Li in Tiantai is what is explicated in the doctrine of "Roots and Traces." In conformity with the Jizang's Three Treatise usage considered above, he is happy to begin by defining Li as Emptiness, and opposing its unity to the diversity of particular beings. The Vimalakirti Sutra states, "All dharmas are established from the root of non-dwelling [從無住本立一切法 cong wuzhuben li yiqiefa]."[21] Zhiyi, in the Fahuawenju, directly equates Li with Non-Dwelling: "Non-dwelling is the Li, all dharmas are the events (shi)." This is consistent with the pre-Tiantai understanding of Li in Chinese Buddhism. For Zhiyi, Li is "Non-Dwelling" in the specific sense of not dwelling in either of the two extremes, a synonym for the Center: not confined to either Provisional Positing or Emptiness, Being or Non-Being, this or that. Li means the absolute, the unconditional, the omnipresent, what is not confined to any simple location, and is thus discoverable everywhere and at all times. He clarifies this by saying, "Li is true Suchness [真如 *zhenru, tathata*], and true Suchness is originally pure. Whether a Buddha exists or not, it is eternal and unchanging, so Li is called the real. Events means mind, attention, and consciousness and so on, which give rise to pure and impure karma. These change and move and are unfixed, so events are called provisional truth [權 *quan*]. Without Li there is nothing by which to establish events, without events there is no way to manifest Li. Events have the power to manifest Li [若非理無以立事。非事不能顯理。事有顯理之功]."[22]

So far this is all standard pre-Tiantai understanding, and even suggests a one-way dependence relation between Li and *shi* (Li "establishes" *shi* but *shi* merely "manifests" Li), and the original purity of Suchness, all doctrines for which later Tiantai will criticize Huayan.[23] For it is just this way of understanding the situation that is supplanted by Zhiyi's treatment here, evident in his the application of the categories of 權 *quan* and 實*shi*, provisional and ultimate truth, which situates the discussion in terms of the epistemology of the *Lotus*. For this move is precisely what is decisive. Hence, Zhiyi goes on in this passage to say, "In the relation between Li and teachings, we say the previously mentioned Li and events [事 *shi*] are *both* Li. For example, both ultimate and conventional truth are called truths—for it is by comprehending them that the Buddhas achieve their sagehood. . . ." Here, both Li and *shi* are collapsed into Li, in that both are "truths," both provisional and ultimate truth are what has to be realized to achieve sagehood. In the new context, the meaning of Li shifts; as compared to the multiplicity of events, the unchanging essence of Suchness is Li, but as opposed to the activity of teaching, the Li is the content of teaching, the ideas to be realized, including both provisional and ultimate truths. These are all Li because these are all liberating coherences: that which must be realized in order to attain value, which in this case is liberation from suffering. As discussed in the previous section, all Conventional Truths, and a mastery of them due to realizing also their interpervasion, are what one realizes, not what one transcends and leaves behind, in enlightenment. Hence each and every coherence, every determination, is a Li.

This is a consequence of the "shifting" structure—a kind of harvesting of Zhuangzi's "slippage and doubt" 滑疑 motif—that can be observed in Zhiyi's discussion of any set of terms. Indeed, we may say that to treat a set of definitions in this shifting, mitosis-producing way is precisely to explicate their Li, their non-dwelling. Zhiyi says:

The root is the one Real-Attribute, while the traces are everything else besides the Real-Attribute of all dharmas. Again, when Li is contrasted to event [*shi*], it is called the root, but once one is speaking of Li and event, *both* are to be called teachings, and thus traces.

Again, both Li and event as teachings are to be called the root, and the practice of this teaching by those who receive it is to be called the trace; it is like a man who leaves footprints in going to his dwelling place: by following the footprints the dwelling place can be found. Again, practice is whereby one realizes substance, and substance is the root; when function arises in accord with this substance, this is the trace. Again, to truly attain substance and function is the root, and to provisionally put forth substance and function (in teachings and practice) is the trace. What manifests today is the root; but what is said in the past and future is the trace. . . . First we will explain root and trace in terms of Li and events. "All dharmas are established from the root of non-dwelling." The Li of non-dwelling is the ultimate truth of the Real-Attribute at the root time [i.e., from the perspective of the root] [本時實相真諦 *benshi shixiang zhendi*]. "All dharmas" here means the manifold of conventional truths at the root time. Because the Real-Attribute ultimate truth root hangs down into the conventional traces, examining these conventional traces reveals the ultimate truth. Although root and trace differ, they are alike in their inconceivability. . . . Second, we explain root and trace in terms of Li and teaching. Both of the two truths perceived in the root time are equally unspeakable, and so both are together called the root. The ancient Buddhas nonetheless spoke them via skillful means, producing the teachings of the Two Truths, and these teachings are called the traces. If there were no Two Truths in the root, there could not exist these two types of teachings. And without the traces revealed in the teachings, how could the truths of the root be revealed? Although the roots and traces differ, they are one in their inconceivability. . . .[24]

On the first level, Li and *shi* are distinguished; but relative to the second level, both Li and *shi* are collectively called Li. The introduction of the categories of root and trace, as abstracted from the *Lotus*, allow for a shifting multiplication of the applicability of the term Li. There is always another level, another more fundamental aspect, even when we are speaking of what is from another perspective the Li which grounds the *shi*. This is how the simple unilateral dependence relation is overcome here. Moreover, it does not simply reduce to a one-way hierarchy, but turns in upon itself. Root and trace mean here what Li and *shi* mean in Huayan—the independent and the dependent, as we shall see presently—but Li itself is merely one level in this development, which continues to mutate and split at each level to which we pay attention.

This indicates that in Tiantai Li is more like an empty-place marker, or a structural token, or an indicator that a certain structure will apply to any content without exception, rather than a term that denotes a particular content. In every relation, one side will be Li. Expanding the context, it is possible that the whole of the previous set, including both terms, will be Li. But Li will necessarily always be present, with some content or another, as a structural necessity. This is consistent with the initial definition of Li as "non-dwelling." The Li that is posited along with any content will be the implicit self-transcendence that is necessarily posited at the same time. In other words, when X is posited as a determinate content—whether this is a concept, a practice, a deluded thought, or a Buddhist teaching—the ambiguity and absoluteness of this X, this X's being non-X (Emptiness) and its being present in and as all other coherences (the Center), will be the corresponding Li. In this way, Li can always be said either to have a content—the Three Truths—or to have no particular content—for a particular content is a "dwelling." Li is also for this reason inescapable whenever any content is posited. Since the Three Truths means that determinacy is ambiguity is absoluteness, any determinacy itself is always also precisely Li, as what has to be realized in order to be liberated from suffering.

The simultaneous deployment of these various levels of meaning entails considerable complexity. We find Zhanran emphasizing the multiple contrasted meanings directly: "It should be understood that deluded sentient beings have only the Li, while the Buddhas have attained the events [shi]; also, deluded sentient beings have only the events, while the Buddhas have realized the Li. Thus sentient beings have only the events and Li within delusion, while the Buddhas fully possess the [same] events and Li within enlightenment. Although they differ as to delusion and enlightenment, the events and the Li are the same entity in both cases."[25]

Sentient beings possess only the Li as "potential" in the qualified sense indicated above, but not the realization of this truth in "events." But Buddhas are the ones who realize this Li, while sentient beings are stuck with only the deluded *shi*. Embracing both of these contrary meanings at the same time, as Zhanran does here, entails a reconfiguration of our understanding of the relation between "potentiality" and "actuality" as such, and this is the real point, for this is the real import of the doctrine of the Three Truths. For, as we saw in the second meaning of Li listed above, to say sentient beings have it "only in Li" means simply that "it is true of sentient beings that they are identical to Buddhas," while having the "event" in this context means that Buddhas are those who ("genuinely") *know* this as a temporal mental act of cognition with a beginning and end. But in the awareness of deluded sentient beings, there are only events—temporal conditioned facts with a beginning and end—and no Li, no inherent omni-present coherences, no experience of the unconditioned: there, experience apprehends only the conditional and thus suffering. The conflation of the two senses yields a distinctive sense of the identity between Li and events. For whether or not one knows this truth about things as a temporal act of cognition, one's "knowing" of it always exists as an inherent eternal fact, that is, in the guise of ("as") whatever coherences one may be aware of. The eternal truth and the temporal events within delusion include the realiza-tion of truth itself as temporal event, while the same eternal truth and the same temporal events within enlightenment include the realization of truth as part of the eternal, always-occurring truth. The event of the Buddha's coming-to-know-the-truth, in other words, exists in both cases, but in one case it is a simply located event with a beginning and end in time and applying only to a certain realm of space, and in the other as itself a Li, a fact that is omnipresent and eternal.

In technical Tiantai terms, this important point, seeing every experi-enceable determination as itself the central unconditional Li that encom-passes all other determinations both as Li and as *shi*, is addressed in Zhiyi's comments and Zhanran's subcomments on a line from Chapter 2 of the *Lotus Sutra*, which in Kumārajīva's brilliant mistranslation states: "This dharma dwells in the dharma-position, and all the characteristics of the world dwell eternally" (是法住法位，　世間相常住 *shifazhufawei, shijianxiangchangzhu*). But to understand the significance of these comments, in particular Zhan-ran's subcomments, we must first take a look at the Huayan understanding of Li and event (*shi*).

APPEARANCE AND REALITY IN HUAYAN AND TIANTAI

Dushun 杜順 (557–640), a slightly younger contemporary of Zhiyi's, is the nominal founder of the Huayan 華嚴 School of Buddhism, supposedly bas-ing itself primarily on the *Avatamsaka Sûtra*. But there is considerable doubt that the doctrinal works attributed to him can really be traced back to this historical Dushun. The "second patriarch" Yunhua Zhiyan 雲華智儼 (602–668) is thought to have established some of the basic doctrines of the school,[26] but Xianshou Fazang 賢首法藏 (643–721) is usually fingered as the de facto founder or at least completer of the doctrinal system of the Huayan School. The works attributed to all of these figures, as well as later Huayan masters, all argue emphatically for mutual pervasion of events. Huayan thinkers developed many formulas for working out the vari-ous directions and implications of this interpervasion, as we shall see, but as a shorthand we can point to the typical Huayan formulation found in the famous slogan "non-obstruction between events" (事事無礙 *shi shi wu ai*, or 事事圓融 *shi shi yuan rong*), and the analogy of Indra's net from the *Avatamsaka Sûtra* itself, developed in the works attributed to Dushun. It is well documented that an important shift in Huayan doctrine takes place in the course of the Tang Dynasty, whereby the concept of the Tathagatagarbha (womb or embryo of the Tathatagata, usually equivalent to the concept of "Buddha-Nature") and the notion of the "Original Pure Mind," largely traceable to the *Awakening of Faith* 大乘起信論 (also probably of Chinese origin), become increasingly dominant. This tendency reaches its zenith in the thought of the "fifth patriarch" of the school, Guifeng Zongmi 圭峰宗密 (780–841), but is already subtly traceable in some of Fazang's writings, and becomes more visible in the thought of the "fourth patriarch," Qingliang Chengguan 清涼澄觀 (738–839). In Zongmi's case, this has been interpreted as a shift from the emphasis on the interpenetration of events with other events to an emphasis on the interpenetration between Li and events (理事無礙 *li shi wu ai*), Li being identified with the Pure Original Mind itself, with the Buddha-nature or Tathagatagarbha.[27] This moves Huayan thought away from the Madhyamika principles used to argue for the omnipresence of every event as presented in Tiantai, not only in its robust idealism but also in establishing a fixed one-way relationship between the pure mind (indeterminate in itself) and all other determinacies (which are both identical to and nonidentical to this pure mind, which serves as their ontological basis). We will explore this problem in depth in the next chapter.

It should be noted, however, that in the works attributed to Dushun, there is no trace of this doctrine of the true essence of mind as the basis for the all-pervading omnipresence of each event. Rather, "Dushun" argues on the basis of a consideration of Emptiness. However, the manner in which this proceeds still differs significantly from the use of the Emptiness—expanded into the Three Truths—in Tiantai, discussed above. The difference can be best understood by reproducing Dushun's argument for omnicentrism in his main work, the "Huayan Fajieguan" 華嚴法界觀.[28]

This work starts by considering the common *Prajnâpâramitâ* slogan, "Form is Emptiness, Emptiness is Form." It gives three senses in which Form is Emptiness, and three senses in which Emptiness is Form. Each of these three senses, in both cases, is presented in the form: "X is identical to Y, because X is *not* identical to Y." This claim is read in three different ways for each of the two cases, the conclusion being that, when finally understood in this complex mediated sense, Form is Emptiness, Emptiness is Form. From this is derived the idea of the mutual pervasion of all particulars, as expressed in a great variety of alternate ways. This is clearly analogous to the Tiantai attempt to establish the Center as both the identity and distinction between Emptiness and Provisional Positing. The Dushun work also takes pains to indicate that the "identicalness" of form and emptiness also includes their difference. But this difference takes on a very non-Tiantai significance here.

The divergence from Tiantai thinking can be noted most clearly in the asymmetry in Dushun's arguments for the claims that "Form is identical to emptiness, because form is not identical to emptiness," on the one hand, and "emptiness is identical to form, because emptiness is not identical to form," on the other. This takes place in the second iteration of each of these claims in the work. "Form is not emptiness" because the characteristic of "being form" and the characteristic of "being emptiness" are distinguishable; this is consistent with Tiantai thinking. But for "emptiness is not form," Dushun suddenly introduces the category of *dependence*: he says that which depends (能依 *neng yi*, i.e., form, etc.) is not the same as that which is depended on (所依 *suo yi*, i.e., emptiness). Fazang uses the same vocabulary in his *Huayanjing zhigui* 華嚴經旨歸 to define Li and events (事 *shi*): "The contrast between Li and *shi* refers to the marks of events arising through dependent co-arising on the one hand, and, on the other hand, the True Li upon which they depend (所依真理 *suo yi zhenli*)."[29] This suggests a one-way relation of dependence between form and emptiness, a sense in which emptiness is ontologically prior to or more fundamental than form. It is implied that emptiness does not require form in order to be emptiness, but form (and all other determinate quiddities) does require emptiness in order to be form. This asymmetry is what opens the door for a new understanding of the omnipresence of each particular that easily merges with the "Original Pure Mind" doctrine found in some forms of Chan, in one reading of the *Awakening of Faith,* and in other Tathagatagarbha works.

This is the only point at which we would want to take exception to Tao Jiang's excellent analysis of the meaning of Li in Huayan, which makes the useful and interesting suggestion that we interpret Li here not as a static whole, since it does not consist of *shi* as its parts, nor as something ontologically distinct from the *shi*, but rather as "activity" as such, "activity without an agent," as opposed to *shi* as determinate "thing" regarded as the product of all such activity. Jiang suggests that Li may be best understood as a *verb*, invoking the inseparability between subject and verb to explain the inseparability and interpenetration of Li and *shi*, each being a partial abstraction from what is always a total situation involving both. Li in Jiang's analysis of Huayan means "the ultimate verb, the absolute self-negating activity of the universe," indivisible, boundless, neither reducible to nor separable from the concrete things that it negates (and establishes): *sunyata* itself. Li as *sunyata* is the self-negating activity which is inseparable from, even constitutive of, the determinateness of any "subject," any noun, the self-affirmation of any definite determination. Li is the omnipresent act of negation itself, which necessarily accompanies any presence. This is a very useful way of approaching Huayan thought, allowing us to see Li as a transcending of every "part" without reifying a resultant totalistic "whole" as a specific and determinate entity. Li is indeed for Huayan the indeterminacy of all finite parts as such, without implying a static and determinate whole of which they are parts. This a crucial amendation to Behuniak's use of "wholeness" simpliciter to interpret Li in Huayan: the type of wholeness we have to do with here is *ironic* wholeness: a whole that is no whole, and which has the genuine functions of wholeness only by its failure to become any specific whole. But Jiang wants to assert that this "predicative" use of Li, as opposed to a substantive one, avoids both the reductionist and essential problems because in this conception the verb and the noun are equally foundational: as opposed to the usual commonsensical notion that the noun is primary and the verb secondary, Jiang's version of Huayan grants perfect symmetry to the two: "There is no subject that is apart from verb and no verb apart from subject."[30] But inseparability does not preclude asymmetry of foundational structure, ontological priority as a dependent/independent relation, and this is the crux of the matter. The asymmetry of the Huayan *nengyi/suoyi* distinction suggests something closer to a straight *reversal* of the standard grammatical view: in actual Huayan writings, the verb is *more fundamental* than the subject, the noun (though they are indeed inseparable). The self-negating activity is *more real* than the defined affirmations it establishes and negates. It is also more important—indeed, what is of sole importance for the project of attaining enlightenment, value. As we shall see, the attempt to focus on concrete particulars is in Huayan actually ends up being a focus only on the *interpenetration itself* of these particulars, not their static isolation; in other words, we are still contemplating pure Li, even, or especially, when we are no longer explicitly referring to it, speaking only of "interpenetration of events." The attempt to establish a perfect symmetry of Li and *shi*, in other words, which Huayan writers are undoubtedly aiming at, and believe they are attaining, is undermined by their own procedure and certain assumptions that show their influence only at particular points of stress in the exposition of the system. Let us now examine these in detail.

It is crucial to note the role of the categories of appearance and reality in this argument. The problem is, above all, epistemological; the difference between Tiantai and Huayan is ultimately a Three Truth versus Two Truth distinction, when all is said and done. Simply stated, adopting Jiang's vocabulary again, we may say that even if charitably we were to read the Huayan position as asserting that the inseparability of the verb and subject is what is to be taken as ultimately real, as opposed to the delusion of verbless nouns or nounless verbs (though as we've seen, and will see again below, there is a definite tendency to assert instead the greater reality of the verbs and ontological priority of verb even in this inseparable noun-verb alloy), we would have the same problem, from a Tiantai point of view: the mutually exclusive relation between illusion and reality, between delusion and enlightenment, between truth and falsehood. This is to be distinguished from the Tiantai Three Truths epistemology, in which all illusions are themselves *upāya* and there is no category of "just plain falsehood" at all: there, "noun" alone would be a delusion, hence a conventional truth, hence the Absolute Truth, as we've seen above. In sharp contrast, interpervasion itself in Huayan is derived from the possibility of distinguishing what each dharma "really is"—namely, the absence of any determinate nature—from what it merely appears to be. When it is claimed that "it" interpenetrates, what is meant is that "what it really is" interpenetrates. "What it appears to be" *does not interpenetrate*, nor does it do anything else, for it simply does not exist. The result is that the only characteristic that really belongs to any dharma, that is, which is so of this dharma intrinsically, inalienably, under all conditions, from all perspectives and at all times, is the character of Emptiness. This "nature" of Emptiness thus constitutes the *whole real* being of each and every particular—not a part of its real being, but its entire real being, inasmuch as this simply means all that is really intrinsic to it. This character of Emptiness is indivisible. It cannot be partially possessed; to have this character is to have it in its entirety. The character of "being susceptible to otherness, to other characteristics" is thus possessed *in its entirety* by every being and state. The whole dharma is thus "really" nothing but this nature, and this nature is indivisible, which means that the dharma is indivisible and everywhere. But this is a mediated type of interpervasion, by which I mean that it must pass through the third term of the real nature, Emptiness. The illusory characteristics (i.e., all the characteristics other than Emptiness per se that the object may seem, from some sentient being's deluded perspective, to possess) do not exist (except qua expressions of Emptiness, i.e., of the active non-exclusivity that takes on any apparent characteristic), and hence as such these characteristics cannot interpenetrate. We may say without hesitation that this is probably a more faithful understanding of the Indian Buddhist notion of appearance versus reality than that found in Tiantai, and perhaps it is worth remembering here that Fazang was fluent in Sanskrit, of which Zhiyi could read not a word.

The role of illusion is given its most systematic exposition in Huayan thinking in Fazang's *Huayan yisheng jiaoyi fenqi zhang* 華嚴一乘教義分齊章. There, borrowing Yogācāra terminology, Fazang defines the "Three natures," each of which has two aspects:

1. The Perfect and Complete Real Nature (*pariniṣpanna*, 圓成實性 *yuanchengshi xing*), which is (a) unchanging (不變 *bubian*), but (b) follows conditions (隨緣 *suiyuan*).

2. The Other-dependently Arising (*paratantra*, 依他起性 *yitaqi xing*) Nature, which is (a) devoid of self-nature (無性 *wuxing*) but (b) appears to exist (似有 *siyou*).

3. The Wholly Imaginary Clung-to Nature (*parikalpita*, 遍計所執 性 *pianji suozhi xing*), which is (a) nonexistent in Li (理無 *liwu*) but (b) existent in the deluded clinging sentiments of sentient beings (情有 *qingyou*).

Fazang tells us that (a) and (b) in each of these categories are actually identical to one another: in each case, (a) is a flip side way of saying the same thing as (b). Further, the (a) aspect in each is identical to the (a) aspect in the other two, and likewise for the (b) aspects in each category. Each refers to the same two aspects, which are really just flip sides of one another, but analyzed in each case in a different way. In 1., the unchanging nature is manifested only because it follows conditions, just as "the bright purity of a mirror is never lost even when it manifests both tainted and pure images . . . the manifestation of the tainted dharmas does not pollute the purity of the mirror; not only do they not pollute it—rather, it is only because of this that the bright purity of the mirror is manifested. . . . It is not only that the purity of the nature is manifested without destroying the taint and purity [of the manifestations]; it is only because the nature is pure that taint and purity come to be."[31] In 2., the same relationship between the side (a) and side (b) pertains. But here, the category of *appearance* (似 *si*) comes into play: it is only because they "in reality" have no self-nature that their existence can be called "merely appearance." So "to be appearance" means the same as "to not-really-exist," because appearance means specifically "merely appearance." The same applies even more clearly to level 3. It is only because they are really "nonexistent in Li" that they can be called "existent [merely] in the perception of clinging deluded beings." Li here means "the truth to be recognized," and more particularly, "what needs to apprehended to attain value: the content of enlightenment." These perceived characteristics that are so prevalent in deluded experience are things that have no part in enlightened experience. They are literally unreal, do not cohere into the total body of truths, and are of no value. Fazang says, "It is as if one deludedly thought one saw a ghost when looking at a wooden table. The ghost ultimately does not exist in the table. If it did exist in the table, one could not call this 'deludedly thinking' a ghost is there, for it would exist in the table, and would not be there only because of deluded thinking. So here since it is deluded thinking, we know it is nonexistent in Li. Only because it is nonexistent in Li can it be called existent due to deluded thinking, and only because it exists due to deluded thinking do we know that it is nonexistent in Li. Hence they are nondual, and one solitary nature."[32] Here, the "identity" between appearance and reality means not that whatever exists in appearance also exists in reality, that the content of the two is the same, much less that being-appearance means the same as being-reality, as in the Tiantai Three Truths, but rather that understanding appearance-as-appearance is the disclosure of the absence of these particular appearances in reality. To see appearance as appearance is to see reality—not because these appearances really pertain to reality, but because they do not. More precisely, appearance as such pertains to reality, and reality is only reality because it produces appearance (as in the production of tainted and pure appearances in the mirror analogy in level 1), but the *specific determinations of each appearance* do not pertain to reality. It is "presentation of appearance" that discloses reality, not "the appearances so disclosed." Fazang finishes his discussion by showing that each of the three natures is to be conceived definitively as neither existent or nonexistent, both or neither, because each has these two aspects, and each pair is ultimately identical in the sense just described.

This way of understanding the matter has profound implications. In the analysis of the "Six Marks" at the end of the same work, Fazang offers his famous analogy of the pillar and the house to explain the interpenetration and omnipresence of particulars. There, Fazang says that the pillar is precisely the house, because the one pillar alone is able to make the house. The reason for this is that if the pillar is lacking, the house cannot come into existence, and whenever the pillar exists, the house exists. This last point depends on a distinction between a "real pillar" and a mere plank of wood, and also on the distinction between a "good house" (好舍 hao she) and a "broken house" (破舍 po she)—the latter meaning not a real house, not a genuine, successful example of a house. This is another manifestation of the point just made about appearance and reality. For Fazang's point is that, in the absence of the existing completed house, the apparent pillar is simply *not a pillar*—it is merely a plank of wood. It cannot be accurately named a pillar unless the whole house is there. The same argument is used to assert that the pillar is also identical to all the other parts of the house, each being identical to the whole house in the same way. For if the pillar is gone, the house cannot exist, and without the house, the walls, roof, and so on are not "really" walls, roof, and so on, but merely chunks of wood. This is a "mediated" identity, mediated by each part's identity with the whole. It rests entirely on the enforcement of an absolute appearance/reality dichotomy. This means that what interpenetrates in each case is not what we normally call a pillar, if we are deluded about interpenetration and think of it as a separable single part of the house. *That* pillar simply does not exist, and cannot interpenetrate with other particulars, or do anything else for that matter. The only pillar that qualifies as a pillar is the one that is already seen to be interpenetrating. Now, we can always move the analysis to other levels, and say that while the pillar-without-a-house is not really a pillar, it is really a plank of wood, and exists interpenetratingly in other totalities that way, namely, qua plank of wood but not qua pillar. But this recourse to "really qualifying to be called X" already introduces a level of final adjudication that limits the possibility of multiperspectivism and surreptitiously posits a metaperspective, with at best a one-way hierarchy of levels of reality and interpervasion.

This has very serious consequences for epistemology. For example, in Fazang's *Huayanjing wenda* 華嚴經問答, we find the following exchange:

Q: "One person practices, and all people attain Buddhahood"—what does this mean?

A: This is said in reference to the one person as dependently co-arising, because in that sense one person simply is all people, and all people are the one person. The same can be said of each practice: each practice is all practices, and all practices are the one practice. Thus they are the same.

Q: But now we see manifestly one person practicing and the rest not practicing. It is just the one person, not anybody else. How can this be?

A: What you are seeing is nothing more than Wholly Imaginary [遍計 *pianji*]. It has nothing to do with the dependently co-arising dharmas. It is not worth talking about [不關緣起之法，不足言也 *buguan yuanqi zhi fa, buzuyanye*].[33]

The deludedly seen dharmas, which exist in clinging imaginary perception but not in or as Li, have nothing to do with dependent co-arising, and are of no account. There is no better way to understand the different epistemologies of Tiantai and Huayan than to compare this response to that given by Zhanran to a similar question in the *Zhiguanyili* 止觀義例:

Q: Here we see manifestly black, yellow, red and white [i.e., separate differentiated things and characteristics]. In what sense are they the Dharma-realm of True Suchness?

A: When you speak of black and so on, this is what is seen by deluded attachment [情 *qing*]. When you speak of the Dharma-realm,

you are talking about according with Li. How can you use deluded
attachment to challenge Li? Our present contemplation is to contravene deluded attachment and contemplate Li. One mustn't go
on to contravene Li and accord with deluded attachment.

Thus far, Zhanran's answer is more or less the same as Fazang's: the
separate, independent, non-interpenetrating things seen by the ordinary
mind are just delusions. One is to ignore them and attend instead to the
interpenetrations of Li. But Zhanran's answer continues:

> Moreover, black and the rest are conventional truth, while the
> Dharma-realm is ultimate truth. Or again, black and the rest are
> a manifestation of a small portion of conventional truth [俗諦之
> 少分 sudizhishaofen], while the Dharma-realm is a manifestation of
> the entirety of the Three Truths [三諦之全分 sandizhiquanfen]. Or
> again, black and the rest are a small portion of what is seen by the
> human and heavenly eyes, while the Dharma-realm is the entirety
> of what is seen by the Buddha-eye. Each eye is inherently equipped
> with (具 ju) all five eyes, so black and the rest inherently entail
> all dharmas. The same applies to the relationship between the one
> truth and the Three Truths. For these reasons, you cannot use [the
> manifestation of] black and the rest to undermine the existence of
> the Dharma-realm. . . .[34]

Here is the crux of the matter, the smoking gun. After the standard
"reality versus appearance" answer, which is framed specifically with reference to the practice of contemplation, Zhanran reframes his answer, first, in
terms of the Three Truths, and second, in terms of *whole and part*. We can
now see what sort of whole and part relation applies in the Tiantai context.
The separable independent things deludedly seen by ignorant beings are not
"nonexistent," but a small portion of the truth of Provisional Positing. Their
interpenetration is the entirety of the Three Truths, which are the identity
between Provisional Positing and Emptiness and the Center. Provisional
Truth is Local Coherence: a deluded experience of a patch of blackness
as an isolated entity is a locally coherent phenomenon, one among a vast
number of conflicting conventional truths. As such, it is a small portion
of the totality of conventional truths, which seen together simply are the
Global Incoherence of Emptiness, which seen correctly is all Three Truths
and each of these initially deluded patches of conventional truth as the
unconditional Center of all other coherences. Significantly, Zhanran then
turns the question toward the perspectivism of different perceivers; the dif-

ferentiated marks are a small portion of what the human and heavenly eye see, subsumed in the greater scope perceived by the Buddha-eye. These perceivers are themselves identical, each eye entails the others, because of the *Lotus Sutra* relation of the practices and cognitions of the human and heavenly vehicles and the Bodhisattva practices and cognitions, the setup/punch line structure of the Four Onenesses discussed above. The independent differentiated things perceived by deluded beings are "opened and revealed" to be the interpenetrative Dharma-realm; they are not rejected as nonexistence, and thus unqualified to be discussed as either interpenetrating or failing to interpenetrate. I think it is safe to say that Fazang could say either that these events are the entirety of Li, or that they are not Li at all, or both, or neither, but he could never say that they themselves are "a small portion" of Li itself. The two-level ontology of Huayan thought entails an all or nothing approach; first, Li and *shi* are separate, given ontologically distinct definitions as the undividable non-self-nature and the differentiated events, respectively, and then they are recombined and shown to be wholly interpenetrating. So each event, seen as really being nothing other than Li, is the entirety of Li; and each event, as being the opposite of Li, is no Li at all. This is exactly what we would expect from a *universal*, a genuine concept, even if it is the undifferentiated "universal universal." Conceptual universals have no parts: they are either instantiated or not instantiated, all or nothing.[35] The Tiantai view, on the other hand, deriving more directly from the indigenous Chinese mereological view derived from a whole/part model, is that each event is itself part of Li itself, and each part of Li is interpenetrative with all of Li. Li divides, Li has differentiations to it, in an important sense there are in fact many Li, which are then sublated, but there is no two-level ontology involved. What has whole and parts is not a concept but a given intuition, an actually present experience. What we have in Tiantai is an omnicentric whole: to be seeing anything is to be seeing a part of it, and to be seeing a part of it is to be seeing all of it. One simply cannot be not seeing it, full stop. Anything seen is a coherence (non-ironic, a seeable) a local coherence which as such is also global incoherence (the irony of this very coherence as it coheres with the "more parts" of the whole) and the interesubsumption of all the parts. The very colors and events we see with our human eyes are themselves Li; to see them is to see Li. We must remember here the basic meaning of Li: it is what must be cohered with to produce further coherences, or, in Buddhist terms, what must be realized and accorded with in order to realize liberation: the unconditional omnipresent that subsumes and manifests itself as all other things and conditions. These particulars we are seeing are what must be known in order to be enlightened.

EXISTENCE AND NONEXISTENCE IN TIANTAI AND HUAYAN

The Huayan notion of reality and appearance allows for a concept of
Non-Being in the absolute sense, the sense ironized by Guo Xiang, as opposed
to the Laozi/Zhuangzi sense, the ironic sense that continues to prevail in
Tiantai. That is, in Tiantai there is no such thing as an entity that may be
adduced, raised for consideration, but which in the end can be concluded
simply to not exist. The binary yes/no does not apply to the category of
existence; it is not true to say that something either exists or it doesn't. Just
being able to be asked about already qualifies it for minimal existence in the
Tiantai sense: anything that any sentient being perceives, however deludedly or however fleetingly. For indeed, by the Three Truths understanding of
upāya on the *Lotus Sutra* model, whatever is entertained in the mind of any
sentient being "exists" in at least that sense. No possibility is rejected on the
basis of being a mere illusion, which "in reality" does not exist. In Huayan,
as we have just seen, there are some possibles that "do not exist" in Li, and
are thus of no account and not a part of enlightenment. These contrasting
ideas of nonexistence play a crucial role in the differing conceptions of "the
mutual identity of particulars" as deployed in the two schools.

Fazang's discussion of "mutual identity" in the *Huayan yisheng jiaoyi
fenqi zhang* focuses on the categories of "Emptiness and existence" (空有
kong you). The crux of his argument is given as follows:

> Because when self exists, the other necessarily does not exist, the
> other is precisely the self. And why? Because the other has no
> self-nature, and is created by the self. Next, because when the self
> is empty, the other necessarily exists, the self is precisely the other.
> And why? Because the self has no self-nature, and is thus created
> by the other. Because these two existences and two nonexistences
> *are never simultaneous*, there is never any "other" out there with
> which one fails to be identical. Because [self] existing and [other]
> not existing, on the one hand, and [self] not existing and [other]
> existing, on the other, are nondual, thus they are forever mutually
> identical.[36]

Existence and nonexistence are *mutually exclusive* here, and the identity between X and Y means the reduction of X to an aspect of Y or of Y to
an aspect of X. Only one can "exist" at any time, or from any perspective.
If X exists, Y does not. If Y exists, X does not. If X is viewed as existing, Y
is merely an aspect of X, and hence there is no Y outside of X that it fails
to be identical with. If Y is viewed as existing, X is merely an aspect of Y,
and there is no X outside of Y that it fails to be identical with. These two

contrary views of the matter "are never simultaneous." This means that we can view it either one way or the other at any given time, but not both, and this is crucial to the argument for identity, since it means that whatever way we happen to be viewing the relationship at any given time, there will not be two coexisting beings counterposed and "other" to one another—"there is never any other out there with which one fails to be identical."

The relation between these two alternate ways of viewing the matter is then described as "nondual." Fazang does not give an explicit reason for this metalevel nonduality, but the implicit argument seems again to depend on non-simultaneity. The two views are reversible, but never simultaneous. This again means that at any given time they can never be in conflict with one another. Moreover, the fact that only one "exists" at any given time is "the same" in either case. In no case is there any other view, or other entity, in conflict with this view or this entity.

This same argument is reiterated, *mutatis mutandis*, for the other aspect of intercausality Fazang wishes to elucidate, namely, mutual entering (相入 *xiangru*), which focuses on "having power and lacking power" (有力，無力 *youli, wuli*). We notice immediately its resonance with the Zhuangzian argument about "this" and "that": there is always only one "this," and when X is "this," non-X becomes "that," and vice versa. But there is also something new and rather strange in this argument. We are told that the two views are never simultaneously entertained, and yet Fazang's own discussion here is precisely a way of simultaneously entertaining them. Fazang has thus surreptitiously introduced a metaperspective, his own, which in fact enunciates a global view that comprehensively embraces the two supposedly mutually exclusive views. Explicit reference to Li has dropped out of the discussion here, as in the Dushun texts, apparently to concentrate directly on the interpervasion of particular events themselves without further mediation by Li. But ironically, what has happened here is that *the suppression of explicit references to Li has allowed a single, synordinate comprehensive view of Li to define the field of discussion.* For the nonduality of the two alternate views is established only within the embrace of this comprehensive view of the true enunciated by Fazang himself. This is a jumping out of perspectivism similar to the transition from the "Inner Chapters" to the "Autumn Floods" version of Zhuangzi's relativism, as discussed in chapter 2 of this book.

The Tiantai conception of mutual identity retains explicit reference to Li, with continually shifting levels of reference, without the assumption of absolute nonexistence as mutually exclusive with presence, and without a metaperspective. It is, I would claim, a more faithful expression of the Zhuangzian perspectivism in the "Inner Chapters." This can be seen again by considering the treatment of identity between the Three Truths. Fazang says that when X exists, it means that non-X does not exist, is subsumed into X because there is no "other" to fail to be identical with. But this would also mean, in the Tiantai view, that *there is no other to be identical with, either.* Indeed, this is precisely the crux of Zhili's later critique of Huayan-inspired explications of the identity between delusion and enlightenment: they end up asserting that "one exists while the other does not" (一有一無 *yiyouyiwu*), and thus there is no actual identity established between *different* entities.[37] The further reversal of the situation does not change the basic structure, but rather complicates matters by introducing an unspoken overriding "principle," which remains unrelativized because it simply never enters that discussion.

In contrast, Zhiyi says that the Three Truths are mutually identical in that when one is Empty, all are Empty (一空一切空 *yikong yiqiekong*). When one is Provisionally Posited, all are Provisionally Posited (一假一切假 *yijia yiqie jia*). When one is the Center, all are the Center (一中一切中 *yizong yiqiezhong*). So there is no Emptiness or Provisional Positing which is not the Center, no Center and Emptiness which are not Provisional Positing, no Provisional Positing and Center which are not Empty.[38] This is a discussion of the relationship between aspects of Li itself, not, it would seem, particular entities. But the point is that for Tiantai, all entities are just determinations, and the "abstract" determinations of the aspects of Li, the Three Truths, are in just the same boat as every other entity not matter how "concrete." Li is, in a word, a "dharma," like anything else: it is something coherently entertained in the experience of some sentient being. Why are the Three Truths "identical"? Not because "[w]hen Emptiness exists, Provisional Positing does not exist," and vice versa, and then the reverse. Among these three, it is not the case that when X exists, the other two, non-Xs, therefore fail to exist, that they must always have opposite valences. Rather, the structure here is just the opposite. If any is X, all are X. If any is Y, all are Y. There is a built-in, constant level jumping here. Emptiness and Provisional Positing and the Center are three discernibly different determinations, but ones that always turn out to be mutually reducible, synonymous. If the determination "Emptiness" is viewed as Empty, this is a disclosure of a way of reading the determinations "Provisional Positing" and "the Center" equally as "Empty," that is, as ambiguous. If the determination "Emptiness" is viewed as a Provisional Posit, the other two are thereby made readable in the same way, namely, as specific determinations. If it is viewed as the Center, the other two determinations are also readable as "the Center," that is, as absolute. "Absoluteness" is a specific, ambiguous, and absolute determination. "Specific determinateness" is a specific, ambiguous, and absolute determination. "Ambiguity" is a specific, ambiguous, and absolute determination. Focus on the ambiguity of any brings to light the ambiguity of all, and so on.

Because "specifically determinate" can never be merely a general determination, this same way of thinking applies to any particular provisional
posit. Hence, we find Zhiyi saying, "The mind is empty: thus all things are
empty. The mind is provisionally posited: thus all things are provisionally
posited. The mind is the Center: thus all things are the Center." Given
that A is B is C, we can say that since X is A, all Ys are A; since X is B,
all Ys are B; since X is C, all Ys are C. X is a ambiguous, so all Ys are also
ambiguous; X is specifically determinate, so all Ys are specifically determinate; X is absolute, so all Ys are absolute. It is not X being specific that
makes all Ys disclose themselves as ambiguous, as we might expect. It is
not that the fixity of one term in the field ambiguates all the other terms.
Rather, when any one term is seen as fixed, this simultaneously fixes the
meanings of all the others. As soon as one term is seen as ambiguous, all
the others are suddenly also unsettled, ambiguated. When the reversibility
and identity of these two, and therefore the absoluteness, is seen for one
term, all other terms are also seen as absolute.

This is the precise opposite of saying, with Fazang: "Given that A and
B are mutually exclusive, we can say that since X is A, all Ys are non-A;
since X is non-A, all Ys are A. Therefore, X is both A and non-A, and Y
is also both A and non-A. The Aness and non-Aness of X and Y are never
simultaneous, and thus never in conflict, although always mutually exclusive.
X is thus Y, Y is thus X." Quite a different logic is at work in this Huayan
formulation. It remains dependent on the relation between "unchanging
and following conditions" (不變隨緣 *bubian suiyuan*) predicated of the
Nature, that is, of Li itself. These are identical only in the qualified sense
that "having changing, differing determinations" is a necessary property of
the "unchanging real nature" of pure non-self-nature, lack of a determinate
character. Any particular determination that might arise from the nature is
always the whole nature in its entirety, disclosing the purity of that unde-
termined nature precisely by its ability to take on determinations, to arise,
to make-present. This determination is a real part of the nature only in
this sense, as "a presentation," and in this sense it subsumes all others, it
exists, while the others don't. Its "existence" here is the existence of the
nature, the undividable whole. As this determination itself, rather than as
determination as such, it is an "existence within passionate attachment"
(情有 *qing you*) only, and does not exist. For it is impossible for the nature
to be in two places at odds with each other; it is entire in this X, and thus
when this X is seen as the nature (as presenting-determination-as-such) all
the other determinations "do not exist." The consideration that this can,
in turn, be applied to all the other determinations is alone what makes
interpenetration work here. But this application of the same consideration

to other determinations remains unthematized, an expression of the meta-perspective of final truth adopted by Fazang himself.

We still have not arrived at the Tiantai argument that X is Y here, however. It depends on the doctrine that establishing not only the "empti-ness of the nature" (性空 *xingkong*) but also the "emptiness of attributes" (相空 *xiangkong*), and the fact that the Truth of Provisional Positing is never refers to just "specificness in general," but always starts with some genuinely particular determination being experienced, as we have already mentioned. This does not mean that every determination can be deduced in advanced from this determination present to me here and now. It means rather that as experience proceeds, as new determinations arise, they are always seen also *retrospectively* as having been preexistent, as being further disclosures of the nature of the initial determination which are not arising anew, but are read-able as eternal and absolute, as identical with every other determination. I will be arguing that this sense of retrospectively apprehended preexistence of particular determinations is precisely what is lacking in the Huayan account of interpenetration, which thus limits its understanding of Li.

What Zhiyi means by the interpenetration as identity can perhaps be understood more clearly from his incidental early works than from his more intricate mature works such as the *Mohezhiguan* 摩訶止觀, which seem to presuppose an understanding of the more basic points made in the earlier texts, expanding upon their implications, and *exemplifying* these doctrines as a method applied on all levels of analysis, rather than expounding them simply as a content of doctrine. In the *Liumiaofamen* 六妙法門—a text that also, unlike the *Mohezhiguan*, has the advantage of having been composed by Zhiyi himself, rather than cribbed from his lectures by his disciple Guanding 灌頂—Zhiyi discusses six types of practice: Counting (數 *shu*) (the breath), Following (隨 *sui*) (the breath), Stopping (止 *zhi*) (the mind), Contemplat-ing (觀 *guan*) (mind and body), Returning (還 *huan*) (i.e., turning back to contemplate the contemplator), and Purity (淨 *jing*) (the elimination of all the fixed differentiations defining the previous steps). He first presents these six steps as successive phases in a meditation program, to be followed in the order given. Then he presents them as each being appropriate as a starting point for practitioners of various differing dispositions. Then he goes on to show how each gate actually encompasses or subsumes all the others, giving a good sense of what Zhiyi means when he says two qualita-tively different dharmas are in fact "identical" to one another: "counting" as such includes following (one is following the breath as one counts it), stopping (one stops thinking of other things when thinking of the breath, and comes to rest [stop] in the breath), contemplating (one contemplates as one counts), returning (one keeps returning to the breath), and purity (all other differentiations and obstacles cease as one counts); to "count" is already to "follow," to "stop," to "contemplate," and so on.[39] The same consideration is spelled out for the other steps: to "contemplate" is already to count, to follow, to stop, and so on. Note that in each case, we are considering a particular characteristic as such: "following" as such, ignoring the question of what is following what. The point is just this very dharma, which one was seeing *as* the quality "counting," can equally be read as the quality "following" and so on. In each case, even the root case, it is only an interpretative act of seeing-as.

After several mutations and combinations, he goes on to describe the relation between these six determinations and a seventh determination: the mind. Zhiyi tells us that this seventh determination, mind, is the "source" of all the others, but then continues to assert that each of them is *identical to* the mind. "Mind is the gate of following" is to be understood here not as an assertion of two separate things, the mind and following, one of which is in some sense the "gate" to the other. Rather, Zhiyi clearly means here that "mindness" is "followingness." The entity formerly identified as "mind" is now recontextualized, looked at from another angle, and seen to be the entity "following." The characteristics that allowed it to be identified as mind—awareness, discernment, etc.—can be redescribed so that they allow it to be identified as following. The coherence "mind" is equally readable as the coherence "number" or "following" or "stopping," and vice versa, always in this same tenuous, metaphorical way; for it was only "mind" in this same tenuous, locally coherent way. It is in this sense that Tiantai conceives inter-pervasion and mutual identity of all dharmas: to exist is to exist-with-others, defined by the border between the inside and the outside, but this border proves impossible to comprehend coherently, so whatever determinations are posited on the outside—encountered in the world, accompanying this coherence in any way—are equally to be found on the inside, as the identity of this coherence. It is not because the existence of the one negates the existence of the other. We will have more to say about this passage, and about the general Tiantai conception of mind, creation by mind, mind-only, and the relationship of mind to Li, in the following chapter.

WAVE AND WATER IN HUAYAN: "BEYOND" LI

The implications for the understanding of Li in the two schools of the above should be to some extent obvious. But we can get a clearer understanding of it by examining the deployment of the key metaphor of the waves and the water in the two schools.

The metaphor of the water and the waves is a well-known trope in Buddhist metaphysics. In the *Laṅkāvatāra Sūtra*, the water represents the pure essence of mind, and the waves the phenomenal realm that disturbs its tranquility, stirring it into determinate discriminating thoughts. The pure essence of the Eighth Consciousness is inseparably present in the other operations of the mind, but the disturbances must be removed for it to return to its pure, calm, unified state, which can reflect the phenomenal realm with mirrorlike clarity. The *Awakening of Faith* uses the metaphor in a similar way, but suggests that the disturbance is now derived from the "wind" of primal Ignorance. The Pure Mind, Suchness, the one, the undifferentiated, is the water. The many, the particular divided thoughts and phenomena as mental events, are the waves. Every experienced event is fully determined by Ignorance, is a wave, but is also a full presencing of the water itself. Yet the essence of mind is free from all thoughts, as the essence of water is free from waves.

This metaphor suggests that, although the waves are not the essence of water, the waves are nonetheless nothing but water. They need not be removed or replaced in order to restore the original character of Suchness. If their undifferentiated essence is seen, their undisturbed state can be attained. This could mean either that the waves must cease, or that seeing the wetness in the waves is itself tantamount to stilling them, even if they continue to exist. The *Awakening of Faith* seems to imply that the motion of the waves is not the real nature of water; its essence is, instead, wetness per se, which is never increased or diminished, no matter what state of waviness it may be in. In Huayan thought, the water represents Li and the waves events. Waves are entirely water, and this one quality of wetness is present *in its entirety* in each of the waves. Further, the water may be entirely waves. In some Huayen writings, it is possible to dismiss the implication that the waves must be stilled, leaving the water flat and calm. Rather, Li is entirely present in every event, and the events—the waves—are the way in which Li is expressed. Hence, each wave gives us the entirety of wetness—Li—which is all that all the waves are. In this sense, all waves are in each wave. Moreover, it is the nature of water to form waves. Li "does not hold onto its nature"—it must form waves. Water is waves and nothing besides, waves are water and nothing besides.

This is considered the apex of nonduality and antitranscendentalism in Huayan thought. Here, the metaphor is used to express what is sometimes called "nature-origination" (性起 *xingqi*). Tiantai writers use this term disparagingly, comparing it to their own doctrine of "inherent entailment" (性具 *xingju*). These Tiantai writers also use the water and waves metaphor, but with an important modification. Rather, starting with Zhanran, we find not a two-termed metaphor, as in Huayan, exploring the relation between (1) wetness (Li, sameness) and (2) wave (event, difference), but rather a three-termed metaphor, exploring the relation between (1) wetness (Li), (2) wave (events), and (3) various degrees of clarity and muddiness of the water (defilement). Through this modification of the metaphor, the Tiantai writers assert not that wetness is unchanging and one, while waves are changing and diverse, but rather that wetness is both one and many, waves are both one and many, and both are equally changing and unchanging, and further, that both defilement and purity are interpenetrating and omnipresent. This relates directly to the doctrine of "inherent entailment": defilement is to be accepted as a brute, unchangeable fact, not an illusion. It is, in fact, omnipresent, indispensable even in Buddhahood. But at the same time, by virtue of this very fact, it is also permeated with purity. To get a grasp on what this means, let us examine the deployments of this trope in detail in the two schools.

Another work attributed to Dushun, the *Huayan wujiao zhiguan* 華嚴 五教止觀, defines Li and 事 *shi* in terms derived from the *Awakening of Faith*: "The Gate of the mind's True Suchness is Li, the Gate of the mind's arising and perishing is *shi*. This refers to the nonduality of Emptiness and Existence [空有無二 *kong you wu er*], self-sufficiently interfused. They are manifested and concealed differently, but ultimately are without any obstruction."[40] We should carefully note the direct association of Li with Emptiness and *shi* with Existence, of both with aspects of "mind," and of the further step asserting their nonobstruction in spite of differences of manifestation (隱顯 *yinxian*). This discussion comes in the third section of a five-part work, corresponding to the "Final Mahayana Teaching" in the Huayan classification of teaching. The same section goes on to connect this idea to the simultaneity of *samatha* and *vipasyana* in terms that suggest that it is an attempt to crystallize the Tiantai teaching—and then perhaps transcend it in the next two sections of the text, in which the discussion of Li drops out entirely, and we have a direct discussion of the interpervasion of event with event, without any further direct reference to Li. This is a crucial point to which I will return. In a nutshell, as has already been touched on in the previous section, my claim here is that the Huayan works of "Dushun" and Fazang commonly attempt to transcend Li altogether, using it as a stepping stone to move into a direct discussion of "the interfusion of event with event" which is supposed to disclose the full attention to the real particulars, but which instead ends up bringing in a surreptitious level of *single-value Li (as standard of value and coherence) as the frame of the discussion*, creating a synordinate one-perspective view, precisely by suppressing the explicit discussion of Li.

The text goes on to introduce a trope that will have a large role to play in later Huayan and Tiantai: the water and the waves. The Dushun text equates water with Li, waves with events. "It is like the metaphor of the water and the waves. The different characteristics and forms of high and low are the waves, the equal nature of wetness is the water. The waves are devoid of any waviness that is other than water, so we illuminate water precisely in the waves. The water is devoid of any water that is other than the waves, so it is precisely the water that becomes the waves. The water and waves are one, but this does not obstruct their difference; they are different, but this does not obstruct their oneness. Because their oneness is unobstructed, when you are in the water you are in the waves. Because their difference is unobstructed, when you are in the waves you are not in the water."[41] The water and the waves are always copresent, so that whenever one is present the other is findable; but one can be aware of one without being aware of the other, so it is possible to say both that "being in the waves is being in the water" and "being in the waves is not being in the water." The latter means that "being in the waves" is ultimately *a different thought* from "being in the water." This amounts to saying that you can think of and experience the waves *exclusively as water*. They are distinguishable in thought, but when closer attention is paid, it is revealed that one always entails the other.

It is to be noted here that the waves represent differentiation, the water unity or equality. Waves stand for the differentiated particulars, water for the unifying omnipresence of the universal universal. Their interpenetration means both are present in every instance of waviness. Fazang uses the metaphor in exactly the same way, expanding further on the implications. As he says in the *Huayanjing tanxuanji* 華嚴經探玄記: "The non-obstruction of Li and events has two meanings: The first is that all the dharmas and teachings are wholly True Suchness [真如 *zhenru*], which does not obstruct the marks of the events being differentiated clearly from one another. The second is that True Suchness is wholly all dharmas, which doesn't obstruct their being of a single flavor, transparently equal. The first is like the fact that although the waves are precisely water, this does not obstruct the characteristic of motion; the second is like the fact that although the water is precisely the waves, it does not lose its wetness. . . . Truly it is all because the events which are wholly Li are neither the same nor different from the Li which is wholly events. Because they are not the same, they are present in one another; because they are not different they are identical to one another."[42] Water represents Li, the still, the equal, the wetness; wave represents *shi*, events, the moving, the different. These are neither the same nor different, and hence both mutually implicative and mutually distinguishable.

This reveals to us the basic notion of Li in Huayan. It should be noted that Fazang hopes to surpass this notion of Li, or see it as self-surpassing into the realm of "the mutual penetration of event with event." This is supposed to be because of the fact that Li is itself emptiness, and thus gets subsumed completely into the particular, and need no longer be a focus of discussion. Fazang takes this idea very far. In the *Huayanjing wenda* 華嚴經問答 we find the following:

Q: What is the difference between event and Li in the Three Vehicle Teaching and in the Universal [i.e., Huayan] teaching?

A: In the Three Vehicles, event means the mind that traces objects and the material form that is obstructive, and so on. Li means the True Suchness that is equal [everywhere]. Although event and Li differ, they are mutually identical and intermelding, and do not obstruct one another or damage one another. But the meaning of event is here still not the same as the meaning of Li [事義非理義 也 shi yi fei li yi ye]. In the Universal Dharma's teaching on event and Li, Li is itself identical to event, and event to Li. Within [the very definition of] Li there is [the meaning of] event; in [the very definition of] event there is [the meaning of] Li [理即事, 事即理, 理中事, 事中理 li ji shi, shi ji li, li zhong shi, shi zhong li]. Identity and being within-one-another are interchangeable [即中 中即 ji zhong zhong zi]. Although event and Li are unmixed, they vanish into one another without duality. Although they exhaust all words completely, words remain completely unexhausted. As Li is to event, so is event to Li. Speaking in terms of mind, all dharmas are mind; speaking in terms of form, all dharmas are form. . . . And why? Because of the Dharani of unobstructed dependently co-arisen dharmas, wherein the adducing of any one at random subsumes all, so that all are free and at ease, since when one is non-existent, all are non-existent. It is not so in the Three Vehicles; when it tries to disregard principle and speak of only events, it ends up involving no [real] events, precisely because the events [for them] are not free and at ease. When they try to speak of the teaching of the one mark, they end up establishing events in accord with deluded attachments, precisely because they don't [really] understand Li thoroughly. . . .

Q: Then how are event and principle defined in the Universal Teaching?

A: In terms of the temporary previous *upāya*, within material form the five-fathom body is defined as an event, while the unobstructedness of this body is defined as Li, and so on. But in the correct contemplation, we can also say that the five fathom body is the Li, and non-obstruction is the event, or the reverse. Within event, we can equally say that mind is defined as the obstructive, and that which traces along an object is defined as material form, and also the reverse. We can speak in whatever way is needed.[43]

In this passage Fazang's treatment is thoroughgoingly reversible, and seems to be very much in accord with the Tiantai treatment of these problems. It should be noted that here the question of identity is treated in the "if one is X, then all are X" mode typical of Tiantai writing, not the "if one is X, then all are non-X" we saw in Fazang's explication of mutual identity of particular events above. No fault could be found with the explication by a Tiantai writer, and it is passages such as this which have caused the greatest difficulty in finding the difference between Tiantai and Huayan treatments of these issues. But we must note here that this is an example of what Tiantai polemicists describe as Huayan using the words for mutual identity without grasping the meaning. We need to soberly consider whether such accusations are anything more than baseless sectarian polemicizing. The general construction of Fazang's argument above suggests that there is something to the Tiantai objection. In particular, even this extreme claim of the interchangeability of Li and event can be understood in terms of the water/wave model of Huayan thought, which it appears to be surpassing, and indeed it is really only comprehensible in this way. What Fazang means, I believe, is that the definitions of event and Li are, in Huayan, mutually implicative. Event always implies and includes Li, Li always implies and includes event. As we have seen in the explication of the Three Natures, to be the unchanging nature (water) is to present various dharmas following conditions (wave). Wave means water, water means wave, in that wave always means water-as-wave, and water always means wave-as-water. The further claim that "unobstructedness" can be called the event, and the five-fathom body the Li is thus still misleading, and mediated. For what is meant here is that the body "is really" itself nothing but the unobstructedness of conditioned co-arising, while unobstructedness "is really" itself nothing but unobstructed dharmas. Hence, we can say that wave is the principle and water is the event. But that this entire discussion still proceeds under the auspices of Emptiness as principle is proved by the further Q and A from this work, already cited, where Fazang says that the empirical difference between different bodies is merely delusion, having nothing to do with *actual* dependently co-arising dharmas. The body that is principle, in other words, is the body-as-dependently-arisen and hence unobstructed, not the deludedly conceived body as separate and obstructed, which is a mere deludely imagined appearance which in reality, and in Li, simply does not exist. "Wave" means principle only because wave is first understood as meaning only "water as wave," not "wave which excludes all other waves." Waviness as waviness itself, to wit, as deludedly conceived as merely itself and no other, does not serve as Li, that is, does not account for the interpenetration of all dharmas, is not what must be seen to attain enlightenment. "Wave" is principle only because "wave" really means "water as wave," and "water" in the same definition means "wave as water."

Fazang states very clearly that interpenetration cannot occur without both differentiation and undifferentiation, without event and Li. As he says in the *Huayan zhigui* 華嚴經旨歸, "If there were only event, there would be mutual obstruction and no mutual penetration. If there were only the Nature of Li, there would be only the one flavor, and again no mutual penetration. But now it is the intermelding of event and Li that entails this unobstructedness. This means that the event, which is non-different from Li, completely subsumes the nature of Li, so that all those many events, also non-different from Li, following that Li *on which they depend* [隨彼所依理 *sui bi suo yi li*], all of them being manifest within any one of them."[44] Note however that the relation of dependence remains unchanged here. The same must be said of Fazang's attempt to restructure his definition of Li and event so that dialectical equivocations are possible: it is not right simply to say that Li is undifferentiated and event is differentiated; rather, for each one must say it is, it isn't, both and neither, precisely because of the inseparability of Li from event. Li is not simply undifferentiated because all Li is also necessarily event, and so on. But in spite of this admirably subtle attempt to avoid one-way transcendence, it must be said that when all is boiled down we have an unchanged relation of dependence of event upon Li. This will become even clearer when we consider the relation of Li to mind in Huayan, below.

WAVE, WATER, AND MUD IN TIANTAI: INHERENT ENTAILMENT AS OMNIAVAILABILITY

This point may seem vague and even perhaps unfair. It can be made clearer, and I think fully persuasive, by considering the way a similar metaphor is deployed in Tiantai. For in Tiantai, starting with Zhanran, we find not a two-termed metaphor as in Huayan, exploring the relation between (1) wetness (= Li, sameness) and (2) wave (= event, difference), but rather a three-termed metaphor, exploring the relation between (1) wetness (= Li), (2) wave (= events), and (3) various degrees of clarity and muddiness of the water (= subjective delusion of sentient beings). Through this modification of the metaphor, the Tiantai writers assert not that wetness is unchanging and one, while waves are changing and diverse, but rather that wetness is both one and many, waves are both one and many, that both are equally changing and unchanging, and further, that both defilement and purity are interpenetrating and omnipresent.

Zhanran offers this metaphor in his discussion of "The Non-Duality of Taint and Purity" 染淨不二門 in the famous *Shibuermen* 十不二門 section of the *Fahuaxuanyishiqian* 法華玄義釋籤:

> If you recognize that the Dharma-nature has since beginning-less time been present only as ignorance, you can comprehend how the ignorance of this present moment is precisely nothing but Dharma-nature. Ignorance *creating* all dharmas everywhere, with the participation of the Dharma-nature, is called taint. The Dharma-nature *responding* to all conditions everywhere, with the participation of Ignorance, is called purity. The water may be muddy or clear, but *both the wave and the wetness* are in any case no different. Although the water's clarity or muddiness is due to conditions, this formation of muddiness has always been going on [濁成本有 *zhuocheng benyou*]. Although the muddiness has always been there, it is in its entire substance clear, because the Li of the two types of wave is omnipresently interconnected [通 *tong*], and the entirety of this substance [體 *ti*] manifests as [each] function [用 *yong*]. Thus all the Three Thousand, in all their various causes and effects, are called simply "dependent co-arising" [緣起 *yuanqi*]. The dependent co-arising of both delusion and enlightenment are inseparable from this present moment. The nature of this moment is eternal; the Li of dependent co-arising is one. But within this one Li there is [forever] a division of the pure and the impure. Looked at in terms of the divisions, six realms [purgatories, animals, hungry ghosts, Asuras, humans, and gods] are impure and [Śrāvakas, pratyekabuddhas, bodhisattvas, buddhas] are pure. But looked in terms of the omnipresence [of each] [通 *tong*], each one of the ten is both pure and impure [or, each is interconnected to both the pure and the impure]. Thus we know that the tainted substance of each moment is pure. . . . How could the person whose six sense organs are purified regard the ten realms as definitively and fixedly [定 *ding*] ten![45]

Zhanran tells us here, first, that Dharma-nature (法性 *faxing*) and Ignorance (無明 *wuming*) are mutually convertible: each one can appear *as* the other. Moreover, even when converted into one form or another, it always continues to function as both. Ignorance can appear as Dharma-nature, or vice versa, but in either case, a full description requires a reference to both. Each dharma always involves both Ignorance and the Dharma-nature. Purity and taint refer to the *relation between them* in any given instance. When Ignorance is central, it derives "assistance" (與 *yu*) from its peripheral other form, Dharma-nature, to *create* all dharmas. In Zhili's interpretation, this means that when the mind is entangled in conceptions of oneness and multiplicity, sameness and difference, as mutually obstructed, so that it dwells in and attaches to each moment of experience as a separate thing, it *transforms and creates* all dharmas: that is, it sees them as arising and perishing, coming into existence anew, standing separate from the continuity of the past and of the activities of the mind. When Dharma-nature is central, it derives assistance from peripheral Ignorance to *respond* to all conditions—i.e., to all the dharmas previously "created" by the tainted mind. Tainted creation is always prior and presupposed. According to Zhili, this purity means the interpenetration of oneness and manyness, sameness and difference, so that each moment of experience is released and abandoned into all others. Although Zhili rightly warns against interpreting this one-sidedly as asserting that, in all contexts, "taint equals creation, while purity equals response," the difference in modality is noteworthy. Purity functions on the presupposition of the prior existence of impurity, by virtue of its contrast, thereby making it an aspect of its own purity. Both the contrast and the subsumption are essential to the function of purity, which thus both preserves and transforms the existence of impurity. I have above described this relation as parallel to that of a setup and punch line of a joke, and this metaphor will be extremely useful here. Impurity is the setup, Purity is the punch line. For it is this model that allows us to see how Zhanran can go on to claim both that the impurity is always there and yet also that it is always also pure, as the setup is necessarily always prior, always unfunny, always contrasted to the funniness of the punch line, but for that very reason enables the setup, which retrospectively pervades even the setup with its funniness.

Moving into the metaphor of the waves and the water, Zhanran tells us that, for both the muddy wave and the clear (i.e., "pure") wave, *both* the waviness and the wetness are unchanged.

"Muddiness" represents taint or impurity: "Ignorance, with the assistance of the Dharma-nature, creating all dharmas." Ignorance is in this case central, Dharma-nature is peripheral, but both are always present. "Clarity" represents purity: "Dharma-nature, with the assistance of Ignorance, responding to all conditions." Dharma-nature is in this case central, Ignorance is peripheral, but both are always present. "Wave"—or better, waviness—represents "event" (*shi*), the conditioned arising of a particular occurrence at a particular time and place. More specifically, it is the Three Thousand causes and effects as "simply located" spatiotemporal events. "Wetness" represents Li, substance, the unchanging nature (理, 體, 性). This is neither one nor many, neither zero nor Three Thousand. It is the Three Truths, local coherence as global incoherence as intersubsumption. As discussed above, the upshot of this for the handling of sameness-difference relations is that all the Three Thousand discernible characteristics are each unchangeable and omnipresent. For this is what the Tiantai term 具 *ju* literally means: to be equipped with, that is, to have access to, to have available for use. Omnipresence here, as we saw was already the case in earliest Confucianism in the previous volume, really means omniavailability. Tiantai doctrine proclaims that "Evil entails goodness": that means evil always has goodness available to it as a possibility and as a resource. "Goodness entails evil": that means goodness always has available to it for its own utilization, can make good use of evil, is equipped with evil as a part of its upayic arsenal. When Tiantai says, "X is inherently equipped with Y," X and Y are not conceived as objects with inert characteristics inhering in them that we observe from outside, over there inertly entailing other objects; these are activities that constitute the very being of all experiences comprising sentient beings, who in Buddhism generally have no inert substantial being, but are rather nothing but their own activities, their karma. We who are contemplating "entailment" are not outside of the object contemplated as entailing other objects: we are ourselves no more and no less than an activity, "a single moment of thought" (一念 *yinian*) "equipped with access to" (具 *ju*) the objects we contemplate, which are themselves aspects of this action. We are inside the system being considered in our description, not outside of it, and our contemplation of all objects addressed in our theorizing is already presaturated with desire and evaluative intentionality. Sentient beings are activities equipped with access to other activities, activities to whom other activities are available. To "entail" in this sense presupposes actively inhabiting, presupposes the activity constituting the sentient being to whom something is available as part of the reality of acting in this way. This is an extension of the tendency to include human subjectivity as part of the constitution of ultimate reality that we have seen also in one way or another in all the pre-Buddhist Chinese traditions we have discussed. The operative assumption is that desire and value are also built into simply being in any position, to "being" something. To be anything is to be an intentional desiring activity equipped with access to all other types of activity, to whom all other things are available for evaluation, use, reinterpretation, subsumption. Now, by our definition, whatever is always available as value, and whose availability is a necessary condition of a given value, is a Li. Each is available everywhere, and each intersubsumes all of the others. Hence, none has a definite identity (it can always be read as any of the others), but all of them are irrevocably available at any locus. Each is everywhere and nowhere. These Three Thousand unchangeable omniavailabilities are Li.

This "one Li" is necessarily always inclusive of, divided into, both the pure and the impure. It is strictly neither one nor many. Conversely, taint and purity each includes all dharmas without exception. Taint is all dharmas, involving both Dharma-nature and Ignorance, seen under the category of "creation." Purity is all dharmas, involving both Dharma-nature and Ignorance, seen under the category of "response."

Both purity and impurity refer to types of event (shi). Both take place at a particular time and place: they are mental activities of sentient beings and buddhas, respectively. Both the muddy wave and the clear wave are waves. Moreover, both involve both "water" and "dirt." They are merely arranged differently in the two cases. A clear wave, after all, is not purely water; it is water and solidity arranged in a certain structure (all the water on top, all the mud packed on the bottom). Without the mud, the solid, there would be no "wave." The wave cannot exist in empty space. A pure wave—Buddhahood—is the copresence of Ignorance and Dharma-nature in a particular structure. The impure wave—delusion—is the copresence of the same two in a different structure (the mud dispersed in the water).

Both types of wave are entirely wetness. Wetness is a way of emphasizing the inseparability of Li, just as in the Huayan use of the metaphor. Wetness is putatively the same everywhere: each wave is not just partially wet, but entirely wet. Wetness is fully, not partially, instantiated in each wave. All wetness is involved in each wave.

All wetness is wavy, is in motion. All substance is function. All substance is involved in each function. The wetness of the clear wave and the wetness of the muddy wave are each omnipresent, fully present in both the clarity and the muddiness. But wetness is really just *motion*: slipperiness, instability, non-solidity—just as, as we saw above, Zhiyi had originally identified Li precisely with "non-dwelling" (無住 *wuzhu*). The sole reason for using this metaphor of wetness is to show the omnipresence of motion *per se*, which, as Zhili says, is a little harder to see, since it is also always particularized in some diverse way. Wetness is just a way of saying "waviness per se," what Zhili calls "just the one nature of motion per se." (*zhi yi dong xing* 只一動性). "Motion" here is another word for "dependent co-arising," which is to say, conditionality, which is to say, instability, finitude, karma, activity, unfinished process, inescapable engagement with otherness, limitedness per se. The one nature all things share is conditionality. And this in turn is why each instantiation thereof must always be readable as both pure and tainted, irreducible to any single characteristic (such as purity). All motions are one motion, as we might say that one wave is all waves, in the manner that applies when, say, a person is throwing a ball: the motion of his arm and the tensing of his ankle are aspects of a single motion. One wave is like the hand, the other like the ankle. They are different, but they are joined—*not* by their static sharing of a single nature analyzed from without, *not* by their static participation as organs in a total organism, which differ but all serve as articulated parts within a larger whole to which they are subordinated. It is neither a shared essence nor membership in a whole that makes them interpenetrate here: rather, it is specifically their "single nature of motion," their *action*, their instability, their waviness, their finitude and impermanence per se. That they move, that they cannot stand still, that they must diverge, that they can never settle into any oneness, is what unifies them. Their differences are all in action at once, fully instantiated in one another. Each activity (of hand, of ankle) must be equipped with all the other activities just to be the activity it is; to be activity X is to have all the other activities available as aspects of what it is already doing, and to be available to all the other activities in the same way.

To clarify this, let us return to the Tiantai explanation of the passage from the *Lotus* quoted previously: "This dharma dwells in the dharma-position, and all the characteristics of the world dwell eternally" (是法住法位, 世間相常住 *shifazhufawei, shijianxiangchangzhu*). For in the discussion of this passage we will find our water/wave metaphor again, related now to the tropes of "position" and "Suchness." Zhiyi had said of this passage:

> [Deluded] sentient beings and the perfect enlightenment [of the Buddha] are but one Suchness, not two. None are outside Suchness, and it is this being-Such of all dharmas which is thus their "position." "All the characteristics of the world dwell eternally," because given that Suchness is the position in which transmundane perfect enlightenment dwells, Suchness is also its characteristics. Both the position [位 *wei*] *and* the characteristics [相 *xiang*] dwell eternally. Similarly, Suchness is also the position in which the mundane deluded sentient beings dwell, and it is also their characteristics. How could those not also dwell eternally?[46]

Suchness is not only the "position" in which dharmas dwell—i.e., that beyond which they never go no matter how they change, what is constant to them, that in which they have their being. Suchness in this sense is a way of indicating the Emptiness of all dharmas, the one universal trait that is always "so, such" of them no matter what modifications they may undergo. But in another sense, Suchness itself is also their mark, their particular characteristics, just as Emptiness is also Provisional Positing, and is, indeed, every particular Provisional Posit. This is because "Suchness" simply means the being-such-and-such-of-dharmas, namely, being exactly as they are, the fact that dharmas are "such" unto themselves. "Being Such" is a way of saying what is unchanging about them, that no omnipresent universal can be attributed to them except the empty "like this," because they are so unstable; but this is also a way of talking about what is most particular and transient about them, the fact that they are so particular that no universal term at all can be predicated of them, nothing can be said but the empty statement that they are "just as they are." "Wetness" is a way of saying what is universal about all waves and also just a way of saying that all waves are thoroughly non-solid, non-dwelling, pure "motion," incapable of assuming any final fixed form, any one single characteristic (even that of "wetness")— i.e., that they have nothing stable or universal about them. Emptiness is Provisional Positing. Suchness is characteristics. Wetness is waviness. The one unchanging fact about things is absolute change.

This may sound like the Huayan point that to be Li (undifferentiated constant Suchness) always implies also to be event (divided, changing particular), and thus "interpenetration" always involves both, but the reasoning is subtly different. For in Tiantai the relation between these two contrasted sides is not mutual implication but recontextualized synonymity. Another way of saying Li, suitable for other contexts, is to say event. To be determinate is to be locally coherent is to be globally incoherent; and equally, to be globally incoherent is already to be locally coherent. There is no global incoherence that *is* not (rather than merely "does not imply") also local coherence. This being-locally-coherent is what never fails to be so of them, that they are always just as they are and exactly like themselves, they are always "Such." To be such is to be "just like this," and hence the "this" is the "such." The difference between "what it is to be this" and "this" *simpliciter* on which the traditional metaphysical establishment of essence and universals depends is here annulled. As A. C. Graham has noted, the term 如 *ru* as a translation of "Suchness," suggests "being as (not what) it is," comparable to isness in the sense of a predicative adjective ("He is tall," in Graham's example) rather than isness as existence ("There is a man").[47] Zhiyi's understanding of the term is consistent with this implication. As we put it above, to be is to be determinate, and to be determinate means not just to be determinate per se, but to be particularly determinate, to be Such, "just like this"—hence absolutely particular and not characterizable at all. To be determinate is to be indeterminate. To be coherent is to be incoherent. Hence, Zhanran comments on Zhiyi here:

> Dharmas never go outside of Suchness, so Suchness is their "position." Precisely this is what is true of deluded sentient beings *in Li* [i.e., as unchangeable omniavailability, though as yet unrealized], while precisely this is what the Buddhas have *realized* [so "precisely this" is what never changes whether one is deluded or enlightened]—this is what is meant by "dwelling." . . . Sentient beings and Buddhas are the dharmas that do the dwelling in it. The single *tainted and pure Suchness* is what they dwell in. *Because it is always limited, differentiated, fixed and determined*, it is called a position.

染淨一如是所住位。分局定限故名為位.

In all cases, they are said to have a "position," and it is for this reason that we speak of "the one Suchness." They never leave Suchness, so they are limited to just this [state of "having a position," i.e., being finite, determinate, locally coherent, and thus apparently simply located]. This limitation is omnipresent, is identical to interpenetration, since it pervades everywhere. It is the utmost limitation, and at the same time the fullest omnipresence.

不出真如故唯局此。此局即通遍一切故。局之極也。通之盛也.

It is like the "position" of a king in the mundane world. A person occupies this position, and the position is also the nature of this person, because it is unchangeable [as per the Tiantai definition of "the nature"], as a person's royal nature remains unchanged whether he is clad in rough cloth or is ascending his throne. [So far, then], the "characteristics" may differ, but the nature is what remains the same.[48]

According to Zhanran, "position" (*wei*) means finitude, determination, and it is "being determined and limited" (and therefore "limited in this particular way"), which is meant by "being-Such." By the argument rehearsed above, this being finite and determined, being (locally) coherent as such and such a particular entity, is identical to being all-pervasive and infinite, precisely by virtue of being finite, of having borders. That is, the position of all things, which they never leave, their constant nature, is the state of "having a position which is finite, simply located, and hence can never be dwelt in constantly." One thing that is determinate and particular about them is *that* they are determinate and particular, but this particular determinate characteristic is true of any contrasting determinacy as well. Their unchanging nature is, in more traditional Buddhist terms, to change, which also implies to be limited (in time), finite (in space) and determinate. The state of being finite is the Suchness (just like this, some specific way) which they never leave, which is thus unchanging, is the case, no matter what specific "position" they may inhabit, which is thus applicable everywhere, is omnipresent, is universal, is infinite. Being is being Such is being finite is being everywhere and everywhen. Suchness is finitude, and finitude is infinity. To be is to be conditional, which is to be empty, which is to be unconditional. Provisional Positing is Empty is the Center, and all are alternate names for conditionality, finitude. This "being-finite" is the unchanging nature of all dharmas.

Up to this point in Zhanran's comment, we still have changing characteristics contrasted to an unchanging nature, and determination-as-such, specificness per se, rather than particular determinations. But this is not all. Zhanran continues:

"The characteristics of the world dwell eternally." "Characteristics" means what can be outwardly flagged [i.e., whatever is distinguishable]. "The position" means what can be dwelled in enduringly. But the characteristics are none other than the position, whether of enlightenment or of delusion. When delusion is made explicit, it is seen to be precisely Li, and Li is precisely what dwells eternally. The Buddhas have already realized this eternity, while sentient beings are identical to it in Li [i.e., "potentially," in terms of its preexistent omniavailability]. Hence both the characteristics and the position—of both sentient beings *and* of Buddhas—dwell eternally. Since *the pure and tainted characteristics and positions* are all one Suchness, the Li of characteristics and the Li of positions must be equivalent. The Buddhas cultivate and realize the supreme Li in accordance with the mundane world, which shows that the mundane world originally possesses this Li.

Q: The position may be one [unchanging] Suchness. But how can the characteristics also be equal [and thus eternal]?

A: The position refers to the Li or Nature, which absolutely can never change. The characteristics refer to the following of conditions, which differ as to taint and purity. Although the conditions may differ, they are all instances of what is called "dependent co-arising." It is like clear and muddied waves; their wetness is no different in either case. Since they are the same in that it is just the wetness that is deemed to be the waves, we say Suchness is their characteristic. Since they are the same in that it is just the waves that are deemed to be the wetness, we say that Suchness is their position. Thus the characteristics also share in the eternity [of the position]. Although they have the same name, since they differ as to taint and purity, *it is necessary to make this distinction with respect to Suchness, the positions, as well.*

The point is that it is not only the "position" or "Suchness" or "the wetness," that is, "the Nature" that is one, everywhere equal, eternal, unchanging, omnipresent, but also the characteristics, the waves. In other words, not just "being-such" is constant, but, since being-such can only mean being finite and limited and determined in *this* particular way, the specific characteristics disclosed in all possible experience are also eternal. Conversely, *Suchness itself is also differentiated*. This is the crucial point; the way the Huayan writers set up this metaphor, and their general system, makes it increasingly difficult for them to make this claim about Li. Zhili comments on this metaphor:

> The muddied water represents the tainted mind in delusion. The clear water represents the pure mind after the attainment of Buddhahood. The waves represent the fact that the Three Thousand are all Function. The wetness represents the fact that the Three Thousand are all Substance [i.e., Li, the Nature]. It must be understood that although the water is muddied in the case of the tainted mind, there too the entire wave is nothing but wetness; when the water is clarified, how could this be some other wave *or* some other wetness? Thus when [Zhanran] says there is no difference between them, he means that *both* the wave and the wetness are always the same. . . . This is to explain how the characteristics of the world dwell eternally. But characteristics are originally what is changing and moving. To make clear in what sense they are nonetheless eternal, it is necessary to elucidate the matter in terms of their "position." The entirety of each characteristic is nothing but the position, so if the position is eternal, the characteristics are also eternal. Hence the text says the position is nothing other than the characteristics. . . . Now I will explain Zhanran's meaning: Since the question he poses for himself asks how each characteristic could be everywhere equal, it is clear that the answer is intended to show this constantly equal presence of the characteristics on the analogy of the omnipresence of having-a-position. . . . The intent is to show the constantly equal presence of the characteristics, but since the characteristics include both the tainted and the pure, their omnipresence is hard to reveal. Thus Zhanran first uses the wetness to talk about the position and its omnipresence, and also to reveal that all characteristics are nothing but the position, the entire waviness is nothing but wetness. The point is to allow us to understand the characteristics by analogy to the position and show how they are *both* equally present at all times. . . . Moreover, if we want to focus on the difference, how could it be that just the characteristics are different, and not the position as well? Thus this section of the text goes on to say, "since they differ as to taint and purity, it is necessary to make a distinctions concerning

Suchness *and concerning the position as well.*" Is this not because the
tainted characteristics necessarily take *entangled* Suchness [在纏真如
zaichan zhenru] as their position, and the pure characteristics take
disentangled Suchness [出纏真如 *chuchan zhenru*] as their position?
In terms of equality, since the clear and muddied waves are both
one single wetness, we can also say they are one single waviness,
because after the [muddied] waviness is purified, *it is still the same
motion and function* [動用 *dongyong*] *as when it was muddied.*[49]

The unchanging Suchness is not only the undepartable "position" of
all dharmas; it is also, precisely, their characteristics as unchanging. Conversely, change and diversity are not only the characteristics of all dharmas;
they are also, precisely, their Suchness as changing and diverse. A characteristic is nothing but a position—i.e., a set of boundaries. To be positioned is
to be conditioned, to have a necessary outside. Conditions differ, but all are
conditional. Any conditionality is a specific, differing conditionality—that
is what it means to be conditional. To be conditional is to be specific, to
be limited, to differ from others. But there is no "differing as such"—that
would not be really differing, but still a universal sameness. To be merely
"determinate as such" is still to be indeterminate. But it is precisely because
this determinate characteristic as such is universal that each characteristic
is all characteristics. Wetness is the unchanging nature of the changing,
differing waves. But the presence of waviness (or *dongyong* 動用, "motion
and function," as Zhili puts it, or finitude, or determinateness, unstable
unfinished other-engaging process, conditioned karmic activity) is also the
same, whether the water is muddied or clear. The universality of wetness
is adduced, Zhili says, merely to illustrate what the universal presence of a
single attribute is like, what a universal is: the real point is to the universality of waviness, which is harder to see because of the difference in the
shape and muddiness of the waves. But the wetness is precisely the waviness, and both remain the same everywhere, both pervade the entire sea.
This is because to be a wave is to be moving, to be always different, and it
is only in this sense that the clarified waviness is the same waviness as the
muddied waviness it used to be. To be a particular wave is to be wetness
is to be waviness is to be non-dwelling, unrestrictable to any simple location, equally discoverable in any location. As Zhanran said, their position
is to have some limited position, be some "suchness," and this position is
never transcended. The muddy wave is the same wave as the clear wave
in exactly the same sense in which even the muddy wave is "the same" as
itself—because "wave" is just a way of indicating "waviness." Hence, Zhili
says clearly that both sameness and difference apply to both the wave (i.e.,

the waviness) and the wetness. As Zhili puts it, "The whole substance is clear, because the two waves, muddy and clear, are just the one motion, just one unchanging nature of movingness."[50]

This "just one" must be understood in the sense of the "Four Onenesses" discussed above. The point is not that there is a single shared essence—motion or waviness or wetness—that is the secret identity of each apparently different wave. Motion, waviness, is indeed the nature of a wave (i.e., its intrinsic characteristic that identifies it as a wave, which is always so of it no matter what changes it may undergo). But being a wave is just being waviness. To be a wave is to be waviness, and even the identification of a single wave in two consecutive moments of muddiness is a partial construal focusing abstractly on the sameness (waviness) at the expense of the difference, both of which are equally applicable, and strictly speaking, synonymous. Any other wave is the "same" wave to just the same extent as "this" wave is the same wave in any two consecutive moments—that is, provisionally—although "different" is an equally accurate description in both cases. Any particular instance of conditionality "co-arises" with all instances. This is because "conditionality" cannot function as a normal universal, which remains other to its instances, which remains unchanging and the same as against its changing, differing instances. With this universal, both the universal and the instances are eternal, and simultaneously, *both* the universal and the instances are constantly changing. The universal too constantly changes, can never be one. Li is also multiple, just as much as it is singular.

Both difference and sameness are applicable at every level here—both purity and taint, both mutability and constancy. The muddiness is there from the beginning, but, as Zhili says, muddiness is not the nature of water. This is not because the nature of water is rather purity or unchangingness, a single pure nature, but because its nature is to be non-dwelling as either muddy or clear, its nature is finitude as interpenetration, determinacy as indeterminacy as the interchangeability of the two—the Three Truths. All the waves are both defiled and pure, because any single wave has the nature of moving, from muddy to clear and from clear to muddy. It is the "same" (different) wave that is muddy or is clear.

In sum, given that the one shared nature is "movingness" (impermanence, dependent origination, conditionality, determinate finitude) itself, both "the nature" and "the characteristics" are eternal. The characteristics are, in the metaphor, the shape of a particular wave, its frothiness, its motion, its history, its progression. The difference between this same characteristic as "pure" and as "muddied" rests simply in how it is seen to be related to other characteristics. Nothing else about it changes. Muddiness here equals simply separation, obstructions, severing of contexts. In this sense, muddiness is "not the nature of water," because "it is not the nature of waves"—the real nature of "movingness" itself. Mud here stands for the inertness, the solidity, the separation of the solid as opposed to the liquid. It is not the nature of "being a characteristic" qua characteristic to be isolated from other characteristics: that is, this is not the nature of being finite, of inhabiting a limited "position." The muddiness is a nondisclosure of the real nature of what limitedness is, that is to say, what a limit is, what finitude is, what conditionality is, what locatedness is, what determinateness is. For to be determinate is, in Tiantai, to be locally coherent, which is to be globally incoherent: to be determinate is to be indeterminate, to be limited is to be connected to all other contexts. To be separated is actually another way of saying to be connected; separation, this thing being itself and none other, is only coherent in the context of its articulation within a group of other things, other characteristics. This thing being itself is a manifestation of its interconnection with other things, its inseparability from them. The Three Truths is a way of showing that the notion of a hard-and-fast border between any two characteristics is ultimately self-contradictory; they can be neither fixedly internal nor external to one another.

In simple terms, this means that the "what" of any event or thing never changes, any more than its "nature" does. This red cup falling to the floor is eternally red, eternally a cup, eternally falling. What changes when the broader contexts are also brought into consideration is not the "what" of the thing, either as to its distinguishing characteristics or its shared nature, but the "how." It is now this same "what" in all the ramifications emerging from its connections with the rest of the waves and their wateriness. It is now red as interpenetrating, cup as interpenetrating, falling as interpenetrating. It is now red as white-ceramic, it is now cup as broken shards, it is now falling as past.

Shall we see this as a second-order dualism? The "how" at least seems to change decisively, and can always be translated back into a "what": it was formerly a fact that these characteristics were viewed qua isolated, while afterward this has been *replaced* by a new fact, the fact that these unchanged characteristics are viewed qua interpenetrating. But this view is a result of again failing to include the subjective inclinations and cognitive states among the phenomena that interpenetrate. This is precisely what Zhanran's passage just quoted aims to prevent. "In terms of their differences, the six realms are defiled and the four realms are pure, but in terms of their omnipresence, all ten realms are defiled and all ten realms are pure." Both sides of this equation must always be included in a complete account. If we imagine a single wave passing through ten stages of increasingly unmuddied water, we could say that the wave at the first position is entirely muddy while at the last position it is entirely clear. But we can also say of this wave and every wave that it is always both muddy and clear. For the whole motion from front to back is the same wave, and at all times part of the wave is the other waves before and behind it. Muddiness, solidity, is not the nature of water, of wetness, of waviness. But to push the metaphor, it of course the motion of the wave that stirs up the mud, that muddies it. And it is the further motion of the wave that finally clarifies it: the wave moves on from the muddy spot, it cannot stay there. And that is why the muddiness dwells eternally!

What we are to imagine in this metaphor, as used in Tiantai, then, is not the usual trope, as found in Indian Buddhist works, in the *Awakening of Faith* and in Huayan, which the Zhili's disciple Kedu 可度 describes well as simply directly taking the waves to represent acquired characteristics, transformation, and function, and the water to represent the nature or the unchanging substance.[51] In the Tiantai version we have not two levels, but three. The clarity and muddiness represent the pure and defiled minds, each of which involves all dharmas, involves both Ignorance and Dharma-nature, structured differently (i.e., with a different "how" but not a different "what"). The waves represent the pure and defiled functions. The wetness represents the *pure and defiled* substance, or Li. Wetness is just a way of speaking of the omnipresence and thoroughgoingness of waviness. To be wet is simply to be wavy, to be slippery, to be in motion thoroughly and in every molecule. Wetness is obviously the same everywhere, but waviness is less clearly a "universal," so this expedient is used to reveal waviness as omnipresent. In other words, Li is just a way of talking about the omnipresence of function, motion, dependent co-arising, conditionality. At every level, considered even in itself alone, we have both purity and defilement, both sameness and difference, both mutability and constancy. We have waves moving through both muddy and clear water. The water does not move, only the waves do. But it would be senseless to think of a "wave" that was simple statically muddy or clear; if we take a cross-section of a wave at a specific moment and free-frame it, cut off the rest of the motion, surrounded not by the rest of the ocean but instead by a blank white space, there is no wave there at all, only a formation of water standing still. This could not be water, but only, say, an ice statue of a wave. To be wet is to be wavy, which means to be moving through both clear and muddy water. To be a wave is to be in one specific place, but also, by definition, not to be only in that one place. Each single wave passes through both muddy and clear water. But it is not simply a matter of integrating the wave into the whole of the ocean, seeing it as part of the whole. Instead, the interconnection is accomplished precisely by the division. For a single unchanging ocean, considered as a static whole, would also not be wavy. For the wave to be a wave, it must be both separate, specific, distinguishable *and* interconnected. Wetness is motion, and motion is separation. Wetness is motion, and motion is interconnection. Separation is interconnection. Dependent co-arising, conditionality, is separation and specificity, being one thing rather than, and contrasted to, another. But dependent co-arising, conditionality, is interconnection, such that being just this thing in isolation would be failing to be this thing. The muddiness stays where it is, and the clarity stays where it is. They are perfectly and completely divided, each finite, dwelling in its own position. It is precisely because each stays right where and how it is, and never changes into the other, that they interpenetrate; indeed, this dwelling in their own position is their interpenetration. Their interpenetration is their division; as Zhanran says in the citation above, "the limitation is identical to interpenetration, since it pervades everywhere; it is the utmost finitude, and at the same time the fullest interpenetration." The wetness is divided into muddied and clear wetness. Each wave is both a muddy and a clear wave, and is every other muddy and clear wave. The muddiness is entirely wet waviness as muddy. The clarity is completely wet waviness as clear.

Hence, to be is to be determined, is to be finite, is to be indeterminable, is to be this particular thing and every particular thing as such, which is to say, as Such. In terms of praxis, this was to be realized in the contemplation of "the Three Thousand as each moment of experience" (一念三千 *yinian sanqian*). Not *in* each moment, not *born from* each moment, but *as* each moment. The Three Thousand are neither prior nor posterior to this experience; they are this determinate experience itself, as the characteristics of a thing, in particular the characteristics of its arising and perishing, are precisely that thing itself.

It is this eternity and omnipresence of X that is meant in Tiantai when X is spoken of as being "inherent in the Nature," or "X qua the Li." It means "X as necessary, eternal and omnipresent." Li in this context means the Three Truths. But here we can assert that any other specific determination is Li in a much more literal and unmediated sense than that put forth by Fazang even in his passage about "the body" above. In Tiantai, each particular, even every deludedly imagined, mutually obstructive particular, is really Li in the sense of what must become intelligible and accorded with in order to achieve enlightenment. It is just this that is at stake in Zhili's insistence on the "two levels of whole and part, in Li and event" (理事兩 重總別 *lishi liangchong zongbie*) To understand this, however, we must first consider the role of "mind" in the two teachings. Before taking that on, however, let us make a summary of the differences between the two schools explored so far, in relation to classifications of teachings in the two traditions, as they relate to the themes developed in this book.

SUMMARY OF DIFFERENCES BETWEEN TIANTAI AND HUAYAN,
AND THE IRONY OF COHERENCE IN THE TIANTAI AND
HUAYAN CLASSIFICATIONS OF TEACHINGS

The Tiantai classification of teachings, in the terminology of Guanding's
(561–632) *Tiantai bajiao dayi* 天台八教大意 ("Overview of the Tiantai
Eight Teachings") and Chegwan's (Ch: Diguan 諦觀 d. 971) *Tiantai Sijiaoyi*
天台四教儀 ("Tiantai's Four Teaching Methods"), systemizing Zhiyi's more
expansive and diffuse treatment in his *Sijiaoyi* 四教義 ("The Meaning of
the Four Teachings"), introduces eight categories, four of which apply to
the contents of the teachings and four of which apply to the methods
of teaching. The first group are "Dharma-teachings which convert beings"
(化法四教 *huafa sijiao*) and are comprised of the Tripitaka Teaching, the
Shared Teaching, the Separate Teaching, and the Integrated Teaching
(藏教, 通教, 別教, 圓教 *zangjiao, tongjiao, biejiao, yuanjiao*). The second
group, the "Four Teaching-Forms of Conversion" (化儀四教 *huayi sijiao*), are
the four methods of the Sudden, the Gradual, the Secret, and the Unfixed
(頓, 漸, 秘密, 不定 *dun, jian, mimi, buding*). These four methods apply
only to the first four of the "five periods of teaching": the Avatamsaka,
the Tripitaka ("Hinayana"), the Vaipulya (方等 *fangdeng*) and the Prajnâpâramitâ. The Integrated Teachings as presented in the *Lotus* and *Nirvana*
sutras are neither sudden nor non-sudden, gradual nor nongradual, and so
on. The Sudden and Gradual mean the "Sudden" and complete disclosure
of the whole truth in the *Avatamsaka*, the "gradual" disclosure in the upayic
teachings. The last two methods refer to the way in which the teachings
are understood differently by different listeners, either beknownst (as in the
Unfixed method) or unbeknownst (as in the Secret method) to one another.

Fazang's classification uses five categories: the Hinayana (*xiaoshengjiao*),
the Beginning Mahayana (*dasheng shijiao*), the Final Mahayana (*dasheng
zhongjiao*), the Sudden (*dunjiao*), and the Integrated (*yuanjiao*). The final
category is further subdivided into the Same-One-Vehicle Integrated Teaching (同教一乘圓教 *tongjiao yisheng yuanjiao*) and the Separate-One-Vehicle
Integrated Teaching (別教一乘圓教 *biejiao yisheng yuanjiao*), the last being
the Huayan teaching and the penultimate more or less equivalent to the
Tiantai teaching. Fazang's categories are equivalent to Zhiyi's Four Dharmas
of Conversion, that is, the four types of content, with the addition of the
"Sudden" teaching, which in Zhiyi had been a name for a method, not a
content. By rearranging the list so that the Sudden is placed in tandem
with the other four Dharmas of Conversion, Fazang creates a parallelism
that changes its implications considerably. For Fazang, the Sudden means
the teaching that is beyond words, which cuts off all determinate thoughts,
where a single moment of nonconceptualization is equivalent to Buddha-

hood, with no gradual stages. The Huayan category of the Hinayana is equivalent to the Tiantai category Tripitaka, the Beginning Mahayana to the Shared, the Final Mahayana to the Separate, the Integrated to the Integrated. This equivalence is directly acknowledged by Chengguan, who remarks, "The reason Tiantai (Zhiyi) did not include the category of the Sudden is simply that for him each of the Four Teachings has a dimension of wordlessness to it. We separate it off now to allow the Sudden to manifest the wordless teaching as a separate category, a method appropriate to those with a capacity to separate from all thoughts, in accordance with the Chan school."[52] But as Dong Ping has pointed out, this redefinition of a method into a content brings certain problems with it.[53] In particular, it has profound implications for how the ironic aspect of coherence is understood in the two traditions. In accordance with the Three Truths doctrine, every determinate content without exception is also ambiguous, is indeterminable, is beyond words, for to be determinate is to be ambiguous, devoid of a univocally discernible identity. This is the aspect of Emptiness that pertains to any Provisional Posit as such. To make "beyond words" itself a content makes of it a particular determination, which would make it another "Provisional Posit." This is, of course, consistent with Three Truths doctrine in that "Emptiness" is in fact a Provisional Posit—is itself specific, and thus is ambiguous, and is absolute. But sectoring it off as a separate content gives a misleading impression of setting up a wordlessness that does not work in the same way as the wordlessness "of" all contents, which is rather itself a content not susceptible to the same considerations as any other content, while also draining the wordless aspect out of the other teachings. Determinate and indeterminate are here set up as mutually exclusive, rejoined only by the integration of the Integrated Teaching. We see here a suggestion of mutual exclusivity of existence and nonexistence, in this case of determinations, which echoes the Huayan treatment of these concepts generally, as discussed above.

This of course has implications for the issue of the "intelligibility" aspect of Li in general. For although Fazang of course also adds "speakable but not speakable, thinkable but not thinkable" to his description of the Integrated Teaching, the mere possibility of a content of teaching that is one and not the other (the "Sudden" Teaching as purely unspeakable) skews the field of discourse significantly. Similarly, in Fazang's division of the Integrated Teaching into two types, the "Same Teaching" Vehicle, generally referring to the *Lotus* and Tiantai, is the Integrated Teaching seen as having no other content than the other teachings as *upāyas*, but reconfigured, while the "Separate Teaching" Vehicle, representing Fazang's own Huayan position, is seen as a new and unique content on its own right. The issue here is really the status of intersubjectivity. If there can be a "Separate" version of the Integrated Teaching, it means that real truth can, at least in principle, be conceived apart from the *upāyas* which led up to and express it in particular intersubjective situations, and indeed that enlightenment can at least be conceived as a content in a particular sentient being's head, which has no necessary relation to the enterprise of communicating that content to other beings. In other words, intersubjectivity is not constitutive and inescapable for Fazang as it is for Zhiyi, and this is in keeping with the former's notion of Li as a single indivisible whole (at least "in principle").

It will be noticed that the structure of this move is similar to several others we have considered. For Fazang, illusion can be separated from reality (that something is taken to exist in illusory clinging does not guarantee its existence in Li), Being from Non-Being (when this dharma is seen as existing, all the others are seen as nonexistent), subjectivity from intersubjectivity (Separate Vehicle), intelligibility from unintelligibility (Sudden Teaching), at least conceptually or in principle. All of these dyads are, on the contrary, strictly inseparable, even interchangeable, for the Tiantai tradition. This puts us in a position to sum up the difference between the notion of coherence/Li in the two schools.

In a nutshell, in Tiantai, coherence *is* incoherence. That is, (local) coherence is (global) incoherence. All coherence, therefore, is "ironic" coherence. Now, "incoherence" itself, if it is anything, if it can be predicated of anything at all in any sense, is just one more coherence. Hence, it is only ironically coherent as "incoherence." This is the meaning of the claim that Emptiness is not decisively (*ding*) Emptiness. This second-order "coherence" (harmonious togetherness, indeed interchangeability, identity) between coherence and incoherence is the Center. All there are anywhere, concretely or abstractly, mentally or physically, are coherences that are incoherences. They are coherent in the sense of "intelligible," incoherent in the sense of "unintelligible," also coherent in the sense of "sticking together" among intelligibles, also in the sense of the "sticking together" of coherence and incoherence. They are also coherence in the sense of the object to be known in order to become enlightened, that is, in order to create further harmonious coherence (salvific Buddha activity, responding to sentient beings, opening up all provisional views to reveal their identity to ultimate truth, etc.). Each event, particularly intelligible coherence (事 *shi*, having a beginning and end, an inside and an outside, and therefore a determinate intelligible) is just this same coherence (Li) seen partially, incompletely, dimly, hastily, unthoroughly. The perception of this table is an event (*shi*) that, if seen (intelligibly) more completely, is this table as Li, as salvific Coherence, as Eternal, Self, Blissful, Pure, (常樂我淨 *chang le wo jing*—i.e., the characteristics of the unconditional) engaged in eternal Bodhisattva activity, and every other type of activity. We have here a multitude of Lis, coherences, which interpenetrate just as the events do, for they are the same Three Thousand, considered either as Three Thousand Li or Three Thousand *shi*. We might speak here of "the nonobstruction of Li with Li," or "principle with principle," "coherence with coherence." We will discuss the implications of this at more length below.

In Huayan, on the other hand, all particular existences are again nothing but coherence, but here in the sense of unobstructed, indivisible togetherness (Li). They are also "coherence itself" in the sense of "intelligibility itself," that is to say, becoming present in awareness, which is where the marriage with mind-only comes in. But this unobstructed, indivisible togetherness which is intelligibility itself (not particular intelligibles), this "coherence itself," is itself incoherent, that is, inconceivable, all-inclusive, hence having no outside; any particular intelligible designation divides this indivisible coherence. Hence "coherence (intelligibility) itself" is ironic, *strictu senso* unintelligible. But *this* "incoherence" is not itself a coherence here, as it is in Tiantai, and remains *non-ironic*. This is precisely because it is posited as a specific content that is supposed to be unproblematically aligned with the contents of the other teachings—i.e., it is definitively, unproblematically intelligible as "unintelligibility." Similarly, Li appears to drop out of the picture in the Huayan Integrated Teaching, because Li as such is ironic, unintelligible as such. Each event is the disclosure of the entirety of Li in the sense that "intelligibility," presencing, unobstructed togetherness of events, is disclosed as every event—but, "ironically," in this seeing of Li completely in each event, Li is really not seen at all—Li is "seeing as such," which cannot itself be seen. Here, we cannot speak of "the interpenetration of Li with Li," principle with principle, for there is no multiplicity of principles—Li is either none (unintelligible, ironic) or One (coherence as such).

SEVEN

MIND, OMNIPRESENCE, AND COHERENCE IN TIANTAI AND HUAYAN

THE PURE MIND AND THE DELUDED MIND IN HUAYAN THOUGHT

We turn now to the treatment of mind in the two schools. For it is in the context of a dispute about the status of the mind, and its relation to Li, that the Tiantai doctrine of the "Three Thousand as Li, Three Thousand as event" (理三千, 事三千 li sanqian shi sanqian) is expounded by Siming Zhili, which is the occasion of the manifestation of the distinctive Tiantai treatment of Li, the culmination of our study. This is not accidental. We have treated the epistemologies and axiologies and theories of mind in the various thinkers already discussed in a passing way, but even there it has been clear that the understanding of Li involves a concealed reference to some kind of picture of what human subjectivity is. Li is a coherence that is knowable, intelligible to a human mind; it needs to harmonize in some way with the human cognitive apparatus to count as Li. Li is a coherence that is valued, wanted by the human mind; it needs to harmonize in some way with human desires to count as Li. The relation between mind and Li becomes more specifically addressed in the Buddhist context, because a particular state of mind is itself regarded as the highest value; indeed, in some forms of Chinese Buddhism, mind per se is value per se. How value is to be apprehended by humans—how mind can apprehend mind, how Li can apprehend Li, and whether it needs to do so—becomes a new kind of dilemma here. The relationship between the seeking of value and intelligibility—the mind that gropes for Li—and the Li so sought now opens up new vistas for controversy. The differing ways in which Li is understood will thus necessarily also involve differing conceptions of the mind—the seeking, knowing, valuing mind, on the one hand, and the mind as value-itself, on the other—and its manner of apprehending Li. These varying conceptions of mind, conversely, can allow us to understand exactly what the implications of these differing conceptions of Li are, and what is at stake in these disagreements.

We can give a schematic summary of the conclusions of the previous chapter here to anticipate the implications of this doctrine for our understanding of Li in the two schools. Zhili will be claiming that any determination, any coherence, any dharma, can be considered in four different ways:

1. As one specific part of the totality of events, one specific event (事別 shibie);

2. As the event that serves as the totality of which all other events are parts (事總 shizong);

3. As one specific part of the totality of Lis, one specific Li (理別 libie);

4. As the Li that serves as the totality of which all other Lis are parts (理總 lizong).

If we compare this to the famous "Four Dharmadhatus" of the Huayan school, we can quickly get a sense of what the issue is here. The Four Dharmadhatus are:

1. The Dharmadhatu of events: all dharmas seen as events (事法界 shifajie);

2. The Dharmadhatu of Li: all events seen as Li (理法界 lifajie);

3. The Dharmadhatu of the nonobstruction of Li and event (理事無礙法界 lishiwuaifajie);

4. The Dharmadhatu of the nonobstruction of event and event (事事無愛法界 shishiwuaifajie).

These are four alternate ways of viewing the totality of all that exists, representing ascending levels of spiritual attainment. All things can be seen as events, as Li, as events-that-are-Li, and as events-that-are-all-other-events. The Third Dharmadhatu here means seeing each event equally as some particular dharma and as itself identical to the one undividable Li. The Fourth Dharmadhatu means seeing each dharma equally as this particular event and as all other particulars subsumed into this event. If we compare the Tiantai and the Huayan schemas, we may say that the first category in the Tiantai scheme is equivalent to the first in the Huayan scheme—the ordinary world of sundered particular events. The second Tiantai category, event as totality, is equivalent to the *fourth* Huayan category: the interpenetration of events. The third Huayan category, which sees each event equally as the total one Li, is equivalent to the fourth Tiantai category: Li as totalizer of all events, which allows them to interpenetrate to form one indivisible whole. But there is no Huayan equivalent for the third Tiantai category, a particular Li as part of the totality of Lis, subsumed into another Li.[1] Indeed, it is senseless, as we have just seen, to speak of a multitude of Lis in a Huayan context. Tiantai, on the other hand, strictly speaking has nothing that corresponds to the second Huayan category, the world as Li only. Peter Gregory has shown that Zongmi shifted the emphasis of the Huayan system from the Fourth category, interpenetration of events, to the third, interpenetration of Li and event, simultaneously identifying Li with the Original Pure Mind, the preexistent Original Enlightenment in all sentient beings. My claim here is that this difference in understanding of Li is what made this shift possible, and that even if an adjustment were made to return the focus to the interpenetration of events with one another, this still would not be equivalent to the Tiantai understanding of the relation between Li and event. The crux of the matter, again, is whether we can speak of *more than one* Li. The importance of this difference will become evident in consideration of the practice of mind-contemplation, to which I now turn.

The treatment of "mind" in Tiantai and Huayan undergoes a strange history. Mind is a much more central and constant topic of discussion in Zhiyi than in Fazang. It does not become a really central term in Huayan thought until Chengguan and Zongmi, probably under the influence of Chan and a particular reading, indeed, of Tiantai. But I will argue here both that the later Huayan treatment of mind is a distortion of the early Tiantai ideas on this topic, following an early Chan direction instead, and also that this reading of mind is overdetermined by Fazang's admittedly ambiguous and scanty treatment of the problem, and the general features of Fazang's thinking about the relation of Li to *shi* as outlined above.

In fact, Fazang's teacher Zhiyan had already defined the contours of Huayan thinking about mind. In his *Huayan yisheng shixuanmen* 華嚴一乘 十玄門, purportedly representing the teaching of Dushun himself and giving the earliest Huayan exposition of the famous "Ten Wondrous Gates" (*shixuanmen*) of interpenetration, the ninth gate is called "Weixin huizhuan shanchengmen" 唯心迴轉善成門 ("Skillful Completion by the Turning of Mind-Only"). Zhiyan says:

> This is expounded with reference to the mind. When we say that it is only mind that turns, we mean that all the previous meanings and teachings are established by the Pure True Mind of the

Nature of the Tathagatagarbha. Both good and evil follow the turnings of this mind, so it is called Skillful Completion by the Turning. Because there is no object outside the mind, it is called Mind-Only. If it turns with the flow [順轉 shunzhuan], it is called Nirvana. . . . If it turns against the flow [逆轉 nizhuan], it is called Samsara. . . . For this reason we cannot definitively say this nature is pure or impure. . . . Q: If there is no object outside the mind, and the existence or nonexistence of each thing is determined completely by the mind, then why is it that when a person first sees something placed beyond a barrier, and afterward someone else moves the thing away, the first person's mind still thinks it exists there? At that time the thing is actually nonexistent there, so how can you say that it is made so or not so by the mind? A: If you are talking about the turnings of the false, deluded mind [虛妄心 xuwangxin] it can be said simultaneously that this thing beyond the barrier turns with the mind and equally the converse, that the mind turns with the presence or absence of the thing. But if you are talking about the True, Real, Pure Mind of the Tathagatagarbha Nature 如來藏性真實淨心 [rulaizangxing zhenshixin], this thing never leaves its original place, and yet its essence responds in all directions, its nature constantly turning. Even if it is moved to a different place, it is [in reality] constantly unmoved in its original place.[2]

Here, a distinction is made between the Pure Mind and the Deluded Mind. All things are "turned" by the former in that it is the essence of all things, which pervades all times and places. It is the real ontological ground of all existence. But the deluded mind can only be said to "turn" things in an ambiguous sense; it both determines and is determined by external things. "Mind-only" is clearly asserted here primarily of the Pure Mind. The relation between these two minds remains a bit unclear; we can assume perhaps that they share the relation between any event and the true nature of Li, that is, they are identical and different from it, and identical because different, and different because identical, in the distinctive Huayan sense delineated by "Dushun" in the Fajieguan. But the reality determined by Mind-only in the strong sense is only the reality of interpervasion, of being everywhere at once, not, again, the divided, differentiated, here-and-not-there of ordinary experience. The existence of the latter is made so by the mind in one sense, namely, in that the deluded mind mistakenly takes them to be here and now rather than there and then, but in another sense it is the mind that is determined by these existences, which in some undisclosed way exist apart from it.

Yang Weizhong has pointed out that a similar ambiguity exists in Fazang's discussions of mind. Fazang uses the term One Mind (一心 yixin) for the Pure Mind that is identical to Li, to the Tathagatagarba, to the Pure "Illumination" (明 *ming*) of the nature and so on. He uses "one's own mind" (自心 *zixin*) for the Deluded Mind, the mind that makes distinctions and "creates" the world only in the weaker sense. According to Yang's analysis, "one's own mind" is used by Fazang to denote a mediator between the One Mind and the external objects of which it is the substance, the "existential condition" of the mind in the moment of the encounter between these two aspects of the True One Mind.[3] Noting that Fazang changes Gate Nine of the Ten Wondrous Gates from Zhiyan's "Mind-Only," just quoted, to "Host and Companion of Perfect Illumination Replete with All Virtues" (主伴圓 明具德門 *zhuban yuanming jude men*), which seems to indicate a turn away from the Mind-only implication of the previous formulation, or from the identification of Li with the Pure Mind as such, Yang goes on to point out that nonetheless the phrase "Perfect Illumination" (圓明 *yuanming*) used in this formulation continues to refer to the "Essence of Perfect Illumination of the Purity of the Self-Nature," which is another name for Zhiyan's Pure Mind, and thus "the sense of an idealistic ontology is not diminished one iota" by this change.[4] While that might be a slight overstatement—it does seem clear that Fazang was uneasy about the one-sided idealistic meaning, and made some efforts to counteract it—I think this judgment is ultimately correct. This can be seen by looking at Fazang's admittedly scarce and ambiguous references to the role of the Pure Mind in his other works.

In the *Huayanjing tanxuanji*, Fazang adopts the language of the *Awakening of Faith* (*Qixinlun*):[5] we have the "gate" of Mind as Suchness (真如門 *zhenrumen*) and of Mind as Arising and Perishing (生滅門 *shengmiemen*), that is, as temporal and conditional, each of which considered alone is said to subsume all dharmas, without being confused. Moreover, the two are themselves intersubsumptive. Significantly, Fazang adopts the metaphor of water and waves, discussed at length in the previous chapter, to explain this identity between two terms which nonetheless remain distinct: "The waves that subsume the water are not for that reason still, and the water which subsumes the waves is not for that reason moving."[6] The opening words of his commentary to the text from which these terms are derived, the *Dasheng Qixinlun yiji*, makes the same equation of the "True Mind" with the unchanging, undifferentiated "water," in other words, with Li.[7] This would suggest that "mind as Suchness" is simply another name for Li, for the Pure Nature. Mind as arising and perishing would then be "one's own mind," maintaining again the two minds spoken of by Zhiyan, and asserting their identity and difference in accordance with the water/wave metaphor. It is "one's own mind" that gives rise to things in the ambiguous second sense of adding differentiations to the undifferentiated nature of Suchness. The transforming, differentiating mind, "one's own mind," is the mind Fazang speaks of as standing in a relationship of *interdependence* with perceived dharmas: "Objects are not objects by themselves; they necessarily depend on the mind in order to be objects. The mind is not the mind by itself; it necessarily depends on objects to be the mind."[8] The interdependence between this mind and all other entities is just like that between any other events, and their interpervasion follows the same contours. It is a 事 *shi* among *shi*. But both this mind and these events exist and pervade due to their identity with Li, which is here equated with the Mind as Suchness. Very near the climactic end of the *Huayan yihseng jiaoyi fenqizhang*, his most systematic work, after already expounding all the variations of interpenetration in his version of the Ten Wondrous Gates, Fazang gives us almost exactly the sentence we had found in the Zhiyan work: "The Gate of the Skillful Completion by the Turning of Mind-Only, this means that all the previous meanings are nothing but the turnings of the One Pure True Mind of the Self-Nature of the Tathagatagarbha."[9] Elsewhere, describing the Ocean Seal Samadhi (海印三昧 *haiyin sanmei*), he says, "This refers to original enlightenment. . . . This Mind subsumes all mundane and transmundane dharmas, and is the Dharma-gate Essence of the One Dharma-realm Universal Mark [總相 *zong xiang*]. It is only because of deluded thoughts that there are any differentiations. If all deluded thoughts are left behind, there is only the One True Suchness."[10] This assertion is, of course, to be contrasted to Zhili's later claim that differentiations exist even in the absence of deluded thoughts.

However, Fazang's "One True Mind" is not to be understood as a monolithic undifferentiated blank. In the *Huayan yisheng jiaoyi fenqizhang*, for example, he explains how the conception of mind differs in the Five Teachings. In the "Sudden Teaching," "all dharmas are just the one Mind of True Suchness, all differentiated marks are obliterated, so it is free of words, cuts off thoughts, is unspeakable." In the Integrated Teaching, "the focus is on the Perfect Illumination [圓明 *yuanming*] of the Ocean of the Nature, the dependent co-arising of the whole Dharma-realm, unobstructed and free, so that one is all, all are one, and host and companion are perfectly intermelded."[11] All differentiations are gone in the sense that everything is now interpenetrating. Note that here the term *mind* is again replaced by "Perfect Illumination," as Yang Weizhong notes, and if not for the context, which is a discussion of "Mind" in each of the Teachings, it would be easy to overlook any reference to a transcendent Mind here at all. The same term is used in the programmatic description of "The One Substance" in the *Xiu Huayan aozhi wangjin huanyuan guan* 修華嚴奧旨妄盡還源觀, usually but not definitively attributed to Fazang. The One Substance, according to this text, means, "the Substance of the Perfect Illumination which is Pure in its Own-nature. But this is precisely the substance of the Dharma-nature within the Tathāgatagarbha, which has from the beginning been perfect and replete in its own nature. Situated within taint it remains unpolluted, in the practice of cultivation it remains unpurified, and thus we call it Pure in its Own-nature. The Substance of this Nature shines everywhere, so that all darknesses are lit up, and hence we call it the Perfect Illumination."[12] It is unchanging and aware, so it is called pure and mindlike. As identical with the True Suchness of Li, this Pure Mind or Perfect Illumination remains the transcendent reason for the interpenetration of event with event. Fazang is sometimes quite explicit about this, as when he states flatly, "As for the many levels of inter-reflection within Indra's Net, all these events and marks are made to be unobstructed because of the Perfect Intermelding of the Mind-consciousness Dharma-nature of the Tathagatagarbha"[13] (皆是心識如來藏法性圓融故， 令彼事相如是無礙 *jie shi xinshi rulaizang faxing yuanrong gu, ling bi shi xiang ru shi wu ai*). Grammatically, it is not absolutely impossible to read this in a more "Tiantai" way, to wit, as "because of the perfect intermelding of the dharma-nature . . . *of* the [deluded] mental consciousness," but the context, and Fazang's other pronouncements on this topic, push us toward the other meaning. But in either case, the causal connection is quite clear, as evident in the blunt usage of the 令 *ling* in this passage; it is the same "*neng yi/suo yi*" (能依， 所依 dependent, depended on) dichotomy between Li and event, understood as the undifferentiated (undividable, interpenetration per se) and the differentiated (separated, sundered), respectively, the asymmetrical dependence relation between Li and *shi* that we observed in Dushun's *Huayan fajieguan*, and this seems never left behind in all the interpenetrations of the Huayan school. Note also that practice here seems to consist in attempting to view this Pure Mind itself functioning in all things, as displayed in their interpenetration.

However understated this stress on an absolute Pure Mind that is the source and ground of all phenomenal appearances is in Fazang, it is brought front and center in the writings of Chengguan and Zongmi, which is the version that comes to influence the Shanwai Tiantai writers of the Song dynasty most directly. This aspect of later Huayan thought is well documented, and we need not belabor the point here. The gist of this way of thinking is summed up succinctly by Chengguan, echoing Fazang's formulation: "Mind is the universal mark [總相 *zong xiang*]. In the state of enlightenment it is called Buddha, completing dependent co-arising of the pure. In the state of delusion it makes sentient beings, completing the dependent co-arising of the tainted. Although there is taint and purity within dependent co-arising, the Substance of Mind does not differ [in them]. When one attains the fruition of Buddhahood one accords with this Mind, and becomes infinite (unendable) just like the True [i.e., Mind, Li]. *Deluded dharmas come to an end (are finite)*, and so they are not spoken of here. The old translation [of the *Avatamsaka* sutra] says, 'Mind, Buddhas and sentient beings—there is no difference among these three.' This would mean that all three are infinite. But 'infinite' is precisely the mark of 'non-differentiation' [無別 *wubie*], so it should say rather that concerning Mind, Buddhas and sentient beings, the *Substance and Nature* [體性 *tixing*] of all of these is infinite and inexhaustible. Because the Substance of delusion is originally the True, it can [in this sense] also be said to be infinite and inexhaustible."[14] This is further clarified by his flat assertion that "awareness is the Substance of mind [知即 心體 *zhi ji xinti*]. Differentiating knowledge is not True Awareness, so True Awareness is uncognizable by ordinary consciousness. The arising of optical defects [creating illusions] is also not the True Awareness, so the latter is not a condition or object of mind [非心境界 *fei xin jingjie*]. The Substance of Mind is free of thoughts [離念 *linian*], there are no thoughts in it to be destroyed, and thus we say that the nature is originally pure."[15]

Mind is here the one Universal mark (總相 *zongxiang*). It is strictly and literally synonymous with Li. It is the Substance, the Nature, the ground of interpenetration and presence of all differentiated dharmas. It "creates" (造 *zao*) both delusion and enlightenment, and is unchanged in either state. It is precisely Non-dwelling, but this is understood as identical with Awareness (知 *zhi*), which is *free of* the transformations of thoughts (念 *nian*). Particular things are a function of these differentiated thoughts that arise and perish, which are infinite and inexhaustible in that their Substance remains always the same unchanging nature of non-dwelling awareness, but which are perishable, having perhaps a beginning but certainly an end, in their marks as particulars. Zongmi's position follows more or less the same lines, as Peter Gregory's extensive analyses have shown.[16] Mind, pure awareness, is the unconditional, the omnipresent, for mind as pure "illumination," as the awareness that does not rise and fall with the temporal coming and going of discrete thought-moments, is simply the fact of not being limited to any possible finite condition or state or perception or conception, the non-dwelling of any particular in itself, shining out always to an other, which it immanently pervades. This illumination, which is the pure and ever-present essence of mind, is itself precisely "nonobstruction between events," interpervasion as such, what presences and unifies all particular things, is in its essence undifferentiated and interpenetrative, and this Mind as such, unchanging awareness, is the coherence of things (omnipresent unifying totality of all interpenetrative particulars) which must be realized in order to realize enlightenment—in other words, Mind as such is Li.

MIND AND THE NATURE IN TIANTAI THOUGHT

Let us now turn to the Tiantai understanding of mind and its role in Buddhist practice. For the doctrine most central to our inquiry into Chinese understandings of Li is Zhili's assertion, in sharp contrast to the Huayan view of Li as undifferentiated totalizing subsumer and *shi* as differentiated subsumed part, that there are "two forms of subsumer and two types of subsumed" (理事兩重總別). Li is both subsumer and subsumed, and event (*shi*) is also both subsumer and subsumed. Each Li can be seen as the whole subsuming all other Lis and all events, or as a Li subsumed into another Li, or subsumed into an event. Similarly, each event can be viewed as both the whole subsuming all other events and all Lis, and also as a part subsumed into all Lis and into all other events.

This doctrine is put forward in the context of a discussion of meditational practice, in controversies about the true meaning of mind-observation (觀心 *guanxin*) and inherence-observation (觀具 *guanju*) in Tiantai. To understand the fourfold schematic of Li/event relations in Tiantai, given above, we must look at the relation between "mind" and "the Nature" in Tiantai praxis. "Mind" is, in this context, the exemplar of an *event*, while "the Nature" is strictly synonymous with Li. That is, in contrast to the Huayan view of mind as Li, for Zhili's Tiantai, mind is a series of *shi*, events that arise and perish in time (these events are *nian* 念, individual thought-instants or moments of sentience). The structure of the Mind/Nature relation is precisely the structure of the *shi*/Li relation. And yet Tiantai accepts all the same extravagant Mahayana scriptural claims about mind as the creator, source, ground of all dharmas that Huayan does. Zhili's position is that all these claims are ultimately pragmatic—as are all claims, statements, and propositions in a Tiantai context: they are true in some sense, they are locally coherent, they are *upāyas*. In this case, they are the Buddha's instructions for a particularly effective form of meditation, the practice of mind-contemplation, in which the Three Thousand Li and the Three Thousand events "both take one moment of [deluded] experience *qua event* as their subsuming whole" (皆以事中一念為總 *jieyishizhongyinianweizong*).[17] As we will see in the final section of this chapter, Li is indeed what *enables* the event—in this case, a moment of mental experience—to subsume all things, but it is not Li directly that is observed doing the subsuming in this practice. Rather, what is to be observed is the untheorized, manifest fact that the mind does in fact subsume all events and all Li, which is, when understood through doctrinal considerations, then seen as manifesting Li, the interpenetration of all Li, and the interpenetration of all Li and all *shi*. The initial fact to be observed is the way one particular even—a moment of experience—turns out to have always been doing this odd subsuming, serving as totalizer, *zong*, to whatever it touches. This subsuming on the level of event is just the noticing that the nature of all consciousness, deluded or otherwise, involves a multiplicity-as-oneness, or a oneness-as-multiplicity, that all distinctions and characteristics experienced as different are possible only as "dwelling together in a single moment of experience" (同居一念 tongjuyinian).[18] As we shall see, this simply means, for example, that whatever the mind turns its attention to, whether an isolated event or fact (i.e., as a shi), or a some particular quality as omnipresent and unconditional (thus, as a Li), it finds that this quality and the seemingly antithetical character of "being-here-and-now-noticing-it"—the quality of mindedness—are copresent, mutually pervasive, coextensive: no boundary can be found separating subject and object, and if one existed, there could be no contact between them and thus no perception of the object by the subject. And yet subjectivity and objectivity are definitionally mutually exclusive. Mind and object of mind are one but different. Similarly, present moment and past and future moments are one but different. Any X and the non-X whose contrast to X allows X to manifest as X are one but different. Merely to experience a characteristic is to experience a difference, and the experience of a difference is only possible as this copresence of contraries and interpenetration, the Li of the Three Truths.

It is on this particular shi/Li relation that the later Tiantai writers lavish the most attention, giving them the opportunity to explain what the "totality of Lis" and so on might mean. More specifically, it is in this context that we find the resources by which to understand the as yet unbroached topic of the relation *between* the four levels in the schematic above. In the Huayan system, as we might expect from its straightforward approach to the Two Truths, we have a simple progression; one's insight develops, through Buddhist practice, from the First Dharmadhatu to the Fourth. In the Tiantai case, we will find Zhili asserting a kind of meta-identity as the ultimate goal of practice: the ability to see the identity *between* the four levels, so that the event as totalizer is seen as the Li as totalizer, and the differentiated events as the differentiated Li. To get at this crucial point, as I said, we must make a detour through the Tiantai descriptions of the relation between the mind and the Nature.

I have in mind in particular the use of the compound terms xinxing 心性 and what this tells us about the Tiantai conception of xing, which is synonymous, in these contexts, with the Tiantai conception of Li. The term xinxing appears frequently in Zhanran's works, and the apparent ambiguity of his usage of this compound served as one of the primary sources of the "Shanjia/Shanwai "debates in the Northern Song dynasty, particular in regard to the understanding of Buddhist praxis. The interpretation of this binome is particularly important to the contested question of how to understand mind-observation. Zhili's "Shanjia" position, which will be my focus here, can be clarified through an examination of his understanding of Zhanran's crucial usage of the term xinxing in the Shibuermen. The following passage is the core text around which this debate revolves:

[All the possible objects of knowledge presented by Zhiyi in the *Fahuaxuanyi*], from the realm of the Ten Suchnesses up to "Non-Truth," can each be understood either in terms of the sub-suming whole or the subsumed parts. The subsuming whole is a single instant of experience, while the subsumed parts are divided into physical and mental. . . . Once one understands the subsumed parts, the parts must be seen as subsumed into the subsuming whole: all dharmas without exception are *xinxing*. There is only this one Nature—but the single Nature is the absence of any Nature. Thereby the Three Thousand particular existences are all there as always. Thus it should be known that since mind-and-matter [qua the Nature] are here *as* the mind,[19] just the mind is what is meant by its transformations. These transformations are what is meant by the creation [by the mind of individual things, which are distinct from and opposed to mind]. Creation [in this sense] is what is meant by [the entire] substance [being expressed *as*] the function. Truly it is for this reason that there is neither mind nor matter, there is both mind and matter, there is only mind, there is only matter.[20]

且十如境乃至無諦。一一皆有總別二意。總在一念。別分色心。
。。。既知別已，攝別入總。一切諸法。無非心性。一性無性。
三千宛然。當知心之色心，即心名變。變名為造。造謂體用。是
則非色非心。而色而心。唯色唯心。良由於此.

The binome *xinxing* in this phrase "All dharmas without exception are *xinx-ing*" can be interpreted in at least the *five* following ways:

1. *Xinxing* means "Mind-nature." This is how the term will prob-ably initially strike the eye of most readers familiar with the way in which this binome is usually used in other schools of Chinese Buddhism in this period of history.[21] Mind-nature would mean the constant defining characteristic or essence of mind, Mindness as such. "All dharmas are Mind-nature" would then mean that all constituents of experienced reality are, when understood truly, reduced to their ultimate essence, nothing but Mind. This means that what they really are, in spite of appearing as matter and other types of non-mind characteristics, is mind, the essence of mind, mindlikeness, mentalness. Saying all dharmas are "mind-nature" is equivalent to saying they are all mind, i.e., are "made of" mind, are reducible to mind-stuff. The true essence of matter, on this reading, is Mind. This, in highly oversimplified form, is more or

less how the Shanwai writers read this passage, and, as shown above, how this term would be understood in a Huayan context.

2. *Xinxing* means "mind's nature." This reading, while sounding very close to the first interpretation in both Chinese and English, actually denotes *precisely the opposite meaning*. "All dharmas are mind's nature" would mean, not that the innermost essence of matter is mind, but conversely that the innermost essence of mind is matter, or all dharmas. The statement then answers the question, "What is the real essence of mind?" rather than, "What is the real essence of all dharmas?" That is, "all dharmas" are the real "nature" of "mind." When the mind is analyzed to ferret out its true essence, this essence is found to be, not mind, but these dharmas, including matter or any other non-mind entity. It would mean that mind is ultimately, in its innermost nature, dharmas, matter, non-mind. This reading is closely related to the way Zhiyi himself had used this binome in certain contexts, to state in his case that the real nature of mind is not mind but rather, for example, Emptiness.[22] Such passages also use this phrase to answer the question, "What is the essence of mind?" rather than, "What is the essence of all apparently non-mind dharmas?"

3. *Xinxing* means "mind and the Nature." This takes the two characters *xin* and *xing* not as a binome, but as two separate terms. "All dharmas are mind and the Nature" could then expand into two separate (although of course intimately related) claims: "All dharmas are mind" and "All dharmas are the Nature."

4. *Xinxing* means "mind, or the Nature." This would mean that "mind" and "nature" are to be understood as synonymous terms, to be read simultaneously. "Mind" and "nature" are in this sense two names for the same thing. In a certain way, this comes close to the first reading: the Nature is Mind itself, and this is what all dharmas are being identified with. But it can also be understood as closely allied to the third reading: All dharmas are mind, and all dharmas are the Nature, and these two *separate* and *different* claims end up being mutually entailing, and ultimately identical to one another. The former (reading 4 as an elaboration of reading 1) indicates the Shanwai interpretation. The latter (reading 4 as an elaboration of reading 3) represents Zhili's Shanjia interpretation.

5. *Xinxing* means "the Nature-as-the-mind." The "as" is what is crucial to this translation, providing a further elaboration of reading

3. "All dharmas are the Nature-as-the-mind" would mean that all components of experience are identical to the Nature, but in the peculiar form of being identical to one's own (deluded, temporally arising) mind. The English term *as* is, as I've said, a particularly useful device for translating Tiantai ideas, meaning here that a given entity has two identities at once; "X as Y" means it is truly X but also truly Y, where Y is one of many forms in which X can legitimately appear or present itself without losing its identity as X, and while also truly being Y. If I say, for example, that I am using a book "as" a doorstop, it can mean that this object remains truly a book, but also that it is really performing the function of a doorstop, is in fact stopping a door, is in reality a doorstop. "The Nature-as-the-deluded-mind" would then mean that it truly remains the Nature, but is just as truly the deluded mind. Concomitant to this claim in this case is the reversed claim, i.e., that all dharmas are also "the deluded-mind-as-the-Nature," which would mean, as we shall see below, this moment of delusion, with all entities as its aspects, as omnipresent and eternal.

The last reading comes closest to Zhili's interpretation. But the question is complicated by the fact that this is a claim about the relation of "all dharmas" to this *xinxing*. The explicit claim in this particular passage is that all dharmas "are" *xinxing*, indicating a relation of identity. But the passage goes on to indicate that this claim implies other relations between all dharmas and *xinxing*. In particular, Zhili's reading requires *six* distinct but related claims, three concerning the relation between dharmas and mind, and three concerning the relation between dharmas and the Nature. That is, all dharmas are:

1. *created* by the (deluded) mind (心造 *xinzao*);

2. *inherently entailed* in the (deluded) mind (心具 *xinju*);

3. *identical to* the (deluded) mind (即心 *jixin*);

4. created by *the Nature* (理造 *lizao*);[23]

5. inherently entailed in the Nature (性具 *xingju*); and

6. identical to the Nature (即性，即空即假即中 *jixing, jikong-jijiajizhong*).

Moreover, all six of these claims must be understood not as independent facts, but as mutually entailing and mutually illuminating, as is made increasingly explicit in the writing of Zhili and his disciples.[24] This means that he understands reading 5 as, so to speak, involving all the four previous readings, which are seen as implying one another. His vociferous rejection of reading 1 (and the first version of reading 4) is due to his conviction that this *alone* is not what the statement "all dharmas are *xinxing*" is stating.

Zhili advocates, famously, the contemplation of the deluded mind (妄心觀 *wangxinguan*), which he explains as meaning "to manifest the Three-Thousand-Nature(s) in the aggregate mind" (於陰心顯三千性 *yu yinxin xian sanqian xing*),[25] as opposed to the contemplation of the "true mind" (enlightened mind, Buddha mind, pure mind) allegedly advocated by the Shanwai masters. That the object of contemplation should be the deluded mind, rather than the true mind, is not difficult to understand, and indeed is one of the least controversial of Zhili's polemical slogans. The point is made quite commonsensically already by Zhiyi in the *Mohezhiguan*, not only in his frequent descriptions of the "one moment of mind arising from sense-object meeting sense organ," but in the explicit Q and A in that text concerning the subject and object of contemplation.[26] But the full implications of this idea become focal in Zhili's polemical writings, hinging on developments made by Zhanran in his reworking of Zhiyi's ideas, introducing new applications of borrowed terminology into the discussion. The treatment of *xinxing* in this passage is a case in point. As suggested in reading 3, Zhili states that "the two characters *xin* and *xing* are not different and yet different (心性二字, 不異而異 *xinxing er zi bu yi er yi*)."[27] Two separated claims then are involved: that all dharmas are mind, and that all dharmas are the Nature. In the opening paragraph of this section I alluded to two Tiantai meditational procedures: "mind-observation" and "inherence-observation." The separation of these two procedures corresponds to the reading of *xin* and *xing* as fully distinct terms in this passage. To understand what is at stake here, however, we have to get a clearer grasp on what the terms *the Nature* and *the mind* denote in the context of Tiantai writings of this period.[28]

We start by considering Zhiyi's teaching of "The Samadhi of Awareness of the Process of Attention" (覺意三昧 *jueyisanmei*), inherited from Huisi's "Samadhi of Following One's Own Attention" (隨自意三昧 *suiziyisanmei*), the centerpiece of the "Four Samadhis" from the *Mohezhiguan* and increasingly the focus of all Tiantai practice for Zhanran and the Song combatants. This particular practice must be understood in the context of two scriptural passages, which I will first consider here.

The *locus classicus* of the doctrine that "all dharmas are created by the mind" is the following passage from the "old translation" of the *Avataṃsaka Sūtra* referred to already in the citation from Chengguan:

> It is like a skilled painter spreading out the various colors [on the canvas], who then deludedly takes them to be different forms [in

the painting]. The four material elements [earth, water, fire, wind] are all the same [in each of the colors]. The four elements are not themselves colors, and colors are not themselves the four elements. And yet there are no other colors apart from the four elements. [In the same way], the mind is not the colors of the painting, and the colors of the painting are not the mind, but apart from the mind there are no colors in the painting, and apart from the colors in the painting there is no mind. That mind does not constantly dwell [in any mark]. It is infinite, difficult to comprehend, manifesting all colors, each of which knows not the others. It is like the skilled painter, who does not know his own painting mind. You must understand that the nature of all dharmas is also like this. The mind is like a skilled painter, painting forth all varieties of the five aggregates [i.e., forms, sensations, conceptions, volitions, discernments]. There is no dharma in all the worlds not created by it. As it is with the mind, so it is with the Buddha. As it is with the Buddha, so it is with all sentient beings. Mind, Buddha, sentient beings—there is no difference between these three. All the Buddhas realize that all is turned by the mind. Whosoever can see it this way sees the true Buddha. . . . The mind creates all the Tathāgatas.[29]

Mind creates all things, and is inseparable from all the things it creates. It is neither identical to nor different from its creations, just as the four elements are neither identical to nor different from the colors that are composed of them. "Element" as such is not "color" as such, and yet there are no colors that are not entirely made up of the elements. The reverse— "no elements without color"—is not asserted in this part of the metaphor. Similarly, "mind" as such is not "all objects" as such, but there are no objects that are not entirely mind; in this case, we are told further that there is no mind separable from the forms it creates. Here, the mind in question seems to be the conditional, ordinary, deluded karma-creating mind, or at least the big M Mind in a state of severe delusion, since it knows not what it is doing, and like the painter "deludedly" takes its own creation for a new reality. It is a mind that is infinitely creative but gets lost in its own creativity. Its creativity seems to be linked to its lack of self-transparency, like that painter's ignorance of his own painting mind, and the ignorance between the various forms of their common source. It must focus on its object, and forget itself, ignore the act of positing the object, in order for that object to be truly posited as an independent object.

This is also linked to the mind's "not-dwelling" in any of the marks it creates. Taken as the deluded mind, of course, the assertion that this mind is "no different" from the Buddha is somewhat startling; this is precisely what Chengguan seeks to remedy in his adoption of the "New Translation," which specifies that it is just the "essence" (體性 *tixing*, literally "substance and nature") of the mind—hence not its deluded creativity—which is infinite and identical to the Buddhas. The Tiantai reading, however, sticks to the literal paradox of the "old" translation; it is the deluded mind that is identical to the Buddhas and to Sentient Beings, and according to Zhili, this means *each* of these three "creates all things like a skilled painter," is inseparable from all things, in a certain sense "is" all things, and so on. The fact that this mind is not transparent to itself, does not thoroughly "know itself" or what it is doing, as in the metaphor of the inspired painter above, is particularly important for the Tiantai system, and also central to the next passage to be discussed.

This second scriptural passage I wish to keep close to the discussion here is from Chapter Five, "Medicinal Herbs" (藥草品), of Kumārajīva's *Lotus* itself. It is not often quoted in the context of the issue at hand here, as the above text is, but I think it sums up something very important in the understanding of reality which structures the Tiantai meditational system. The passage runs:

> The teachings preached by the Tathagata are all of one mark and one flavor, what is known as the mark of liberation, the mark of freedom, the mark of cessation. Ultimately all these teachings lead to the Knowledge of All Modes [i.e., the Buddha's perfect enlightenment]. When a sentient being hears any of these preachings of the Tathagata, and remembers, reads, recites and practices them, the merit he thereby gains is unknown to himself. And why? Because only the Tathagata knows what the type, mark, essence and nature of this sentient being is, what he is thinking of [念何事 *nian he shi*], what he is cogitating, what he is practicing; how he is thinking [云何念 *yunhe nian*], how he is cogitating, how he is practicing; by virtue of what dharma he is thinking [以何法念 *yi hefa nian*], cogitating or practicing, and by what dharma he is attaining what dharma. Only the Tathagata knows without obstruction, accurately and clearly what stage a sentient being may be dwelling in.[30]

Leaving aside for the moment the local purposes this type of rhetoric might play in the context of the religious argument the sutra is making, it makes one essential assertion that is crucial to the focus of Tiantai meditation, already hinted at in the previous passage: the minds of sentient beings are not "transparent" to themselves. It is not just that we don't know what reality is; it is that we don't even know what we think reality is. We are not aware of the meaning of our own thoughts. We do not know what we are thinking; we may think we are thinking about X, but in fact be mistaken, and actually be thinking about Y. We don't even know what the object we are currently making judgments about is, or what those judgments might be. In other words, we may believe that we are deeming S to be P, but in fact this is not at all the activity we are engaged in. We are rather, in fact, deeming S to be non-P, or T to be L, or N to be G. We may think we believe X, but in fact be mistaken about this; our belief in X may be known by the Buddha to actually be a belief in Y. The very activity of deeming, of judging, is not a bare transparent datum. It is not a brute fact that "I judge S to be P." Neither the thinker, the thought-of object, nor the thought itself has a decidable nature. The disambiguating act of thinking is itself ambiguous. This is the premise for Tiantai "awareness to attention."

It should be stressed that the mature Tiantai conception admits no function of mind above and beyond (念 nian), the forming of determinate thoughts; there is no room here for the kind of "space between thoughts," or the indeterminate background behind all these particular thoughts, the space in which thoughts occur, which is invoked in many types of Buddhist practice, including certain forms of Chan, and even in the Huisi text just mentioned.[31] There is a crucial change on this point between Huisi, if indeed this text is correctly attributed to him, and Zhiyi's mature position. The space between thoughts would be, for Zhiyi, merely another thought, another phase with a specific beginning and end. The "non-thought" here is always only an aspect of a particular thought, just as Emptiness (global incoherence) is always also some specific Provisional Posit (local coherence). Indeed, the "mind" itself is merely an aspect of a thought. The "mind" contemplated in Tiantai mind contemplation is the mind described in the *Foshuo guan puxian pusa xingfa jing* 佛說觀普賢菩薩行法經, an apocryphal scripture apparently of Chinese composition, frequently quoted by Zhiyi, and often attached to the *Lotus* as its "Afterword," in which we find a passage used in the Tiantai practice of the Lotus Repentance, during which Zhiyi is said in some sources to have had a major "enlightenment experience."

> The mind means the thinking [念 nian] of all sorts of non-goods, creating the ten types of evil karma, and the five evils leading to the uninterrupted purgatories. It is like a monkey and also like glue, sticking covetously to everything everywhere in the six sense organs. The karma of these six organs spreads like branches and twigs and flowers and leaves outward to fill the Three Realms, the 25 types of being, all places of birth, with the ability to increase the twelve types of suffering from ignorance to old age and death, so that one goes through all the eight perversions and all the eight disasters. . . . Contemplate the mind as no mind, as arising from deluded thinking. Think of the mind with this mark of having arisen

from deluded thought as resembling a wind blowing through empty space, having no dwelling place. Such a dharma and its attributes are neither born nor perish—what then is called sin, what merit? My mind is itself empty, and both sin and merit have no owner. All dharmas are the same way. They neither dwell nor perish. This kind of repentance is the contemplation of the mind as no mind, dharmas as not dwelling within dharmas, all dharmas as liberated, the Noble Truth of Cessation and quiescence.[32]

Note that here it is the "deluded sinful mind" that creates all existence—the existence of suffering and delusion and karma. It is active, purposive "thinking" (nian), particularized mental activity, as opposed to the quiescent awareness of the Huayan True Mind, which is said to be "free of thoughts" (離念 linian), as in the Awakening of Faith. This active, purposive, biased thinking is the mind that is here contemplated as "no mind," as "arising from deluded thinking." A particular thought is the disambiguating "master signifier" that makes all other existences coherent and determinate. This depends on the determinateness of this thought itself. But this determinateness too is arbitrarily posited in the same act, is a by-product of this act of determining. This act itself, however, can be seen, when recontextualized by a further thought, as itself ambiguous (Empty). The act of determining itself and all other existences is itself indeterminate. Mind, the creator and owner of thoughts, is itself created by and owned by thoughts. That is, thoughts posit their own determinate substratum, from which they putatively emerge and to which they putatively accrue, but this is an erroneous, or at best provisional, positing. Thoughts posit the reference point in relation to which they have their meaning (the determinate nature of this particular act of determining, or the mind, the enduring owner of thought which brings these thoughts together into a single meaningfully coherent system), but this implies a delusory circularity—their positing of this reference point is itself not meaningfully established without the reference point so posited.

As we shall see, mature Tiantai praxis analyzes the mental process as going through the four phases of "not-yet-thinking," "about-to-think," "thinking," and "done-thinking," but it is made very clear that this always refers to some specific mental act, thinking of some particular object: "not-yet-thinking" does not refer, in Zhiyi at least, to any blank quiescent state of awareness prior to the arising of all thought. It means simply all the thoughts prior to the one in question, that is, whatever was going on when one was "not-yet-thinking" about this particular object. Moreover, all four of these phases are ontologically in the same boat, all are to be analyzed as Empty, Provisionally Posited, and the Center, and for exactly the same reason: all four phases have a beginning and end, are temporal events, and the ostensible borderlines between themselves and whatever precedes and succeeds them—which define them as being what they are and nothing besides—cannot be intelligibly understood, cannot possibly exist as simply located entities.[33] The "not-yet-arisen" is really an aspect seen from *within* some particular arisen moment of thought, not some putative other state that is entirely free from any thoughts. Moments of experience are not isolated atoms; indeed, they cannot be. If they were, on the Tiantai view, they would not be experienceable at all. The past moment, the not-yet that precedes this moment, is present here within this moment, internal to it, perceivable from within it. There is inexorable multiplicity within the apparent singularity of this moment. As we shall see, this necessary copresence of multiplicity and singularity is the essence of the Tiantai practice of mind-contemplation.

It must be understood, then, to state it plainly, that when Tiantai writers state that "the mind creates all dharmas," they do *not* mean that the mind—either the deluded mind or the putative pure mind—literally creates all dharmas, or any dharmas at all, in the normal sense of the term. "Create" here cannot mean to bring a previously nonexistent entity into existence *ex nihilo*. Indeed, in the strict sense, Tiantai denies that any entity at all is created, by mind or by any other agent; there is no genuine transition from nonexistence to existence, nor vice versa; both of these concepts, "existence" and "nonexistence," are regarded by Tiantai doctrine as merely provisionally coherent, and having no correspondence to ultimate reality. However, in the key passage of the *Mohezhiguan* on the "Mind as the Inconceivable Object," Zhiyi starts by introducing the theme of *creation* (造 *zao*) by mind, quoting the *Avatamsaka Sutra* passage just cited: "The mind is like a skilled painter, creating all different varieties of the five aggregates." He then enumerates these various types of aggregates, the ten realms of sentient beings, in all their aspects, stating in each case that "the mind" *inherently entails* (具 *ju*) all of these aspects. But after stating categorically that the mind inherently entails all Three Thousand aspects of reality, he hastens to add that this does not mean that the mind is prior to these Three Thousand in any sense; rather, he states that their relation is like that between an object and the "eight characteristics" (八相 *baxiang*) that constitute its process of becoming (i.e., greater and lesser characteristics of arising, dwelling, changing, vanishing). This relation between identity, determinacy, and the *process* of arising and perishing is again to be noted here. The claim that "the mind creates all things" is thus immediately glossed as "the mind inherently entails all things," which is then quickly amended to "precisely the mind *is* all dharmas, precisely all dharmas *are* the mind." A moment later, Zhiyi indicates the implications of this claim for his previous statement about creation, that is, the way in which it undermines it: he states categorically that it is no more correct to say that "mind creates and entails all things" than to say "the objective conditions [緣 *yuan*] create and entail all things and cognitions." Both of these statements are locally coherent (假 *jia*), but globally incoherent (空 *kong*); they fall under the "Four Propositions" (四句: 我生, 他生, 共生, 離生, i.e., that anything arises from itself, from another, from both or from neither) rejected by Nāgārjuna.[34] After a lengthy refutation of all possible positions, filtered through the standard Tiantai Three Truths epistemology, Zhiyi states, "If one grasps this meaning, all these descriptions are valid, and all descriptions are invalid. However, if one goes with the most convenient [i.e., useful, for meditative purposes] description, one should say that Ignorance gives determinate form to the Dharma-nature [無明法法性 *wuming fa faxing*], and this is what produces all dharmas. It is like the dharma of sleep giving determinate form to the mind, and thus producing all the events in a dream. The mind and external conditions join, and thus all the Three Thousand natures and characteristics of the world arise from the mind."[35] Note the unusual verbal use of the word *fa* here; it is to be understood as a transitive verb not in the more usual sense of "to imitate, model oneself upon," but rather in accordance with Zhiyi's discussion of the term in the *Fahuaxuanyi*, where its primary meaning is "trackable" (可軌 *kegui*),[36] that is, capable of being tracked or followed, capable of serving as a model, or, more broadly, determinable, determinate. As a transitive verb, it means to make determinate, to make knowable, to give recognizable form to. Note also that the particular description of all things as "created and entailed by the mind," then, is chosen as an expedient for the purpose of Buddhist practice, for mind-observation, after making clear that it is not to be taken literally. The term *ignorance* is here explicitly synonymous with the term *mind*, and the creation of all dharmas by the mind is here merely the way in which ignorance "gives determinate form" to the absolute reality, the Dharma-nature. It disambiguates by filtering down a preexistent overabundance of content, the Three Thousand. The multiplicity and particularity of this content is *not* a result of Ignorance or delusion; the distinctions themselves preexist in the ultimate reality. As Zhili says conclusively, "Even when Ignorance is removed, distinctions still exist [除無明有差別 *chuwuming youchabie*]."[37] This is of course what is meant by the Tiantai "inherent entailment" of the Three Thousand in the Nature (性具三千 *xingju sanqian*). Where does this content, in all its intricate particularity, ultimately come from? Strictly speaking, no possible answer can be given to this search for a single unambiguous "source" of any kind. It is "beyond thought and comprehension," and more specifically it is created neither by the Dharma-nature (法性), nor by Ignorance(無明), nor by both (共), nor by neither (離): it is not what is so, nor what is not so, nor both, nor neither. It is extremely important to see the sense in which this attribution of "creativity" to the mind is connected with the mind's delusion, and how this connects to the question of truth and appearance in Tiantai epistemology. To say the mind is creating what it sees is to say that it is deluded.

Zhanran clarifies the implications of this view in several of the other self-posed questions and answers in his *Zhiguanyili*:

> Q: [Zhiyi's Mohezhiguan] says, "Believe only in the Dharma-nature; do not believe in anything else." There is only the Dharma-nature; nothing else exists. But then what are all the diverse dharmas we see before us? And why is it also said that the Dharma-nature inherently entails all the many dharmas? A: Because sentient beings for long aeons have been exclusively attached to the diverse dharmas, and did not believe in the Dharma-nature, this statement is made as a corrective to destroy this ancient prejudiced way of calculating, so that in all the diverse dharmas they will see purely and only the Dharma-nature. But to see the Dharma-nature is to see that the Dharma-nature is purely and only all the diverse dharmas. This Nature that is also all the diverse dharmas is originally without either the one name or the other. It is called either [diverse] dharmas or [one] Nature in accordance with the need to refute or establish upayically.[38]

Neither unity nor diversity is primary. It is not the case that the world appears to be multiform, deluded, and biased but is in reality one. Rather, either of these ways of stating the case is equally biased, and either is also equally valid, to be applied as a corrective to a previous bias. But it is the mind's power to disambiguate this neither-same-nor-different into some determinate scheme of samenesses and differences that is the delusion that is to be focused on in Tiantai meditation:

> Q: All the texts say that mind and material form are nondual. But if we want to contemplate this, how do we set up our contemplation? A: Mind and material form are one substance; neither precedes the other. Each is the entire dharma-realm. But in the sequence of contemplation, we must start with the internal mind. Once the internal mind is purified, this pure mind will encounter all dharmas, and naturally meld with them all perfectly. Moreover, we must first understand that all dharmas are mind-only, and only then begin contemplating the mind. If you can comprehend all dharmas to the end, you will see that all dharmas are nothing but mind, and that all dharmas are nothing but material form. You must understand

that every existence comes from the distinctions made by one's own mind. When have dharmas themselves ever declared that they were the same as or different from one another? Hence the *Zhanchajing* says, "There are two types of contemplation. The first is Consciousness-only [唯識 *weishi*]. The second is of the Real-Attribute [實相 *shixiang*, i.e., of the ultimate reality]." The Real-Attribute [practice] is the contemplation of Li while the Consciousness-only [practice] works through individual events [事 *shi*]. Although Li and events are nondual, the ways for contemplating them are to be slightly separated. Only one who is able to understand this can be spoken to about the Way.[39]

Again, reality is ultimately neither material nor mental. But the contemplation of mind is made primary for the sake of Buddhist praxis, precisely because it is mind that is the source of the problem of delusion and suffering for sentient beings. All is mind, all is matter. But in what sense are things said to be "mind" from the point of view of praxis? The mark of mind is the making of distinctions. Dharmas themselves do not distinguish themselves from one another, do not predicate sameness or difference of themselves. Zhanran here quotes a Chinese apocryphal sutra, the full title of which is *Zhancha shan'e yebao jing* (占察善惡業報經 "The sutra of prognostication and investigation of good and evil karmic retribution"), which gives a fuller exposition of the practice of the "contemplation of consciousness-only," as follows:

In all times and places, wherever physical, verbal or mental karma is being created, you should observe and know that it is all mind only. This goes also for all objects and states: whenever the mind fixes its attention in some object of cognition, you should notice and be aware of it, never letting the mind go obliviously chasing after objects without noticing its own activity. Rather, observe each and every movement of the attention. Whenever the mind traces or attends to something, you should return it to make the mind follow after that act of attention itself, so the mind is aware of it. Know that your own inner mind is what is producing thoughts and acts of attention; it is not the objects themselves that have thoughts or make distinctions. That is to say, the inner mind produces countless views of long and short, beautiful and ugly, right and wrong, gain and loss, decay and advantage, existence and nonexistence and so on, while the objects themselves have never had thoughts which give rise to such distinctions. You should know that all objects are themselves devoid of any thoughts and distinctions, so they are themselves neither long nor short, neither beautiful nor ugly, and so forth, up to neither existent nor nonexistent. In themselves they are free of all marks. Thus you should observe that all dharmas are born from the thoughts of the mind. In the absence of this mind, there is no dharma and no mark that could view itself as being different from anything else. You should hold and attend to [this operation of] your inner mind, and know that there are only these deluded thoughts and no real external objects. Attend to it without cease. This is called cultivating and learning the contemplation [that all is] mental consciousness only. If the mind is inattentive and does not realize that its own attention is operating, it believes there to be external objects before it. This is no longer called the contemplation [that all is] mental consciousness only.[40]

The function of the mind is to make distinctions, which is what it is to make predications, including those of existence and nonexistence, that is, that there even is or is not an object here to be cognized, about which some predications might be made. It is fundamentally a faculty of dividing. It divides itself from the objects before it, reifying both, and simultaneously separates out the objects from one another, identifying them as this or that, and cognizing various characteristics inhering in them by which to distinguish them. Where it makes a border, it posits a determinate thing within the border. The act of cognition is here regarded in a way very consistent with indigenous Chinese epistemological theories: knowing is a skill in dividing things out of a larger context. Where there is no dividing, there is no thing. To be aware of a thing is here not conceived according to the metaphor of a receiving of an impression, or the lighting up of what was in darkness, or a clearing away of a blockage; it is not a kind of disclosing or illuminating, not a revealing or a reception, but rather a dividing. Where there is any quiddity or characteristic of any kind, there is a distinction, a parsing, a forming of boundaries between "this" and "another." Without this bordering, no characteristics can exist. But things do not border themselves; it is a particular biased perspective and cognitive apparatus of a sentient being that decides to divide up the world in one way or another, setting the limits to how much of the given counts as "this thing" and how much as "that thing," where things begin and end. This is what constitutes the world of shapes, colors, entities, characteristics. When contemplating mind, then, where is mind to be found? Mind cannot directly be an object of mind. By mind-contemplation, the attentiveness to, say, the stream of words and emotions through one's "interior monologue" is not meant. These are mental objects, not the distinguishing function of mind as subject and perceiver. All these things are distinguishable, are perceivable, hence all belong to the realm of objects. Rather, wherever one notices a characteristic of any kind, any sort of definitive presence, one is to see the activity of mind. The greenness of green, the redness of red, the bookness of book, the spaciness of space: these are mind. And this mind is not the pure mind, but the deluded mind, the mind that makes arbitrary and biased distinctions. This deluded mind is the creator of all particular things, including the Buddha, and it is this deluded mind that is to be the object of contemplation in Tiantai practice.

But as we saw in the previous chapter, delusion in Tiantai means partial truth, not pure illusion, and further, by the Three Truths, that each partial truth is, on the one hand, completely false in the sense of failing to correspond to anything in reality, but also, on the other hand, definitely pragmatically useful in overcoming attachments (including the attachment to itself) in some contexts, and further, therefore, a revelation of the absolute and complete unconditional truth. Mind creates deludedly, because it is conditional and partial itself, situated in a certain way, predisposed in a certain way. I do not see the red of this flower as an ant crawling on it would see it, or as a bee coming to pollinate it would see it. What I see here is determined by my cognitive apparatus, the structure of my sense organs, and the kind of framing and focusing I am involved in at the moment due to my preoccupations, the desire-oriented project I am engaged in. I do not see the ultraviolet or infrared wavelengths that are present here, and so on; what I see is a small portion of what is actually present, as Zhanran said about the colors seen by the ordinary human eye in the passage cited in the previous chapter. It is not an *ex nihilo* mirage, but a narrowing down of what is really there to yield a very partial picture. By being here and being what I am, structured and disposed as I am right now, I create the phenomenal appearances that are manifesting to me. On the other hand, I do not create these determinacies out of thin air, based on nothing real. They are indeed a part of the real—but a part of the real, seen without reference to all its relevant contexts, is not exactly what that same part would appear to be if seen together with all relevant contexts. We have here again the "selecting out" process we've seen in earlier Chinese thought: delusion here means to "deem to be definitively same or different," when in fact the reality before is both same and different, that is to say, is such that the mutually exclusive categories sameness and different do not accurately represent it. Hence, this moment of coming-to-see-as-X is "not created by the Dharma-nature, nor by ignorance, nor by both, nor by neither." Dharma-nature would be the absolute truth, the total apprehension of the whole reality. Ignorance would be a purely arbitrary creation of something that is just plain false, which is in no sense at all really there. Neither of these is the case; what I see is neither truth nor illusion, which as we have seen are, taken without qualification, meaningless terms in Tiantai epistemology. It is a provisional posit, a local coherence, that is being created by this disambiguating moment of attention, of seeing-as. This is the truth and not the truth. What is crucial here, in the Tiantai sense, is that provisionally positing (*jia*), the characteristic of "Conventional Truth," has to be understood in several different senses (not only as having different contents). As Zhili puts it, there is the "provisional positing" of conditional arising (緣生之假 *yuansheng zhi jia*), characteristic of the Tripitaka and Common teachings; this is standard mereological reductionism of early Buddhism and its refinements and further reversals and entailments in Indo-Tibetan Madhyamika; then there is the provisional positing of "establishing" (建立之假 *jianli zhi jia*), which refers to the Separate Teaching, encompassing both the positive creation of *upāyas* by Bodhisattvas and the type of claim found in Nagarjuna (*MMK* 24:20) that without Emptiness, nothing could exist; and finally there is "the wondrous provisional positing," "the provisional positing identical to inherent entailment" (妙假, 具即是假 *miaojia, ju jishi jia*) of the Integrated Teaching.[41] *Jia* of course means first and foremost "false," but in the context of the Three Truths it also means, "upayically put forth" (temporary) and, further, "inherently entailed," which is to say, the Center, the absolute, the whole truth This asserts the inextricability from any truth, fact, appearance—ultimate or provisional—of any other truth, fact, appearance, opinion: all are absolute truths in the precise sense of *juedai* 絕待 given by Zhiyi in the *Fahuaxuanyi*:[42] they are instantiated everywhere, even in their own negation, in whatever is excluded by the contrast by means of which they are determinate at all. As Zhili says, 須即陰說具三千方為妙假: "We need to be able to speak of all Three Thousand as inherently entailed in the aggregates themselves before we can call it the Wondrous Provisional Positing."[43] We have here a further development of the "whole/part" epistemology, centered on the process of *selecting out* samenesses and differences from an overabundant set of present alternatives, that undermined the Nominalism/Realist split all the way back to Mencius, Zhuangzi, and Xunzi.

   Now we can understand the relation of mind and the Nature, which is the relation between event and Li. Zhili spells out his understanding of the relation of *xin* and *xing*, what he means by "not different and yet different," with a quote from Zhanran's *Zhiguandayi* 止觀大意 which makes a very creative adaptation of Fazang's terms 隨緣 *suiyuan* (following conditions) and 不變 *bubian* (unchanging). Zhanran says: "Although present in some particular, conditioned way, it is unconditioned and unchanging. Hence it is 'the Nature.' Although unconditioned and unchanging, it follows conditions [and hence manifests as this particular, conditioned presence]. Hence it is 'the mind' [隨緣不變故為性, 不變隨緣故為心]."[44] *Bubian*, unchanging, or as Zhili puts it, "what is originally there and is never altered"

(本有不改 *benyoubugai*),[45] the unconditional, is the primary denotation of the term *the Nature*. "Mind," on the other hand, is used here to denote what does change, what "follows conditions," the conditional, or rather a particular conditional event, the arising of a state of consciousness following upon the contact between a sense organ and a sense object. Zhili stresses that in fact "mind" here could be replaced by *any* particular conditional (i.e., determinate) object; we could equally say, "Although unconditioned and unchanging, it follows conditions. Hence it is 'sentient beings,'" or "Although unconditioned and unchanging, it follows conditions. Hence it is 'the Buddha.'" Only this full reversibility will match the claim, made in the *Avatamsaka Sutra* passage cited above, that "[t]here is no difference between mind, Buddha and sentient beings." In the present case, mind is singled out because of its special relevance for meditation.[46] But in the distinctive Tiantai formulation used here, these two terms, the conditional and the unconditional, are such that they entail and imply one another. That is, both "mind" (or "the Buddha" or "sentient beings") and "the Nature" are terms that include two opposed but mutually encompassing poles, with a difference in emphasis. Each name implies both meanings, and ultimately refers to the same double-faceted fact, as when we use "equilateral triangle" and "equiangular triangle" to refer to the same triangle, each term necessarily implying the other, but with the emphasis temporarily on one side or the other. The two opposed but ultimately mutually entailing poles in this case are "the conditioned particular (in this case, a moment of sentience, a particular temporal mental event)" and "the unconditioned omnipresent universal." The unconditioned, the Nature, means what is findable everywhere, which is presencing under any and every condition (the "unchanging").

Xin and *xing*, then, are, among other things, *opposite* terms, and the declaration that all dharmas are *xinxing* must be understood as a deliberate paradox. This point must be stressed, as it is easily overlooked, and is certainly not the case for the usage of the term *xinxing* in most other schools of Chinese Buddhism. In Tiantai, as we shall see in more detail below, this statement is akin to saying "All things are square-circle," or perhaps more to the point: "all things are finite-infinite," or, "all things are permanent-impermanent" or "all things are conditioned-unconditioned" or "all things are relative-absolute." All things are Ignorance-Dharmanature. All things are Samsara-Nirvana. All things are the event-Li, the Li-event.

Thus, the deluded mind "creates" particular dharmas by selecting out from the ever-present ambiguity, the Three Thousand that are actually available at every possible locus, filtering out everything except some particular single entity, excluding all the others. It "creates" them by disambiguating them, deeming them, and itself, to be genuinely susceptible to the bivalent predicates "same" and "different." This creation comes in two forms.

Zhanran had said, "Creation [造 *zao*] of dharmas by the mind comes in two kinds: The first is in the context of Li, where creation means precisely inherent entailment [造即是具 *zao jishi ju*]. The second is in the context of events, which is a description of the transformations and creations of the ordinary people and the sages of past, present and future. . . . In all cases, it is only because these things are inherently entailed in Li that it can be created as a phenomenon [有理具方有事造 *you liju fang you shizao*]."[47] First there is "creation" in terms of Li. This doesn't mean that an entity called Li creates things. It means that any entity is in one sense the Center, the omnipresent unconditional, "non-dwelling" not as such but the impossibility of this coherence being only this coherence, in isolation from all other coherences, free of all ambiguity. X is determined as X (provisional positing) by setting up boundaries around itself, but these prove to be ambiguous, rendering it impossible to give a determinate inside-outside division, means its identity as X is itself undermined (Emptiness), whereby it becomes impossible to exclude X from being read as any other coherence: its overflows into every other possible determination, which turn out on examination to be synonyms for it "in some sense." As such, that specific entity, that determination, inherently entails all other determinations, which cannot be separated from it. That coherence in this way brings all other coherences into coherence with it; it is the union of all coherences. It is an activity that is inherently equipped with them as always-available dimensions of its own action. It creates all the others in the sense that it is readable as any of them. Hence, the equilateral triangle "creates" the equiangular triangle, for these are two names for one and the same triangle. This just means that the determination "equilateral," correctly understood and thought through, leads unavoidably to the determination "equiangular," and vice versa. Creation in Li is just another name for inherent entailment. Inherent entailment just means "non-dwelling": the impossibility of dwelling in any particular form, the continual spilling over of any determination, its continual necessity to be something other than any particular determination that might be assigned to it.

In fact, a Li is just a "non-dwelling root." It is something that "transcends" its ingression in any particular form, that is, can be comprehended outside of these particular ingressions, remains what it is no matter what form it appears in. It "transcends" any particular determinate form, does not "dwell" in/as any of them. It is a "root" in that these particular determinations are nonetheless dependent—in the sense of inseparable, not in the sense of logical or temporal priority—on it for their existence or appearance in experience. The latter are reducible to it, grow out of it, such that, in fact, this non-dwelling root manifests completely in a particular form, with nothing left over. The wetness is just the waviness. But there is not some particular entity or nonentity called the non-dwelling root, as against a bunch of other entities that are dwelling (fixed determinacies, which can appear only in one time and place) and merely, as it were, "branches," that is, dependent offshoots with no further productivity. Rather, every one of the Three Thousand Quiddities is the non-dwelling root to all other dharmas, and every other dharma also plays the role of the rooted and the fixed that express the non-dwelling root. Thus, we can continue to say, "looked at in terms of a dung beetle, all these things are the dung beetle's realized functions," to use another of Zhili's formulations. Li is a non-dwelling root, and a non-dwelling root is a Center.

Then there is the creation in event, which means that this present moment of thought leads to further moments of thoughts, and the contents thereof; creation in events is the filtering out and parsing activity of the mind, the setting of limits which disambiguates this interpenetrative Li in any given instance. This specific manner of appearing conditions other specific manners of appearing, in a real-time sequence of events. The same two types of creation will apply equally to any dharma, mind or matter. It is not so much that Li creates events, but rather that Li means "inherent entailment of all entities in each entity," the eternal availability of all entities as dimensions of the action that constitutes any entity, the fact that each action is inherently equipped with all the others while they are also equipped with it, that to act is to have available for subsumption all other actions which in turn makes oneself available for subsumption into them, and so this fact about dharma X will be what enables dharma Y to be dharma Y also. Dharma X's Li (or, more strictly, dharma X *as* Li) in this sense "creates" dharma Y, and vice versa. Their creation in event, on the other hand, is a way of singling out this same specific intentional disambiguating mental activity, and the world as it appears through the filter of this activity. The creation in activity is *conditioned* by inherent entailment in Li, but not single-handedly *caused* by it. The conditioned is conditioned but not caused by the unconditioned, for the unconditioned is, because unconditioned, not determinable as a single entity, and thus not capable of being a cause, that is to say, something single-handed capable of making any determinate fact "so." Thus, as Zhili says, we must not one-sidedly cling to Zhanran's statement that "it is only because these things are inherently entailed in Li that it can be created as a phenomenon" to set up a doctrine of the Pure Original Mind, or the Li per se, actually creating all dharmas. Instead, he says, we should know that Zhanran's meaning is that the deluded phenomenal mind is itself Li, to wit, the function of Li.[48] The "function of Li" (理之用 *li zhi yong*) is another combination of opposite terms, equivalent to *xinxing* interpreted to mean "the Nature as the deluded mind," "the mind as filtering down of the Nature," the conditioned-unconditioned. Each event is the unconditioned-conditioned, the conditioned-unconditioned, the unchanging that follows conditions, the following of conditions that is unchanging.

This does not mean the nature is prior and the appearance is posterior. When Zhili or Zhanran says, "It is only because there is inherent entailment of this thing in the nature that there can possibly be transformation into or creation of this thing in phenomena,"[49] they do not in any way imply a foundational priority of the nature over phenomenal events. Rather, they mean an induction similar to what we do when we come to realize that a certain triangle has three equal angles; we conclude that it must have three equal sides, because only if it had three equal sides could it possibly have three equal angles. This is not because the sides come first and the angles after, or vice versa; they are simultaneous, and mutually implicative. Whichever one we can realize first assures us of the existence of the other. So principle and phenomena are simultaneous, neither is the final ground of the other. But in Buddhist practice we look at our own mind as a deluded phenomenon, and from that see the structure of the rest of the situation, the mind and all dharmas as mutually subsumptive phenomena and as mutually subsumptive eternal objects.

Li, the Buddha-nature, Truth, Ultimate Reality, Original Enlightenment, the Non-dwelling root are not to be construed as some preexisting (in)determinate ground that single-handedly creates or emanates to form all phenomenal existences, the literal "source of all things." Indeed, it would be more accurate to say that for Zhili *each* dharma-as-a-Li, not "Li as such," is a condition of all experience in the precise sense of a Kantian a priori category. Zhili says the "one nature" is not a "fixed single nature," which is equivalent to saying also that this "same nature" is not a "fixedly same nature." It is not definitively "the same." Rather, it is the nature in the sense of unchanging, but unchanging only in the sense of non-dwelling, which is the only sense in which it can serve as a ground or "root." In fact, we can say it is a multitude of alternate "Ones" or different "Samenesses." *Which* particular version of Li is now functioning, however, is entirely a function of what's going on with my delusion at this moment: Li is loneliness right now because I am lonely. This is what Zhili says, that both the Three Thousand as-events and the Three Thousand as-Lis are unified by a single moment of deluded attention, by a particular event. It is the totality as event that unifies all Lis and all events, and also unifies Lis and events, such that they too are intersubsumptive. This moment of deluded determinateness is ineradicable, and is the premise for the rest of the contemplation. We start where we are. There is no limitedness as such: rather, as Zhanran says, "The Real-Attribute is necessarily all dharmas, and all dharmas are necessarily the Three Thousand" (實相必諸法, 諸法必三千 *shixiang bi zhufa, zhufa bi sanqian*). Limitedness includes this particular limit; all the other limits, the

Three Thousand, are correlative to this limit I now deludedly experience as this determinate state.

That is, when one thing is determined as X, all other things are also Xish, no matter what X is. The universe is an infinity of *alternate* Onenesses. The Non-dwelling "One" nature is that by virtue of which all things are readable as "of the same nature as" *whatever* X might be adduced. This is the "one same nature"—*not some particular characteristic that is "the same" in all cases, but the characteristic of "sameness-as-difference" as such.* It is that all dharmas are the Same as *any* X that reveals their Emptiness; it is not that their sameness or inclusion in mind in particular is Emptiness, or that Emptiness is Mind. Emptiness is ambiguity, which means their ability to be something besides what they are. Emptiness is seen by means of their ability to converge as anything, not by whatever it is they happen to be converging as. Provisional Positing is the fact that in spite of converging into something, they remain themselves. The Center is the fact that these are one fact, not two facts, about them. Hence, at the next level both this sameness and this difference are the same for all dharmas, and moreover both are eternally different for all dharmas. This is the Three Truths all over again. For all Three Thousand are in one sense "the same" in all cases, applying everywhere as categories, as we'll discuss in more detail momentarily. "Sameness" is one of the characteristics that is "the same" for all things, shared in all cases. "Difference," however, is another one. But Zhili here points to the shared characteristic of *"allowing all difference to be unified or read as the same one, no matter what that one is"* as Li, because it is what allows us to come to see the undecidability, and hence the interpervasion, of all the other shared characteristics. In contemplation of the mind, we see that the phenomenal, determinate, simply located moment of mental experience unifies all other dharmas, that all dharmas converge here as this moment of experience and share its nature, that the border between this quality and the others which are internal-external to it can never be established. All dharmas have the nature of this moment of experience, which means they all have the characteristic of "being able to assimilate to and form a part of this determinate experience without ceasing to be what they are." Matter is experienceable as mental, mind as material—in either case, what is important is their undecidability. That is, they are experienced here *as* this moment but also as something distinct from this moment ("converging as this moment" and "not losing their own essences"). This is the "event as totalizer," sameness on the level of phenomenal occasions. The deluded mind transforms into and creates all things: this means that as soon as my mind becomes X, it makes all things appear as aspects of X, converge as X, as X's inside-outside. This reveals something about both this experience and about all other things, as phenomenal occurrences. *It reveals that X is X in spite of being nothing but non-X. It also reveals that all non-Xs can be Xish without changing in the least, without ceasing to be non-Xish.* This reveals that *all* of them are Li, that is, the Three Truths, which is to say, determinate only as undecidable, which is to say, categories, determinacies which are nowhere and everywhere, as we shall see below. The one Li may also be described as Three Thousand different, but intersubsuming, Lis. We may indeed say that all things are creations or aspects of some one particular—of mind, or of delusion, or of the Buddha-nature—but only to the extent that we are seeing this X as precisely also non-X, as subsuming all its internal-external conditions, thus, seeing it as principle. Mind creates all dharmas because mind is not only mind, but rather mind-matter, mind/non-mind. Thus, it can fulfill the "multiple conditions" stipulation of the doctrine of dependent co-arising. All things are produced by X because X can never be just X.

All things are *xinxing*, says Zhanran. In terms of mind-contemplation, for reasons too complicated to go into here, this is taken to mean that each perceived coherence is a function of the mind, hence an intrinsic unchangeable aspect of mind, hence the sole essence of mind, what mind really is and always has been, and thus equally what all other entities really are and have always been.[50] But in that case, Zhanran continues, all these natures, since they are all findable everywhere, are one and the same nature. Otherwise, there would be change from one to another; none of them would be truly unchangeable and findable everywhere if something were truly "other" to it, if the appearance of something could displace it. There cannot be multiple unconditioned existences, because in that case each would be limited—excluded—by the "condition" of the presence of the other. However, this means that there is no particular coherence one could point to that is unchangeable, that must be appearing *simpliciter* everywhere, or even anywhere. That means there cannot be only one specific unconditioned coherence. We have here a pure form of ironic coherence: it is one because it is none because it is many, it is many because it one because it is none. For the very same reason that they are all one nature, there is no specifiable nature at all: as Zhanran says, "one nature is no nature" (一性無性 *yixingwuxing*). For although a given X may be the nature, unchangeable and present everywhere, since X is equally Y, X need not be present anywhere at all as X itself, it might be present *only* as Y. There is no X one could point to that is unconditioned and present everywhere, that can be found under all conditions, except in the form of other coherences. Zhanran's meaning here is clarified in his *Zhiguanyili* with a useful metaphor:

> The clinging mind is originally itself all dharmas. In contemplating this clinging mind, we see that it is empty and false. The Three Thousand within this falseness are in their own essence devoid of

nature. They are themselves the inconceivable perfect Three Truths of the nature of mind. It is like the images of flowers in the sky. There is no difference in substance between the flowers and the empty sky. But this empty sky does not match either the name of "flower" or the name of "empty sky," for the latter was originally posited in contradistinction to the flowers. This emptiness has no name. You should carefully extend this comparison in detail—it applies to all things.[51]

We might be tempted to think of the emptiness of the sky as the unconditioned: it is everywhere, it is present even in its absence, it is unremovable, it encompasses all things and indeed is present even where it appears to be displaced, in the filled-in spaces occupied by non-space things, such as the flowers. But *for this very reason*, we cannot use the name "empty sky" as a determinate name for the unconditional, because this discernible name "empty sky" was posited in contrast to the filled in spaces, the flowers. "Non-flowers" is internal to the original meaning of "empty sky," and this contrast alone gives it its meaning. Once these are seen to be identical, because the objects doing the filling-in are in their substance also empty sky, empty sky is no longer a legitimate name for this nature, since it has nothing with which to be contrasted. As Zhanran says, this is the basic structure applying to everything in Tiantai thinking: precisely by succeeding in pervading, this determinate item—in this case, sky—is no longer that which is pervading; it annuls itself by its very success. So whatever name, characteristic, essence or "nature" is chosen for "the Nature" ipso facto ceases to be a legitimate name for the Nature. One nature is no nature. No specific nature can be the one unconditioned nature, and at the same time any particular coherence that appears in experience must be the entirety of this one nature. Hence, Zhanran concludes that each function is the entirety of the Nature, is in fact all Three Thousand quiddities appearing *as* this particular thing. The quiddity "mind" that pervades and is findable in all experienced entities, by virtue of its "creation" and "inherent entailment" of them, ceases to be meaningfully determinable as "mind" by virtue of that very fact, since mind is, by definition, what is set up in opposition, separated from, these quiddities. Thus, as our Zhanran concludes, one can say that there is mind and there is matter (the two names are contrasted), or that there is neither mind nor matter (no name fits the case), or that there is only mind, or that there is only matter (any name will equally do). To be a Li is to be unconditional. To be unconditional is to be omnipresent. To be omnipresent is to intersubsume all other determinations, copresent in and as all of them. Thus, as Zhili says, "the Substance/Nature," this Li, is not a "Nature of oneness": rather, it is a "Three Thousand Nature" (此性體非謂一性，蓋三千性也).[52] That is, it is Three Thousand intersubsuming Lis.

THE THREE THOUSAND LIS AND THE THREE THOUSAND EVENTS

In the Northern Song, as we have noted, some Tiantai writers, later called the "Shanwai," began to express this eternity and omnipresence in terms of the privileging of "Awareness" (知 *zhi*) or Mind, which characterizes later Huayan thought (i.e., Chengguan and Zongmi, although, as we have seen, even in Fazang a similar tendency is discernible) and early Chan. Here, the Mind is a transcendent category that produces all phenomena, and of which all phenomena are transformations. It is in this sense at least conceptually prior to them, and is their ontological base, although it is not a definite objective entity. It is pure indeterminacy, pure subjectivity itself. Realizing this all-pervasive awareness as all things is awakening, and so this Mind is called Principle (Li). Praxis for the Shanwai writers means to see "the Three Thousand Quiddities" as this present moment of mind, which is the transformation of mind as such, with nothing left out. Principle is mind as the all-embracing "whole," which is uniquely capable of producing, determining, containing, and unifying all differentiated existences. It is the only true category, the only universal, all-pervasive and undifferentiated. Some of the later Shanwai, such as Gushan Zhiyuan 孤山智圓 (976–1022), adopt Zhili's critique of the *xingqi* doctrine attributed to Huayan: the idea that all dharmas "arise from" but are not "inherently included in" the Nature, that is, in Li. But for the Shanwai, the Three Thousand are inherently included not in "mind-and/or/as-the-nature" but only in "the nature of mind"—awareness as such—and the one-way ground-grounded relation between principle as such and the Three Thousand quiddities remains.

Zhili opposes this doctrine by asserting that the Three Thousand must be understood in two different senses, or levels, and that this alone expresses Zhiyi's original meaning, as opposed to the Huayan and Chan versions which are verbally so similarly. Zhili writes:

> You should understand that the categories "subsuming whole" and "subsumed part" [總別 *zong bie*] each apply to both the Three Thousand as Lis and the Three Thousand as events. Only when these two [i.e., the subsuming whole and the subsumed parts of the Three-Thousand-as-Lis, on the one hand, and both of these for the Three-Thousand-as-events, on the other] are seen as identical is the Wondrous Contemplation accomplished.[53]

Here we have the *locus classicus* for Zhili's doctrine of the relation *between* the different levels of Li and event. Each of the Three Thousand coherences is to be simultaneously construed in four different ways, as Li-totality, as Li-particular, as event-totality, and as event-particular. Whether we are speaking in terms of Li or of events, there is interpervasion such that all the different particulars are subsumed into each other part, the latter serving in any given case as the unifying totality. But event-interpervasion is not the same as Li-interpervasion, although it is a one-sided revelation of the latter. Event-interpervasion is what we see in the creation by mind of all dharmas: there remains a one-sided relationship of creator to created, or of disambiguator and disambiguated. All other events are subsumed *into* the mind, not yet vice versa. If another event is considered, then all events are subsumed into this event and not vice versa. Li-interpervasion is not merely subsumption, but the further fact that all subsumption is also intersubsumption. To be subsumed is to subsume, and vice versa. When these *two* types of interpervasion are seen as one and the same interpervasion, when these Three Thousand are seen to be the selfsame Three Thousand, enlightenment is accomplished. This means the one-way subsumption of all coherences by this moment of spuriously creative experience, the interpervasion of events exemplified in "creation" by mind, which is one-sided in that "the mind" is the disambiguator and the external dharmas are the disambiguated, comes to be seen as none other than the bilateral intersubsumption of all Lis. For a Li is what both subsumes all particulars and is subsumed in all particulars.

Buddhist practice, then, begins with noticing that external objects are de facto internal to the mind, that mind in its ordinary operations subsumes all its objects. This subsumption of objects into mind is not enlightenment, but on the contrary, precisely the opposite: it is the very definition of delusion. The point of the practice is to see that *this* form of deluded subsumption turns out to have always already been identical to the *other* kind of subsumption: the subsumption of Lis, which is necessarily intersubsumption. Seeing the copresence of same and different in the de facto subsumption of conditional objects by conditional mind is what reveals that they are, in fact, not simply-located finite objects at all, but can only be provisionally posited as empty as the Center, that is, unconditional and intersubsumptive Lis. The mind thus discovers, in the process of this transition whereby the two forms of subsumption are seen to be identical, that it itself—this conditional event of mentation—is an unconditional Li, instantiated omnipresently even in and as its very absence, in the fashion of the self-forgetting of the *Lotus Sutra*; but more importantly, that all its conditional phenomenal objects are themselves also Lis, which in turn subsume it, and instantiate themselves in it, the phenomenal mind, by means of their very self-negation: each object too is provisionally posited as empty as the Center.

Zhili goes on to define how these terms are to be understood:

Above the "subsumed parts" were specified in accordance with the
fact that all the dharmas retain their own essences [when they are
unified into a "subsuming whole"]. Now we specify the "subsuming whole" by virtue of the fact that [all these parts] converge as
a single moment of experience. They unceasingly maintain their
own essences, and yet are unceasingly converging as some single
moment. Thus the subsuming whole and the subsumed parts are
mutually subsumptive, in terms of both all dharmas as inherent in
the Nature [i.e., as eternal and omnipresent, as Lis], and all dharmas
dependently co-arising [as events located at a particular time and
place]. This does not mean that the subsumed parts are the phenomena and the subsuming whole is the Li. Moreover you should
understand that the "subsuming whole" for both all-dharmas-as-Lis
and all-dharmas-as-events is a single event, a *phenomenal* moment
of experience.[54]

It is not the case that the Li refers to the identical, the undifferentiated,
the Universal, or the whole, as opposed to events as the diverse, the differentiated, the Particular or the parts, as Chengguan had stated. Rather,
Li means all particular things *as* eternal and omnipresent, as universal
and necessary, but still retaining their own identities, inasmuch as, by the
Three Truths, their particularity is precisely their nonparticularity, which
is precisely their all-pervasion. In the Tiantai use of the metaphor of the
waves, we may recall, Li is represented by the wetness of the water, which
is divided into muddy wetness and clear wetness, representing entangled
Suchness and disentangled Suchness. Differentiation is thus inherent to Li
as such; Li is differentiated. Phenomena means these same occasions viewed
as having simple location, as having a definite beginning and end in time
(arising at moment X and perishing at moment Y) and in space (whether
physical or "conceptual"—i.e., as filling only the expanses between certain
definite borders that determinate it). This means both necessary mutation
or process, and also necessary finiteness. These are the waves, muddy and
clear. The oneness, sameness, or unity of these differentiated particulars is in
both cases, in Buddhist practice, to be found in one phenomenal moment
of experience, that is, one particular quiddity conceived as having a definite
beginning and end, fluent and finite, contingently encountered, occurring
right now, at this particular time and place—a particular muddy waviness.

But Zhili asserts that these two different forms of subsumption are
"identical" to one another. This means that they must finally be seen to be
both distinguishable and ultimately intersubsumptive, mutually reducible,

themselves versions of one another. The two forms of subsumption subsume one another. This is only possible on the distinctive Tiantai premise of the Three Truths, which tell us that "to be determinate" really means just "locally coherent," which means "globally incoherent," which means indeterminate. This applies equally to the dharmas and to the relationships between them. It is this that makes possible the double status of all dharmas, such that each functions both as a Li and as event.

To understand this, let us look further into Zhili's text:

> "Mind" [or any other phenomenal dharma] and "the Nature" are both different and non-different. Since [Zhanran] says, "Mind means the conditioned manifestation of the unchanging," we have here an event which is identical to Li. "The nature means the unchangingness of [each] conditioned appearance" thus means Li that is identical to each event. The two terms are used together here [i.e., in Zhanran's text, which asserts that all dharmas, whether mental or material, are "the Mind/Nature"] in order to reveal Li precisely as the event itself. On this precedent we can also make the same assertion about any phenomenon in place of "Mind," e.g., Buddha or Sentient Beings. You should understand that each of these is simultaneously to be known as-Li and as-event. This differs from the other [Shanwai] explanation, which holds that mind is specified as referring to Li, which is regarded as the subsuming whole, while Buddhas and Sentient Beings are specified as referring to events, which are regarded as the subsumed parts. . . . *Although the nature is called one, it is not a definite single nature* [無定一之性 *wu dingyi zhi xing*]. [I.e., there is no one definite single Li.] This is what allows all Three Thousand forms of matter and mind in all their specific appearances to remain just as they are. This is what [the *Vimalakīrti Sūtra*] means when it says "all dharmas are established from the non-dwelling root." You should understand that this applies equally whether we are speaking in terms of Li or in terms of events. Thus Zhanran explains this by saying, "[Seeing all Three Thousand Quiddities] from the point of view of Li, they are the conditioning and illuminating cause of Buddha-nature as inherent properties [i.e., as eternal and omnipresent]. From the point of view of events, they are the threefold Buddha-nature[55] as cultivated [i.e., phenomenal, simply located, dependently co-arising] properties. From the point of view of delusion, these are the cycle of the Three Paths (karma, delusion, and suffering). From the point of view of enlightenment, these are the supreme function of realized Buddhahood. All four

levels of analysis are established on the basis of the Ultimate Reality within delusion."

> Let me now interpret this passage. The Ultimate Reality within delusion is "the non-dwelling root." This is what the present text [i.e., Zhanran's "Ten Gates of Non-duality," upon which Zhili is here commenting] refers to as "the one nature that is no-nature." The four levels Zhanran indicates are "the establishment of all dharmas," or what the present text calls "the Three Thousand appearing just as they are." On the first level [i.e., seeing all things qua Lis], since the Buddha-nature as conditioning and illuminating cause plays the role of "all dharmas," we must take the implication to be that the Buddha-nature as cause proper is playing the role of "the non-dwelling root." In the three other levels [i.e., all dharmas in terms of events, either deluded or enlightened], phenomenal cultivations, as according with or violating the nature, play the role of "all dharmas," so "the Three Buddha-natures collectively as the Nature [or as a Li, i.e., as eternal and omnipresent] must be what is playing the role of the "non-dwelling root." Here we have the two types of subsuming whole and subsumed parts, so that these categories apply equally both to all things regarded as Li, and to all things regarded as events.[56]

Let us interpret this dense and complex passage. First, Zhili makes clear that mind is here merely an example of a particular phenomenon, stressed only for its convenience in the Buddhist practice of mind-contemplation in meditation. It has no special status; whatever can be said about it can also be said about any other phenomenal datum. What matters about it is that it is conditional, finite, temporal, fluent. It is indeed identical to Li, but not because it is somehow infinite or all-pervasive without also being finite, in contradistinction to all other dharmas, which are finite and simply located only, such that mind would be the totalizing whole and all other dharmas would be the subsumed parts. Rather, it is identical to Li in that, like any other finite fluent thing, this moment of experience is necessarily also readable as *a Li*, as eternal and omnipresent, or better, as categorical, as necessary and literally universal, as a value-bearing coherence with which it is valuable to cohere. Initially, as pure event, this moment of experience is evil—conditional, contingent, an instance of necessary suffering, whether it is pleasant or unpleasant. It subsumes all other events, in the manner of spurious mind-creation, the inalienable "in"-ness of all coherences within this coherence of "this moment of attention": all "dwell together in this moment of attention" while also "retaining their individual essences." As such, *all* of these events are still evil, still contingent, still conditional, still necessary suffering. This particular piece of suffering subsumes all other pieces of suffering, which turn out to be aspects of itself, and indeed unchangeably identical with itself. But with the experience of this one-way subsumption of all these instances of suffering, a turnaround occurs: this moment of attention, since it has the ability to appear as all other forms of suffering, is itself a Li. But the other events with which it is identical are thus also each a Li. I am sitting here feeling lonely. Loneliness is a conditional, contingent piece of suffering. But my loneliness subsumes its whole loneliness-surrounding world of coherences: the desolate coffee shop, the lingering words of rejection, the possibilities of not-being-lonely to which it is contrasted and for which it longs, which give it its coherent identity as loneliness. If these are contrasted to it, they are in relationship with it. If they are in relation to it, they must overlap with it somewhere. If they overlap with it, they must be "in" it. If they are "in" it, without simply replacing it so that no contrast and hence no identity-establishment is possible, then they must be identical to it: they must be it. Now, even "non-loneliness," as a conditional fact ever-threatened by the loneliness to which it is contrasted, is still a form of suffering, an evil. But when the two are seen to be two names for the same nameless thing, when this loneliness is seen to be inextricable even from its contrasted non-loneliness, it is known not to be conditional at all, to be a the transcendence of conditionality, to be the overcoming of suffering sought by Buddhists: it is seen to be a Li. But what Li? We cannot call this Li "loneliness" or "mind" or "me" only—it is equally accurate to call this Li "non-loneliness" or "matter" or "you." Each of these Li is the "Center" which subsumes all the others. The one-way subsumption of all beings by this moment of mind is seen to actually be the intersubsumption of all Lis. When these two are seen to be intersubsumptive, the contemplation is complete.

Hence, Zhili tells us that the "one nature" that is identical in all things is not a fixed single nature; it is not itself something determinate, or even determinately indeterminate. It is what Zhili later calls "not the one nature, but the Three-Thousand Nature"—or the Three Thousand Lis. These Three Thousand Lis are intersubsumptive: each is a name for all the others. But differentiation, multiple nameability, is inalienable even in the realm of Li. Like the wetness of the water, differentiation is applicable to it to exactly the same extent as to the phenomena; Suchness is divided in itself into entangled and disentangled, the wetness is also either muddy or clear, and Li too is not an undifferentiated unity. It is the "non-dwelling root." Non-dwelling here means ambiguous, or capable of appearing in every possible form, *as* any particular dharma. It is a "root" because no matter what level of analysis is adopted, we can always locate this level of indeterminateness grounding the determinacy and expressed *as* the determinacy. There is always something playing this role; this "level of indeterminateness" is not some separate dharma in its own right, but one role that all dharmas play in relation to all other dharmas. It is simply the indeterminate relation of all other dharmas-as-principle to this particular dharma-as-phenomena.[57] It is called a "root" because it is what is expressing itself *as* these other, different dharmas, forming the foundation of their being and the ultimate meaning to which they are reducible (i.e., they can be viewed "as" forms of this root, as modes of its expression), readable into and discoverable in this apparently "other" determinacy, as its necessary inside-outside ground. Each thing, again, plays this role for all other things. When all things are looked on as eternal and omnipresent, as necessary and universal, this role is played by the Cause Proper Buddha-nature as omnipresent and eternal, expressing itself *as* the Conditioning Cause and Illuminating Cause Buddha-natures as omnipresent and eternal. It is "non-dwelling" because it can be viewed indeterminately as either of these forms. It is a "root" because it is the ground of their being, to which they are reducible and hence identical. When all things are looked at as finite conditional phenomena, the Three Buddha-natures collectively are the non-dwelling root, which can appear indeterminately as any particular phenomena (and hence is non-dwelling), and stand as their root. Zhili here stops his analysis at this level, but the principle is also to be extended further, consistently with general Tiantai treatment of the repeated applicability of all categories at all levels. So while Zhili says the Buddha-nature as a whole is the non-dwelling root of all phenomenal reality, it is equally implied that when all things are seen as delusion, it is karma, delusion, and suffering that pervade all times and places, assuming indefinitely any possible form, standing as the basis as all, while when these same things are seen as enlightenment, it is the function of realized Buddhahood that plays this role. Karma and delusive cognitive-emotional disturbances (*klesha*) are necessary and universal, as are enlightenment and liberation, as are my shoe and that patch of red. As Zhiyi says in the *Sinianchu* 四念處, "Delusive disturbance pervades all times and places, and thus all times and places are enlightenment. If one abandons this enlightenment, where else can enlightenment be sought? Similarly, the truth of samsaric suffering pervades all times and places, and all are [thus] Nirvana."[58] Zhanran picks up this crucial point in the *Jingangpi* 金剛錍, stressing again that it is only because the delusively disturbed mind pervades all times and places (i.e., is eternal and omnipresent) that we can conclude that the pure mind of enlightenment pervades all times and places.[59] Similarly, in mind-contemplation, a single moment of conditional experience is seen as the non-dwelling root of all other dharmas, *as* which they are appearing, and vice versa.

Hence, Zhili goes on to clarify the difference between his claim and the Shanwai/Huayan claim that Li, Emptiness, Pure Mind is the only subsuming whole, in spite of his willingness to admit that Li is what is revealed by every act of subsumption, as the necessary condition of that subsumption. The question again reverts to oneness and difference, easier to put in English than Chinese; is it *the* Li that subsumes, or is it *any* Li that subsumes? Zhili asserts the latter, and that any event is, just by being an event, *a* Li (not *the* Li). Zhili says:

> Q: Since you end up positing the Real-Attribute within delusion as the One Nature, as opposed to the Three Thousand as the subsumed parts, you are precisely reading Li as the subsuming whole. Why do you take such pains to refute the other view [of the Shanwai, which adopts a version of the Huayan view, which also takes Li as the subsuming whole]?
>
> A: Because all dharmas share the same nature, when they are seen as conditioned as various particular dharmas, any one among them can be selected at random to be the universal whole that unifies all the others as its parts. The entirety of sentient beings have been in delusion since beginningless time. So if we just talk directly about the true nature or the subsuming whole, how will they be able to realize how each particular phenomenon inherently entails and absorbs all others into itself? . . . But if we show how a single phenomenal moment of experience unifies in itself all other dharmas, this allows us to reveal that they all share the same single true nature. . . . *You must understand that it is only because they share the same single nature that it is possible for them to dwell together as a single moment of experience.* Hence we are using the observed fact that they dwell together as a single moment of experience to conclude [inductively] that they share the same single true nature. We are not simply taking this one moment of experience and calling it the ultimate truth. For is it not also true that they all dwell together as a single particle of matter, and does this not equally reveal the ultimate truth? The text earlier asserts that "the one nature is the universal subsuming whole"; later it says, "one moment of experience is the universal subsuming whole." This reveals how Lis and events mutually illuminate each other. These two lines precisely reveal the reason that the subsumed parts are integrated into the subsuming whole. Because the one nature has no fixed nature, the Three Thousand as Li and as events are established. *The two levels of Three Thousand, the Three Thousand as Lis and the Three Thousand*

as events, dwell together as a single moment of experience. How could this be the same as their doctrine which straightaway identifies one moment of Mind as the True Nature itself?[60]

The difference between the subsumption on the level of event and subsumption on the level of Li is that the latter involves the premise that subsumption is always intersubsumption. The subsumption of one content by another, for example, objects by mind, presents itself as a one-way includer/included relation. This same relation is seen to be the *zong* and *bie* of Li when this one-sided one-way subsumption is seen to be identical to mutual subsumption, where each is included and each is includer. These two are seen to be identical: the spurious deluded one-way subsumption of all things by the deluded mind is the self-negated form, the set-up, by which the intersubsumption of mind and all objects, and the intersubsumption of all objects, accomplishes its omnipresence. This metalevel setup-punch line identity-as-difference between delusion and enlightenment is the crux of the Tiantai position. The intersubsumption of all objects, such that each is an omnipresent Li, is present here as its own negation, the spurious one-way subsumption of objects by mind, the domineering self that possesses and controls its world. Reversibility is the key.[61] The latter is now seen as a *upāya*, a *miaojia* 妙假, which is the very self-negating conditional manner in which the unconditional manifests itself, and which is thus itself seen to be inherently included and itself unconditionally omnipresent, a Li: what must be realized in order to end suffering.

Zhili sums up his point as follows:

No single one of the Three Thousand mental or physical phenomena can ever change, and so *each one* is called "the Nature." . . . So the subsuming whole and subsumed parts pertaining to Li (the Nature) are as follows: the originally inherent Three Thousand [i.e., the Three Thousand different but intersubsumptive Li, each of which is thus eternal and omnipresent] are the subsumed parts, and a single moment of phenomenal experience is the subsuming whole [本具 三千為別，剎那一念為總 *benjusanqian wei bie, chana yinian wei zong*]. This is because the Three Thousand share the same single nature, which makes it possible for a single moment of experience to serve as the subsuming whole. . . .

The subsuming whole and the subsumed parts pertaining to phenomena are as follows: the transforming and created Three Thousand events are the subsumed parts, and, again, one moment of phenomenal experienced event is the subsuming whole [變造 三千為別，剎那一念為總 *bianzao sanqian wei bie, chana yinian wei zong*]. This is also because the Three Thousand share the same nature, which allows them all to converge and reduce to a single moment of experience. . . . This nature and substance does not mean some single unified nature. We mean rather the "Three Thousand-Nature(s).[62]

Now we can see what Zhili means when he says, in the passage cited at the beginning of this section, "Only when these two [i.e., the subsuming whole and the subsumed parts of the Three Thousand-as-Li, on the one hand, and both of these for the Three-Thousand-as-phenomena, on the other] are seen as identical is the Wondrous Contemplation accomplished." It is clarified by Zhili's very pithy summary of Tiantai faith in his *Xiuchanyaozhi* 修懺要旨: "All dharmas are originally entailed [i.e., unchangeable Lis] in the mind itself, and are generated [as temporal phenomena] by the entirety of the mind. *Temporal generation of dharmas requires no separate Li [outside of original entailment]: each is generated due to this original entailment itself. Entailment is not some separate entailment [outside of generation]; in each case it is just dependent co-arising itself*" (生無別理, 並由本具. 具無別具, 皆是緣生 *sheng wu bie Li, bing you benju. Ju wu bie ju, jie shi yuansheng*).[63] The two italicized sentences here give a strong restatement of what Zhili means by "the identity between Li and events," and with it, the identity between Li-as-part-and-whole and event-as-part-and-whole. It is not that there exists an eternal set of forms or universals, an atemporal template of possible determinacies, which arise as temporal phenomena at a given time and place according to some additional principle or factor. Rather, temporal generation is itself the mutual entailment of the various Lis themselves, their mutual embrace as whole and part. X-as-event generates Y-as-event because X-as-Li entails (i.e., is another name for) Y-as-Li. The "slide" between X being present and Y being present is just like the seeing of, for example, a picture of two faces sliding into seeing a picture of a vase between them (in the popular gestalt drawing), according to the changes in attention and desire. "Faces" generates "vase" because of the original entailment of vase in faces; further, the act of seeing-as-faces generates the act of seeing-as-vase in just the same way. Conversely, there is no repository of the eternal universals stored up somewhere outside the flow of dependent co-arising. Rather, dependent co-arising itself is the storing up of all dharmas in each dharma. No second realm is required outside of the transient temporal occurrences of events to guarantee the eternal presence of each event, their universal presence as Lis. The very process of occurring of any event is the presencing of all dharmas-as-Lis. When an event occurs and absorbs all past, present, and future events as aspects of itself, this is at the same time their pervasion of all these temporal events as mutually entailing

Lis. Temporal arising of dependently co-arising events *is* the original entailment of these very determinacies as Lis, as universals being instantiated in
events.

Now we can perhaps understand more fully the Tiantai conception
of Li, and its manner of apprehension by the human mind. Li is still and
always value, coherence (totalizing), intelligibility, and the ironic effacement
of intelligibility (ambiguity). The mind in Tiantai remains the anti-value par
excellence, that which seeks value because it lacks it, and thereby posits and
determines the nature of that value. Its essence is temporality, simple location, arising and perishing, conditionality, other-dependence. Concomitant
to this is its function of seeking value—desiring, attaching, hating—and
parsing the world to make it intelligible to its desire, making distinctions
and separations, reifying possible objects of desire and avoidance. This state
of mind is anti-value per se. The Li that alone can satisfy it is the unconditionality of all possible objects of experience in the manner described above:
their value, coherence, intelligibility, and nonintelligibility. This anti-value
mind, the deluded mind, apprehends this Li by realizing its identity to
it, their intersubsumption. It is by virtue of its very conditionality that it
intersubsumes the unconditional, realizes itself as an unconditioned quiddity in its own right, pervading all other conditions. The deluded mind is
present as the truth to be realized, and the truth so realized is itself present
as the deluded mind. It is in the recognition of its own conditionality that
the deluded mind sees the truth, and that the truth sees the deluded mind.
We can say equally that Li thinks, desires, sees, and suffers, as that suffering, seeing, desire, and thinking are themselves Lis.[64] As Zhili says, Tiantai
insists that we can legitimately say that the universe is not only mind-only,
or form-only, or scent-only, or arising-only, or perishing-only, but also "false
views-only, attachment-only" (唯見唯愛 *weijian wei'ai*).

Phenomenal experience is thus a constant succession of new delusions,
which are, ipso facto, the constant emergence of *new Li*. This means that
every experience is a disclosure of a new cosmos, with a new set of rules,
and even new a priori categories of experience and understanding, new ways
of unifying all previous unifying conditions of experience. The Principle of
Emptiness is not "a single, same principle," as in Huayan, nor is there a
fixed set of categories of understanding as in Kant, or of Reason as in Hegel,
nor even the "primordial nature of God," which possesses a certain set of
eternal objects and no others, as the basic overall activity of creativity, the
general activity that is not an occasion but rather analogous to Spinoza's
substance, assuming a primal determinateness, as in Whitehead. Rather, in
a very real sense, as in the *Lotus Sutra* doctrine of universal Buddhahood,
there is in Tiantai *a new and different God*, a new foundation and new telos

of all possible activity, with each moment of experience. Every moment is a new Li, which by being deludedly dreamt to exist right here and right now ipso facto everywhere exists, has existed, will exist, for all eternity.

Bringing the discussion back to the issue of ironic and non-ironic coherence, we may say that the Pure Mind position, whether of Chan, Huayan, or the Shanwai, attempts to incorporate irony directly into the immediate subsumption of events by mind via the notion that mind is itself Empty, that is, devoid of any positive identity of its own: this coherence of all things is a non-coherence, has no intelligible characteristics. This subsumption—this dominance, this possession—is for this reason seen as a non-subsumption, non-dominance, non-possession, revealing instead the free unconditionality of all events, all characteristics. At the final Huayan stage, there are supposedly only events interpervading unobstructedly. Explicit reference to Li disappears: this cosmos of interpenetrating events is itself the beatific vision that ends suffering. But precisely as such, *this* vision is itself Li, one that locks in as a definite point of view that excludes other points of view, all the more entrenched for being invisibly embedded in the framing of what defines events, that is to say, what serves as the standard by which to determine what is "real" and what merely "appearance." The mind is a *shi*, but manifests the nonobstruction of event and event directly: this nonobstruction of events is itself the only Li, the only real coherence, and it is supposed to contain a built-in guarantee against becoming a non-ironic coherence due to its intrinsic emptiness of identity. A non-ironic coherence, in the ironic traditions of which we speak, is of course a form of dominance, a definite rule, a coercion, a lack of unconditionality. The mind is supposed to be unbiased, unconditional, because, seen and experienced correctly, it is perfectly empty, it is emptiness itself, a mirrorlike pure awareness that manifests anything precisely because it holds to no identity of its own. Zhili's Tiantai position, in contrast, is that this is a sham. That is, the phenomenal mind is a *shi*, and as such is necessarily conditional, and as such is necessarily biased and delusional. Its emptiness is never separable from its biased conditional particularity, and any claim it may make to be viewing or subsuming things from a positionless position is just a subterfuge: the claim to be free from bias is itself always biased. Rather, the self-undermining of non-ironic coherence to achieve the real, ironic, coherence, Li, must be achieved through this very bias. The very bias is accomplished only through the de facto overlapping copresence of sameness and difference in ordinary deluded perception, its ceaseless subsumption of whatever it encounters, the very thing that made it feel, erroneously, that it was in control of whatever it encounters. It is this copresence of self and other, of sameness and difference, in any perception which reveals the multilocality and multi-identity of any local coherence, its ambiguity, its unconditional omnipresence. This in turn reveals the unilateral subsumption of things by mind to necessarily entail an intersubsumption of the mind itself by things. The very act of disambiguation, the deluded mind itself, is the mechanism for revealing the failure of disambiguation, and the upayic necessity of this failure to its own self-overcoming. The result is the intersubsumption of all possible coherences, always manifesting upayically also as their own opposites, and thus revealed as all equally unconditional, all equally the locus of absolute value, all equally the ironic unity of all things that ends suffering by remaining inextricably copresent in suffering: each and every possible characteristic appearing anywhere is, not "in reality" or "in essence" *the* one Li, but is, rather, itself, precisely as this specific appearance, *a* particular Li. Zhiyi had said it already, but now we are in a position to understand it: 一色一香無非中道 (*yise yixiang wufei zhongdao*) "Each sight or smell is itself the Middle Way."[65]

CONCLUSION

The Vertex of the Vortex

In *Ironies of Oneness and Difference*, and again in the introduction to this book, I raised the several issues as a way of framing the problem of Li. We were looking for how the Chinese traditions handled the questions of repeatability, set membership, apodictic knowledge, part and whole relations, omnipresence, contextualization, determinateness, conditionality, ironic and non-ironic coherence, pragmatism, value, nominalism/realism, and normativity. At the heart of all these issues was a question about sameness and difference: What happens to all these conceptions if neither sameness nor difference, neither oneness nor manyness, can be an ultimate ontological fact about anything? How can we think about how early Chinese thinkers might have thought about entities that were neither same nor different, or that were both same and different? We attempted to make some headway on this issue by considering early Chinese notions of coherence, both ironic and non-ironic, as ways of conceiving a neither/nor/both/and mode of understanding for what we would otherwise call sameness and difference; and in this volume, we have looked at the term Li as an increasingly important marker of a kind of second-order relation between certain kinds of coherences, which cohere again so as to end up being again neither definitively the same coherence nor definitively different coherences. The term Li, we said, would play a crucial role in configuring these issues, which are approached in quite different ways in the various strands of occidental philosophy. Li, I suggested, means a harmonious coherence, which, when a human being becomes harmoniously coherent with it, leads to further harmonious coherence. We have come to see how all these meanings are combined in the Tiantai conception of Li as Centrality. We are now in a position to see how "centrality" and "coherence" converge into the meaning of Li, and how this sort of notion developed through various partial prefigurements in Confucian and Daoist thought. Let us review these findings briefly.

In the *Analects*, we found that Confucius was said to have no "constant teacher," and yet to find his teacher everywhere. He himself was the "center," which here meant the determinant of the coherence, the "pattern," the "principle," the sustainable intelligible unity with the past and the future, the value. But he was depicted as neither subjectively creating this value *ex nihilo* nor acting as a mere passive mirror of an objectively existing truth. The value he creates is a coherence, a readable converging, of aspects available everywhere, combined by the selective filter of Confucius's own responses and evaluations. His discernment is a selective frame which creates/discerns coherence, the value-endowed style of culture, which is omniavailable, present in more than one place, not strictly reiterable except in the special sense of being continuable. We have here already the sprout of a model of a multiple instantiation that is neither nominalist nor realist, manifesting in a cognition that is neither objective nor subjective.

In the *Mencius*, we had the selective definition of which of the inborn capabilities of the human animal are to be properly named "the Nature" (性 *xing*) with a more explicit set of criteria: precisely those spontaneous human tendencies that allow for coherence, that is, those that are appealing (valued) and discernible to other humans, and that create cohesion among humans, are to be called the Nature. These were the desires that can be satisfied independently of external material conditions, that allow for the other (for example, material) desires to also be nurtured and developed, the enjoyment of which is increased rather than decreased when shared, and so on. The material desires were to be called "the Decree," because they are not conducive to coherence in this sense: they isolate, they create strife because their satisfaction depends on external material resources, which may be in short supply, their enjoyment is decreased when shared, and so on. The class name *Human Nature* was there also neither objective nor subjective, neither nominalist nor realist; and there again we had a "center" embodied by a living human agent, the sage, whose manifestation of these virtues makes him the organizing hub, around which this style of being, humanity, converges. The human virtues manifested by the presence of this center, by drawing others to cohere with them and emulate them, literally actualized the coherence "humanity." Once picked out, it is seen to have always been there, and always to have been operating as a genuine multiply instantiated coherence, really present as something with actual and identifiable causal effects in all the members it includes. But the act of picking it out, prioritizing, and naming it in this way is itself an example of it, decisively instantiating it and simultaneously revealing its instantiation elsewhere, even in the past.

In the *Xunzi*, we had a seeming conflict between a nominalistic and a realist theory of naming, which was resolved once again by recourse to a human center, in this case the tradition of the sages and exemplary persons who literally give order to the cosmos through mandated ritual. But this too was neither creation *ex nihilo* nor passive reflection of coherence: Xunzi recognized an overabundance of real distinctions, groupings, coherences in the world, among which the sages serve as a selective filter, enforcing their standardized names in the same way that weights and measures are to be enforced in the marketplace. Omnipresence was found in the "Greatest Coherence" (大理 *dali*), the value present in all parts of the organized whole, which resulted from the noble man's selective ritual regulations of which of the really occurring groupings of nature may be grouped into a valued whole, that is to say, a whole that maximizes the satisfaction of human desires. This Greatest Coherence, a second-order coherence relation between a certain subset of prior coherences both human and nonhuman, operated as a genuine whole inclusive even of the natural world, viewed as having a real determinative power to instantiate its characteristics of "order and value" fully in each of its component participants. These characteristics turned out, once they were established in any time and place, to be really there, really efficacious, really multiply instantiated, extending to all relevant times and places.

In the *Laozi* tradition, we have the advent of ironic coherence: a valued togetherness, which is necessarily also unintelligible, unreadable. When all is together, nothing is discernible, and this is the ultimate cohering, also the ultimate value, from which lesser (intelligible, non-ironic) values/coherences emerge. The motif of the center is here transformed from the exemplary center of Confucianism, the model that inspires those around it to modify themselves because it is seen and valued, to the invisible center, which attracts, creating togetherness and value, precisely by not being seen, not being valued. To be valued is to inspire imitation, which is to inspire competition, which is to create strife, which is to undermine ultimate coherence. To be seen is to be cut out from a background that is unseen, which means again a loss of the greatest coherence. Coherence is "ironic" in that the true coherence (value, togetherness, the unhewn or devalued from which the valued grows, which is inseparable from the valued, which accounts for the cycle of reversal from value to anti-value, and which is omnipresent in both the valued and the devalued) is by definition incoherent (indiscernible, invisible).

In the writings of Zhuang Zhou, we had an overabundance of perspectives, each positing its own standard of rightness (是 *shi*), which were filtered down moment by moment not according to tradition or sagacity, but by virtue of the mere fact that each perspective was in fact a perspective, a "this." Being a "this," it posits its "that," which is also a "this," and hence its own new perspective. Zhuang Zhou's "wild card" perspective reflects and affirms the "rightness" presented by each new situation, but does not consider it in conflict with the opposite perspective, the opposed *shi/fei* 是非.

Shi is "this," which is coherence, value, intelligibility; but in positing its own negation, which in turn negates "this," every coherence is also necessarily an incoherence, which again affirms Laozi's ironic coherence: value which is togetherness which is unintelligibility: "the radiance of drift and doubt" (滑疑之耀 *guyi zhi yao*). The "togetherness" here comes in not as an overriding convergence of all things in a single vision (as in Xunzi's "Greatest Coherence") but resides in a new application of the motif of the center, already prefigured in Mencius's discussion of "not clinging to the center." Zhuang Zhou introduces the idea of the pivot of Dao (道樞 *daoshu*), which is also the pivots of daos: the point where opposed *shi/feis* are not opposed, not mutually exclusive, precisely because of their mutual positing, and hence, in "responding but not storing" (應而不藏 *ying er bu cang*) like a mirror, they flow freely into one another. The center allows one to "travel two roads at once" (兩行 *liangxing*): this special kind of value bilocality is Zhuang Zhou's distinctive contribution to the problematic of coherence, universality, and omnipresence in Chinese thought.

In *Liji* texts such as the "Yueji," "Daxue," and "Zhongyong," as also in the Yin-Yang systems of the commentaries to the *Zhouyi* and Yang Xiong's *Taixuanjing*, we found a domestication of the ironic notion of the coherence and center—the unseen, the unmanifest, the unintelligible—as a creator of observable order and consistency. Overall coherence works through local pockets of invisibility or ironic coherence: the as-yet-unseen sprouts, the unmanifest but constant Inner Coherence (誠 *cheng*), which reveals itself in all individual affects and actions but never shows itself *simpliciter*, the Yin side of a Yin-Yang dyad, which however works toward and is subordinated to the manifestation and purposes of the Yang. The role of the unintelligible, the background, the unreadable togetherness in which value is rooted is here acknowledged and integrated into the system of Greatest Coherence.

Moving into the present volume, examining the later parts of the *Zhuangzi*, and the *Hanfeizi* commentary to the *Laozi*, we found an ironic appropriation of the non-ironic sense of coherence, where local forms of coherence—predictability, intelligibility, constancy—coexisted with the overriding incoherence of the whole, the ironic value/togetherness of the valueless, the unreadable whole. These horizontal forms of coherence were necessarily tentative, approximate, non-rigorous, and all structured basically as expansions of the Laozian point about reversal. What is knowable about things is their tendency to revert to the Dao, which is formulable in vague terms for general tendencies, but is not strictly predictive for individual events. The value of knowing these "principles" lies not in allowing us to control or understand all the events in the world, but in creating a state of mind that takes into account the centripetal action of the Dao, for living with minimal strife and worry. Knowing the Li of reversal and transformation ("Community Words"), of perspectival relativism ("Autumn Floods"), or of yielding (*Hanfeizi* commentary) in a general way allows for an easier handling of things in general, without requiring specific knowledge about particular entities as such.

In Wang Bi, we see the introduction of another way of combining the ironic and non-ironic traditions, with the introduction of Li not as the determinate counterpart and opposite of the indeterminate Dao, the determinate parts of an indeterminate whole, as in the *Hanfeizi* commentary, but Li as mini-Daos, as the scarcest elements of a given situation, concretized indeterminacies that structure the determinate situation around them. The least evident aspects of the situation bear the same relation to that situation that the Dao bears to the universe as a whole; they are the empty space in that situation toward which the other elements converge. First-order harmony here is specifically the harmony between a desire and its object: the predominant elements desire what they lack, and are thereby ruled and organized by it. In observing the situation, we harmonize with this kind of harmony: to understand and master the situation is to harmonize with (com-prehend) its harmony (convergence of desires of its elements toward the mini-Dao, the Li, that rules and determines it, the quantitatively least-represented element). This is done in order to create another harmony: the harmony between what we, the knowers, may want, and the outcome of the situation. Here, we have an attempt at a more concrete kind of information about specific situations, determined in a broad variety of individual ways. Predictability and knowability are now direct expressions of the localized instances of unknowability.

In Guo Xiang, the ironic sense of coherence is pushed to its extreme, such that all apparent principles are in reality only one Li: the self-so, the negation of all principles. It is a Li because it is still a harmony—i.e., a cohering of elements "vanishing into" the present situation, moment, or entity, where their harmony is guaranteed by the fact that no traces emerge; and it is a value—the one thing "worth noticing" in order to ensure maximum human effectiveness in responding to the situation. This is the second-order harmony, the harmony with human interests: not conscious teleological desires any more, but merely the form of living that is most in accord with the basic nature of the human event, most conducive to the full free function of the self-so and its self-forgetting. "No principle" still fits our definition of "Li." But Guo also equates this self-forgetting, this Li of self-so, with the earliest concept of Li as a cutting, a limitation. The self-so is whatever an event may be prior to its interference from traces, from things lying outside its limits, defined as whatever requires knowing and willing to attain. The complete isolation, limitedness, separation of any event is its Li, its self-so, but this is at once the unintelligible, the unknowable, the merging of all elements in the incoherent ironic coherence formerly reserved for the whole. Hence, Guo creates a singularity between the non-ironic Li as intelligible separation and ironic Li as unintelligible omnipresence.

In Huayan Buddhism, we have what looks an expanded sense of one side of Guo's Daoism: the one real principle is Emptiness, which is Li in all the senses delineated above: it is all-inclusive (cohering, harmonizing), it is universally applicable, it is what needs to be paid attention to in order to attain maximum value for human beings (second-order harmony, harmony with human needs). As in Guo, this involves a turnaround and negation of Li, a turning back to events, to individual instances outside the top-down control of any higher-order principles. But as in Guo also, this amounts to the redundant repetition of one and the same principle, namely, the principle of "no-principle." That is all that Emptiness qua interpenetration means here, and it retains the full sense of a truth to be recognized, against which alternate perceptions can only be counted as illusions and errors.

In Tiantai, developing the other aspect of Guo's work—coherence and incoherence converging to a point of being completely coextensive—this epistemological stance is altered: there are no errors, only *upāyas*. Moreover, the notion of Li is diversified: it is not just that there is one principle-of-no-principle, which then empties out into the interpenetration of events. Rather, there are infinite principles, infinite Lis, which interpenetrate infinite events. These Lis are neither simply given as facts in the objective world (realism) nor merely projected onto a blank canvas by subjective whim or convention (nominalism). Rather, they are "inherently entailed" in the sense delineated by the Three Truths: always identifiable, but always ambiguous, and thus readable *into* all locations and times, but equally readable *out* of the initial instance, the apparently "given" occurrence of this quiddity. Yet each of them is genuinely omnipresent and omnitemporal, playing a non-negligible part in every event occurring at any time or place, and demanding to be recognized as a nonnegotiable attribute instantiated in every event; neglect of this attribute in any event anywhere is an obstacle to the realization of the highest value, the only complete satisfaction of sentient desire, namely, the end of suffering in the state of Buddhahood as Tiantai conceives it. Each one is an omnipresence which must be recognized to attain the satisfaction of human aspiration: a second-order coherence, an omnipresence (coherence) which must be known (coherence between a mind and a cognitive object) in order to bring satisfaction (coherence between desire and object desired): in short, a Li. Li is "Centrality," so that the claim that "all dharmas are Li" means that "all dharmas revert to and are reducible to each dharma; each dharma is the omnipresent unconditional center of the universe, subsuming all qualities in itself, and as itself; thus each is the Middle Way, the end of suffering." Every content is also a

category that subsumes all other contents; every category is also a content
subsumed by every other category. It is in this sense that Li are valued coherent harmonies to be harmonized with: all things "cohere" in them, they are
"readable" (coherent) and all things are readable in them, and this reading
of all coherences in each coherence is a harmonizing that itself constitutes
liberation from the existential condition of suffering, conceived as a function
of conceiving the self (and correlatively, all entities) as finite, simply located
in one time or place rather than any other, hence impermanent, sundered
from one another, and hence constitutively saturated with suffering.

Each thing, each imaginable characteristic, is in Tiantai a "Li." These
Li are neither subjective nor objective, imply neither realism nor nominalism. The desires of sentient beings are what underwrite the biased perspectives that disambiguate the observed world into specific, simply located
entities. These desires are in one sense simply "given"—they have been
going on since beginningless time—but the doctrine of "inherent evil" (性
惡 xing'e), stipulating that all evils are ineradicably present in all times and
places, even in Buddhahood,[1] implies that they themselves are also part of
the valued coherence, what must be comprehended in order to be liberated,
the Li. The use of the term Three Thousand for the totality, rather than
simply all dharmas, brings with it also the "traditionalism" of the non-ironic
tradition—i.e., these are the ten realms and ten suchnesses that are pointed
out by the Buddha in the scriptures as being particularly relevant for human
practice. The contemplation of "inherent entailment" (具 ju), then, means
simply seeing each thing not only as a display of the capacity of my mind
to produce this effect, but to see it as literally unconditioned, preexistent,
like a universal category, incapable of causal arising from any particular set
of conditions. Ironically, this is ensured precisely because it is nothing but
conditional.

In the preceded pages, we have experimented with many motifs and
models in an attempt to maximize our appreciation for the nuances of many
related but distinct ways of thinking about problems of sameness, difference,
coherence, incoherence, and omnipresence, and found each of them to have
their own distinctive ways of handling and organizing some of these key
motifs that we have found to gather around the term Li. The Tiantai position
just summarized may perhaps be considered the most intricate and extensive
development of the tendency to make Li a marker of omnipresence, but
at the same time to maintain its original sense of division and particularity, along with its focus on value and its performatively self-instantiating
character. The attempt at a detailed exposition of the premises and nuances
involved in that highly counterintuitive system provides, I hope, something
interesting to think about, and allows us to think many new thoughts,
which I would suggest, if pressed, is the sole and real point of intellectual

endeavors such as the one currently before the reader: to provide the power to think a greater number of more greatly differing thoughts. This has been the driving desideratum of this work, quite apart from questions of getting things either historically or philosophically "right," although as I indicated in the introduction to the prequel, those labors are necessary to maximize the real goal, which is always the literal ability or power to think more thoughts. Truth is important, but it is important only because it makes things so much more interesting. I hope at least that the journey has been interesting for those who like the activity of thinking, take pleasure in the expansion of thinking into new powers and operations, and have some prior interest in thinking about these particular types of issues. I hope, in other words, that reading one's way through the ins and outs of all these texts has given you some interesting new thoughts, whether right or wrong. (If not, your time has been wasted, and in that case, dear reader, you are certainly owed an apology.)

One who feels at home in goals and methods of this kind will naturally tend to read texts somewhat as an "insider" in each case, however diverse those cases might be: wallowing in each of them for the intrinsic rewards of doing so, opting for total immersion, motivated by love of the game itself, wanting to see what possibilities for alternate ways of seeing the world might open up from inside each orientation, implication after implication, and without much interest in gathering these moves and expansions into handy "results" to be harvested for ulterior uses. But taking a step back from this gallery of related philosophical positions in which we've tried to immerse ourselves, we might ask ourselves how these ideas that might look to someone in more of a hurry, what form they might assume in takeaway shorthand models, for application to other truth projects or goodness projects of whatever kind. In our discussion we've had to try on and fling off various models and analogies to explore individual points of oddness, without worrying too much about squaring them with one another. These models seem to lend themselves to incessant invention and modification and revision, precisely because in this term Li something interestingly strange is being denoted. But the "outsider" will justifiably want to compare and crystallize and refine these models for some kind of conclusion. We moderns, for example, may be tempted to compare the weird ubiquitous co-presence of intersubsumptive but conflicting Li in Tiantai doctrine to, say, the presence of radio waves pervading space. All the stations are playing in all locations at the same time, but only one comes forth, due to the way a particular radio receiver is tuned. Perhaps an even better metaphor would be that of various prisms and lenses. All the colors are present everywhere, copresent in each locus. But a particular prism or lens breaks this light up, making one or another color appear at a particular locus. All the colors are in fact present at each locus, but only one is manifest. A moment of experience is like the lens that selects out and manifests some of the Three Thousand at this locus rather than others, while in fact each is present everywhere. This metaphor must be modified by the further consideration that each of the particular colors subsumes all the others; it is not just white that is composed of all the other colors, but each particular color does likewise: it is as if red light could be broken up by a particular lens into all the other colors of the spectrum, plus white itself. This consideration is what is meant by "intersubsumption of Lis." The unique role of white light in physical reality as we presently conceive it would be a case of "the exclusive Mean": a fixed relationship exists between that which is the subsumed and that which is the subsumer. In the Tiantai case, each is the subsumer and each is the subsumed.

But there is still something profoundly wrong with these metaphors. They are too "Platonic." That is, they suggest a two-tiered ontology: lenses are lenses, light is light. To correct this, we would have to make a mental adjustment that seems to make the metaphor quite unworkable. For to really correspond to the Tiantai position, we would need a situation where light was, as it were, made of not waves or particles, but of *lenses*. The light pervading all space would have to be just lenses and nothing more; perhaps tiny lenses, or waves that are themselves distortions of space, which function themselves as lenses. This would mean that light passes through light, as it were; that is, that the lens bending the light is itself made out of light. Perhaps we could imagine this by picturing light threaded through itself, so that we have a difference in scale, something like a knot; light loops around to form a construct through which other light may pass, and be filtered and distorted; or microlevel coherences of light passing through macrolevel coherences.

All this is very confusing, and perhaps it is not constructive to continue to modify our metaphor; it has, in effect, broken down. To make it work, we would have to speak of a certain inherent "nodalizing" capability inherent in the nature of a "ray." That is, rays would have to also serve as nodes of other rays, rather than being evenly distributed universal presences with no built-in centers of gravity—or in the Tiantai case, the constant ability to serve as a nodal center of gravity for other rays. But the problem that arises here is indicative of the big issue we are confronting in this book. In a word, rather than a two-tiered ontology, we would suggest that we think here of a vortex with a center of gravity: a certain kind of center-periphery ontology, a kind of modified offshoot of Qian Mu's pendulum or Hall and Ames's focus/field model, which we might call the vortex-vertex model. *Li are the vertices of vortices.* Like essences, universals, or Platonic Forms, the Li have the character of (1) multilocal or omnipresent instantiation; (2) transcendence; (3) determining (content-providing); (4) inclusivity, and

(5) normativity. But each of these must be understood by means of this vortex whirling around its vertex, rather than the two-tiered light/lens model or the two-tiered universal/particular model or Form/Matter model. That is:

> Multilocal or Omnipresent Instantiation: The Li must pervade a given span of particular instantiations not as light pervades a space, nor as a universal Form is repeated identically in its instantiations, but as the center of gravity, the vertex, is discernible everywhere in the vortex. Note that we do not say here that there is one entity, the vertex, and another entity, the vortex, and then a third entity, which we call the "influence" of the vertex on the vortex. For this way of speaking presupposes a strict simple-location ontology, which multiplies entities in order to bridge the gap of relation between these sundered entities, and in fact, as Whitehead pointed out, is correlative to an ontology of universals and particulars. Rather, wherever the influence of something is discernible, that something is itself present in that certain form. Since the identity of an entity is here a matter of continuity—coherence—rather than repeatability of a selfsame essence, we have the manifestation of the same coherence in different forms rather than the influence of one thing on another. Hence, to indicate a few of the models for this idea, the Way of Wen and Wu was "present" all around Confucius; the "influence" of the sage's human nature is present as the humanness of the people influenced and grouped by him (Mencius); the Ritual is present in its various, apparently contrary expressions (Xunzi); the Dao is the source but also the stuff and the course of things, it is what they are made of and also what they come from and go to, and again what charts their motion (Laozi); the wild card is present as whatever perspective it is mirroring (Zhuangzi); the Inner Coherence ("sincerity," 誠 cheng) "is" the various emotions that manifest in accordance with it ("Zhongyong"), and so on. This is the distinctive matrix of omnipresence in these traditions, as opposed to the derivation from the concept of universality in occidental traditions. The vertex is present in the vortex. As we saw in the Tiantai case, the ultimate issue of this way of thinking is that the vortex is present as the vertex.
>
> Transcendence: The Li must be beyond any particular determination not as white light is beyond any particular color, nor as a universal or Form is beyond any of its instantiations, but as a center of gravity is not any of the elements that are organized around it, nor the entirety of the vortex, but a virtual point that

may be empty of contents. It is present *as* them, but it is not any of them *simpliciter*. To be a center that joins two extremes, it must not itself be either of the two extremes; it must exclude them, be beyond them. Transcendence here means simply negation (to "not" be X is to be entirely "beyond" X), but negation in this case turns out to imply inclusion: the center is not the two extremes precisely because it is the one place that is both of the two extremes, their only point of contact and copresence. More to the point, the center is the sole intelligibility of the whole, the totality of relations. Outside of the whole, there is nothing. Hence, there is nothing for that totality to be related to. Thus, precisely because everything is constituted by its relations and is nothing besides, each thing, qua center, is transcendent, is beyond all relations. Put another way: if all is relation (nontranscendent), then there are no relata, and if there are no relata, there are no relations. Each thing subsumes all beings as aspects of itself, each is nothing but the totality of all relations, each is the whole, outside of which there is nothing. Each thing stands alone beyond all otherness, dependent on no "other" being, transcendent to all other beings. Total immanence implies total transcendence.

Determination (content-providing): The Li must determine and provide the content of events not as light provides the content of the various colors, nor as a universal or Form provides the content of particulars, but as a vertex determines the position of the elements in a vortex, and the character of the vortex itself.

Inclusivity: The Li include all their exemplars not as light includes all colors, nor as a universal or Form includes the essence of all its instantiations, but as a center of gravity at the vertex is expressed by the behavior of all elements in the vortex, the point from which they are all derivable.

Normativity: The Li are normative not as definitional forms but as the point of equilibrium to which an internal pull can be felt in all elements of a vortex, if these are viewed as elements in the whole vortex rather than separate events. But this normativity will only hold if human welfare, desire in the broad sense, is also one of the elements in the vortex. That is, we must presuppose that we are ourselves wind-sailors, who study these vortices with the specific interest of knowing how to maintain our equilibrium in sailing through them, utilizing them for sailing power, and so on. To know where the vertices or centers of gravity lie is the essential thing we need to know to make our way through the vortices and keep from capsizing. Not every vortex-around-a-vertex is a Li: only those that are "edible" to us, as it were, qualify.

The earliest usage of the character Li was as a verb: to divide, as one divides plots of land for farming. This is a particular kind of cutting: the treatment of jade is also a process of cutting away, but one that creates a finished product that has a certain value to human beings. To divide in this way is also to group. It is to divide raw material into groups according to certain value requirements. As a noun, this comes to mean the contours of the natural material along which it can be so divided. It suggests the perforations that guide effective cutting, leaving the material grouped in a way that is coherent for human valuation.

Thinking in terms of the vertex-vortex model, these perforations are the vertices which, when chosen as guides for our grouping divisions, form coherent vortices around themselves. A ready model from Chinese medicine would be the acupuncture meridians and their pressure points (穴道 xuedao). One cuts or presses into the body at certain places, and this divides and channels the energies of the body into coherent groupings, making the body a more harmonious totality. The division in the body thus further unifies the body. It is in this sense that dividing and uniting are combined in the conception of Li.

I will now repeat verbatim the chart given earlier, noting the three distinct levels of harmonious coherence are thus necessary for any item, X, to qualify as Li:

1. The harmonious coherence (togetherness) of

    a. the parts of X with one another, and

    b. X as a whole with its environment.

2. The harmonious coherence between X and a desiring human perceiver:

    a. The given desires of the human being must harmoniously cohere with X; that is, X must satisfy some human desire.

    b. Human awareness harmoniously coheres with X; that is, X is intelligible to human awareness.

3. The harmonious coherences that result when 1 above harmoniously coheres with 2 above. These can be of any number of types:

    a. Marketability or social utility of X (X adheres with economic demand and market desires);

b. Harvest of crops (nutrition available to humans, which harmoniously cohere with their needs);

c. Continuation of the species (harmonious coherence of past and present);

d. Grouping together of the species (harmonious coherence of its members);

e. Skill in human relations, or practical prowess or skill of any kind (coherence of ends and means);

f. Liberation from suffering (Nirvana), and enlightenment to further intelligible coherences ("wisdom").

Li is any harmonious coherence of the type described in 1 that can harmoniously cohere with human beings in the sense of 2, leading to further harmonious coherences of the type described in 3. Li is all about *what goes where*, not about what is and what is not, or a world of laws hidden either behind or inside existent things. Li refers to those vortices-around-vertices that are capable of serving as an element in the prior vortex-around-a-vertex, which is a human being, such that it either increases the harmony or expanse of that human vortex, or makes it an element in some larger vortex. It is hoped that running some such considerations through one's mind will provide more than randomly probable assistance to anyone involved, for whatever reason, in thinking about coherence, incoherence, value, omnipresence, or the meaning of the term Li in classical Chinese philosophical texts.

TOWARD LI IN NEO-CONFUCIANISM

This is not the place to conduct a comprehensive analysis of the Neo-Confucian conceptions of Li. It would require another book, or possibly several, to exhaust the vast and sometimes contradictory utterances of even one of the main Neo-Confucian thinkers, let alone the various possible interpretations offered in the growing body of secondary literature. However, it might be worthwhile to take a quick and tentative glance at the direction such a work might take, on the basis of these considerations of the prehistory of Li. We have been groping for models with which to think about describing values and accounting for the identities and relations of existing entities without recourse to mutually exclusive notions of one and many, or of sameness and difference. Applying the takeaway models of center and periphery, of vertex and vortex, of second-order coherences between coherences, of intelligibility as cohesion, of negation (transcendence) as inclusion (immanence), and so on, to the formative moves in the development of Neo-Confucianism, attempting also a somewhat oversimplified account of the immensely complex and hotly contested question of Zhu Xi's (朱熹, 1130–1200) understanding of the relation between Li and "material force" (氣 qi), we can perhaps gain some insight into some of the peculiarities of this mode of thinking, some of which were mentioned in passing at the beginning of this work.

I choose to focus on Zhu Xi not only for the obvious reason of his historical and philosophical importance and influence, but also because Cheng-Zhu Neo-Confucianism is often viewed as the place to look for a decisive rift in the tradition, where something much closer to European dualistic metaphysics somehow makes its appearance in China. Zhu Xi seems closer to the two-tiered model, with his ontology of Li and qi. Moreover, he sometimes says Li is static as opposed to the dynamism of qi, that it is eternal and unchangeable, and that it preexists qi, has determining influence on qi, provides values, and so on—all of which stinks of metaphysical dualism. But here too, we must make the adjustment to the vertex-vortex model. This helps clear up some of the confusions about oneness and many-ness, or sameness and difference, among the Li.

We may start by considering the very beginning of this shift in the conception of Li in the work of Cheng Hao 程顥 (Cheng Mingdao 程明道, 1032–1085). For it was Cheng who famously is said to have declared himself the initiator of a new understanding precisely of Li: "Though much in my learning was received from tradition, my understanding of the two characters 天理 tianli are derived from my own experience."[1] This seems to suggest that Cheng believed he had arrived at a radically new understanding about "Heavenly Li" at least, which becomes the guiding concept for the more comprehensive innovations and expansions of the Neo-Confucian concept of Li *simpliciter*, always a shorthand for *tianli* in this context, to follow in the thought of his younger brother Cheng Yi 程頤 (Cheng Yichuan 程伊川, 1033–1107) and of Zhu Xi. It is thus perhaps useful to look at Cheng Hao's first deployments of the term. In my view, Cheng's short essay "Shi ren pian" (識仁篇 "Essay on Recognizing *Ren*") is extremely illuminating in this connection. That work opens with the following words:

> The first thing we must do is recognize what *ren* 仁 is. *Ren* means to form a single undivided body with things. Rightness [義 *yi*], Ritual [禮 *li*], Wisdom [智 *zhi*], and Good Faith [信 *xin*] are all *ren*. Once you have recognized *this* Li [*ci Li*], simply attend respectfully to it and preserve it with Sincerity [*cheng*]; there is no need for caution or control, for extensive searching. The only thing to guard against is laziness of mind. If the mind is not lazy, what need one guard against? Extensive searching is necessary only when the Li is not understood. But if it is preserved long enough it will become clear spontaneously; then what search is necessary? This Dao means not to stand over against things as their opposite [與物無對 *yuwuwudui*]; "vastness" is really inadequate to describe it. All the functions of the world are then my own function. Mencius said that for "all things to be complete in me" requires "finding the genuinely sincere in oneself upon self-examination," and that this is the greatest joy. If in self-examination you find a lack of genuine sincerity, then you are still standing over against things as their opposite. To try to use such a self to then unite with things is impossible—what joy then can there be in it?[2]

Cheng here does not speak of Li in general; instead he is speaking about a specific Li: the Li of *ren*, which he calls "*this* Li" (此理 *ci li*). It seems that Li is, initially, a shorthand for *ren* itself. *Ren* in classical Confucian texts is variously translated as "benevolence," "humaneness," "humanity," "co-humanity," "Goodness," "authoritative humanity," and so on. It is one of the four traditional Mencian virtues, Benevolence, Rightness, Ritual, and Wisdom (sometimes, as here, supplemented by the fifth, Good Faith, which fills out the fivefold parallelism with the Five Phases (五行 *wuxing*) and all the other correlative sets of five). But here we note that *ren* is defined specifically as *coherence*, in two specific ways. First, it is the unity with all things: coherence as togetherness, on an organistic model of "forming one body." All things, including the self, are to be viewed as part of a single undivided living body. Cheng will famously compare *ren* to *feeling*, as opposed to numbness, of the parts of a body, and this is what he has in mind here: the ability to feel what other things feel, rather than standing over them as an opposite, externally to them. This may be regarded as a metaphysical expansion of the traditional Confucian association of *ren* with "reciprocity," 恕 *shu*, putting oneself in the shoes of the other in any relationship. The use of *ti* 體 here should remind us not only of Mencius's use of the term in the older sense of "parts" with reference to the organs of a single human body, and with a similar interest in expansion of embodiment and concern (6A14–15), but also of the verbal use of the term in Wang Bi and thereafter, meaning "to embody" but in the specific sense of standing in the shoes of the other, as well as Guo Xiang's occasional use of the metaphor of the spontaneous connection and mutual service of the various parts of the body, all unknowingly joining vanishingly into the accomplishment of any event. Secondly, *ren* is another kind of coherence: the unifier of the other, apparently different and even opposed Confucian virtues of Rightness, Ritual, Wisdom, and Good Faith. *Ren* is simultaneously one item in the list of virtues and the totality of the list. It is not simply one among them, it is what is expressed in all of them. It is both whole and part. It is both one and many. Zhu Xi will make much of this idea, as we shall see. For the moment, let us note simply that *ren* is what expresses itself even when not apparent, which is present even when seemingly replaced by its opposite (for example, "Rightness"), as its own apparent absence, and is at the same time thought to thereby be what gives real value to all the virtues and to bring them together into a living and embodied unity. To be *ren* is (1) to be unified with all things, feeling and functioning with and for and as them all, and (2) to be unified with all virtues, activating and functioning as them all. Cheng Yi will associate *ren* more directly with two further qualities: the endless production of life (生生不息 *shengsheng buxi*), as in the *Zhouyi* commentaries, associated now with *ren* as the germ within a seed, and 公 *gong*, impartiality, that is, what applies equally in all places, unbiased toward any one expression or position. We must, I think, understand both of these ideas specifically in terms of the initial idea of Li as *ren* first developed by Cheng Hao, although Cheng

Yi and Zhu Xi will add some decisive twists to the implications of this move.

It is also, as the title of the essay suggests, something that functions as an object of knowledge, coherence as intelligibility; indeed, Cheng Hao stresses that merely recognizing it and remaining aware of it, keeping it in view, continuing to feel it as such, is the heart of Confucian self-cultivation. *Ren* is the recognizable vertex of the virtues and of the accomplished sense of oneness with the total body of all things, giving them their value when they are recognized as the vortex around this vertex.

Li as *ren* is value, but it incorporates one dimension of the ironic conception of coherence as value: the inclusion of both good and evil. The need to overcome "oppositeness," the true togetherness of all things, still trumps the need for a clear-cut value dualism, just as in the ironic tradition. To be one body with all things, without opposing any, involves accepting both good and evil things as parts of this totalistic body. Good and evil, as part of the one harmonious coherence of the body of *ren*, are also "not two opposed things produced within the original nature"—as embraced within the original nature of *ren*, they are not actually opposites at all.[3] This would be a sticking point for later Neo-Confucians in the Cheng-Zhu tradition, but we can perhaps understand it as part of the entailment of Li as coherence and the incorporation of the ironic elements that were now entrenched in the tradition (and we will see a similar idea reasserted by Wang Yangming). But Cheng Hao gives us a new example of the non-ironic incorporation of this ironic motif, which allows him to embrace this inclusion of good and evil in Li without undermining his commitment to the Good, conceived specifically as the coherence of *ren* as Li, as value. It is accomplished in this case by Cheng Hao's conception of *ren* as Li as explicitly *nonreversible*. In spite of the importance of the notion of reciprocity in *ren*, close examination reveals that the affect of reciprocity is accomplished all from one side: unreciprocated reciprocity. The structure is quite similar to the Huayan approach. Cheng says, "For there to be both good and evil events is all the Li of Heaven. It is necessary that the things within the Li of Heaven include both good and evil. For it is the natural condition of things to be uneven. We should only understand this, but refrain from entering into evil ourselves, lest we devolve into a mere thing."[4] The point here is that the active experience of the oneness of all things in the single body of *ren* as value is a specific prerogative and responsibility of human beings; humans are the unifier, all things are merely the unified. That which is unified must include both the good and the evil for it to qualify as the ultimate coherence of all things in one body, but since good is defined precisely by the ability to *actively form* one body with all things, to recognize and realize this oneness, this ironic form of value is incorporated into the non-ironic value of the *Ren* person. To be evil would be to devolve into a mere thing: that is, something that "stands over against its opposite," isolated, incoherent, sealed up in its own borders and thus unable to be unbiased, failing to form one body with all other things (although still part of the one body of all things formed by the *ren* sage). The unifier is good, the unified includes both good and evil. Failing to unify all would undermine the goodness of the unifier. This sort of appropriation of an ironic motif into a non-ironic framework should be familiar to us by now.

But something quite decisively new does happen with Cheng Yi's appropriation of his brother's ideas, as Graham and others have suggested. This is where the idea of the Li as both one and many really comes to the fore, with a new emphasis on the specific Lis of individual things. The germ of this idea is already present in Cheng Hao in the notion of *ren*'s relation to the other virtues, and by extension in its copresence in all members of the one body of all things. But Li still remains for Cheng Hao, when all is said and done, a single Li: the Li, the second-order coherence, that is *ren*. Cheng Hao has suggested a structure by which it can remain itself and yet "manifest" as diverse specific virtues, but in the final analysis it seems that he thinks of Li everywhere primarily as the same Li with the specific characteristics, unchanged, of being *ren*: empathetically forming one body with things, feeling with them, as expressed in all the virtues. It seems that the notion of specific individual Lis as providing some explanation of "why they are so" and "how they should be" is the contribution of Cheng Yi, who stresses the many more than the one, albeit with his brother's overriding single Li perhaps lurking the background.

Cheng Yi's notion of Li brings with it a stronger sense of the "conditions for the possibility" of the existence, and the value, of a particular thing. We have seen that Li has already taken on the sense of a potentiality, something unrealized, a fact to be recognized but as yet not explicitly recognized, the preexistent perforations along which cuts might be made for maximal value. Playing on the ordinary usage of Li as "possibility," I would suggest that Cheng Yi's Li might be well translated with Leibniz's term, "Compossibility." It is a precondition for the appearance of anything in reality: if there is no specific Li for a thing, that thing cannot exist. When something is impossible, Cheng says, "There is no such Li," or, "How could there be such a Li?" When admitting something to be marginally possible, though unconfirmed, he will say that there is this Li. That means that, given what else exists, it has no place to fit in. It cannot be. But the key to understanding the one-many implications of this notion comes in the prefix: Li is not just possibility, it is compossibility: it is the possibility of coexistence. This "co-" is where our notion of coherence comes into the picture. Li is, as we remarked in the Conclusion, a question of what goes where, how a thing functions within the whole, of properly playing of its roles in the overall web of coherence. Li is not just the "logical" possibility of a thing's existence, it is the possibility, given the existence of everything else that exists, of this thing also existing. "Existence" here would also imply value, as in all the cases we've examined: it must exist sustainably, in interaction with things around it in a way that provides enough value for them to motivate their continued interchange with it, its sustenance and propagation. We might think here of Cheng Chung-ying's suggestion of "well-placedness" as a translation of Li.[5] So when Cheng talks about, say, some poems by Du Fu as a Li that exists, he means that these poems are proved by the fact that they were written to be possible in the context of all that exists, to have a place there, to not impinge on other existence to the extent of excluding them, so that it is not impossible for someone to suddenly perceive them in a delirium, in spite of never having read them. Compossibility, however, is thus also *ren*, is also *gong* (impartiality), is also *sheng* (generativity). The compossibility of X to exist in the whole is also the compossibility of X and Y in the whole itself, and the compossibility of Y. The compossibility of any given thing is by definition also the compossibility of other things; one compossibility is simultaneously many compossibilities. It is the same, impartial (*gong*) compossibility everywhere, and yet for this particular item it is this particular item's (com)possibility. It is the forming of one body with all things in mutual reciprocity, manifesting also as its own other: it is *ren*. And it is the sustainable continuation of this life into another life, the production of life: the future (com)possibility of the existence of Y as it is present in the existence of X. It is the compossibility of the two diverse things X and Y that allows X to be what contributes to the production of Y, which would otherwise be in exclusionary opposition to it.

Zhu Xi follows this trend. Zhu's remarks on the relation of *ren* to the other virtues, picking up on Cheng Hao's definition above, provides our best model of how to understand the oneness and manyness of Li. Zhu Xi says:

> The word *ren* cannot be understood until you see that it includes rightness, ritual and wisdom. "Benevolence" per se refers to the original substance of benevolence. Ritual is the patterned regulations of benevolence. Rightness is the decisive cuttings and limitations of benevolence. Wisdom is the differentiations of benevolence. For example, although the four seasons differ, they all emerge from the spring. Spring is the generativity of the impulse of generation, summer is the growth of the impulse of generation, autumn is the completion of the impulse of generation, and winter is the storing up of the impulse of generation. The four can be reduced to two, the two to one, so their unity has a ruling source and their

togetherness an origin. . . . Benevolence is the head/beginning of the four fonts, while wisdom is what allows them to start and to finish. It is like the four virtues of the *Zhouyi*, "origin" is the elder of the four, but it starts not in itself but in "firmness." For the transformations of heaven and earth cannot expand and go forth unless they have first gathered and congealed. The transition from wisdom to benevolence is the seed and axle of all transformations.[6]

And again:

> Spring is benevolence, which has the sense of an impulse of generation to it. In the summer, a sense of penetration and unobstructedness is seen in it. In autumn, a sense of realness and fruition is seen in it. In winter, a sense of firmness is seen in it. How can it be said that the impulse of generation has ceased for one moment in the times of summer, autumn and winter? Even when the roots are barren, the impulse of generation exists in them. For generally speaking, there is only one Li between heaven and earth, which divides off into many different names depending on where it arrives.[7]

And, bringing out the way in which the "one" principle expresses itself not only as different, but even as opposite characteristics:

> Q: Benevolence, I think, means the impulse for ceaseless generation. It is only because people are stopped by selfish intentions that this impulse of generation cannot flow freely. If one overcomes his selfishness, the entirety of the substance produces the great function, and it is constantly flowing. A: This is the common theory of the mass of people, which misses the essential point. What is needed here is to understand the meaning of the word *benevolence*, which can only become clear when you look at the four virtues of benevolence, rightness, ritual, and wisdom together. When you understand what each of these means you will understand the meaning of the word *benevolence*. If you just look at benevolence by itself, it will become increasingly unclear the more you examine it. . . . In general the virtue-nature of human beings has four aspects: benevolence, which is a warm, harmonious impulse; rightness, which is a severe, fierce, hard, and decisive impulse; ritual, which is an expressing and disclosing impulse; and wisdom, which is an impulse of collecting and turning inward which leaves no traces. These four exist within the nature, but the sagely teaching stresses seeking the meaning of benevolence as the most urgent

matter, because benevolence is the first of the four. If you can
constantly preserve this warm and kind impulse here, you will
naturally be able to express and disclose when the times comes for
expressing and disclosing; when it's time to be hard and decisive,
you will naturally be able to do so; when it's time to gather and
turn inward, you will be able to do so naturally.[8]

Summing up the relation to the Li of human beings, Zhu says:

> Love is a feeling of empathy, and empathy is a feeling, but its Li
> is called *ren*. . . . The reason human beings are human beings is
> that their Li is the Li of heaven and earth, and their *qi* is the *qi*
> of heaven and earth. Li has no traces and cannot be seen, so it
> must be viewed in *qi*. If you want to know the meaning of *ren*, it
> is an undivided *qi* of warmth and harmony; its *qi* is the Yang *qi* of
> heaven and earth in spring, and its Li is heaven and earth's heart/
> mind of generating living things.[9]

Ren is generativity, the origin, the spring of all things. But *ren* is also the
collective name for all four of the Mencian virtues: *ren* itself (= benevolence), rightness, ritual, and wisdom. Each of these is "benevolence," the
generativity, appearing in a different way in a different context, just as we
might say that "summer" is the further development or expression of what
was started as "spring," autumn its harvesting, winter its fallow period of
self-restoration, storage of energy, consolidation of gains, turning inward for
replenishment.

We can see here a development of the "compossibility" of Cheng Yi's
notion of Li. The "co-" is still very much to the fore here. But Zhu Xi's
more detailed explications sometimes seem to bring out the more active
determinative sense of Cheng Yi's "possibility." Zhu's more robust sense of
preexistence and priority of Li perhaps tips the implication one step further,
to what we might call a kind of "co-potentiality." We may ponder this in
considering the following exchange:

> Q: How is it that a dry and withered thing also has the Nature?
> A: It has always had this Li, which is why we say that there is
> nothing in the world outside the Nature. (When they went walking
> in the street, he said) A brick has the Li of a brick. (When they
> sat, he said) A bamboo chair has the Li of a bamboo chair. A dry
> and withered thing can be said to lack the impulse of life, but it
> cannot be said to lack the Li of life. For example, a rotten piece
> of wood may be useless, so that it can only be put in the furnace.

This is what it means to lack the impulse of life. But when you burn a specific kind of wood, a specific Qi-force is produced, each one different. This is because the Li of each is thus.[10]

Li is still ultimately rooted in *ren*, generativity (*sheng*) and unity ("one body" as inter-feeling) as such, and its unbiased omnipresence in various apparently non-*ren* manifestations. But "generation" means "co-generation," and the sort of "life" generated here includes *any function*, any distinctive way of functioning within the whole, any way of affecting other things that is of potential value to those things in their own continued coherence with one another. The "co-potentiality of life" is just a "co-potentiality of mutually useful activity." It is a kind of *co-activity*. The dried and withered thing has the potential to act in concert with other things, to perform a role in the totality: it can produce energy. That is its co-potential for value. The Li of each thing is specific to that thing as that thing's function within the whole, in relation to other things and to its potential values. This value means specifically value to the human, or at least to the sage among humans who sees all things as his own undivided body, who, as possessor of the most balanced and unobstructed *qi*, manifests the totality of *ren*, of Li. When asked about the Li of specific inanimate things, Zhu Xi cites the *potential functions* of things: "A boat can only move on water, a cart can only move on land."[11] Contrast the case of the cart to the case of the rotten wood. The latter *has no other function* than the potential energy it will produced when burned. If it were still a decent piece of wood, it might function as part of a cart or a boat, and then would manifest the coherence of that part of that vehicle. Being rotten, it reverts to its minimal function *for human beings*. Zhu does not say that "to burn and produce heat" is part of the Li of the cart, although it can be burned for fire. That is not the Li of cart qua cart, but the Li of the wood. We may think here of Fazang's distinction between the complete building and the "broken building." The point is that Li is the possibility of functioning ("it *can* only move . . .") in the context of how it coheres both with other things (land, water) and also, crucially, with human beings, themselves conduits of the unbiased and unceasing generative fullness of *ren*.

Discerning Li is for Zhu Xi a matter of finding the parts that fit together, the co-potentials:

For Heavenly Li is never in all the ages extinguished in any human being; no matter how it is covered over or confined, Heavenly Li is always constantly there just as ever, emerging from within selfish desire at every moment without cease—it is just that human beings are not aware of it. It is exactly like [fragments of] bright pearl or of a large shell mixed in together with sand and gravel, successively flashing forth here and there. Just recognize and gather these scattered pieces of the Way and its coherences [*daoli*] right where they appear, joining the fragments until they gradually become an integral whole. After your own good intentions grow and increase by the day and the month, Heavenly Li will naturally become pure and firm in you. What you formerly called selfish desires will naturally retreat and scatter, until finally they no longer sprout up at all.[12]

The parts that don't fit into this overall network of coherence, that do not cohere, are ipso facto "selfish (i.e., biased, non-*ren*) desires. The parts that do are always flashing forth, and need only be retained and put in tandem with one another to spring into a fully coherent Gestalt.

Zhu's description of Li as a kind of network of roads has led to the translation of the term as "pattern," associated with the array of veins in a piece of jade. This is a useful consideration. In Zhu's recorded conversations we do indeed find some provocative materials on this point:

> Q: What is the difference between Dao and Li? A: Dao is a road, and Li is its pattern and coherence. Q: Like the pattern in wood? A: Yes. Q: So it is just like that? A: Dao is a vastly inclusive term, while Li is the coherent veins in this Dao. (He also said) Dao is vast, Li is dense.[13]

> Q: What is the difference between *ren* and Dao? A: Dao is a collective name, while benevolence specifies it as one particular thing. It is a like a road, with many paths and subdivisions, but which are all a single road.[14]

Note that *ren* is still the general synonym for Li as such here. The Dao/Li relation here still bears the traces of the *Hanfeizi* conception: Dao as the all-inclusive term, Li as the term for the individual divisions. But the oneness-manyness relation has been modified: one road also connects to the totality of roads, and Dao is no longer the material outside the roads, what's left out of the coherent divisions and groupings created by the cutting, but rather the totality of cuts in their interfusion. But that is not the whole story: what is crucial is that a Li per se is a center, a sustainable vertex of contrasting but converging forces. The Cheng-Zhu way of thinking about Li seems to shift the focus from the vortex-around-a-vertex to the vertex itself, the vertex as such. I would suggest that if we must picture this network of roads analogy that we do so not as flat mapping of a "pattern," but rather as a system of ravines or valleys. They are intrinsically centers

of gravitational pull, vertices of possible movements. With this emendation, Graham's description, cited earlier, of the Li as channels along which
qi moves is quite helpful. Zhu's conception of Li is very explicitly that of
a Center, like the Tiantai notion. It is the Taiji (太極 "Great Ultimate")
that forms the pivot and interface between Yin and Yang, determining their
movement, forming the template on the macrolevel of the each microlevel
vortex: like slicing a magnet, every portion separated off ends up having
the same positive-negative polarity as the original whole. Thus, it is also
explicitly linked to "the Mean," or Center (中 zhong), expressed as the
"warmth and harmony" (溫和 wenhe), which is the characteristic of ren. The
further linkage of ren and the Center is crucial here, for the idea of centrality helps explain the oneness-manyness problem, and also the peculiar form
of omnipresence characteristic of Cheng-Zhu Neo-Confucianism. Wherever
there is a thing—a vortex of qi—there is a vertex, a center, which makes it
what it is and provides the norm to which it tends to, and should, adhere
in order to remain itself, that is, to sustain the coherence among its own
parts and between itself and its characteristic functions in its interactions
with the things in its environment. Centrality itself is precisely a kind of
co-potentiality: it enables the continued function of the two extremes in
their relation to one another. This maintenance of balance is what allows it
to take its place in the larger context of its external relationships, to be an
identifiable member of a larger whole. This principle of centrality is present
in every thing, but although the specific centers may be differently determinable, they are all Li because they are centers, because of their function
as the vertex of the vortex. They produce coherence both internally and
externally. But this does not separate off into a set of definitively distinct
centers in that to be is to be centered, to cohere around a center, to have a
center of gravity that provides equilibrium and intelligibility as this or that
(coherence). The Center is precisely sustainable intelligibility, as in Qian
Mu's pendulum: without the coherence provided by the center, the vertex
would not be anything, would be random movement in all directions never
collected back into a finite range, incoherent, unintelligible, inaccessible to
cognition. But it must be identifiably and coherently "something" in order
to function as a part—one extreme—of another pendulum swing. The same
applies for the role of this large whole as one extreme of another swing,
another vortex. Here again, there is a constant reference to the human
being—"embodying Li in its completeness"—who is himself metaphysicalized
and made an intrinsic standard of value within the cosmos. Those centers
that are digestible to the centering processes of humans—the most excellent qi in the cosmos, which allows Li to function unobstructedly within it,
where Li can manifest in its most balanced and comprehensive way—count
as Li. The center is a value: it is the value of life, "continual generation"

(生生不息 *shengshengbuxi*), which Zhu Xi also characterizes as *ren*, the subsuming virtue of "harmony and warmth."

It should be noted that Zhu's one-many structure here follows what might be called a Huayan rather than a Tiantai structure: there is one specific privileged center of centers, called Benevolence, which is identical to the other virtues and underwrites their mutual identity. The issue is again whether there is a single selfsame Li serving as the coherence of all and each, or if there many distinct and specific Lis each providing its own kind of coherence, and how to understand the relation between this one and this many. If Cheng Hao tended toward a clearly "Huayan" notion of a single selfsame Li, *ren*, which served as the coherence of all and each, Cheng Yi and Zhu Xi add a real diversification into the specific Li, which are nonetheless also all the one Li expressed in various ways, which might seem to tilt more toward the Tiantai vision of Three Thousand intersubsumptive but specific Lis. But this is still here, as in Huayan, a consequence of the specific qualities of that one all-inclusive Li: in the Huayan case, because Li was Emptiness, a "principle of no-principle," it necessarily involved both self-emptying openness to otherness and indivisibility, the pure undivided reflectivity or interactivity per se. Li is just the single idea "interpervasion," and its apparent multiplicity as the immanent principle of each thing follows from this characteristic, which remains foundational and unchanged; as in Guo Xiang, the seeming diversity of principles ends up meaning only that the same principle-of-no-principle is repeated everywhere. *Ren* as a foundational principle has some of the same features, namely, a built-in mandate to extend into otherness, to overcoming dividedness, to generate and sustain life. It is just the same thing, the one and only fact of co-potentiality, which applies to the whole as a whole and to each individual existent thing: the Li of the whole is Co-poteniality, and the specific Li of a cart is the same Co-potentiality of the cart qua cart; the Li of the boat is the same Co-potentiality of the boat qua boat. It is the same Li that is all these different Lis, not, as in Tiantai, genuinely different Lis that are intersubsumptively all the "same" Li, a different "same" in each case (i.e., the Li that is the valued coherence of all things is the specific Li of boatishness per se, but also and alternatively it is the specific Li of cartishness per se that is the Li of all things). As such, any manifestation of life, integration, centrality, coherence may be viewed as a further flowering of the single principle or *ren*. This is further complexified by the explicit use of the Yin-Yang model to comprehend balance, which allows for apparently diametrically opposed functions to be seen as parts of a single process, playing out a single purpose and exemplifying a single overall character, as in the case of spring and autumn, which "are" both spring, or *ren* and *yi*, which are opposites but are both still "really" *ren*. The ultimacy of the one of the pair remains unshaken. The one Li that is one and present everywhere is the Li of "becoming one with all things and being present everywhere." The Tiantai structure would require that he say not only, "Rightness, Ritual and Wisdom are all alternate expressions of Benevolence, which is their real essence and to which they are all reducible," but also, to begin with, "Benevolence, Rightness and Wisdom are all alternate expression for Ritual, which is their real essence and to which they are all reducible." Further, we would need an emendation of Cheng Hao's one-way concept of inclusion in the one body of all things, his stricture against becoming a "mere thing": thinghood as such, the very separation into self-enclosure, would have to be seen as a mode of being one with all other things, and to be a specific Li in its own right, pervading and grounding all other things, including the expansive benevolent mind of the sage. Reversibility is again the issue here: full and exceptionless intersubsumption. Occasionally, we do find Zhu making a move in this direction, as for example in the following passage:

> Benevolence (*ren*) and rightness are like Yin and Yang, a single *Qi*. Yang is the *Qi* in the process of growth, and Yin is the *Qi* when it has just begun retreating. *Benevolence is rightness which is just in the process of being generating, while rightness is benevolence which is turning back and collecting itself.* . . . If you can [truly] see Yang, you can see Yin; if you can [truly] see Yin, you can see Yang. If you know one, you know the other.[15]

In the sentence I have italicized here, Zhu allows for a reversibility between substance and function: rightness is a function of benevolence, but that fact can also be expressed by saying that benevolence is a function of rightness. This is the Tiantai structure of relation between various Lis. Some of the consequences of his willingness to apply this structure can be seen in similar passages, for example:

> Q: What is the difference between the substance and function concerning benevolence, rightness, ritual and wisdom? A: From the point of view of Yin and Yang, benevolence and ritual are Yang, while rightness and wisdom are Yin. The first two are function, the latter two are substance. Spring and summer are Yang, autumn and winter are Yin. In terms of benevolence and rightness alone, things begin in spring and grow in summer, which is benevolence. They are harvested in autumn and stored in winter, which is rightness. In terms of all four virtues, spring is benevolence, summer is ritual,

autumn is rightness, winter is wisdom. Benevolence and ritual are putting forth and spreading out, while rightness is severe, killing, decisive and judgmental, and wisdom is a collecting and storing up.[16]

Again:

Benevolence and rightness are the substance and function of one another, the motion and stillness of one another. The substance of benevolence is still, but its function flows without end. The function of rightness is originally moving, but its substance is that each thing finds rest in its proper place.[17]

And again:

Someone asked about the saying that Benevolence is yielding while Rightness is firm. He answered: "Benevolence is yielding in its substance but firm in its function, while Rightness is firm in its substance and yielding in its function." . . . [On another occasion, though, he said], "The substance of benevolence is firm but its function is yielding; the substance of rightness is yielding but its function is firm." Guang asked, "Is it that speaking from the point of view of the motion of the Great Ultimate, benevolence is firm and rightness is yielding, but from the Yin and Yang within a single object, the function of benevolence is yielding while the function of rightness is firm?" He said, "That's right too. Benevolence is an impulse of flowing, moving, emerging and transcending, but its function is kind and yielding. Rightness is a sense of measuring and weighing to follow what is proper, but its function is decisive and disjunctive."[18]

The flexibility of the categories of *ti* and *yong*, and the reversibility of subject and predicate it allows, is deployed to good effect here.[19] Of course, this interpenetration only applies to the predetermined human values, the virtues: it does not extend, as in Tiantai, to apparent evils, nor to the entirety of the phenomenal world. But this is because of a differing conception of human welfare. In both cases, a Li must be "edible" to humans to count as a Li, must be useful for specifically human ends. Tiantai, working within the framework of infinite rebirths and infinitely multifarious bodhisattva work, regards all possible vortices as materials that will prove useful to this project. Zhu Xi, with a more modest conception of human spiritual diges-tion, sees only the Confucian virtues as edible, that is, transformable into the energy and activities of human social, political, and emotional life. Zhu

Xi's conception is oligocentric, not omnicentric: there are a limited number of reversible centers—benevolence, rightness, etc.—which are capable of subsuming all events; but reversibility only pertains to these centers, not to all possible elements of the periphery, as in Tiantai.

The reversibility of subject and predicate can be found also in Wang Yangming 王陽明 (Wang Shouren 王守仁, 1472–1529), who quite frequently and self-consciously deployed the subject-predicate reversibility motif, and at the most comprehensible level, asserting, for example, Li is the orderliness of *qi*, and *qi* is the function of Li: "Li is the orderliness of *qi*, *qi* is the function of Li. Without this orderliness, the function would be impossible, and without the function, there would be no means by which to see the orderliness."[20] Note that these are presented here in definitional form: Li *is* the orderliness of *qi*, *qi is* the functioning of Li. Li is just something about *qi*, but *qi* is also just something about Li. The "center" can be wherever one likes, wherever one chooses to start. Neither is in this sense more foundational than the other. Indeed, we seem to have here the structure of the Tiantai "Non-Exclusive Center" (不但中 *budanzhong*): rather than saying both "order" and "function" are two alternate ways of describing a *tertium quid* that enables both but is exclusively identifiable with neither ("The Exclusive Center" 但中 *danzhong*), Wang directly uses each of the two extremes as the name for the substantial Center of which the other is an attribute, eliminating the neutral "middle" man entirely. This appears to be a "Tiantai" move. Note, however, the next line, which echoes exactly the typical Huayan *nengyi/suoyi* 能依／所依 distinction, where apparent interdependence reveals itself to be an asymmetrical unilateral dependence: *qi* depends on Li ontologically, it cannot function at all without it, while Li depends on *qi* only epistemologically, which is to say, doesn't really depend on it to exist, but only to be seen or manifested. Wang also shows a tendency toward privileging a particular determination or anti-determination, "of which" everything else is made the expression: the Innate Knowledge (良知 *liangzhi*), the substance of mind. But Wang also provides a loophole, in his claim that "the mind has no substance of its own: it takes the feeling and response of the rights and wrongs of all things as its substance" (心無體，以萬物之是非感應為體 *xinwuti, yiwanwuzhi shifeiganying wei ti*).[21] Here, "all things" becomes, for once, the real substance of which mind is instead the function: the usual substance of which all things are the expression—the mind—has instead become the predicate, the expression, of all things. This is also clear in Wang's extended polemic against the Cheng-Zhu conception of Li, which he claims is mistaken in seeking a particular "fixed Li" (定理 *dingli*) in each particular thing. Instead, he says, the mind itself is Li: not a fixed Li, but the "Li-ing" of whatever it encounters, precisely the "feeling and response of the rights and wrongs of all things." These cannot be known in advance and cannot be exhaustively catalogued or systematized even after the fact. Here we have the inclusion of "coherence with human cognition and desires," which has always been implicit in the notion of Li as coherence, made explicit again. "The mind is Li" means that the mind is the decisive vertex creating a unique vortex around itself whenever it wills, defining thereby a set of determinate "things" that are the components from which its endeavor is to be compounded, which it endeavors to form into a coherent vortex. Thus it is that all things are mind, and mind is the Li of all things, but there is nonetheless no "fixed" Li which is the mind: for the mind is both what constitutes things as things, and is itself nothing but the process of centering and cohering *of* those things.

But this full reversibility is the exception rather than the rule in both Zhu and Wang. For Zhu, the ultimate center of centers is The Great Ultimate, which is the Non-Ultimate, which is generativity, which is Benevolence, which is warmth and harmony—the vertex of the vortex, which brings it together as this particular vortex, holds it together as such, and makes it function. For Wang, the ultimate center of centers is the mind, which includes all things as its substance, standing as their equilibrium, their mutual adjustment, the feeling and response of liking and disliking, right and wrong, between them, and yet is also beyond it ("the substance of mind has no good or evil")—the vertex-vortex of all things and of each thing it encounters.

Zhu's doctrine of the relation between Li and *qi* reflects this structure. Asked whether there is a priority between Li and *qi,* Zhu says:

> Originally there is no prior and posterior between them. But if you insist on searching out the origin, you must say that the Li is first. But Li is also not some separate thing; it exists here within this *qi*. Without this *qi,* the Li has no other place that can carry it. *Qi* refers to metal, wood, water and fire, while Li means benevolence, rightness, ritual and wisdom.[22]

Again:

> Someone asked about the theory that Li precedes *qi*. [Zhuxi] said, "One cannot say that. Can we know that, as things appear at present, Li precedes *qi,* or *qi* precedes Li? Neither can be found out. But if we speculate on it, it seems that this *qi* always moves in dependence on this Li, and wherever this *qi* gathers, Li is also present. Now *qi* can congeal and create things, while Li has no sentiment or intention, no plan, no calculation, no creation. But wherever *qi* congeals, Li is within it. It is perhaps like the plants

and animals and people in the world; none is born without a root; and it is certain that nothing grows in unplanted land from no seed. All of this is *qi*. As for Li, it is just a pure, unobstructed realm, without form or trace. It cannot create, while *qi* can ferment and congeal to generate things. But wherever this *qi* is, Li is within it."[23]

Here, Li and *qi* are determined in a relation of root and branch, although Zhu goes on to qualify this with his assertion—rejected by many later Neo-Confucians—that Li per se cannot create, and to this degree is unlike a seed or root. Li is the vertex determining the vortex, not the coherence of the vortex-around-a-vertex; it does not create the vortex, and there remains a kind of rogue element, not strictly determined, in the behavior of the vortex, although it cannot exist as such without its orientation around the vertex. Qi has some degree of autonomy, a "mind of its own," which allows for Zhu's "theodicy," as it were. He specifies that Heaven has no intention to create sages, and that Li's governance is not an exact arrangement, but more like the pouring out of water on the ground, which *more or less* follows certain predictable patterns. We may think here of iron filings flung over a magnetic pattern: they will more or less cling to the shape of the pattern, making it discernible, but there will always be a few scattered bits out of place.

Where does the *qi*, the obstructing element that is flung, which arranges itself so as to give more or less complete reflections of Li, come from? Zhu sometimes asserts that this "flinging" is itself a function of Li—it is a Li that there be *qi* at all. This is as far as his "theodicy" goes, and while it cannot provide a final explanation of evil—which for Zhu means simply the one-sidedness and obstruction in the expression of Li—in the world, none is really necessary. We may here again make a fruitful comparison to the Tiantai case. The parallel terms in Tiantai would be Li as inherent entailment—all-pervasiveness in time and space—and "dependent co-arising," that is, *shi*, the temporal functions of arising and ceasing in particular times and places, simple location and temporal process. Zhili says, "When events are generated, there is no separate generation: it is all from inherent entailment in Li. Inherent entailment is no separate inherent entailment: is it all just dependent co-arising."[24] Here we see the full mutually reversibility of the two realms, Möbius-like, where each is entirely reducible to the other: there is no arising-and-perishing other than inherent entailment itself, and no inherent entailment other than arising-and-perishing itself. Arising-and-perishing is another word for ineradicable presence (in the modified form of readability-into); ineradicable presence is another name for arising-and-perishing. They are related like equilaterality and equiangularity of a triangle. This is a consequence of the Three Truths doctrine:

conditionality itself is unconditionality, local coherence is global incoherence is intersubsumption. Needless to say, Zhu Xi neither wants nor needs anything quite so radical for his purposes. It is enough simply to assert that it is a part of Li—the vertex or center of gravity that allows man, the best vortex around the most fully expressed vertex, to flourish, to generate ceaselessly—that there be such a thing as *qi* continually generated. It might also be a good thing if *qi* more obediently reflected Li—although sometimes Zhu suggests that it would not be—but that is not relevant to the question. The question is just whether the process of edible-to-man centerings includes the fact of ceaseless production of malleable overgrowing flung *qi*, the medium through which it is, in fact, expressed. The answer is yes. Li does not have to mean "the best possible order," but only "what among existing configurations is most nourishing to mankind in his own pattern of ceaseless generation, benevolence, balance." It would be possible to say that even the disorder is an expression of Li, pantheistically, inasmuch as the random flinging, the constant production, of *qi* is also an aspect of Li. But this misconceives the concept of Li as we have disclosed it here: it misses the unalterable connection to human welfare that is built into the concept of Li. At most, it allows Zhu to say, characteristically, that "in a sense" the existence of disorder and evil is also Li, in that this "flinging" is a necessary part of the ordering process which is genuinely beneficial to human welfare—benevolence, rightness, generativity, etc.—but in another sense—i.e., as disorder considered as such—it is not Li. In one sense everything is Li—hence good—and in another there is both good and evil, something needing to be corrected. We may recall here the passage from Zhu's commentary to the *Zhouyi*, quoted in our discussion of that text; in one sense, yin and yang are to be balanced, but in another sense, yang is to be promoted and yin suppressed. Only to the extent that these disordered elements are seen as subsumed into the prescribed centers are they Li; as ends in themselves they are obstructions to Li. This seeming prevarication is found very often in Zhu's pronouncements on this topic, and make perfect sense if we keep this basic definition of Li in mind. Hence:

> Q: Each thing possesses the entire Great Ultimate—thus the Li is complete in all of them, yes? A: You can say it is complete, but you can also say it's one-sided. From the point of view of Li itself, it is complete in all, but from the point of view of *qi*, it is impossible for them not to be one-sided in some way.[25]

Again:

> If we are discussing the single origin of all things, we can say that they are the same in terms of Li, but differ in terms of *qi*. But exam-

ining the different bodies of all things, we see that the *qi* is similar but the Li absolutely different. As for the saying that all things are the same in terms of Li, but differ as to *qi*, this is directed at the beginning of all things, when the heavenly mandate is flowing, and it is all of one type, so we say the Li is the same. Because there are pure and impurity, unmixed and mixed combinations of the *qi* of the Yin-Yang and the five processes [wood, fire, earth, metal, water], we say the *qi* are different. But the contrary claim is made with reference to all things as already existing, for then, although they differ as to purity and impurity, they all are made of the *qi* of Yin-Yang and the five processes, so we say they are similar in their *qi*; but because the differences between their levels of turbidity and brightness, openness and cloggedness differ greatly, we say the Li is absolutely different. . . . The similarity of *qi* is seen in the fact that all creatures understand cold and warmth, hunger and satiety, love life and hate death, approach benefit and avoid harm—this is the same in humans and in other creatures. They differ in Li; for example, the lord and servant relation among bees and ants just means they have a little spark of illumination of the [principle of] rightness. The father and son relationship among tigers and wolves just means they have a little spark of illumination of the [principle of] benevolence. But they are unable to push it farther to the rest of [principle]. It is just like a mirror which is dark all over except from one or two little points in the middle.[26]

Zhu Xi makes very free use of this "in one sense same, in one sense different" structure, and the reversibility it entails, in designating the precise relation between Li and *qi*. But this reversibility itself is not Li, as it is for Tiantai. Li is for Zhu Xi the vertices of the coherences that aid human coherence when cohered with. Human coherence revolves around the vertex of equilibrium expressed most directly as benevolence, the warm and harmonious process of constant generation, which necessarily also expresses itself through the proper measure of harshness, coldness, inward turning, and death. In this, Zhu's conception of Li, although having its own distinctive contents in accordance with his conception of the desiderata constitutive to its criterion, nevertheless accords closely with the way the term Li is used in other contexts throughout the Chinese intellectual tradition. As with the acupuncture points, and *pace* Dai Zhen's critique, there is still a conception of division in Zhu's conception of unity. It is the vertices of centrality, the centers of gravity, that divide and group the energies of heaven and earth in such a way as to make them coherent entities (that is, to generate beings), which, when taken as a guide for our own acts of grouping, allow us to maximize the equilibrium and generativity (value) of these beings.

Looking back to the wide range of usages of the term Li in both philosophical and ordinary discourse, we can perhaps now discern what is behind it. Both Neo-Confucian philosophers and ordinary modern Chinese speakers can say, "There is no such Li," to mean something that could be translated as either, "That's not the right thing to do," or, "There is no such thing as that." More exactly, though, it means in both cases something like, "There is no compossibility for that," which, expanded, means something like, "There is no acupuncture point right there, so by cutting there you fail to create any coherent groupings." Coherent groupings means here groupings that are both discernible as some particular things to a human being—hence coherence coherent with some specific human cognition—and also integrable into human purposes without obstructing the coherence with more fundamental and comprehensive human purposes. The perception and the valuation are inseparable, a point made more explicitly in Wang Yangming's thought than perhaps anywhere else, where an "object" is constituted as such only by being the orienting target of a volition. It is important to remember here the notion of "being" as synonymous with "a coherent grouping." The yes/no Parmenidean relation between being and nonbeing has never been palatable to Chinese thinkers, and after the many centuries it took to finally even frame it, it was decisively overcome by Guo Xiang in his very adoption of it. Rather, to say something "exists" is to say that it is coherently, discernibly, usefully grouped, integrated intelligibly into some whole. A goofy but effective way of grasping this idea is to consider the modern Chinese usage of the word ling 零 for "zero," and its relation to terms such as lingjian 零件, meaning "spare parts." Spare parts, as of an automobile, are fragments not currently integrated into some larger whole, particularly the whole that is of some use to human purposes, such as the automobile. To be "zero," nothing, is to be like a spare part, unintegrated, incoherent. At best, these spare parts might "exist" as integrated into some other whole—e.g., the mechanic's workshop—but the criterion for existence is still going to be some human purpose or other. The idea of absolute existence contrasted to absolute nonexistence is lacking here. So, "There is no such Li" means simply, "There is no such coherence—it does not exist, and/or in its current unintegrated state it is useless: it is not compossible with the other things we are doing, have done, and want to do."

The same basic sense is operative when someone says he has gotten a hold of a Li to mean that he has understood a point that is made, or an idea. It means, "I see where the vertices are that make the vortices coherent; I have a sense of where the acupuncture points lie; I can now group these materials in a way that is coherent with my ultimate needs." The "I see" here is a further coherence between human cognition and the array of vertices. When someone is asked to "talk Li" in the sense of "be reasonable," it means, "The words you are using now are pressing on points that are not acupuncture points, further disorganizing the body of material; they impede other possibilities; they fail to cohere with the other coherences that exist; they are incompossible. Divide along the acupuncture points instead." When someone is money managing (*licai*) or cutting hair (*lifa*), he is grouping the money or the hair in such a way as to form vertices that make useful vortices, imposing divisions along the acupuncture points of the money or hair, so that it coheres with the human desire for increased wealth or beauty. When someone is told, "Don't Li him," in the sense of "pay no attention to him," it means, "Don't try to integrate him into your practice of grouping the world along its acupuncture points, for it will not yield any coherent-to-human-value-and-cognition groupings to do so: no useful vortices can form for you which take him as a vertex." A similar analysis can be made for all of the examples given earlier in this book.

Things get more complicated when the ironic usage of the term is involved, but the same basic structure still applies. When Li in the ironic sense is invoked, it means, "Pay attention to the fact of illegibility: this will bring all elements of your existence into harmony." The "division" here is purely on the cognitive side: don't pay attention to all those particular readable characteristics of things, but rather to the background, the outline, the self-contradictoriness, the ambiguity, or the overarching raw material into which they resolve and from which they begin. Making this divide in your cognition is the application of the needle to the acupuncture point, which brings the cognition and the rest of the human person into a harmony with itself and with its highest possible values. All things are brought into the vortex of this vertex. When Buddhist intellectuals speak of "realizing the Li of Emptiness," it means, "Of all the various aspects of a thing you might concentrate on, concentrate on this sense in which it is Empty of self-being, and keep concentrating on this same aspect of whatever thing you encounter: for activation of that acupuncture point groups your cognitions in the form most useful to you: the way that eliminates desire and suffering." When Huayan Buddhists say, "Li and events are unobstructed," they mean, "The aspect of things which it is most liberating to concentrate on is their ultimate lack of any characteristics of their own. It is equally findable—in its entirety—in any perceived event. This indeterminateness is what is most reliably present in any event. Since indeterminateness cannot be cognized as such, it is this interpenetration of each event with all other events to which attention is to be paid. That concentrating on this one fact will divide consciousness in such a way as to unify it, and unify the person with the highest values, forming a vertex which makes all things its vortex." When Tiantai Buddhists speak of the Three Thousand Li, they mean: "Any of the Three Thousand determinate events, when concentrated upon and fully realized, divides the world like an acupuncture point; it can serve as the vertex of a vortex which unifies all the parts of the individual, all possible theories and practices, and all events, such that all of these are, in vortexing around this vertex, thereby vortexing around the highest value. This event is both the vertex and the vortex, and all the elements in its vortex are thus also vertices in their own right. Every point is an acupuncture point—as long as it is pressed hard enough. Each event is Li, if its defining division is made sharply enough, if the event is made explicit and articulated enough."

It is hoped that these investigations into the implications of the term Li can help us grasp how it is that the Chinese tradition was able to get along without any notions of an intelligible realm, or a two-tiered metaphysic consisting of eternal supersensory laws, universals, Ideas, or forms on the one hand and temporal sensory events, particulars, instantiations on the other—indeed, without any idea of mutually exclusive sameness and difference, oneness and manyness, as ultimate ontological facts. Instead, what holds individual events and generalizable multilocal facts together is a coherence or a metacoherence between coherences, always involving the irreducible co-presence of unity and diversity at even the most primitive level. This does not solve the problem of induction, because this problem is stated in terms of the presupposition of the existence of genuinely distinct particulars and universals and, as stated, is unsolvable. But these reflections can perhaps help us see why the problem need not be so posed. There is, as I've indicated, a Tiantai solution to the problem of induction, but it is not useful for fulfilling the purposes that normally bring this problem into focus. The Tiantai solution is that all possible inductions are performatively true. If, having seen X here, I infer that X is also equally present somewhere else, I am correct; the act of seeing it so is what makes it equally so in all other places and times (including all pasts and futures), hence makes it true that it always has and always will be so. But the opposite will also be correct. Whatever I was reading into the "here" can also be, equally correctly, read into the "somewhere else," and in neither case will it be a mere subjective projection; it is "inherently entailed," and it is this doctrine alone among traditional Chinese philosophies that can, strictly speaking, solve the problem of induction. As a criterion for *which* inductions are legitimate, however, this is quite useless. In the context of the Tiantai epistemology, it is more than adequate; whatever one-sided induction I am making, it is an *upāya* that can be used to lead beyond itself, finally to the emptying-out of the original X, the realization of its local-coherence-*sive*-global-incoherence-*sive*-intersubsumption, its status as a Center, a Li, and this will attain the practical goal of cognition as conceived in Tiantai: liberation, Buddhahood. But in terms of specific inductions about the future, what will or will not be so in real time in a singly ordered world, none of the conceptions of Li in the tradition can be of any use. It is simply not possible to know exactly what will be eternally so, in all cases, based on what is happening here and now. However, it is also not necessary. One need only know that existence is vortices around vertices, which can be, at certain times, places where dividing pressure needs to be applied so as to order all the surrounding vortices around it more coherently. This is the only needed a priori assumption. A good doctor knows, however, that all bodies are different; with experience, and reference to precedent, he can make an educated guess about where the acupuncture points may lie. But in the end, some trial and error is necessary; each body must be treated on a case by case basis. There may be general categories of bodies into which individuals are grouped, but they are not to be considered hard and fast rules or laws.

Similarly, the fact/value problem cannot be solved as usually stated, as Hume showed. The ultimate values in terms of which coherence is defined in Chinese traditions—human virtuosity, freedom from suffering, or the enabling harmony and equilibrium supporting generative power of human beings, or of coherent beings in general—is never defended on objective grounds, and never could be. Even the most "objectivist" school of Neo-Confucianism, as represented here by Zhu Xi, justifies its claims for what constitutes Li as value by means of its assertion that human beings, and ultimate human aspirations, have a special representative place in the cosmos. This claim itself is not, and cannot be, justified objectively. This may seem to pose another version of the problem of induction: even if we grant that human aspirations have a special status, which human inclinations count as the truly human, which are highest or ultimate, what forms of coherence represent the truly human such that their perpetuation is a criterion for what counts as Li? Of all the possible types of humanity, what kind of flourishing is defined as truly "human" flourishing? But the only answer that can be given to these questions is a version of Zhuangzi's answer, as reinterpreted through the non-ironic conception of sociality and tradition. "Our" aspirations are the truly human aspirations, and it is the continued equilibrium and flourishing of "us" that constitutes value—we Neo-Confucians, for example, or anyone who can read and understand what we're saying. This vague "us" is as far back as we can go: it is indistinctly bordered, but not unintelligible. And to join this community requires, not the repetition of a pattern or the application of a rule, but the coherence with the tradition of this community in the past, continuing it in some new way. Perhaps the easiest way to formulize this is to consider the distinction between law and ritual made in early Confucianism, discussed in the prequel, and the continued influence of this conception throughout the tradition in its many permutations. We noted there the peculiar combination of normativity and allowance for exceptions that marked this conception of ritual, reducible to neither the nominalist nor realist notion of universality, which we have traced elsewhere in Chinese thought. We might then say simply that what all these conceptions of Li share is this overall assumption: there are no *laws* of nature. There are, instead, only *rituals* of nature. There are no universals as such. There are only local traditions of coherence. Each such tradition of coherence, however, is not something to which preexistent members are merely added, fully constituted members that join a fully constituted coherence from outside. Rather, it actually makes these members what they are by so adding them, and they make it what it is by being so joined. It is something that, though never the same, remains fully present in each of its differing places of instantiation, and has the real causal power of binding its members to one another to form a totality, thereby actually determining what they are, namely, actual instantiations of this very totality, which however is constituted by these instantiations. Each is a vertex to the vortex of members that constitutes it as a vertex, and yet the intelligibility of those members as any specifically discernible entities at all is provided only by the ever-shifting vertex itself. They are present as intelligible entities only to the extent that they are members of this vortex, constituting and yet constituted by this vertex, which is the sole content of their intelligibility, which is all they really "are." The world we are asked to contemplate here would be one that has no single ruling order, and yet is also not unruly, neither controlled by an omnipresent law nor anarchic, neither pervaded by organizing universals nor devoid of real unities and harmonies, neither centered nor centerless. What harmonies there are in Li always in one way or another fold in the ironic dimensions long integrated into Chinese thinking about coherence, the cosmos being a "Great Harmony" (太和 *taihe*) only in the sense described by Zhang Zai 張載 (1020–1077), in one of the foundational and defining declarations standing at the beginning of the new Neo-Confucian metaphysics: it qualifies as "harmonious" if and only if it is an unstable mass of confusion, like "an agitated cloud of dust raised by a stampede of wild horses" (不知野馬絪蘊, 不足謂之太和 *buru yema yinyun,bu zu wei zhi taihe*). Li, as a second-order coherence, points toward the always unsteady form of "harmony" and "peace" that Zhuangzi had described as the "Turbulent Tranquility" (攖寧 *yingning*), which is always both destroying and forming coherences, both making and dissolving harmonies—indeed, not only as two distinct acts, but explicitly as forming them only *by* disturbing them, formation accomplished only through disturbance itself (攖而後成者也 *ying er hou chengzhe ye*). What is omnipresent is the process of cohering itself: a centerless cosmos where centerings and decentering for further recenterings are going on everywhere.

NOTES

INTRODUCTION

1. Throughout this book whenever I leave "Li" capitalized and unitalicized, I mean this term: 理.

2. Think not only of all the obvious Daoist examples—無為 *wu wei* and the like—and the ceaseless iterations of things such as True Emptiness as Wondrous Being (真空妙有 *zhenkong miaoyou*), Non-Attribute (無相 *wuxiang*), Non-Dwelling (無住 *wuzhu*), No-Mind (無心 *wuxin*), No-Thought (無念 *wunian*) and such in Chinese Buddhism, but also the inevitability with which each line even of Confucian thought always seems to end up with something like Zhou Dunyi's 無極而太極 *wuji er taiji* ("the limitless/standardless and yet the ultimate limit/standard!") or Wang Yangming's 無善無惡是心之體 *wushanwu e shixinzhiti* ("the absence of both good and evil—that is the substance of mind") considered as a synonym for the "ultimate good" 至善 *zhishan*.

3. Qian Mu, *Hushang xiansi lu* (Taipei: Dongda tushu gongsi, 1988), 42–44.

4. Qian's own way of thinking here clearly reflects the influence of Cheng-Zhu Neo-Confucianism, along with its interpretation of the version of coherence that takes shape in the Yin-Yang theory rooted in the *Zhouyi*. As such, it is most closely fitted to what we will be calling the non-ironic sense of coherence, along with the systems we are calling "non-ironic incorporations of the ironic."

5. The other argument used by Aristotle and his followers is even less satisfying. The Law of Non-Contradiction is admitted to be undemonstrable, because circular: any attempt to demonstrate it assumes it in advance. But then, lo and behold, this circularity, which in all other cases is used as an argument *against* the validity of a claim, is used as an argument for its absolute certainty. First there is some name-calling and threats against those who deny it: they are uneducated, they are fools, they are not worth our time. Then there is the suggestion that it is an axiom that must be accepted on faith, like the axioms of mathematics—you can't prove everything, gosh! For it is claimed that the law of non-contradiction is assumed in argument, and that no discussion can proceed without assuming it. This may be true. But it amounts to no more than saying that when certain North American contractors buy and sell lumber by the foot, they are also assuming twelve inches to the foot, and otherwise no business could be done. Other people talk differently at other times—poets, madmen, non-logicians—and their talk proceeds and has effects

in the world just as much as do the discussions of those who, temporarily and in some contexts, decide to adhere to the law of non-contradiction.

Sometimes it is argued that for someone to argue for a position at all, and therefore to be involved in the conversation, presupposes that he believes there is a difference between his opponent accepting his view and not accepting it.

Sometimes it is claimed that the behavior of people proves that they do accept the law of non-contradiction. The care I take when I cross the street seems to mean that I accept that there is a real difference between being hit by a car and not being hit by a car. But this is not denied by the denier of the law of non-contradiction. All that is denied is that this cannot coexist with a simultaneous belief that there is no relevant difference between the two. If I want X and also don't want X, my behavior may sometimes, under some conditions (random or non-random) display my desire for X. The claim is simply that this is not the whole story about what I desire. It is far from implausible to say, for example, that I both desire to die and desire to avoid death. This is where the metaphysical version of the LNC comes in: its defender will say "I desire to die in one respect—or at some times—and I desire not to die in other respects, or at other times." So again, the psychological version of the LNC depends on the ontological version, and its feasibility depends entirely on what is defined as a "respect" and as a "time." I claim that these are defined with reference to contradiction itself, and so the entire principle collapses into meaningless gerrymandering. This of course rests on the claim that any other attempt to specify what constitutes a "time" and a "respect" in isolation of an explicit appeal to non-contradictoriness will, when closely examined, reveal that it presupposes a prior acceptance of non-contradiction in the definitions of each proposed criterion—something I can only assert but not exhaustively demonstrate in the limited space allotted here.

6. See David L. Hall and Roger Ames, *Thinking from the Han: Self, Truth, and Transcendence in Chinese and Western Culture* (Albany: State University of New York Press, 1998), 76; and David L. Hall, *Eros and Irony* (Albany: State University of New York Press, 1983), 113–148.

7. As is noted in the *Zhuangzi*, "To forget the feet indicates the fitness (or comfort, 適 *shi*) of the shoes; to forget the waist indicates the fitness of the belt; when consciousness forgets right and wrong it indicates the fitness of the mind. . . . He who begins in fitness/comfort and is never unfit/uncomfortable has the comfort of forgetting even comfort." 50/19/62–64.

8. My translations-cum-interpretations here of course require some explanation. See in particular the discussion of "The Five Meanings of the Unhewn: Omnipresence and Ironic Coherence in the *Laozi*," in *Ironies of Oneness and Difference*, 146–62.

CHAPTER ONE. LI 理 AS A FUNDAMENTAL CATEGORY IN CHINESE THOUGHT

1. Fung Yulan, *A History of Chinese Philosophy*, trans. Derk Bodde (Princeton: Princeton University Press, 1953), vol. 2, 537.

2. I owe this crucial point to A. C. Graham, *Two Chinese Philosophers* (LaSalle: Open Court, 1992), 16, quoting *Chengshi yishu*, 49, 1–6.

3. This useful phrase is derived from Donald J. Munro, *The Concept of Man in Early China* (Ann Arbor: Center for Chinese Studies, University of Michigan, 2001).

4. Graham, op. cit., 18.

5. I am paraphrasing here from the translation of Leibniz's text by Rosemont and Cook, in Leibniz, *Discourse on the Natural Theology of the Chinese* (*Monographs of the Society for Asian and Comparative Philosophy, no. 4*), trans. Henry Rosemont Jr. and Daniel J. Cook (Honolulu: University Press of Hawaii, 1977), 60–67.

6. Ibid., 71.

7. I will list a few here, with translations of the meaning of the whole phrase and literal renderings of the character or characters yoked to Li in each phrase. However, the term *Li* will be left untranslated, here as throughout most of this book:

Lixing (理性 "inborn characteristic of Li"): reason, rationality

Lun2li (倫理 "human relationships Li"): ethics

Lun4li (論理 "discourse Li"): logic

Daoli (道理 "Li of [and?] the Way"): principle, idea, a valid point made or understood

Guanli (管理 "to control and Li"): manage, management

Chuli (處理 "to position oneself in and Li [something]"): to deal with, handle (a situation)

Jiangli (講理 "to speak Li"): to talk or listen to reason

Dili (地理 "terrain Li"): geography

Wenli (文理 "patterned ornament and Li, or the Li of patterned ornament"): pattern

Wuli (物理 "Li of things or matter"): physics

Lijie (理解 "to Li and untangle"): to understand

Likui (理虧 "Li lacking"): to be in the wrong

Heli (合理 "coming together with Li"): reasonable

Zhenli (真理 "genuine Li"): truth

Licai2 (理財 "to Li wealth"): money management

Lifa (理髮 "to Li hair"): get a haircut, or cut hair

Licai3 (理睬 "to Li and see?"): to notice. Li can be used by itself as a verb in this sense: "Don't 'li' it" means something like, "Don't pay any attention to it," i.e., don't bother to try to integrate it into your awareness, judge it, make any adjustments of it or the rest of the world to make them fit together in some desirable way.

Xiuli (修理 "to cultivate and Li"): to fix, as a car or a person (by humiliating and cutting him down to size)

Huli (護理 "to protect and Li"): medical nurse, or nursing

Liizhi (理智 "Li wisdom"): reason, rationality

Linian (理念 "Li thought"): an idea, sometimes in the Platonic sense

Lixing2 (理型 "Li form"): a Platonic idea or form

Lixiang (理想 "Li thinking"): an ideal

Shengli (生理 "life Li"): physiology, physiological

Gongli (公理 "everywhere-available or unbiased Li"): an axiom

Dingli (定理 "fixed Li"): a theorem

Tiaoli (條理 "stripelike Li"): order

Zhi4li3 (治理 "to govern and Li"): to govern

Lilun (理論 "Li discourse"): a theory

Lihui (理會 "to Li and meet") to pay attention to (synonymous with Licai3) or to understand

Tongli (同理 "same Li"): "by the same token. . . ."

Changli (常理 "constant or usual li"): common sense, general principle

Jingli (經理 "to go through comprehensively and to Li"): to manage, a manager

Liyou (理由 "Li come-from"): a reason (for doing something)

Liao4li3 (料理 "raw materials Li-ed"): to manage or deal with; also, cuisine, cooking, e.g., Italian cuisine, Japanese cuisine, etc. (originally Japanese, current in Taiwan)

Yuanli: (原理 "origin Li"): principle

Gongli: (共理 "shared Li"): a Universal; sometimes 共相 *gongxiang*, shared characteristic, is also used for a Universal in the philosophical sense

Qingli (清理 "to purify and Li"): to clean up

Tuili (推理 "to push Li"): to infer or deduce, to reason, as in solving a puzzle or a murder mystery

Zhaoli (照理 "to reflect or shine on Li, or to accord with Li"): by rights, it would be reasonable to expect that. . . .

Jianbuduan, Lihuanluan (剪不斷, 理還亂 "cut, they do not break; Li'ed, they return to chaos"): unmanageable and persistent, as of unruly emotions (from a Li Houzhu poem)

Lichu touxu (理出頭緒 "to Li-out the end of the thread"): to find a way to make sense of

Li suo dang ran (理所當然 "what should be so by virtue of Li, what matches that which belongs to Li"): to be taken for granted as what should be so, requiring no further argument

Qi you ci li (豈有此理 "How could there exist such a Li?"): how unreasonable, how absurd, how outrageous

Shunlichengzhang (順理成章 "to follow Li and form a coherent insignia"): reasonable behavior according to de facto precedent

Lizhiqizhuang (理直氣壯 "Li straight qi [life-force] strong"): to be fearless because one is in the right

    8. Tang Junyi, *Zhongguo zhexue yuanlun: Daolunpian* (Taipei: Taiwan xuesheng shuju, 1986), 21–89.

    9. Ibid., 212; italics in the original.

    10. Tang Junyi, op. cit., 31.

    11. I translate this term in accordance with the suggestion of Scott Cook, in his unpublished paper, "The Term Li in Chinese Treatises on Literature and the Arts."

12. Duan Yucai, *Shuwenjiezizhu* (Shanghai: Shanghai guji chubanshe, 1982), 32.

13. Joseph Needham, *Science and Civilization in China* (Taipei: Caves Books, 1985), Vol. 2, 302.

14. David Hall and Roger Ames, *Anticipating China* (Albany: State University of New York Press, 1995), 269.

15. Ibid., 213.

16. See Chad Hansen, *Language and Logic in Ancient China* (Ann Arbor: University of Michigan Press, 1983), 30–54.

17. Ibid., 112.

18. A. C. Graham, "Relating Categories to Question Forms in Pre-Han Chinese Thought," in *Studies in Chinese Philosophy and Philosophical Literature* (Singapore: Institute of East Asian Philosophies, 1986), 382–83. The case of the Mohist is obviously quite relevant to the question at hand. For here we have the closest case in the tradition of an attempt to give an abstract and comprehensive "logical" treatment to the question of how predicates attach to multiple instances, the equivalent of the problem of universals. I have nothing to add to Graham's analysis of the Mohist's, except to note the relevance of his analysis in the present context.

19. Graham, 343–44.

20. For example, a sentence such as, 不內相教而外相謗者，是謂不足親也 *bunei xiangjiao er wai xiangbangzhe, shi wei bu zu qin ye* ("To slander a person in public without first instructing him in private is to be unworthy of associating with"), from the "Guidelines of Governing" chapter of Liu Xiang's 劉向 *Shuoyuan* 說苑，政理. Note that in this chapter title I translate X Li as "guidelines of X," i.e., lines to be followed in treating X so as to make it desirably coherent (i.e., a coherence that is coherent with our desires). With that understanding of the intended meaning, I would have no objection to translating this sort of usage of Li directly as "principles," as the content of the chapter really is concerned with those types of coherences which in English we would call principles, i.e., precepts to guide behavior.

21. For example, in Kumārajīva's rendering of the *Saddharmapundarikasutra* (*Miaofalianhuajing*), we often find structures like the following: 不復為貪欲所惱，亦復不為瞋恚愚癡所惱，亦復不為憍慢嫉妒諸垢所惱 (T33.954c.): "He will no longer be afflicted with greed, not will he be afflicted by anger and delusion, nor will he be afflicted by other defilements such as arrogance and envy." To passively "be afflicted by X" rather than actively "to afflict X" is here indicated with a *wei* X *suo* afflict construction: to "be" that which X afflicts.

22. Graham, "The Cheng-Chu Theory of Human Nature," in *Studies in Chinese Philosophy*, 421.

23. Ibid.

24. Ibid., 422.

25. Ibid., 423–24.

26. Ibid., 426–27.

27. Ibid., 431.

28. Willard Peterson, "Another Look at Li," *Bulletin of Sung-Yuan Studies* 18 (1986): 14.

29. Ibid., 15.

30. Ibid., 17–18.
31. Ibid., 18.
32. Ibid., 19.
33. Ibid., 20.
34. Ibid., 21.
35. Ibid., 23.
36. Ibid.
37. Ibid., 27.
38. These points allow Peterson to provide solutions to the six "problem areas" concerning Neo-Confucian Li raised by Wittenborn (Allen Wittenborn, "Li Revisited and Other Explorations," *The Bulletin of Sung-Yuan Studies* 17 [1981]: 32–48):

1. "How do we, or can we know li?" The problem here is that there is no independent standard of what a thing's li is outside of its actual behavior; so if I think the li of this cart is "to travel on land," and this is discomfirmed by the fact that it later does something not specified by this characterization, such as be used as a boat to float on water, how can I ever know if I have correctly ascertained any thing's li? Peterson answers that both the floating and land-travel are part of a single coherence, which includes, again, both a thing's actual and potential connections, without thereby fading immediately into all possible connections and thus meaninglessness.

2. "Is li prior to ch'I, and, if so, what does this mean?"

3. Is li subjective or objective?"

4. "Is li a form of what things are or a standard of what they should be?"

5. "What accounts for the differentiation of things?" Peterson grants that li gives no answer to the question of what *causes* things to be differentiated; they are so of themselves, if this question is meant to be answered in terms of efficient causality.

6. "What is the scope of li?" This question is concerned with the li of purely mental concepts, such as dreams, memories, numbers, beliefs, actions, and emptiness. Peterson answers that coherence applies to the "sticking together" also of particular sets of electrical characters in a particular part of our brain and events in the world.

39. Ibid., 29.
40. Hall and Ames, *Anticipating China*, 303, note 65.
41. Ibid., 136.
42. Ibid., 140.
43. Ibid., 213.
44. Ibid., 214–15.
45. Ibid., 215.
46. Indeed, we could almost translate Li simply as ""guideline" or "useful information," as long as we gloss this by saying that "useful" presupposes a given set

of human goals and desires, the coherence with which makes something useful, and that "information" means an intelligible fitting between a symbol, a cognitive apparatus, a background set of linguistic or symbolic usages, and a context, in such a way as to be transferable between contexts. With this translation, "useful information" becomes equivalent to our previous definition of Li, i.e., a harmonious coherence that, if cohered with, leads to further such coherences.

CHAPTER TWO. THE ADVENT OF LI, IRONIC AND NON-IRONIC

1. *Ironies of Oneness and Difference*, 201.
2. See *Xunzi*, 21/102/5–21/107/17.
3. 7/3/17. Cf. the almost identical usage at 18/7/21.
4. 14/5/36.
5. 51/13/42.
6. 64/17/47, 82/20/80.
7. 56/15/67–68.
8. 94/26/3.
9. See *Ironies*, 199–220, particularly the discussion of the taxonomy of whales and fish on p. 209.
10. Thanks are due here to Paul Goldin's sublimely hostile review of the first volume of this series, which nicely illustrates both the attractions and the dangers of isolating Xunzi from his own context and immediately assimilating him into ours. Looking at this single example in isolation, outside of its place in the development of relevant positions earlier and later in our particular way of narratizing Chinese thought here, it might indeed be convenient to look at Xunzi's position, and some of the others in early Confucian and Daoist thinking, as founded on a straightforward assumption of a kind of "underdetermination," in the modern sense of that term, which seems to make the human action of adding explanatory theoretical concepts or linguistic systems the disambiguating factor that provides the determinations, hence resulting in a kind of nominalism, as he suggests. But such a move, though convenient, arouses some worry about too quickly integrating the Confucian and Daoist problematic into an existing conversation, with its own set of concerns and assumptions, which obscures some of the relevant connections to some of the distinctive trajectories and concerns animating the prior and subsequent Chinese traditions, as sketched out in our discussion. The key point is again the question of sameness and difference, both of which I contend must be regarded as ontologically real and genuinely mutually exclusive, on some level or other of abstraction or concreteness, for any nominalism or realism to be true in the strict sense. My claim is that for Xunzi, in contrast, the pre-theorized facts must be such that the theoretical explanation pertaining to their essence, however conceived, cannot be either entirely extraneous to them, making them genuinely different from this imputed essence or explanation and leaving them unchanged by its application, nor a denotation of some genuinely shared and unchangeably iterable fact about them. Their shared name denotes the inherence of a whole in which they cohere. But they cohere in a way that is not limitable to only one such whole. Indeed, it seems that clarity might be

better served here by inventing an alternate term which reverses the emphases so as to avoid any implication that there is a neutral substratum of fact about the real state of the natural world, prior to human theorizing, that is ultimately to be thought of as devoid of the determinations subsequently foisted upon it. The nature of the smallest units of fact to be theorized here are after all themselves functions of the alternate theories, and all these incompatible facts, generated by alternate holisms of meaning, are really to be found as always having been available, ineradicably, both before and after these alternate groupings pick them out and synthesize them in one particular way. A term such as, say, *overperforation* would perhaps do a better job of stressing this overabundance of asynordinate determinations and their ineradicable availability than the accepted term *underdetermination,* which prima facie seems to put stress instead on the paucity of theoretical determinations and the contrastive presupposition of their ultimate absence from the facts to be discovered. Admittedly, though, this is mainly a matter of emphasis; the choice of one term over another depends on pragmatic rhetorical considerations. "Overperforation" is recommended for the express purpose of facilitating linkages to other positions in our exposition, rather than participating in an ongoing conversation within the philosophy of science, however worthy that purpose might be.

11. 78/21/1.

12. 82/21/78–83.

13. 28/9/63.

14. 77/20/33–34.

15. 7/3/28.

16. 21/8/31–32.

17. 7/3/6–7.

18. I am interpreting the notorious "*qiong ren yu*" (窮人慾) in a controversial manner here, flying in the face of thousands of years of commentary; Neo-Confucians take the *qiong* to mean "to extend to the limit," thereby reading a strong contrast between "Heavenly coherence" and "human desires" into the passage. I think this is clearly incorrect. The "proper Way of man" and "the desires of their nature" are all positively valued here, and seem to refer not to the excessive but to the proper desires of man, those which are in accord with the "stillness" of human nature when it has not yet been "transformed" by things. Note also that the word *qiong* is consistently used to mean "exhaust," not "extend to the limit," in this text. As we note in our discussion of the *Zhuangzi*, *qiong* is generally the opposite of 達 *da,* meaning failure as opposed to success, blockage as opposed to reaching the goal. I take the meaning here to be "makes human desires fail (to reach satisfaction)."

19. Translation adapted from Scott Cook, "The Term Li in Chinese Treatises on Literature and the Arts," (unpublished paper), 33.

20. It is also worth noting that this conception can be boiled down into an *immanent* axiology, i.e., that an attempt is made to derive value simply from existence as such, without applying a heteronomous valuation from without which would in principle designate some portion of being as good and another portion as bad. This is equal to saying also that it is tautological, or that it leads to an infinite regress. It rests on the base assumption that being (or rather, continuous creation) is good as such.

21. There are many instances of such a situation in the hexagrams themselves. For example, Hexagram #24, Return (復 *Fu*), is one of the most auspicious overall hexagrams in the system, and is traditionally regarded as the reassertion of the power of Yang. It consists of one Yang line, on the bottom, and five Yin lines. The "ruling line" of the hexagram, the fifth from the bottom, which should "ideally" be occupied by a Yang line, is here occupied by a Yin line, which moreover does not have the virtue of "responding" with the second line, since the latter is also Yin. Structurally, this hexagram doesn't have much going for it, according to the general rules applied to hexagram interpretation. And yet it is highly auspicious and moreover emblematic of a Yang situation because the single Yang line comes "at the beginning," is perfectly playing its pure role of initiation, a turning point (associated with the winter solstice) where a small bubbling up of Yang force is enough to ensure subsequent "responses" and "finishes" from the Yin elements present (structurally, this response would come especially from the fourth line), and thereby to serve the process of continuance. Another example is the final hexagram, #64, Before Completion (未濟 *Wei Ji*). Here *every* line is in the wrong place. But this too is one of the most auspicious of hexagrams, since its disequilibrium implies of state of incompletion that will function, holistically, as an initiation for later completion. The total hexagram is thus Yangish, although it is quantitatively equally Yin and Yang and structurally perfectly wrong, with a Yin ruler. Here we see a non-ironic incorporation of the ironic implications of coherence: it is still value, it is still intelligibility, it is still a kind of sticking together or harmony of elements, but now value and intelligibility reside in the harmony between valued intelligibility and non-valued unintelligibility.

22. Legge's amusingly outraged comments on the "silliness" of this "drivel" are still well worth consulting.

CHAPTER THREE. THE DEVELOPMENT OF LI IN IRONIC TEXTS

1. 41/16/1–3.
2. 44/17/50–52. 天在內，人在外，德在乎天。知天人之行，本乎天，位乎得。。。。曰何謂天？何謂人？北海若曰：牛馬四足，是謂天；落馬首，穿牛鼻，是謂人.
3. 15/6/3–4. 庸詎知吾所謂天之非人乎、所謂人之非天乎.
4. 6/2/66. 庸詎知吾所謂知之非不知邪、庸詎知吾所謂不知之非知邪.
5. 16/6/20.
6. 42/17/6–7.
7. 43/17/37–39.
8. 44/17/45–46.
9. 44/17/48–50.
10. 22/8/33. 上不敢為仁義之操，而下不敢為淫僻之行也。.
11. 30/12/37–41.
12. 58/22/16–20.
13. 59/22/36–39.
14. 25–26/11/8–9.
15. 40/15/10–12.

16. 72–73/25/59–82.

17. Reading 小 *xiao* for 水 *shui*, in accordance with Yu Yue's amendment, preserving the parallelism with the previous line.

18. Thus at least do I understand the import of Graham's remark that this passage argues that "infinity is more than the sum of finite quantities" (Graham, *Disputers*, 209).

19. I take the parallelism to break up at this line, with 合并 *hebing* as two parallel verbs, rather than a verb and object as in the previous two lines, which seems to me an impossible reading for this line. I take the omitted object to be simply "things."

20. Reading 私 *si* for 賜 *si* throughout this passage, in accordance with the suggestion of Chen Guying, quoting Ma Xulun (Chen Guying, *Zhuangzi jinzhu jinshi*, vol. 2 [Taipei: Taiwan shangwu yinshuguan, 1989], 755). I justify this not only by the greater coherence it gives the passage, and the alternating use of the *si* for *partial* in two of the four examples given, but also by the last use of the *si* for *bequeath*, which is followed by an explicit claim about "completeness," which seems to me to be posed in clear contrast to partiality. The senses various illustrious commentators have wrenched out of the passage reading the character as it stands, meaning to bequeath, ingenious as they sometimes are, do not seem to me compelling.

21. Supplying 殊材 *shu cai*, in accordance with the suggestion of Xuan Ying (see Wang Shuming, *Zhuangzi jiaoquan* [Taipei: Academia Sinica, Academy of History and Linguistics, 1988], 1033–34).

22. Glossing 度 *du* as 居 *ju*, as suggested by Lu Wenchao, cited in ZZJS, 912.

23. Before discussing the implications these lines have for our overall interpretation, we should note that they could also be read in other ways. For example, we could take these lines to mean: "Whenever one thing is thwarted, another is suited. . . . When one thing is just right, another is deficient," as most commentators and translators do. Indeed, there is much to recommend this reading, and it is not to be ruled out, especially if we take the overall context to be a description of the totality of Dao's operation. Moreover, following this reading, the line about individual things going in their own directions seems to lead naturally into the statement that some are right and some deficient at any time, echoing the flow of disaster and prosperity alluded to above. But I have adopted the above reading because it better emphasizes the peculiar relation of part to whole being suggested here, on which the entire argument rests. This part/whole paradigm makes it very appropriate that this paradoxicality or unity of opposites be true not only of the totality, but of every part within it, which will have a number of contrary points of view available to it, an extension of the value of relativism put forward elsewhere in the text.

Another possibility, adopted by Watson, is to take this section as referring to the individual's (wrong) attitude: "Bad and good fortune, tripping and tumbling, come now with what repels you, now with what you welcome. Set in your own opinion, at odds with others, now you judge things to be upright, now you judge them to be warped. But if you could only be like the great swamp . . ." Burton Watson, *The Complete Works of Chuang Tzu* (New York: Columbia University Press, 1968), 291. This too is possible, although somewhat less persuasive than the other alternative, since it demands certain additions which have no basis in the text (for example, there is no explicit reference to the partiality of the individual's view anywhere in the passage; on the contrary, the only individual explicitly referred to is the Great Man, who joins things into impartiality), and seems to violate the general force of the larger context, in whatever way we may interpret it.

Nonetheless, I do not wish to completely dismiss these readings, as it seems to me that, in spite of the larger interpretative difference behind them, they complement each other and my own reading well, each adding a dimension to the sense of the passage, albeit from different perspectives. I am compelled to the reading adopted in my own translation not only by concerns for thematic consistency, but also by grammatical considerations: the 者 *zhe* in the middle of each of these phrases seems to militate against reading them to mean simply, "There are some who are thwarted, some who are suited," for which meaning we would expect either no *zhe* or a *zhe* following both verbs. The single *zhe* in each phrase seems to me to suggest at the very least a conditional, and more likely a full nominalization, a subject-predicate sentence: "One who possesses what thwarts him (also) possesses what suits him," and so on. However, it is to be noted that the 而 *er* in the first line breaks up the parallelism, hence interfering with this subject-predicate reading, which works better in the second line. It is likely that the text is corrupt here, and there should either be an *er* in both lines or in neither. If it appeared in both, I would change my reading; if in neither, my reading would be supported.

24. My translation here is potentially controversial, so I shall say a few words to justify it. The first impulse may be to translate this phrase to mean, "Dao is their unity, or impartiality," taking the 為 *wei* as a copula. Grammatically, however, we would normally expect a possessive 其 *qi* rather than a 之 *zhi* in that case. Another possibility is to read the *wei* in the fourth tone, and the *zhi* as a pronoun referring to the previously adduced items, i.e., Heaven, Earth, Yin and Yang, yielding, "Dao serves as their impartiality," or something of the sort. But this too is not as convincing as taking the phrase as strictly parallel to the preceding two phrases, which forces us to take the 為 *wei* as a nominalized verb, meaning, "all activity, all deeming, all purpose." As Heaven and earth were the vast among forms, and Yin and Yang the vast among forces, Dao is the *gong* among *weis*.

25. Some of the choices in this translation are perhaps a bit controversial, so I will try to justify them. I take both *gong* and Dao to be the provisional names that are permitted provisionally but not accepted as adequate; *gong*, as we noted before, is the quintessential "community word," and the description of what words do: they universalize. The name *Dao* indicates the ultimate universality that is not partial to heaven or earth, to Yin or Yang, to forms or forces, nor to any one principle or meaning. Words and Dao (which also has the meaning "to speak") share this feature. I take 比 *bi* to mean both compare and contrast, i.e., both to group similar members together into a class and to contrast this class to another class; as we noted above, this is precisely what happens in the use of particular words, which simultaneously name a universal class ("dog" for example groups all individual dogs together) and distinguish this class from every other category (the universal "dog" gets its meaning through its contrast to the universal "horse" et al.). To have meaning, it must indicate more than one thing and less than all things.

26. Taking 以 *yi* as equivalent to 相 *xiang*, as suggested by Xuan Ying.

27. Strangely, the image of the bridge, so vividly depicting this state of dependence on the joining of opposites, has been read as a mistaken character by most commentators, in spite of its reappearance later in the passage and the very good sense it makes as is.

28. According to *Zhuangzi*, ch. 17, these were stock propositions among the debaters of the time.

29. This whole section could perhaps be taken as a critique of the "Daoism" ascribed to Shen Dao, Tian Pian, and Peng Meng in the "Tianxia" chapter, which held that "Dao can include but cannot differentiate," and advocated "Universality with no favoritism" (公而不黨 *gong er bu dang*). This would be a commitment to the total universality of namelessness and nonaction, which ignores the concrete particularity of individual occurrences.

30. Reading 之 *zhi* as 其 *qi* throughout, as suggested by Ma Xulun, quoted in Wang Shuming, 1041.

CHAPTER FOUR. THE ADVENT OF LI AS A TECHNICAL PHILOSOPHICAL TERM

1. *Ironies of Oneness and Difference*, 131–38.

2. Guo Moruo 郭沫若 seems to have been the first to advance this theory, considering all four chapters to be derived from Song Xing 宋鈃 and Yi Wen 尹文 at the Jixia Academy in the state of Qi, and his conclusion is supported by the work of such scholars as Liu Jie 劉節, Pan Fu'en 潘富恩, and Shi Changdong 施昌東. Others, such as Zhu Bokun 朱伯崑 and Qiu Xigui 裘錫圭, suggest Shen Dao 慎到 or Tian Peng 田駢, or members of their school, as the author, while others, such as Feng Youlan 馮友蘭, Ren Jiyu 任繼愈, Li Jinquan 李錦全, and Wu Guang 吳光 endorse the notion of these works as coming from "Daoist" writers associated with the Jixia Academy of Qi but without venturing to name a specific author. See Wu Menghong 巫夢虹, "Guanzi sipian sixiangyanjiu" ("Research on the Thought of the 'Four Chapters' of the *Guanzi*" 《管子》四篇思想研究, Master's Thesis, Taiwan National Central University 國立中央大學, 2004, for a good overview of the scholarship on this issue and a valiant attempt to give a comprehensive outline of the doctrines of these four chapters read as a single integrated whole.

3. Reading *chu* for *ai*, as suggested by Wang Niansun, and adopted by Chen Guying. See Chen, 95.

4. ZZJC, vol. 5, 269.

5. Ibid., 219.

6. 人皆欲智，而莫索其所以智乎。智乎智乎，投之海外無自奪，求之者不得處之者，夫正人無求之也，故能虛無，虛無無形謂之道。化育萬物謂之德。君臣父子人間之事謂之義。登降揖讓，貴賤有等，親疏之體，謂之禮。簡物小未一道，殺僇禁誅謂之法.

7. ZZJC, vol. 5, 270. This phrase is a "false cousin" to the more modern usage, which would interpret this last phrase as "this is the principle of attaining oneness," which is suggested by the form "xx 之理 *zhi li*." I think this is a later grammatical form depending on a more fully developed concept of Li. Here we should translate literally as I have attempted. The case is similar to that in the first

line of the received *Laozi*: *feichang* should be read literally, character by character, not in its later and modern sense of "extraordinary."

8. Ibid., 272. My reading follows Chen Guying's interpretation. See Chen, 118.

9. The later "Baixin" echoes this idea, spelling out the idea of continuance more explicitly: "With harmony, one can long persist." (和則能久 *he ze neng jiu*) ZZJC, vol. 5, 224.

10. Ibid., 272.

11. ZZJC, vol. 4. 219. See also Chen, 147. I follow his emendation of 執 *zhi* to 勢 *shi*, but not his replacement of 不 *bu* with 而 *er*.

12. See *Ironies*, 139–99.

13. Following the interpretation of Wang Yinzhi. See Chen, 141.

14. Reading 識 *shi* for 職 *zhi*.

15. Bamboo, measure, fullness and emptiness, straightness, strength, etc.

16. 道在天地之間也，其大無外，其小無內，故曰不遠而難極也。虛之與人也無間。唯聖人得虛道，故曰並處而難得。。。。天之道，虛其無形。虛則不屈，無形則無所位「，無所位「，故遍流萬物而不變。德者道之舍，物得以生。生知得以職道之精。故德者得也，得也者，其謂所得以然也，以無為之謂道，舍之之謂德。故道之與德無間。故言之者不別也。間之理者，謂其所以舍也。義者，謂各處其宜也。禮者，因人之情，緣義之理，而為之節文者也。故禮者謂有理也，理也者，明分以諭義之意也。故禮出乎義，義出乎理，理因乎宜者也。法者所以同出，不得不然者也。故殺僇禁誅以 ‧之也，故事督乎法，法出乎權，權出乎道。ZZJC, vol. 5, 220–21. Wang Yinzhi suggests that this phrase should be rearranged to read, "禮出乎理，理出乎義，義因乎宜 *li chu hu li, li chu hu yi, yi yin hu yi*," (ritual derives from Li, Li derives from rightness, rightness follows along with what is appropriate) which follows the exposition more directly. I prefer to follow the more garbled and intricate version given in the received text. See Chen, 141.

17. This line of thought appears to have been common in "HuangLao" thought: the categorical claim that "Dao produces laws" (道生法 *dao sheng fa*) is found in the texts discovered at Mawangdui, which many scholars, somewhat questionably, take as representative of HuangLao thought, the "Four Canons of the Yellow Emperor" 黃帝四經.

18. This is signaled by the expression 人之情 *ren zhi qing*, which at this point means "what is real in people" as opposed to potentially deceptive appearances, with *qing* meaning the real state of something, as for example, the true facts in a legal case. The emphasis is on what is so prior to any specific, one-sided, deliberate manipulation. Hence, I translate as "unpremeditated human responses" and the like. The phrase *ren qing* later comes to mean simply "human emotions," and is a common antonym of Li in both Buddhism and Neo-Confucianism, which is one further reason we should pay special attention to this connection here.

19. See Kwong-loi Shun, "Mencius and Human Nature," *Philosophy East and West* 47 (January 1997), for a good summary of early usages of this term. Shun agrees with Graham's analysis of the term, as "what a thing is genuinely like," but takes exception to Graham's further equation of the term with "essence" in the Aristotelian sense. As Shun points out, the term can mean simply refer to "certain

characteristic features . . . that are particularly conspicuous, pervasive, and difficult to alter, without necessarily having the connotation of what is essential as opposed to accidental." I agree with Shun, and add that the stress is on "genuine" in the sense of "what it is like prior to deliberate manipulation for some special purpose," rather than "genuine" in the sense of objective as opposed to a subjective illusion.

20. ZZJC, vol. 5, 222.

21. 原始計實。本其所生。知其象，則索其形，緣其理，則知其情。索其端，則知其名。ZZJC, vol. 5, 224.

22. John Makeham, "Names, Actualities, and The Emergence of Essentialist Theories of Naming in Classical Chinese Thought," *Philosophy East & West* 41, no. 3 (July 1991), p. 347. Makeham claims here that "Relative to the concepts each is paired with, 'form,' 'distinguishing marks,' and 'starting point' are all manifest and apparent." But this makes havoc of the parallelism of the passage, which lines up not "form" but "image" with distinguishing marks and starting point. Just the opposite is the case: these three (象，理，端 *xiang, li, duan*) are precisely the *non*-manifest beginnings of the terms they are paired with. The "image" is the not-fully-actualized beginning of the palpable form (not, as Makeham alleges, its mental representation). The "Li" are the limited particular channels of fitting together that can later become manifest as the genuine condition of a thing. The "starting points" are the unmanifest sprouts that eventually can blossom into a named—renowned, eminent, valued, definite presence. Makeham has to add the "If you want to . . ." clause to the beginning of each phrase to make his meaning come out, but this gives a very forced meaning to the connective *ze*.

23. Shun has gathered useful examples from early sources: "[I]t is the ch'ing of the senses to desire their ideal objects (*LSCC* 5/9b.6–10a.1) and the ch'ing of human beings to desire life and honor and have an aversion to death and disgrace (*LSCC* 5/10a.7–8, 8/ 4b.2–5). Sometimes the ch'ing of x's can be certain characteristic features of x's as a class, without such features obtaining of each individual x. For example, that the common people have different abilities is described as the ch'ing of the common people (*ST*, 250, no. 33), and the distinction between genders is described as the ch'ing of human beings (*MT* 6/35). But, often, the ch'ing of x's includes characteristic features that obtain of x's as a class in virtue of their obtaining of each individual x, as when 'ch'ing' is used to refer to the tendency of the senses to seek their ideal objects, or to refer to the desires and aversions that human beings have" (Kwong-loi Shun, op. cit.).

24. Scholars disagree about the authorship of this commentary, whether it comes from the same author as the rest of the *Hanfeizi* text, and whether the thought expressed therein is compatible with the Legalism of the rest of the *Hanfeizi*. It has been suggested that it is a work of Hanfei's early years, or that it comes from another brush entirely. The facts of the matter, if we had them, would certainly be helpful in interpreting the text; given the distinctive Legalist reading—some would say twisting—of other Laozian themes (e.g., the idea of the unknown ruler, taken by Hanfeizi as a recommendation that the ruler not let his preferences be known by his ministers, the better to test and surveille them), we might indeed wonder whether the interpretation of Dao and its relation to Li in this text can really be

taken as representative of the ironic tradition. In fact, *Hanfeizi's* Legalism in general can perhaps be considered a non-ironic appropriation of ironic motifs. But the passage under discussion here provides a valuable window into the way the terms Dao and Li are to be related, in a way that seems to develop the line of thinking we've seen in the above ironic appropriations of non-ironic motifs. The general attitude toward this relation seems to be shared by the "HuangLao" Daoism represented by the unearthed "Four Canons of the Yellow Emperor" 黃帝四經 as well; the "Sidu" 四度, for example, tells us, "Success and failure share the same Dao but are different Lis" (逆順同道而異理 *nishun tongdao er yili*). Sameness pertains to Dao, which participates in both positive and negative events, while differentiation pertains to Li.

25. The term *ji* is sometimes glossed as meaning "coming together" (cohering) and sometimes as "examining" (making intelligible). I include both meanings here, in line with the internal connection we have discerned between intelligibility and coherence in the tradition so far.

26. 道者，萬物之所然也，萬理之所稽也。理者，成物之文也；道者，萬物之所以成也。故曰：「道，理之者也。」物有理不可以相薄，物有理不可以相薄故理之為物之制。萬物各異理，萬物各異理而道盡。稽萬物之理，故不得不化；不得不化，故無常操；無常操，是以死生氣稟焉，萬智斟酌焉，萬事廢興焉。。。道與堯、舜俱智，與接輿俱狂，與桀、紂俱滅，與湯、武俱昌。。。凡道之情，不制不形，柔弱隨時，與理相應。萬物得之以死，得之以生；萬事得之以敗，得之以成。道譬諸若水，溺者多飲之即死，渴者適飲之即生。。。故得之以死，得之以生，得之以敗，得之以成.

。。。。凡理者，方圓、短長、麤靡、堅脆之分也。故理定而後可得道也。故定理有存亡，有死生，有盛衰。夫物之一存一亡，乍死乍生，初盛而後衰者，不可謂常。唯夫與天地之剖判也具生，至天地之消散也不死不衰者謂常。而常者，無攸易，無定理，無定理非在於常所，是以不可道也。。。。。短長、大小、方圓、堅脆、輕重、白黑之謂理。理定而物易割也。*Hanfeizi*, "Jielaopian," *Zhuzijicheng*, vol. 5, 107–108.

27. *Shi* 勢, as in the Wang Bi text; but the Mawangdui text B has 器 "*qi*," utensils or palpable objects, which also works here.

28. I am following the Mawangdui texts here, both of which lack the character *de* in this line, so that Dao remains the subject for the verb "to husband," in contrast to the first line of the chapter, where Dao is what generates while Virtuosity is what husbands. The other two agents listed in the first line—"things" and "tendencies"—drop out here in all versions of the text, which might be taken as support for the Mawangdui reading, but in either case the point is the same; although the verbs "to form" and "to complete" are not used, which are what was done by "things" and "tendencies" respectively, their function seems to be covered by the following six verbs: to grow, to nourish, to house, to mature, to feed, to shelter. These are simply another way of describing the process of being "formed" and "completed," but when looked at not as the actions of things and tendencies, but of Dao and/or Virtuosity, the latter in any case being the presence of the formlessness of Dao in the formed thing. What matters is the double vision of agency: on the one hand things and tendencies make things what they are, but on the other precisely in so doing it is Dao (and/or Virtue) that, by not doing so, is making things what they are.

29. 故任一人之能，不足以治三畝之宅也。修道理之數，因天地之自然，則六合不足均也.

30. 3/2/9.

31. See Harold D. Roth, *The Textual History of the Huai-nan Tzu* (Ann Arbor: Association of Asian Studies Monograph, 1992), 9–26.

32. 故任一人之能，不足以治三畝之宅也。修道理之數，因天地之自然，則六合不足均也.

33. Roth et al., *Huainanzi*, 55.

34. Ibid., 53, n. 17.

35. 所謂後者，非謂其底滯而不發，凝結而不流，貴其周於數而合于時也。夫執道理以耦變，先亦制後，後亦制先。是何則？不失其所以制人，人不能制也.

36. 所謂無形者，一之謂也。所謂一者，無匹合於天下者也。卓然獨立，塊然獨處，上通九天，下貫九野。員不中規，方不中矩。大渾而為一，棄累而無根。懷囊天地，為道開門。穆忞隱閔，純德獨存，佈施而不既，用之而不勤。是故視之不見其形，聽之不聞其聲，循之不得其身；無形而有形生焉，無聲而五音鳴焉，無味而五味形焉，無色而五色成焉。是故有生於無，實出於虛，天下為之圈，則名實同居。音之數不過五，而五音之變，不可勝聽也；味之和不過五，而五味之化，不可勝嘗也；色之數不過五，而五色之變，不可勝觀也。故音者，宮立而五音形矣；味者，甘立而五味亭矣；色者，白立而五色成矣；道者，一立而萬物生矣。 是故一之理，施四海；一之解，際天地。其全也，純分若樸；其散也，混分若濁。濁而徐清，沖而徐盈.

CHAPTER FIVE. LI AS THE CONVERGENCE OF COHERENCE AND INCOHERENCE IN WANG BI AND GUO XIANG

1. See Mizoguchi Yûzô, "Liqilun de xingcheng," trans. Li Changli, in *Zhongguo guannian shi*, ed. Yuan Shuya (Zhengzhou: Zhongzhou guji chubanshe, 2005), 147.

2. Ibid.

3. 夫象者，何也？統論一卦之體，明其所由之主者也。 夫眾不能治眾,治眾者,至寡者也。夫動不能制動,制天下之動者,貞夫一者也。 故眾之所以得咸存者,主必致一也; 動之所以得咸運者,原必(無)二也。 物(無)妄然,必由其理。統之有宗,會之有元,故繁而不亂,眾而不惑. 故六爻相錯,可舉一以明也; 剛柔相乘,可立主以定也.．．．．夫少者,多之所貴也; 寡者,眾之所宗也。 一卦五陽而一陰,則一陰為之主矣; 五陰而一陽, 則一陽為之主矣! 夫陰之所求者陽也, 陽之所求者陰也, Wang Bi, *Zhouyilueli*, "Mingduan."

4. Tang Junyi, *Zhongguo zhexue yuanlun: yuandaopian*, volume 3 (Taipei: Xuesheng shuju, 1986), 336.

5. Ibid., 350–53.

6. Ibid., 370.

7. *Zhouyi zhu*, Qiangua, Wenyan.

8. Tang Junyi, "Wang Bi zhi you Yixue yi tong Laoxue zhi dao," in *Zhongguo zhexue yuanlun: Yuandao pian, Volume 2* (Taipei: Xuesheng shuju, 1986), 355–58.

9. Alan K. L. Chan, *Two Visions of the Way: A Study of the Wang Pi and the Ho-shang Kung Commentaries on the Lao-tzu* (Albany: State University of New York Press, 1991), 66.

10. For example, in such usages as *li yi yi zhangyou yue de* 禮以體長幼曰德 ("Using ritual propriety to give form to ["embody"] the [distinction between] elder and younger is called Virtue." (*Liji*, "Xiangyinjiuyi").

11. We see this sense of "completeness," ironically, even in the earliest usages of *ti* as a noun, the literal meaning of which is "part," as in a limb or other portion of the body, rather than the entire body. See, for example, *Shijing*, Daya, "Xingwei": *niuyang wu jianlu fangbao fangti* 牛羊勿踐履，方苞方體 ("Let not the cows and sheep trample [on the rushes], which have just now grown and fully formed"). *Ti* here seems to mean, literally, to be endowed with [all its proper] parts. See also Shijing, Gufeng, "Xiang Shu,": *xiang shu you ti, ren er wu li* . . . 相鼠有體，人而無理。。。 "See the mouse, with [all this] limbs—and yet here is a man lacking ritual propriety . . ." The connection with ritual is often picked up in later writings, implying also this sense of completion, for example, Liji, "Liqi," *liyezhe youtiye. Ti bubei junzi weizhi buchengren* 禮也者猶體也。體不備，君子謂之不成人 ("Ritual is like body parts. If one lacks the complete array of [all] the body parts, the gentleman calls one an incomplete person").

12. This has an ethical sense of "empathizing," "being considerate," i.e., seeing things from the position of the other—the famous Confucian virtue of "reciprocity." For example, in such usages as *gongzu zhi zui, suiqin buyifan, yousizhengshuye, suoyi ti baixing* 公族之罪，雖親不以犯、有司正術也，所以體百姓也 ("When any of the ruler's clan are guilty of an offense, although they are close kin, he does not for this reason allow them their offense, for there are proper procedures of the authorities in charge. This is how he *puts himself in the place of/forms one body with* the common people" (Liji, "Wenwan shizi"). *Ti* here means to take the common people as part of his own body, but not in the sense of regarding them as organs to be used for his own self-centered purposes, like one's limbs, but rather in the ethical sense of "consideration of their position," "seeing things as they do, from their point of view." A similar sense is found in modern Chinese usages such as *titie* 體貼 ("considerate"), *tiliang* 體諒 ("forgive," in the sense of "understanding" the offender's predicament), and also in the sense of bodily going through an actual experience in compounds such as *tiyan* 體驗 ("to experience") and *tihui* 體會 ("experiential understanding"). We may think here of Mengzi's remark that the sages "did not practice Benevolence and Righteousness; rather, they proceeded from Benevolence and Righteousness." *buxing renyi, you renyixing* 不行仁義，由仁義行。 For a comprehensive and insightful analysis of the implications of some of these points for the broader overview of Chinese metaphysics and onto-cosmology, see Chung-ying Cheng, "On the Metaphysical Significance of *Ti* (Body-Embodiment) in Chinese Philosophy: *Benti* (Origin-Substance) and *Ti-Yong*," *Journal of Chinese Philosophy* 29, no. 2 (June 2002): 145–61.

13. *Shishuo xinyu*, Chapter 4, Item 8: 王輔嗣弱冠詣裴徽，徽問曰：「夫無者，誠萬物之所資，聖人莫肯致言，而老子申之無已，何邪？」弼曰：「聖人體無，無又不可以訓，故言必及有；老、莊未免於有，恒訓其所不足. See Yu Jiaxi, ed., *Shishuo xinyu jianshu* (Taipei: Huazheng shuju, 2002), 199.

14. Tang Junyi, *Zhongguo zhexue yuanlun: Yuandao pian*, Volume 2, 373–74.

15. Wang Bi, *Laozizhu*, Ch. 5. The same sentiment, stressing the ironic sense of ordering as non-ordering, or the true overall coherence as simply the reciprocal ordering, limiting, making coherent of individual things, is found in Wang's comments to Chapters 36 and 38.

16. Ibid., Ch. 47.

17. ZZJS, 251.

18. Ibid., 111.

19. Ibid., 662.

20. Ibid., 200.

21. Ibid., 50.

22. *Huran*. This term, which normally means simply "suddenly," has a rather extended meaning in Guo Xiang. The *hu* here also implies to not pay attention, to neglect, unconsciousness. Moreover, the *ran* has a sense of both being-so and affirming, embodying a particular point of view.

23. ZZJS, 754.

24. Mizoguchi, op. cit., 154.

25. *Zhuangzi jishi*, ed. Guo Qingfan (Taipei: Muduo Press, 1983), 74. Henceforth cited as ZZJS.

26. Ibid., 277.

27. Ibid., 245.

28. Ibid., 583.

29. Ibid., 585.

30. Ibid., 570.

31. Ibid., 58–59.

32. This is why Guo does sometimes sound as though he considers the determinacy of things to be fixed, for example when he says, "This passage means to say that the determinacies of things have their different allotments and roles [*fen*]; thus the intelligent await their end holding on to their intelligence, while the stupid await death embracing their stupidity; how could they change their innate determinacy in the middle?" (Guo 1983, 59). But in the light of his entire system, his emphasis on change and transformation, his admission of unfixity of worldly conditions that alone express determinate differences, we may rather interpret such assertions to mean that at any given moment one is just what one is and cannot be otherwise, that one's determinacy in that moment is self-so and absolute, not that one must literally be the same in every subsequent moment. For Guo makes it abundantly clear elsewhere that *xing* does not mean something eternally fixed: "Benevolence and Righteousness are the determinate nature [性 *xing*] of man; but man's determinate nature changes [人性有變 *ren xing you bian*], it is different in the past and in the present" (Guo 1983, 519). Whatever changes happen to occur to one's determinacy are also self-so, and hence are also one's "nature." "To follow one's present determinacy and move directly forward [直往 *zhiwang*] is self-so. To so move and harm that determinacy, and the fact that the determinacy [性 *xing*] once hurt can change, are also self-so" (Guo 1983, 281). Here we see clearly that *xing* is something that can and does change; in fact, in light of Guo's general view of the uninterrupted all-pervasiveness of change, it must change.

33. ZZJS, 588.

34. Ibid., 225.

35. Guo's thought bears a striking resemblance also to the more radical variety of Chan Buddhism as represented to works associated with the Linji school. They share the idea of total merging with each moment of experience, relinquishment of all clinging to particular identity, and an anti-explanatory tendency. What distin-

guishes them are two crucial points. First, Guo's epistemology is based on his "traces" idea, whereas the Buddhist epistemology follows the Two Truths structure of Indian Mahayana. The traces are an inadvertent by-product of the self-so, and are usually, although not always, considered harmful by Guo Xiang; they are a mistake made by deluded people who cling to bygone traces and make ideals of them, thereby distorting their own self-so of each moment. The Buddhist picture attributes a positive salvific meaning to the misapprehensions of the Buddha's activities and teachings, which he also underwrites with his own compassion. Although the nonintentionality of the Buddha's work comes to be stressed more and more in Chinese Buddhism, in accordance with Guo's thinking, the basic Two Truths structure continues to alter the structure. Second, Guo has no theory of karma, even in a conventional truth sense. For him, what one encounters and what one does are exactly equal, and treated in exactly the same way. For Chan, what one encounters is the result of one's past karma, and is, initially, sharply distinguished from the Buddha-nature's constant relinquishment. One is still counseled to accept each encounter wholeheartedly and without resistance, as in Guo Xiang, but a different reason is given. It is still "done by oneself," but in a quite different sense. Chan moves closer to Guo's position when it claims that this karmic determinacy can be completely overcome by means of one's present attitude in accepting it; for Guo, the very idea that what one is encountering is some particular event, identifiable as this rather than that, is a result of trace-thinking, and a similar idea comes to play a part in Chan. But again, the original structure of the karmic idea prevents a full convergence of the two positions.

36. ZZJS, 225.
37. Ibid., 257.
38. Ibid., 280.
39. Ibid., 206. See also 156.
40. Ibid., 213.
41. Ibid., 323–24.
42. Ibid., 5.
43. Ibid., 406.
44. Ibid., 4.
45. See my *The Penumbra Unbound: The Neo-Taoist Philosophy of Guo Xiang* (Albany: State University of New York Press, 2003).
46. ZZJS, 213.
47. Ibid., 471.
48. Ibid., 549.
49. Ibid., 273.
50. Ibid., 638.
51. Ibid., 855.
52. Cf., among many other examples: "At the point where principle reaches its ultimate, outside and inside [the realm of social rules] vanish (into) one another; there has never been one who roams outside [i.e., in the self-so] who does not at the same time vanish (into) the inside [i.e., morality]. Thus the sage constantly roams outside the realm to vanish (into) what is inside it, following along with existence with no deliberate mind, and hence although his body is waving about all day long, his spirit and breath remain unchanged, looking above and below along with ten thousand different circumstances, and yet calmly constant and self-like" (ZZJS, 99).

Or again, "Although the sequence of precedence and following is the work of man, it comes from within the perfect principle [of the self-so], and is not the doing of the sage" (ZZJS, 470).

53. Ibid., 72.

54. A mutation of *duhua*.

55. ZZJS, 99.

56. Wing-tsit Chan, *A Source Book in Chinese Philosophy* (Princeton: Princeton University Press, 1973), 317.

CHAPTER SIX. BEYOND ONE AND MANY

1. *Yinwenzi; Guanyinzi* 尹文子, 關尹子 (Taipei: Taiwan Zhonghuashuju, 1979), *Guanyinzi*, 1.

2. Aramaki Noritoshi 荒牧典俊," Zhongguo fojiao de jieshou Li de yida bianhua," "中國對佛教的接受—"理" 的一大變化," in *Shijiezongjiaoyanjiu* 世界宗教研究. 1988.01.01: 37–43.

3. Kan'no Hiroshi, 菅野博史, 道生撰『妙法蓮花経疏』における「理」の概念について ("On the Concept of Li" in Daosheng's *Commentary to the Lotus Sutra*"), in 創価大学人文論集 3 (March 1991): 119–43.

4. *Taishōshinshūdaizōkyō* 大正新脩大藏經 ("The Chinese Buddhist Canon as Compiled in the Taishō Reign," ed. and compiled Takakusu Junjirō, Watanabe Kaigyoku et al. [Tokyo: Taishō Issaikyō Kankō Kai, 1924–1934]), vol. 45, 19, top fascicle. Henceforth this collection will be cited as "T," followed by volume number, page number, and top, middle, and bottom fascicle of the page indicated as "a, b, c," respectively. Hence, this citation would be: T45.19a.

5. See James Behuniak Jr., "*Li* in East Asian Buddhism: One Approach from Plato's Parmenides," *Asian Philosophy* 19, no. 1 (March 2009): 31–49.

6. It should be noted as well that the endeavor to end suffering is itself something one may choose to embark upon or not; Buddhism is good and true only to the extent that the liberation from suffering is one's goal. It may be that all goals can be (not "must be") reduced to this goal—all human activity can be seen (not "must be seen") as various attempts to reduce suffering in one way or another. But this is different from asserting that something that is useful for this goal is true or good outside of the context of having adopted this goal explicitly.

7. See T25.59b17–61b18. The four siddhantas (literally, "tenets" or "doctrines" with an implication of something firmly established or held to; roughly, "established authorized teachings") are (1) the Worldly Siddhanta, which corresponds directly to the category of "Conventional Truth" on a non-Upayicized understanding of that doctrine: it is the Buddha's teaching in terms generally accepted by the world; (2) the Individually Adapted Siddhanta, which means that the Buddha may preach things that conform to the preconceptions of a particular sentient being, no matter how misguided, but that conform neither to the first Siddhanta (ordinary Conventional Truth) nor to Ultimate Truth; (3) the Counteractive Siddhanta, which takes the particular beliefs of either the world in general or of some individual subset of sentient beings, even if only a single one, and rather than speaking in terms of these preconceptions, instead speaks in a way designed specifically to undermine and refute them; (4) the Supreme Meaning Siddhanta, which corresponds to the

preaching of Ultimate Truth on a Two Truths scheme: the preaching of non-self, emptiness, and so on.

8. 性欲無量故，說法無量；說法無量，義亦無量。無量義者，從一法生；其一法者，即無相也。如是無相，無相不相，不相無相，名為實相。T9.385c–386a.

9. Ibid.

10. It will be noted here that the Tiantai writers thus do not recognize a difference between what Westerhoff has called "essence-svabhava" and "substance-svabhava"—which is perhaps not surprising, given the lack of a substance ontology in pre-Buddhist China against which to argue. See Jan Westerhoff, *Nāgārjuna's Madhyamaka: A Philosophical Introduction* (Oxford: Oxford University Press, 2009). On the Tiantai view, the rejection of substance-svabhava entails the rejection of essence-svabhava, as we shall see.

11. In this story, Śāriputra compares himself, and the other śrāvakas, to a son who, while still a youth, has been separated from his father, gone off on his own, become lost. The father searches all over for him, but finally gives up in despair; he can find him nowhere. Instead, he settles in a certain town and becomes very rich. Meanwhile, the son has to fend for himself, and lives hand to mouth in extreme poverty, taking whatever odd jobs come his way. In his wanderings, quite by chance, he eventually comes to the gate of his father's opulent mansion. He is greatly intimidated by the splendor of this palatial estate, seeing nothing there that seems remotely relatable to his own condition; this is someone as different from himself as imaginable, someone with whom he has nothing at all in common. Indeed, he fears this must be a king of some sort, a person of great authority and might who will force him into military service or corvee labor if he doesn't flee as quickly as possible. The father, instantly recognizing this broken impoverished man at the gate as his own long lost son, is overjoyed. He sends his servants to apprehend him—but the son is terrified, and falls into a faint. Realizing that his son has forgotten his own identity and is in no condition to take in the news, he devises a "skillful means": the son is allowed to return to the poor part of town, and two ragged looking messengers are sent, pretending to be looking randomly for cheap day laborers, paid at the minimum wage. This the son can accept; it accords with his own concept of himself and his worth. He takes the job, and works shoveling out manure for twenty years. For Zhiyi's interpretation, see *Fahuawenju*, especially T34.279c, and passim.

12. This is of course a very abbreviated summary of Zhiyi's favorite method of meditative inquiry. This method, described in greatest detail in the *Mohezhiguan*, T46.63b–66c, argues as follows: "Whenever a single moment of experience arises, all three types of Provisional Positing (elements, succession, conceptual contrasts) are present. . . . One should ask of this one moment of experience, Is this mental event created by itself? Does the facing object produce this mental event? Do the organ and object combine to form this mental event? Is this mental event born in separation from organ and object? If the mental event creates itself, we are taking the previous mental event as the organ and the subsequent mental event as the consciousness born from this organ. Is the mental event born from the organ or from the consciousness? If the organ can produce the consciousness, does the organ have consciousness existing antecedently within it, or no consciousness within it?

If there is consciousness already within the organ, organ and consciousness coexist, and there is no relation of the generator and the generated between them (as claimed). If there is no consciousness within the organ, and yet it can generate consciousness, why does this organ produce consciousness when all other objects, also equally lacking consciousness within them, cannot? Or is it that although there is no actual consciousness within the organ, it can generate consciousness because it has within it the "potential for consciousness"? But is this "potential for consciousness" existent or nonexistent? If it is existent, it is already consciousness coexisting with the organ—in what sense is it to be called merely a potential? If it is nonexistent, on the other hand, it can do no generating of consciousness. Moreover, is this potential for consciousness the same as consciousness or something other than consciousness? If they are the same, the potential is the consciousness, then there is no possible relation of generator and generated between them. If they are different, then we have here another case of generation from an other, not from itself. If we reason in this way, we find that the mental event is not generated from mind itself.

"[A similar argument can be made to refute the contention that the mental event is generated by the object]: is this object mental, and thus capable of generating the mental, or non-mental, and thus capable of generating the mental? If it is mental, it is not an object, and not outside, and the refutation goes the same as the refutation of generation from self. Moreover, in this case the organ and object would be two coexistent mentals, and no generator/generated relationship would exist between them. If the object is non-mental, we refute as above. If you say that there is the potential for generation of consciousness within the object, again we ask if this potential is existent or nonexistent. If it is existent, it coexists with the object, and there is no generator/generated relationship. If it is nonexistent, it can do no generating. From this we conclude that the mental event is not produced by the object.

"If the claim is made that the mental event is generated by the combining of the organ and object, we ask if this is because they both are mental, or both are non-mental? If both are mental, we have the coexistence of two mentals when they come together, and the case is refuted as before. If they are both non-mental, in their coming together they remain devoid of the mental. For example, when a mirror confronts a face, is it because both have this visage that the image appears, or because both lack this visage? If they both have this visage, there should be two visages when they come together. If neither has this visage, they cannot produce one just by being juxtaposed. If you say that it is in uniting the mirror and the image into a unity that the image is produced, we note that in reality they do not form a unity, and if they did there would be no image [i.e., we would be back to the case of self-production, already refuted]. . . . [Thus generation from a finite combination is refuted].

"If it is claimed that the mental event is generated in separation from both organ and object, with no cause at all, we ask: is this "separation" something that exists or does not exist? If it exists, then we still have a particular cause here; in what sense is it free of conditions? If it does not exist, it can do no producing. Or if it is claimed that this detachment from organ and object has the potential for consciousness, is this potential existent or nonexistent? . . . Thus we see that this mental event is not generated by detachment from organ and object."

This is the refutation of the first type of Provisional Positing. Next, Zhiyi takes on succession, focusing on the four states of not-yet-arisen, about-to-arise, arisen, and gone, for any mental event. This angle is expounded most commonly and at most length in Zhiyi's works, and seems to be of particular use in meditative practice. But the argument is the same for each type of Provisional Positing. In each case, attention is drawn to the interface between the "this" and the "not-this," either spatially, temporally or conceptually, and the impossibility of construing this boundary coherently is made apparent. The "this" arises necessarily with some "non-this," but the generation of the one by the other cannot be understood if cause and effect are assumed to be simply located entities.

13. T46.29c.

14. T46.10b.

15. T8.332a–333c. For a paradigmatic instance of Zhiyi's deployment of this motif in the discussion of the Three Truths, *Miaofalianhuajing xuan yi*, in T33.702c, and *passim*.

16. T46.13c.

17. T33.691b.

18. T46.60c.

19. T9.11c.

20. T33.p0763c. 既以大乘果為大理。何不用小乘果為小理。彼救云。小果非真。故不以其果為理。若爾權教及權行人。何嘗是實。既立權教行人。何不立權理。又權若無理。俗不應稱諦.

21. T14.547c.

22. T34.37c.

23. Indeed, it is no accident that later Tiantai writers, such as Boting Shanyue 柏庭善月 (1149–1241) in his brilliant *Taizong shilei yinge lun*, make a point of restating the Li/*shi* relationship in strictly bilateral terms. In explaining Zhanran's comment that "It is only because of inherent entailment in Li that there can be function as event [*shi*]," he states. "Without *shi*, Li has nothing to depend on; without Li, *shi* has nothing to be rooted in [理無事無依，事無理無本 *liwushiwuyi, shiwuli wuben*]. For Li absorbs *shi*, and *shi* subsumes Li." Shanyue, 台宗十類因革論 *Taizong shilei yinge lun*, juan 2, XZJ 95.907b. Li here *depends on shi*; it is not merely "manifested by" *shi*. Li is the root (本 *ben*) of *shi*, while *shi* is the thing depended on (*yi*) by Li. These are basically equivalent terms, implying that the two are strictly mutually dependent, allowing no one-way dependence relationship between them. This is to be recalled when we consider the split between *shi* as 能依 *nengyi* (that which depends) and Li as 所依 *suoyi* in Huayan, below. This restatement of the relation in Tiantai is not mere latter-day gerrymandering; it shows a grasp of the real meaning of Zhiyi's way of setting up the problem, in spite of the superficial similarity to the later Huayan way of speaking.

24. T33.764b.

25. T46.784c

26. For a full account, see Robert Gimello, *Chih-Yen and the Foundations of Hua-Yen Buddhism*, PhD dissertation, Columbia University, 1976.

27. Peter N, Gregory, *Tsung-mi and the Sinification of Buddhism* (Princeton: Princeton University Press, 1991), 157–65.

28. The text of this work appears at T45.672-683, with Chengguan's commentary.

29. T45.594a.

30. See Tao Jiang, "The Problematic of Whole-Part and the Horizon of the Enlightened in Huayan Buddhism," *Journal of Chinese Philosophy* 28, no. 4 (December 2001): 457–75, 467.

31. T45.499a–b.

32. T45.499b–c.

33. T45.600b–c.

34. T46.451c.

35. Compare Kant's remarks in the Transcendental Aesthetic regarding space: "We present space as an infinite *given* magnitude. Now it is true that every concept must be thought as a presentation that is contained in an infinite multitude of possible presentations (as their common characteristic) and hence the concept contains these presentations *under itself*. But no concept, as such, can be thought as containing an infinite multitude of presentations *within itself*. Yet that is how we think space (for all parts of space, *ad infinitum*, are simultaneous). Therefore the original presentation of space is an a priori *intuition*, not a concept." Kant, *Critique of Pure Reason*, Unified edition (with all variants from the 1781 and 1787 editions), trans. Wener S. Pluhar (Indianapolis: Hackett, 1996), 79. The same point is made concerning time: "Time is not a discursive or, as it is called, universal concept; rather, it is a pure form of sensible intuition. Different times are only parts of one and the same time; and the kind of presentation that can be given only through a single object is intuition" (86).

36. T45.503b.

37. T46.707a–b.

38. T46.55b. The order is rearranged for clarity.

39. *Liumiaofamen*, T46.551c.

40. T45.511b.

41. T45.511c.

42. T35.119a.

43. T45.598c.

44. T45.595b.

45. T46.703c.

46. T34.58a.

47. A. C. Graham, "'Being' in Western Philosophy Compared with *Shih/fei* and *yu/wu* in Chinese Philosophy," in *Studies in Chinese Philosophy and Philosophical Literature* (Singapore: Institute of East Asian Philosophies, 1986), 348.

48. T34.247a–b.

49. T46.716b–c.

50. T46.716c.

51. Fazang used the metaphor in precisely this way, for example, at T45.638b–c: "The function is the waves, roiling and jumping, but the entire true substance is what is moving and changing. The substance is mirror-pure clear water, all of it following conditions and gathering it all into quiescence." Sometimes Fazang, in elaborating the Huayan metaphor of the "Ocean Seal Samadhi," compares the substance to the water when the waves are gone, and the function to the images that appear on the still surface of the water. See T45.647b. Zhanran, on the other

hand, states rather emphatically, "There is no water without waves, and no wave that is not wet."

52. Chengguan, *Dafang guangfo Huayanjing shechao xuantan*, ch. 15.

53. See Dong Ping, *Tiantai zong yanjiu* (Shanghai: Shanghai guji chubanshe, 2002), 173–75.

CHAPTER SEVEN. MIND, OMNIPRESENCE, AND COHERENCE IN TIANTAI AND HUAYAN

1. On this point see Ōtake Susumu 大竹　晋. 「理理相即」と「理理円融」：『花厳止観』論攷 ("Riri sousoku to riri enyuu: kegon shikan ronkou") ("A Study on the Li-Li concepts in Hua-Yan Buddhism"). *Tsukube*: 筑波大学哲学・思想学会, 哲学・思想論叢 17 (January 31, 1999): 23–34, for a fascinating overview of later medieval Japanese and Korean recountings of Huayan (Kegon) thought which, doubtless under Japanese Tendai influence, attempt to find some concept of interidentity and interpervasion of multiple Lis in Huayan thought, and the futility of the search for any trace of a doctrine of multiple Lis in Chinese Huayan sources.

2. T45.518b–c.

3. Yang Weizhong, *Xinxing yu Foxing: Zhongguo Fojiao xinxinglun ji qi xiangguan wenti yanjiu*. PhD Dissertation, Nanjing University, Department of Philosophy, 1998, published as Volume 12 of *Zhongguo Fojiao xueshu lundian* (Gaoxiong: Foguangshan, 2001), 368–69.

4. Ibid., 370.

5. See T32.576a.

6. T35.440c.

7. T44.240c.

8. T45.627b.

9. T45.507a.

10. T45.637b.

11. T45.485b.

12. T45.637b.

13. *Tanxuanji*, T35.347.

14. T35.658c.

15. T35.612b–c.

16. See Peter Gregory, *Tsung-mi and the Sinification of Buddhism* (Princeton: Princeton University Press, 1991), esp. 162–72 and 224–52.

17. T46.708c.

18. T46.710a.

19. Literally, "with respect to the mind-and-matter "of" mind," i.e., the mind-and-matter that *are* this moment of mind.

20. Zhanran, *Shibuermen* (originally excerpted from *his Fahuaxuanyi shiqian*), T46.703a.

21. For a good overview of the scope of usages in the broader tradition, see Yang Weizhong, *Xinxing yu foxing: Zhongguo fojiao xinxinglun jiqi xiangguan wenti yanjiu* (Gaoxiong, Taiwan: Foguangshan wenjiao jijinhui, 2001).

22. For example, in the discussion of Mind-observation in the 六妙法門 *Liumiaofamen*, Zhiyi says, "When observing the mind, the practitioner should understand that the *xinxing* is forever quiescent, and thus all dharmas are also quiescent" (T46.554a). This means "the innermost nature of the mind is quiescent, and so, since all dharmas are nothing but this mind, they are also quiescent." Note that this is stating not that all dharmas are mind, but that whatever is so of mind is so of all dharmas; that all dharmas are mind had been established in the preceding two steps of the discussion, without reference to the Nature. In fact, the point here is that the mind is non-mind (as stated in the next phrase: "since it is quiescent, there is no thought," not that dharmas are non-dharmas (i.e., that dharmas are mind).

23. It is noteworthy that this expression seems to be consistently used, rather than the synonymous *xingzao*, which I have never seen in any Tiantai work. The stylistic or rhetorical reasons for this would be well worth investigating; but it is not difficult to demonstrate that *li* and *xing* are doctrinally synonymous in this context, even if it can be shown that each term is consistently used in certain particular contexts and not others.

24. Shanyue (1149–1241), a seventh-generation dharma-descendant of Zhili's, explains the relations between identity and entailment very effectively: "Any discussion of 'identity' [*ji*] or "entailment" [*ju*] coming from our [Tiantai] school must illuminate both of them simultaneously before it can be considered to have correctly grasped the meaning. What does this mean? For example, the *Mohezhiguan* explains that each single moment of experience *entails* the Three Thousand, but also that the Three Thousand *are identical to* each single moment of experience and vice versa, so that neither is prior or posterior. This is the greatest example of both identity and entailment. It still must be understood that "identity" must not lack "entailment," and "entailment" must not lack "identity." Identity without entailment is not the Integrated identity; entailment without identity is not the Sudden entailment. The Sudden entailment means identity to all dharmas without exception. The Integrated identity means entailment of all dharmas without exception. Even if both entailment and identity are each explained separately, but without showing how they complete one another and make one another possible, this is still something the one-sided teachings are capable of speaking about. Only when entailment and identity are both explained at the same time can it be considered the Integrated explanation. . . . Hence we speak of identity in such a way that identity is always identical to entailment; we speak of entailment in such a way that entailment is always said in reference to identity. It is only because we speak of identity in such a way that identity is always identical to entailment that our claims about the Three Thousand as unchangeable meritorious qualities of the Nature (*xingde sanqian*) mean not only the inherent entailment of their Natures, but even of the marks arising within temporal events. It is only because we speak of entailment in such a way that entailment is always said in reference to identity that our claims that the Three Thousand as events within temporal practice (*xiuzhong sanqian*) are identical to the Principle-Nature do not obstruct the fact that all marks remain just as they are . . ." (Shanyue, *Taizong shilei yingelun*, juan 2, XZJ95.908a–b.) The same reasoning applies to the question of "creation," which Zhili explains at length in section four of his *Shiyishu*, entitled, "Refutation of the Shanwai's failure to distinguish between the

creation in terms of event and creation in terms of principle [*bubian shili erzao*]."
There, he states: "In terms of creation in the as a function of temporal events, we
select out the aggregate of ignorant consciousness as the creator and the ten realms,
both sentient beings and their environments, as the created. In terms of creation
as a function of principle, creation is identical to inherent entailment. Since each
dharma, created or creating, is identical to principle, each one, just as it is, inherently
entails all the Three Thousand as meritorious properties of the Nature" (T46.841a).

25. *Simingshiyishu*, T46.832b.

26. "Q: The Five Aggregates are all the objects of contemplation; is the
subject doing the contemplating then something outside of mind and body? A: In
the Inconceivable Object and Wisdom, precisely the contemplated aggregates are
themselves the subject doing the contemplating. But a distinction can also be made.
The non-good and neutral aggregates are the object, while the good five aggregates
are the subject doing the contemplating. When this contemplation reaches purity
and maturity, there are seen to be no non-good or neutral aggregates (outside the
contemplating 'good' aggregates); there are only the good aggregates. The good aggregates become the upayic aggregates, which become the flawless [no-outflows] aggregates, which become the Dharma-nature aggregates, which are called the unequalled
unsurpassed aggregates. In this sense, can it not also be said that there is thus a
contemplator outside the [original, ordinary] aggregates?" (T46.51b). Here we have
a nutshell version, in Zhiyi's plainer style, of what Zhili argues for so insistently.
Initially, there is a distinction between the relatively good aggregates—i.e., Buddhist practices and cognitions, the deliberate endeavor of the contemplation and
its concomitant doctrines—which view the deluded mind and body as its objects.
Ultimately, both of these are deluded, but in relative terms, the viewer is "good"
and the viewed is the "not-good." The object viewed is the aggregates running their
natural deluded karmic course, uninformed by Buddhist practices. The contemplation
succeeds when these deluded aggregates are seen to be empty, provisionally posited,
and central; that is to say, as ambiguous, locally coherent, and expressible as all
other entities. Since the contemplating "good aggregates" have seen these deluded
aggregates as lacking any definitive and separable self, the former see the latter also
to be expressing itself as the former themselves, as the "good" aggregates, so that
"there is no longer any non-good or neutral aggregate"—not because these contents
have been eliminated, but because these selfsame elements, unchanged, have been
absorbed into aspects of the contemplating "good" mind. Both viewer and viewed
are seen to be the whole, and both are thereby sublated. When this occurs, there is
a qualitative change, such that ultimately this subject that is also object, or object
which is also subject, can no longer be simply identified with the pre-contemplation
aggregates, which by definition were either exclusively subject or exclusively object.
This is what Zhili means by "manifesting the Three Thousand Natures within the
aggregate mind."

27. *Shibuermenzhiyaochao*, T46.709c.

28. The first of these is well known, but the second is less commonly noticed
as a further aspect of distinctively Tiantai meditation, and for good reason; it is
certainly not named as a separate category of practice in Zhiyi's writings. But that
in contrast these two procedures are conceived as distinct by Zhanran, and that this

distinction is considered of great importance, is demonstrated quite clearly in a passage of his *Zhiguanfuxingzhuanhongjue*: "Q: Since one [moment of] mind inherently entails [all dharmas], one need only observe the mind [觀心 *guanxin*]. What need is there to observe inherence [觀具 *guanju*]? A: The method of meditation adopted in our [Tiantai] school is forever different from that of all other theories. Its covering and integration of all the ten direction and the three times, of ordinary and the sagely, of all causes and all effects is truly only because of inherence-observation [*guanju*]. Inherence is precisely Provisional Positing, and Provisional Positing is precisely Emptiness and Centrality. Although the Nature of Principle inherently entails all, if one does not observe it but speaks only of observing mind, this will fail to fully accord with the principle. Do not even the Hinayanists observe the mind? It is just that they confusedly fail to realize that this one mind inherently entails all dharmas" (T46.289c). Inherence-observation is thus clearly, for Zhanran, a further step beyond mere mind-observation, and Zhili exploits this point, not unconvincingly, to support his claim that we must read *xin xing* as suggesting two separate referents.

29. T9.465c–466a. The "new translation" of the same passage, in the 80 juan version of the sutra, on which Fazang himself worked, reads as follows: "It is like a skilled painter, spreading out various colors, and then deludedly taking them to be different objects [in the painting]. The elements [of which the colors are composed] have no differences. The elements have no colors in them, nor do the colors have elements in them, but neither are there any colors obtainable apart from the elements. The mind has no colors or paintings in it, nor do the colors and paintings have the mind in them, but neither are there any colors or paintings obtainable apart from the mind. That mind is eternally non-dwelling, infinite in measure, difficult to understand. It manifests all colors, none of which are aware of one another. Just as the skilled painter is unable to know his own mind and yet paints because of his mind, so it is with the nature of all dharmas. The mind is a skilled painter, able to paint various worlds. All the five aggregates are generated from it. There is no dharma it does not create. As it is with the mind, so it is with the Buddha. As it is with the Buddha, so it is with all sentient beings. *You should know that the Substance and Nature of the Buddha and the Mind are all infinite.* If a man knows the activities of the mind, and how it creates all worlds, this man sees the Buddha, comprehends the true nature of the Buddha." The italicized passage reflects the Huayan understand later expressed by Chengguan. The specification that it is "the Substance and Nature" that is infinite, and the exclusion of "sentient beings" (which would include delusion) are to be noted here, as they accord precisely with Chengguan's later remarks.

30. T9.19b–c.

31. "The Bodhisattva, when he practices, [moves from] not-yet-raising his foot to being about-to-raise his foot, from not-yet-generating a thought to being about-to-generate a thought. He first contemplates this mind, which has not yet had a thought and which is about to have a thought. When a thought has not yet arisen, there are no mental conceptions, no mind, no concomitants of mind. This is called the mind-nature. This mind-nature is neither generated nor destroyed, is neither illuminated nor benighted, neither empty nor provisionally posited, neither cut-off nor eternal. It has no marks or appearance, nothing which can be attained,

and so it is called the mind-nature. It is also called the pure mind of the self-nature."
Suiziyi sanmei, XZJ98.689a.

32. T9.392c–393a.

33. Zhanran makes this point eminently clear: "Q: Of the four phases of the [experience of any of the] Ten Realms [not-yet-arisen, about-to-arise, arisen, already-gone], the arisen has marks that are easy to know. But how can the not-yet-arisen and the *already-gone* be contemplated? A: Although the already-gone and the not-yet-arisen do not refer exclusively and precisely to one single mental state, *they necessarily take shape within the arisen state of mind.* Thus, one comes to know which realm the arisen state of mind belongs to; looking to what preceded it from within this perspective, we have what in this context takes the role of the already-gone, and looking ahead, we have the not-yet-arisen. Thus the already-gone and the not-yet-arisen can be contemplated from within the perspective of the about-to-arise and the arisen" (T45.452b–c).

34. T46.54a.

35. T46.55a.

36. T33.685c, 741b.

37. T46.715b.

38. T46.452a.

39. Ibid.

40. T17.908a.

41. T46.836a.

42. T33.696b–697c.

43. T46.836a. Note that "the Three Thousand" means not only a single univocal set of facts, but all views and opinions, all "misconceptions," all perspectives on the world. See the explanation of the "three worlds" 三世間 from the *Dazhidulun* that go into this equation: we have both "sentient beings" and "the five aggregates," counted *twice*: once as "real" (實) and once as provisional (假): both the "true" mereological reductionist view of sentient beings as the five aggregates and the "false" conventional view of them as sentient beings are counted among the Three Thousand that must be inherently entailed in each moment of experience.

44. Zhanran, *Zhiguan dayi*, T46.460b.

45. Zhili, *Sibuermenzhiyaochao*, T46.713a.

46. T46.710a.

47. T46.293a.

48. T46.835b.

49. T46.710b

50. For a more detailed analysis of the conception of mind-creation here, see my "Mind and its 'Creation' of all Phenomena in Tiantai Buddhism," *Journal of Chinese Philosophy* 37. no. 2 (June 2010): 156–80.

51. T46.452c.

52. T46.712c.

53. Siming Zhili, *Sibuermen zhiyaochao*, T46.708b.

54. Ibid., T46.708b–c.

55. In Tiantai, the Buddha-nature is described as threefold, corresponding to the Three Truths. The Buddha-nature as conditioning cause of Buddhahood is

the practices and conditions that make possible the mental state of wisdom and realization (including meditation, morality, etc., and all the other conditions which make these possible). The Buddha-nature as illuminating cause is this mental state of wisdom which realizes the truth. The Buddha-nature as cause Proper is this truth itself which is realized, the truth about all things which is thus present in them from the beginning, and hence can be construed as a "mere potential" waiting to be realized. It is the Buddha-nature as conditions and illuminating that do the realizing, and the Buddha-nature as cause proper which is realized. A further twist is that, since these three are related as the Three Truths are related to each other, the content of the cause proper is nothing but the interchangeability of the first two, i.e., the fact that the illuminating is precisely the conditioning cause, that practices and conditions on the one hand and the awareness that results from them are identical-as-contrasted. In this passage from Zhanran, the threefold Buddha-nature is seen both in terms of principle and in terms of phenomena, and in both cases all three are seen to be operative.

56. Ibid., T46.709c–710a.

57. But this same dharma-as-principle has a *determinate* relationship to this particular dharma-as-*Li*, which is simply a way of restating the interchangeability of determinacy and indeterminacy entailed by the Three Truths.

58. T46.575a.

59. T46.783b.

60. "問: 「既以迷中實相為一性, 對三千為別, 正當以理為總, 何苦破他?」 答: 「以三千法同一性故, 隨緣為萬法時, 趣舉一法總攝一切也。眾生無始全體在迷, 若唯論真性為總, 何能事事具攝諸法? 而專舉一念者, 別從近要立觀慧之境也。若示一念總攝諸法, 則顯諸法同一真性。故《釋籤》云, 俗即百界千如, 真則同居一念。須知同一性故, 方能同居一念, 故以同居一念用顯同一真性, 非謂便將一念名為真諦, 豈同居一塵非真諦邪? 今文以一性為總, 前後文以一念為總, 蓋理事相顯也。此之二句, 正出攝別入總之所以也, 由一性無性立理事三千故, 故兩重三千同居一念也, 豈同他釋直以一念名真性邪? T46.710a–b.

61. This is why the *reversibility of subject and object* is so crucial to the Tiantai conception of Li, and why object must also understood to observe subject. Zhanran in his *Zhiguanyili* makes this point as quite emphatically: "Q: [Zhiyi's] *Fahuaxuanyi* says that the object is able to contemplate the subject. Although many scriptures are quoted to prove it, this Li is hard to understand. A: If we follow the merely upayic teachings, this Li is incomprehensible. But from the point of view of the ultimate teaching, the principle/coherence is quite easy to integrate. We take mind itself as the object, while mind is also the subject that is doing the contemplating. Thus subject and object are both mind, and the essence of mind pervades everywhere. *Each state of mind reflects on another state of mind*—the Li is here is quite clear. Thus at the beginning of the section on the Inconceivable Object it says, 'The inconceivable object is itself precisely the subject doing the contemplating.' From this we can derive four different but equally accurate descriptions: the object is aware of [lit. illuminates, shines on] the object, the object is aware of the subject, the subject is aware of the object, the subject is aware of the subject. . . . Thus it is different from what people of the world normally think of, namely, an inert object

as that which we are aware of, and also differs from the idea of a partial, small mind as the subject that contemplates. Nor is it the same as the idea of artificially setting up Suchness as the object of contemplation. These differences applying to the object also apply to the subject—let there be no confusion on this" (T46.452b). Zhili gives a more expansive account of the implications of this idea: "Thus we can say that all the sentient beings and all the Buddhas of the past, present and future, throughout the ten directions of space, and also their constituent environments, are the object being contemplating, and also that all the sentient beings and all the Buddhas of the past, present and future, throughout the ten directions of space, and also their corresponding environments, are the viewing wisdom as subject doing the contemplating [neng guan zhi]. The object and the viewing wisdom are two names for the same entity. Thus subject and object are two and not two . . . [So we can say equally that] the object perceives the object, or that the object perceives the viewing wisdom, or that the wisdom perceives the wisdom, or that the wisdom perceives the object." 是故得云三世十方生佛依正為所觀境。三世一方生佛依正為能觀智。境智名別其體不殊。是故能所二而不二。境照於境。境照於智。智照於智。智照於境 (T39.145c). This is also the key insight underlying Zhanran's claim that "insentient beings also have the Buddha-nature" (無情有性 wuqing youxing) as expounded in the Jingangpi 金剛錍.

62. T46.710a–b, 712c.

63. T46.868b.

64. Hence Zhili says, "The Real-attribute is the Li of the Middle Way [i.e., the Center]. The entirety of this Li of the Middle and the Real is the active wisdom that is doing the contemplating, the contemplating wisdom, and this is what is called the Wisdom of the Real-attribute. The Real-attribute itself is the wisdom; it is not that there is some other wisdom that is given this name because of the object that it reflects upon." 實相者。 中道理也。全中實理為能觀慧。名實相慧。實相即慧也。非別有慧。從其所照得實相名. T39.125a.

65. T46.1c.

CONCLUSION

1. For a comprehensive discussion of this doctrine in Tiantai, see my *Evil and/or/as the Good: Omnicentrism, Intersubjectivity, and Value Paradox in Tiantai Buddhist Thought* (Cambridge: Harvard University Press, 2000).

EPILOGUE

1. Wang Xiaoyu, ed., *Erchengji* (Beijing: Zhonghua shuju), 424.

2. 學者須先識仁。仁者，，渾然與物同體，義、禮、智、信皆仁也。識得此理，以誠敬存之而已，不須防檢，不須窮索。若心懈，則有防；心苟不懈，何防之有！理有未得，故須窮索；存久自明，安待窮索！此道與物無對，「大」不足以明之。天地之用，皆我之用。孟子言「萬物皆備于我」，須「反身而誠」，乃為大樂。若反身未誠，則猶是二物有對，以己合彼，終未有之，又安得樂！。。。See Wang Xiaoyu, ed., *Er Cheng ji* (Beijing: Zhonghua shuju, 1991), 16–17.

3. Wang Xiaoyu, ed., *Er Cheng ji* (Beijing: Zhonghua shuju, 1991), 10.

4. 事有善有惡皆天理也。天理中物須有善惡。蓋物之不齊，物之情也。但當察之，不可自入于惡，流于一物。 Ibid., 17.

5. Chung-ying Cheng, "Categories of Creativity in Whitehead and Neo-Confucianism," *Journal of Chinese Philosophy* 6 (1979): 262.

6. *Zhuzi yulei,* compiled by Li Jingde, in Eight Volumes (Taipei: Zhengzhong shuju, third edition, 1973), Vol. 1, 175–76.

7. Ibid., 168.

8. Ibid., 177–78.

9. Ibid., 90 (ibid., 179). In another place, Zhu expands on this thought as follows: "Man's ability to speak and move and think and act is all qi, but Li exists within it. When these develop into filiality, brotherliness, loyalty, good-faith, benevolence (*ren*), rightness, ritual and wisdom, this is all Li. . . . Human beings obtain a qi which is balanced and unobstructed, while other things obtain a qi which is one-sided and clogged. Because only man has balanced [*qi*], this Li penetrates it without being clogged. Because other things have one-sided [*qi*], this Li is obstructed and they have no knowledge [of it]" (ibid., 105–106). Compare also ibid., 90: "In the case of human nature, we speak of darkness and brightness; in the case of the natures of other creatures, there is only one-sidedness and obstruction. Darkness can be made bright, but what is already one-sidedly obstructed cannot be made open and unobstructed."

10. Ibid., 98. 桔槔之物，亦有性，，是如何？曰：＂是他合下有此理，故云天下無性外之物。＂因行街，云：＂階磚便有磚之理。＂因坐，云：＂竹椅便有竹椅之理。枯槁之物，謂之無生意，則可；謂之無生理，則不可。如朽木無所用，止可付之爨灶，是無生意矣。然燒甚麼木，則是甚麼氣，亦各不同，這是理元如此。＂ 「問：理是人物同得於天者。如物之無情者，

11. Ibid. 「問：理是人物同得於天者。如物之無情者，亦有理否？曰：固是有理，如舟只可行之於水，車只可行之於陸。」。 朱子語類⊠卷第四，性理一》(台北：文津，1986 年12月)，頁61。

12. Ibid., Vol. 8, 4476–77. 蓋天理在人，恆萬古而不泯；任其如何蔽錮，而天理常自若，無時不自私意中發出，但人不自覺。正如明珠大貝，混雜沙礫中，零零星星逐時出來。但只於這箇道理發見處，當下認取，簇合零星，漸成片段。到得自家好底意思日長月益，則天理自然純固；向之所謂私欲者，自然消磨退散，久之不復萌動矣 (朱子語類卷第一百一十七)。

13. Ibid., Vol. 1, 159.

14. Ibid., 161.

15. Ibid., 195.

16. Ibid., 169–70.

17. Ibid., 194.

18. Ibid., 195.

19. See Antonio Cua, "On the Ethical Significance of the Ti-Yong Distinction," *Journal of Chinese Philosophy* 29, no. 2 (June 2002): 163–70) for some useful reflections on the functions of this kind of *ti* and *yong* flexibility and context-dependence in Neo-Confucian moral reflection. See also Charles Muller, "Essence-Function and Interpenetration: Early Chinese Origins and Manifestations," *Toyogakuen*

XXX, no. 7 (1999), and "Tiyong and Interpenetration in the Analects of Confucius: The Sacred as Secular," *Toyogakuen* XXX, no. 8 (2000).

20. 理者氣之條理,氣者理之運用。無條理則不能運用,無運用則亦無以見其所謂條理者矣. Wang Yangming, *Chuanxilu* (Taipei: Junshi shicuishe, 1985), juan 2, 81–82.

21. Ibid., juan 3, 137.

22. *Zhuzi yulei*, op. cit., Volume 1, 4.

23. Ibid., 4–5.

24. T46.868b.

25. Ibid., 91–92.

26. Ibid.

BIBLIOGRAPHY

Andō Toshio 安藤俊雄. *Tendai seigu shisō ron* 天台性具思想論 ("The Tiantai/Tendai Theory of Inherent Entailment"). Kyoto: Hōzōkan, 1953.

———. *Tendaigaku: konponshisō tosono tenkai* 天台学─根本思想とその展開 ("Tendai Studies: The Fundamental Doctrines and their Developments") Kyoto: Heirakujishoten, 1982.

Aramaki Noritoshi 荒牧典俊. "Zhongguo fojiao de jieshou Li de yida bianhua," "中國對佛教的接受─"理"的一大變化" ("A Major Change in the Chinese Buddhist Reception of Li"), in *Shijiezongjiaoyanjiu* 世界宗教研究 (Jan. 1, 1988): 37–43.

Behuniak Jr., James. *Mencius on Becoming Human*. Albany: State University of New York Press, 2005.

———. "*Li* in East Asian Buddhism: One Approach from Plato's Parmenides," *Asian Philosophy* 19, no. 1 (March 2009): 31–49.

Chan, Alan K. L. *Two Visions of the Way: A Study of the Wang Pi and the Ho-shang Kung Commentaries on the Lao-tzu*. Albany: State University of New York Press, 1991.

Chan, Wing-tsit. *A Source Book in Chinese Philosophy*. Princeton: Princeton University Press, 1973.

Chang, Garma C. C. *The Buddhist Teaching of Totality: The Philosophy of Hwa Yen Buddhism*. University Park: State University of Pennsylvania Press, 1971.

Chang, Leo S., and Yu Feng. *The Four Political Treatises of the Yellow Emperor: Original Mawangdui Texts with Compete English Translations and an Introduction*. Honolulu: University of Hawaii Press, 1998.

Chen Guying 陳鼓應. *Zhuangzijinzhujinshi* 莊子今注今釋 (*The Zhuangzi with Modern Commentary and Explanations*). Taipei: Taiwan Shangwuyinshuguan, 1989.

———. *Guanzisipianquanshi; jixiadaojiadaibiaozuo* 管子四篇詮釋；稷下道家代表作 (*An Exegesis of the "Four Chapters" of the* Guanzi: *The Representative Work of Jixia Academy Daoism*). Taipei: Sanminshuju, 2002.

Chen Yingshan 陳英善. *Tiantai yuanqizhongdao shixiang lun* 天台緣起中道 實相論 (*Tiantai's Theory of the Ultimate Reality Middle Way Dependent Co-arising*). Taipei: Dongchu chubanshe, 1995.

———. *Huayan wujin fajie yuanqilun* 華嚴無盡法界緣起論 (*Huayan's Theory of the Infinite Dependent Co-arising of the Dharma-Realm*). Taipei: Huayan lianshu chuban, 1996.

———. *Tiantai xingju sixiang* 天台性具思想 (*Tiantai's Theory of Inherent Entailment*). Taipei: Dongda tushu, 1996.

Cheng Chung-ying, "Categories of Creativity in Whitehead and Neo-Confucianism," *Journal of Chinese Philosophy* 6 (1979): 262.

————. "On the Metaphysical Significance of Ti (Body-Embodiment) in Chinese Philosophy: Benti (Origin-Substance) and Ti-Yong," *Journal of Chinese Philosophy* 29, no. 2 (June 2002).

Cook, Francis H. *Hua-yen Buddhism: The Jewel Net of Indra.* University Park: Pennsylvania State University Press, 1973.

Cook, Scott. "YueJi (Introduction, Translation, Notes, and Commentary)," *Asian Music* XXVI, no. 2 (Spring/Summer 1995): 19–24.

————. "The Term Li in Chinese Treatises on Literature and the Arts." Unpublished paper.

Csikszentmihalyi, Mark. *Material Virtue: Ethics and the Body in Early China.* London: Brill, 2004.

————, and Philip J. Ivanhoe, eds. *Religious and Philosophical Aspects of the Laozi.* Albany: State University of New York Press, 1999.

Cua, Antonio. "On the Ethical Significance of the Ti-Yong Distinction," *Journal of Chinese Philosophy* 29, no. 2 (June 2002): 163–70.

Dewoskin, Kenneth J. *A Song for One or Two: Music and the Concept of Art in Early China.* Ann Arbor: Center for Chinese Studies, 1982.

Ding Yuanzhi 丁源植. *GuodianzhujianLaozishixiyuyanjiu,* 郭店竹簡老子釋析與研究 (*Analysis and Research into the Guodian Bamboo Strip Laozi*). Taipei: Wanjuanlou tushu youxian gongsi, 1999.

Dong Ping 董平. *Tiantaizongyanjiu* 天台宗研究 (*Researches on the Tiantai School*). Shanghai: Shanghai gujichubanshe, 2002.

Donner, Neal, and Daniel B. Stevenson. *The Great Calming and Concentration: A Study and Annotated Translation of the First Chapter of Chih-I's* Mo-ho chih-guan. Honolulu: University of Hawaii Press, 1993.

Duan Yucai 段玉裁. *Shuwenjiezizhu* 說文解字注 (*Commentary to the* Explanation of Graphs and Explanations of Characters). Shanghai: Shanghai gujichubanshe, 1982.

Eno, Robert. *The Confucian Creation of Heaven.* Albany: State University of New York Press, 1990.

Etani Ryūkai 惠谷隆戒. *Tendaikyōgakugairon* 天台教學概論 (*Overview of Tiantai/ Tendai Doctrine*). Kyoto: Bukkyōdaigaku, 1986.

Fang Dongmei 方東美. *Huayanzong zhexue* 華嚴宗哲學 (*The Philosophy of the Huayan School*). Taipei: Liming wenhuashiyegongsi, 1981.

Fung Yulan. *A History of Chinese Philosophy,* trans. Derk Bodde. Vol. 2. Princeton: Princeton University Press, 1953.

Geaney, Jane. *On the Epistemology of the Senses in Early Chinese Thought.* Honolulu: University of Hawaii Press, 2002.

Gimello, Robert. *Chih-Yen and the Foundations of Hua-Yen Buddhism.* PhD dissertation, Columbia University, 1976.

Goldin, Paul Rakita. *Rituals of the Way: The Philosophy of Xunzi.* Chicago: Open Court, 1999.

Graham, Angus Charles. *Later Mohist Logic, Ethics and Science.* Hong Kong: Chinese University Press, 1978.

————. *Chuang-tzu: The Seven Inner Chapters and Other Writings from the Book* Chuang-tzu. London: George Allen and Unwin, 1981.

————. *Studies in Chinese Philosophy and Philosophical Literature*.Singapore: Institute of East Asian Philosophies, 1986.

————. *Disputers of the Tao*. La Salle: Open Court, 1989.

————. *Two Chinese Philosophers*. La Salle: Open Court, 1992.

Gregory, Peter N. *Tsung-mi and the Sinification of Buddhism*. Princeton: Princeton University Press, 1991.

————. *Inquiry Into the Origin of Humanity: An Annotated Translation of Tsung-Mi's Yuan Jen Lun with a Modern Commentary*. Honolulu: University of Hawaii Press, 1995.

Guo Chaoshun 郭朝順. *Tiantai Zhiyi de quanshi lilun* 天台智顗的詮釋理論 (*Tiantai Zhiyi's Hermeneutic Theory*). Taipei: Liren shuju, 2004.

Guo Qingfan 郭慶蕃. *Zhuangzijishi* 莊子集釋 (*ZZJS*). Taipei: Muduochubanshe, 1983.

Hagen, Kurtis. *The Philosophy of Xunzi: A Reconstruction*. Chicago: Open Court, 2007.

Hall, David L. *Eros and Irony*. Albany: State University of New York Press, 1983.

————, and Roger Ames. *Thinking Through Confucius*. Albany: State University of New York Press, 1987.

————. *Anticipating China: Thinking Through the Narratives of Chinese and Western Culture*. Albany: State University of New York Press, 1995.

————. *Thinking from the Han: Self, Truth, and Transcendence in Chinese and Western Culture*. Albany: State University of New York Press, 1998.

Hamar, Inre, ed. *Reflecting Mirrors: Perspectives on Huayan Buddhism*. Wiesbaden: Harrassowitz Verlag, 2007.

Hansen, Chad. *Language and Logic in Ancient China*. Ann Arbor: University of Michigan Press, 1983.

————. "A Tao of Tao in Chuang Tzu." In *Experimental Essays on Chuang Tzu*, ed. Victor Mair. Honolulu: University of Hawaii Press, 1983.

————. *Language and Logic in Ancient China*. Ann Arbor: University of Michigan Press, 1983.

————. *A Daoist Theory of Chinese Thought: A Philosophical Interpretation*. Oxford: Oxford University Press, 1992.

Hegel, Georg Wilhelm Friedrich. *Logic. (Encyclopedia Logic)*. Trans. William Wallace. Oxford: Clarendon Press, 1975.

————. *Phenomenology of Spirit*. Trans. A. V. Miller. Oxford: Oxford University Press, 1977.

————. *The Science of Logic*. Trans. A. V. Miller. Atlantic Highlands: Humanities Press International, 1989.

Henricks, Robert G. *Lao-tzu Te-Tao Ching*. New York: Ballantine Books, 1989.

Hong Ye 洪業, NieChongqi 聶崇岐, Li Shuchun 李書春, and Ma Xiyong 馬錫用, eds. *Zhuzi Jicheng* 諸子集成 (*The Complete Classical Philosophers*) (In Eight Volumes). Shanghai: Shanghai ShudianChubanshe, 1996.

Huainanzi 淮南子. Taipei: Zhonghuashuju, 1983.

Hurvitz, Leon. *Chih-I (538–597): An Introduction to the Life and Ideas of a Chinese Buddhist Monk*. Bruxelles: L'Institut Belges des Hautes Etudes Chinoises, 1962.

Ishizu Teruji 石津照璽. *Tendai jissōron no kenkyū* 天台實相論の研究 (*Studies of the Tiantai/Tendai Theory of Ultimate Reality*). Tokyo: Kōbundōshobō, 1947.

Jiang, Tao. "The Problematic of Whole-Part and the Horizon of the Enlightened in Huayan Buddhism," *Journal of Chinese Philosophy* 28, no. 4 (December 2001): 457–75.

Jiao Hong 焦宏. *Laoziyi* 老子翼 (*Wings to the Laozi*). Taipei: Guangwenshuju, 1962.

Kameya Seikei, and Kōno Hōun 龜谷聖馨, 河野法雲. *Kegon hattatsushi* 華嚴發達史 (*History of the Development of Huayan/Kegon*). Tokyo: Meikyō Gakkai, 1913.

Kant, Immanuel. *Critique of Pure Reason*. Unified edition (with all variants from the 1781 and 1787 editions). Trans. Werner S. Pluhar. Indianapolis: Hackett, 1996.

Kannō Hiroshi 菅野博史. "Dosei sen myōhō renge kyō shō ni okeru ri no gainnen ni tsuite" 道生撰『妙法蓮花経疏』における「理」の概念について ("On the Concept of Li in Daosheng's Commentary to the *Lotus Sutra*"). *Sōka daigaku jinbun rongi* 創価大学人文論集 3 (March 1991): 119–43.

Kataoka Gidō 片岡義道. *Yichinensanzen no gendaiteki igi* 一念三千の現代的意義 (*The Contemporary Significance of [Tendai's Docrine of] One Moment of Experience as Three Thousand*). Tendaigakuhō. 天台學報. Tokyo: Tendai gakkai, 1995.

Kawada Kumatarō and Nakamura Hajime 川田熊太郎, 中村 元. *Kegon shisō* 華嚴思想 (*Huayan/Kegon Thought*). Kyoto: Hōzōkan, 1960.

Kjellberg, Paul, and Philip J. Ivanhoe. *Essays on Skepticism, Relativism, and Ethics in the Zhuangzi*. Albany: State University of New York Press, 1996.

Kline, T. C., and Philip J. Ivanhoe. *Virtue, Nature, and Moral Agency in the Xunzi*. Indianapolis: Hackett, 2000.

Knaul, Livia. "Kuo Hsiang and the Chuang Tzu." *Journal of Chinese Philosophy* 12, no. 4 (1985): 429–47.

Kohn, Livia, and Michael LaFargue. *Lao-tzu and the Tao-te-ching*. Albany: State University of New York Press, 1997.

Kong Yinda 孔穎達. *Zhouyi Zhengyi* 周易正義 (*The Book of Changes, with Corrected Meanings*). Taipei: Zhonghua shuju, 1986.

Laozi Wangbizhu, Boshu Laozi, Yiyin, Jiuzhu, HuangdiSijing 老子王弼注,帛書老子, 伊尹,九主, 黃帝四經 (*The Laozi with the Wang Bi Commentary, The Silk Manuscript Version of the Laozi, the Yiyin, the Nine Masters, and the Four Scriptures of the Yellow Thearch*). Taipei: Tianshi chubanshe, 1982.

Leibniz, Gottfried Wilhelm. *Discourse on the Natural Theology of the Chinese (Monographs of the Society for Asian and Comparative Philosophy, no. 4)*. Trans. Henry Rosemont Jr. and Daniel J. Cook. Honolulu: University Press of Hawaii, 1977.

Li Disheng 李滌生, ed. *XunziJishi* 荀子集釋 (*The Xunzi, with Collected Explanations*). Taipei: Xueshengshuju, 1979.

Li Jingde 黎靖德, compiler, *Zhuzi yulei* 朱子語類, in Eight Volumes. Taipei: Zhengzhong shuju, third edition, 1973.

Li Silong 李四龍. *Tiantaizhizhe yanjiu—jianlun zongpai fojiao de xingqi* 天台智者研究——兼論宗派佛教的興起 (*A Study of Tiantai Zhizhe—And On the Origin of Sectarian Buddhism*). Beijing: Beijing daxue chubanshe, 2003.

Liang Qichao 梁啟超. *MojingJiaoshi* 墨經校釋 (*Text Criticism and Explanations of the Mohist Canon*). Taipei: Xinwenfeng chubanshe, 1975.

Lijiyinde. 禮記引得 (*Index to the* Record of Ritual) Shanghai: Shanghai gujichuban-she, 1983.

Lin Shuen-fu 林順夫. "The Language of the 'Inner Chapters' of the Chuang Tzu." In *The Power of Culture: Studies in Chinese Cultural History*, ed. Peterson, Plaks, and Yu, 47–69. Hong Kong: Chinese University Press, 1994.

Liu Guijie 劉貴傑. *Huayanzong rumen* 華嚴宗入門 (*Introduction to the Huayan School*). Taipei: Dongda tushugongsi, 2002.

Liu Ming-wood. "The *Lotus Sutra* and *Garland Sutra* According to the T'ien-t'ai and Hua-yen Schools in Chinese Buddhism." *T'oung Pao*, Vol. 74, 1988.

———. *Madhyamaka Thought in China*. Leiden: Brill, 1994.

Lynn, Richard John. *The Classic of Changes: A New Translation of the I Ching as Interpreted by Wang Bi*. New York: Columbia University Press, 1994.

Machida Saburō 町田三郎. "Kan Shi shi hen nitsuite" 管子四篇似ついて ("On the 'Four Chapters' of the Guanzi"), *Shin Kanshiso no kenkyu* 新漢思想の研究. Tokyo: Sobunsha, 1985.

Makeham, John. "Names, Actualities, and The Emergence of Essentialist Theories of Naming in Classical Chinese Thought," *Philosophy East & West* 41, no. 3 (July 1991): 341–63.

———. *Name and Actuality in Early Chinese Thought*. Albany: State University of New York Press, 1994.

Mou Zongsan 牟宗三. *Foxing yu Bore* 佛性與般若 (*Buddha-nature and Prajna*). Taipei: Taiwan xuesheng shuju, 1977.

Mizoguchi, Yûzô 溝口雄三. "Liqilun de Xingcheng" 理氣論的形成 ("The Formation of the Theory of Li and Qi"), trans. Li Changli. In *Zhongguo Guannian Shi*, ed. Yuan Shuya. Zhengzhou: Zhongzhou guji chubanshe, 2005.

Mozisuoyin. 墨子索引 (*Index to the* Mozi) Chinese Studies, Ancient Chinese Texts Concordance Series, Chinese University of Hong Kong. Hong Kong: The Commercial Press, 1994.

Muller, Charles. "Essence-Function and Interpenetration: Early Chinese Origins and Manifestations." *Toyogakuen* XXX, no. 7 (1999).

———. "Tiyong and Interpenetration in the Analects of Confucius: The Sacred as Secular." *Toyogakuen* XXX, no. 8 (2000).

Munro, Donald J. *The Concept of Man in Early China*. Stanford: Stanford University Press, 1969.

———. *The Concept of Man in Contemporary China*. Ann Arbor: The University of Michigan Press, 1977.

———. *Images of Human Nature: A Sung Portrait*. Princeton: Princeton University Press, 1988.

———, ed. *Individualism and Holism*. Ann Arbor: Center for Chinese Studies, 1995.

———. *The Concept of Man in Early China*. Ann Arbor: Center for Chinese Studies, University of Michigan, 2001.

Needham, Joseph. *Science and Civilisation in China*. Taipei: Caves Books, 1985.

Nivison, David S. *The Ways of Confucianism: Investigations in Chinese Philosophy*. Ed. with an Introduction by Bryan W. Van Norden. Chicago: Open Court, 1996.

Ng Yu-kwan 吳汝鈞. *Tien-t'ai Buddhism and Early Madhyamika*. Honolulu: University of Hawaii Press, 1993.

———. *Tiantai Zhiyi de xinling zhexue* 天台智顗的心靈哲學 (*Tiantai Zhiyi's Philosophy of Spirit*). Taipei: Taiwan shangwu yinshuguan, 1999.

———. *Fahua xuanyi de zhexue yu gangling* 法華玄義的哲學與綱領 (*The Philosophy and Outline of the* Fahuaxuanyi). Taipei: Wenjin chubanshe, 2002.

Nylan, Michael. *The Canon of Supreme Mystery By Yang Hsiung: A Translation with Commentary of the* T'aihsüanching. Albany: State University of New York Press, 1993.

———, and Nathan Sivin. "The First Neo-Confucianism: An Introduction to Yang Hsiung's 'Canon of Supreme Mystery' (T'aihsuanching, c. 4 B.C.)." In *Chinese Ideas about Nature and Society: Studies in Honour of Derk Bodde*, ed. Charles Le Blanc and Susan Blader. Hong Kong: Hong Kong University Press, 1987.

Ōtake Susumu 大竹 晋. "Riri sōsoku to riri enyū: kegon shikan ronkō 「理理相即」と「理理円融」: 『花嚴止観』論攷 ("A Study on the Li-Li concepts in Hua-Yan Buddhism"). Tsukuba: Tsukuba daigaku tetsusgaku shiso ronsō 筑波大学哲学・思想学会, 哲学・思想論叢, Issue 17, January 31, 1999, 23–34.

Pan Guiming 潘桂明. *Zhiyi pingzhuan* 智顗評傳 (*Critical Biography of Zhiyi*). Nanjing: Nanjing daxue chubanshe, 1996.

———, and Wu Zhongwei 吳忠偉. *Zhongguo Tiantaizong tongshi* 中國天台宗通史 (*Comprehensive History of the Tiantai School in China*). Nanjing: Jiangsu guji-chubanshe, 2001.

Peng Guoxiang 彭國翔. *Rujia chuantong de quanshi yu sibian: cong xianqin Rujia Song-Ming lixue dao xiandai xin Ruxue* 儒家傳統的詮釋與思辨：從先秦儒家，宋明理學到現代新儒學 (*Hermeneutics and Thinking in the Confucian Tradition: From Pre-Qin Confucianism and Song and Ming Neo-Confucianism to Modern New Confucianism*). Wuhan: Wuhandaxue chubanshe, 2012.

Peterson, Willard. "Another Look at Li," *Bulletin of Sung-Yuan Studies* 18 (1986).

Puett, Michael. *The Ambivalence of Creation: Debates Concerning Innovation and Artifice in Early China*. Stanford: Stanford University Press, 2001.

———. *To Become a God: Cosmology, Sacrifice, and Self-Divinization in Early China*. Cambridge: Harvard University Press, 2004.

Qian Mu 錢穆. *Zhuang Lao tongbian* 莊老通辨 (*Comprehensive Discernments Concerning Zhuangzi and Laozi*). Hong Kong: Xinya yanjiusuo, 1957.

———. *SongMing lixue gaishu* 宋明理學概述 (*An Overview of Song and Ming Neo-Confucianism*). Taipei: Xuesheng shuju, 1977.

———. *Zhongguo sixiang shi* 中國思想史 (*A History of Chinese Thought*). Taipei: Xuesheng shuju, 1985.

———. *Zhuangzi Zuanjian* 莊子纂箋 (*The Zhuangzi, with Compiled Commentaries*). Taipei: DongdaTushuGongsi, 1986.

———. *Hushang xiansi lu* 湖上閒思錄 (*A Record of Leisurely Lakeside Thoughts*). Taipei: Dongda tushu gongsi, 1988.

Rickett, W. Allyn. *Guanzi: Political, Economic and Philosophical Essays from Early China*. Princeton: Princeton University Press, 1998.

Rosemont Jr., Henry, ed. *Chinese Texts and Philosophical Contexts: Essays Dedicated to Angus C. Graham*. La Salle: Open Court, 1991.

Roth, Harold D. *The Textual History of the Huai-nan Tzu*. Ann Arbor: Association of Asian Studies Monograph, 1992.

———. *Original Tao: Inward Training (Nei-yeh) and the Foundations of Taoist Mysticism*. New York: Columbia University Press, 1999.

Sakamoto Kôhaku 坂本廣博. "Shishuzanmai—tokunihikôhizazanmai to zuigiikakuizanmainitsuite" 四種三昧一特に非行非坐三昧と随自意、覚意三昧につい て. In *Tendaikyôgaku no kenkyû* 天台教学の研究, 159–77. Tokyo: Sankibôbutsushorin, 1990.

Sekiguchi Shindai 關口真大. *Tendai shikan no kenkyū* 天台止觀の研究 (*Studies of Tiantai/Tendai Concentration and Contemplation*). Tokyo: Iwanami shōten, 1969.

———. *Tendai kyōgakukenkyū* 天台教學の研究 (*Studies of Tiantai/Tendai Doctrine*). Daitō shuppansha, 1978.

Schopenhauer, Arthur. *The World as Will and Representation*. Trans. E. F. J. Payne. New York: Dover, 1969.

Schwartz, Benjamin I. *The World of Thought in Ancient China*. Cambridge and London: Belknap Press, 1985.

Shen Haiyin. "Chih-I's System of Sign Interpretation." *Chung-Hwa Buddhist Journal* 15 (2002): 495–584.

Shi Kaihua 施凱華. *Tiantai Zhizhe jiaopan sixiang* 天台智者教判思想 (*Tiantai Zhizhe's Conception of Classification of Teachings*). Taipei: Wenjin chubanshe, 2006.

———. *Tiantai zhongdao shixiang yuandun yisheng sixiang* 天台中道實相圓頓一乘思想 (*Tiantai's Philosophy of the Middle Way Ultimate Reality Integrated Sudden Single Vehicle*). Taipei: Wenjin chubanshe, 2009.

Shi Xingguang 釋性廣. *Yuandun zhiguan tanwei* 圓頓止觀探微 (*Detailed Exploration of [Tiantai's] "Perfect and Sudden Concentration and Contemplation"*). Taipei: Fajie chubanshe, 2011.

Shi Yisan 石一參, ed. *Guanzi Jinquan* 管子今詮 (*The Guanzi, with a Modern Interpretation*). Changsha: Shangwu yinshuguan, 1938.

Shun, Kwong-loi. "Mencius and Human Nature." *Philosophy East and West* 47 (January 1997).

———. *Mencius and Early Chinese Thought*. Stanford: Stanford University Press, 1997.

Slingerland, Edward. *Effortless Action: Wu-wei as Conceptual Metaphor and Spiritual Ideal in Early China*. Oxford: Oxford University Press, 2003.

Sommer, Deborah. "Boundaries of the *Ti* Body." *Asia Major*, Third Series, Vol. XXI, Part 1, Institute of History and Philology, Academia Sinica, Taiwan, 2008.

Spinoza, Baruch. *On the Improvement of the Understanding, The Ethics, Correspondence*. Trans. Elwes. New York: Dover, 1955.

———. *The Ethics and Selected Letters*. Trans. Shirley. Indianapolis: Hackett, 1982.

Strawson, P. F. *Individuals: An Essay in Descriptive Metaphysics*. London and New York: Routledge, 1959.

Sun Yirang 孫詒讓. *MoziJiangu* 墨子閒詁 (*The Mozi, with Substitutions and Glosses*). Taipei: Taiwan ShangwuYinshuaguan, 1983.

Swanson, Paul. *Foundations of T'ien-t'ai Philosophy: The Flowering of the Two Truths Theory in Chinese Buddhism*. Berkeley: Asian Humanities Press, 1989.

Taishōshinshūdaizōkyō 大正新脩大藏經 (*The Chinese Buddhist Canon as Compiled in the Taishō Reign*). Ed. and compiled by Takakusu Junjirō, Watanabe Kaigyoku et al. Tokyo: Taishō Issaikyō Kankō Kai, 1924–1934. (Cited as "T").

Takamine Ryōshū 高峯了州. *Kegon shisōshi* 華嚴思想史 (*History of Huayan/Kegon Thought*). Tokyo: Kōkyō Shoin, 1942.

Tamaki Kōshirō 玉城康四郎. *Shinhasokunotenkai* 心把捉の展開 (*The Development of the Begriff of Mind*). Tokyo: Sankibōbutsushorin, 1961.

Tan Yuanping 談遠平. *Lun Yangming zhexue zhi yuanrong tongguan* 論陽明哲學之圓融統觀 (*On Wang Yangming's Global View of Complete Interpenetration*). Taipei: Wenshizhe chubanshe, 1993.

Tang Junyi 唐君毅. *Zhongguo zhexue yuanlun: yuandaopian* 中國哲學原論:原道篇. Vol. 3. (*Essays Tracing the Sources of Chinese Philosophy: Tracing the Origins of Dao*). Taipei: Xueshengshuju, 1986.

———. *Zhongxi zhexue sixiang zhi bijiao lunwenji* 中西哲學思想之比較論文集 (*A Collection of Essays on Comparative Topics in Chinese and Western Philosophical Thought*). Taipei: Xueshengshuju, 1988.

———. *Zhongguo zhexue yuanlun: yuanxingpian* 中國哲學原論:原性篇 (*Essays Tracing the Sources of Chinese Philosophy: On the Origins of Theories of Human Nature*). Taipei: Xueshengshuju, 1989.

Tang Yongtong 湯用彤. *HanWei liangJin NanBeichao fojiao shi* 漢魏兩晉南北朝佛教史 (*History of Buddhism in the Han, Wei, Jin, Northern, and Southern Dynasties*). Two Volumes. Beijing: Zhonghua shuju, 1983.

Tu Wei-ming. *Confucian Thought: Selfhood as Creative Transformation*. Albany: State University of New York Press, 1985.

Van Norden, Bryan. *Virtue Ethics and Consequentialism in Early Chinese Philosophy*. Cambridge: Cambridge University Press, 2007.

Yinwenzi; Guanyinzi 尹文子, 關尹子. Taipei: Taiwan Zhonghuashuju, 1979.

Wang Fuzhi 王夫之. *Du sishu quanshuo* 讀四書全說 (*Complete Explanations for Reading the Four Books*). Beijing: ZhonghuaShuju, 1975.

———. *Zhuangzi tong, Zhuangzijie* 莊子通,莊子解 (*Comprehending the Zhuangzi; Explanations of the Zhuangzi*). Taipei: LirenShuju, 1984.

Wang Guangqi 王光祈. *Zhongguoyinyue Shi* 中國音樂史 (*History of Chinese Music*). Hong Kong: Taiping Shuju, 1963.

Wang, Robin. "Dong Zhongshu's Transformation of Yin-Yang Theory and Contesting of Gender Identity," *Philosophy East and West* 55, no. 2 (2005): 209–31.

Wang Shumin 王淑岷. *Zhuangzi jiaoquan* 莊子校詮 (*The Zhuangzi, with Collations and Explanations*). Taipei: Academia Sinica, 1988.

Wang Xiaoyu 王孝魚, ed. *Er Cheng ji* 二程集 (*Collected Works of the Two Cheng Brothers*). Beijing: Zhonghua shuju, 1981.

Wang Yangming 王陽明. *Chuanxilu* 傳習錄 (*Record of Practicing What Is Transmitted*). Taipei: Junshi shicuishe, 1985.

Watson, Burton. *The Complete Works of Chuang Tzu*. New York: Columbia University Press, 1968.

Wei Daoru 魏道儒. *Zhongguo Huayanzong tongshi* 中國華嚴宗通史 (*Comprehensive History of the Huayan School in China*). Zhonghe, Taipei County: Kongting shuyuan, 2007.

Wei Hanjie 韋漢傑. *Tiantai zhiyi de foxue sixiang: fajie yuanrong* 天台智顗的佛學思想: 法界圓融 (*Tiantai Zhiyi's Buddhist Thought: The Perfect Integration and Intermelding of the Dharma-realm*). Taipei: Wenjin chubanshe, 2010.

Wei Qipeng 魏啟鵬. *ChujianLaoziJianshi* 楚簡老子柬釋 (*Selections and Explanations of the Chu Bamboo Strip Version of the* Laozi). Taipei: Wanjuanlou tushu youxian gongsi, 1999.

Wenzi 文子. Taipei: ZhonghuaShuju, 1978.

Westerhoff, Jan. *Nāgārjuna's Madhyamaka: A Philosophical Introduction.* Oxford: Oxford University Press, 2009.

Whitehead, Alfred North. *Process and Reality.* New York: Harper and Row, 1929.

———. *Adventures of Ideas.* New York: Free Press, 1956.

———. *Science and the Modern World.* New York: Macmillan, 1967.

Wittenborn, Allen. "Li Revisited and Other Explorations," *The Bulletin of Sung-Yuan Studies* 17 (1981).

Wu Kuang-ming. *Chuang Tzu, World Philosopher at Play.* New York: Crossroad, 1982.

———. *The Butterfly as Companion.* Albany: State University of New York Press, 1990.

Wu Menghong 巫夢虹. *Guanzisipiansixiangyanjiu* 《管子》四篇思想研究 (*Research on the Thought of the "Four Chapters" of the* Guanzi). Master's Thesis, Taiwan National Central University國立央大學, 2004.

Wu Zhen 吳震. *Yanming houxue yanjiu* 陽明後學研究 (*A Study of the Latter-Day Wang Yangming School*). Shanghai: Shanghai renminchubanshe, 2002.

Xu Fuguan 徐復觀. *Liang-Han sixiangshi* 兩漢思想史 (*Intellectual History of the Han Dynasty*). Hong Kong: Xianggangzhongwendaxue, 1975.

Xunziyinde 荀子引得 (*Index to the Xunzi*). Shanghai: Shanghai gujichubanshe, 1986.

Yang Changzhen 楊長鎮. *Xunzi Lei De CunyoulunYanjiu* 荀子類的存有論研究 (*An Investigation of the Ontology of Types in the Xunzi*).Taipei: WenjinChubanshe, 1996.

Yang Weizhong 楊維中. *Xinxingyu Foxing: ZhongguoFojiaoxinxinglunji qi xiangguanwentiyanjiu* 心性與佛性；中國佛教心性論及其相關問題研究 (*Mind-nature and Buddha-nature: Researches into Theories of the Nature of Mind in Chinese Buddhism and Related Questions*). PhD Dissertation, Nanjing University, Department of Philosophy, 1998, published as Volume 12 of *ZhongguoFojiaoxueshulundian* (Gaoxiong: Foguangshan, 2001).

Yang Xiong 楊雄. *Fayan* 法言. Taipei: Zhonghuashuju, 1983.

———. *Taixuanjing* 太玄經. Taipei: Zhonghuashuju, 1983.

Yinwenzi; Guanyinzi 尹文子、關尹子. Taipei: Zhonghuashuju, 1979.

You Huizhen 尤惠貞. *Tiantaizong xingju yuanjiao zhi yanjiu* 天台宗性具圓教之研究 (*A Study of the Integrated Teaching of Inherent Entailment of the Tiantai School*). Taipei: Wenjin chubanshe, 1993.

———. *Tiantai zhexue yu fojiao shijian* 天台哲學與佛教實踐 (*Tiantai Philosophy and Buddhist Practice*). Jiayi: Nanhua daxue, 1999.

Yu Jiaxi 余嘉錫, ed. *Shishuo xinyu jianshu* 世說新語箋疏 (*The Shishuo xinyu, with Notes and Comments*). Taipei: Huazheng shuju, 2002.

Yuan Shuya 苑淑婭, ed. *Zhongguo guannianshi* 中國觀念史 (*History of Chinese Concepts*). Zhengzhou: Zhongzhou guji chubanshe, 2005.

Zhang Dainian 張岱年. *Zhongguo zhexueshi shiliaoxue* 中國哲學史史料學 (*Studies of Historical Materials in the History of Chinese Philosophy*). Beijing: Sanlianshuju, 1982.

Zhang Yangming 張揚明. *Laozi jiaozhengyishi* 老子斠證譯釋 (*The Laozi, with Critical Translations and Explanations*). Taipei: WeixinShuju, 1973.

Zhang Zhan 張湛. *Liezi zhushi* 列子注釋 (*The Liezi, with Explanatory Commentary*). Taipei: HualianChubanshe, 1969.

Zhu Xi 朱熹. *Zhuzi yulei* 朱子語類, in Eight Volumes. Li Jingde 黎靖德, compiler. Taipei: Zhengzhong shuju, third edition, 1973.

———. *Zhouyi benyi* 周易本義 (*The Book of Changes in Its Original Signification*). Taipei: Guangxue She Yinshu Guan, 1975.

ZZJS. See Guo Qingfan 郭慶藩, ed. *Zhuangzijishi*. Taipei: Muduo Press, 1983.

Zhuzi Yinde. Laozi, Zhuangzi 諸子引得: 老子莊子 (*Indices to the Philosophers: Laozi and Zhuangzi*). Taipei: ZhongqingTushuChubanGongsi, 1986.

Ziporyn, Brook. "Anti-Chan Polemics in Post-Tang Tiantai," *Journal of the International Association of Buddhist Studies* 17, no. 1: 26–63.

———. "The Self-so and Its Traces in the Thought of Guo Xiang," *Philosophy East and West* 43, no. 3 (July 1993): 511–39.

———. *Evil and/or/as the Good: Omnicentrism, Intersubjectivity, and Value Paradox in Tiantai Buddhist Thought.* Cambridge: Harvard University Press, 2000.

———. *The Penumbra Unbound: The Neo-Taoist Philosophy of Guo Xiang.* Albany: State University of New York Press, 2003.

———. *Being and Ambiguity: Philosophical Experiments with Tiantai Buddhism.* Chicago: Open Court, 2004.

———. "Mind and Its 'Creation' of All Phenomena in Tiantai Buddhism," *Journal of Chinese Philosophy* 37, no. 2 (June 2010): 156–80.

———. *Ironies of Oneness and Difference.* Albany: State University of New York Press, 2012.

INDEX

Made in the USA
Coppell, TX
30 November 2020

42510966R10256